FERM'S FAST FINDER

FERM'S FAST FINDER

14th Edition,
Revised and Expanded Guide
to the 2017 *National Electrical Code*

International Association of Electrical Inspectors
Richardson, Texas

Notice to the Reader

This book has not been processed in accordance with NFPA Regulations Governing Committee Projects. Therefore, the text and commentary in it shall not be considered the official position of the NFPA or any of its committees and shall not be considered to be, nor relied upon as a formal interpretation of the meaning or intent of any specific provision or provisions of the 2017 edition of NFPA 70, *National Electrical Code.*[1]

Publishers do not warrant or guarantee any of the products described herein or perform any independent analysis in connection with any of the product information contained herein. Publisher does not assume, and expressly disclaims, any obligation to obtain and include information referenced in this work.

The reader is expressly warned to consider carefully and adopt all safety precautions that might be indicated by the activities described herein and to avoid all potential hazards. By following the instructions contained herein, the reader willingly assumes all risks in connection with such instructions.

THE PUBLISHERS MAKE NO REPRESENTATIONS OR WARRANTIES OF ANY KIND, INCLUDING, BUT NOT LIMITED TO, THE IMPLIED WARRANTIES OF FITNESS FOR PARTICULAR PURPOSE, MERCHANTABILITY OR NON-INFRINGEMENT, NOR ARE ANY SUCH REPRESENTATIONS IMPLIED WITH RESPECT TO SUCH MATERIAL. THE PUBLISHERS SHALL NOT BE LIABLE FOR ANY SPECIAL, INCIDENTAL, CONSEQUENTIAL OR EXEMPLARY DAMAGES RESULTING, IN WHOLE OR IN PART, FROM THE READER'S USES OF OR RELIANCE UPON THIS MATERIAL.

[1]*National Electrical Code* and *NEC* are registered trademarks of the National Fire Protection Association, Inc., Quincy, MA 02169.

Resources 6

How to Use the Index 7

A 8

B 18

C 33

D 61

E 72

F 82

G 94

H 106

I 114

J 121

K 124

L 125

M 136

N 148

O 153

P 164

Q 173

R 175

S 186

T 205

U 218

V 221

W 223

X 230

Y 231

Z 231

Table of Conents

[1]The following are registered trademarks of the National Fire Protection Association, Inc., Quincy, MA 02269.

NFPA 20, *Standard for the Installation of Stationary Fire Pumps for Fire Protection*

NFPA 30, *Flammable and Combustible Liquids Code*

NFPA 30A, *Code for Motor Fuel Dispensing Facilities and Repair Garages*

NFPA 33, *Standard for Spray Application Using Flammable and Combustible Materials*

NFPA 34, *Standard for Dipping and Coating Processes Using Flammable or Combustible Liquids*

NFPA 54, *National Fuel Gas Code*

NFPA 70, *National Electrical Code* 2002, 2005, 2008, 2011, 2014, 2017.

NFPA 70-E, *Standard for Electrical Safety in the Workplace*

NFPA 72, *National Fire Alarm Code*

NFPA 79, *Electrical Standard for Industrial Machinery*

NFPA 88A, *Standard for Parking Structures*

NFPA 99, *Standard for Health Care Facilities*

NFPA 101, *Life Safety Code*

NFPA 220, *Standard on Types of Building Construction*

NFPA 303, *Fire Protection Standard for Marinas and Boatyards*

NFPA 325, *Guide to Fire Protection Hazard Properties of Flammable Liquids, Gases, and Volatile Solids contained in the NFPA "Fire Protection Guide to Hazardous Materials*–2001 edition"

NFPA 497, *Recommended Practice for the Classification of Flammable Liquids, Gases, or Vapors and of Hazardous (Classified) Locations for Electrical Installations in Chemical Process Areas*

NFPA 499, *Recommended Practice for the Classification of Combustible Dusts and of Hazardous (Classified) Locations for Electrical Installations in Chemical Process Areas*

NFPA 780, *Standard for the Installation of Lightning Protection Systems*

The following are registered trademarks of the Institute of Electrical and Electronics Engineers New York, NY 10016-5997.

ANSI C2, *National Electrical Safety Code*

ANSI 18, *Shunt Power Capacitors*

ANSI Z535.4, *Product Safety Signs and Labels*

IEEE 835-1994 IEEE Standard Power Cable Ampacity Tables

The *NEC–IRC Cross References*, used in Section 3, are registered trademarks of the International Code Council, and are used with permission.

The following are registered trademarks of Underwriters Laboratories Inc. Northbrook, IL 60062-2096.

Fire Resistance Directory

UL Product Spec

Ferm's Fast Finder Index is an alphabetized index of important words and phrases within the 2017 *National Electrical Code*. It also contains cross-references to other codes that are referenced within the *NEC*.

Look for the tab with the letter associated with the main section of what you are looking for. For example, Luminaires are located under "L." The main subheads are in bold and are flush against the left margin of the page. Any indented text under the main subheads are subsections of that group.

Example:

LUMINAIRES . . . . **Art. 410**	◄————————	**Main Category**
As a Raceway 410.64	◄————————	**First subsection of main category**
Ballast Type (Electric Discharge and LED)		
Calculations, Inductive and LED Loads . . . . . . 220.18(B)	◄————————	**Subsection of the first subsection.**

Under each main category heading are:

- references in the 2017 *National Electrical Code*, NFPA 70

- references to other NFPA standards and documents that are included in fine print notes throughout the *NEC* 2017. These include their numbers and editions.

- UL Guide Card letters for all references to the UL ProductSpec, available online at http://productspec.ul.com/index.php.

- references to additional codes and standards, such as those by ANSI and IEEE.

Readers may contact the National Fire Protection Association at (617) 770-3000 to verify current dates or proposed revisions.

For further information on ordering UL publications, write or call:

Underwriters Laboratories, Inc.

Attn: Publications Stock

333 Pfingsten Road

Northbrook, IL 60062-2096

(847) 272-8800, ext.42899

A

ABANDONED CABLES & WIRING

Abandoned Audio Distribution Cable . . . . 640.6(C)

   Definitions 640.2

Abandoned Class 2, Class 3, and PLTC Cables 725.25

   Definition 725.2

Abandoned Coaxial Cable 820.25

   Definition 820.2

Abandoned Communication Cable 800.25

   Definition 800.2

Abandoned (Data Processing) Information Technology Cables

. . . . 645.5(G)

   Definition 645.2

Abandoned Fire Alarm Cable 760.25

   Definition 760.2

Abandoned Network-Powered Broadband Communication

Systems 830.25

   Definition 830.2

Abandoned Optical Fiber Cable 770.25

   Definition 770.2

     Abandoned Premises-Powered Broadband

     Communications Systems 840.25

Circuit Conductors

   Cellular Concrete Floor Raceways 372.18

   Cellular Metal Floor Raceways 374.18

   Underfloor Raceways 390.8

Temporary Wiring . . . . 590.3(D)

ABOVEGRADE, RACEWAYS, WET LOCATIONS

1000 Volts or Less 300.9

Over 1000 Volts 300.38

AC RESISTANCE & REACTANCE . . . . . .   Chapter 9 Table 9

AC SYSTEMS

Conductor to be Grounded 250.26

Conductors of the Same Circuit . . . . 300.3(B)

   Class 1 Circuits . . . . 725.48(A)

   Underground . . . . 300.5(I)

Grounding Electrode Conductor, Size 250.66

Grounding of 250.20

Grounding Separately Derived Systems 250.30

Grounding Service-Supplied Systems 250.24

Induced Currents in Ferrous Metal Enclosures or

Ferrous Metal Raceways 300.20

ACCESS & WORKING SPACE

Boxes Behind Electric-Discharge Luminaires (Lighting Fixtures) . . . . 410.24(B)

Behind Panels Designed to Allow Access to

   Electrical Equipment 300.23

   Audio Signal Processing, Amplification and Reproduction .

   . . . . 640.5

   Cables. . . . . 300.4(C)

   CATV and Radio Distribution Systems 820.21

   Class 1, 2, and 3 Remote-Control, Signaling, and

   Power-Limited Circuits 725.21

   Communications Circuits 800.21

   Fire Alarm Systems 760.21

   Optical Fiber Cables and Raceways 770.21

   Network-Powered Broadband Communication Systems . . .

   . . . . 830.21

   Premises-Powered Broadband Communications Systems . .

   . . . . 840.21

Cable Trays . . . . 392.18(E) & (F)

Cranes and Hoists 610.57

Dedicated Space . . . . 110.26(E)

Duct Heaters 424.66

   Limited Access Working Space . . . . .110.26(A)(4)

Elevators, Dumbwaiters, etc. 620.5

Energized Parts, Service Equipment 230.62

Hydromassage Bathtub Electrical Equipment. 680.73

Manholes . . . . 110 Part V

   Access to 110.75

   Cabling Work Space 110.72

   Equipment Work Space 110.73

Metal Poles, to Supply or Cable Terminations . . . . 410.30(B)

Panels Designed to Allow Access. 300.23

Over 1000 Volts

   Entrance and Access to Work Space 110.33

   Controlled by Various Means 110.31

   Guarding to Prevent Access, Temporary Installations . 590.7

   Work Space and Guarding 110.34

   Work Space About Equipment. 110.32

Overcurrent Devices. 230.93

   Access to Occupants . . . . 230.72(C)

   Occupant to Have Ready Access. . . . . 240.24(B)

Solar Photovoltaic System Boxes 690.34

Splices and Taps

   Cellular Concrete Floor Raceways 372.56

   Cellular Metal Floor Raceways 374.56

Metal Wireways 376.56

Surface Metal Raceways 386.56

Surface Nonmetallic Raceways 388.56

Surface Metal Raceways . . . . .386.10(4)

Surface Nonmetallic Raceways . . . . .388.10(2)

Vaults and Tunnels 110.76

Wireways, Metal . . . . 376.10(4)

Nonmetallic . . . . 378.10(4)

Working Space 600 Volts, Nominal, or Less . . . . . 110.26(A)

ACCESSIBLE

Attics (Wiring in)

Armored Cable 320.23

Concealed Knob-and-Tube Wiring 394.23

Metal Clad Cable 330.23

Nonmetallic-Sheathed Cable. 334.23

Open Wiring on Insulators. 398.23

Service Entrance Cable . . . . 338.10(B)(4)(a)

Underground Feeder and Branch-Circuit Cable . .340.10(4)

Boxes Behind Electric-Discharge and LED Luminaries . . . . .
. . . . 410.24(B)

Cable Trays . . . . 392.18(E) & (F)

Conduit Bodies, Junction, Pull and Outlet Boxes 314.29

Over 1000 Volts . . . . 314.72(D)

Definition of . . . . .Art. 100 Part I

Disconnect for Cord- and Plug-Connected Appliances . 422.33

Grounding Electrode Connection . . . . 250.68(A)

HACR Receptacle Outlet 210.63

Handhole Enclosures 314.29

Handhole for Metal Poles Supporting Lighting Luminaires
(Fixtures) . . . . 410.30(B)

Intersystem Bonding Connection 250.94

Limited Access Working Space . . . . .110.26(A)(4)

Metallic Water Pipe Bonding Jumper . . . . .250.104(A)

Other Metal Piping Bonding Jumper . . . . .250.104(B)

Overcurrent Devices, Integrated Electrical Systems . . . 685.10

Raised Floors, Wiring Under . . . . 645.5(E)(1)

Sealoffs, Hazardous (Classified) Locations . . . . .501.15(C)(1)

Class II, Divisions 1 and 2 . . . . 502.15

Class I, Zones 0, 1, and 2 . . . . 505.16(D)(1)

Sign Ballasts, Transformers and Power Supplies . . . 600.21(A)

Sign Outlet . . . . .600.5(A)

Solar Photovoltaic System Overcurrent Devices . . . . 690.9(B)

Splices & Taps

Auxiliary Gutters . . . . 366.56(A)

Cable Trays — Accessible and above side rails 392.56

Strut-Type Channel Raceway 384.56

Surface Metal Raceways 386.56

Surface Nonmetallic Raceways 388.56

Wireways

Metal Wireways . . . . 376.56(A)

Nonmetallic Wireways 378.56

Structural Steel Bonding Jumper Connection . . . .250.104(C)

Supplementary Overcurrent Protection . . . . . . .422.11(F)(1)

Overcurrent Protective Devices . . . . 424.22(C)

System Grounding Connection. . . . . .250.24(A)(1)

ACCESSIBLE (READILY ACCESSIBLE)

Arc-Fault Circuit-Interrupter Protection 210.12

Definition of . . . . .Art. 100 Part I

Disconnecting Means for

Agricultural Buildings . . . . 547.9(A)(8)

Air Conditioning or Refrigeration Equipment 440.14

Information Technology Equipment Rooms 645.10

Carnival Ride and Concession . . . . 525.21(A)

Crane or Hoist Runway Conductor . . . . .610.31(1)

Electric Vehicle Charging System 625.42

Electrically Driven Irrigation Machines . . . . 675.8(B)

Electrified Truck Parking Space Supply Equipment . . . . .
. . . . 626.22(D)

Elevator, Dumbwaiters, Escalators, etc. . . . . . . 620.51(C)

Fuel Cell Systems 692.17

More Than One Building or Other Structure 225.32

Motor and Controller Disconnecting Means. 430.107

Outside Feeder Taps . . . . 240.21(B)(5)(4)

Outside Secondary Conductors . . . . .240.21(C)(4)(4)

Over 1000 Volt Service Conductors. 230.205

Permitted to be Not Readily Accessible . . . . 230.205(A)

Phase Converters . . . . .455.8(A)

Portable Switchboards 520.51

Room Air Conditioners 440.63

Service Disconnecting Means . . . . .230.70(A)(1)

Shore Power Connections . . . . 555.17(B)

Solar Photovoltaic Systems . . . . 690.13(A)

Storage Batteries . . . . 480.7(A)

Swimming Pool, Spa, Hot Tub, etc. 680.12

Emergency Switch for Spas and Hot Tubs 680.41

Wind Electric Systems . . . . .694.22(A)(1)

X-Ray Equipment, Medical . . . . 517.72(B)

    Non-Medical 660.5

Dispensing Equipment, Motor Fuel 514.11

Ground-Fault Circuit-Interrupter Protection for Personnel . .
. . . . 210.8

    GFCI for Appliances 422.5

Locked Service Overcurrent Devices 230.92

Overcurrent Devices. . . . . 240.24(A)

    Fuel Cell Systems . . . . 692.9(B)

Receptacle Outlets in Guest Rooms of Hotels and Motels . . .
. . . . 210.60(B)

Switches and Circuit Breakers . . . . 404.8(A)

Transformers and Transformer Vaults 450.13

AC-DC GENERAL USE SNAP SWITCHES

Marking. 404.20

Motor Controllers . . . . .430.83(C)(1)

Motor Disconnecting Means . . . . .430.109(C)(1)

Ratings, Type Loads 404.14

ADA STANDARDS FOR ACCESSIBLE DESIGN

ADA Accessibility . . . . .110.1 Info. Note

ADA Standards for Accessible Design . . Informative Annex J

ADJUSTABLE SPEED DRIVES

Adjustable Speed Drive (Definition of) . . . . . . Article 100

Adjustable Speed Drive System (Definition of) . . Article 100

Adjustable Speed Drive Systems . . . . Art. 430 Part X

Branch-Circuit Short-Circuit and Ground-Fault Protections

    Several Motors or Loads 430.131

    Single Motor Circuits 430.130

Bypass Circuit/Device . . . . .430.130(B)

Conductors 430.122

Disconnecting Means 430.128

Motor Overtemperature Protection 430.126

Overload Protection 430.124

ADMINISTRATION AND ENFORCEMENT . . . .
. . . . **Informative Annex H**

AERIAL CABLE

CATV and Radio Distribution Systems 820.44

Coaxial Cables 840.46

Communication Wires and Cables. 840.45

Identification . . . . 200.6(A)(8)

Instrumentation Tray Cable . . . . 727.4(6)

Messenger Supported Wiring . . . . Art. 396

Network-Powered Broadband Communications Systems . . .
. . . . 830.44

Nonmetallic Extensions . . . . 382.12(2)

Optical Fiber Cables 840.44

Type MC Cable . . . . 330.10(A)(8)

AFCI

    See ARC-FAULT CIRCUIT INTERRUPTERS   Ferm's Finder

AGRICULTURAL BUILDINGS . . . .**Art. 547**

Bonding. . . . . 547.10(B)

    Site-Isolating Device . . . . 547.9(A)(4)

Distribution Point, Definition 547.2

Electrical Supply

    Feeders to Two or More Buildings or Structures . . . .
. . . . Art. 225 Part II

    From Distribution Point 547.9

    Service Disconnecting Means & Overcurrent Protection at
the Building(s) or Structure(s). . . . . 547.9(B)

    Service Disconnecting Means & Overcurrent Protection at
the Distribution Point . . . . 547.9(C)

Equipment Enclosures, Boxes, Conduit Bodies, and Fittings .
. . . . 547.5(C)

Equipment Grounding Conductor . . . . 547.5(F)

Equipotential Plane 547.10

    Definition 547.2

    Where Required Indoors/Outdoors . . . . 547.10(A)

Ground-Fault Protection for Receptacles . . . . 547.5(G)

Identification — Where More Than One Distribution Point . .
. . . . 547.9(D)

Luminaires (Lighting Fixtures) 547.8

    See LUMINAIRES (LIGHTING FIXTURES) . Ferm's Finder

Marking of Site-Isolation Device . . . . 547.9(A)(10)

Motors 547.7

    See MOTORS . . . . Ferm's Finder

Physical Protection of Wiring and Equipment . . . . . 547.5(E)

Site Isolating Device . . . . 547.9(A)

    Definition 547.2

Wiring Methods 547.5

AIR-CONDITIONING & REFRIGERATING EQUIPMENT . . . . .
Art. 440

Branch-Circuit Conductors. . . . . 440 Part IV

Branch-Circuit, Short-Circuit and Ground-Fault Protection . .
. . . . 440 Part III

Note: If nameplate calls for fuses as the overcurrent protection then fuses must be used.

Conductor Ampacity & Rating 440.6

Controllers for Motor-Compressors . . . . 440 Part V

Disconnecting Means . . . . 440 Part II

    Cord Connected Room Air Conditioners 440.63

    Information Technology Equipment Rooms 645.10

Grounding and Bonding 440.9

    Cord- and Plug-Connected 250.114

    Fixed 250.110

    Fixed (Specific) 250.112

    Non-threaded fittings (EGC Required for Rooftops) . . 440.9

    Room Air Conditioners 440.61

    See GROUNDING, Fixed Equipment . . . . . Ferm's Finder

Hermetic Refrigerant Motor-Compressor, Definition . . . . . .
. . . . Art. 100

Highest Rated (Largest) Motor 440.7

Lighting Outlet Required . . . . 210.70(C)

Nameplate and Marking Requirements 440.4

    For Controllers 440.5

    Not Permitted to be Obscured by Disconnect Switch . . . . .
. . . . 440.14

Overload Protection . . . . 440 Part VI

Protection Devices 440.65

    Arc-Fault Circuit Interrupter . . . . .440.65(2)

    Heat Detecting Circuit Interrupter . . . . .440.65(3)

    Leakage-Current Detector-Interrupter . . . . . . .440.65(1)

Rated Load Current 440.2

Receptacle Required 210.63

Recreational Vehicles, Pre-Wired. . . . . 551.47(Q)

Room Air Conditioners . . . . 440 Part VII

    As a Single Motor Unit . . . . 440.62(A)

    Maximum Loads . . . . 220.18(A)

    Total Marked Rating . . . . 440.62(B)&(C)

Short-Circuit Current Rating 440.10

AIRCRAFT HANGARS . . . . Art. 513

Aircraft Electrical Systems . . . . 513.10(A)

Battery and Charging . . . . 513.10(B)

Classification of Locations 513.3

Equipment in Class I Locations 513.4

Equipment Not within Class I Locations 513.7

External Power Sources for Energizing Aircraft . . . 513.10(C)

Grounding and Bonding 513.16

Bonding in Hazardous (Classified) Locations 250.100

Class I, Division 1 and 2 . . . . 501.30

Class I, Zone 1 and 2 . . . . 505.25

Main and System Bonding Jumpers 250.28

Method of Bonding at the Service . . . . 250.92(B)

Mobile Servicing Equipment . . . . 513.10(D)

Pendants. . . . . 513.7(B)

    Class I, Division 1 Locations . . . . 501.130(A)(3)

    Class I, Division 2 Locations . . . . 501.130(B)(3)

Sealing. 513.9

Sealing and Drainage 501.15

Wiring Methods in Class I Locations 513.4

Wiring Not within Class I Locations 513.7

Wiring Under Hazardous Areas 513.8

    Raceways Embedded in or under a Concrete Floor . 513.8(A)

    Uninterrupted Raceways Embedded in or under a Concrete Floor . . . . 513.8(B)

See HAZARDOUS (CLASSIFIED) LOCATIONS . . . .
. . . . Ferm's Finder

AIR-HANDLING SPACES, PLENUM 300.22

Definition of Plenum . . . . Art. 100 Part I

AIRPORT RUNWAYS

Airfield Lighting Cables . . . . 300.37 Ex.

Minimum Cover Requirements . . . . Table 300.5

Minimum Cover Requirements Over 1000 Volts . . Table 300.50

ALARM INDICATION OR SYSTEMS

Burglar Alarm Systems . . . . Art. 725

Class 1, 2 and 3 Circuits . . . . Art. 725

    See CLASS 1, 2 & 3 REMOTE CONTROL CIRCUITS. . . .
. . . . Ferm's Finder

Common Area Branch Circuits . . . . 210.25(B)

Conductors, Separation from Electric Light and Power, Class 1, etc. 725.136

    With Optical Fiber Cables . . . . 770.133(A)

Emergency Systems 700.6

    See EMERGENCY SYSTEMS . . . . Ferm's Finder

Fire Alarm Systems . . . . Art. 760

    See FIRE ALARM SYSTEMS . . . . Ferm's Finder

Fire Pump Circuits . . . . .695.4(B)(3)(e)

Fixed Electric Heating Equipment for Pipelines and Vessels . .
. . . . 427.22

Generator Overload Indication. . . . . 445.12 Ex.

Hazardous (Classified) Locations

Class I Locations 501.150

Class II Locations 502.150

Class III Locations 503.150

Health Care Facilities . . . . 517 Part VI

Connection to Life Safety Branch . . . . 517.43(C)

Legally Required Standby Systems 701.6

Motor Circuit Over 1000 Volts . . . . 430.225(A), Ex.

Motor Orderly Shutdown 430.44

Motors and Generators, Class I, Division 1 . . . . . 501.125(A)

Optional Standby Systems 702.6

Outside Wiring of Alarm Systems 800.1

See Life Safety Code, NFPA 101 . . . . NFPA 101

See National Fire Alarm Code, NFPA 72 . . . . NFPA 72

ALTERNATE POWER SOURCE **517.2**

Critical Operations Power Systems (COPS) . . . . . 708 Part III

Direct Current Microgrids . . . . Art. 712

Emergency Systems . . . . Art. 700

Energy Storage Systems . . . . Art. 706

Legally Required Standby Systems . . . . Art. 701

Optional Standby Systems. . . . . Art. 702

Stand-Alone Systems . . . . Art. 710

ALUMINUM CONDUCTORS **310.106**

Aluminum to Copper Connections 110.14

Ampacity of 310.15

Bars in Sheet Metal Auxiliary Gutters . . . . . . 366.23(A)

CO/ALR Marking on

Receptacles . . . . 406.3(C)

Snap Switches . . . . 404.14(C)

Dimensions of

Conductors . . . . Chapter 9 Table 8

Compact Conductors . . . . Chapter 9 Table 5A

See Aluminum Conductor Dimension, Compact. . . . . .
Ferm's Charts and Formulas

Insulated Conductors . . . . Chapter 9 Table 5

Dwelling Service and Feeder . . . . 310.15(B)(7)

See Dwelling Unit Services . . . . Ferm's Charts and Formulas

Minimum Size and Rating

Outside Branch Circuits and Feeders, Overhead Spans . . .
. . . . 225.6(A)

Overhead Service Conductors . . . . 230.23(B)

Underground Service Conductors . . . . 230.31(B)

Oxide Inhibitor on Aluminum Terminations

Where Required by Listing . . . . 110.3(B)

Where Used 110.14

See (ZMVV) . . . . *UL Product Spec*

See (DVYW) . . . . *UL Product Spec*

Properties of . . . . Chapter 9 Table 8

Restrictions Where Used as Grounding Electrode Conductor .
. . . . 250.64(A)

Terminals, Identified for . . . . 110.14(A)

ALUMINUM CONDUIT AND FITTINGS

Fittings and Enclosures with

Corrosive Environments . . . . 358.10(B)

Dissimilar metals 358.14

Intermediate Metal Conduit 342.14

Steel Rigid Metal Conduit 344.14

Installation in Concrete or in Contact with Earth

See (DYWV) . . . . *UL Product Spec*

Protection against Corrosion . . . . 300.6(B)

Suitable for Installation Condition . . . . 344.10(B)

ALUMINUM DUST

Class II, Group E . . . . 500.6(B)(1)

Class II Locations . . . . Art. 502

ALUMINUM SIDING, GROUNDING OF . . **250.116 Info. Note**

AMBIENT TEMPERATURE . . . **310.15(A)(3) Info. Note No. 1**

Correction Factors for Conductor Ampacities 0-2000 volts

Calculation. . . . . .310.15(B)(2)

Table . . . . .Tables 310.15(B)(2)(a) & (b)

Correction Factors for Conductor Ampacities 2001 to
35,000 volts

Calculation. . . . . 310.60(B)(4)

Table . . . . Table 310.60(C)(4)

Correction Factors for Raceways and Cables Exposed to

Sunlight on or Above Rooftops . . . . .Table 310.15(B)(3)(c)

Electrical Nonmetallic Tubing, Uses Not Permitted . 362.12(3)

High Density Polyethylene Conduit, Type HDPE, Uses Not
Permitted . . . . .353.12(4)

Liquidtight Flexible Metal Conduit, Uses Not Permitted . . . .
. . . . .350.12(2)

Liquidtight Flexible Nonmetallic Conduit, Uses Not Permitted
. . . . .356.12(2)

Nonmetallic Auxiliary Gutters, Indoor and Outdoor 366.10(B)

Other Space Used for Environmental Air . . . . .300.22(C)(3)

Rigid Polyvinyl Chloride Conduit: Type PVC,

Uses Not Permitted . . . . 352.12(D)

Reinforced Thermosetting Resin Conduit: Type RTRC

    Uses Not Permitted . . . . 355.12(D)

Solar Photovoltaic Circuit Requirements . . . . . . .690.7 & 8

Surface Nonmetallic Raceways, Uses Not Permitted . .388.12(6)

AMBULATORY HEALTH CARE OCCUPANCY 517.2

Essential Electrical System 517.45

AMPACITY, DEFINED . . . . **Art. 100**

AMPACITY OF

Aluminum Conductors, Allowable. . . . .

    . . . . Tables 310.15(B)(16) through (B)(21)

Aluminum Conductors, Allowable, 2001 to 35000 Volts . . . .

    . . . . Tables 310.60(C)(68) through (C)(86) (even numbered)

Armored Cable. 320.80

Bare or Covered Conductors . . . . .310.15(B)(4)

Bus Bars and Conductors in Auxiliary Gutters 366.23

Cable (in Cable Tray)

    2000 Volts or Less . . . . 392.80(A)

    2001 Volts or Over – Type MC and Type MV . . . 392.80(B)

    Power and Control Tray Cable. 336.80

    Type MC Cable 330.80

Cablebus 370.20

Conductors for Individual Dwelling Unit or Mobile Home . . .

    . . . . .310.15(B)(7)

Continuous Load at 125 Percent

    Branch Circuit. . . . . 210.19(A)(1)(a)

    Feeders .215.2(A)(1)(a)

    Services. .230.42(A)(1)

Copper Conductors, Allowable . . . .

    . . . . Tables 310.15(B)(16) through (B)(21)

Copper Conductors, Allowable, 2001 to 35000 Volts. . . . . . .

Tables 310.60(C)(67) through (C)(85) (odd numbered)

Crane & Hoist Conductors . . . . Table 610.14(A)

Derating Allowable Ampacity

    Ambient Temperature Correction Factors . . . .

    . . . . .Tables 310.15(B)(2)(a) & (b)

    Flexible Cords and Cables . . . . 400.5(A)

    Grounding or Bonding Conductor . . . . . . .310.15(B)(6)

    Neutral Conductor . . . . .310.15(B)(5)

    Nonmetallic Sheathed Cable 334.80

    Number of Conductors. . . . . 310.15(B)(3)(a)

    Solar Photovoltaic Systems . . . . 690.31(E)

    Wiring above Heated Ceilings

        Electric Space-Heating Cables 424.36

Electric Radiant Heating Panels and Heating Panel Sets. . .

    . . . . 424.94

    Wiring in Walls . . . . 424.95(B)

Determination of 310.15

    2001 to 35,000 Volts. 310.60

Feeder to Dwelling Unit . . . . .310.15(B)(7)

    See Allowable Ampacity Tables of 0 to 2000 Volts . . .*Ferm's Charts and Formulas*

Feeder to Mobile Home . . . . .310.15(B)(7)

    Allowable Demand Factors 550.31

    Capacity and Rating. . . . . 550.33(B)

    See DEMAND FACTORS . . . . Ferm's Finder

Fire Alarm (NPLFA) Circuits. 760.43

Fire Alarm (NPLFA) Circuit Conductors . . . . 760.49(A)

    NPLFA Conductors (Allowable) 18 AWG & 16 AWG . . . .

    . . . . .Table 402.5

        Larger than 16 AWG. 310.15

    NPLFA Circuits and Class 1 Circuits in Same Raceway . . .

    . . . . 760.51(A)

    NPLFA and Power-Supply Conductors in Same Raceway . .

    . . . . 760.51(B)

(Fixture) Luminaire Wire . . . . Table 402.5

Flexible Cords and Cables (Adjustment Factors) 400.5

    Flexible Cords and Cables (Allowable) . . . Table 400.5(A)(1)

    Types SC, SCE, SCT, PPE, G, G-GC, and W . . . .

    . . . . .Table 400.5(A)(2)

Fuel Cell Systems

    Conductors . . . . 692.8(B)

    Grounded or Neutral Conductor . . . . 692.8(C)

Generator Conductors to First Overcurrent Device . . . 445.13

High Voltage Conductors, 2001 to 35, 000 Volts . . . 310.60(B)

Integrated Gas Spacer Cable 326.80

Machine Tool Wire . . . . .310.15(A)(1) IN 2

    See *Electrical Standard for Industrial Machinery, NFPA 79* . .

    . . . . NFPA 79

Metal-Clad Cable. 330.80

    Allowable, 14 AWG and Larger, 0 through 2000 Volts . . . .

    . . . . 310.15

    Allowable, 14 AWG and Larger, 2001 to 35,000 Volts . . . .

    . . . . 310.60

    Allowable, 18 AWG and 16 AWG 402.5

    Installed in Cable Tray . . . . 330.80(A)

    Single Conductors Grouped Together . . . . 330.80(B)

Mineral-Insulated Cable, Metal-Sheathed Cable 332.80

    Installed in Cable Tray . . . . 332.80(A)

Single Conductors Grouped Together . . . . . . 332.80(B)

Mobile Home (Service or Feeder) . . 215.2(A)(4), 310.15(B)(7)

Modifications to Tables 310.15(B)(16) through 310.15(B)(21) . . . . 310.15(B)(1)–(7)

Modifications to Tables 310.60(C)(67) through 310.60(C)(86) 310.60

Nonmetallic Sheathed Cable 334.80

Overhead Service Conductors . . . . 230.23(A)

Single Insulated Conductors in Free Air 60 to 90°C . . . . .Table 310.15(B)(17)

Single Insulated Conductors in Free Air 150 to 250°C . . . . .Table 310.15(B)(19)

Service-Entrance Cable: Types SE . . . . .338.10(B)(4)

Solar Photovoltaic System . . . . 690.9(B)

Flexible Cords and Cables . . . . 690.31(E)

Tray Cable . . . . 392.80(A)

Power and Control Tray Cable 336.80

Type MV and Type MC Cables (2001 Volts or Over) . . . . 392.80(B)

Underground Feeder and Branch-Circuit Cable (Type UF) 340.80

AMERICANS WITH DISABILITY ACT
ADA Accessibility . . . . .110.1 Info. Note

ADA Standards for Accessible Design . . Informative Annex J

AMMONIA
Hazardous (Classified) Locations

Class and Division

Class I, Group D . . . . 500.6(A)(4) Info Note 2

Refrigerant Machinery Rooms . . . . 500.5(A)

Zones

Group IIA . . . . 505.6(C)

Refrigerant Machinery Rooms. . . . . 505.5(A)

AMPACITY CALCULATION APPLICATION INFORMATION . .
. . . . **INFORMATIVE ANNEX B**

ANESTHETIZING LOCATIONS, INHALATION . . .517 Part IV
Battery-Powered Lighting Units . . . . 517.63(A)

ANNEXES *See* **Informative Annexes** . . . . Ferm's Finder

ANTENNA DISCHARGE UNITS
Receiving Stations 810.20

Transmitting Stations 810.57

ANTENNA SYSTEMS, RADIO & TELEVISION . . . . . .Art. 810
Grounding Devices to be Listed, Where Required 810.7

Lead-In Protectors 810.6

Used in Audio Systems . . . . 640.3(K)

APPLICATOR, DEFINED. 665.2

APPLIANCES . . . . .Art. 422
Attachment Fitting. 422.33

Branch Circuit Installation . . . . 422 Part II

See CALCULATIONS . . . . Ferm's Finder

Branch Circuit Ratings 422.10

Branch Circuits Required 210.11

Ceiling Fans. 422.18

Central Vacuum Outlet Assemblies 422.15

Cord- and Plug-connected Appliances Subject to Immersion 422.41

Cord Connected 422.16

Disconnecting Means . . . . 422 Part III

Cord- and Plug-Connected Appliances. 422.33

Motor-Driven Appliances . . . . 422.31(C)

Permanently Connected Appliances 422.31

Electric Drinking Fountains (water coolers) . . . . . 440.3(C)

Ground-Fault Circuit-Requirement

Accessibility (Readily Accessible) 422.5

Drinking water coolers . . . . 422.5(A)(2)

High-Pressure Spray Washers . . . . 422.5(A)(3)

Tire Inflation (For Public Use). . . . . 422.5(A)(4)

Type. . . . . 422.5(B)

Vacuum Machines (Automotive For Public Use) . . . . 422.5(A)(1)

Vending Machines . . . . 422.5(A)(5)

Grounding of . . . . 250 Part VI

Cord Connected Equipment. 250.114

Fixed Equipment – General 250.110

Fixed Equipment – Specific 250.112

Mobile Homes 550.16

Park Trailers . . . . 552.56(F)

Ranges & Dryers 250.140

Recreational Vehicles . . . . 551.55(F)

Household Cooking Used in Instructional Programs . . . . 220.14(B)

Installation of . . . . 422 Part II

Listing 422.6

Load Calculations . . . . Art. 220

See CALCULATIONS . . . . Ferm's Finder

Commercial Cooking Equipment 220.56

Demand Factors (Four or More) 220.53

Dryers (Clothes). 220.54

Electric Heat 220.51

Laundry Load . . . . 220.52(B)

New Restaurants. 220.88

Ranges 220.55

Small Appliance (Dwellings) . . . . 220.52(A)

Marking . . . . 422 Part V

Mobile Homes 550.14

Overcurrent Protection of 422.11

48 Ampere Maximum Load . . . . 422.11(F)

Park Trailer 552.58

Polarity in Cord- and Plug-Connected Appliances . . . 422.40

Recreational Vehicles 551.57

Vending Machines . . . . 440.3(C)

APPROVED **90.4**

Approval 110.2

Definition of . . . . Art. 100 Part I

Examination of Equipment for Safety 90.7

Installation and Use . . . . 110.3(B)

Labeled, Definition of . . . . Art. 100 Part I

Listed, Definition of . . . . Art. 100 Part I

ARC ENERGY REDUCTION

Documentation. . . . . 240.87(A)

Fuses. 240.67

How it Operates . . . . 240.87(B) Info Note 2

Method to Reduce Clearing Time . . . . 240.87(B)

ARC WELDERS . . . .**Art. 630 Part II**

See WELDERS, Electric . . . . Ferm's Finder

ARCS & ARCING PARTS **110.18**

Aircraft Hangers . . . . 513.7(C)

Arcing or Suddenly Moving Parts 240.41

Arc Lamps 520.61

Portable Arc Lamps 530.17

Bulk Storage Plants. . . . . 515.7(B)

Commercial Garages . . . . .511.7(B)(1)(a)

Conduit Seals, Class I Divisions 1 & 2 . . . . .501.15(C)(5)

Health Care Facilities . . . . .517.61(B)(2)

Motion Picture Projectors. . . . . 540.11(A)

Motors. 430.14(B)

Spray Application, Dipping and Coating . . . . 516.7(B)

ARC-FAULT CIRCUIT INTERRUPTERS **210.12**

Branch Circuit Extensions and Modifications, Dwelling Units . . . . 210.12(D)

Combination Type . . . . 210.12(A)

Definition of . . . . Art. 100

Direct Current 690.11

Dormitory Units . . . . 210.12(B)

Dwelling Units . . . . 210.12(A)

Branch Circuit Extensions or Modifications . . . . 210.12(D)

Outlets and Devices (supplying). 210.12

Extensions and Modifications . . . . 210.12(D)

Guest Rooms and Guest Suites . . . . 210.12(C)

Mobile Homes and Manufactured Homes. . . . . . 550.25(B)

NPLFA Circuit Power Source Requirements . . . . 760.41(B)

Outlet Type Device . . . . 210.12(A)

PLFA Circuits, Power Sources for . . . . .760.121(B)

Readily Accessible Location 210.12

Receptacles

Branch Circuit Protections. . . . . 406.4(D)(4)

Dormitory Units . . . . 210.12(B)

Dwelling Units . . . . 210.12(A)

Extensions and Modifications . . . . 210.12(B)

Replacement . . . . 406.4(D)

Readily Accessible Location . . . . 406.4(D)

Replacement Impracticable . . . . 406.4(D)(3)Ex.

Room Air Conditioners 440.65

Solar Photovoltaic Systems (Direct Current) 690.11

ARC FLASH HAZARD WARNING **110.16**

ARC LAMPS, PORTABLE **530.17**

AREA IN CIRCULAR MILLS OF CONDUCTORS . . . .**Chapter 9 Table 8**

AREA IN SQUARE INCHES

Auxiliary Gutters 366.22

Cable Trays 392.22

Compact Copper and Aluminum Conductors . . . . Chapter 9 Table 5A

Concentric Conductors . . . . Chapter 9 Table 5

Conduit Fill Tables

See Compact Copper and Aluminum . . . .

A

. . . . *Ferm's Charts and Formulas*

See Conduit and Tubing . . . . *Ferm's Charts and Formulas*

See Dwelling Services . . . . . *Ferm's Charts and Formulas*

See Equipment Ground, with . . *Ferm's Charts and Formulas*

For Conductors of the Same Size . . . Informative Annex C

Percent of Cross Section . . . . Chapter 9 Table 1

Conduit or Tubing . . . . Chapter 9 Table 4

Strut-Type Channel Raceway 384.22

Wireways, Metal . . . . 376.22(A)

Wireways, Nonmetallic 378.22

ARENAS

Emergency Systems . . . . 700.2 IN

Places of Assembly . . . . Art. 518

Theaters, Audience Areas, Performance Areas, etc. . . . Art. 520

ARMORED CABLE, TYPE AC . . . . Art. 320

Bending Radius 320.24

Boxes and Fittings 320.40

Equipment Grounding Conductor 320.108

Exposed Work 320.15

Grounding 320.108

In Accessible Attics 320.23

Listing Requirements 320.6

Protection against Physical Damage 300.4

Exposed Work 320.15

Through or Parallel to Framing Members 320.17

Securing and Support of 320.30

Uses Not Permitted 320.12

Uses Permitted 320.10

See (AWEZ) . . . .*UL Product Spec*

ARMORIES . . . . .518.2(A)

General Lighting Load . . . . Table 220.12

Wiring Methods 518.4

ARRAY, SOLAR PHOTOVOLTAIC SYSTEMS 690.2

Installation and Service . . . . Art. 690

ARRESTERS, SURGE — OVER 1000 VOLTS . . . . Art. 280

Bonding and Grounding at Mobile Homes 820.106

Communications Circuits . . . . 800 Part III

Network-Powered Broadband Communications Systems . . . .
. . . . 830.90

Premises-Powered Broadband Communications Systems . . . .
. . . . 840.90

Surge Protection, Class I Locations 501.35

Surge Protection, Class II Locations 502.35

See (VZQK) . . . .*UL Product Spec*

ARTICLES AND PARTS IN *NEC*

Arrangement of .90.3

Listing of (Front of *National Electrical Code*) . . . . . .Contents

ASKAREL

Definition of . . . . .Art. 100 Part I

Transformers 450.25

ASSEMBLY HALLS .518.2(A)

General Lighting Load . . . . Table 220.12

Temporary Wiring 518.3

Wiring Methods 518.4

ASSEMBLY TYPE CORD, LISTED . . . . 400.10(A)(11)

ASSURED EQUIPMENT GROUNDING CONDUCTOR
PROGRAM . . . . .590.6(B)(3)

ATTACHMENT PLUGS (CAPS)

Class I Locations 501.145

Class II Locations 502.145

Class III Locations 503.145

Definition of . . . . Art. 100

Grounding-Pole Identification . . . . 406.10(B)

Grounding Requirements on Flexible Cord 400.24

Grounding Type 406.9

Listing and Marking 406.7

Polarized Terminal Identification . . . . 200.10(B)

Where Required on Flexible Cords . . . . 400.10(B)

ATTICS

Access to Working Space . . . . 110.33(B)

Armored Cable in 320.23

Knob-and-Tube Wiring in 394.23

Lighting Outlet

All Occupancies . . . . 210.70(C)

Dwelling Units . . . . .210.70(A)(3)

Metal Clad Cable in 330.23

Nonmetallic Sheathed Cable in 334.23

Open Wiring in 398.23

Service Entrance Cable . . . . 338.10(B)(4)(a)

Sign Transformers in . . . . 600.21(E)

AUDIO SIGNAL PROCESSING, AMPLIFICATION, AND REPRODUCING EQUIPMENT . . . . **Art. 640**

Access to Equipment Behind Access Points 640.5

Abandoned Audio Distribution Cables . . . . 640.6(C)

Audio Systems Near Bodies of Water 640.10

Combination Systems (with Fire Alarm Systems) . . . 640.3(J)

Covered by Article . . . . 640.1(A)

Definitions 640.2

Flexible Cords and Cables

    Permanent Installations 640.21

    Temporary Installations 640.42

Grounding 640.7

    Isolated Ground Receptacles . . . . 640.7(C)

    Separately Derived Systems, 60 Volts to Ground . . 640.7(B)

Grouping of Conductors 640.8

Mechanical Execution of Work 640.6

Near Bodies of Water 640.10

Neat and Workmanlike Manner . . . . 640.6(A)

    Distribution Cables . . . . 640.6(B)

    Identified for Future Use . . . . 640.6(D)

Not Covered by Article . . . . 640.1(B)

Other Articles 640.3

Output Wiring and Listing of Amplifiers . . . . 640.9(C)

Permanent Installations . . . . 640 Part II

    Conduit or Tubing 640.23

    Loudspeakers, in Fire Resistance-Rated Walls, etc. . . 640.25

    Use of Flexible Cords and Cables 640.21

    Wireways, Gutters, and Auxiliary Gutters 640.24

    Wiring of Equipment Racks 640.22

Portable and Temporary Installations . . . . 640 Part III

    Environmental Protection of Equipment 640.44

    Equipment Access 640.46

    Multipole Branch-Circuit Cables Connectors 640.41

    Protection of Wiring 640.45

    Use of Flexible Cords and Cables 640.42

    Wiring of Equipment Racks 640.43

Protection of Equipment 640.4

Use of Audio Transformers and Autotransformers . . 640.9(D)

Wiring Methods 640.9

AUDITORIUMS **518.2**

General Lighting Load . . . . Table 220.12

Wiring Methods 518.4

AUTOMATIC, DEFINED . . . . **Art. 100**

AUTOMOTIVE

Tire Inflation Machines (For Public Use) . . . . . . 422.5(A)(4)

Vacuum Machines (For Public Use) . . . . 422.5(A)(1)

AUTOTRANSFORMERS **450.4**

Audio Systems . . . . 640.9(D)

Ballast for Lighting Units 410.138

Branch Circuits 210.9

Feeders 215.11

Grounding 3-Phase, 3-Wire Systems 450.5

Motor Starting . . . . 430.82(B)

Motor Disconnecting Means . . . . 430.109(D)

Not Permitted

    Park Trailers . . . . 552.20(E)

    Recreational Vehicles . . . . 551.20(E)

Overcurrent, Protection of . . . . 450.4(A)

See BALLASTS . . . . Ferm's Finder

AUXILIARY GROUNDING ELECTRODES **250.54**

AUXILIARY GUTTERS . . . . **Art. 366**

Audio Systems 640.24

Clearance, Bare Live Parts . . . . 366.100(E)

Conductors of the Same Circuit . . . . 300.3(B)(4)

Corrosion Protection 300.6

Definition

    Metallic Auxiliary Gutter 366.2

    Non-Metallic Auxiliary Gutter 366.2

Deflection of Conductors . . . . 366.58(A)

Grounding 366.60

Nonmetallic

    Ampacity of Conductors . . . . 366.23(B)

    Indoor Use . . . . 366.10(B)(2)

    Number of Conductors . . . . 366.22(B)

    Outdoor Use . . . . 366.10(B)(1)

    Securing and Supporting . . . . 366.30(B)

Sheet Metal

    Ampacity of Conductors . . . . 366.23(A)

    Indoor and Outdoor Use . . . . 366.10(A)(1)

    Number of Conductors . . . . 366.22(A)

    Securing and Supporting . . . . 366.30(A)

    Wet Locations . . . . 366.10(A)(2)

Splices and Taps 366.56

Used as Pull Boxes . . . . 366.58(B)

Wire Bending Space . . . . 366.58(A)

B

Available Fault Current 110.24

   Emergency Systems 700.4

   Industrial Control Panel 409.22

   Irrigation Machines 670.5

   Legally Required Standby Systems 701.4

   Modular Data Centers 646.7

   Series Ratings, Breakers 240.86

   Surge Protective Devices 285.6

   Transfer Equipment 702.5

AVAILABLE FAULT CURRENT 110.24

   Emergency Systems 700.4

   Field Marking . . . . 110.24(A)

   Industrial Control Panel 409.22

   Interconnected Electric Power Production Sources . . . .

   . . . . 705.12(B)(2)(e)

   Irrigation Machines 670.5

   Label

      Arc-Flash Hazard Warning 110.16

      Service Equipment 110.24

   Legally Required Standby Systems 701.4

   Modifications . . . . 110.24(B)

   Modular Data Centers 646.7

   Motor Control Centers 430.99

   Series Ratings, Breakers 240.86

   Surge Protective Devices 285.76

   Transfer Equipment 702.5

B

BACK-FED OVERCURRENT DEVICES

   Equipment Over 1000 Volts, Nominal 490.25

   In Panelboards . . . . 408.36(D)

   Interconnected Electric Power Production Sources . . . .

   . . . . 705.12(B)(2)(3)(b)

   Stand Alone Systems . . . . 710.15(E)

BACK-FED DUE TO LOSS OF PRIMARY SOURCE OF POWER

   Electric Vehicle Charging Systems 625.46

   Electrified Truck Parking Places 626.26

BACKFILL . . . . 300.5(F)

   Underground Conductors, Over 1000 Volts . . . . . 300.50(E)

BALCONIES, DECKS, AND PORCHES RECEPTACLE OUTLETS REQUIRED . . . . 210.52(E)(3)

BALLASTS

   Calculations of Load . . . . 220.18(B)

   Conductors within 75 mm (3 in.) of a Ballast Must Be

   Rated Not Lower Than 90°C 410.68

   Electric-Discharge Lighting Systems 1000 Volts or less 410 Part XII

      Disconnecting Means for . . . . .410.130(G)

   Electric-Discharge Lighting Systems

      More than 1000 Volts . . . . 410 Part XIII

   Luminaire (Fixture) Mounted on Fiberboard . . . . .410.136(B)

   High-Intensity Discharge Luminaires (Fixtures) . . .410.130(F)

   Sign Ballasts Listed and Thermal Protection 600.22

   Sign Ballasts, Locations 600.21

   Thermal Protection of Fluorescent Luminaires (Fixtures) . . . .

   . . . . .410.130(E)

   Wired Luminaire (Fixture) Sections . . . . 410.137(C)

   See LUMINAIRES, Ballast Type . . . . Ferm's Finder

BARE CONDUCTOR

   Ampacity . . . . .310.15(B)(4)

   Auxiliary Gutters . . . . 366.56(B)

   Basic Requirement . . . . 310.106(D)

   Contact Conductors, Permitted . . . . 610.13(B)

      Installation, Cranes and Hoists . . . . 610 Part III

   Definition of . . . . Art. 100

   Dimensions . . . . Chapter 9 Table 8

   Lighting Systems Operating at 30 Volts or Less . . . . 411.6(C)

   Service Entrance, Types SE, USE 338.100

   Service-Entrance Conductors . . . . 230.41 Ex.

   Underground Service Conductors, Grounded Conductor . . .

   . . . . 230.30(A)Ex.

BARE LIVE PARTS

   Auxiliary Gutters . . . . .366.100(E)

   Cabinets, Cutout Boxes, etc. . . . . .312.11(A)(3)

   Clearances .110.26(A)(1)

   Guarding 110.27

      Over 1000 Volts 110.34

   Guarding, within Compartments 490.32

   Guarding, within Compartments, Low Voltage 490.33

   Minimum Space Separation 490.24

   Switchboards or Panelboards 408.56

BARE NEUTRAL (Permitted) . . . . **310.106(D)**

Over 1000 Volts . . . . 250.184(A) Ex. 1 & 2

   Grounded Neutral Conductor . . . . 250.184(A) Ex. 3

Overhead Service Conductors . . . . 230.22 Ex.

Service-Entrance Conductors . . . . 230.41 Ex.

Underground Service Conductors . . . . 230.30(A) Ex.

BARRIERS

Box Volume Calculations . . . . 314.16(A)

Busways, Over 1000 Volts . . . . .368.234(B)

Cabinets, Cutout Boxes and Meter Sockets . . . . . 312.11(D)

Cable Tray, Cables Rated Over 1000 Volts . . . . .392.20(B)(2)

Emergency System Feeder Wiring . . . . .700.10(D)(1)(3)

ENT and RNC, Places of Assembly . . . . 518.4(C)

ENT, Thermal Barrier 362.10

Fire Barriers 300.21

Nonmetallic-Sheathed Cable, Thermal Barrier, Types III, IV, V Buildings . . . . .334.10(3)

Motor Control Center . . . . 430.97(A) Ex.

   Service-Entrance Motor Control Centers . . . . . 430.97(E)

Permanent Barriers in Boxes . . . . 314.28(D)

Service Conductors in Cable Trays . . . . 230.44 Ex.

Service Switchboards . . . . 408.3(A)(3) Ex.

Spas, Hot Tubs, Bonding, Indoor . . . . 680.43(D)

Spas, Hot Tubs, Receptacles, Indoor . . . . . . .680.43(A)(4)

Swimming Pool Covers, Electrically Operated . . 680.27(B)(1)

Swimming Pool Junction Boxes . . . . 680.24(A)(2)(b)

   Other Enclosures . . . . 680.24(B)(2)(b)

Swimming Pool Switching Devices . . . . 680.22(C)

Swimming Pool Receptacles . . . . 680.22(A)(53)

Transformer, Dry-Type, Not Over 112½ kVA . . . . . 450.21(A)

Transformer, Oil-Insulated Installed Outdoors 450.27

Voltage Between Adjacent Devices — Receptacles . . . 406.5(J)

Voltage Between Adjacent Devices — Switches . . . . 404.8(B)

BASEMENT

Armored Cable in 320.15

Nonmetallic Extensions Not Permitted in . . . . . . 382.12(1)

Nonmetallic Sheathed Cable in . . . . 334.15(C)

Receptacles in

   GFCI Protection Required, Unfinished . . . . . 210.8(A)(5)

   Required . . . . .210.52(G)(3)

BATHROOM(S)

Branch Circuit Required . . . . .210.11(C)(3)

Definition of . . . . .Art. 100 Part I

GFCI Protection of Receptacles

In Dwellings . . . . 210.8(A)(1)

   Other Than Dwellings . . . . 210.8(B)(1)

Lighting Outlet, Wall Switched in Dwelling . . . .210.70(A)(1)

Luminaires (Fixtures) in, ... 410.10(D)

   Mobile and Manufactured Homes . . . . 550.14(D)

Overcurrent Devices Not Permitted in . . . . 240.24(E)

Receptacles Prohibited in Bathtub and Shower Space . . . . 406.9(C)

   Mobile and Manufactured Homes . . . . 550.13(F)(1)

   Park Trailers .552.41(F)(1)

   Recreational Vehicles . . . . 551.41(C)

Receptacles Within 6 feet of Bathtub or Shower Stall, GFCI Protection . . . . 210.8(A)(9)

Requirement for Receptacle Outlets in Dwellings . . 210.52(D)

   Required in Mobile and Manufactured Homes . . . . 550.13(D)(9)

Service Equipment Not Permitted in . . . . .230.70(A)(2)

BATHTUBS

Hydromassage . . . . 680 Part VII

   Definition 680.2

Luminaires (Fixtures), Ceiling Fans . . . . 410.10(D)

   Mobile and Manufactured Homes . . . . 550.14(D)

Mobile and Manufactured Homes, Receptacle Not Permitted

   In Tub or Shower Space . . . . .550.13(F)(1)

   Recreational Vehicles Tub or Shower Space . . . . 551.41(C)

Receptacle Not Permitted in Tub or Shower Space . . . 406.9(C)

Receptacles Within 6 feet of Bathtub or Shower Stall, GFCI Protection . . . . 210.8(A)(9)

BATTERIES (Storage) . . . . **Art. 480**

Aircraft Batteries . . . . .513.10(A)(2)

Battery and Cell Terminations 480.4

Battery System (Definition) . . . . Art. 100

Commercial Garages . . . . 511.10(A)

Critical Operations Power Systems (COPS) . . . . . . 708.20(E)

   For Generator Sets . . . . .708.20(F)(4)

Diesel Engine Drives for Fire Pumps . . . . 695.12(C)

Disconnecting Means 480.6

Emergency System Power Source . . . . 700.12(A)

   For Generator Sets . . . . .700.12(B)(4)

   Maintenance . . . . 700.3(C)

Emergency System Unit Equipment . . . . 700.12(F)

B

B

Energy Storage Systems . . . . Art. 706

    Battery Interconnections 706.32

    Charge Control 706.23

    Disconnect and Overcurrent Protection 706.7

    Dwellings. 706.30(A)

    General 706.50

    Installation 706.30

  IEEE Standards . . . . 480.1 Info. Note

  Legally Required Standby System Power Source . . . 701.12(A)

    For Generator Sets . . . . .701.12(B)(5)

    Tests and Maintenance . . . . 701.3(C)

  Legally Required Standby System Unit Equipment. . 701.12(G)

  Less Than 50 Volts 720.9

  Listed 480.3

  Overcurrent Protection . . . . 240.21(H)

  Recreational Vehicles . . . . 551.30(C)

  Solar Photovoltaic Systems . . . . Figure 690.1(b)

  Ventilation

    Locations. 480.10(A)

    Electric Vehicles 625.52

  Vents (Cells) 480.10

  Wind Electric Systems . . . . Figure 694.1(b)

BELL CIRCUITS . . . . Art. 720

  Class 1, 2 & 3 Circuits . . . . Art. 725

  See Articles 501, 502, 503, for Installation within Hazardous
(Classified) Locations . . . . *Ferm's Charts and Formulas*

  See CLASS 1, 2 & 3 REMOTE CONTROL CIRCUITS . . . . .
. . . . *Ferm's Finder*

BENDING CONDUIT AND TUBING

  Electrical Metallic Tubing. 358.24

  Electrical Nonmetallic Tubing 362.24

  Flexible Metal Conduit 348.24

  Flexible Metallic Tubing, Fixed . . . . 360.24(B)

    Infrequent Flexing Use . . . . 360.24(A)

      High Density Polyethylene Conduit 353.24

  Intermediate Metal Conduit 342.24

  Liquidtight Flexible Metal Conduit 350.24

  Liquidtight Flexible Nonmetallic Conduit. 356.24

  Nonmetallic Underground Conduit with Conductors . . . . .
. . . . 354.24

  Reinforced Thermosetting Resin Conduit (Fiberglass) Type
RTRC 355.24

  Rigid Metal Conduit 344.24

  Rigid PVC Conduit 352.24

BENDING SPACE, CONDUCTORS

  Auxiliary Gutters . . . . 366.58(A)

  Bus Enclosures, Entering 408.5

  Cabinets, Cutout Boxes and Meter Sockets 312.6

  Manholes 110.74

  Motor Control Centers . . . . 430.97(C)

  Motor Controllers . . . . 430.10(B)

  Motor Terminal Housings . . . . 430.12(B)

  Over 1000 Volts 300.34

  Panelboard Construction 408.55

  Panelboards and Switchboards . . . . 408.3(G)

  Pull and Junction Boxes 314.28

    Power Distribution Blocks . . . . .314.28(E)(3)

  Switches . . . . 404.3(A)

  Switches, Construction . . . . 404 Part II

  Transformers 450.12

  Under 600 Volts . . . . 110.3(A)(3)

  Wireways

    Metal . . . . 376.23(A)

      Power Distribution Blocks . . . . 376.56(B)(3)

    Nonmetallic . . . . 378.23(A)

BENDS

  Cables, in

    Armored Cable, Type AC 320.24

    High Voltage Cable 300.34

    Integrated Gas Spacer Cable 326.24

    Metal-Clad Cable, Type MC 330.24

    Mineral-Insulated Cable, Type MI 332.24

    Nonmetallic-Sheathed Cable (Type NM) 334.24

    Power and Control Tray Cable. 336.24

    Service-Entrance Cable. 338.24

    Underground Feeder and Branch-Circuit Cable (Type UF) .
. . . . 340.24

  Number of Bends Permitted in

    Electrical Metallic Tubing 358.26

    Electrical Nonmetallic Tubing 362.26

    Flexible Metal Conduit 348.26

    High Density Polyethylene Conduit 353.26

    Integrated Gas Spacer Cable 326.26

    Intermediate Metal Conduit 342.26

    Liquidtight Flexible Metal Conduit 350.26

Liquidtight Flexible Nonmetallic Conduit 356.26

Nonmetallic Underground Conduit with Conductors 354.26

Reinforced Thermosetting Resin Conduit 355.26

Rigid Metal Conduit 344.26

Rigid PVC Conduit 352.26

BLOCK (City, Town or Village)

Definition of for Communication Circuits 800.2

Definition of for Network-Powered Broadband Circuit . . 830.2

Primary Protector Requirements Broadband Systems . . . . . .
. . . . 830.90(A)

Primary Protector Requirements Communication Circuits. . .
. . . . 800.90(A)

Underground Block Distribution. . . . . 800.47(B)

BOAT HOISTS

GFCI Protection Required, Dwelling Unit Locations . . . . . .
. . . . 210.8(C)

BOATYARDS AND MARINAS . . . . Art. 555

Branch Circuits. . . . . .555.19(A)(3)

Demand Factors 555.12

Disconnecting Means for Shore Power Connections . . 555.17

Distribution System 555.4

Electrical Connections 555.9

Electrical Datum Plane 555.9

Definition 555.2

Transformer Enclosures 555.5

Enclosures 555.10

Equipment Grounding Conductor, Type of Conductor . . . . .
. . . . 555.15(B)

Feeders and Services, Load Calculations 555.12

Floating Buildings, Covered by Code . . . . 90.2(A)(1)

Floating Buildings . . . . Art. 553

GFCI Protection 555.3

Other Than Shore Power . . . . .555.19(B)(1)

Grounding 555.15

Motor Fuel Dispensing Stations . . . .

Classification of Locations . . . . 514.3(C)

Hazardous (Classified) Locations 555.21

Portable Power Cables . . . . .555.13(B)(4)

Receptacle Location 555.19

Service Equipment Location 555.7

Shock Hazard. 555.24

Shore Power Receptacles . . . . 555.19(A)

Signage 555.24

Splices of Conductors 555.9

Transformers 555.5

Wiring Methods . . . . 555.13(A)

Installation. . . . . 555.13(B)

See Fire Protection Standard for Marinas and Boatyards,
NFPA 303 . . . . .NFPA 303

BOILERS

Branch Circuits

Electrode Type. 425.82

Resistance Type . . . . 425.72(D)

Electrode-Type, 600 Volts or Less . . . . 424 Part VIII

Electrode-Type, Over 1000 Volts . . . . 490 Part V

Fixed Industrial Process Resistance-Type Boilers. . 425 Part VI

Fixed Industrial Process Electrode-Type Boilers . . 425 Part VII

Resistance-Type . . . . 424 Part VII

Resistance-Type in ASME Stamped and Rated Vessel . . . . . .
. . . . .422.11(F)(3)

BONDING . . . . 250 Part V

Agricultural Buildings . . . . 547.10(B)

Bonding Conductors and Jumpers 250.102

Conductor Sizing Load Side 250.122

Conductor Sizing Supply Side 250.66

Definition . . . . Art. 100

Main Bonding Jumper 250.28

Other Than Service Enclosures . . . . 250.96(A)

Over 250 Volts. 250.97

Service Equipment Enclosures. 250.92

System Bonding Jumper 250.28

System Bonding Jumper . . . . .250.30(A)(1)

Supply-Side Bonding Jumper . . . . .250.30(A)(2)

Definition. 250.2

Size of on Load Side of Service . . . . 250.102(D)

Size of on Supply Side of Service. . . . . 250.102(C)

Sizing of . . . . Table 250.102(C)(1)

To Other Systems 250.94

Note: Installing supplementary equipment grounding
conductors in metal raceways is no substitute for effectively
bonding those raceways . . . . 250.96(B) IN

Cable Trays . . . . 392.60(A)

Where Permitted as Equipment Grounding Conductor . . .
. . . . .392.60(B)(4)

CATV Systems . . . . 820.100(D)

B

Bonding at Mobile Homes . . . . .820.106(B)

Communications Circuits 250.94

    Bonding of Electrodes . . . . 800.100(D)

    Bonding at Mobile Homes . . . . .800.106(B)

Concentric and Eccentric Knockouts . . . . 250.92(B)

    Over 250 Volts. 250.97

Conductor Sizing

    Line Side of Service Equipment . . . . .250.102(C)

        Installation .250.102(E)

        Minimum Size . . . . Table 250.66

    Load Side of Service Equipment . . . . 250.102(D)

        Installation .250.102(E)

        Minimum Size . . . . Table 250.122

Connections 250.8

Definition of . . . . Art. 100

Electrically Conductive Materials and Other Equipment

    Grounded Systems . . . . 250.4(A)(4)

    Ungrounded Systems . . . . 250.4(B)(3)

Electrical Equipment

    Grounded Systems . . . . 250.4(A)(3)

    Ungrounded Systems . . . . 250.4(B)(2)

Enclosures for Grounding Electrode Conductors . . 250.64(E)

Expansion Fittings 250.98

Exposed Structural Steel . . . . .250.104(C)

Flexible Metal Conduit for Service . . . . 230.43(15)

Floating Buildings 553.11

Fountains 680.53

    Signs in, ... 680.57(E)

Grounding Electrode System 250.50

Grounding Electrodes Together 250.58

    CATV Systems. . . . . 820.100(D)

    Communications Circuits . . . . 800.100(D)

    Intersystem 250.94

    Network-Powered Broadband Communications Systems . .
    . . . . 830.100(D)

    Radio and Television Equipment . . . . 810.21(J)

    Use of Strike Termination Devices 250.60

Hazardous (Classified) Locations 250.100

    Class I Locations . . . . 501.30(A)

    Class I, Zone 0, 1, and 2 Locations . . . . 505.25(A)

    Class II Locations . . . . 502.30(A)

    Class III Locations . . . . 503.30(A)

    Intrinsically Safe Systems 504.60

Health Care Facilities (Panelboard) 517.14

Critical Care (Category 1) Spaces, Equipment Grounding and
Bonding . . . . 517.19(E)

Critical Care (Category 1) Spaces, Patient Vicinity in
(Optional) . . . . 517.19(D)

Hydromassage Bathtubs. 680.74

Installed With Circuit Conductors, General . . . . . . 300.3(B)

Installed With Circuit Conductors, Underground . . . 300.5(I)

Intersystem . . . . 250.94(A)

    Communication. . . . . 800.100(B)(1),(2) and (3)

    Community Antenna Television and Radio Distribution
    Systems. . . . . 820.110(B)(1), (2) and (3)

    Network-Powered Broadband Communications Systems . .
    . . . . 830.100(B)(1),(2) and (3)

    Optical Fiber Cables . . . . 770.100(B)(1),(2) and (3)

    Radio and Television Equipment . . 810.21(F)(1),(2) and (3)

Jumper, Supply-Side 250.2

Liquidtight Flexible Metal Conduit 350.60

    Used for Service Entrance . . . . .230.43(15)

Loosely Jointed Metal Raceways 250.98

Main Bonding Jumper

    Definition . . . . Art. 100

    Installation. 250.28

    Serviced-Supplied AC Systems 250.24

    Size 250.102

Manufactured Buildings 545.11

Metal Raceways

    Enclosing Grounding Electrode Conductors. . . . 250.64(E)

    Used for Other Than Service Entrance 250.96

    Used for Service Entrance 250.92

Metallic Piping Systems

    Other Piping Systems. . . . . 250.104(B)

    Water Piping Systems . . . . 250.104(A)

        In Multiple Occupancy Buildings . . . . . .250.104(A)(2)

        In Multiple Buildings Supplied from a Feeder or Branch
        Circuit. . . . . .250.104(A)(3)

        Separately Derived Systems . . . . .250.104(D)(1)

Mobile Homes . . . . 550.16(C)

Multiple Raceways

    Load Side. . . . . 250.102(D)

    Supply Side . . . . 250.102(C)

Other Systems 250.94

    CATV and Radio Distribution Systems. . . . . . 820.100(D)

    Communications Circuits . . . . 800.100(D)

    Network-Powered Broadband Communication Systems . . .
    . . . . 830.100(D)

Radio and Television Equipment . . . . .810.21(J)

Over 250 Volts to Ground 250.97

Park Trailers 552.57

Portable and Vehicle-Mounted Generators 250.34

Premises-Powered Broadband Communications Systems

    Mobile Homes . . . . .840.106(B)

Recreational Vehicles 551.56

Separate Building 250.32

Separately Derived Systems 250.30

Service Equipment Enclosures . . . . 250.92(A)

    Common Grounding Electrode 250.58

    Concentric or Eccentric Knockouts . . . . 250.92(B)

    Equipment Bonding Jumpers . . . . 250.102(C)

    Main Bonding Jumper 250.28

    Metal Enclosures Protecting Grounding Electrode Conductor
. . . . 250.64(E)

        Installation . . . . 250.64(E)

    Switchboards and Panelboards Used for Service . . . 408.3(C)

Service Equipment

    Main Bonding Jumper 250.28

    Neutral Must Be Bonded to Service Equipment 250.24

    Size on Line Side, Calculation . . . . .250.102(C)

    Size on Line Side, Table . . . . Table 250.66

    Use of Grounded Circuit Conductor on Line Side of Mains
. . . . .250.92(B)(1)

Sizing Table . . . . .250.102(C)(1)

Solder Not Permitted in Bonding Connection(s) . . . . 250.8(B)

Spas & Hot Tubs Outdoor Locations . . . . 680.42(B)

    General Requirements 680.26

Spas and Hot Tubs Indoor Locations . . . . 680.43(D)

    Methods . . . . 680.43(E)

Swimming Pools 680.26

    Cord-Connected Equipment . . . . 680.8(B)

    Lifts, Electrically Powered 680.83

    Underwater Lighting . . . . .680.26(B)(4)

    Underwater Audio Equipment . . . . 680.27(A)

    See SWIMMING POOLS, Grounding . . . . . Ferm's Finder

System Bonding Jumper

    Definition . . . . Art. 100

    Installation 250.28

Therapeutic Pools & Tubs

    Permanently Installed Therapeutic Pools 680.61

    Therapeutic Tubs (Hydrotherapeutic Tanks) . . . .
. . . . .680.62(B) & (C)

Unions in Water Line . . . . .250.52(A)(1)

    Effective Bonding Path . . . . 250.68(B)

Water Meter or Filter . . . . 250.53(D)(1)

    Effective Bonding Path . . . . 250.68(B)

Water Pipe (Metal) . . . . 250.104(A)

    Permitted Connection Locations . . . . 250.68(C)

See GROUNDING, Separately Derived Systems . . . .
Ferm's Finder

BONDING JUMPER

Conductor or Jumper . . . . Art. 100

Connections 250.8

Electrode System . . . . .25053(C)

Equipment . . . . Art. 100

Fences 250.194

Main . . . . Art. 100

Material .250.102(A)

Piping Systems 250.104

Receptacle to Box 250.146

Service . . . . 250.92(B)

Sizing Table . . . . 250.102(C)(1)

Supply Side (Definition) 250.2

System . . . . Art. 100

BORED HOLES THROUGH STUDS, JOISTS . . . . 300.4(A)(1)

BOWLING LANES .518.2(A)
Wiring Methods 518.4

BOXES & FITTINGS . . . . .Art. 314
6 mm (¼ in.) Setback or Flush Mounting Walls and Ceilings . .
. . . . 314.20

Accessible 314.29

Accessible After Electric-Discharge and LED Luminaires
    (Fixtures) Installed . . . . 410.24(B)

Barrier . . . . 314.16(A)

Boxes at Ceiling-Suspended (Paddle) Fan Outlets . . 314.27(C)

Cables Entering Boxes 314.17

Ceiling Fan Outlet . . . . 314.27(C)

Ceiling Outlet . . . . .314.27(A)(2)

Conductors Entering Boxes 314.17

    Bushings on Intermediate Metal Conduit 342.46

    Bushings on Rigid Metal Conduit 344.46

    Bushings on Rigid Nonmetallic Conduit 352.46

    Insulated Fittings on Raceways . . . . 300.4(G)

B

Conductors Entering Cabinets, Cutout Boxes, and Meter Socket Enclosures. 312.5

    Conductors 4 AWG and Larger . . . . 300.4(G)

Conductors, Number in 314.16

Conduit Bodies, Where Required 300.15

    Splices and Taps, Electrical Metallic Tubing 358.56

    Splices and Taps, Electrical Nonmetallic Tubing. . . . 362.56

    Splices and Taps, Flexible Metal Conduit. 348.56

    Splices and Taps, Flexible Metallic Tubing 360.56

    Splices and Taps, High Density Polyethylene Conduit 353.56

    Splices and Taps, Intermediate Metal Conduit. 342.56

    Splices and Taps, Liquidtight Flexible Metal Conduit 350.56

    Splices and Taps, Liquidtight Flexible Nonmetallic Conduit 356.56

    Spices and Taps, Nonmetallic Underground Conduit With Conductors 354.56

    Splices and Taps, Type RTRC Conduit 355.56

    Splices and Taps, Rigid Metal Conduit 344.56

    Splices and Taps, Rigid PVC Conduit 352.56

Conduit Bodies 314.1

    Accessible 314.29

    Conductors Entering 314.17

    Definition . . . . Art. 100

    Number of Conductors . . . . .314.16(C)(1)

    Over 1000 Volts . . . . 314 Part IV

    Size of . . . . 314.28(A)

    Unused Openings . . . . 110.12(A)

Continuity of Metal Enclosures 250.90

    Bonding Other Enclosures. 250.96

    Class I, Divisions 1 & 2 Locations . . . . 501.30(A)

    Class I, Zone 0, 1, and 2 Locations . . . . 505.25(A)

    Class II, Divisions 1 and 2 Locations . . . . 502.30(A)

    Class III, Divisions 1 and 2 Locations. . . . . . . 503.30(A)

    Couplings and Connectors, EMT 358.42

    Couplings and Connectors, IMC 342.42

    Couplings and Connectors, RMC 344.42

    Electrical Continuity 300.10

    Hazardous Locations 250.100

    Loosely Jointed Raceways 250.98

    Mechanical Continuity 300.12

    Method of Bonding at the Service. . . . . 250.92(B)

    Over 250 Volts. 250.97

Threaded Conduit Hazardous Locations . . . . 500.8(E)(3)

Covers and Canopies 314.25

    Construction of 314.41

    Extensions from . . . . 314.22 Ex.

    For Pull and Junction Boxes . . . . 314.28(C)

    For Systems Over 1000 Volts. . . . . 314.72(E)

    Grounding of . . . . 314.25(A)

    Manholes. . . . . 110.75(D)

    Requirement For, Completed Installations 410.22

Cutout . . . . Art. 312

Drainage Opening, Field Installed 314.15

Emergency Systems, Identification . . . . 700.10(A)

Extension Rings . . . . 314.16(A)

    Surface Extensions 314.22

Fill Calculations . . . . 314.16(B)

Floor Boxes . . . . 314.27(B)

Free Length of Conductor in 300.14

Free Length of Conductor in, Electric Heat Cables . . . . 424.43(B)

Free Length of Conductor in, Deicing & Snow-Melting . . . . 426.23(A)

Free Length of Conductor in, Pipeline Heating . . . 427.18(A)

Grounding . . . . 250 Part IV

    Continuity and Attachment to Boxes 250.148

    Electrical Continuity 300.10

    Methods of Equipment Grounding . . . . 250 Part VII

    Other Than Service Enclosures 250.86

    Requirement for Grounding Metal Boxes 314.4

    Service Enclosures 250.80

Hazardous (Classified) Locations *See* Articles 500 through 517

High Voltage Systems . . . . 314 Part IV

    See OVER 1000 VOLTS, NOMINAL . . . . . Ferm's Finder

Luminaire (Lighting Fixture) or Lampholder Outlets . . . . 314.27(A)

    Ceiling Outlets . . . . .314.27(A)(2)

    Maximum Luminaire (Fixture) Weight. . . . . . . 314.27(A)

    Means of Support . . . . 410.36(A)

Metallic Boxes

    Conductors Entering . . . . 314.17(B)

    Conductor Openings . . . . 314.17(A)

    Corrosion Resistant. . . . . 314.40(A)

    Equipment Grounding Conductor Connection . . . . .250.148(A)&(C)

    Grounded 314.4

Grounding Provisions . . . . 314.40(D)

Mounting . . . . 110.13(A)

Securing Raceways or Cables to . . . . 314.17(B)

Supports 314.23

Thickness of Metal . . . . 314.40(B)

Over 1650 cm³ (100 in.³). . . . . 314.40(C)

Thickness of Metal, Cabinets and Cutout Boxes . 312.10(B)

Unused Openings . . . . 110.12(A)

Minimum Depth of Boxes 314.24

Nonmetallic Boxes

Arrangement of Grounding Conductors . . . . . 250.148(D)

Conductor Openings . . . . 314.17(A)

Mounting. . . . . 110.13(A)

Permitted. 314.3

Securing Permitted Wiring Methods to. . . . . . 314.17(C)

Support. 314.23

Provisions for Support. 314.43

Unused Openings . . . . 110.12(A)

Number of Conductors in 314.16

Required 300.15

Round Boxes (Not Always Permitted) 314.2

Separable Attachment Fittings . . . . 314.27(E)

Sizing of Outlet, Device and Pull & Junction Boxes and Conduit Bodies 314.16

Sizing of Pull and Junction Boxes 314.28

Over 1000 Volt Systems 314.71

Conductor Bending Radius 300.34

Sizing of Cabinets and Cutout Boxes. 312.6

Snap Switches and Adjacent Devices, Over 300 Volts Between . . . . 404.8(B)

Support of Ceiling-Suspended (Paddle) Fans . . . 314.27(C)

Weight Limits 314.27

Support of, General . . . . 110.13(A)

Support of Luminaires (Lighting Fixtures) . . . . 410.36(A)

Designed for . . . . 314.27(A)

Weight Limits . . . . 314.27(A)(1)&(2)

Support of, Means 314.23

Under Roof Decking. . . . . 300.4(E)

Unused Openings Boxes and Conduit Bodies . . . 314.17(A)

Unused Openings Closed, General . . . . 110.12(A)

Utilization Equipment . . . . 314.27(D)

Vertical Surface . . . . 314.27(A)(1)

Volume Required Per Conductor . . . . Table 314.16(B)

Wall or Ceiling Use 314.20

Wet Locations 314.15

Cabinets and Cutout Boxes 312.2

Corrosion Protection 300.6

Cabinets and Cutout Boxes . . . . 312.10(A)

Enclosures for Switches or Circuit Breakers 404.4

Nonmetallic Conduit Systems and Boxes 352.100

See SWIMMING POOLS, Junction Boxes Feeding. . . . . Ferm's Finder

See SWIMMING POOL, Underwater Lighting. . Ferm's Finder

BOXLESS DEVICES . . . . **300.15(E)**

Fitting Only . . . . 300.15(F)

Flat Conductor Cable 324.42

Manufactured Buildings 545.10

Mobile Homes . . . . .550.15(I) Ex.

Nonmetallic-Sheathed Cable . . . . 334.30(C)

Devices of Insulating Material . . . . 334.40(B)

Devices with Integral Enclosures . . . . 334.40(C)

Nonmetallic-Sheathed Cable Interconnector . . . . 334.40(B)

Park Trailers . . . . .552.48(I)

Component Interconnections . . . . 552.48(N)

Receptacles, Self-Contained . . . . 334.40(B)

Recreational Vehicles . . . . .551.47(J)

Component Interconnections . . . . 551.47(O)

Switches, Self-Contained . . . . 334.40(B)

BRANCH CIRCUITS . . . . **Art. 210**

Air Conditioners . . . . 440 Part IV

Room Air Conditioners 440.62

Arc-Fault Circuit-Interrupter Protection 210.12

Appliances

Installation of for Appliances . . . . 422 Part II

Number Required, Small Appliances . . . . . . .210.11(C)(1)

Outlets Served, Small Appliances . . . . 210.52(B)

Small Appliance Loads Dwellings . . . . 220.52(A)

Specific Appliances . . . . 220.14(A)

Balanced Load . . . . 210.11(B)

Bathroom Circuit Required, Dwelling Units . . . .210.11(C)(3)

Busways as . . . . 368.17(C)

Overcurrent Protection. . . . . 368.17(D)

Calculations of 220.10

See Also CALCULATIONS . . . . Ferm's Finder

Classification & Rating of 210.3

Ratings of . . . . 210 Part II

B

Color Coding

  Conductor Identification 310.110

  Equipment Grounding Conductor 250.119

  Grounded Conductor 200.6

  High-Leg 110.15

  Identification 210.5

  Intrinsically Safe Systems . . . . 504.80(C)

  Isolated Power Systems . . . . 517.160(A)(5)

  Sensitive Electronic Equipment . . . . 647.4(C)

Common Area (Branch and Dwelling Unit Branch) Circuits . .
. . . . 210.25

Conductors (Ampacity & Size) . . . . 210.19(A)

  Over 600 Volts . . . . 210.19(B)

Continuous Loads . . . . .210.19(A)(1)

  Overcurrent Protection . . . . 210.20(A)

    Individual Appliance Branch Circuit . . . . . . 422.10(A)

Critical Care (Category 1) Spaces, Health Care Facilities . . . .
. . . . 517.19(A)

Direct-Current Ungrounded Conductor Identification . . . . .
. . . . 210.5(C)(2)

Dryers, Demand Loads 220.54

Dwellings, Required in

  Bathroom Receptacle Outlets . . . . .210.11(C)(3)

  Central Heating Equipment 422.12

  General Lighting 220.12

  Laundry Equipment . . . . .210.11(C)(2)

  Minimum Number . . . . 210.11(A)

  Small Appliance . . . . 210.11(C)(1)

Electric Vehicle, For Charging Purposes 625.40

Electrified Truck Parking Space Wiring Systems 626.10

Emergency Systems

  Emergency Lighting 700.17

  Emergency Power 700.18

  Limitations on Loads Supplied 700.15

  Wiring of 700.10

Extensions (Grounding of) . . . . .250.130(C)

Fixed Electric Space Heating 424.3

  Electric Pool Water Heaters 680.10

Garage Branch Circuits . . . . .210.11(C)(4)

General Care (Category 2) Spaces, Health Care Facilities . . . .
. . . . 517.18(A)

Ground-Fault Circuit-Interrupter Protection (GFCI)

  Bathtubs, Hydromassage 680.71

  Boat Hoist . . . . 210.8(C)

Commercial Garages 511.12

Construction Sites 590.6

Definition of . . . . Art. 100

Dwellings . . . . 210.8(A)

Elevator Pits, Cartops, etc 620.85

Feeders, Protection in Lieu of Branch Circuit Protection . . .
. . . . 215.9

Fountains . . . . 680.51(A)

  Cord- and Plug-Connected Equipment . . . . . 680.56(A)

  Signs within Fountains . . . . 680.57(B)

HACR Equipment Receptacles installed Outdoors . . 210.63

HACR Equipment Receptacles installed Outdoors
(Dwellings) . . . . 210.8(A)(3)

Health Care Facilities Critical Care (Category 1) . . . 517.21

Health Care Facilities Therapeutic Pools and Tubs . . . . . .
. . . . 680.62(A)

    Receptacles within 1.83 m (6 ft) . . . . 680.62(E)

    Therapeutic Tubs . . . . 680.62(A)

Health Care Facilities Wet Locations . . . . 517.20(A)

High Pressure Spray Washers . . . . 422.5(A)(3)

Hotels 210.18

Hot Tubs Outdoors 680.44

  See SWIMMING POOLS . . . . Ferm's Finder

Hot Tubs Indoors

  Luminaires (Lighting Fixtures), Outlets, and Ceiling Fans
. . . . .680.43(B)(1)

  Receptacles for Hot Tubs . . . . .680.43(A)(3)

  Receptacles within 3.0 m (10 ft) . . . . . . .680.43(A)(2)

  Required Protection 680.44

Hydromassage Bathtub 680.71

Marinas & Boat Yards . . . . .555.19(B)(1)

Mobile Homes . . . . 550.13(B)

Mobile Home Service Equipment . . . . 550.32(E)

Other Than Dwelling Units . . . . 210.8(B)

Overcurrent Protective Device, definition . . . . . . Art. 100

Park Trailers . . . . 552.41(C)

  Pipe Heating Cable Outlet . . . . 552.41(D)(3)

Receptacle Replacement . . . . .406.4(D)(2) and (3)

Recreational Vehicles

  Shower Luminaires (Fixtures) . . . . 551.53(B)

  Specific Outlets . . . . 551.41(C)

  With One Circuit . . . . 551.40(C)

Recreational Vehicle Park 551.71

Residential Occupancies . . . . 210.8(A)

See (KCXS) . . . . .UL Product Spec

Signs (Outdoor Portable) . . . . .600.10(C)(2)

    at Fountains. . . . . 680.57(B)

Spas Indoors

    Luminaires (Lighting Fixtures), Outlets, and Ceiling Fans
    . . . . .680.43(B)(1)

    Receptacles for Spas . . . . .680.43(A)(3)

    Receptacles within 3.0 m (10 ft) . . . . . . .680.43(A)(2)

    Required Protection 680.44

Spas Outdoors 680.44

    See SWIMMING POOLS. . . . . Ferm's Finder

Swimming Pools

    Electrically Operated Pool Covers . . . . . .680.27(B)(2)

    Luminaires (Lighting Fixtures), Outlets, & Ceiling Fans .
    680.22(B)

    Motors. . . . . 680.21(C)

    Receptacles Protected . . . . 680.22(A)(1) through (A)(4)

    Separation of Conductors for Underwater Lighting from
    GFCI .680.23(F)(3)

    Storable Pool Luminaires (Lighting Fixtures)

        Over the Low Voltage Contact Limit to 150 Volts . . . .
        . . . . 680.33(B)

        Note: Open-neutral protection required by this section

    Storable Pools 680.32

    Types Permitted 680.5

    Underwater Luminaires (Fixtures) More than the Low
    Voltage Contact Limit . . . . .680.23(A)(8)

    Underwater Luminaires (Fixtures) Relamping680.23(A)(3)

    Therapeutic Pools & Tubs . . . . 680.62(A)

Identification of Circuits 110.22

    In Panelboards 408.4

Identification of Conductors

    Equipment Grounding Conductors 250.119

    Equipment Grounding Conductors, Branch Circuits . . . . .
    . . . . 210.5(B)

    General Rules 310.110

    Grounded Conductor of Branch Circuit . . . . . 210.5(A)

    Grounded Conductors 200.6

    Ungrounded Conductors, All Branch Circuit . . . 210.5(C)

Individual (Branch Circuit)

    Definition of . . . . .Art. 100 Part I

    Overcurrent Protection. 210.20

    Permissible Loads. 210.23

    Rating or Setting Motor Circuit 430.52

    Receptacle Rating . . . . .210.21(B)(1)

Required

    Central Heating Equipment 422.12

    Electric Signs . . . . 600.5(A)

    Electrode-Type Boiler Over 1000 Volts . . . . . 490.72(A)

    Elevator Car Air Conditioning and Heating . . 620.22(B)

    Elevator Car Lighting . . . . 620.22(A)

    Elevator Machine Room. . . . . 620.23(A)

    Hoistway Pit Lighting and Receptacle(s) . . . . 620.24(A)

    Hydromassage Bathtubs 680.71

    Isolated Power System, Health Care Facility . . . .
    .517.31(C)(2)

    Marinas and Boatyards Shore Power Receptacles . . . . .
    .555.19(A)(3)

    Office Furnishings . . . . 605.9(B)

    Transport Refrigerated Units (TRUs) 626.30

Isolated Power Systems, Health Care Facilities 517.160

Laundry Area (Dwellings) Required . . . . .210.11(C)(2)

    Load Calculation . . . . 220.52(B)

    Load for Electric Dryers 220.54

    Location, Appliance Receptacle within 6 Feet . . . 210.50(C)

    Not Required . . . . .210.52(F) Ex. 1&2

Maximum Loads 220.18

    Summary. 210.24

Maximum Voltage 210.6

    120 Volts Between Conductors . . . . 210.6(B)

    277 Volts to Ground. . . . . 210.6(C)

    600 Volts Between Conductors . . . . 210.6(D)

    Between Adjacent Switches and Devices . . . . . . 404.8(B)

    Elevators, etc. 620.3

    Lighting Equipment Outdoors 225.7

    Occupancy Limitations. . . . . 210.6(A)

    Over 600 Volts Between Conductors . . . . 210.6(E)

Minimum Ampacity & Size

    Appliances 422.10

    Electric Radiant Heating Panels and Sets . . . . . 424.95(B)

    Electrically Driven or Controlled Irrigation Machines . . . .
    . . . . 675.9

    Electrode-Type Boilers 424.82

    Elevators, etc. . . . . 620.12 & 13

    Fixed Electric Heating Equipment for Pipelines and Vessels
    . . . . 427.4

    Fixed Electric Space-Heating Equipment . . . . . 424.3(B)

    Fixed Outdoor Electric Deicing and Snow-Melting
    Equipment. 426.4

    Household Ranges and Cooking Appliances . .210.19(A)(3)

B

Information Technology Equipment . . . . 645.5(A)

Multi-Receptacle Circuits . . . . .210.19(A)(2)

Not Over 600 Volts . . . . .210.19(A)(1)

Other Loads . . . . .210.19(A)(4)

Over 600 Volts. . . . . 210.19(B)

X-Ray Equipment, Non-Medical . . . . 660.6(A)

Motor Circuit Conductors . . . . 430 Part II

Multioutlet Assembly, Calculations of . . . . 220.14(H)

Multioutlet Branch Circuits, Rating 210.3

Conductors .210.19(A)(2)

Outlet Devices. . . . . .210.21(B)(2) &(3)

Permissible Loads 210.23

Protection of Conductors 240.4

Summary. 210.24

Multiple Circuits 210.4

Equipment Grounding Connections 250.144

Simultaneous Disconnecting Means 210.7

Devices or Equipment . . . . 210.4(B)

Size of Equipment Grounding Conductors . . . .250.122(C)

Multiwire Branch Circuits 210.4

Definition of . . . . .Art. 100 Part I

Neutral Continuity Must Not Be Dependent

on Device Connections . . . . 300.13(B)

Simultaneous Disconnecting Means Required

(Line-to-Line Loads). . . . . 210.4(C)

Circuit Breaker as Overcurrent Device . . . . . 240.15(B)

Devices or Equipment on Same Yoke 210.7

Tapped from Grounded Systems 210.10

Not More Than One Dwelling Unit 210.25

Number of, Required 210.11

Central Heating Equipment 422.12

Calculation of Loads to Determine Number   Art. 220, Part II

Permissible Load 210.23

Number of, Supplied to More Than One Buildings. . . . 225.30

Outside . . . . Art. 225

Overhead, Over 1000 Volts . . . . 399.10(2)

See OUTSIDE BRANCH CIRCUIT & FEEDERS . . . .

. . . . Ferm's Finder

Overcurrent Protection 210.20

Outlet Devices. 210.21

Protection of Conductors 240.4

Protection of Equipment 240.3

Patient Bed Location

Critical Care (Category 1) Spaces . . . . 517.19(A)

General Care (Category 2) Spaces . . . . 517.18(A)

Permissible Loads 210.23

Computation of Loads . . . . Art. 220, Part II

Loads Evenly Proportioned . . . . 210.11(B)

Maximum Load 220.18

Outlet Devices. 210.21

Specific Circuits 210.23

Summary. 210.24

Ranges . . . . .210.19(A)(3)

Branch Circuit Rating. . . . . 422.10(A)

Computations . . . . 220.14(B)

Demand Loads, Dwelling Units 220.55

Demand Loads, Other Than Dwelling Units 220.56

Neutral Load 220.61

Rating & Classification of 210.3

Branch Circuit Ratings . . . . Art. 210, Part II

Required 210.11

See LIGHTING OUTLETS REQUIRED . . . Ferm's Finder

See RECEPTACLE, Outlets Required . . . . . Ferm's Finder

Sign Circuit . . . . 600.5(A)

Requirements General 210.11

Requirements Summary 210.24

Selection Current, Hermetic Refrigerant Motor-Compressors .

. . . . 440.4(C)

Definition . . . . Art. 100

Small Appliance (Dwelling Units) . . . . .210.11(C)(1)

Load for Calculation . . . . 220.52(A)

Outlets Served. . . . . 210.52(B)

Specific Purpose 210.2

Air Conditioning & Refrigeration 440.6

Branch Circuit Conductors, General. 440.31

Room Air Conditioners 440.62

Single Motor-Compressor. 440.32

Busways 368.17

Class 1, 2 & 3 Remote Control . . . . Art. 725

Cranes & Hoists . . . . 610 Part II

Overcurrent Protection 610.42

Deicing & Snow-Melting Equipment (Continuous Load) . .

. . . . 426.4

Dryers (Location), Receptacle Outlet Within 6 Feet 210.50(C)

Loads 220.54

Dumbwaiters . . . . Art. 620

Electric Heat (Space) 424.3

Elevators . . . . Art. 620

Escalators. . . . . Art. 620

Fire Alarms . . . . Art. 760

Heating Equipment for Pipelines and Vessels (Continuous Load) 427.4

Induction & Dielectric Heating . . . . Art. 665

Information Technology Equipment 645.5

Infrared Heating Equipment 422.48

    Branch Circuits. 424.3

Low Voltage Systems . . . . Art. 720

Low Voltage Lighting Systems 411.7

Marinas & Boatyards . . . . .555.19(A)(3)

Mobile Homes . . . . Art. 550

Motion Picture & TV Studios . . . . Art. 530

Motors . . . . 430 Part II

Moving Walks . . . . Art. 620

Office Furnishings, Fixed-Type 605.7

Office Furnishings, Freestanding-Type 605.8

Office Furnishings, Freestanding-Type Cord & Plug . . 605.9

Pipe Organs . . . . Art. 650

Ranges . . . . .210.19(A)(3)

    Demand Load 220.55

    Overcurrent Protection Branch Circuit . . . . . 422.11(B)

    Rating of Receptacle . . . . .210.21(B)(4)

Recreational Vehicles 551.42

Refrigeration (HACR) Equipment Receptacle 210.63

Signaling Systems . . . . Art. 725

    Fire Alarm Systems. . . . . Art. 760

Signs 600.5

Sound Recording Equipment . . . . Art. 640

Space Heating Equipment 424.3

Switchboards & Panelboards Instrument Circuits . . 408.52

Systems Over 1000 Volts . . . . Art. 110 Part III

    Conductors 310.60

        Outdoor Overhead Conductors. . . . . Art. 399

    Conductor Ampacity . . . . 210.19(B)

    Equipment . . . . Art. 490

    General . . . . Art. 300 Part II

    Motors. . . . . .Art. 430 Part XI

    Outside Branch Circuits. . . . . .Art. 225 Part III

Systems Under 50 Volts . . . . Art. 720

Theaters . . . . Art. 520

    Fixed Stage Equipment . . . . 520 Part III

    Fixed Stage Switchboard . . . . 520 Part II

    General 520.9

Portable Stage Equipment . . . . 520 Part V

Portable Stage Switchboard . . . . 520 Part IV

Water Heaters . . . . 422.10(A)

    Pool Heaters 680.10

    Storage-Type 422.13

Welders . . . . Art. 630

    Arc Welders (Motor and Nonmotor Generator) . . . . 630 Part II

    Resistance Welders. . . . . 630 Part III

X-Ray Equipment, Medical . . . . 517 Part V

X-Ray Equipment, Nonmedical . . . . Art. 660

    Fixed and Stationary Equipment . . . . 660.4(A)

    Over1000 Volts. . . . . 660.4(C)

    Portable, Mobile, and Transportable . . . . 660.4(B)

    Rating of Supply Conductors . . . . 660.6(A)

Specific Requirements . . . . 210 Part II

    Summary 210.24

Supplementary Overcurrent Protection 240.10

    Definition . . . . .Art 100, Part I

    Motor Control Circuits. 430.72

    Protection of Flexible Cords and Fixture Wires 240.5

Taps Permitted

    Conductor Protection. 210.20

    Conductor Protection. . . . . 240.4(E)

    Motor Circuits. . . . . 430.53(D)

    Other Loads. . . . . 210.19(A)(4) Ex. 1

    Overcurrent Protection. . . . . 240.21(A)

    Protection of Flexible Cords and Fixture Wires . . . 240.5(B)

    Ranges and Cooking Appliances . . . . . 210.19(A)(3) Ex. 1

    Temporary Installations . . . . 590.4(C)

Uses Permitted of Type SE Cable . . . . 338.10(B)

    Frames of Ranges and Clothes Dryers 250.140

Voltage Drop on . . . . 210.19(A) IN 4

    Fire Pumps. 695.7

    Not Considered for Ampacity Considerations . . . . .310.15(A)(1) IN 1

Sensitive Electronic Equipment . . . . 647.4(D)

    Cord-Connected Equipment . . . . 647.4(D)(2)

    Fixed Equipment. . . . . 647.4(D)(1)

    Utilization Equipment. . . . . 110.3(B)

Note: Manufacturers of electrical luminaires and other equipment will often specify the minimum acceptable operating voltage for their product to function correctly.

Voltage Limitations 210.6

B

B

Elevators, etc. 620.3

Water Heaters . . . . 422.10(A)

Pool Heaters 680.10

Storage-Type 422.13

BRANCH CIRCUITS & FEEDERS

Calculation of Loads . . . . Art. 220

    See CALCULATIONS . . . . Ferm's Finder

Outside Wiring . . . . Art. 225

    Attached to Buildings or Structures 225.11

    Circuit Exits and Entrances 225.11

    Clearance Overhead Conductors and Cables 225.18

        Over 1000 Volts. 225.60

    Clearance from Windows . . . . 225.19(D)(1)

    Clearance above Roofs . . . . 225.19(A)

    Clearance over Swimming Pools 680.9

    Conductor Covering 225.4

    Entering a Building or Structure 225.11

    Exiting a Building or Structure 225.11

    Minimum Size Conductor 225.5

        Festoon Lighting . . . . 225.6(B)

        Overhead Spans . . . . 225.6(A)

        Over 1000 Volts. 225.50

    More Than One Building or Other Structure . . . 225 Part II

    Open-Conductor Spacing 225.14

    Outdoor Overhead Conductors over 1000 Volts. . . Art . 399

    Point of Attachment . . . . 225.16(A)

    Vegetation Not Permitted as Means of Support 225.26

        Temporary Wiring . . . . 590.4(J)

    Wiring on Outside of Building 225.10

        In Raceways 225.22

        Installation of Types SE and USE Service Cable . . . . . . 338.10(B)(4)(b)

        Mounting Supports 230.51

        Multiconductor Cables 225.21

        Protecting Open Conductors and Cables 230.50

        Use Permitted for Service Entrance Cable. . . . 338.10(B)

    See BRANCH CIRCUITS . . . . Ferm's Finder

    See FEEDERS . . . . Ferm's Finder

BREAKERS & FUSES . . . . **Art. 240**

Accessibility 240.24

    Access to Service Disconnecting Means . . . . . . 230.72(C)

    Circuit Breakers Used as Switches . . . . 404.8(A)

Location . . . . 230.70(A)

Backfed Overcurrent Devices . . . . 408.36(D)

    Solar Photovoltaic Systems . . . . 710.15(E)

Breakers Used as Switches, Lighting Loads

    HID. . . . . 240.83(D)

    SWD . . . . 240.83(D)

Continuous Loads

    Branch Circuits . . . . 210.20(A)

    Feeders . . . . 215.2(A)(1)

    Fixed Electric Heating Equipment for Pipelines and Vessels 427.4

    Fixed Electric Space-Heating Equipment . . . . . 424.3(B)

    Fixed Outdoor Electric Deicing and Snow-Melting Equipment 426.4

    Non-Motor Operated Appliance . . . . 422.10(A)

    Pool Water Heaters 680.10

    Solar Photovoltaic Systems . . . . 690.8(B)

    Water Heaters 422.13

Definitions of Different Types . . . . Art. 100 Part I

Delta Breakers (Not Permitted) . . . . 408.36(C)

Grounded Conductor, Overcurrent Device Not in, General 240.22

    Service Equipment . . . . 230.90(B)

Identification of 110.22

    Circuits in Switchboards and Panelboards 408.4

In Parallel (Not Permitted) 240.8

Interrupting Capacity 110.9

    Cartridge Fuses & Fuse Holders . . . . 240 Part VI

    Circuit Breakers . . . . 240 Part VII

    Impedance and Other Characteristics 110.10

    See Short-Circuit Calculations Formula (Point to Point) . . . . *Ferm's Charts and Formulas*

    See Short-Circuit Current in Amperes Tables. . . . . *Ferm's Charts and Formulas*

    Series Ratings 240.86

        Selected Under Engineering Supervision, Existing Installations. . . . . 240.86(A)

Locked or Sealed 230.92

    Specific Circuit Permitted to Be Locked 230.93

Mounting Height . . . . 240.24(A)

Next Higher Size Permitted . . . . 240.4(B)

    Autotransformers . . . . 450.4(A)

    Motor Circuits. . . . . .430.52(C)(1)

    Transformers 450.3

Plug Fuses, Fuseholders, and Adapters. . . . . 240 Part V

Standard Ratings . . . . 240.6(A)

    Adjustable-Trip Circuit Breakers . . . . 240.6(B)

    Restricted Access . . . . 240.6(C)

Tie Bars (Handle Ties) Required

    Multiwire Branch Circuits Temporary Installations . . . . . .
. . . . 590.4(E)

    Multiwire Circuits, Dwelling Units . . . . 210.4(B)

    Multiwire Circuits, General 210.7

    Multiwire Circuits Other Than Line-to-Neutral Loads . . . .
. . . . 210.4(C) Ex. 2

    Permitted for Specific Line-to-Line Loads . . . . . 240.15(B)

    Service Disconnects, Not Over 1000 Volts 230.74

    Service Disconnects, Over 1000 Volts. . . . . . . 230.205(B)

    Single-Pole Units for Service Disconnects . . . . 230.71(B)

    Taps From Grounded Systems 210.10

Up Position — On 240.81

    Circuit Breakers Used as Switches 404.7

Wet Locations 240.32

    Installation of Cabinets or Cutout Boxes 312.2

    In Enclosure or Cabinet 404.4

Wire Bending Space

    At Terminals . . . . 312.6(B)

    Enclosures for Motor Circuits . . . . 430.10(B)

    Enclosures for Switches and Circuit Breakers . . . . 404.3(A)

    In an Enclosure Containing a Panelboard 408.55

    Industrial Control Panels . . . . 409.104(B)

See FUSES. . . . . Ferm's Finder

See Circuit Breakers (DHJR) . . . . *UL Product Spec*

See Fuses (JCQR) . . . . *UL Product Spec*

See OVERCURRENT PROTECTION . . . . Ferm's Finder

BTU/HR TO TONS FORMULA . . *Ferm's Charts & Information*

BTU/HR TO WATTS FORMULA . . *Ferm's Charts & Information*

BUCK AND BOOST TRANSFORMERS

Audio Systems . . . . 640.9(D)

Autotransformers 450.4

Ballast for Lighting Units 410.138

Branch Circuits 210.9

Feeders 215.11

Grounding Autotransformers 450.5

Motor Starting . . . . 430.82(B)

Overcurrent, Protection of 450.4

See AUTOTRANSFORMERS. . . . . Ferm's Finder

BULK STORAGE PLANTS . . . . **Art. 515**

Class I Locations, General . . . . 500.5(B)

Class I Locations, Specific 515.3

Conductors (Gas & Oil Resistant) 501.20

    See (ZLGR) . . . . *UL Product Spec*

Gasoline Dispensing at Bulk Stations 515.10

    *See Code for Motor Fuel Dispensing Facilities and Repair
Garages, NFPA 30A* . . . . NFPA 30A

Gasoline Dispensing General . . . . Art. 514

Grounding & Bonding. . . . . Art. 250

    Grounding Regardless of Voltage 515.16

    In Class I, Division 1 & 2 Locations 501.30

    In Class I, Zone 0, 1, & 2 Locations 505.25

    In Hazardous Locations 250.100

    Using Nonmetallic Wiring Methods . . . . 515.8(C)

Lightning Protection (Surge Arresters over 1 kV) . . . Art. 280

    *See Standard for the Installation of Lightning Protection
Systems, NFPA 780* . . . . NFPA 780

    Surge Protection. 501.35

Sealing, General 501.15

Sealing, Specific 515.9

Static Protection

    See Flammable and Combustible Liquids Code, NFPA 30 . . .
. . . . NFPA 30

Wiring Methods

    Above Class I Locations 515.7

    Class I, Division 1 & 2 Locations . . . . Art. 501

    Class I, Zone 0, 1, & 2 Locations. . . . . Art. 505

    Farms, *See Flammable and Combustible Liquids Code,
NFPA 30* . . . . NFPA 30

    Underground Wiring 515.8

        Seals 515.9

    Within Class I Locations 515.4

See HAZARDOUS (CLASSIFIED) LOCATIONS Ferm's Finder

BULL SWITCH (Definition) **530.2**

Current-Carrying Parts . . . . 530.15(D)

BURGLAR ALARMS . . . . **Art. 725**

Dwelling Units- Not GFCI Protected . . . 210.8(A)(5) Ex to (5)

Not Covered by Article 640 . . . . 640.1(B)

Outside Wiring. . . . . Art. 800

See ALARM INDICATION OR SYSTEMS . . . . Ferm's Finder

BURIED CONDUCTORS

Ampacity Calculations, 0 to 2000 Volts Under

Engineering Supervision . . . . 310.15(C)

Application Information. . . . . . . .Informative Annex B

Ampacities, 2001 to 35,000 Volts. . . . . 310.60(B)

Backfill for 1000 Volts and Above . . . . 300.50(E)

Backfill for Under 1000 Volts . . . . 300.5(F)

Bushing on Open End of Conduit . . . . 300.5(H)

Conductors of Same Circuit. . . . . 300.5(I)

Cover

   Less Than 1000 Volts . . . . Table 300.5

   1000 Volts and Above . . . . Table 300.50

Directional Boring. . . . . 300.5(K)

Earth Movement . . . . 300.5(J)

   Conductors 1000 Volts and Above . . . . 300.50(C)

Identified for Such Use . . . . 310.10(F)

   1000 Volts and Above. . . . . 300.50(A)

   1000 Volts and Above (Shielding) . . . . 310.10(E)

   See OVER 1000 VOLTS, NOMINAL . . . . . Ferm's Finder

Protection of Conductors

   Less Than 1000 Volts . . . . 300.5(D)

   1000 Volts and Above. . . . . 300.50(C)

Sealing Underground Raceways, Feeders 225.27

Sealing Underground Raceway, Services 230.8

   Sealing Underground Raceways, 1000 Volts and Above . . . . 300.50(F)

   Sealing Underground Raceways, Under 1000 Volts . . . . 300.5(G)

Splicing of, 1000 Volts and Above . . . . 300.50(D)

Splicing of, Under 1000 Volts . . . . 300.5(E)

Swimming Pools, Fountains and Similar Installations . . 680.11 . . . . and Table 300.5

UF Cable . . . . Art. 340

   See (YDUX) . . . . .UL Product Spec

Under Buildings . . . . 300.5(C)

   Service Conductors 230.6

Under Bulk Storage Plants 515.8

   Sealing 515.9

Under Swimming Pools 680.11

USE & UF. . . . . Table 310.104(A)

USE, Type. 338.2

   See (TXKT) . . . . .UL Product Spec

BUSBARS

Aboveground Wiring Method 1000 Volts and Above . . 300.37

Ampacity for Service Entrance . . . . 230.42(A)

Ampacity of Conductors, Auxiliary Gutters. .366.23(A) and (B)

Busways . . . . Art. 368

Clearance in Switchboards 408.5

Expansion and Contraction . . . . .366.100(E)

Grounding Electrode Conductor Installations . . . . .250.64(C)(2)

Mounting in Switchboards 408.3

   Rigidly Mounted 408.51

Phase Arrangement, Switchboards and Panelboards. . . . . 408.3(E)

Support and Arrangement 408.3

Support and Arrangement, Motor Control Centers . 430.97(A)

   Phase Arrangement . . . . 430.97(B)

BUSHINGS

At Boxes

   Cabinets, Cutout Boxes, and Meter Socket Enclosures . . . . 312.6(C)

   Metal Boxes or Conduit Bodies . . . . 314.17(B)

   On Armored Cable 320.40

   On Electrical Nonmetallic Tubing. 362.46

   On High Density Polyethylene Conduit 353.46

   On Intermediate Metal Conduit 342.46

   On Nonmetallic Underground Conduit with Conductors 354.46

   On Reinforced Thermosetting Resin Conduit 355.46

   On Rigid Metal Conduit 344.46

   On Rigid Polyvinyl Chloride Conduit 352.46

At Box Covers & Fittings for Flexible Cord 314.42

   Protection from Damage, Flexible Cords and Cables . 400.14

Fixed Outdoor Electric Deicing and Snow-Melting Equipment . . . . 426.22(C)

Insulating (4 AWG Conductors & Larger) . . . . . . 300.4(G)

Open End of Conduit Entering Equipment . . . . 300.16(B)

Open End of Conduit for Support . . . . 300.15(C)

Open End of Conduit Underground . . . . 300.5(H)

BUSWAYS . . . .**Art. 368**

Ampacity for Service Entrance . . . . 230.42(A)

Branches from 368.56

Definition 368.2

Disconnects . . . . 368.17(C)

Expansion Joints

   Over 1000 Volts 368.244

   Provisions for in Auxiliary Gutters 366.44

Grounding 368.60

Overcurrent Protection (General) 368.17

  Rating for Branch Circuits . . . . 368.17(D)

  Rating for Feeders. . . . . 368.17(A)

  Where Required for Reduction in Size . . . . . . 368.17(B)

  Where Used as Feeder or Branch Circuit. . . . . 368.17(C)

Over 1000 Volts, Nominal. . . . . 368 Part IV

  Aboveground Wiring Methods 300.37

  Switches 368.239

  See OVER 1000 VOLTS, NOMINAL . . . . . Ferm's Finder

  Reduction in Ampacity . . . . 368.17(B)

Sealing of, Over 1000 Volts, Nominal . . . . 368.234(A)

  Prevent Accumulation of Flammable Gases 368.238

Service-Entrance Conductors. . . . . 230.43(9)

  Permitted as Wiring Method, Over 1000 Volts. . . . .

  . . . . .230.202(B)

Support of 368.30

Terminations and Connections Over 1000 Volts 368.238

Use Permitted. 368.10

Uses Not Permitted 368.12

See (CWFT) . . . .*UL Product Spec*

"BX CABLE," *See* **Armored Cable, Type AC** . . . . **Art. 320**
See ARMORED CABLE, TYPE AC . . . . Ferm's Finder

BYPASS ISOLATION SWITCH
Critical Operations Power Systems. . . . . 708.24(B)

  Definition . . . . .Art. 100 Part I

  Emergency Systems . . . . 700.5(B)

  Legally Required Standby Systems . . . . 701.5(B)

CABINETS, CUTOUT BOXES & METER SOCKET ENCLOSURES . . . . **Art. 312**
Conductors Entering 312.5

Conductors Entering, 4 AWG and Larger . . . . 300.4(G)

Insulating Bushings . . . . 312.6(C)

Mounting of 110.13

Wet Locations 312.2

  Enclosures for Overcurrent Devices 240.32

  Enclosures for Switches and Circuit Breakers 404.4

    Flush-Mounted. . . . . 404.4(B)

    Surface-Mounted. . . . . 404.4(A)

    Tub and Shower Enclosures. . . . . 404.4(C)

Wire Bending Space . . . . 312.6(B)

  Conductor Bending Radius Over 1000 Volts. 300.34

CABLE END FITTINGS **300.16**

CABLE, ENTERING BOXES **314.17**
Entering Cabinets and Cutout Boxes . . . . 312.5(C)

  Cables 4 AWG and Larger . . . . 300.4(G)

Insulated Fittings . . . . 300.4(G)

CABLE LIMITERS . . . . **230.82(1)**
Permitted without Disconnecting Means 240.40

See (CYMT). . . . .*UL Product Spec*

CABLE MANAGEMENT SYSTEM
Electric Vehicle Supply Equipment 625.2

Electrified Truck Parking Spaces 626.2

CABLE, PHYSICAL PROTECTION
Agricultural Buildings . . . . 547.5(E)

Carnival and Amusement Rides . . . . 525.20(A)& (G)

CATV Systems 820.24

  Grounding Conductor . . . . .820.100(A)(6)

Class 1, 2, & 3 Circuits 725.24

  Safety-Control Circuits . . . . 725.31(B)

Communication Circuits 800.24

  Grounding Electrode Conductors. . . . . . . .800.100(A)(6)

Elevators, Not Required to be in Raceway. . . . . . . 620.21 Ex.

Equipment Grounding Conductors Smaller Than 6 AWG . . .

. . . . .250.120(C)

Fire Alarm Systems, Mechanical Execution of Work . . 760.24

Fire Pump Control Wiring . . . . 695.14(A)

Fire Pump Engine Controllers and Batteries 695.12

Fire Pump Power Wiring . . . . 695.6(D)

Fitting Required Cables Entering or Exiting Conduit . . . . . .

. . . . 300.15(C)

General 300.4

Grounding Electrode Conductors . . . . 250.64(B)

Network-Powered Broadband Systems 830.24

Open Wiring . . . . 398.15(C)

Optical Fiber Cables and Raceways 770.24

Service Entrance Cable . . . . .338.10(B)(4)

Service Entrance Conductors and Cables Aboveground . . . .

. . . . 230.50(B)

Service Entrance Conductors, Underground . . . . . 230.50(A)

Solar Photovoltaic Systems (PV) . . . . 690.31(E)

Temporary Locations . . . . 590.4(J)

Type AC Cable .320.12(1)

Type AC Cable Exposed Work 320.15

Type AC Cable in Accessible Attics 320.23

Type MC Cable .330.12(1)

Type MC Cable in Accessible Attics 330.23

Type MC Cable Through or Parallel to Framing Members . . .
. . . . 330.17

Type MI Cable Through or Parallel to Framing Members. . . .
. . . . 332.17

Type NM Cable Exposed Work. . . . . 334.15(B)

Type NM Cable in Accessible Attics 334.23

Type NM Cable in Crawl Space. . . . . 334.15(C)

Type NM Cable Through or Parallel to Framing Members . . .
. . . . 334.17

Type NM Cable in Unfinished Basements and Crawl Spaces . .
. . . . 334.15(C)

Under Roof Decking. . . . . 300.4(E)

Underground Installations . . . . 300.5(D)

Underground Service Lateral 230.32

Wind Electric Systems . . . . 694.30(B)

CABLE ROUTING ASSEMBLY

Defined . . . . Art. 100

CABLE, SECURING AND SUPPORTING OF

Armored Cable. 320.30

Communication Circuits 800.24

Exiting From Cable Trays . . . . 392.18(G)

In Vertical Raceways 300.19

Messenger Supported Wiring . . . . Art. 396

Metal-Clad Cable 330.30

Mineral-Insulated, Metal-Sheathed Cable 332.30

Nonmetallic-Sheathed Cable 334.30

PV Cables . . . . 690.4 & 690.31

Temporary Locations . . . . 590.4(J)

CABLE TIES AND CABLE ACCESSORIES

Armored Cable. 320.30(A)

Audio Signal Processing Cables . . . . 640.6(A)

Class 1, Class 2, and Class 3 Circuits 725.24

Communication Circuits,

   Mechanical Execution 800.24

   Plenum Rated . . . . .800.170(C)

Community Antenna Television and Radio Distribution

Systems 820.24

Electrical Nonmetallic Tubing . . . . 362.30(A)

Fire Alarm Cables . . . . 760.24(A)

Flexible Metal Conduit . . . . 348.30(A)

Liquidtight Flexible Metal Conduit 350.30

Liquidtight Flexible Nonmetallic Conduit. 356.30

Low-Voltage Suspended Ceiling Power Distribution Systems. .
. . . . 393.14(A)

Medium Voltage Cable 328.30

Metal-Clad Cable. . . . . 330.30(A)

Motion Picture and TV Studios

   Portable Wiring . . . . 530.12(B)

Multiple Circuits (Neutral Identifications) . . . . . . 200.4(B)

Nonmetallic-Sheathed Cable 334.30

Network-Powered Broadband Communications Systems . . . .
. . . . 830.24

Nonmetallic, Ducts and Plenums . . . . .300.22(C)(1)

Optical Fiber Cables 770.24

Photovoltaic Systems (Conductor Grouping) . . . .690.31(B)(2)

Signs

   Class 2 (Cables) . . . . .600.33(B)(1)

Temporary Installations (Support) . . . . 590.4(J)

CABLE TRAYS . . . . Art. 392

Above Side Rails Permitted, Splices 392.56

Accessible Splices. 392.56

Airfield Lighting Cable Tray . . . . 392.10(E)

Ampacity of Cables

   2000 Volts or Less . . . . 392.80(A)

   2001 Volts or Over . . . . 392.80(B)

Combination of Multi and Single Conductor Cables

   2000 Volts or Less . . . . .392.80(A)(3)

   2001 Volts or Over . . . . .392.80(B)(1)

Fill Calculations 392.22

   Dividers (applied to each side). . . . . 392.22(A)

Grounding and Bonding of 392.60

Installation of Cables . . . . 392.18(B)

Installation of Tray . . . . 392.18(A)

Labeling Where Service and Non-Service Conductors are
Present 230.44

Marking-Over 600 Volts . . . . 392.18(H)

   Industrial Establishments . . . . 392.18(H) Ex.

   Requirements for Marking Labels. . . . . 110.21(B)

Mixture of Multiconductor Cables

2000 Volts or Less . . . . .392.80(A)(3)

2001 Volts or Over . . . . .392.80(B)(1)

Number of Multiconductor Cables

2000 Volts or Less . . . . .392.80(A)(3)

2001 Volts or Over . . . . .392.80(B)(1)

Number of Single Conductors

2000 Volts or Less . . . . .392.80(A)(2)

2001 Volts or Over . . . . .392.80(B)(2)

Over 600 Volts in Same Cable Tray . . . . 230.44 Ex.

Power & Control Tray Cable . . . . Art. 336

Service Entrance Conductors 230.44

Single Conductors (1/0 AWG or Larger) . . . . .392.10(B)(1)

Splices Permitted 392.56

Temporary Wiring in Assembly Occupancies . . . 518.3(B) Ex.

Under 600 Volts in Same Cable Tray . . . . 230.44 Ex.

Used as Supports . . . . 392.18(G)

Uses Not Permitted 392.12

Uses Permitted 392.10

Welding Cables 630.42

CABLEBUS . . . . **Art. 370**

Ampacity 370.80

Definition of 370.2

Fittings 370.42

Grounding 370.60

Marking 370.120

Overcurrent Protection 370.23

Support . . . . 370.30(A)

Conductor . . . . 370.30(B)

Uses, Not Permitted 370.12

Uses, Permitted 370.10

CABLES

Abandoned

Abandoned Audio Distribution Cable . . . . 640.6(C)

Definition 640.2

Abandoned Class 2, Class3, and PLTC Cable 725.25

Applications 725.154

Definition 725.2

Abandoned Coaxial Cable 820.25

Applications 820.154

Definition 820.2

Abandoned Communication Cable 800.25

Applications 800.154

Definition 800.2

Abandoned Fire Alarm Cable 760.25

Applications 760.154

Definition 760.2

Abandoned Optical Fiber Cable 770.25

Applications 770.154

Definition 770.2

Circuit Conductors

Cellular Concrete Floor Raceways 372.58

Cellular Metal Floor Raceways 374.58

Temporary Wiring . . . . 590.3(D)

Under Raised Floors . . . . 645.5(G)

Aerial Entrance . . . . 820.133(B) Ex.

Lead-in Clearance . . . . 820.44(A)(4)

Aerial, Network-Powered Broadband Systems 830.44

Armored, Type AC . . . . Art. 320

Border Lights, Theater 520.44

Bundled

Definition of 520.2

Derating Required . . . . 310.15(B)(3)(a)

Cable Trays 392.10

Carnivals, Circuses, Fairs and Similar 525.20

Circuit Integrity Cables (Communications Cables) 800.179(G)

Circuit Integrity Cables, (Communications, Definition of) 800.2

Circuit Integrity Cables (Fire Alarm Cables) . . . . .760.176(F)

Circuit Integrity Cables, (Fire Alarm, Definition of) . . . 760.2

Circuit Integrity Cables (Remote Control and Signal Cables) .
. . . . .725.179(F)

Circuit Integrity Cables, (Definition of) 725.2

Class 1, 2 & 3 Remote Control and Signaling . . . . . Art. 725

Community Antenna TV & Radio Distribution Systems . . . .
. . . . Art. 820

Continuity 300.12

Electric Vehicle Charging Systems 625.17

Elevators, Not Required in Raceways . . . . 620.21 Ex.

Fire Alarm System Cables . . . . Art. 760

Flat Cable Assemblies, Type FC . . . . Art. 322

Flat Conductor, Type FCC . . . . Art. 324

Grouped 520.2

Heating, *See* HEATING CABLES . . . . Ferm's Finder

Installed Under Floor Coverings 424.45

Installed Under Roof Decking . . . . 300.4(E)

Instrumentation Tray Cable, Type ITC . . . . Art. 727

Medium Voltage Cable, Type MV . . . . Art. 328

C

Metal-Clad, Type MC . . . . Art. 330

Mineral-Insulated, Metal-Sheathed Type MI . . . . . . Art. 332

Nonmetallic Extensions . . . . Art. 382

Nonmetallic-Sheathed Cable, Types NM, NMC and NMS . . . . Art. 334

Optical Fiber . . . . Art. 770

Power and Control Tray, Type TC . . . . Art. 336

Protection Against Physical Damage 300.4

Roof Decking, Installed Under . . . . 300.4(E)

Rooftops, Sunlight and Ambient Temperature Correction . . . . 310.15(B)(3)(c)

Sealing, Hazardous (Classified) . . . . 501.15(D)&(E)

Secured . . . . 300.11(A)

Service Entrance Cable, Types SE and USE . . . . . . Art. 338

Shallow Grooves . . . . 300.4(F)

Splices in Boxes 300.15

Stage . . . . 530.18(A)

Supported from Cable Trays . . . . 392.10(A)

Through Studs, Joists, Rafters 300.4

Underground . . . . 230 Part III

General 300.5

Identified for Such Use . . . . 310.10(F)

Over 1000 Volts 300.50

Splicing Means Listed . . . . 110.14(B)

Underground Feeder and Branch-Circuit, Type UF . . Art. 340

Under Floor Coverings (Space Heating) 424.45

CALCULATIONS . . . . Art. 220

Air Conditioning Equipment . . . . Art. 440

Branch Circuit Loads . . . . Art. 440 Part IV

Ampacity Calculation Application Information . . . . Informative Annex B

Appliance Loads 210.23

Branch Circuit Computations 220.10

Branch Circuit Ratings 422.10

Dryers, Dwelling Units 220.54

Laundry Circuit, Dwellings . . . . 220.52(B)

Maximum Loads 220.18

More Than Four, Dwelling Units 220.53

Ranges, Dwelling Units 220.55

Small Appliance Loads, Dwelling Units. . . . . . . 220.52(A)

Storage-Type Water Heaters 422.13

Ballasts . . . . 220.18(B)

Commercial Kitchen Equipment 220.56

Optional Calculation New Restaurants 220.88

Continuous Loads (Definition) . . . . Art. 100 Part I

Branch-Circuit Conductors . . . . 210.19(A)(1)

Branch-Circuit Overcurrent Device . . . . 210.20(A)

Electric Vehicle Supply Equipment 625.17

Feeder Conductors . . . . 215.2(A)(1)

Feeder Overcurrent Device 215.3

Fixed Electric Space-Heating . . . . 424.3(B)

Individual Branch Circuit, Appliances . . . . . . 422.10(A)

Pool Water Heaters 680.10

Storage-Type Water Heaters 422.13

Wind Electric Systems 694.12

Cranes & Hoists . . . . 610.14(E)

Demand Factors

Appliance and Laundry Loads (Dwellings) 220.52

Four or More on Same Circuit 220.53

Permitted to Apply Table 220.42 . . . . 220.52

Commercial Cooking Equipment . . . . Table 220.56

Optional Calculation New Restaurant 220.88

Cranes and Hoists . . . . Table 610.14(E)

Dryers, Clothes (Dwellings) 220.54

Elevators 620.13

Feeder Demand Factor 620.14

Motor Circuit Conductors . . . . 430 Part II

Farm Loads

Dwelling Unit . . . . 220.102(A)

Other Than Dwelling Unit . . . . 220.102(B)

Total 220.103

Household Electric Range . . . . Table 220.55

LED . . . . 220.18(B)

Lighting Load Demand Factors . . . . Table 220.42

Marinas and Boatyards 555.12

Mobile Home Parks . . . . Table 550.31

Mobile Homes 550.18

Motors . . . . 430 Part II

Multifamily Dwellings, More Than Three Units (Optional) . . . . Table 220.84

Park Trailers 552.47

Park Trailers DC Converter Rating . . . . 552.20(B)

Receptacle Loads (Dwellings) . . . . Table 220.12

Dwelling Occupancies . . . . 220.14(J)

Included with General Lighting Loads . . . . Table 220.42

Small Appliance & Laundry Included in General Load 220.52

Receptacle Loads (Non-Dwelling) . . . . .220.14(I)

   Demand Factor Receptacles Only . . . . . . .Table 220.44

   Permitted Demand Factor with General Lighting 220.44

   Permitted To Include with General Lighting . . . . Table 220.42

   Unit Loads . . . . .Table 220.12 Note

Recreational Vehicles DC Converter Rating . . . . 551.20(B)

Recreational Vehicle Parks . . . . .Table 551.73(A)

Restaurants, New (Optional) 220.88

Schools, Service Conductors or Feeders (Optional) . . 220.86

Schools, Service Conductors or Feeders (Standard)220 Part II

See Additional Loads

   All Occupancies, Optional 220.87

   Dwellings, Optional 220.82

   Dwellings, Standard (Additions to Existing Installations) . . . . 220.16(A)

   Other Than Dwellings, Standard (Additions to Existing Installations) . . . . .220.16(B)

   See Optional Calculations . . . . 220 Part IV

Studio or Stage Set Lighting 530.19

Welders

   Arc Welders. 630.11

   Resistance Welders. 630.31

Dwelling Unit . . . . Art. 220

   Additional Loads to Existing Unit (Standard) . . . 220.16(A)

      Optional Method. 220.83

      Permitted 220.87

   Optional Method . . . . 220 Part IV

      Multifamily, Three or More Units 220.84

      Single Unit 220.82

      Two Units 220.85

   Standard Method . . . . 220 Part II

Electric Heat 220.51

   Optional Dwelling Units . . . . 220.82(C)

   Optional for Adding Loads in Existing . . . . . . 220.83(B)

   Optional, Multifamily. 220.84

   See ELECTRIC HEAT (SPACE) . . . . Ferm's Finder

Electric Vehicles . . . . Art. 625

   Other Applicable Articles . . . . Table 220.3

Elevators, Escalators, Dumbwaiters & Moving Walks 620.13

   Feeders 620.14

   Motor-Circuit Conductors . . . . 430 Part II

Motor Controller Rating 620.15

Examples . . . . Informative Annex D

Farm Loads . . . . 220 Part V

Feeders . . . . 220 Part II

   Examples. . . . . Informative Annex D

   Optional Methods. . . . . 220 Part IV

      Fractions of an Ampere . . . . 220.5(B)

Hotels 220.12

   General Lighting Demand Factors 220.42

Laundry Loads (Dwellings) . . . . 220.52(B)

   Electric Dryers. 220.54

Lighting Loads 220.12

      Permissible Demand Factors 220.42

Lighting, Track . . . . 220.43(B)

Marinas and Boatyards 555.12

Mobile Homes 550.18

Mobile Home Parks 550.31

Motels 220.12

   General Lighting Demand Permitted 220.42

Motors . . . . 430 Part II

Multifamily Dwelling (Optional Method) 220.84

Multioutlet Assemblies . . . . 220.14(H)

Neutral Feeder Load 220.61

   Adjustment Factor . . . . .310.15(B)(3)

      When Considered Current-Carrying . . . . .310.15(B)(5)

Noncoincident Loads 220.60

Ranges (Household) . . . . .210.19(A)(3)

   Branch Circuit Loads . . . . 220.14(B)

   Commercial 220.56

   Individual Circuits . . . . 422.10(A)

   Optional Calculation New Restaurants 220.88

   Permissible Demands (Dwelling Units) 220.55

   Receptacles . . . . .210.21(B)(4)

Receptacle Outlets

   Dwelling Units . . . . .220.14(J)

   Nondwelling Units . . . . .220.14(I)

      Demand Factor Permitted. 220.44

      See Note [b] Under Table 220.12 . . . . 220.14(K)

Recreational Vehicle Parks 551.73

Recreational Vehicles 551.42

Schools (Optional Method) 220.86

Show Windows . . . . 220.14(G)

   Load Per Linear Foot . . . . 220.43(A)

Signs and Outline Lighting . . . . 220.14(F)

Solar Photovoltaic Systems . . . . 690 Part II

Track Lighting . . . . 220.43(B)

Voltages . . . . 220.5(A)

Water Heaters

Individual Circuit for . . . . 422.10(A)

    Pool Water Heaters 680.10

    Storage-Type. 422.13

Welders, Electric . . . . Art. 630

    Arc Welders 630.11

    Resistance Welders 630.31

Wind Electric Systems. 694.12

See DEMAND FACTORS . . . . *Ferm's Finder*

CAMPING TRAILER (Definition of)

. . . . 551.2

CANOPIES

Attachment Methods (Screws) 314.25

Boxes and Fittings 314.25

    Box Fill Calculation. . . . . 314.16(B)(1) Ex.

Combustible Finishes

    Canopies at Boxes. . . . . 314.25(B)

    Canopies at (Fixtures) Luminaires 410.23

Conductors, Space for 410.20

Cover, at Boxes 410.22

Electric Discharge Luminaires (Fixtures) . . 410.62(C)(1)(2)(c)

Live Parts Exposed 410.5

See Capacitance (Formulas) . . . . *Ferm's Charts and Formulas*

CAPACITORS

. . . . Art. 460

1000 Volts and Under . . . . 460 Part I

    Ampacity of Conductors . . . . 460.8(A)

    See . . . . *Ferm's Charts and Formulas*

    Discharge of Stored Energy 460.6

    Disconnecting Means . . . . 460.8(C)

    See . . . . *Ferm's Charts and Formulas*

    Grounding 460.10

    Marking 460.12

    Motor Overload Device 460.9

    Overcurrent Protection . . . . 460.8(B)

    With Motors 430.27

Accidental Contact. . . . . 460.2(B)

Containing More than 11 L (3 Gal) Flammable Liquid . . . . . 460.2(A)

Hazardous (Classified) Locations

Class I 501.100

Class II 502.100

Class III 503.100

Over 1000 Volts . . . . 460 Part II

    Grounding 460.27

    Identification 460.26

    Means for Discharge 460.28

    Overcurrent Protection. 460.25

    Switching. 460.24

        Isolation . . . . 460.24(B)

        Load Current . . . . 460.24(A)

        Series Capacitors . . . . 460.24(C)

See (CYWT) . . . . *UL Product Spec*

CARNIVALS, CIRCUSES, FAIRS, AND SIMILAR EVENTS . . . . Art. 525

Attractions Using Pools, Fountains, etc. . . . . 525.3(D)

Disconnecting Means . . . . 525.21(A)

GFCI Protection 525.23

    General-Use 15- and 20-ampere, 125-volt . . . . 525.23(A)

    Not Permitted . . . . 525.23(C)

    Not Required . . . . 525.23(B)

    Receptacles Supplied by Portable Cords . . . . . 525.23(D)

Grounding and Bonding . . . . 525 Part IV

    Equipment Bonding 525.30

    Equipment Grounding 525.31

    Equipment Grounding Conductor Continuity Assurance 525.32

Overhead Conductor Clearances 525.5

    Portable Structure Clearances

        Over 600 Volts . . . . 525.5(B)(2)

        Under 600 Volts . . . . 525.5(B)(1)

    Vertical Clearances . . . . 525.5(A)

Permanent Amusement Attractions . . . . Art. 522

Portable Distribution or Termination Boxes 525.22

Portable Wiring Inside Tents and Concessions . . . . 525.21(B)

Power Sources 525.10

Protection of Electrical Equipment 525.6

Wiring Methods . . . . 525 Part III

    Boxes and Fittings . . . . 525.20(H)

    Cord Connectors . . . . 525.20(E)

    Flexible Cord . . . . 525.20(A)

    Open Conductors . . . . 525.20(C)

    Protection . . . . 525.20(G)

Single-Conductor . . . . 525.20(B)

Splices . . . . 525.20(D)

Support . . . . 525.20(F)

CARTRIDGE FUSES . . . . **240 Part VI**

Class I, Division 2 Locations . . . . 501.115(B)(3)

Lighting (Fixtures)Luminaires . . . . 501.115(B)(4)

Classification of 240.61

Disconnecting Means 240.40

Marking . . . . 240.60(C)

Maximum Voltage, 300-Volt Type . . . . 240.60(A)

Noninterchangeable . . . . 240.60(B)

Renewable Fuses . . . . 240.60(D)

Supplementary Overcurrent Protection, Fixed Electric Space
Heating . . . . 424.22(C)

CATV SYSTEMS . . . . **Art. 820**
See COMMUNITY ANTENNA TELEVISION AND RADIO
DISTRIBUTION SYSTEMS. . . . . Ferm's Finder

CAUTION SIGNAGE
Electric Deicing and Snow-Melting Equipment, Fixed
Outdoor 426.13

Engineered Series Combination Systems . . . . . . 110.22(B)

High-Impedance Grounded Neutral AC System . . 408.3(F)(3)

High-Leg Identification . . . . 408.3(F)(1)

Lighting Systems Operating Over 1000 Volts 410.146

Pipeline and Vessels, Fixed Electric Heating 427.13

Requirements . . . . 110.21(B)

Resistively Grounded DC Systems . . . . 408.3(F)(5)

Tested Series Combination Systems . . . . 110.22(C)

Ungrounded AC Systems . . . . 408.3(F)(2)

Ungrounded DC Systems . . . . 408.3(F)(4)

Ungrounded Systems . . . . 250.21(C)

Unqualified Persons . . . . 110.31(B)(1)

**CEILING GRID, LOW-VOLTAGE SUSPENDED POWER
DISTRIBUTION SYSTEMS**
Conductor Sizes and Types 393.104

Connections 393.57

Connectors . . . . 393.40(A)

Definitions 393.2

Disconnecting Means 393.21

Enclosures . . . . 393.40(B)

Grounding 393.60

Installation 393.14

Interconnection of Power Sources . . . . 393.45(B)

Listing Requirements 393.6

Overcurrent Protection . . . . 393.45(A)

Reverse Polarity . . . . 393.45(C)

Scope 393.1

Securing and Supporting 393.30

Splices 393.56

Uses Not Permitted 393.12

Uses Permitted 393.10

CEILING OUTLET (BOX) . . . . **314.27(A)(2)**

CEILING-SUSPENDED (PADDLE) FANS
Bathtubs and Shower Areas, Above . . . . 410.10(D)

Outlet Box, Support of . . . . 314.27(C)

Spare Separately Switched Ungrounded Conductors . . . . . .
. . . . 314.27(C)

Spas and Hot Tubs, Indoor . . . . 680.43(B)(1)

Support of 422.18

Swimming Pools . . . . 680.22(B)

CELL
Cellular Concrete Floor Raceways

Definition 372.2

Cellular Metal Floor Raceways

Definition 374.2

Electrolytic Cells . . . . Art. 668

Fuel Cell Systems . . . . Art. 692

See FUEL CELL SYSTEMS. . . . . Ferm's Finder

Solar Cell, Definition of 690.2

Storage Batteries . . . . Art. 480

CELL LINE, ELECTROLYTIC CELLS . . . . **Art. 668**

CELLARS *See* **BASEMENT** . . . . Ferm's Finder

CELLULAR CONCRETE FLOOR RACEWAYS . . . . . . **Art. 372**
Connection to Cabinets and Other Enclosures . . . . 372.18(B)

Definitions 372.2

Discontinued Outlets 372.58

Header . . . . 372.18(A)

Inserts . . . . 372.18(D)

Installation 372.18

Junction Boxes . . . . 372.18(C)

Markers . . . . 372.18(E)

Number of Conductors 372.22

C

Size of Conductors 372.20

Splices and Taps 372.56

Uses Not Permitted 372.12

    Installation of Conductors with Other Systems 300.8

CELLULAR METAL FLOOR RACEWAYS . . . . Art. 374

Construction Specifications. 374.100

Definitions 374.2

Discontinued Outlets 374.58

Inserts . . . . 374.18(C)

Installation 374.18

Junction Boxes . . . . 374.18(B)

Markers . . . . 374.18(D)

Number of Conductors 374.22

Size of Conductors 374.20

Splices and Taps 374.56

Uses Not Permitted 374.12

    Installation of Conductors with Other Systems 300.8

CENTER PIVOT IRRIGATION MACHINES *See* **ELECTRICALLY DRIVEN OR CONTROLLED IRRIGATION MACHINES . . . . . . Art. 675**

CENTIGRADE TO FAHRENHEIT . . . .
. . . .**Tables 310.15(B)16 through 20**

CHAIR LIFTS . . . . Art. 620

CHILD CARE FACILITIES

Definition 406.2

Tamper-Resistant Receptacles . . . . 406.12(3)

CHURCHES . . . . Art. 518

CINDER FILL

Electrical Metallic Tubing . . . . 358.10(C)

Intermediate Metal Conduit . . . . 342.10(C)

High Density Polyethylene Conduit Type HDPE. . . 353.10(3)

Nonmetallic-Underground Conduit with Conductors . . . . .
. . . . .354.10(3)

Reinforced Thermosetting Resin Conduit . . . . . 355.10(C)

Rigid Metal Conduit . . . . 344.10(C)

Rigid PVC Conduit . . . . 352.10(C)

CIRCUIT BREAKERS . . . . 240 Part VII

Accessibility and Grouping, Where Used as Switches . . . . . .
. . . . .404.8(A)

Adjustable Trip . . . . 240.6(B)

Restricted Access Adjustable-Trip. . . . . 240.6(C)

Applications, 1-Phase, 3-Phase, Slash Rating 240.85

Ampere Ratings . . . . Table 240.6(A)

Adjustable-Trip Circuit Breakers . . . . 240.6(B)

Fuses and Fixed-Trip Circuit Breakers . . . . 240.6(A)

Restricted Access Adjustable-Trip Circuit Breakers   240.6(C)

Table for Standard Ampere Ratings . . . . . . Table 240.6(A)

Back Fed Breakers

Overcurrent Protection. . . . . 408.36(D)

Solar Photovoltaic . . . . 710.15(E)

Back Fed due to Loss of Primary Source of Power

Electric Vehicle Charging Systems 625.46

Electrified Truck Parking Places. 626.26

Circuits Over 1000 Volts . . . . 490.21(A)

Definition of . . . . .Art. 100 Part I

Disconnection of Grounded Conductors . . . . . . 404.2(B)

For Dispensing Equipment . . . . 514.11(A)

Enclosures . . . . 404.3(A)

Interrupting Rating 110.9

Required Marking. . . . . 240.83(C)

Marking 240.83

Nontamperable 240.82

Overcurrent Device, as . . . . 240.15(B)

Overcurrent Protection Over 1000 Volts . . . . . 240 Part IX

Parallel, Use in 240.8

Rating, Nonadjustable Trip . . . . 240.6(A)

See BREAKERS AND FUSES . . . . Ferm's Finder

See (DHJR) . . . .*UL Product Spec*

Series-Combination Ratings, Identification 110.22

Series Ratings 240.86

Short-Circuit Current Rating 110.10

Transformers, Circuit Breaker Ratings. 450.3

1000 Volts and Less . . . . .Table 450.3(B)

Over 1000 Volts . . . . Table 450.3(A)

Transient Voltage Surge Suppressor

See (DIMV) . . . .*UL Product Spec*

Used As Switches, Lighting Loads

HID. . . . . 240.83(D)

SWD . . . . 240.83(D)

CIRCUIT, CONTROL *See* **CONTROL CIRCUITS . . . .**
. . . . **Ferm's Finder**

CIRCUIT INTEGRITY CABLE

Definition

    Class 1, Class 2, and Class 3 Circuits 725.2

    Communication Systems 800.2

Fiber Optic Cables . . . . 770.179(E)(1)

Listing for PLTC . . . . 725.179(F)(1)

Mechanical Execution of Work . . . . 760.24(B)

Power Limited Fire Alarm Circuits . . . . 760.176(F)(1)

Survivability Characteristics, Communication Circuits . . . . .
. . . . 800.179(G)(1)

CIRCUITS

Identification of 110.22

    In Switchboards and Panelboards (Field Required) . . . . . .
. . . . 408.4

Low Voltage

    Class 1, 2 & 3 Systems . . . . Art. 725

    Communications Circuits . . . . Art. 800

    Fire Alarms . . . . Art. 760

    Less than 50 Volts . . . . Art. 720

    Low Voltage Lighting . . . . Art. 411

    Sound Recording . . . . Art. 640

    See LOW VOLTAGE SYSTEMS . . . . Ferm's Finder

Number Per Building

    Allowed, General 225.30

    Required, Dwelling Unit Bathroom . . . . .210.11(C)(3)

    Required, Dwelling Unit Laundry . . . . . . .210.11(C)(2)

    Required, Dwelling Unit Small-Appliance . . . .210.11(C)(1)

    Required, General 210.11

    Use of Demand Factors Not for Number of 220.42

See BRANCH CIRCUITS . . . . Ferm's Finder

CIRCULAR MIL AREA OF CONDUCTORS . . . .
Chapter 9 Table 8

See BUSBARS . . . . Ferm's Finder

CIRCUSES . . . . Art. 525

See CARNIVALS, CIRCUSES, FAIRS, AND SIMILAR
EVENTS . . . . Ferm's Finder

CLAMP FILL, BOXES . . . . .314.16(B)(2)

CLAMPS, GROUND 250.8

Electrodes, Connection to 250.70

Protection of Attachment 250.10

CLASS I, II, AND III LOCATIONS (HAZARDOUS)

See HAZARDOUS (CLASSIFIED) LOCATIONS . . Ferm's Finder

CLASS 1, 2 & 3 REMOTE CONTROL CIRCUITS . . . . Art. 725

Abandoned Cables 725.25

Applications in Buildings 725.154

Circuit Identification 725.30

Classification, General Definition 725.2

    Class 1 . . . . 725.41

    Class 2 & 3 .725.121

Conductors

    Copper Conductors for Control Circuit Devices . . . .
. . . . 430.9(B)

Definitions 725.2

Grounding . . . . Art. 250

Physical Protection . . . . 725.31(B)

Power Source Limitations . . . .
Chapter 9 Tables 11(A)&(B)

Safety-Control Equipment 725.31

Class 1 Circuits . . . . 725 Part II

    Circuits Beyond Building 725.52

    As Messenger Supported Wiring . . . . Art. 396

    Different Systems in Same Enclosure or Raceway . . . 725.48

    Mechanical Execution of Work 725.24

    Motor Control Circuits . . . . 430 Part VI

        Copper Conductors . . . . 430.9(B)

        Mechanical Protection of Conductors Physical Damage . .
. . . . 430.73

        Overcurrent Protection 430.72

        Ungrounded for Integrated Electrical Systems . . . 685.14

        Where Not Required to Be Grounded 250.21

    Number in Raceway, and Derating 725.51

    Overcurrent Protection 725.43

        Device Location 725.45

    Size . . . . 725.49(A)

    Wiring Methods 725.46

Class 2 & 3 Circuits . . . . 725 Part III

    Applications of Listed Cables 725.154

    Circuit Marking 725.124

    Different Systems in Same Enclosure 725.139

    Industrial Establishments . . . . .725.135(J)

    Installation 725.133

    Limits – Voltage & Current 725.121

    Listing and Marking of 725.179

    Power Limitations (AC) . . . . Chapter 9 Table 11(A)

Power Limitations (DC) . . . . Chapter 9 Table 11(B)

Separation of Circuits. 725.136

Uses Permitted and Substitutions . . . . .725.154(A)

Vertical Support for Fire-Rated Cables and Conductors . . .
. . . . 725.3(I)

Wiring Methods, Load Side of Power Source 725.130

Wiring Methods, Supply Side of Power Source 725.127

Cable Routing Assemblies. . . . . .725.3(M)

Communications Raceways. . . . . .725.3(N)

Identification of Circuits 725.30

Installation Requirements. 725.135

Limited Power (LP) Cables . . . . 725.179(I)

Listing Requirements . . . . .Art. 725 Part IV

Class 2, Class 3 and PLTC Cables 725.179

Equipment (Powered Devices). 725.170

Mechanical Execution of Work. 725.24

See LOW VOLTAGE SYSTEMS . . . . Ferm's Finder

Transmission of Power and Data. 725.144

CLASS 2 & 3 TRANSFORMERS

See (XNWX) . . . . .UL Product Spec

CLEAN SURFACES, GROUNDING 250.12

CLEARANCES

Clearance & Head Room about Equipment 110.26

Switchboards and Panelboards. 408.18

Clearance of Outside Branch Circuits . . . . Art. 225

From Buildings 225.19

For Overhead Conductors and Cables 225.18

Clearance of Service Drops

Carnivals, Circuses, etc. 525.5

Clearances to Portable Structures. . . . . 525.5(B)

Vertical Clearances. . . . . 525.5(A)

From Building Openings. . . . . 230.9(C)

Other Than Service Cables on Insulators. . . . . . 230.51(B)

Overhead Service Drop Conductors 230.24

Point of Attachment Below Service Head . . . . . 230.54(C)

Recreational Vehicles 551.79

Swimming Pools. 680.9

Communication Systems . . . . 680.9(B)

Network-Powered Broadband Communication Systems .
. . . . .680.9(C)

Power, (Not in and Enclosed Raceway) . . . . . . 680.9(A)

Elevation & Clearance of Electric Signs 600.9

Fire Ladders . . . . 225.19(E)

High Voltage 490.34

See Life Safety Code, NFPA 101 . . . . NFPA 101

Live Bare Parts

Bus Enclosures 408.5

In Auxiliary Gutters. . . . . .366.100(E)

In Cabinets, Cutout Boxes and Meter Enclosures312.11(A)(3)

Over 1000 Volts 110.34

Minimum Separation 490.24

Under 600 Volts 110.26

Switchboards and Panelboards. 408.56

Overhead Conductors

Carnivals, Circuses, etc. 525.5

In Recreational Vehicle Parks 551.79

Clearance from Ground 225.18

Railroad Tracks . . . . 230.24(5)

Overhead Open Conductors 225.14

Carnivals, Circuses, etc. 525.5

CATV Systems. . . . . 820 Part II

Communications Systems . . . . 800 Part II

From Buildings 225.19

From Ground 225.18

Network-Powered Broadband Systems . . . . 830 Part II

Overhead Feeder Conductors and Cables 225.18

Overhead Service Drop Conductors 230.24

Individual Open Conductors . . . . Table 230.51(C)

Point of Attachment Below Service Head and Goosenecks. .
. . . . 230.54(C)

Recreational Vehicles 551.79

Radio and Television Equipment . . . . 810 Part II

Amateur Station Antenna Systems . . . . 810 Part III

Swimming Pools. 680.9

Communication Systems . . . . 680.9(B)

Network-Powered Broadband Communication Systems .
. . . . .680.9(C)

Power (Not in an Enclosed Raceway) . . . . . . 680.9(A)

Over 1000 Volts

Entrance to Work Space 110.33

From Non-Electrical Pipes and Ducts . . . . 110.34(F)

Work Space (General) 110.34

Work Space about Equipment 110.32

See Life Safety Code, NFPA 101. . . . . .NFPA 101

Underground Wiring from Swimming Pools . . . 680.11, 300.5

CLINICS . . . . **517 Part II**

Essential Electrical Systems, in 517.45

Example of (Health Care Facilities) . 517.2 Informational Note

See HEALTH CARE FACILITIES . . . . Ferm's Finder

See Standard for Health Care Facilities, NFPA 99 . . . . NFPA 99

Tamper-Resistant Receptacles . . . . .406.12(5)

CLOCK OUTLET . . . . **210.52(B)(2) Ex. 1**

CLOTHES CLOSET

Definition . . . . Art. 100

Luminaire (Fixture) Types Not Permitted . . . . . . 410.16(B)

Luminaire (Fixture) Types Permitted . . . . 410.16(A)

Location of Luminaires (Fixtures) . . . . 410.16(C)

Overcurrent Devices Prohibited . . . . 240.24(D)

Storage Space, *See* Clearance from Different Types of
Luminaires . . . . 410.2 Fig.

CLOTHES DRYERS

Calculations for Dwelling Units 220.54

Calculations for Other than Dwelling Units . . . . . 220.14(B)

Feeder Demand Factors . . . . Table 220.54

Grounding the Frame of 250.140

Grounding by Grounded Conductor. . . . . . .250.142(B) Ex 1

Mobile Homes, Wiring Methods . . . . 550.15(E)

Insulated Neutral . . . . 550.16(A)

Park Trailers . . . . 552.55(C)

Recreational Vehicles, Insulated Neutral. . . . . . . 551.54(C)

CLOTHING MANUFACTURING PLANTS (Ignitable Fibers) . .
. . . . **500.5(D)**

Hazardous (Classified) Locations (Class III) . . . . . . Art. 503

CO/ALR MARKING

Receptacles . . . . .406. 3(C)

See (RTRT) . . . .*UL Product Spec*

Switches . . . . 404.14(C)

See(WJQR). . . . .*UL Product Spec*

COAXIAL CABLE

CATV Systems . . . . Art. 820

Communications Systems . . . . Art. 800

Definition . . . . Art. 100

Fire Alarm Systems . . . . 760.179(H)

Network-Powered Broadband Communication Systems . . . .
. . . . Art. 830

Radio and Television Equipment . . . . Art. 810

CODE ARRANGEMENT . . . . **90.3 and FIGURE 90.3**

COLOR CODING

Equipment Grounding Conductor . . . . 210.5(B)

Conductor Identification 200.6

Equipment Grounding Conductors 250.119

For Branch Circuits . . . . 210.5(B)

Flexible Cords . . . . 400 Part II

Grounded Conductors 200.6

For Branch Circuits . . . . 210.5(A)

Means of Identifying 200.6

Heating Cables 424.35

Higher Voltage to Ground (Delta), General 110.15

Delta Service, Midpoint Grounded 230.56

Intrinsically Safe Systems . . . . 504.80(C)

Mobile Home Power Supply

Cord (Power Supply) . . . . 550.10(B)

Feeders . . . . 550.33(A)

Mast Weatherhead or Raceway . . . . .550.10(I)

Multiwire and Individual Branch Circuits. . . . . . . 210.5(C)

Park Trailer Power Supply

Cord (Power Supply) . . . . 552.43(B)

Feeders . . . . 552.43(A)

Mast Weatherhead or Raceway . . . . 552.43(C)

Sensitive Electronic Equipment . . . . 647.4(C)

Trailing Cable, Marina Hoists, Cranes, etc. 555.23

Ungrounded Conductors . . . . 210.5(C)

Isolated Power Systems, Health Care Facilities. . . . .
. . . . .517.160(A)(5)

COMBUSTIBLE DUSTS . . . . **Art. 502**

Definition . . . . Art. 100

General . . . . 500.6(B)

COMMERCIAL GARAGES . . . . **Art. 511**

Battery Charging Equipment . . . . 511.10(A)

Class I Locations . . . . 500.5(B)

Area Classification 511.3

Electric Vehicle Charging . . . . 511.10(B)

Elevators & Escalators in 620.38

Equipment above Class I Locations . . . . 511.7(B)

Equipment in Class I Locations 511.4

Fuel Dispensing Units . . . . 511.4(B)(1)

Ground-Fault Circuit-Interrupter Protection 511.12

Grounding and Bonding . . . . Art. 250

C

Grounding 511.16

Hazardous (Classified) Locations 250.100

Special Requirements 501.30

Portable Hand Lamps . . . . 511.4(B)(2)

Sealing 501.15

At Horizontal and Vertical Boundaries 511.9

Process Sealing 501.17

Surge Protection Class I Locations 501.35

See Standard for the Installation of Lightning Protection Systems, NFPA 780 . . . . NFPA 780

Wiring Methods

Above Class I Locations . . . . 511.7(A)

In Class I Locations (General) 501.10

In Class I Locations . . . . 511.4(A)

Major Repair Garages . . . . 511.3(D)

Major and Minor Repair Garages . . . . 511.3(C)

Underground Wiring 511.8

Modifications to Classification . . . . 511.3(E)

Parking Garages . . . . 511.3(A)

Repair Garages with Dispensing . . . . 511.3(B)

Underground Wiring 511.8

Under Hazardous Areas . . . . 511.4(A)

See HAZARDOUS (CLASSIFIED) LOCATIONS . . . .
. . . . Ferm's Finder

See Code for Motor Fuel Dispensing Facilities and Repair Garages

COMMON AREA BRANCH CIRCUITS . . . . 210.25(B)

COMMON GROUNDING ELECTRODE 250.58

Agricultural Buildings . . . . 547.9(B)(3)

Bonding of Made and Other Electrodes 250.50

Bonding to Other Systems 250.94

CATV Systems . . . . 820.100(D)

Communication Circuits . . . . 800.100(D)

Grounding Electrode System 250.52

Intersystem Bonding Termination, CATV Systems . . . .
. . . . .820.100(B)

Intersystem Bonding Termination, Communications Circuits .
. . . . .800.100(B)

Intersystem Bonding Terminations, Network-Powered Broadband . . . . .830.100(B)

Lightning Protection Systems 250.106

Air Terminals (Strike Terminal Devices) 250.60

See also *Standard for the Installation of Lightning Protection Systems, NFPA 780* . . . . NFPA 780

Network-Powered Broadband Systems . . . . 830.100(D)

Radio and Television Equipment . . . . .810.21(J)

Separately Derived Systems . . . . 250.30(A)(5 and 6)

Size of Conductor 250.66

COMMON NEUTRAL (Not Permitted)
Office Furnishings, Cord- and Plug-Connected . . . . 605.9(D)

COMMON NEUTRAL CONDUCTOR (Permitted)
Continuity in Branch Circuits, Device Removal . . . 300.13(B)

Feeders 215.4

In Metal Raceways or Enclosures . . . . 215.4(B)

Neutral Load 220.61

Number of Sets Permitted . . . . 215.4(A)

Lighting Equipment Installed Outdoors . . . . 225.7(B)

Multiwire Branch Circuits 210.4

See NEUTRAL OR GROUNDED CONDUCTOR . . . . . .
. . . . Ferm's Finder

Where Considered Current-Carrying . . . . .310.15(B)(5)

See NEUTRAL OR GROUNDED CONDUCTOR . . . .
. . . . Ferm's Finder

COMMUNICATIONS CIRCUITS . . . . Art. 800
Abandoned Cables 800.25

Access to Electrical Equipment 800.21

Bonding at Mobile Homes . . . . .800.106(B)

Bonding of Electrodes . . . . 800.100(D)

Cable Assemblies, see (DUNH) . . . .*UL Product Spec*

Cable Routing Assemblies,

Listed 800.182

Marked 800.182

Support . . . . .800.110(C)

Cable Substitution 800.154

Cable Ties and Cable Assemblies, Nonmetallic 800.24

Cable Ties for Use in Plenums . . . . .800.170(C)

Circuit Integrity Cable . . . . .800.179(G)(1)

Circuits Requiring Primary Protectors 800.50

Conductors

Applications of Listed Conductors 800.154

Other Conductors with . . . . 800.133(A)

Overhead 800.44

Temperature Limitations . . . . 800.3(H)

Within Buildings . . . . 800 Part V

Community Antenna Television and Radio Distribution
Systems . . . . .820.110(C)

Definition of 800.2

Dwelling Unit Communications Outlet 800.156

Electrical Circuit Protective System, Defined 800.2

Fire Resistance 800.179

Fire-Resistive Cable . . . . .800.179(G)(2)

Grounding

    Cables 800.93

    Devices 800.180

    Mobile Homes 800.106

    Methods 800.100

Grounding of Entrance Conduits Containing Communication
Circuits 800.49

Innerduct, Defined 800.2

Installation, Listing Required 800.113

    Abandoned Cables 800.25

    Intersystem Bonding Termination . . . . 800.100(B)(1)

Lightning Conductors Separated by at least 6 Feet 800.53

Listing Required (Equipment) 800.170

Listing Required (Wires and Cables) 800.179

Listing Required (Communications Raceways) 800.154

Listing Required (Grounding Devices) 800.180

Listing Required (Installed in Buildings) 800.113

Mechanical Execution of Work 800.24

Network-Powered Broadband Communications Systems . . . .
. . . . .830.110(C)

Optical Fiber Cable . . . . 770.110(C)(1) and (2)

Plenum Grade Cable Ties . . . . .800.170(C)

Primary Protector Grounding at Mobile Homes 800.106

Protection . . . . 800 Part III

    Devices 800.90

    Grounding 800.100

    Requirements

    Application, Primary Protector . . . . 800.90(A)

    Hazardous (Classified)Location, Primary Protector 800.90(C)

    Location, Primary Protector . . . . 800.90(B)

    Requirements, Secondary Protector . . . . 800.90(D)

    Spread of Fire or Products of Combustion 800.26

Temperature Limitations . . . . .800.3(H)

Types of Cable 800.179

Underground Circuits Entering Buildings 800.47

Unlisted Cables Entering Buildings 800.48

COMMUNICATIONS RACEWAY, DEFINED . . . . Art. 100

COMMUNITY ANTENNA TELEVISION AND RADIO
DISTRIBUTION SYSTEMS . . . . Art. 820

Abandoned Coaxial Cable, Definition 820.2

Abandoned Cables 800.25

Access to Electrical Equipment 820.21

Cable Substitution 820.154

Cable Ties and Accessories, Nonmetallic 820.24

Cables Outside and Entering Buildings . . . . 820 Part II

Cables within Buildings . . . . 820 Part V

    Cable Routing Assemblies . . . . .820.110(C)

    Innerduct for Coaxial Cables . . . . .820.110(A)(3)

    Raceway Fills . . . . .820.110(B)

    Types . . . . .820.110(A)

Definitions 820.2

Grounding Methods . . . . 820 Part IV

Grounding Metallic Entrance Conduits 820.49

Intersystem Bonding Termination . . . . .820.100(B)

Listing, Marking, and Installation of Cables 820.113

    Alternate Wiring Methods of Art. 830 Permitted . . 820.3(I)

Mechanical Execution of Work 820.24

Power Limitations 820.15

Protection . . . . 820 Part III

Wiring in Ducts . . . . 820.3(B)

See (DVCS) . . . . .UL Product Spec

Unlisted Cable Entering Buildings 820.48

COMPACT CONDUCTORS . . . . Chapter 9 Table 5A
Compact Stranding, Definition of . . . . Notes to Tables
. . . . Informative Annex C

Wire-Bending Space (Terminals) . . . . .Table 312.6(A) and (B)

COMPRESSOR MOTORS
See AIR-CONDITIONING & REFRIGERATING
EQUIPMENT . . . . Ferm's Finder

COMPUTER ROOMS . . . . Art. 645
See INFORMATION TECHNOLOGY EQUIPMENT . . . . .
Ferm's Finder

CONCEALED (Definition of) . . . . Art. 100 Part I

CONCENTRIC KNOCKOUTS
Bond Around, Service . . . . 250.92(B)

Bonding for Over 250 Volts 250.97

CONCRETE
Concrete Encased Electrodes . . . . .250.52(A)(3)

    DC Systems, Sole Connection Size . . . . 250.166(D)

Concrete Walls Considered Grounded . . . .

Table 110.26(A)(1) Note

Metal Raceways, Equipment in . . . . 300.6(A)(3)

Use with Minimum Cover Requirements . . . . . Table 300.5

Wet Location, (Definition of) . . . . Art. 100 Part I

CONDUCTORS . . . . Art. 310

Aluminum Conductors, Material 310.106

Note: Use oxide inhibitor where required

    Compact Conductors. . . . . Chapter 9 Table 5A

    Dwelling Unit Services and Feeders . . . . . . .310.15(B)(7)

    Not Permitted to Terminate Within 450 mm (18 in.) of Earth or Masonry Walls for Grounding . . . . 250.64(A)

    See Aluminum Conductor Terminations. . . . . *Ferm's Charts and Formulas*

Aluminum to Copper, Limited Connections 110.14

Ampacity of, 0 – 2000 Volts (General) 310.15

    Calculated Under Engineering Supervision . . . . 310.15(C)

      See Informative Annex B for Formula Applications . . . . Informative Annex B

    Determined from Tables . . . Tables 310.15(B)16 through 21

    See AMPACITY . . . . Ferm's Finder

Ampacity of, 2001- 35,000 Volts (General) 310.60

    Calculated Under Engineering Supervision . . . . 310.60(C)

    Determined from Tables . . . Tables 310.60(C)67 through 86

    See Informative Annex B for Formula Applications . . . . . Informative Annex B

Ampacity of Bare or Covered Conductors. . . . . .Table 310.15(B)(21)

    Limits, Used with Insulated Conductors . . . . .310.15(B)(4)

Ampacity of Busways, Maximum Allowed . . . . . . 230.42(A)

Application & Insulation . . . . Table 310.104(A)

    Over 1000 Volts . . . . Tables 310.104(B) through (E)

Area in Circular Mils . . . . Chapter 9 Table 8

    See Busbars . . . . *Ferm's Charts and Formulas*

Area in Square Inches . . . . *Ferm's Charts and Formulas*

Backfill . . . . 300.5(F)

    Over 1000 Volts . . . . 300.50(E)

Bare Bus Bars in Sheet Metallic Auxiliary Gutters . . 366.23(A)

Bare, Covered, Insulated Conductor (Definition of) . . . . .Art. 100 Part I

Bending Space

    Auxiliary Gutters, in 366.58

    Bending Radius Over 1000 Volts 300.34

    Enclosures for Motor Controllers and Disconnects, in . . . . 430.10(B)

Examination of Equipment. . . . . 110.3(A)(3)

Manholes. 110.74

1000 Volts, Nominal, or Less. . . . . 110.74(A)

Over 1000 Volts, Nominal . . . . 110.74(B)

Pull and Junction Boxes Not Over 600 Volts, in 314.28

Pull and Junction Boxes Over 1000 Volts, in 314.71

Switch or Circuit Breaker Enclosures, in . . . . . . 404.3(A)

    How Measured (wire-bending space) 404.28

Switchboards and Panelboards, in — Wire Bending Space. . . . . 408.3(G)

    Clearance Entering Bus Enclosures. 408.5

    Provisions for 408.55

Terminals of Cabinets, Cutout Boxes, Meter Sockets . . . . 312.6(B)

Wireways, in Metal . . . . 376.23(A)

Wireways, in Nonmetallic . . . . 378.23(A)

Bundled as to Ambient Temperature . . . . .310.15(B)(2)

Buried (General) 300.5

    Bushing on Open End of Conduit. . . . . 300.5(H)

    Over 600 Volts (Shielding) . . . . 310.10(E)

    Over 1000 Volts (Other Nonshielded Cables) . .300.50(A)(3)

    See OVER 1000 VOLTS, NOMINAL. . . . . Ferm's Finder

Type Identified for the Purpose . . . . 310.10(F)

Cable (In Cable Tray)

    Ampacity of, 2000 Volts or Less . . . . 392.22(A)

    Ampacity of, 2001 Volts and Over . . . . 392.22(C)

    Ampacity of Type TC Cable 336.80

    Number of, Cables 2001 Volts and Over . . . . . 392.22(C)

    Number of Multiconductor Cables 2000 Volts of Less . . . . 392.22(A)

    Number of Single Conductor Cables 2000 Volts or Less . . . . 392.22(B)

Circular Mil Area of . . . . Chapter 9 Table 8

    See COLOR CODING . . . . Ferm's Finder

Combination of, in Raceway

    Conductor Properties . . . . Chapter 9 Table 8

    Dimensions of Compact Aluminum Building Wire. . . . . Chapter 9 Table 5A

    Dimensions of Insulated Conductors and Luminaire (Fixture) Wires . . . . Chapter 9 Table 5

    Percent Area Conduit and Tubing. . . . . . Chapter 9 Table 4

    Percent of Cross-Sectional Area Allowed. . Chapter 9 Table 1

Compact Conductors (Aluminum) . . . . . Chapter 9 Table 5A

    Compact Stranding, Defined . . Table C.A(A) (Below Table)

Conductor Fill in Class 1 Sealing Fittings . . . . . .501.15(C)(6)

Connection to Terminals 110.14

   Motor Control Circuit Devices 430.9

Continuous Loads (Definition). . . . . Art. 100 Part I

   Branch Circuit Conductors . . . . .210.19(A)(1)

   Feeder Conductors . . . . 215.2(A)(1)

   Fixed Electric Space-Heating . . . . 424.3(B)

   Individual Branch Circuit, Appliances . . . . . . 422.10(A)

   Pool Water Heaters 680.10

   Storage-Type Water Heaters 422.13

Copper Conductors 110.5

   Agricultural Buildings

      Bonding and Equipotential Plane 547.10

      Equipment Grounding Conductor, Underground (Direct Buried) . . . . 547.5(F)

      Wiring Methods 547.5

   Ampacity of, 0 – 2000 Volts (General) 310.15

      Calculated Under Engineering Supervision . . . 310.15(C)

      Determined from Tables. . Tables 310.15(B)16 through 21

      For Short-Time Rated Cranes and Hoists . . . . 610.14(A)

      See Informative Annex B for Formula Applications . . . . Informative Annex B

      See AMPACITY . . . . Ferm's Finder

   Ampacity of, 2001- 35,000 Volts (General). 310.60

      Calculated Under Engineering Supervision . . . 310.60(C)

      Determined from Tables. . . . . Tables 310.60(C)(67) through 86

      See Informative Annex B for Formula Applications . . . . Informative Annex B

   Class I, Zone 0, 1, and 2, Protection "e" Field Wiring . . . . 505.18(A)

   Copper to Aluminum Permitted 110.14

   Dimensions & Percent Area of. . . . . . . Chapter 9 Table 5

      Conductor Properties . . . . Chapter 9 Table 8

   Dwelling Unit Services and Feeders . . . . . .310.15(B)(7)

   Fire Alarm Systems

      NPLFA Circuit Conductors 760.49

   Health Care Facilities . . . . 517 Part II

      Critical Care (Category 1) Spaces, Patient Bed Locations 517.19

      Equipment Grounding Conductor, Patient Care . . . . 517.13(B)

      General Care (Category 2) Spaces, Patient Bed Locations 517.18

      Panelboard Bonding Normal and Essential Circuits 517.14

      Panelboard Grounding, Critical Care (Category 1) Spaces . . . . 517.19(E)

   Low-Voltage Wiring, Park Trailers . . . . . . .552.10(B)(1)

   Marinas and Boatyards, Equipment Grounding . . . . 555.15(B)&(C)

   Material Not Specified Means Copper 110.5

   Motor Controllers. . . . . 430.9(B)&(C)

   Properties of . . . . Chapter 9 Table 8

   Required for Type MI Cable Conductors 332.104

   Swimming Pool, Fountains, and Similar Installations

      Bonding Conductor . . . . 680.26(B)

      Fountains . . . . 680 Part V

      Hydromassage Bathtubs, Bonding 680.74

      Permanently Installed Pools. . . . . 680 Part II

      Shall Be Long Enough (Replacement Pump Motor) 680.74

      Spas and Hot Tubs . . . . 680 Part IV

      Therapeutic Pools and Tubs . . . . 680 Part VI

      Underwater Audio Equipment 680.27

      Underwater Luminaires (Lighting Fixtures) 680.23

Correction Factors . . . . Tables 310.15(B)(2)(a)&(b)

Crane & Hoist Conductors . . . . 610.14(A)

Deflection of, *See* CONDUCTORS, Bending Space . . . . Ferm's Finder

Derating Allowable Ampacity

   Ambient Temperature . . . . . . Tables 310.15(B)(2)(a)&(b)

   Class 1 Circuit, Overcurrent Protection for 725.43

   Class 1 Circuit Conductors 725.51

   Grounding or Bonding Conductors Not Considered . . . . .310.15(B)(6)

   Heated Ceilings 424.36

   Neutral Conductor . . . . .310.15(B)(5)

   Number of Current-Carrying Conductors, Adjustment Factors .310.15(B)(3)(a)

      Metal Wireways 376.22

      Nonmetallic Wireways 378.22

Different Systems in Same Enclosure

   1000 Volts, Nominal or Less . . . . 300.3(C)(1)

   Cable Trays

      Cables Over 1000 Volts . . . . 392.20(B)

      Multiconductor Cables 1000 Volts or Less. . . . 392.20(A)

   CATV and Radio Distribution Systems 820.133

   Class 1 Remote Control, Signaling Circuits 725.48

   Class 2 & 3 Remote Control, Signaling Circuits . . . 725.136

   Communications Circuits 800.133

   Elevators, Dumbwaiters, etc. 620.36

C

Emergency System Wiring . . . . 700.10(B)

Essential Electrical System, Life Safety Branch . . 517.42(D)

Fire Pumps, Independent Routing . . . . . . .695.6(A)(2)(a)

Generator Control Wiring . . . . 695.14(F)

Grounded Conductors, Identification . . . . 200.6(D)

Intrinsically Safe Systems 504.30

Legally Required Standby Wiring 701.10

Network-Powered Broadband Systems 830.133

Non-Electrical Systems Prohibited 300.8

Non-Power-Limited Fire Alarm (NPLFA) Circuits . . 760.48

Optical Fiber Cables 770.133

Optional Standby Wiring. 702.10

Over 1000 Volts, Nominal . . . . 300.3(C)(2)

   Requirements for 300.32

Power-Limited Fire Alarm (PLFA) Circuits 760.133

Different PLFA Circuits

   Prohibition of with Service Conductors 230.7

   Solar Photovoltaic Systems. . . . . 690.31(B)

   Surface Metal Raceways 386.70

   Surface Nonmetallic Raceways 388.70

Dimensions & Area of . . . . Chapter 9 Table 5

   Compact Aluminum Wire . . . . Chapter 9 Table 5A

   Conductor Properties . . . . Chapter 9 Table 8

Dwelling Unit Services & Feeders . . . . .310.15(B)(7)

   Individual Unit Feeder Conductors . . . . . . .310.15(B)(7)

Equipment Grounding Conductors

   Box Fill . . . . .314.16(5)

   Identification. 250.119

   Installation. .250.120

   Sectioned. . . . . 250.122 and 310.10(H)(5)

   Size 250.122

   Increased Due to Voltage Drop . . . . .250.122(B)

Exposed to Direct Sunlight . . . . 310.10(D)

Feeder Identification

   Direct-Current Systems . . . . .215.12(C)(2)

   Equipment Grounding Conductor . . . . 215.12(B)

   Grounded Conductor Identification . . . . 215.12(A)

   Ungrounded Conductor Identification

      Alternating-Current Systems . . . . .215.12(C)(1)

Feeder to Mobile Home . . . . .310.15(B)(7)

   Conductor Size . . . . .310.15(B)(7)

   Minimum Capacity 550.33

      Allowable Demand Factors 550.31

Fill within Boxes, Conductors 314.16

Fine Stranded Conductors 110.14

Fire Alarm Systems . . . . Art. 760

   Nonpower-Limited Circuits (NPLFA) . . . . 760 Part II

   Power-Limited Circuits (PLFA) . . . . 760 Part III

Fire Pumps . . . . Art. 695

Flexible Cords . . . . Art. 400

Free Length at Boxes 300.14

   Deicing and Snow-Melting Equipment . . . . . 426.23(A)

   Fixed Electric Space Heating Cables 424.43

   Pipeline and Vessel Heating Equipment . . . . . 427.18(A)

Gasoline & Oil Resistant (General) . . . . 310.10(G)

   Class I Locations 501.20

   See (ZLGR) . . . .*UL Product Spec*

High Voltage, Rated 2001 to 35,000 Volts 310.60

   . . . . Tables 310.60(C)67 through 86

   Grounding Conductor Continuity . . . . 200.2(B)

   Requirements for . . . . 300 Part II

   See OVER 1000 VOLTS, NOMINAL . . . . . . Ferm's Finder

Identification of

   Branch Circuit Conductors 210.5

   Equipment Grounding Conductors, General . . . . 210.5(B)

   Equipment Grounding Conductors. 250.119

   Flexible Cords . . . . 400 Part II

   Grounded Conductors . . . . 210.5(A)

      (Fixture) Luminaire Wires 402.8

      Means of Identifying. 200.6

      Use of White or Gray 200.7

   Heating Cables. 424.35

   Higher Voltage to Ground (Delta), General 110.15

      Service Conductors 230.56

   Intrinsically Safe Systems 504.80

   Isolated Power Systems . . . . .517.160(A)(5)

   Mobile Home Power Supply

      Cords, Power Supply . . . . 550.10(B)

      Feeders . . . . 550.10(A)

      Mast Weatherhead or Raceway . . . . .550.10(I)

   Multiwire Branch Circuits and Individual Branch Circuits .

   . . . . 210.5(C)

   Park Trailer Power Supply

      Cords, Power Supply. . . . . 552.43(B)

      Feeder . . . . 552.43(A)

      Mast Weatherhead or Raceway . . . . 552.43(C)

   Ungrounded Conductors . . . . 210.5(C)

Induction, Arrange Wiring to Prevent . . . . 300.3(B)

  In Metal Raceways and Enclosures 300.20

    Over 1000 Volts. 300.35

  Installation in Cable Trays 392.46

  Single Cables of Type MI Cable 332.31

  Three-Way and Four-Way Switch Wiring . . . . . 404.2(A)

  Underground Installations . . . . 300.5(I)

Inserting in Raceways

  Completed Runs. 300.18

  General Rules 300.3

  Number and Size of (General) 300.17

  Requirements for Stranded Conductors . . . . . .310.106(C)

Integrated Gas Spacer Cable 326.104

Low Voltage & High Voltage in Same Enclosure . . . 300.3

  Cable Trays

    Cables Over 1000 Volts . . . . 392.20(B)

    Multiconductor Cables 1000 Volts or Less . . . 392.20(A)

  CATV and Radio Distribution Systems. 820.133

  Class 1 Circuits 725.48

  Class 2 & 3 Circuits . . . . .725.136(A)

  Communications Circuits . . . . 800.133(A)(1)

  Network-Powered Broadband Systems . . . . .830.133(A)(1)

  NPLFA Circuits 760.48

  Optical Fiber Cables 770.133

  PLFA Circuits 760.136

Luminaire (Fixture) . . . . Art. 402

  Allowable Ampacity 402.5

  Ampacity of . . . . 240.4(A)

  Overcurrent, Protection of 240.5

  Supplementary Overcurrent Protection 240.10

  Taps. . . . . .210.19(A)(4)

    To Branch Circuit Conductor. . . . . 240.5(B)(2)

    To Luminaire (Fixture) Outlet Box . . . . . . .410.117(C)

    Manufactured Wiring Systems . . . . .604.100(A)(2) Ex. 1

  Types . . . . Table 402.3

  Whips . . . . .210.19(A)(4)

    Flexible Metal Conduit . . . . .348.20(A)(2)

    Flexible Metallic Tubing . . . . 360.20(A) Ex. 2

    Length and Size of Luminaire (Fixture) Wire . . . .

    . . . . 240.5(B)(2)

    Liquidtight Flexible Metal Conduit . . . .

    . . . . 350.30(A) Excs. 3 and 4

    Liquidtight Flexible Nonmetallic Conduit . . . .356.30(2)

    Type AC Cable . . . . 320.30(D)(3)

    Type MC Cable . . . . 330.30(D)(2)

    Type NM Cable . . . . .334.30(B)(2)

    Wiring of . . . . 410 Part VI

Machine Tool Wire

  Ampacity of . . . . 310.15(A)(1) Info. Notes 2

  Application and Insulation . . . . Table 310.104(A)

  See Electrical Standard for Industrial Machinery NFPA 79 . .

  . . . . .NFPA 79

Material Not Specified Means Copper 110.5

Metal Clad Cable . . . . Art. 330

  Ampacity of Conductors 330.80

  Conductor Material and Size 330.104

  Insulation 330.112

Mineral-Insulated, Metal-Sheathed Cable . . . . Art. 332

  Ampacity of Conductors 332.80

  Insulation within 332.112

  Type of Conductors 332.104

  See MINERAL-INSULATED, METAL-SHEATHED CABLE

  Ferm's Finder

Minimum Size (General) . . . . .310.106(A)

  Branch Circuits . . . . 210 Part II

  Equipment Grounding Conductor 250.122

  Feeders 215.2

    600 Volts and Less . . . . 215.2(A)

    Over 600 Volts . . . . 215.2(B)

  (Fixture) Luminaire Wire 402.6

  Flexible Cords and Cables 400.21

    Portable Cables Over 600 Volts . . . . . 400 Part III, 400.31

  Grounding Electrode Conductor 250.66

  Outside Branch Circuits and Feeders 225.6

  Parallel Conductors . . . . 310.10(H)

  Services

    Minimum Permitted for Dwellings. . . . . . .310.15(B)(7)

    Overhead Service Drop 230.23

    Service Entrance 230.42

    Underground Service-Lateral . . . . 230.31(B)

Mobile Home Service or Feeder . . . . .310.15(B)(7)

  Minimum Permitted Size . . . . .310.15(B)(7)

  Neutral, Definition of . . . . Art. 100

Number of, in

  Auxiliary Gutters 366.22

  Boxes 314.16

  Cable Trays

    Multiconductor Cables 2000 Volts or Less. . . . 392.22(A)

Single Conductor Cables 2000 Volts or Less. . . 392.22(B)

Type MV and MC Cables (2001 Volts and Over) 392.22(C)

Cellular Concrete Floor Raceways 372.22

Cellular Metal Floor Raceways 374.22

Combination of, in Raceways . . . . Chapter 9 Table 1

  Areas of Conduit or Tubing for . . . . . . Chapter 9 Table 4

  Dimensions for . . . . Chapter 9 Table 5

  Dimensions for Compact Aluminum Building Wire. . . .
  . . . . Chapter 9 Table 5A

Conduit Bodies . . . . 314.16(C)

Electrical Metallic Tubing 358.22

  Conductors of the Same Size . . . .
  . . . . Informative Annex C, Table C1

  Conductors of the Same Size (Compact) . . . .
  . . . . Informative Annex C, Table C1A

Electrical Nonmetallic Tubing 362.22

  Conductors of the Same Size . . . .
  . . . . Informative Annex C, Table C2

  Conductors of the Same Size (Compact) . . . .
  . . . . Informative Annex C, Table C2A

Elevators . . . . Art. 620

  Conductors in Raceways 620.33

  Conductors in Wireways 620.32

(Fixture) Luminaire Wires 402.7

Flexible Metal Conduit 348.22

  Conductors of the Same Size . . . .
  . . . . Informative Annex C, Table C3

  Conductors of the Same Size (Compact) . . . .
  . . . . Informative Annex C, Table C3A

  3/8" Flexible Metal Conduit . . . . Table 348.22

General Installations 300.17

Intermediate Metal Conduit 342.22

  Conductors of the Same Size . . . .
  . . . . Informative Annex C, Table C4

  Conductors of the Same Size (Compact) . . . .
  . . . . Informative Annex C, Table C4A

Liquidtight Flexible Metal Conduit 350.22

  Conductors of the Same Size . . . .
  . . . . Informative Annex C, Table C7

  Conductors of the Same Size (Compact) . . . .
  . . . . Informative Annex C, Table C7A

Liquidtight Flexible Nonmetallic Conduit 356.22

  Conductors of the Same Size (Compact) (FNMC-A)

  . . . . Informative Annex C, Table C6A

  Conductors of the Same Size (Compact) (FNMC-B)

  . . . . Informative Annex C, Table C5A

Conductors of the Same Size (Type FNMC-A) . . . .
. . . . Informative Annex C, Table C6

Conductors of the Same Size (Type FNMC-B) . . . .
. . . . Informative Annex C, Table C5

Nipples (60% Fill) . . . . Chapter 9, Note 4

Nonmetallic Underground Conduit with Conductors . . . .
. . . . 354.22

Outlet Boxes 314.16

Rigid Metal Conduit 344.22

  Conductors of the Same Size . . . .
  . . . . Informative Annex C, Table C8

  Conductors of the Same Size (Compact)
  . . . . Informative Annex C, Table C8A

Rigid PVC (Type A). 352.22

  Conductors of the Same Size . . . .
  . . . . Informative Annex C, Table C11

  Conductors of the same Size (Compact)
  . . . . Informative Annex C, Table C11A

Rigid PVC (Type EB) 352.22

  Conductors of the Same Size . . . .
  . . . . Informative Annex C, Table C12

  Conductors of the Same Size (Compact)
  . . . . Informative Annex C, Table C12A

Rigid PVC (Schedule 40 & HDPE) 352.22

  Conductors of the Same Size . . . .
  . . . . Informative Annex C, Table C10

  Conductors of the Same Size (Compact) . . . .
  . . . . Informative Annex C, Table C10A

Rigid PVC Conduit, Schedule 80 (PVC) 352.22

  Conductors of the Same Size . . . .
  . . . . Informative Annex C, Table C9

  Conductors of the Same Size (Compact) . . . .
  . . . . Informative Annex C, Table C9A

Skeleton Tubing, Field-Installed . . . . 600.31(C)

Surface Raceways (Metal) 386.22

Surface Raceways (Nonmetallic) 388.22

Underfloor Raceways 390.6

Wireways (Metal) 376.22

Wireways (Nonmetallic) 378.22

Oil & Gasoline Resistant (General) . . . . 310.10(G)

  Class I Locations 501.20

  See (ZLGR). . . . . UL Product Spec

Operating Over 1000 Volts . . . . 300 Part II

  Conductor Construction and Applications 310.104

Overcurrent Protection of 240.4

  Over 1000 Volts . . . . 240 Part IX

Protection of Flexible Cords and Luminaire (Fixture) Wires
. . . . 240.5

Service Entrance Conductors 230.90

See OVERCURRENT PROTECTION . . . . . Ferm's Finder

Parallel Conductors 1/0 AWG and Larger Permitted . . .310.10(H)

Auxiliary Gutters (within and grouped) 366.20

Control Power . . . . 310.10(H)(1) Ex. 1

Existing Installations, 2 AWG Permitted . . . .
. . . . 310.10(H)(1) Ex. 2

Grounding (Equipment) . . . . .250.122(F)

Underground . . . . 300.5(I)

Point, Neutral Point, Definition of . . . . Art. 100

Power and Control Tray Cable . . . . Art. 336

Properties of . . . . Chapter 9 Table 8

Protection of, Physical Damage (General) 300.4

Cables in Accessible Attics 320.23

Equipment Grounding Conductors Smaller Than 6 AWG . .
. . . . .250.120(C)

Grounding Conductors

Communications Circuits . . . . .800.100(A)(6)

Community Antenna Television and Radio Distribution
Systems . . . . .820.100(A)(6)

Network-Powered Broadband Communication Systems .
. . . . .830.100(A)(6)

Radio and Television Equipment . . . . 810.21(D)

Grounding Electrode Conductors . . . . 250.64(B)

Multiconductor NPLFA Cables . . . . 760.53(A)

Open Wiring on Insulators 398.15

In Accessible Attics 398.23

Over 1000 Volts

Metal-Sheathed Cables 300.42

Underground Installations . . . . 300.50(B)

PLFA Circuits . . . . 760.130(B)

Safety Control Circuits . . . . 725.31(B)

Service Entrance Conductors Aboveground 230.50

Sleeves . . . . 300.15(C)

Types NM, NMC, and NMS Cables . . . . 334.15(B)

Types NM, NMC, and NMS Cables (In Unfinished
Basements) . . . . 334.15(C)

Underground Installations . . . . .300.5(D)

Underground Service-Laterals 230.32

Protection of, at Boxes

Boxes, Conduit Bodies, or Fittings 314.17

Cabinets, Cutout Boxes, and Meter Socket Enclosures . 312.5

Covers of Outlet Boxes and Conduit Bodies 314.41

Intermediate Metal Conduit 342.46

High Density Polyethylene Conduit, Type HDPE . . . 353.46

Nonmetallic Underground Conduit with Conductors 354.46

Reinforced Thermosetting Resin Conduit, Type RTRC 355.46

Rigid Metal Conduit 344.46

Rigid PVC Conduit 352.46

Radius of Bends

Manholes 110.74

Nonmetallic Underground Conduit with Conductors 354.24

Over 1000 Volts Nominal 300.34

Pull and Junction Boxes 314.28

Over 1000 Volts 314.71

Service Entrance Cable: Type SE and USE 338.24

Type AC Cable 320.24

Type IGS Cable 326.24

Type ITC Cable 727.10

Type MC Cable 330.24

Type MI Cable 332.24

Type NM Cable 334.24

Type TC Cable 336.24

Type UF Cable 340.24

See Also, BENDS . . . . Ferm's Finder

Resistance of . . . . Chapter 9 Table 8

AC Resistance and Reactance . . . . Chapter 9 Table 9

Rooftops, Sunlight and Ambient Temperature Adjustments . .
. . . . .310.15(B)(3)(c)

Sealing Underground Raceways

600 Volts and Under . . . . 300.5(G)

Over 1000 Volts . . . . 300.50(F)

Branch Circuits and Feeders 225.27

Service Raceways 230.8

Service Drop Conductors . . . . 230 Part II

Allowable Ampacity for

Single Conductor Free Air 60 - 90°C . . .Table 310.15(B)17

Single Conductor Free Air 150 - 250°C . . . .
. . . . .Table 310.15(B)19

Clearances 230.24

Means of Attachment 230.27

Size and Rating 230.23

Shielding, Over 2000 Volts . . . . 310.10(E)

Direct Burial Conductors 310.60

Shielding, 2001 to 35,000 Volts . . . . .310.60(B)(1)

Direct Burial Conductors . . . . .310.60(B)(2)

See OVER 1000 VOLTS, NOMINAL . . . . . . Ferm's Finder

C

Single Conductor . . . . 300.3(A)

    In Cable Trays . . . . 392.22(B)

    Nonheating Leads of Electric Space-Heating Cables . 424.43

    Solar Photovoltaic Systems. . . . . 690.31(C)

    Underground . . . . 300.5(I)

Small Motors . . . . 430.22(G)

Splice Not Permitted of or in

    Flexible Cord Initial Installation. 400.13

    Grounding Electrode Conductor . . . . 250.64(C)

    Raceways (General) . . . . 300.13(A)

    Raceways (*See* Specific Raceway Article)

    Sealing Fittings . . . . .501.15(C)(4)

    Swimming Pool Lighting Ground Wire . . . . .680.23(F)(2)

Splices of or in . . . . 110.14(B)

    Auxiliary Gutters 366.56

    Boxes Required 300.15

        See BOXLESS DEVICES. . . . . Ferm's Finder

        Temporary Wiring . . . . 590.4(G)

    Cable Trays. 392.56

    Cellular Concrete Floor Raceway 372.56

    Cellular Metal Floor Raceway 374.56

    Conduit Bodies (General) 300.15

        When Permitted . . . . .314.16(C)(2)

    Direct Burial Cables. . . . . 300.5(E)

    Enclosures for Switches and Overcurrent Devices . . . . . .

    . . . . 312.8(A)

    Flexible Cords

        For Repair Only 400.13

        Temporary Wiring . . . . 590.4(G)

    Heating Cables

        For Pipelines and Vessels . . . . 427.19(B)

        Outdoor Deicing and Snow-Melting. . . . . . 426.24(B)

        Space-Heating Cables, Cannot Alter Length . . . 424.40

        Space-Heating Cables, Embedded . . . . 424.41(D)

    Insulation of . . . . 110.14(B)

    Service Entrance Conductors 230.46

    Under-Floor Raceway 390.7

    Wireways, Metal 376.56

    Wireways, Nonmetallic 378.56

Stranded Required . . . . 310.106(C)

Suitable For Wet Locations . . . . 310.10(C)

    Weatherproof, Definition of . . . . .Art. 100 Part I

    Wet Location, Definition of . . . . .Art. 100 Part I

Supply Conductors, Described . . . .250.102(C)(2) Info. Note

Supporting in or by

    Festoon Lighting . . . . 225.6(B)

    Messenger . . . . Art. 396

    Open Wiring on Insulators. 398.30

    Pull & Junction Boxes. . . . . 314.28(B)

    Vertical Raceways 300.19

Swimming Pools

    Bonding 680.26

    Equipment Grounding . . . . 680 Part II

    Wet-Niche Luminaires (Fixtures) . . . . .680.26(B)(4)

Temperature Rating of Insulation . . . . .310.15(A)(3)

    Allowable Ampacity for . . . Tables 310.15(B)16 through 21

    Conductor Application and Insulation . . . Table 310.104(A)

    Fixture Wire . . . . .Table 402.3

    Luminaire (Fixture) Outlet Boxes 410.21

    Over 2000 Volts Rating

        Allowable Ampacity for . . .Table 310.60(C)67 through 86

Terminations 110.14

    CO/ALR Marking

        Receptacles . . . . 406.3(C)

        Switches . . . . 404.14(C)

    Grounding Conductor Connections

        Connection to Electrodes 250.70

        Equipment Grounding Conductor at Receptacles 250.146

        Equipment Grounding Conductors at Boxes . . . 250.148

        Grounding and Bonding Equipment. 250.8

        Suitable for the Purpose 110.14

        See (AALZ) . . . .*UL Product Spec*

    See (AALZ) . . . .*UL Product Spec*

Tray Cable . . . . Art. 336

    Ampacity of 336.80

    Installation of, in Cable Trays 392.20

UF, Type . . . . Art. 340

    See (YDUX). . . . .*UL Product Spec*

Under Buildings, In Raceway. . . . . 300.5(C)

    When Considered Outside Building 230.6

Underground

    Aircraft Hangars, Under Hangar Floor 513.8

    Bulk Storage Plants

        Underground Wiring Below Class I Locations 515.8

    Dispenser, Sealing at 514.9

    Motor Fuel Dispensing Facilities 514.3

    Sealing of Conduits Under Hangar Floor 513.9

    See BURIED CONDUCTORS. . . . . Ferm's Finder

See HAZARDOUS (CLASSIFIED) LOCATIONS, Wiring Under . . . . Ferm's Finder

See UNDERGROUND WIRING . . . . Ferm's Finder

Under Swimming Pools 680.11

Use Oxide Inhibitor Where Required 110.3

USE, Type . . . . Art. 338

   See (TYLZ) . . . .*UL Product Spec*

Voltage Drop of Branch Circuits . . . . 210.19(A) Info. Notes 4

   Conductors . . . . .310.15(A)(1) Info. Notes 1

   Feeders . . . . 215.2(A)(1) Info. Notes 2

   Fire Pumps 695.7

   Sensitive Electronic Equipment . . . . 647.4(D)

   See VOLTAGE DROP . . . . Ferm's Finder

Volume Required Per . . . . 314.16(B)

Wet Locations . . . . 310.10(C)

CONDUIT

Aluminum

   Be Sure It Is Suitable for the Condition 300.6

   Corrosion Protection . . . . 344.10(B)

   Shall Not Be Used in Concrete or Earth Burial

      Without Supplementary Corrosion Protection

   See (DYWV) . . . .*UL Product Spec*

See BENDS . . . . Ferm's Finder

See CONDUIT BODIES . . . . Ferm's Finder

Note: Boxes such as FS & FD or larger cast or sheet metal boxes are not classified as conduit bodies. *See* definition of . conduit body in Article 100 Part I.

Burial Depth 600 Volts and Less 300.5

Burial Depths Over 1000 Volts 300.50

Continuity of Run

   Bonding in Hazardous Locations 250.100

   Bonding Loosely Jointed Metal Raceways 250.98

   Bonding of Other Enclosures . . . . 250.96(A)

   Bonding of Service Raceways 250.92

   Bonding Over 250 Volts 250.97

   Class I Locations . . . . 501.30(A)

      Zone 0, 1, & 2 Locations . . . . 505.25(A)

      Zone 20, 21, & 22 Locations . . . . 506.25(A)

   Class II Locations . . . . 502.30(A)

   Class III Locations . . . . 503.30(A)

   Complete Runs . . . . 300.18(A)

   Electrical Continuity Metal Raceways 300.10

   Electrical Metallic Tubing 358.42

   Intermediate Metal Conduit 342.42

   Isolated Grounding Circuits . . . . 250.96(B)

   Mechanical Continuity 300.12

   Method of Bonding at Service . . . . 250.92(B)

   Rigid Metal Conduit 344.42

   Threaded Conduit within Hazardous Locations . . 500.8(E)

Dimensions & Percent Area . . . . Chapter 9 Table 4

   Conduit Fill Tables . . . . Informative Annex C

Enclosures with Devices or (Fixtures) Luminaires Supported by . . . . 314.23(F)

Enclosures without Devices or (Fixtures) Luminaires Supported by . . . . 314.23(E)

Exposed to Sunlight on Rooftops . . . . 310.15(B)(3)(c)

Field-Cut Threads . . . . 300.6(A) Info. Notes

Fitting (Definition) . . . . Art. 100 Part I

   See (DWTT) . . . .*UL Product Spec*

Flexible Metal Conduit . . . . Art. 348

   See FLEXIBLE METAL CONDUIT . . . . . . Ferm's Finder

High Density Polyethylene Conduit, Type HDPE . . . Art. 353

Intermediate Metal Conduit . . . . Art. 342

   See INTERMEDIATE METAL CONDUIT . . . Ferm's Finder

Liquidtight Flexible Metal Conduit . . . . Art. 350

   See LIQUIDTIGHT FLEXIBLE METAL CONDUIT . . . . . Ferm's Finder

Liquidtight Flexible Nonmetallic Conduit . . . . Art. 356

   See LIQUIDTIGHT FLEXIBLE NONMETALLIC CONDUIT Ferm's Finder

Nonmetallic Underground Conduit with Conductors . Art. 354

   See NONMETALLIC UNDERGROUND CONDUIT WITH CONDUCTORS . . . . Ferm's Finder

Number of Bends Permitted in

   Flexible Metal Conduit 348.26

   High Density Polyethylene Conduit Type HDPE . . . 353.26

   Intermediate Metal Conduit 342.26

   Liquidtight Flexible Metal Conduit 350.26

   Liquidtight Flexible Nonmetallic Conduit 356.26

   Nonmetallic Underground Conduit with Conductors 354.26

   Reinforced Thermosetting Resin Conduit, Type RTRC 355.26

   Rigid Metal Conduit 344.26

   Rigid PVC Conduit 352.26

   See BENDS . . . . Ferm's Finder

Number of Conductors Permitted in

   See CONDUCTORS, Number of, in . . . . . . Ferm's Finder

Note: Conduit fill tables apply only to complete conduit systems and are not intended to apply to sections of conduit

used to protect exposed wiring from physical damage. . . . .
Chapter 9, Note 2

Radius of Bends

Flexible Metal Conduit 348.24

Flexible Metal Tubing. 358.24

High Density Polyethylene Conduit, Type HDPE . . . 353.24

Intermediate Metal Conduit 342.24

Liquidtight Flexible Metal Conduit 350.24

Liquidtight Flexible Nonmetallic Conduit 356.24

Nonmetallic Underground Conduit with Conductors . . . .
. . . . 354.24

Reinforced Thermosetting Resin Conduit, Type RTRC. . . .
. . . . 355.24

Rigid Metal Conduit 344.24

Rigid PVC Conduit 352.24

Reaming & Threading

Electrical Metallic Tubing 358.28

Intermediate Metal Conduit 342.28

Rigid Metal Conduit 344.28

Rigid Metal Conduit . . . . Art. 344

See RIGID METAL CONDUIT. . . . . Ferm's Finder

Rigid PVC Conduit . . . . Art. 352

See RIGID PVC CONDUIT . . . . Ferm's Finder

Risers Not Over 75 mm (3 in.) under Floor Standing Panels   .
. . . . 408.5

Supports of or from

Cables or Nonelectrical Equipment, Not Permitted . . . . . .
. . . . 300.11(B)

Flexible Metal Conduit 348.30

Intermediate Metal Conduit 342.30

Liquidtight Flexible Metal Conduit 350.30

Liquidtight Flexible Nonmetallic Conduit 356.30

Nonmetallic Rigid Conduit 352.30

Support of (Fixtures) Luminaires or Other Equipment
Prohibited. . . . . 352.12(B)

Reinforced Thermosetting Resin Conduit, Type RTRC . .
. . . . 355.30

Rigid Metal Conduit 344.30

Welding Not Permitted . . . . 300.18(B)

Trimming

Flexible Metal Conduit 348.28

Liquidtight Flexible Nonmetallic Conduit 356.28

Nonmetallic Underground Conduit with Conductors . . . .
. . . . 354.28

Rigid PVC Conduit 352.28

Wet Locations 300.6

Rigid PVC Conduit . . . . 352.10(D)

See RIGID PVC CONDUIT. . . . . Ferm's Finder

Electrical Metallic Tubing . . . . Art. 358

See ELECTRICAL METALLIC TUBING . . Ferm's Finder

Electrical Nonmetallic Tubing . . . . Art. 362

See ELECTRICAL NONMETALLIC TUBING . . . .
Ferm's Finder

Flexible Metallic Tubing . . . . Art. 360

See FLEXIBLE METALLIC TUBING . . . . Ferm's Finder

CONDUIT BODIES (Where Required) 300.15

Conductors Entering 314.17

Cross-Sectional Area. . . . . 314.16(C)

Installation and Use (General) 314.1

Number of Conductors, General . . . . .314.16(C)(1)

With Splices, Taps, or Devices . . . . .314.16(C)(2)

To Be Accessible 314.29

Unused Openings . . . . 314.17(A)

Used As Pull or Junction Boxes. 314.28

CONDUIT AND TUBING FILL TABLES . . . .
. . . . INFORMATIVE ANNEX C

CONTINUITY

Auxiliary Gutters . . . . 366.100(A)

Cellular Metal Floor Raceways 374.100

Conductors, Mechanical and Electrical 300.13

Electrical Continuity Metal Raceways and Enclosures . 300.10

Equipment Grounding Conductor 250.148

Ground Path Not to Rely on Water Meters or Filtering
Equipment . . . . 250.53(D)(1)

Grounding Electrode Conductor . . . . 250.64(C)

Mechanical, Raceways and Cables 300.12

Neutral of Multiwire Branch Circuits . . . . 300.13(B)

Service Conductors 230.46

Service Equipment

Bonding of 250.92

Continuity of Enclosures 300.10

Method of Bonding . . . . 250.92(B)

See CONDUIT, Continuity of Run . . . . Ferm's Finder

Connected to an Equipment Grounding Conductor . . 250.134

Note: This phrase is used throughout the *Code* to give more
specific direction as to how electrical equipment is to be
grounded.

CONNECTIONS

Aluminum to Copper Conductors 110.14

Cellular Metal Floor Raceways to Cabinets and Extensions . . . . 374.18(A)

Essential Electrical Systems

  Automatic to Life Safety Branch 517.43

  Equipment Branch to Alternate Power Source 517.35

  For Clinics, Medical and Dental Offices 517.45

  To Equipment Branch 517.44

Feed-Through Connections of Neutral Conductors . . . . 300.13(B)

Grounding and Bonding Conductors 250.8

  Equipment Grounding Conductor, Multiple Circuit Connections 250.144

  Grounding Electrode Conductor

    Method of Connection 250.70

    Size of Conductor 250.66

    Metallic Water Pipe and Structural Metal . . . . 250.68(C)

    To Grounding Electrode. 250.68

Grounding Connection AC Systems . . . . 250.24(A)

Grounding Connection DC Systems. 250.164

Grounding Connection Ungrounded Systems . . . . 250.24(E)

High-Impedance Grounded Neutral System 250.36

Integrity of . . . . 110.12(B)

Multiple Circuit, *See* MULTIPLE ENCLOSURE SERVICES . . . . Ferm's Finder

Point of Interconnected Power Production Sources . . . 705.12

Splices . . . . 110.14(B)

Switches 404.2

Temperature Limitations . . . . 110.14(C)

Terminals, General Provisions . . . . 110.14(A)

  Location of in Switchboards and Panelboards . . . . 408.3(D)

  See (AALZ) . . . . *UL Product Spec*

Torque (tightening connection) . . . . 110.14(D)

Under-Floor Raceways to Cabinets and Wall Outlets . . 390.15

X-Ray Installations 517.71

CONNECTORS

Armored Cable (Type AC) 320.40

Cabinets and Cutout Boxes . . . . 312.5(C)

Cable, Theater 520.67

Electric Vehicle 625.10

Electrical Metallic Tubing 358.42

Flexible Metal Conduit 348.42

General Requirement for . . . . 300.15(C)

Listed for Specific Wiring Method 300.15

Intermediate Metal Conduit 342.42

Liquidtight Flexible Metal Conduit 350.42

Liquidtight Flexible Nonmetallic Conduit. 356.42

Portable Switchboards on Stage. . . . . 520 Part IV

Pressure (Solderless) Connector, Definition of . . . . . Art. 100

Rigid Metal Conduit 344.42

Rigid PVC Conduit 352.48

Single-Pole Separable

  Definition of 530.2

  Portable Distribution or Termination Boxes, Carnivals. . . . . 525.22(D)

  Use of in Motion Picture and Television Studios . . . 530.22

  Use of in Theaters . . . . 520.53(I)

Solar Photovoltaic Systems . . . . Art 690

  Component Interconnections. 690.32

  Connectors 690.33

  Flexible, Fine Stranded Cables . . . . 690.31(E)

  Grounding Connection Connectors 690.47

See (ECIS). . . . . *UL Product Spec*

CONNECTOR STRIPS . . . . 520.44(B)

CONSTRUCTION SITES

See TEMPORARY INSTALLATIONS . . . . Ferm's Finder

CONSTRUCTION, TYPES OF . . . . .Informative Annex E

CONTINUOUS DUTY

Definition of .Art. 100 Part I

Motor and Branch-Circuit Overload Protection . . 430 Part III

Motor Circuit Conductors . . . . 430 Part II

CONTINUOUS INDUSTRIAL PROCESS

Electrical System Coordination 240.12

Ground-Fault Protection of Equipment (Branch Circuits) . . . . 210.13 Ex. 1

Ground-Fault Protection of Equipment (Feeders) . . . . 215.10 Ex. 1

Ground-Fault Protection of Equipment (Services) 230.95

Integrated Electrical Systems . . . . Art. 685

Orderly Shutdown 430.44

Power Loss Hazard. . . . . 240.4(A)

CONTINUOUS LOAD

Branch-Circuit Conductor Ratings . . . . .210.19(A)(1)

C

Overcurrent Protection . . . . 210.20(A)

Branch-Circuit Ratings, Appliances . . . . 422.10(A)

Branch-Circuits, Electric Space Heating . . . . 424.3(B)

Definition of . . . . Art. 100

Electric Pool Water Heaters 680.10

Feeder Conductor Ratings . . . . 215.2(A)(1)

Overcurrent Protection 215.3

Storage-Type Water Heaters 422.13

CONTROL CIRCUITS

Definition . . . . Art. 100

Fire Pumps 695.14

Industrial Control Panels . . . . Art. 100

Motors . . . . 430 Part VI

AC Systems 50-1000 Volts Not Required to be Grounded . .
. . . . 250.21(A)(3)a, b, c

Arrangement of 430.74

Class 1, 2, and 3 Remote Control Circuits . . . . . Art. 725

Copper Conductors Required . . . . 430.9(B)

Definition of Control Circuit . . . . Art. 100

Disconnecting Means 430.75

Mechanical Protection 430.73

Ungrounded 685.14

Overcurrent Protection

Conductors . . . . 430.72(A)&(B)

Control Circuit Transformers . . . . 430.72(C)

Class 1 Circuits 725.41

Location of Overcurrent Device 725.45

Class 2 or 3 Power Source, Supply Source 725.121

Class 2 or 3 Circuits . . . . Chapter 9 Tables 11(A) & (B)

Cranes 610.53

For Specific Conductor Applications . . . . 240.4(G)

Maximum Rating . . . . Table 430.72(B)

Motors 300% or 400% . . . . Table 430.72(B)

Orderly Shutdown, Motors 430.44

Torque Requirements . . . . 430.9(C)

See CLASS 1, 2 & 3 REMOTE CONTROL CIRCUITS . . . . .
. . . . Ferm's Finder

See DIFFERENT SYSTEMS IN SAME ENCLOSURE . . . . . .
. . . . Ferm's Finder

CONTROL SYSTEMS FOR PERMANENT AMUSEMENT
ATTRACTIONS . . . . Article 522

CONTROLLED RECEPTACLE

Building Automation . . . . 406.3(E)

Energy Management . . . . 406.3(E)

Marking . . . . Figure 406.3(E)

CONTROLLER, MOTOR . . . . 430 Part VII
See MOTOR CONTROLLERS . . . . Ferm's Finder

CONVERSION TABLE, AC CONDUCTOR . . Chapter 9 Table 9

CONVERTERS

Definition for Phase Converters 455.2

See PHASE CONVERTERS . . . . Ferm's Finder

Definition of, for Recreational Vehicles and Park Trailers . . . .
. . . . 551.2 and 552.2

Voltage Converters Park Trailers 552.20

Voltage Converters Recreational Vehicles 551.20

COOKING UNIT, COUNTER-MOUNTED

Branch Circuits . . . . .210.19(A)(3)

Definition of . . . . Art. 100 Part I

Load Calculations 220.55

COOLING OF EQUIPMENT (General) . . . . 110.13(B)
Ventilation for Transformers 450.9

COORDINATION (SELECTIVE)

Critical Operations Power Systems (COPS) 708.54

Definition .Article 100

Elevators 620.62

Emergency Systems 700.32

Fire Pumps . . . . 695.3(C)(3)

Information Technology Equipment 645.27

Legally Required Standby Systems 701.27

COORDINATION OF ELECTRICAL SYSTEMS

Elevator Feeders, Selective Coordination 620.62

Emergency Systems, Selective Coordination 700.32

Essential Electric System . . . . 517.30(G)

Health Care Facilities . . . . 517.17(C)

Legally Required Standby Systems, Selective Coordination . . .
. . . . 701.27

Orderly Shutdown 240.12

COPPER CONDUCTORS, *See* CONDUCTORS, Copper . . . .
Ferm's Finder

(COPS) CRITICAL OPERATIONS POWER SYSTEMS . . . .
. . . .**Informative Annex F**
See CRITICAL OPERATIONS POWER SYSTEMS . . . . . .
. . . . Ferm's Finder

CORD SETS & POWER SUPPLY CORDS
Green Outer Cover or Jacket Permitted 400.23
Ground-Fault Circuit-Interruption Protections . . 590.6(A)(1)
Mobile and Manufactured Homes 550.10
Park Trailers 552.43
Recreational Vehicles 551.46
Temporary Installations
GFCI Protection for Personnel 590.6
Not on Floor or Ground . . . . 590.4(J)
See (ELBZ) . . . .*UL Product Spec*

CORDS . . . . Art. 400
Air Conditioners, Room 440.64
Ampacity of Flexible Cord
Derating for More Than 3 Current-Carrying Conductors . .
. . . . 400.5
Engineering Supervision . . . . 400.5(C)
Flexible Cables . . . . Table 400.5(A)(2)
Flexible Cords and Cables . . . . Table 400.5(A)(1)
General 400.5
Supply Cord of Listed Appliance or Portable Lamps . . 240.5
Appliances
Cord- and Plug-Connected Subject to Immersion . . 422.41
Disconnection of Cord- and Plug-Connected 422.33
General . . . . 422.16(A)
Polarity in Cord- and Plug-Connected 422.40
Range Hoods. . . . . .422.16(B)(4)
Specific Appliances . . . . 422.16(B)
Between an Existing Receptacle Outlet and an Inlet . . . .
. . . . .400.10(A)(11)
Bushings Required 400.14
Busways, Branches from. . . . . 368.56(B)
Trolley-Type Busways, Branches from . . . . 368.56(C)
Carnivals, Circuses, Fairs, Wiring Method 525.20
Color Coding, Grounded Conductor 400.22
Color Coding, Equipment Grounding Conductor 400.23
Counter-Mounted Cooking Units . . . . .422.16(B)(3)
Dishwashers . . . . .422.16(B)(2)
Electric Vehicle Charging System 625.17
Elevators, Not Required to be in Raceway. . . . . . . 620.21 Ex.

Emergency Unit Equipment . . . . 700.12(F)
Range Hoods. . . . . .422.16(B)(4)
Flexible Cord, Uses Permitted (General) . . . . 400.10(A)
Adjustable (Fixtures) Luminaires . . . . 410.62(B)
Attachment Plug Required . . . . 400.10(B)
Branches from Busways . . . . 368.56(B)
Elevators, Dumbwaiters, Escalators, etc.
Car Wiring. . . . . .620.21(A)(2)
Escalators. . . . . .620.21(B)(3)
Hoistways . . . . .620.21(A)(1)
Machine Room and Space, Equipment Components. . . .
. . . . .620.21(A)(3)
Electric Discharge (Fixtures) Luminaires Supported Inde-
pendently. 410.24
Electric Discharge (Fixtures) and LED Luminaires 410.62(C)
Motor Disconnecting Means. . . . . .430.109(F)
Motors on General-Purpose Branch Circuit . . . . 430.42(C)
Hazardous (Classified) Locations
Aircraft Energizers, Ground Support Equipment513.10(C)(3)
Aircraft Mobile Servicing Equipment. . . . . . 513.10(D)(2)
Class I, Division 1 & 2 Locations, Basic Requirements . . . .
. . . . .501.140
Class II, Division 1 & 2 Locations, Basic Requirements . . .
. . . . .502.140
Class III, Division 1 Locations, Basic Requirements. . . . . .
. . . . .503.140
Class I, Division 1 Locations, Flexible Connections. . . . . .
. . . . .501.10(A)(2)
Class I, Division 2 Locations, Flexible Connections . . . . .
. . . . .501.10(B)(2)
Class II, Division 1 Locations, Flexible Connections
. . . . .502.10(A)(2)
Class II, Division 2 Locations, Flexible Connections . . . . .
. . . . .502.10(B)(2)
Class III, Division 1 Locations, Flexible Connections. . . . .
. . . . .503.10(A)(3)
Class III, Division 2 Locations, Flexible Connections . . . .
. . . . 503.10(B)
Pendant Luminaires (Fixtures) Class II, Division 1 . . . . . .
. . . . .502.130(A)(3)
Pendant Luminaires (Fixtures) Luminaires) Class II, Division
2. . . . . 502.130(B)(4)
Pendants Above Class I Locations, Garages . . . 511.7(A)(2)
Pendants Not in Class I Locations, Hangars . . . . . 513.7(B)
Portable Equipment Not in Class I Locations, Hangars. . . .
. . . . 513.10(E)
Portable Lighting Equipment used in Commercial

C

Garage, Class I Locations . . . . 511.4(B)(2)

Process Control Instruments, Class I, Division 2 Locations .
. . . . 501.105(B)(6)

Heater Cords & Other Heating Appliances . . . .422.43(A), (B)

High Voltage Cable (Portable) . . . . 400 Part II

Immersion Heaters 422.44

Kitchen Waste Disposers . . . . .422.16(B)(1)

Legally Required Standby Unit Equipment . . . . . 701.12(G)

Listed Assembly Type . . . . 400.10(A)(11)

Manufactured Wiring Systems . . . . 604.100(A)

Markings

    Standard . . . . 400.6(A)

    Optional . . . . 400.6(B)

Mobile Home Feeder Supply . . . . 550.10(B)

Mobile Home Length of Cord . . . . 550.10(D)

Motion Picture and TV Studios . . . . 530 Part II

Motion Picture Projectors. 540.15

Motors

    Disconnecting Means. . . . . .430.109(F)

    Overload Protection Cord- and Plug-Connected Motors. . .
    . . . . 430.42(C)

Office Furnishings

    Freestanding-Type Partitions 605.9

    Lighting Accessories . . . . 605.6(B)

    Partition Interconnections 605.5

Overcurrent Protection 240.5

    Allowable Ampacity Cables . . . . Table 400.5(A)(2)

    Allowable Ampacity Flexible Cords and Cables . . . . . Table
    . . . . 400.5(A)(1)

    Cords Approved for Specific Appliances 400.13

Park Trailers Connection and Length of Cord 552.44

Park Trailers Feeder Supply . . . . 552.43(A)&(B)

Pendants

    Aircraft Hangars . . . . 513.7(B)

    Bathtubs and Shower Areas, Not within Zone . . . 410.10(D)

    Clothes Closets, Not Permitted in. . . . . 410.16(B)

    Commercial Garages . . . . 511.7(A)(2)

    Conductors 410.54

    Dressing Rooms, Lampholders Prohibited 520.71

    Hazardous (Classified) Locations

        Aircraft Hangars . . . . 513.7(B)

        Class I, Division 1 Locations . . . . .501.130(A)(3)

        Class I, Division 2 Locations . . . . .501.130(B)(3)

        Class II, Division 1 Locations . . . . .502.130(A)(3)

        Class II, Division 2 Locations . . . . .502.130(B)(4)

        Class III, Division 1 & 2 Locations . . . . . . 503.130(C)

        Commercial Garages. . . . . 511.7(A)(2)

        Hospitals, Above Hazardous Location . 517.61(B)(3) Ex. 2

        Hospitals, Other-Than-Hazardous Location . . . .
        . . . . 517.61(C)(1) Ex.

    Makeup Rooms, Not permitted in 520.71

    Permission Required by AHJ (if not in Table 400.4) 400.4

    Rating or Setting of Breakers for Cords (General) 240.5

        For Cables by Type . . . . .Table 400.5(A)(2)

        For Flexible Cords and Cables by Type . . . Table 400.5(A)(1)

    Range Hoods . . . . .422.16(B)(4)

    Recreation Vehicle Feeder Supply . . . . 551.46(A)

    Recreation Vehicle Length of Cord . . . . 551.46(B)

    Room Air Conditioners . . . . 440 Part VII

    Show Cases and Show Windows, Types Allowed. 400.11

    Show Cases 410.59

    Splices, on Construction Sites . . . . 590.4(G)

        Permitted for Repair Only 400.10

    Support of, at Terminations for Busways . . . . 368.56(B)

    Swimming Pools, Fountains, etc.

        Equipment Other Than an Underwater Luminaire (Lighting
        Fixture) 680.8

        Fountains . . . . 680 Part V

        Luminaires (Lighting Fixtures) Other Than Underwater . . .
        . . . . .680.22(B)(5)

        Motors 680.21

        Spas and Hot Tubs . . . . 680 Part IV

        Storable Pools . . . . 680 Part III

        Strain Relief Required . . . . 680.24(E)

        Wet-Niche Luminaires (Fixtures) . . . . 680.23(B)

    Temporary Locations

        Assured Equipment Grounding Conductor Program . . . .
        . . . . 590.6(B)(2)

        Ground-Fault Circuit-Interrupter Protection . . 590.6(A)(1)

        Physical Protection . . . . .590.4(H)

        Support. . . . . 590.4(J)

    Theaters

        Border Lights . . . . 520.44(C)

        Dressing Rooms, Not Permitted in 520.71

        Luminaire Supply Cords 520.68

        Other Portable Stage Equipment . . . . 520 Part V

        Permitted for Portable Equipment . . . . 520.5(B)

    Trash Compactors (Length of Cord). . . . . . . .422.16(B)(2)

Travel Trailer (Length of Cord) . . . . 551.46(B)

Types . . . . Table 400.4

Uses Not Permitted 400.12

Uses Permitted 400.10

   Application Use . . . . Table 400.4

   Class I, Division 1 & 2 . . . . 501.140

   From Busways in Industrial Establishments 400.10

   To Connect Lampholders and (Fixtures) Luminaires . 410.62

   To Connect Motors . . . . 430.42(C)

      Attachment Plug As Disconnect for . . . . . . .430.109(F)

Water Resistant Cord 400.4

   For Fountain Equipment 680.56

See Flexible Cords, (ZJCZ) . . . .*UL Product Spec*

CORRECTION FACTORS, AMBIENT TEMPERATURE

For Allowable Ampacity Values . . . . Table 310.15(B)(2)

CORROSION AND DETERIORATION

Class 1, Class 2, and Class 3 Circuits . . . . 725.3(L)

Deteriorating Agents. 110.11

Protection, General . . . . 300.6(A) and (B)

   Bushings at Motors 430.13

   Cable Trays. 392.100(C)

   Cellular Metal Floor Raceways . . . . .374.12(1)

   Conductors . . . . 310.10(G)

   Deicing and Snow-Melting Equipment

      Resistance Heating Elements 426.26

      Skin Effect Heating. 426.43

   Electrical Metallic Tubing . . . . 358.10(B)

   Equipment Enclosures, etc., Agricultural Buildings. . . . . .

   . . . . 547.5(C)(3)

   Field-Cut Threads . . . . 300.6(A) Info. Notes

   Intermediate Metal Conduit . . . . 342.10(B)

   Luminaires (Light Fixtures) . . . . 410.10(B)

   Metal Boxes, Conduit Bodies, and Fittings. . . . . 314.40(A)

   Metal-Clad Cable 330.12

   Metal Wireways . . . . 376.12(2)

   Mineral-Insulated, Metal-Sheathed Cable 332.12

   Mobile and Manufactured Homes, Power Supply . 550.10(H)

   Nonmetallic Extensions . . . . .382.12(3)

   Nonmetallic-Sheathed Cable, Type NMC . . . .334.10(B)(1)

   Nonmetallic Wireways . . . . 378.10(2)

   Open Wiring on Insulators. . . . . 398.15(B)

   Pools- Swimming 680.14

Pull and Junction Boxes Over 1000 Volts. . . . . . 314.72(A)

Rigid Metal Conduit . . . . 344.10(B)

Rigid PVC Conduit . . . . 352.10(B)

Strut-Type Channel Raceway . . . . 384.10 & 12

Surface Metal Raceways . . . . 386.12(3)

Swimming Pools, Fountains and Similar Installations 680.14

Under-Floor Raceways . . . . 390.3(B)

See Electrical Metallic Tubing (FJMX) . . . .*UL Product Spec*

See Intermediate Metal Conduit (DYBY). . .*UL Product Spec*

See Rigid Ferrous Metal Conduit (DYIX). . .*UL Product Spec*

See Rigid Nonferrous Metal Conduit (DYWV). .*UL Product Spec*

See Rigid PVC Conduit (DZYR). . . . .*UL Product Spec*

COUNTERTOP OUTLETS — Receptacles

Face-Up Position, Not Permitted. . . . . 406.5(G)

Listed Receptacle Assemblies, Face-Up Permitted . . . 406.5(H)

Location and Placement, Dwelling Units

   Bathrooms . . . . 210.52(D)

   Countertop Receptacles not considered required by

   210.52(A). . . . . 210.52(A)(4)

   General . . . . 406.5(E)

   Kitchens . . . . 210.52(C)

On Small Appliance Branch Circuits . . . . .210.11(C)(1)

COVE LIGHTING **410.18**

COVER FOR DIRECT BURIAL WIRING METHODS

Definition of . . . . Table 300.5 Note 1

Minimum Cover . . . . .Table 300.5

Over 1000 Volts, Nominal, Definition Table 300.50 Superscript Note 1

   Industrial Establishments . . . . Table 300.50, Note 3

   Minimum Cover . . . . .Table 300.50

   Protected by Concrete . . . . Table 300.50, Footnote d

Swimming Pools, Fountains and Similar Installations . . . . . .

. . . . .680.11 and Table 300.5

COVERS

Auxiliary Gutters . . . . 366.100(D)

Boxes

   Attachment Methods (Screws) 314.25

   Construction. 314.41

   Over 1000 Volts . . . . 314.72(E)

   Required, General . . . . 314.28(C)

      Luminaire Outlets 410.22

Extensions From . . . . 314.22 Ex.

Handholes. . . . . 314.30(D)

Manholes . . . . 110.75(D)

CRANES & HOISTS . . . . **Art. 610**

Ampacity of Conductors . . . . 610.14(A)

    Contact Conductors . . . . 610.14(D)

    Minimum Size. 610.14(C)

    Secondary Resistor Conductors . . . . 610.14(B)

Class III Hazardous (Classified) Locations 503.155

Common Return. 610.15

Contact Conductors . . . . 610 Part III

Control Circuits . . . . 610 Part VI

Demand Factors . . . . Table 610.14(E)

    Application of . . . . 610.14(E)

Disconnecting Means . . . . 610 Part IV

    Runway Conductors . . . . 610.31 Ex.

Grounding and Bonding 610.61

Operating, Class III Locations 503.155

Overcurrent Protection . . . . 610 Part V

Runway Conductors, Disconnecting Means . . . . . 610.31 Ex.

Ungrounded Supply Circuit Over Class III Locations   250.22(1)

See (ELPX) . . . .*UL Product Spec*

CRAWL SPACES

Lighting Outlets

    GFCI Protection. 210.8(E)

Nonmetallic-Sheathed Cable (Exposed). . . . . . . 314.15(C)

Receptacles

    GFCI Protection

        Dwelling Units . . . . 210.8(A)(4)

        Other Than Dwelling Units . . . . 210.8(B)(9)

CRIMP TOOLS, CLASSIFIED FOR USE WITH SPECIFIC WIRE CONNECTORS

See (ZMLS) . . . .*UL Product Spec*

CRITICAL OPERATIONS POWER SYSTEM (COPS) . . . **Art. 708**

Accessible to Authorized Persons Only 708.50

Availability and Reliability/Development and Implementation/ Functional

Performance Testing. . . . . Informative Annex F

Branch Circuit (Circuit Wiring) 708.10

Branch Circuits Supplied by COPS 708.30

Capacity of Power Sources 708.22

Commissioning 708.8

Definitions 708.2

Emergency Operations Plan 708.64

    Equipment 708.11

Feeder (Circuit Wiring) 708.10

Ground-Fault Protection of Equipment 708.52

Identification of Boxes and Enclosures . . . . 708.10(A)

Generators

    Outdoor, Permanently Installed . . . . 708.20(F)(5)(a)

    Outdoor, Portable. . . . . 708.20(F)(5)(b)

Overcurrent Protection . . . . .Art. 708 Part IV

Physical Security 708.5

Risk Assessment 708.4

Scope 708.1

Selective Coordination 708.54

Selectivity . . . . 708.52(D)

Sources of Power 708.20

Surge Protection . . . . 708.20(D)

Testing and Maintenance 708.6

Transfer Equipment 708.24

Ventilation 708.21

Wiring of Feeders and Branch Circuits 708.10

See . . . . Informative Annex F

CROSS-SECTIONAL AREAS

Compact Aluminum . . . . .Chapter 9 Table 5A

Conductors . . . . Chapter 9 Table 5

    Bare. . . . . Chapter 9 Table 8

Conduit .Chapter 9 Table 4

CURRENT LIMITING

Cartridge Fuses, Marking . . . . 240.60(C)

Circuit Breakers, Marking 240.83

    See (DIRW) . . . .*UL Product Spec*

Circuit Impedance, Short Circuit Current Ratings and Other Characteristics 110.10

Interrupting Rating 110.9

Overcurrent Device, Definition of 240.2

Series Ratings 240.86

See Cartridge Fuses, Nonrenewable(JDDZ). . .*UL Product Spec*

See Cartridge Fuses, Renewable (JDRX). . . . .*UL Product Spec*

DAMP OR WET LOCATIONS

Agricultural Buildings . . . . 547.5(C)(2)

Receptacles . . . . 547.5(G)

Boxes and Fittings 314.15

Cabinets, Cutout Boxes, and Meter Socket Enclosure . . . 312.2

Class 1, Class 2, and Class 3 Circuits . . . . 725.3(L)

Definition of . . . . Art. 100

Deteriorating Agents 110.11

Drainage Openings, Field Installed (Boxes, etc.) 314.15

Electric Signs and Outline Lighting . . . . 600.9(D)

   Electrode Connections . . . . 600.42(G)

Equipment Connected by Cord and Plug . . . . 250.114(4)(F)

Fixed Electric Space Heating Equipment . . . . . . 424.12(B)

Grounding Equipment in . . . . 250.110(2)

Lampholders 410.96

Luminaires in Specific Locations (Fixtures) . . . . . . 410.10(A)

Marinas and Boatyards . . . . .555.13(B)(5)

Materials to Be Identified for the Use 110.11

Open Wiring 398.10

Overcurrent Protection 240.32

Panelboards 408.37

Receptacles, Weather Resistant 406.9

Signs, Portable and Mobile . . . . 600.9(D)

Switches 404.4

Temporary Installations . . . . 590.6(A)(3)

Switchboards 408.16

DANCE HALLS (ASSEMBLY OCCUPANCIES) . . . . . . Art. 518

DATA PROCESSING (INFORMATION TECHNOLOGY) EQUIPMENT . . . . Art. 645
See INFORMATION TECHNOLOGY EQUIPMENT. . . . . . Ferm's Finder

D.C. SYSTEMS . . . . 250 Part VIII

Branch Circuit Identification of Ungrounded Conductor . . . . 210.5(C)(2)

Combination Electrical Systems

   Park Trailers 552.20

Recreational Vehicles 551.20

Concrete Encased Electrodes . . . . 250.166(D)

Equipment Grounding Conductor . . . . . . .250.134(B), Exc. 2

Grounded System Required 250.162

   Sizing 250.166

Ground-Fault Detection

   Grounded Systems . . . . .250.167(B)

   Marking . . . . .250.167(C)

   Ungrounded Systems . . . . 250.167(A)

Integrated Electrical Systems 685.12

Overcurrent Protection Generator Systems 445.12

Point of Connection 250.164

Signage, Caution

   Resistively Grounded DC Systems . . . . 408.3(F)(5)

   Ungrounded DC Systems . . . . 408.3(F)(4)

Size of Bonding Jumper 250.168

Size of Grounding Electrode Conductor 250.166

Storage Batteries . . . . Art. 480

Theaters, Motion Picture and Television Studios, and Similar Locations

   Over 1000 Volts, Direct Current Switchboards 530.64

Solar Photovoltaic (PV) Systems . . . . Art. 690

   AFCI Protection 690.11

   Circuit Requirement 690.7

   Circuit Sizing and Current 690.8

   Disconnecting Means 690.13

   Grounding 690.41

   Grounding Electrode System . . . . 690.47(A)

   Marking . . . . 690 Part VI

   Overcurrent Protection . . . . 690.9(B)

   Over 1000 Volts . . . . 690 Part IX

   Self-Regulated PV Charge Control (Battery) 690.72

   Wiring Method . . . . 690.31(G)

Ungrounded Conductor Identification . . . . 210.5(C)(2)

Ungrounded Separately Derived Systems 250.169

Use of Grounded Conductor for Load Side Equipment . . . . 250.142(B) Ex. 3

Wind Electric Systems . . . . Art. 694

   Charge Control (Battery) . . . . Art. 480

   Disconnecting Means 694.20

   Overcurrent Protection 694.15

   Storage Batteries . . . . Art. 480

   Wiring Method 694.30

DEAD ENDS

Busways 368.58

Cablebus . . . . .370.42(2)

Flat Cable Assemblies . . . . 322.40(A)

Metal Wireways 376.58

Nonmetallic Wireways. 378.58

DEAD FRONT

Attachment Plugs . . . . 406.7(A)

Definition . . . . .Art. 100 Part I

Informative Annex A, Enclosed and Dead Front SwitchedUL 98

Mobile and Manufactured Homes, Distribution Panelboards. 550.11

Panelboards 408.38

Park Trailers, Distribution Panelboards . . . . 552.45(C)

Recreational Vehicles

    Definition 551.2

    Distribution Panelboard . . . . 551.45(C)

Theaters, Motion Picture and Television Studios, and Similar Locations

    Stage Switchboards, Fixed 520.21

    Over 1000 Volts, Substations. 530.64

DEDICATED

Branch Circuits

    Bathrooms (Dwellings). . . . . .210.11(C)(3)

    Central Heating Equipment Other Than Electric . . . 422.12

    Fire Alarm or Burglar System . . . . .210.8(A)(5)Ex

    Laundry (Dwellings) . . . . .210.11(C)(2)

    Receptacle for Deicing or Snow-Melting Equipment,

        Exempt from GFCI . . . . 210.8(A)(3) Ex.

    Small Appliance . . . . .210.11(C)(1)

        Disconnect for HVAC Equipment 645.10

        Fire Pump Transformers, Sizing of Dedicated . . 695.5(A)

    Signs . . . . 600.5(A)

    Unfinished Basements Appliances That Occupy. . . . . 210.8(A)(5)

    Wind Electric Systems . . . . 694.7(D)

Equipment Space

    Indoor. .110.26(E)(1)

    Outdoor. .110.26(E)(2)

Feeder

    Fire Pump. . . . . 695.3(A)(3)

DEFINITIONS

NOTE 1: Many of the categories listed below have additional definitions that are specific to that general subject. These additional definitions are also found in the respective ".2" sections.

NOTE 2: Article 100 includes only those definitions that are considered to be essential to the proper application of the *NEC*. In general, only those terms used in two or more articles are defined in Article 100. The definitions included here are provided in the article in which they are used. In some cases, these may be referenced in Article 100.

Air-Conditioning and Refrigerating Equipment 440.2

Aircraft Painting Hangar 513.2

Arc-Fault Circuit-Interrupter (AFCI) . . . . Art. 100

Armored Cable 320.2

Audio Signal Processing, Amplification and Reproduction

    Equipment 640.2

Busways 368.2

Cable Tray 392.2

Cablebus 370.2

Cellular Concrete Floor Raceways (Cell) 372.2

Cellular Metal Floor Raceways 374.2

Class l, II, & III Locations (General Area Classifications) . 500.5

Class I, Zone 0, 1, & 2 Locations 505.2

    General Area Classifications 505.5

Communication Circuits 800.2

Community Antenna TV and Radio Distribution Systems 820.2

Concealed Knob-and-Tube Wiring 394.2

Control Circuit, Motor . . . . Art. 100

Controller, Motor 430.2

Cover (Direct Burial) . . . . Table 300.5, Note 1

    Over 1000 Volts . . . . Table 300.50, Superscript Note a

Electric-Discharge Lighting. . . . . Art. 100

Electric Signs . . . . Art. 100

Electric Vehicle Charging Systems 625.2

Electrical Metallic Tubing. 358.2

Electrical Nonmetallic Tubing 362.2

Electrically Driven or Controlled Irrigation Machines. . . 675.2

Electrolytic Cells 668.2

Elevators, Dumbwaiters, Escalators, Etc. 620.2

Fire Alarm Circuit 760.2

Fire Alarm Circuit Integrity Cable 760.2

Fire Alarm Systems 760.2

Fixed Outdoor Electric Deicing and Snow-Melting Equipment 426.2

Fixed Electric Heating Equipment for Pipelines and Vessels 427.10

Flat Cable Assemblies 322.2

Flat Conductor Cable 324.2

Flexible Metal Conduit 348.2

Flexible Metallic Tubing 360.2

Floating Buildings 553.2

Fuel Cell Systems 692.2

General, Not Over 1000 Volts, Nominal . . . . . Art. 100 Part II

Grounding 250.2

Hazardous (Classified) Locations . . . . Art. 100

Health Care Facilities 517.2

High Density Polyethylene Conduit, Type HDPE 353.2

Induction and Dielectric Heating Equipment 665.2

Industrial Control Panels . . . . Art. 100

Industrial Machinery 670.2

Instrumentation Tray Cable 727.2

Integrated Gas Spacer Cable 326.2

Interconnected Electric Power Production Sources 705.2

Intermediate Metal Conduit 342.2

Intrinsically Safe Systems . . . . Art. 100

Inverter (Interactive) . . . . Art. 100

Liquidtight Flexible Metal Conduit 350.2

Liquidtight Flexible Nonmetallic Conduit 356.2

Manufactured Buildings 545.2

Manufactured Wiring Systems 604.2

Medium Voltage Cable 328.2

Messenger Supported Wiring 396.2

Metal Wireways 376.2

Metal-Clad Cable 330.2

Mineral-Insulated, Metal-Sheathed Cable 332.2

Mobile Equipment . . . . Art. 100

Mobile Homes, Manufactured and Mobile Home Parks . . 550.2

Motion Picture and TV Studio & Similar Locations 530.2

Motion Picture Projectors 540.2

Motor Fuel Dispensing Facilities 514.2

Natural and Artificially Made Bodies of Water 682.2

Network-Powered Broadband Communication Systems . 830.2

Nonmetallic Extensions 382.2

Nonmetallic Sheathed Cable 334.2

Nonmetallic Underground Conduit with Conductors . . . 354.2

Nonmetallic Wireways 378.2

Non-Power-Limited Fire Alarm Circuit (NPLFA) 760.2

Open Wiring On Insulators 398.2

Optical Fiber Cables and Raceways 770.2

Over 1000 Volts, Nominal (General) . . . . Art. 100 Part II

    High Voltage 490.2

Park Trailers 552.2

Phase Converters 455.2

Power and Control Tray Cable 336.2

Power-Limited Fire Alarm Circuit (PLFA) 760.2

Radiant Heating Panels 424.91

Radiant Heating Panel Sets 424.91

Radio and TV Equipment 810.2

Recreational Vehicles and Recreation Vehicle Parks 551.2

Remote Control Signaling, and Power Limited Circuits
Class I, 2 & 3 . . . . 725.2

Retrofit Kit . . . . Art. 100

Service Entrance Cable 338.2

Sign Body 600.2

Section Sign 600.2

Skeleton Tubing 600.2

Solar Photovoltaic Systems 690.2

Storage Batteries 480.2

Surge Arresters . . . . Art. 100

Surge-Protective Device (SPD) . . . . Art. 100

Swimming Pools, Fountains, etc. 680.2

Tap Conductor 240.2

Theaters,

    Motion Picture and Television Studios, and Similar Locations 520.2

Transformer 450.2

Underfloor Raceway 390.2

Wind Electric Systems 694.2

X-Ray Equipment,

    Medical 517.2

    Nonmedical 660.2

        Zone 20, 21, & 22 Locations 506.2

DEFLECTION FITTINGS . . . . **.300.7(B)**

DEFLECTION OF CONDUCTORS

See CONDUCTORS, Bending Space . . . . Ferm's Finder

DEICING & SNOW-MELTING . . . . **Art. 426**

Ampacity and Size . . . . 210.19(A)(4), Ex. 1(e)

Branch-Circuit Sizing 426.4

Control & Protection . . . . 426 Part VI

Controllers 426.51

Corrosion Protection

   Resistance Heating Elements 426.26

   Skin-Effect Heating 426.43

Disconnecting Means 426.50

Expansion Joints

   Embedded Nonheating Leads . . . . 426.22(D)

   Embedded Resistance Elements . . . . 426.20(E)

   Exposed Resistance Elements . . . . 426.21(C) & (D)

Free Conductors at Boxes

   Resistance Heating Elements, Embedded. . . . . 426.22(E)

   Resistance Heating Elements, Exposed . . . . . . 426.23(A)

Grounding

   Impedance Heating 426.34

   Resistance Heating Elements. 426.27

   Skin-Effect Heating 426.44

Ground-Fault Protection of Equipment, Resistance Units. . . .

. . . . 426.28

Impedance Heating . . . . 426 Part IV

Installation . . . . 426 Part II

Overcurrent Protection . . . . 240.4(B)

   Setting of (Continuous Load) 426.4

Resistance Heating Elements . . . . 426 Part III

Skin-Effect Heating . . . . 426 Part V

Tap Conductors . . . . 210.19(A)(4), Ex. 1(e)

DELTA BREAKERS (Prohibited in Panelboards) . . . .

. . . . **408.36(C)**

DELTA CONNECTED (HIGH-LEG)

High-Leg Marking, General. 110.15

Phase Arrangement in Switchboards and Panelboards 408.3(E)

Service Conductor Identification. 230.56

DEMAND FACTORS

See CALCULATIONS, Demand Factors. . . . . . Ferm's Finder

DENTAL CLINICS AND OFFICES

Defined, Health Care Facilities 517.2

Essential Electrical System 517.45

Wiring and Protection . . . . 517 Part II

See HEALTH CARE FACILITIES . . . . Ferm's Finder

See Standard for Health Care Facilities, NFPA 99 . . . .

. . . . NFPA 99-2012

DERATING AMPACITY

Auxiliary Gutters. . . . . 366.22(A)

   When Applicable 366.23

Cable Trays

   Conductors Rated 2000 Volts or Less 392.22

   Conductors Rated 2001 Volts or Over . . . . 392.22(C)

Fire Alarm Systems

   NPLFA Circuits . . . . 760 Part II

   PLFA Circuits Using NPLFA Methods . . . 760.130(A) Ex. 3

Parallel Conductors . . . . 310.10(H)(4)

Remote Control, Signaling Circuits, Class 1. . . . . . . 725.51

Strut-Type Channel Raceway 384.22

Surface Metal Raceway 386.22

See Also AMPACITY OF, Derating Allowable Ampacity . . . .

. . . . Ferm's Finder

See Also CONDUCTORS, Derating Allowable Ampacity . . . .

. . . . Ferm's Finder

DETERIORATING AGENTS **110.11**

Integrity of Equipment and Connections . . . . 110.12(B

DEVICE

Defined . . . . Art. 100

Nonmetallic-Sheathed Cable Interconnector . . . . . 334.40(B)

Self-Contained . . . . 334.40(B)

DEVICE OR EQUIPMENT FILL FOR BOXES . . . **314.16(B)(4)**

DIAGRAMS (FIGURES)

Adjustable Speed Drive Control . . Informative Annex D, D10

Autotransformer Overcurrent Protection 450.4

Bulk Storage (Marine Terminal) 515.3

Branch Circuit, Feeder, and Service Calculation Methods. . . .

. . . . 220.1

Cable Installation Dimension Details Over 2001 Volts . . . . .

. . . . 310.60

   For Use under Engineering Supervision Informative Annex B

   . . . . Table B.310.15(B)(2) (1 – 10)

Cable TV Substitutions (Coaxial Type Cables Only). . .820.179

Class I, Zone 0, 1, and 2 Locations, Marking . . . . 505.9(C)(2)

Class 2 and Class 3 Cable Substitutions . . . . .725.154(A)

Class 2 and Class 3 Circuits 725.121

Closet Storage Space 410.2

Code Arrangement. 90.3

Control Drawings, Required for Intrinsically Safe System

Equipment . . . . 504.10(A)

Elevators, Dumbwaiters, Escalators, etc.. . . . . 620.13

Control System 620.2

Feeders, Diagrams If Required 215.5

Fire Alarm System Cable Substitutions . . . . .760.154(A)

Generator Field Control. . . . . Informative Annex D, D9

Grounding and Bonding 250.1

Grounding Symbol. .250.126

For Receptacles . . . . .406.10(B)(4)

Hospital Essential Electrical Systems. . . . .
. . . . .IN Figure 517.30 No.1 & 2

Mobile Home Power Supply Configurations . . . . . 550.10(C)

Motors, Article 430 Contents 430.1

Motor Fuel Dispensing Facilities 514.3

Nursing Homes and Limited Care Facilities. . . . .
. . . . Info. Note Figure 517.41(B) No. 1 & 2

Optical Fiber Cable Substitutions . . . . . . Table 770.154(b)

Park Trailer Power Supply Configurations . . . . . 552.44(C)

Recreational Vehicle Power Supply Configurations . 551.46(C)

Service. 230.1

Solar Photovoltaic Systems

Identification of System Components. . . . . Figure 690.1(a)

Identification of System Components in Common System

Configurations. . . . . Figure 690.1(b)

Spray Applications . . . . Figure 516.4

Swimming Pools, Conductor Clearances . . . . Figure 680.8(A)

Wind Electric Systems

Components, Interactive System . . IN Figure 694.1 No. 1(a)

Components, Stand-Alone System . IN Figure 694.1 No. 2(b)

DIFFERENT SYSTEMS IN SAME ENCLOSURE

See CONDUCTORS, Different Systems in Same Enclosure. . .
Ferm's Finder

DIMENSIONS & PERCENT AREA OF CONDUCTORS

See CONDUCTORS, Dimensions & Area of . . . Ferm's Finder

DIMENSIONS & PERCENT AREA OF CONDUIT . . . .

. . . . **Chapter 9 Table 4**

See . . . . Conduit Fill Tables, Chapter 9 Table 5

See . . . . . . For Compact Conductors, Chapter 9 Table 5A

DIMMERS

Device Fill for Boxes . . . . .314.16(B)(4)

Grounding of . . . . 404.9(B)

In Fixed Stage Switchboards 520.25

DIP TANKS (PAINT) .Art. 516

See SPRAY APPLICATIONS, DIPPING, COATING & PRO-
CESSES . . . . Ferm's Finder

DIRECT BURIAL

See BURIED CONDUCTORS . . . . Ferm's Finder

See CABLES, Underground . . . . Ferm's Finder

See CONDUCTORS, Underground . . . . Ferm's Finder

DIRECT CURRENT MICROGRIDS . . . . Art. 712

Circuit Requirements . . . . Art. 712 Part II

Definitions 712.2

Directory 712.10

Disconnecting Means . . . . Art. 712 Part III

Identification of Circuit Conductors. 712.25

Interrupting and Short-Circuit Ratings 712.72

Listing and Labeling 712.4

Marking . . . . Art. 712 Part V

Overcurrent Protection 712.70

Protection. .Art. 712 Part VI

Systems over 1000 Volts . . . . Part VII

System Voltage 712.30

Wiring Methods . . . . .Art. 712 Part IV

DIRECT CURRENT SYSTEMS

See D.C. Systems . . . . Ferm's Finder

DIRECTLY CONTROLLED LUMINAIRES 700.24

DIRECTORY SEE LABELING. . . . . .Ferm's Finder

See MARKING . . . . Ferm's Finder

DISCHARGE STORED ENERGY

Capacitors Under 1000 Volts 460.6

Capacitors Over 1000 Volts 460.28

DISCONNECTING MEANS

Agricultural Buildings. . . . . 547.9(B)(C)

Air Conditioning & Refrigeration . . . . 440 Part II

For Cord-Connected Equipment 440.13

For Dedicated HVAC in Information Technology Room. . .
645.10

Location of. 440.14

Room Air Conditioners 440.63

Appliances . . . . 422 Part III

Cord-Connected 422.33

Motor-Driven . . . . 422.31(C)

D

Permanently Connected 422.31

Unit Switch(es) 422.34

Batteries. 480.6

Capacitors . . . . 460.8(C)

   Over 1000 Volts, Nominal 460.24

Carnivals, Circuses, Fairs and Similar Events . . . . . 525.21(A)

Circuits, Motor Fuel Dispensing Facilities. 514.11

Computers 645.10

   See INFORMATION TECHNOLOGY EQUIPMENT. . . .

   . . . . Ferm's Finder

Cord-and-Plug, Exemption for Lockable . . . . . . 110.25 Ex.

Cranes and Hoists . . . . 610 Part IV

Definition of . . . . Art. 100 Part I

Deicing and Snow-Melting Equipment . . . . . . 426 Part VI

Duct Heaters 424.65

Electric Vehicle Charging System 625.43

   Branch Circuit. 625.40

   Disconnecting Means. 625.43

   Overcurrent Protection. 625.41

   Rating. 625.42

Electrolytic Cells 668.13

Electroplating. 669.8

Elevators . . . . 620 Part VI

   Car HVAC 620.54

   Car Lights, Receptacles, and Ventilation 620.53

   Power from More Than One Source. 620.52

   Single Disconnecting Means Each Unit. 620.51

   To Disconnect Normal and Emergency Power. . . 620.91(C)

   Utilization Equipment 620.55

Fire Pumps . . . . .695.4(B)(1)(3)

Fixed Electric Heating Equipment for Pipelines and Vessels . .

. . . . 426.50

Fixed Electric Space-Heating Equipment 424.19

Fuel Cell Systems. . . . . 692 Part III

Fuses & Cutouts 240.40

   Readily Accessible. 240.24

Generators 445.18

Heating Equipment (Induction & Dielectric) 665.12

Heating Equipment (Space) . . . . 424 Part III

   Location for Duct Heater. 424.65

   Required 424.19

   Thermostats as. 424.20

Heating Equipment for Pipelines and Vessels . . . . 427 Part VII

High Voltage Systems

Mobile and Portable Equipment. . . . . 490.51(D)

Overcurrent Device as 230.206

Service Disconnecting Means 230.205

See OVER 1000 VOLTS, NOMINAL . . . . . Ferm's Finder

Hot Tubs & Spas 680.13

Emergency Switch for Nondwelling Units 680.41

Identification of (General) 110.22

   Circuits in Panelboards. 408.4

Industrial Machinery . . . . 670.4(B)

Information Technology Equipment 645.10

See INFORMATION TECHNOLOGY EQUIPMENT . . . .
Ferm's Finder

Interconnected Electric Power Production Sources

   Disconnect Device 705.22

   Disconnecting Means, Equipment 705.21

   Disconnecting Means, Sources 705.20

Irrigation Machines 675.8

Lockable. 110.25

   Air-Conditioning and Refrigerating Equipment . . . 440.14

   Appliances . . . . 422.31(B)

   Carnivals, Circuses, Fairs and Similar Events

      Rides, Tents, Concessions 525.21

      Services 525.10

   Cranes and Hoists. . . . . .610.31 and 610.32

   Electric-Discharge Lighting, More than 1000 Volts . . . . . .

   . . . . .410.141(B)

   Electric Vehicle Charging System 625.43

   Electrically Driven or Controlled Irrigation Machines . . . .

   . . . . 675.8(B)

   Electrified Truck Parking Spaces

      Parking Space. . . . . 626.24(C)

      Supply Wiring . . . . 626.22(D)

      Transport Refrigerated Units 626.31

   Elevators, Etc.

      Car Light, Receptacle(s), and Ventilation Disconnecting
      Means 620.53

      Disconnects, General 620.51

      Heating and Air-Conditioning Disconnecting Means . . .
      620.54

      Utilization Equipment Disconnecting Means 620.55

   Equipment Over 1000 Volts, Circuit Breakers 490.46

   Equipment Over 1000 Volts, Interrupter Switches. . . 490.44

   Feeder Disconnecting Means . . . . 225.52(C)

   Fire Pumps. 695.4

   Fixed Electric Space-Heating Equipment. . . . .

. . . . .424.19(A) and (B)

Fixed Outdoor Electric Deicing and Snow-Melting
Equipment. . . . . 426.51(A) and (D)

Generators 445.18

Induction and Dielectric Heating Equipment 665.12

Motors . . . . .430.102(A) and (B)

Motors, Over 1000 Volts 430.227

Motors with More Than One Source of Power 430.113

Outdoor Lamps 225.25

Sensitive Electronic Equipment, Lighting Equipment. . . . .
. . . . 647.8(A)

Signs . . . . 600.6(A)

Transfer Equipment. 702.5

Transformers. 450.14

Marinas and Boatyards, Shore Power Connection 555.17

Mobile and Manufactured Homes 550.11

Interconnection . . . . 550.19(B)

Service Equipment 550.32

Motors & Controllers . . . . 430 Part IX

All Disconnects in Circuit to Comply 430.108

Ampere Rating and Interrupting Capacity 430.110

Both Controller and Disconnecting Means 430.111

Energy from More Than One Source 430.113

Grounded Conductors 430.105

Location of. 430.102

Motors Served by Single Disconnecting Means . . . 430.112

Operation 430.103

Over 1000 Volts 430.227

Readily Accessible. 430.107

To Be Indicating. 430.104

Type of 430.109

See MOTORS . . . . Ferm's Finder

Motor Control Circuit 430.75

Motor Fuel Dispensers

Circuits. 514.11

Provisions for Maintenance and Servicing 514.13

Multiple-Occupancy Building

Grouping of 230.72

Location in or on Premises. . . . . 240.24(A)

Locked Service Overcurrent Devices 230.92

Maximum Number of 230.71

Separate Service Disconnects Grouped One Location . . . .
. . . . 230.40 Ex. 2

Outside Branch Circuits and Feeders

Access to Occupants 225.35

Construction of 225.38

Grouping of 225.34

Identification of 225.37

Location of. 225.32

Maximum Number of 225.33

Over 1000 Volts . . . . 225 Part III

Isolating Switches 225.51

Location of . . . . 225.52(A)

Not Readily Accessible. . . . . 225.52(A)

Type of. 225.52(B)

Rating of 225.39

Supplying More Than One Building or Structure . . . 225.31

Type. 225.36

To Be Suitable for Service Equipment. 225.36

Park Trailers . . . . 552.45(C)

Phase Converters. 455.8

Readily Accessible

Air-Conditioning and Refrigerating Equipment. . . . 440.14

Carnivals, Circuses, Fairs and Similar Events

For Rides, Tents, and Concession 525.21

Cranes and Hoists

Cranes and Monorail Hoists 610.32

Rating of. 610.33

Runway Contact Conductor . . . . 610.31(1)

Definition of . . . . .Art. 100 Part I

Electric Vehicle Supply Equipment 625.43

For Motors and Controllers 430.107

In or On Premises. 240.24

Induction and Dielectric Heating 665.12

Information Technology Equipment 645.10

More than One Building or Structure Supplied 225.32

Service Disconnecting Means . . . . .230.70(A)(1)

Solar Photovoltaic Systems . . . . 690.13(A)

Spas and Hot Tub Emergency Switch 680.41

Switches and Circuit Breakers . . . . 404.8(A)

Recreational Vehicles . . . . 551.45(C)

Site Supply Equipment . . . . 551.77(B)

Sensitive Electronic Equipment, Luminaires . . . . . . 647.8(A)

Sensitive Electronic Equipment, Three Phase Systems . . 647.5

Separate Buildings

Supplied by Branch Circuit or Feeder

See DISCONNECTING MEANS, Outside Branch. . . . . .
Ferm's Finder

Supplied by Service 230.70

See DISCONNECTING MEANS, Service Equipment . . .
. . . . Ferm's Finder

Service Equipment . . . . 230 Part VI

   Available Short-Circuit Current 110.9

   Cartridge Fuses and Fuseholders 240.60

   Circuit Breakers 240.83

   Circuit Impedance and Other Characteristics 110.10

   Combined Rating 230.80

   Connection to Terminals. 230.81

   Equipment Connected to Supply Side 230.82

   Grouping of 230.72

      Additional Service Disconnecting Means . . . . 230.72(B)

   Labeled, Definition of . . . . Art. 100

   Listed, Definition of . . . . Art. 100

   Location of. . . . . 230.70(A)

   Marked as Suitable for Use as Service Equipment . . . 230.66

   Maximum Number of 230.71

   Minimum Size and Rating 230.79

   Mobile Home Disconnecting Means . . . . 550.32(F)

   Mounting Height Switches and Circuit Breakers 404.8

      Multiple Branch Circuits (Simultaneous Disconnection)
. . . . 210.7

   Multiple Occupancy Building

      Each Occupant to Have Access . . . . 240.24(B)

      Grouping of. 230.72

      Location, Relative to Overcurrent Protection 230.94

      Locked Service Overcurrent Devices 230.92

      Two to Six Separate Enclosures, Grouped . . . 230.40 Ex. 2

   Number of Permitted . . . . 230.71(A)

   Provisions for Disconnecting the Grounded Conductor . . .
. . . . 230.75

   Provisions to Bond the Grounded Conductor to the Main

      Service Equipment . . . . 250.24(B)

      Load Side Grounding Connections . . . . . .250.24(A)(5)

   Rating of 230.79

   Simultaneous Opening of Poles 230.74

   Supply-Side, Marking 230.82

   See SERVICE EQUIPMENT, Main Disconnect Ferm's Finder

Signs and Outline Lighting 600.6

Solar Photovoltaic Systems . . . . 690 Part III

   Energy Storage Systems. 706.7

   Type 690.15

   Storage Batteries. 480.7

Spas & Hot Tubs 680.13

   Emergency Switch for 680.41

Swimming Pool Equipment 680.13

Transformers 450.14

Welders

   Arc Welders 630.13

   Resistance Welders 630.33

Wet Locations

   Cabinets and Cutout Boxes 312.2

   Switch and Circuit Breaker Enclosures 404.4

   Switchboards 408.16

Wind Electric Systems . . . . Art. 694 Part III

   Storage Batteries 480.6

X-Ray Equipment

   In Health Care Facilities 517.72

   Independent Control, Nonmedical 660.24

   Other Uses, Nonmedical 660.5

DISCONTINUED OUTLETS

Cellular Concrete Floor Raceways 372.58

Cellular Metal Floor Raceways 374.58

Under-Floor Raceways 390.8

DISHWASHERS

Arc-Fault Circuit-Interrupter Protection . . . . 210.12(A)

Booster Heaters, Nondwelling Load Demand Factors . . 220.56

Cord Connected . . . . .422.16(B)(2)

Disconnecting Means . . . . 422 Part III

Ground-Fault Circuit-Interrupter Protection . . . . . 210.8(D)

Grounding of, Cord- and Plug-Connected 250.114

Grounding of, Permanent Wiring Methods 250.110

Maximum Load 220.18

Minimum Branch Circuit 422.10

Mobile Homes (Portable Appliance) . . . . . 550.2 Info. Note

Permissible Load 210.23

DISPOSER, KITCHEN WASTE

Arc-Fault Circuit-Interrupter Protection . . . . 210.12(A)

Cord Connected . . . . .422.16(B)(1)

Disconnecting Means . . . . 422 Part III

Ground-Fault Circuit-Interrupter Protection, Within 6 feet of
Sink . . . . 210.8(A)(7)

Grounding of, Cord- and Plug-Connected 250.114

Grounding of, Permanent Wiring Methods 250.110

Maximum Load 220.18

Minimum Branch Circuit 422.10

Permissible Load 210.23

DISSIMILAR METALS (General) **110.14**

Electrical Metallic Tubing 358.14

Ground Clamps Listed for Electrode & Conductor Materials .

. . . . 250.70

Intermediate Metal Conduit 342.14

Rigid Metal Conduit 344.14

Stainless Steel (and fittings) 344.14

Tower Grounding Connections . . . . 694.40(B)

DOCUMENTATION

AC and Refrigerating Equipment . . . . 440.10(B)

AHJ (Waive Requirements) . . Informative Annex H, 80.13(15)

Arc Energy Reduction 240.87

Circuit Breakers . . . . 240.87(A)

Fuses . . . . 240.67(A)

Critical Operations Power Systems 708.1

Transfer Equipment . . . . 708.24(E)

Emergency Systems . . . . 700.5(E)

Hazardous (Classified) Locations . . . . 500.4(A)

Industrial Control Panels . . . . 409.22(B)

Integrated Electrical System 685.1

Intrinsically Safe Systems . . . . 504.10(C)

Large-Scale Photovoltaic Electric Power Production Facility . .

Arc-Fault Mitigation 691.10

Conformance to Engineered Design 691.7

DC Operating Voltage 691.8

Engineered Design 691.6

Fence Grounding 691.11

Legally Required Standby Systems . . . . 701.5(D)

Manholes . . . . 110.70 Ex.

Manufactured Buildings, Building System 545.2

Motor Fuel Dispensing Facilities . . . . . 514.3(D) Ex. 1 and 2

Outdoor Overhead Conductors Over 1000 Volts 399.30

Series Ratings . . . . 240.86(A)

Substations 490.48

Zone 0, 1, and 2 Locations . . . . 505.4(A)

Zone 20, 21, and 22 Locations . . . . 506.4(A)

DORMITORIES

Arc-Fault Circuit Interrupter Protection . . . . 210.12(C)

Overcurrent Protection, Not in Bathrooms . . . . . . 240.24(E)

Receptacle Outlet Placement Requirements . . . . . 210.60(B)

DOORS

Clearances from, Outside Branch Circuits and Feeders . . . . .

. . . . 225.19(C)

Clearances From, Services . . . . 230.9(A)

Door Stops 490.38

Enclosures, Over 1000 Volts . . . . .110.31(A)(3)

Flexible Cords Prohibited . . . . .400.12(3)

Garage Vehicle Door . . . . .210.70(A)(2)

Locks, Over 1000 Volts . . . . .110.31(A)(4)

Panic Hardware, Listed

Over 1000 Volts . . . . .110.33(A)(3)

Battery Support Systems 480.9

Under 600 Volts . . . . .110.26(C)(3)

Personnel, Electrical Vaults, Over 1000 Volts . . . .110.26(C)(3)

Personnel, Over 1000 Volts . . . . .110.33(A)(3)

Pools . . . . .680.26(B)(7)

Transformer and Transformer Vaults 450.43

Unqualified Access, Over 1000 Volts 490.35

Vaults and Tunnels, Over 1000 Volts . . . . 110.76(B)

Working Space . . . . .110.26(A)(2)

DOUBLE LOCKNUTS

Bonding Over 250 Volts to Ground . . . . 250.97 Ex

Mobile Homes Wiring Methods . . . . 550.15(F)

Not for Hazardous Areas (Bonding) 250.100

Class I, Division 1 & 2 . . . . 501.30(A)

Class I, Zone 0, 1, & 2 . . . . 505.25(A)

Class II, Division 1 & 2 . . . . 502.30(A)

Class III, Division 1 & 2 . . . . 503.30(A)

Not Recognized for Service Raceway Bonding . . . 250.92(B)

Park Trailers . . . . 552.48(B)

Recreation Vehicles Wiring Methods . . . . 551.47(B)

Under Wholly Insulating Bushings Not Used to Secure Raceway

. . . . 300.4(G)

DRAINAGE

Boxes, Outlet, Devices and Junction (Approved Openings) . .

. . . . 314.15

Capacitor Charge, see DISCHARGE STORED ENERGY . . . .

. . . . Ferm's Finder

Conduit Bodies (Approved Openings) 314.15

Equipment in Hazardous (Classified) Locations

Class I, Division 1 & 2 Locations . . . . 501.15(F)

Class I, Zone 0, 1, & 2 Locations . . . . 505.16(E)

Oil-Insulated Transformers, Outdoors 450.27

Raceways on Exterior Surfaces 225.22

Service Raceways 230.53

Swimming Pool Equipment Rooms & Pits 680.12

Transformer Vaults 450.46

DRESSING ROOMS

Motion Picture and Television Studios. 530.31

Theaters and Similar Locations

    Lamp Guards 520.72

    Pendant Lampholders Prohibited 520.71

    Switches Required 520.73

DRIP LOOPS AT WEATHERHEAD

Lowest Point for Conductor Clearance . . . . . . .230.24(B)(1)

Outside Branch Circuits and Feeders 225.11

Overhead Service Locations . . . . 230.54(F)

    Individual Conductors 230.52

DRIVEWAYS

Clearance of Conductors 225.18

Clearance of Service Drop . . . . 230.24(B)

Cover Requirements . . . . Table 300.5

Overhead Aerial Cables . . . . 830.44(C)

DROP BOXES

Definition 520.2

Listed . . . . 520.44(B)

DRY LOCATION (Definition of) . . . . **Art. 100**

Conductors . . . . 310.10(A)

Deteriorating Agents 110.11

Switchboards 408.20

DRYERS, CLOTHES

Disconnecting Means . . . . 422 Part III

Flexible Cord and Cables Ampacity . . . . 400.5(A)

Grounding of 250.140

    By Connection to Grounded Conductor . . 250.142(B) Ex. 1

    In Mobile Homes 550.16

    In Park Trailers 552.55

    In Recreational Vehicles 551.55

Minimum Load Branch Circuits (5000 VA), Dwelling Units . .
. . . . 220.54

Receptacle Location . . . . 210.50(C)

Wiring Methods, Mobile and Manufactured Homes 550.15(E)

DRYWALL SCREWS

Covers and Canopies, Not to be Used 314.25

Grounding and Bonding Connection, Not to be Used . 250.8(5)

Receptacles, Not to be Used 406.5

Switches, Not to be Used . . . . 404.10(B)

DRY-TYPE TRANSFORMERS . . . . **Art. 450**

Accessibility 450.13

Grounding 450.10

In Vaults (Over 35,000 Volts) . . . . 450.21(C)

Installed Indoors 450.21

Installed Outdoors 450.22

Marking of 450.11

Not Covered by Article 450 (for Specific Applications) . . 450.1
Exceptions

Overcurrent Protection 450.3

Ventilation 450.9

See (XQNX). . . . .*UL Product Spec*

DUCT HEATERS . . . . **424 Part VI**

Equipment and Wiring in Ducts . . . . 300.22(B)

Limited Access (Working Space) . . . . .110.26(A)(4)

Working Space Requirements 424.66

See (KOHZ) . . . .*UL Product Spec*

DUCTS & HOODS

Bonded

    Recreational Vehicles . . . . 551.56(F)

    Park Trailers . . . . 552.57(F)

Cable Ties and Other Cable Accessories, Nonmetallic . . . . .
. . . . .300.22(C)(1)

Heaters in . . . . 424 Part VI

Luminaires (Lighting Fixtures) in . . . . 410.10(C)

Network-Powered Broadband Communications Systems . . . .
. . . . 830.24

Not to Infringe on Dedicated Space . . . . .110.26(E)(1)

Wiring In

    Audio Signaling Process, Amplification and Reproduction
    Equipment . . . . 640.3(B)

    CATV Systems . . . . 820.3(B)

    Class 1, 2, and 3 Remote Control Circuits . . . . . . 725.3(C)

    Classification for Spray Applications 516.5

    Communications Circuits 800.154

    Community Antenna Television and Radio Distribution
    Systems . . . . 820.3(B)

    Fire Alarm Systems . . . . 760.3(B)

General 300.22

Network-Powered Broadband Systems . . . . 830.3(B)

Premises-Powered Broadband Communications Systems . . . . 840.3(B)

Optical Fiber Cables and Raceways . . . . 770.3(B)

Spread of Fire 300.21

To Be Suitable for the Environment 110.11

Note: Cable type wiring methods are required to be listed for plenum application. Refer to the Listing, Marking, and

Application sections within the specific system articles referenced above.

DUMBWAITERS . . . . Art. 620

See ELEVATORS, etc. . . . . Ferm's Finder

DUST-IGNITIONPROOF . . . . Art. 502

Definition . . . . Art. 100

Enclosures for Control Transformers and Resistors . . 502.120

Enclosures for Switches, Circuit Breakers, etc. 502.115

Protection Technique, Class II Locations . . . . 500.7(B)

DUSTTIGHT

Class II Locations . . . . Art. 502

Definition . . . . Art. 100

Enclosures for Control Transformers and Resistors . . 503.120

Enclosures for Switches, Circuit Breakers, etc. 503.115

Protection Technique, Class II and Class III . . . . . 500.7(C)

Wiring Methods Class III Locations 503.10

DUTY CYCLE

Arc Welders 630.11

Elevators

    Duty Rating . . . . 620.61(B)

    Feeder Demand Factors . . . . Table 620.14 Note

Explanation of (Term) . . . . 630.31(B) Info Note 3

Motors . . . . Table 430.22(E)

Resistance Welders . . . . 630.31(A)

DWELLING UNIT

AFCI Requirements 210.12

    Branch Circuit Extensions and Modifications . . . 210.12(B)

    Locations Required . . . . 210.12(A)

Branch Circuit Requirements

    Bathroom . . . . .210.11(C)(3)

    Central Heating Equipment Other Than Electric . . . 422.12

    Garage . . . . .210.11(C)(4)

General Lighting 220.12

Kitchens . . . . .210.11(C)(1)

    2 or More Branch Circuits. . . . . .210.52(B)(1)

    Small Appliance Branch Circuits . . . . .210.11(C)(1)

Laundry . . . . .210.11(C)(2)

Small Appliances . . . . .210.11(C)(1)

    See BRANCH CIRCUITS. . . . . Ferm's Finder

GFCI Requirements

    Accessory Buildings . . . . 210.8(A)(2)

    Bathrooms . . . . 210.8(A)(1)

    Boat Hoists. . . . . 210.8(C)

    Boathouses. . . . . 210.8(A)(8)

    Crawl Spaces . . . . 210.8(A)(4)

        Lighting Outlets . . . . 210.8(E)

    Dishwashers . . . . 210.8(D)

    Garages . . . . 210.8(A)(2)

    Kitchens . . . . 210.8(A)(6)

    Outdoors . . . . 210.8(A)(3)

    Sinks, Other than Kitchens. . . . . 210.8(A)(7)

    Unfinished Basements . . . . 210.8(A)(5)

Lighting Requirements

    Bathrooms . . . . 210.70(A)(1)

    Closets 410.16

    Equipment Space . . . . 210.70(A)(3)

    Garages (Attached) . . . . 210.70(A)(2)

    Garages (Detached with Electric Power) . . . . 210.70(A)(2)

    Guest Rooms and Guest Suites. . . . . 210.70(B)

    Hallways . . . . 210.70(A)(2)

    Habitable Rooms . . . . 210.70(A)(1)

    Stairways . . . . 210.70(A)(2)

    Storage Space . . . . 210.70(A)(3)

Receptacle Location Requirements

    Accessory Buildings . . . . 210.52(G)(2)

    Balconies . . . . .210.52(E)(3)

    Basements . . . . .210.52(G)(3)

    Bathrooms . . . . 210.52(D)

    Countertop Receptacles

        Not Considered . . . . 210.52(A)(4)

    Decks . . . . 210.52(E)(3)

    Floor Receptacles . . . . 210.52(A)(3)

    Foyers. . . . . .210.52(I)

    Garage . . . . .210.52(G)(1)

    Guest Rooms, Guest Suites, Dormitories and

    Similar Locations . . . . 210.60(B)

Hallways . . . . 210.52(H)

Kitchens . . . . .210.52(B)(3)

   Island Spaces . . . . .210.52(C)(2)

   Peninsular Spaces . . . . .210.52(C)(3)

   Receptacle Outlet Locations. . . . . .210.52(C)(5)

   Separate Spaces . . . . .210.52(C)(4)

General Provisions . . . . 210.52(A)

Laundry Areas . . . . 210.52(F)

Outdoor Outlets

   Balconies, Decks, and Porches . . . . .210.52(E)(3)

   Multifamily Dwellings. . . . . .210.52(E)(2)

   One and Two-Family . . . . .210.52(E)(1)

Porches. . . . . .210.52(E)(3)

Spacing. . . . . .210.52(A)(1)

Wall Space . . . . .210.52(A)(2)

Receptacle Replacement Requirements . . . . 406.4(D)

Arc Fault Circuit Interrupter Protection . . . . 406.4(D)(4)

Ground-Fault Circuit Interrupters . . . 406.4(D)(3)

Grounding-Type Receptacles . . . . 406.4(D)(1)

Non-Grounding Type Receptacles . . . . 406.4(D)(2)

Tamper-Resistant Receptacles . . . . 406.4(D)(5)

Weather-Resistant Receptacles. . . . . 406.4(D)(6)

Tamper-Resistant Receptacles

   Dormitories . . . . 406.12(7)

   Dwellings . . . . 406.12(1)

   Guest Rooms and Suites . . . . 406.12(2)

Voltage Limitations . . . . 210.6(A)

ECCENTRIC KNOCKOUTS
Bonding Over 250 Volts to Ground . . . . 250.97 Ex.

Bonding Service Equipment . . . . 250.92(B)

EFFECTIVE GROUND-FAULT CURRENT PATH . . . . ART. 100

ELBOWS, METAL, PROTECTION FROM CORROSION . 300.6

ELECTRIC DISCHARGE LAMP CONTROL
See (FKOT) . . . . .UL Product Spec

ELECTRIC DISCHARGE LIGHTING
1000 Volts or Less . . . . 410 Part XII

Auxiliary Equipment, Lamps 410.104

Conductors within 75 mm (3 in.) of a Ballast Branch Circuit
and Feeder 410.68

   Note: See Table 310.104 on page 168-170 in NEC for Special
Application of Type THW

Connection of Electric-Discharge and LED Luminaires
(Fixtures) 410.24

Disconnecting Means for Ballasted Luminaires (Fixtures) . . .
. . . . .410.130(G)

   Metal Halide Lamp Containment . . . . 410.130(F)(5)

Definition . . . . Art. 100

Dwellings

   Open-Circuit Voltage Exceeding 1000 Volts Prohibited . . .
. . . . .410.140(B)

   Open-Circuit Voltage Over 300 Volts 410.135

Flush and Recessed Luminaires (Fixtures) . . . . . 410 Part XI

Luminaire (Fixture) Mounting 410.136

Marking Required for More Than 1000 Volts 410.146

Maximum Load for Branch Circuits . . . . 220.18(B)

More Than 1000 Volts . . . . 410 Part XIII

Voltage Limitations 210.6

   Outdoor Equipment 225.7

See Categories under Luminaires (IEXT) . . . .UL Product Spec

ELECTRIC HEAT (SPACE) . . . . Art. 424
Baseboard (Receptacle Outlet in) 210.52

   In Lieu of Required Wall Receptacles 424.9

Boilers

   Electrode Type . . . . 424 Part VIII

   Resistance Type . . . . 424 Part VII

Branch-Circuit Conductors 424.3

   Disconnect, More than One Supplying Equipment . . 424.19

   Sizing of . . . . 424.3(B)

   Supplying Supplementary Overcurrent Devices . . . .
. . . . 424.22(D)

Cables . . . . 424 Part V

   Area Restrictions 424.38

   Clearance from Other Objects and Openings 424.39

   Color Coding 424.35

   Derating and Clearances of Branch-Circuit Conductors . . .
. . . . 424.36

   Finished Ceiling Materials 424.42

   Installation in Concrete or Poured Masonry Floors. . 424.44

     GFCI Protection . . . . 424.44(E)

   Installation on Dry Board, in Plaster and on Concrete

     Ceilings 424.41

   Listing Required 424.6

Low-Voltage Fixed Electric Space-Heating Equipment

Branch Circuits 424.104

Energy Sources 424.101

Installation 424.103

Listed Equipment. 424.102

Scope 424.100

Non-heating Leads 424.43

Not Permitted in or below Pool Decks . . . . . .680.27(C)(3)

Space-Heating (Installation) 424.45

Concrete or Poured Masonry 424.44

Expansion Joints . . . . 424.45(B)

GFCI Protection . . . .

Concrete or Masonry . . . . 424.44(E)

Under Flooring . . . . 424.45(E)

Under Floor Coverings . . . . 424.45(A)

Splices in, Length Cannot Be Altered 424.40

Calculations of Load on Feeder 220.51

Dwelling Unit (Optional Method) 220.82

Existing Dwelling, Additional Loads (Optional Method) 220.83

Multifamily Dwelling (Optional Method) 220.84

Control & Protection . . . . 424 Part III

Deck Area Heating (Pools) . . . . 680.27(C)

Disconnecting Means 424.19

Lockable Disconnect 424.19

Rating of Disconnect, 125% of total load 424.19

Thermostat Serving as 424.20

Unit Switch(es) . . . . 424.19(C)

Duct Heaters . . . . 424 Part VI

Limited Access. . . . . .110.26(A)(4)

With Heat Pumps and Air Conditioners 424.61

Working Space Requirements 424.66

See(KOHZ). . . . . .UL Product Spec

Feeder

More than One Supplying Equipment 424.19

Sizing. 220.51

Heating Panels . . . . 424 Part IX

Infrared Lamp Industrial Heating Appliances 425.14

Branch Circuits . . . . 210.23(C)

Overcurrent Protection. . . . . 422.11(C)

Inspection and Tests 424.46

Labels 424.47

Low-Voltage Fixed Electric Space-Heating Equipment . . . . 424 Part X

Energy Source 424.101

Installation 424.103

Listed Equipment 424.102

Scope 424.100

Overcurrent Protection 424.22

48 Amperes Maximum Load . . . . 422.11(F)

Boilers Not Contained in ASME Rated Equipment. . . . . 424.72(B)

Resistance Elements . . . . 424.22(B)

120 Amperes Maximum Load

Boilers ASME Rated . . . . 424.72(A)

Permanently Wired Radiant Heaters at Pools . . .680.27(C)(2)

Radiant Heating Panels and Sets . . . . 424 Part IX

Derating of Branch-Circuit Conductors

In Ceilings 424.94

In Interior Walls 424.95

Expansion Joints . . . . 424.98(B)

Nonheating Leads 424.97

Space Heating Cables, Marking and Color Code 424.35

Supplementary Overcurrent Protective Device

Definition of . . . . Art. 100

General 424.22

Not As Substitute for Branch-Circuit Devices 240.10

Resistance-type Boilers . . . . 424.72(C)

Thermostats for 424.20

Unit Heaters Pool Areas. . . . . .680.27(C)(1)

Unit Switch(es) as Disconnecting Means . . . . . . 424.19(C)

See Heating & Cooling Summary Ferm's Charts and Formulas

See (LZLZ) . . . . .UL Product Spec

See (LZFE) . . . . .UL Product Spec

ELECTRIC POWER PRODUCTION AND DISTRIBUTION NETWORK. . . . . Art. 100

ELECTRIC POWER PRODUCTION SOURCES

Fuel Cell Systems . . . . Art. 692

Generators . . . . Art. 445

Interconnected Electric Power Production Sources . . Art. 705

Permitted for Fire Pumps . . . . 695.3(A)(2)

Solar Photovoltaic Systems . . . . Art. 690

Wind Electric Systems. . . . . Art. 694

ELECTRIC SIGNS AND OUTLINE LIGHTING . . . . . . Art. 600

See SIGNS, ELECTRIC AND OUTLINE LIGHTING . . . . Ferm's Finder

E

E

ELECTRIC SPACE HEATING CABLES . . . .**Art. 424 V**

Clearances

From Objects and Openings 424.39

From Wiring (Ceilings). 424.36

Construction 424.34

Inspection and Tests 424.46

Installation (Concrete or Masonry) 424.44

Installation (Under Floor Coverings) 424.45

Installation (Walls and Ceilings) 424.41

GFCI Protection Required

Concrete and Masonry . . . . 424.44(E)

Under Floor Covering . . . . 424.45(E)

Label Requirements 424.47

Marking. 424.35

Restrictions (Area) 424.38

ELECTRIC TRUCK SPACE PARKING EQUIPMENT . . . **Art. 626**

ELECTRIC UTILITIES

Connections, Meter Enclosures 230.82

Fire Pump. . . . . 695.3(A)(1)

Ground-Fault Protection for Personnel 590.6

Installations Covered by *NEC*. . . . . 90.2(A)

Installation Not Covered by *NEC*. . . . . 90.2(B)

Special Permission . . . . 90.2(C)

Transfer Equipment 702.5

ELECTRIC VEHICLE CHARGING SYSTEM EQUIPMENT . . . . **Art. 625**

Branch Circuit 625.40

Definitions 625.2

Disconnecting Means 625.43

Installation . . . . 625 Part III

Listed 625.5

Load Calculation . . . . Table 220.3

Marking. 625.15

Overcurrent Protection 625.41

Personnel Protection System 625.22

Plug-In Hybrid Electric Vehicle (Defined) 625.2

Rating 625.42

Rechargeable Energy Storage System (Defined) 625.2

Supply Equipment

Equipment Construction . . . . 625 Part II

Locations 625.50

Ventilation Not Required . . . . 625.52(A)

Ventilation Required . . . . 625.52(B)

Voltages (Supply Equipment) 625.4

Wireless Power Transfer . . . . Part IV

Construction. 625.102

Grounding. .625.101

Wiring Methods 625.44

ELECTRIC VEHICLE CHARGING SYSTEM

Branch Circuit, For the Purpose of Charging 625.40

Additional Feeders or Branch Circuits . . . . . . 225.30(A)

Cords and Cables. 625.17

Coupler 625.10

Definitions 625.2

Individual Branch Circuit 625.40

Marking 625.15

Overcurrent Protection 625.41

Premise Wiring, Cord- and Plug-Connected 625.44

Ventilation 625.52

Wireless Power Transfer Equipment . . . . 625 Part IV

Construction. 625.102

Grounding 625.101

ELECTRIC WELDERS

See WELDERS . . . . Ferm's Finder

ELECTRICAL EQUIPMENT

Dedicated Space . . . . 110.26(E)

Definition . . . . Art. 100

Hazard Markings . . . . .110.21(A)(2)

Illumination . . . . 110.26(D)

Limited Access . . . . .110.26(A)(4)

Marking . . . . 110.21(A)

Reconditioned . . . . .110.21(A)(2)

Torquing Requirements . . . . 110.14(D)

Working Space . . . . 110.26(A)

ELECTRICAL CIRCUIT PROTECTIVE SYSTEM

Communication Circuits (Defined) 800.2

ELECTRICAL METALLIC TUBING . . . . **Art. 358**

Bends, How Made 358.24

Bends, Number in One Run 358.26

Construction of 358.100

Corrosion Protection . . . . 358.10(B)

Couplings and Connectors 358.42

Dimensions and Percent Area of . . . . Chapter 9 Table 4

Dissimilar Metals. 358.14

Installation in Hazardous Locations . . . . 358.10(A)

Made of 358.100

Marked 358.120

Minimum and Maximum Sizes 358.20

Not as a Means of Support for Cables or

Nonelectrical Equipment (General) . . . . 300.11(B)

   CATV Wiring .820.133(B)

   Class 2 or 3 Remote Control Circuits 725.143

   Communications Wires and Cables. . . . . . . .800.133(B)

   Fire Alarm Circuits, PLFA 760.143

   Network-Powered Broadband Communication Cables . . .

   . . . . .830.133(B)

Number of Conductors 358.22

   Combination of Conductors (General) . . Chapter 9 Table 1

   Conductors and Fixture Wires, Same Size . . . .

   . . . . Tables C.1 & C.1(A)

Reaming of . . . . 358.28(A)

Securing and Supporting 358.30

Splices and Taps 358.56

Threads on, Prohibited . . . . 358.28(B)

Uses Not Permitted 358.12

Uses Permitted 358.10

Wet Locations, in . . . . 358.10(C)

See (FJMX) .UL Product Spec

ELECTRICAL NOISE (ELECTROMAGNETIC INTERFERENCE)

Currents That Introduce, Not Considered Objectionable . . . .

. . . . 250.6(D)

Grounding

   Isolated Grounding Circuits . . . . 250.96(B)

   Isolated Grounding Receptacles . . . . 250.146(D)

   Isolated Ground Receptacles. . . . . 406.3(D)

      For Audio Systems . . . . 640.7(C)

      For Sensitive Electronic Equipment . . . . 647.7(B)

   Isolated Receptacles. . . . . 250.146(D)

   Lighting Equipment 647.8

   Panelboards . . . . 408.40 Ex.

Sensitive Electronic Equipment

   Use of Separately Derived System 647.3

   Use of With Audio Systems . . . . 640.7(B)

ELECTRICAL NONMETALLIC TUBING . . . . Art. 362

Bends, How Made 362.24

Bends, Number in One Run 362.26

Bushings 362.46

Construction 362.100

Dimensions and Percent Area of . . . . Chapter 9 Table 4

Finish Grade Use Requirements 362.10

   Uses of in Places of Assembly . . . .

   . . . . 518.4(C) & (Informational Note)

Fished, Securing Not Required . . . . .362.30(A) Ex., (3)

Joints 362.48

Marking 362.120

Maximum and Minimum Size 362.20

Number of Conductors 362.22

   Combination of Conductors (General) . . Chapter 9 Table 1

   Conductors and Luminaire (Fixture) Wires, Same Size . . . .

   . . . . Tables C.2 & C.2(A)

Securing and Supporting 362.30

Splices and Taps 362.56

Trimming 362.28

Uses Not Permitted 362.12

Uses Permitted 362.10

See (FKHU) .UL Product Spec

ELECTRICAL SERVICE AREAS 210.64

ELECTRICALLY ACTUATED FUSE

Feeders, Additional Requirements 240.101

Over 1000 Volts (Defined) . . . . Art. 100, Part II

Transformers, Overcurrent Protection. . Table 450.3(A) Note 4

Under 600 Volts (Defined) . . . . Art. 100, Part I

ELECTRICAL CIRCUIT PROTECTIVE SYSTEM

Class 1, Class 2, and Class 3 Circuits . . . . 725.179(F)(2)

Critical Operations Power Systems. . . . . .708.10(C)(2)

Definition

   Communication Circuits. 800.2

   Fiber Optic Cables 770.2

Emergency Systems . . . . .700.10(B)(1)

Fiber Optic Cables and Raceways . . . . .770.179(E)

Fire-Rated Cables and Conductors . . . . 300.19(B)

Fire Alarm Systems

   Listing . . . . 760.176(F)(2)

   Other Article. . . . . 760.3(I)

Fire Pumps . . . . .695.6(H)

Fire-Resistive Cable Systems Considered This Protection . . .

. . . . .728.4 Info. Note 2

See (FHIT) . . . . .UL Product Spec

E

ELECTRICALLY DRIVEN OR CONTROLLED IRRIGATION MACHINES . . . . **Art. 675**

ELECTRICALLY OPERATED POOL COVERS
Bonding of Metal Parts of . . . . .680.26(B)(3)
Definition 680.2
Ground-Fault Circuit Interrupter Required . . . . .680.27(B)(2)
Motors and Controllers . . . . .680.27(B)(1)

ELECTRICALLY POWERED POOL LIFTS . . . . . **680 Part VIII**
Bonding 680.83
Definition 680.2
Equipment Approval 680.81
Nameplate Marking 680.85
Protection 680.82
Switching Devices 680.84

ELECTRICAL SERVICE AREAS . . . . **.210.64**

ELECTRIFIED TRUCK PARKING SPACES . . . . **Art. 626**
Definitions of 626.2
Electrical Wiring Systems . . . . 626 Part II
General Requirements . . . . 626 Part I
Supply Equipment . . . . 626 Part III
Transport Refrigerated Units . . . . 626 Part IV

ELECTRODES, GROUNDING . . . . **250 Part III**
At Agricultural Buildings . . . . 547.9(A)(5)
CATV and Radio Distribution Systems . . . . .820.100(B)
Common Electrode for Building Services 250.58
Communications Circuits . . . . .800.100(B)
Direct-Current Sizing 250.166
Electrodes Permitted, Types 250.52
Electrode System Installation 250.53
For Separately Derived Systems 250.30
Fuel Cell Systems 692.47
Grounding Electrode System, Elements of 250.50
Intersystem Bonding Termination, Communications . . . . .
 . . . . .800.100(B)
Intersystem Bonding Termination, CATV . . . . . .820.100(B)
Intersystem Bonding Termination, Network Powered
Broadband . . . . .830.100(B)
Irrigation Machines 675.15
Lightning Protection Systems Bonded to 250.106
Network-Powered Broadband Systems . . . . .830.100(B)
Permanently Installed Generators 250.35

Radio and Television Equipment/Intersystem Bonding
Termination . . . . 810.21(F)
Restrictions on Use of Water Piping . . . . .250.52(A)(1)
Rod, Pipe, or Plates, Augment If Resistance to Ground over
 25 Ohms . . . . 250.53(A)(2) Ex.
Sensitive Electronic Equipment . . . . 647.6(A)
Solar Photovoltaic Systems 690.47
Supplementary Electrodes 250.54
Two or More Buildings from Common Service 250.32
Use of Strike Termination Devices in Lieu of,
Prohibited 250.60
Water Pipe Prohibited for Electrolytic Cells 668.15
Water Piping System Used to Ground a System Must Be
 Supplemented . . . . 250.53(D)(2)
See GROUNDING ELECTRODE CONDUCTORS . . . .
 . . . . Ferm's Finder
See (KDER) . . . .*UL Product Spec*

ELECTROLYTIC CELLS . . . . **Art. 668**
Application of Other Articles Limited 668.3
Cell Line Working Zone (Area Encompassed) 668.10
Circuit Protection, Cell Line Working Zone . . . . . 668.30(D)
Cranes and Hoists in Working Zone 668.32
Definitions 668.2
Fixed and Portable Not Required to Be Grounded 668.30
Isolated Circuits Required . . . . 668.21(A)
Portable Equipment Not to Be Grounded . . . . 668.20(A)
 Isolating Transformers to Supply Branch Circuits 668.20(B)
Runway Conductors, Disconnecting Means . . . . 610.31 Ex.

ELECTRONIC COMPUTER . . . . **Art. 645**
See INFORMATION TECHNOLOGY EQUIPMENT . . Ferm's
Finder

ELECTROPLATING . . . . **Art. 669**
Branch-Circuit Conductor Ampacity 669.5
Disconnecting Means 669.8
Overcurrent Protection 669.9
Warning Signs 669.7
Wiring Methods 669.6

ELEVATOR EQUIPMENT
See (FQKR) . . . .*UL Product Spec*

ELEVATORS, DUMBWAITERS, ESCALATORS, MOVING WALKS, PLATFORM LIFTS, AND STAIRWAY CHAIR LIFTS . . . . Art. 620

Adjustable Speed Drive Systems . . . . Article 430 Part X

Available Short-Circuit Current

    Field Marking . . . . 620.51(D)(2)

Branch Circuits Required

    Car Air-Conditioning and Heating Source . . . . . 620.22(B)

    Car Lights, Receptacles, Ventilation . . . . 620.22(A)

    Hoistway Pit Lighting and Receptacles 620.24

    Machine Room/Space Lighting, Receptacles 620.23

Calculation of Feeder and Branch Circuit 620.13

    Emergency and Standby . . . . 620.91(C)

Multiple Disconnecting Means 620.52

Conductors . . . . 620 Part II

    Ampacity of 620.13

    Installation . . . . 620 Part IV

    Minimum Size of 620.12

Control . . . . 620 Part VI

Control Room, Definition of 620.2

Control Space, Definition of 620.2

Cords and Cables, Not Required in a Raceway . . . . 620.21 Ex.

Definitions of Special Elevator Terms 620.2

Demand Factors 620.14

    Other Than Continuous Load . . . . 430.22(E)

    Feeders 430.26

    Single Motor 430.22

Different Systems in Cable or Raceway 620.36

Disconnecting Means 620.51

    Car Air-Conditioning and Heating 620.54

    Car Light, Receptacle(s) and Ventilation 620.53

    Utilization Equipment 620.55

Emergency and Standby Power Systems . . . . 620 Part X

    General Requirements for Systems . . . . Art. 700

    Hospitals

        Connection of Equipment to Life Safety Branch . . . . 517.33(G)

        Equipment for Delayed Automatic or Manual Connection to Alternate Power Source . . . . 517.35(B)(2)

    Nursing Homes & Limited Care Facilities

        Automatic Connection to Life Safety Branch 517.43

        Connection to Equipment Branch 517.44

Flexible Cords and Cables . . . . 620 Part III

GFCI Protected Receptacles 620.85

Pit Lighting, Machine Space Lighting Not on Load Side . . . . 620.23 & 24

Grounding . . . . 620 Part IX

Hoistway Wiring Methods . . . . .620.21(A)(1)

Hybrid System, Descending Elevator not a . . . . Art. 100

Machine Room . . . . 620 Part VIII

Machine Room, Definition of 620.2

Machine Space, Definition of 620.2

Overcurrent Protection . . . . 620 Part VII

    Selective Coordination 620.62

Power from More than One Source 620.52

Selective Coordination 620.62

Short-Circuit Current Rating 620.16

Surge Protection . . . . 620.51(E)

Traveling Cables . . . . 620 Part V

Voltage Limitations . . . . 620.5(A)

Wiring Methods . . . . 620 Part III

See GRAIN HANDLING & STORAGE AREAS . Ferm's Finder

EMERGENCY SYSTEMS . . . . Art. 700

Additional Service Allowed for . . . . 230.2(A)(2)

    Grouping of Disconnects . . . . 230.72(A) Ex.

    Location of Disconnects . . . . 230.72(A)

    Service Installed Sufficiently Remote . . . . 230.72(B)

    Permitted As Source of Power . . . . 700.12(D)

Automatic Load Control Relay, Defined 700.2

Boxes and Enclosures for (Identification) . . . . 700.10(A)

Branch Circuit Emergency Lighting Transfer Switch. . . 700.25

Capacity of, Load Shedding & Peak Load Shaving 700.4

Circuits for Lighting . . . . 700 Part IV

    Control . . . . 700 Part V

    See Life Safety Code NFPA 101 . . . . NFPA 101

Clinics 517.45

Cord Connected Unit Equipment . . . . 700.12(F)

Definitions 700.2

Dimmer and Relay Systems 700.23

Fire Protection of

    Equipment for Feeder Circuits . . . . 700.10(D)(2)

    Feeder Circuit Wiring . . . . 700.10(D)(1)

    Sources of Power 700.12

Fuel Cells as Source . . . . 700.12(E)

Ground-Fault Indication . . . . 700.6(D)

Ground-Fault Protection of Equipment 700.31

Identification

E

Grounded Circuit Conductor Connection . . . . . . 700.7(B)

Permanently Marked (Components) . . . . 700.10(A)

Receptacles (Distinctive Color) . . . . 700.10(B)

Illumination 700.16

Independent of Other Wiring . . . . 700.10(B)

Luminaires, Directly Controlled 700.24

Maintenance . . . . 700.3(C)

Multiwire Branch Circuits 700.19

Places of Assembly . . . . 518.3(C)

Selective Coordination 700.32

Signs

    Emergency Source . . . . 700.7(A)

    Grounding . . . . 700.7(B)

    Illumination and Exit Required 700.16

Surge Protection 700.8

Switch Locations 700.21

Maintenance 700.3

Transfer Switch(es)

    Branch Circuit Emergency Lighting 700.25

    General 700.5

    Listing Required . . . . 700.5(C)

    Short-Circuit Current Rating . . . . 700.5(E)

    With Generator Set . . . . 700.12(B)(1)

    See (WPWR) . . . . *UL Product Spec*

Unit Equipment . . . . 700.12(F)

    Components . . . . 700.12(F)(1)

    Installation . . . . 700.12(F)(2)

    Remote Heads . . . . 700.12(F)(2)(6)

Wiring Design and Location . . . . 700.10(C)

See Life Safety Code, NFPA 101 . . . . NFPA 101

ENCLOSURES

Arcing Parts 110.18

Bonding, Service . . . . 250.92(A)(2)

Bonding Other Enclosures 250.96

Busways . . . . Art. 368

Cabinets, Cutout Boxes, and Meter Socket Enclosures   Art. 312

Circuits in, Number of . . . . 90.8(B)

Definition of . . . . Art. 100 Part I

Elevators, Dumbwaiters, Escalators, Moving Walks,

    Wheelchair Lifts, and Stairway Chair Lifts . . . 620 Part VIII

For Grounding Electrode Conductors . . . . 250.64(E)

Grounding of . . . . 250 Part VI

High-Intensity Discharge Lamp Auxiliary Equipment . . . . . .

. . . . 410.104(A)

Induction and Dielectric Heating 665.20

Installations Over 1000 Volts, Nominal 110.31

    Equipment Over 1000 Volts – Specific Provisions   490 Part II

Intrinsically Safe Conductors in . . . . 504.30(A)(2)

Manholes and Other Enclosures for Personnel Entry   110 Part V

Panelboards 408.38

Radio Equipment . . . . 810.71(A)

Signs and Outline Lighting (General) 600.8

    Enclosures Used as Pull Boxes . . . . 600.5(C)(2)

    Neon Tubing Electrode, Listed for the Purpose . . 600.42(C)

Subsurface . . . . 110.12(B)

Switches 404.3

Types of Enclosures, NEMA . . . . Table 110.28

Underground 110.28

ENERGY CODE

Lighting Load, Design and Constructed . . . . . . 220.12 Ex.

ENERGY MANAGEMENT SYSTEM

Alternate Power Source 750.20

Building Automation . . . . 406.3(E)

Controlled Receptacle . . . . 406.3(E)

Definitions 750.2

Field Marking 750.50

Load Management 750.30

Marking . . . . Figure 406.3(E)

Recreational Vehicles . . . . 551.42(C) Ex. 2

Scope 750.1

ENERGY STORAGE SYSTEMS (ESS) . . . . Art. 706

Batteries . . . . Art. 706 Part III

    Flow Battery . . . . Art. 706 Part IV

    Installation 706.30

    Interconnections 706.32

    Terminations 706.31

Charge Control 706.23

Circuit Requirements . . . . Art. 706 Part II

Connection to Other Energy Sources 706.8

Definitions 706.2

Directory 706.11

Disconnecting Means 706.7

Electrochemical Energy Storage Systems . . . . Art. 706 Part III

Energy Storage System (Defined) 706.2

Equipment 706.5

Flow Battery Energy Storage Systems . . . . . .Art. 706 Part IV

Illumination . . . . 706.10(E)

Listed 706.5

Locations 706.10

Multiple Systems 706.6

Other Energy Storage Technologies . . . . Art. 706 Part V

Overcurrent Protection 706.21

System Classifications 706.4

Ventilation . . . . 706.10(A)

ENFORCEMENT OF CODE 90.4

Administration and Enforcement . . . . .Informative Annex H

Note: See Informative Annex H, 80.5 for specific adoption Informative

. . . . Annex H Section 80.5

EQUIPMENT

Acceptable Only If Approved 110.2

Approval of 90.4

Cooling of . . . . 110.13(B)

Definition of .Art. 100 Part I

Examination of 90.7

Examination, Identification, Installation, and Use 110.3

Grounding . . . . 250 Part VI

Hazard Markings . . . . 110.21(B)

Identification of Engineered Combination Systems . . . .

. . . . 110.22(B)

    Engineered Combination Systems . . . . 240.86(A)

Installation, General Provisions . . . . Art. 110

Installation, General Provisions, Over 1000 Volts . . . Art. 490

Listing of . . . . 110.3(C)

Marking 110.21

Mounting of . . . . 110.13(A)

Product Safety Standards . . . . Informative Annex A

Reconditioned . . . . .110.21(A)(2)

Wireless Power Transfer Equipment 625.101

    Construction 625.102

    Definitions 625.2

    Grounding 625.101

EQUIPMENT GROUNDING CONDUCTOR

Air Conditioning Equipment on Rooftops 440.9

Agricultural Buildings, Separate Conductor, Copper
or Aluminum . . . . 547.5(F)

Underground to, Insulated, Copper or Aluminum . . . . . .
. . . . 547.5(F)

Boatyards and Marinas . . . . 555.15(B)

Bonded to Well Casing . . . . 250.112(M)

Bonding Metal Piping and Exposed Structural Steel to . . . . .
. . . . .250.104

Box, Conductor Fill . . . . .314.16(B)(5)

Cable Trays 392.60

Carnivals, Circuses, Fairs and Similar 525.31

    Continuity Assurance 525.32

Conductors of Same Circuit, with, General . . . . . . 300.3(B)

Conductors of Same Circuit, with, Metal Raceways . 300.20(A)

Conductors of Same Circuit, with, Underground. . . . .
. . . . 300.5(I) Ex. 1

Connections 250.130

Continuity of 250.124

Cord- and Plug-Connected Equipment (General) . . . 250.138

Cord- and Plug-Connected Equipment (Specific) . . . 250.114

Definition of .Art. 100 Part I

Earth Not Used As Effective Ground-Fault Current Path . . . .
. . . . 250.4(A)(5)

Earth Not Used As Effective Ground-Fault Current Path
for Supplementary Electrodes 250.54

Electrical Nonmetallic Tubing, in 362.60

Equipment Fastened in Place 250.134

Feeder Identification . . . . 215.12(B)

Flexible Metal Conduit 348.60

Floating Buildings 553.8

Identification of, General . . . . 310.110(B)

    Feeder . . . . 215.12(B)

    Identification Methods 250.119

Impedance Grounded Neutral Systems Over 1 kV . . . .
. . . . 250.187(D)

Increased In Size .250.122(B)

Installation of 250.120

Insulated Conductor for Isolated Ground Receptacles . . . . .
. . . . 250.146(D)

Isolated Grounding Circuits . . . . 250.96(B)

Luminaires (Lighting Fixtures)

    Exposed Conductive Parts 410.42

    Means for Attaching Equipment Grounding Conductor . . .
    . . . . 410.46

    Methods of Grounding 410.44

Liquidtight Flexible Metal Conduit 350.60

Liquidtight Flexible Nonmetallic Conduit, in 356.60

Marinas and Boatyards . . . . 555.15(B)

Messenger Supported Wiring. . . . . 396.30(C)

Motor Terminal Housings, Means of Attachment . . 430.12(E)

Panelboards 408.40

   Bonding in Patient Vicinity 517.14

Parallel Conductors . . . . .250.122(F)

Patient Care Spaces . . . . 517.13(A)

   Additional Requirements for . . . . 517.13(B)

Rigid PVC Conduit, in 352.60

Signs and Metal Parts of Outline Lighting. 600.7

Size of 250.122

Sizing . . . . Table 250.122

   Increased in Size. . . . . .250.122(B)

Spliced or Joined in Boxes 250.148

Surface Metal Raceways 386.60

Surface Nonmetallic Raceways 388.60

Swimming Pools, Equipment to Be Grounded 680.6

   Methods of Grounding

      Cord and Plug-Connected Equipment. 680.8

      Feeders 680.25

      Fountains 680.55

      Motors, Permanently Installed . . . . . . .680.21(A)(1)

      Pumps, Storable Pools 680.31

      Underwater Luminaires (Lighting Fixtures) .680.23(F)(2)

Switches, Connected to EGC . . . . 404.9(B)

Switchgear, Connected to EGC . . . . 250.112(A)

Transformers 450.10

Tunnel Installations Over 1000 Volts . . . . 110.54(B)

Types of 250.118

Wireways

   Nonmetallic 378.60

See BONDING . . . . Ferm's Finder

See GROUNDING . . . . Ferm's Finder

EQUIPMENT GROUNDING CONDUCTOR FILL FOR BOXES . . 314.16(B)(5)

EQUIPMENT SPACE, DEDICATED

Indoor . . . . .110.26(E)(1)

Outdoor . . . . .110.26(E)(2)

EQUIPOTENTIAL BONDING

Class1, Division 2 . . . . 501.125(B) Info. Note 2

Hot Tubs and Spas, Indoor Not Required 680.43 Ex. 2 and Ex. 3

Hydromassage Bathtubs. 680.74

Performance, Pools . . . . 680.26(A)

Perimeter Surface . . . . .680.26(B)(2)

Pool Water . . . . 680.26(C)

Swimming Pools . . . . 680.26(B)

Zone 0, 1 and 2 Locations . . . . 505.20(C) Info. Note 2

EQUIPOTENTIAL PLANE

Bonding. . . . . 547.10(B)

Definition, Agricultural Buildings 547.2

Definition, Natural and Artificially Made Bodies of Water 682.2

Installation 547.10

Natural and Artificially Made Bodies of Water 682.33

Receptacle Locations within . . . . 547.5(G)(1)

Required

   Indoors . . . . .547.10(A)(1)

   Outdoors . . . . .547.10(A)(2)

ESCALATORS . . . . Art. 620

See ELEVATORS, ETC. . . . . Ferm's Finder

ESSENTIAL ELECTRICAL SYSTEM

Branches for Hospitals 517.30

   Independent Power Sources . . . . 517.30(A)

   Location of Components . . . . 517.30(C)

   Types of Power Sources. . . . . 517.30(B)

Branches for Nursing Homes 517.41

   Independent Power Sources . . . . 517.41(A)

   Location of Components . . . . 517.41(C)

   Types of Power Sources. . . . . 517.41(B)

Defined 517.2

Health Care Facilities . . . . .Art. 517 Part III

Transfer Switched

   Hospitals . . . . 517.31(B)

   Nursing Homes . . . . 517.42(B)

See HEALTH CARE FACILITIES . . . . Ferm's Finder

EXAMPLES . . . . Informative Annex D

Cable Tray Calculations . . . . Example D13

   Multiconductor Cables 4/0 and Larger . . . Example D13(a)

   Multiconductor Cables Smaller than 4/0 . . Example D13(b)

   Single Conductor Cables 1/0 through 4/0 . Example D13(c)

   Single Conductor Cables 250 through 900 kcmil . . Example D13(d)

Feeder Ampacity for Adjustable Speed Drive Control   Example D10

Feeder Ampacity for Generator Field Control . . . Example D9

Industrial Feeders in a Common Raceway . . . Example D3(a)

Mobile Home. . . . . Example D11

Motor Circuit Conductors, Overload Protection, etc. . . . . Example D8

Multi-Family (Optional, at 208Y/120, Volts, Three-Phase . . . . Example D5(b)

Multi-Family Dwelling (Optional) . . . . . . Example D4(b)

Multi-Family Dwelling . . . . Example D4(a)

Multi-Family Served at 208/Y/120 Volts, Three-Phase   Example D5(a)

One-Family (Optional, Air-Conditioning Larger Than Heat). . . . . Example D2(b)

One-Family (Optional, Heat Larger Than Air-Conditioning). . . . . Example D2(a)

One-Family (Optional, with Heat Pump) . . . . Example D2(c)

One-Family Dwelling (Basic). . . . . Example D1(a)

One-Family Dwelling (Plus Air-Conditioning & Appliances) . . . . Example D1(b)

Park Trailer . . . . Example D12

Range Loads . . . . Example D6

Sizing of Service Conductors for Dwellings. . . . . Example D7

Store Building. . . . . Example D3

EXIT LIGHTS

Emergency Illumination 700.16

Places of Assembly, Emergency Systems . 700.2 Informational Note

See EMERGENCY SYSTEMS . . . . Ferm's Finder

See Life Safety Code, NFPA 101 . . . . NFPA 101

EXOTHERMIC WELDING (Splicing Method)

Connection of Grounding and Bonding Equipment . . . 250.8

Installation of Grounding Electrode Conductor, Continuous . 250.64(C)

Methods of Connection to Electrodes 250.70

Not Required to be Accessible when Fireproofed. . . . . 250.68(A) Ex. 2

Swimming Pool Bonding (Equipotential Bonding Grid) . . . . 680.26(B)

EXPANSION JOINTS

Bonding Around 250.98

Busways, Over 1000 Volts 368.244

Deicing and Snow-Melting

    Protected from Expansion, Nonheating Leads, Embedded . . . . 426.22(D)

    Protected from Expansion, Resistance Heating Elements . . . . 426.20(E)

Heating Cables

    Under Floors. . . . . 424.45(B)

    Within Concrete or Masonry . . . . 424.98(B)

Heating Panels and Heating Panel Sets

    Under Floors. . . . . .424.99(B)(1)

    Within Concrete or Masonry . . . . 424.98(B)

Pipelines and Vessels. 427.16

    Flexural Capability 427.17

Raceways . . . . 300.7(B)

Rigid PVC Conduit 352.44

    Expansion Characteristics . . . . Tables 352.44

Structural Joints . . . . 300.4(H)

Type RTRC Conduit . . . . 355.44, Table 355.44

EXPLANATORY MATERIAL (Informational Notes) . . 90.5(C)

EXPLOSIONPROOF EQUIPMENT

Class I, Zone 0, 1, and 2 Locations, Sealing . . . . .505.16(B)(2)

Class I, II, and III, Zone 20, 21, and 22 Locations, Sealing. 506.16

Class II Locations 502.1

Definition of . . . . Art. 100 Part I

Protection Technique, Class I, Division 1 & 2 . . . . . 500.7(A)

EXPLOSIONPROOF

Explosionproof (Equipment) . . . . Art. 100

See HAZARDOUS (CLASSIFIED) LOCATIONS . Ferm's Finder

See (FTRV) . . . .*UL Product Spec*

EXPOSED

Clearance for Live Parts 110.26

Definitions of (as applied to live parts) . . . . . .Art. 100 Part I

Extensions, Boxes and Fittings 314.22

Structural Steel, Bonding . . . . 250.104(C)

Work Space and Guarding, Over 1000 Volts 110.34

EXTENSION CORD SETS

Assured Equipment Grounding Conductor Program . 590.6(B)

On Construction Sites Utilizing GFCI Protection . . . 590.6(A)

Overcurrent Protection of 240.5

Temporary Installations, Support Not Required . . . . 590.4(J)

EXTENSION RINGS

Exposed Surface Extensions 314.22

F

For Box Volume Calculations . . . . 314.16(A)

See (QCIT) . . . .*UL Product Spec*

EXTENSIONS

Auxiliary Gutters . . . . 366.12(2)

Boxes and Fittings, Exposed 314.22

Cellular Concrete Floor Raceways (uses not permitted)   372.12

Cellular Metal Floor Raceways (uses not permitted) . . 374.12

Flat Cable Assemblies, Type FC . . . . 322.40(D)

Nonmetallic Extensions . . . . Art. 382

Surface Metal Raceways . . . . 386.10(4)

Surface Nonmetallic Raceways . . . . 388.10(2)

Wireways

    From Metal 376.70

    From Nonmetallic 378.70

    Metal, Extension through Walls . . . . 376.10(4)

    Nonmetallic, Extension through Walls . . . . . . 378.10(4)

EXTRA-DUTY OUTLET BOXES. . . . . .406.9(B)(1)

EXTRACTS FROM OTHER NFPA CODES AND STANDARDS

See Informational Notes that immediately follow the listed sections or titles of the following articles: Art. 500; Art. 505; Art. 511; Section 513.1; Art. 514; Art. 515; Art. 516; Art. 517; Art. 695.

See also NEC Style Manual and NFPA *Manual of Style* for further information regarding extracts

F

FACEPLATES

Covers and Canopies 314.25

Flush-Mounted Installations 314.20

Flush Mounting, Receptacle Enclosure . . .406.5(B), (C), & (E)

Grounding Required 250.110

    Grounding Provisions . . . . 404.9(B)

    In Patient Care Spaces . . . . 517.13(B)(1) Ex. 1 to (3)

    Insulated Equipment Grounding Conductor . . . 517.13(B)

    Metal Covers in Completed Installations . . . . . 314.25(A)

    Metal or Non-Metallic, for Receptacles — Thickness . . . . .

    . . . . 406.6(A)

Integral Night Light and/or USB Charger . . . . 406.6(D)

Isolated Ground Receptacles, for . . . . 406.3(D)(2) Ex.

Position of, for Receptacle . . . . 406.5(D)

Receptacles, for 406.6

Repair of Noncombustible Surface 314.21

Snap Switches, for 404.9

Switches (Snap) . . . . 404.9(A)

USB Charging . . . . 406.6(D)

FAHRENHEIT TO CENTIGRADE . . . .
. . . . **Tables 310.15(B)(16) through (21)**

FAIRS, *See* **CARNIVALS, CIRCUSES, FAIRS & SIMILAR EVENTS**
. . . . **Ferm's Finder**

FANS, CEILING-SUSPENDED (PADDLE)
See CEILING-SUSPENDED (PADDLE) FANS . Ferm's Finder

FARM BUILDINGS

Agricultural Buildings . . . . Art. 547

    See AGRICULTURAL BUILDINGS . . . . . . Ferm's Finder

    Wiring Methods 547.5

Bonding and Equipotential Plane 547.10

    GFCI Protection for Receptacles . . . . 547.5(G)

Clearance of Service Conductors from Building Openings . .230.9

Calculating Loads . . . . 220 Part V

Disconnecting Means

    And Overcurrent Protection (Site Isolation), Where Located

    . . . . 547.9

    Grouping of 230.72

    Location, General 230.91

    Maximum Number of 230.71

    More than One Building or Structure . . . . 225 Part II

    Service Equipment, General 230.90

    Service, Location . . . . 230.70(A)

Grounding . . . . 547.9(B)

    Common Grounding Electrode 250.58

    Grounding Electrode System 250.50

    Two or More Buildings from Common Service 250.32

Outside Branch Circuits and Feeders . . . . Art. 225

Service Drop Conductors 230.22

See Flammable and Combustible Liquids at Farms and Isolated Sites . . . . Ferm's Finder

See Motor Fuel Dispensing Facilities . . . . Ferm's Finder

FAULT CURRENT, AVAILABLE **110.24**

Field Marking . . . . 110.24(A)

Modifications . . . . 110.24(B)

See SHORT-CIRCUIT CURRENT AVAILABLE . . . .
. . . . Ferm's Finder

FEEDERS . . . . **Art. 215**

Additional Loads on (Standard Calculation) 220.14

   (Optional Calculation) 220.87

Attached to Buildings or Structures 225.11

Busways, Installation 368.10

  Taps . . . . 240.21(E)

  Uses Not Permitted of As Feeder 368.12

  Uses Permitted of As Feeder 368.10

Calculations . . . . Art. 220

  See CALCULATIONS . . . . Ferm's Finder

Clearance for Overhead Feeder Conductors 225.18

Continuous and Noncontinuous Loads . . . . 215.2(A)

Conductor Ampacity (Over 600 Volts) . . . . 215.2(B)

Definition of (Feeder) . . . . Art. 100

Direct-Current Systems, Supplied From . . . . . 215.12(C)(2)

Dwellings, Size of . . . . .310.15(B)(7)

  Number of Feeders 225.30

  Permitted Size of Feeders . . . . .310.15(B)(7)

Entering a Building or Structure 225.11

Essential Electrical Systems, Alternate Power Source 517.30(F)

Exiting a Building or Structure 225.11

Farm Buildings . . . . 220 Part V

Floating Buildings 553.7

Ground-Fault Protection of Equipment 215.10

Ground-Fault Protection (Health Care) 517.17

Ground-Fault Circuit Interrupter (Personnel) 215.9

Grounding Means 215.6

  In Panelboards 408.40

  Marinas and Boatyards . . . . 555.15(E)

  Swimming Pools 680.25

  See GROUNDING, Fixed Equipment . . . . . Ferm's Finder

High-Leg (Identification) 110.15

  Alternating-Current Systems, Ungrounded Conductors . . .
  . . . . .215.12(C)(1)

  Direct-Current Systems, Ungrounded Conductors . . . . . .
  . . . . .215.12(C)(2)

  Equipment Grounding Conductor . . . . 215.12(B)

  Grounded Conductor . . . . 215.12(A)

In Same Metallic Enclosure . . . . 215.4(B)

Kitchen Equipment, Commercial 220.56

Kitchen Equipment, Dwellings 220.55

Marinas and Boatyards 555.13

Minimum Size & Rating . . . . 215.2(A)

Minimum Size & Rating (Over 600 Volts) . . . . . . 215.2(B)

  Calculated Load . . . . Art. 220

Mobile Home (Four Insulated Conductors) 550.10

  Conductor Size . . . . .310.15(B)(7)

  Installation and Capacity 550.33

  Permitted Size of Conductors . . . . .310.15(B)(7)

  See MOBILE HOMES . . . . Ferm's Finder

More than One Building or Structure . . . . 225 Part II

  Number of Supplies 225.30

Motors

  Circuit Conductors . . . . 430 Part II

  Short-Circuit and Ground-Fault Protection . . . 430 Part IV

  See MOTORS . . . . Ferm's Finder

Neutral (Feeder Load) 220.61

  Common Neutral 215.4

  Considered Current-Carrying . . . . .310.15(B)(5)

  Supplying Outside Lighting . . . . 225.7(B)

Noncoincident Loads 220.60

Outside . . . . Art. 225

  Ampacities of Conductors 310.15

  General . . . . Art. 240

  Over 1000 Volts . . . . 240 Part IX

  Overcurrent Protection 225.3

  See OUTSIDE BRANCH CIRCUITS AND FEEDERS . . . .
  . . . . Ferm's Finder

Recreational Vehicles 551.73

Restaurants, New (Optional) 220.88

Sizing (General) 215.2

  Ampacities of Conductors 310.15

  Calculations . . . . Art. 220

  Mobile Homes, *See* FEEDERS, Mobile Homes . . . .
  . . . . Ferm's Finder

  Motion Picture and TV Studios 530.19

  Recreational Vehicles, Minimum Size 551.73

  See CALCULATIONS . . . . Ferm's Finder

Supervised Industrial Installations . . . . 240 Part VIII

Swimming Pools 680.25

Taps, Overcurrent Protection and Definition . . . . . 240.4(E)

  Location of Overcurrent Protection . . . . 240.21(B)

  Motors 430.28

  Transformer Secondary Conductors . . . . . . .240.21(C)(6)

  See TAPS . . . . Ferm's Finder

Ungrounded Identification

  Alternating-Current Systems . . . . .215.12(C)(1)

  Direct-Current Systems . . . . .215.12(C)(2)

Use of SE Cable 338.10

FEED-THROUGH CONNECTIONS OF NEUTRAL — PIGTAILING . . . . **300.13(B)**

FENCES (Metal)
Grounding and Bonding, Over 1000 Volts . . . . . 250.194(A)
Around the Vicinity of Transformers . . . . 450.10(B)

FERROMAGNETIC ENCLOSURE . . . . **.300.20(A) Ex.2**

FERROMAGNETIC ENCLOSURE, SKIN EFFECT **426.2**

FERROUS METALS
Agricultural Buildings . . . . 547.5(C)(3) Ex.2
Cable Tray Systems. . . . . .392.100(C)
Electrically Continuous . . . . 250.64(E)
Electrical Metallic Tubing. 358.2
Electrical Metallic Tubing, Corrosion Protection. . . 358.10(B)
Enclosures for Grounding Electrode Conductors . . 250.64(E)
Faceplates, Receptacles . . . . 406.6(A)
Faceplates, Switches . . . . 404.9(C)
Field-Cut Threads . . . . 300.6(A) Info. Notes
Fixed Outdoor Electric Deicing and Snow-Melting Equipment 426.26
Induced Currents 300.20
Metal Equipment . . . . 300.6(A) Info. Notes
Protection from Corrosion 300.6
Rigid Metal Conduit 344.2
Solely Protected by Enamel, Rigid Metal Conduit . . 344.10(4)
Solely Protected by Enamel, Strut-Type Channel Raceway . . . . .384.10(8)
Strut-Type Channel Raceway, Uses Not Permitted . 384.12(2)
Underfloor Raceways, Uses Not Permitted . . . . . 390.3(B)

FESTOON LIGHTING
Conductor Covering 225.4
Conductor Size and Support . . . . 225.6(B)
Definition. . . . . Art. 100
Outdoor Lampholders 225.24
Theaters and Audience Areas. 520.65

FIBER BUSHINGS
AC Cable Ends 320.40
Raceways . . . . .300.4(G)

FIBER OPTICAL CABLES & RACEWAYS
See Optical Fiber Cables and Raceways . . . . Art. 770
See OPTICAL FIBER CABLES AND RACEWAYSFerm's Finder

FIBERS, LINT, FLYINGS, IGNITIBLE . . . . **Art. 506**

FIELD APPLIED HAZARD MARKINGS . . . . **110.21(B)**
See . . . . . ANSI Z535.4-2011, Product Safety Signs and Labels

FIELD-CUT THREADS . . . . **300.6(A) Info. Notes**

FIELD EVALUATION BODY (FEB)
Definition . . . . Art. 100
Field Labeled (Evaluation Reports) . . . . Art. 100

FIELD IDENTIFICATION REQUIRED (Switchboards and Panelboards) **408.4**

FINE PRINT NOTES (Now Informational Notes) (Info. Note) . . . . **90.5(C)**

FINELY STRANDED CABLES AND CONDUCTORS, TERMINATING **110.14**

FINISH RATING
Definition of . . . . 362.10 Ex to (2) Info. Note
ENT, Uses Permitted, More Than Three Floors . . . . .362.10(2)
Places of Assembly 518.4

FINISHING PROCESSES . . . . **Art. 516**
Class I and II Locations 516.4
   Special Precautions . . . . 500.4(B) Info. Note
   Specific Occupancies 500.9
Electrostatic Equipment . . . . 516.6(E)
   Hand Spraying Equipment . . . . 516.10(B)
   Use of . . . . 516.6(E)
Grounding 516.16
Grounding & Bonding (General) . . . . Art. 250
   In Class I Locations 501.30
   In Class II Locations 502.30
   In Hazardous (Classified) Locations 250.100
Sealing
   In Class I Locations 501.15
   In Class II Locations 502.15
Wiring Methods
   Above Class I and II Locations 516.7
   Equipment in Class I Locations 516.4
   In Class I Locations 501.10
   In Class II Locations 502.10
See . . . . . Standard for Dipping and Coating Processes Using Flammable or Combustible Liquids

See HAZARDOUS (CLASSIFIED) LOCATIONS . . . . Ferm's Finder

See . . . . . *Standard for Spray Application Using Flammable and Combustible Materials*

FIRE ALARM SYSTEMS . . . . Art. 760

AFCI Protection Prohibited. . . . . 760.41(B)

Abandoned Cables 760.25

Access to Electrical Equipment 760.21

Ahead of Mains, Service Connection . . . . 230.82(5)

   For Emergency System, Prohibited 700.12

   Relative Location of Service Overcurrent Device 230.94 Ex. 4

Branch Circuit (PLFA Circuits). . . . . .760.121(B)

Cable Routing Assemblies. . . . . 760.3(L)

Circuit Integrity (CI) Cable, Definition 760.2

   Circuits Extending Beyond One Building 760.32

   Fire Conditions of Survivability . . . . .760.179(F)

   Listing and Marking, NPLFA . . . . 760.176(D)

   Listing and Marking, PLFA 760.179

   Mechanical Execution of Work . . . . 760.24(B)

Circuit Requirements 760.35

Communication Raceways . . . . .760.3(M)

Conductors

   Non-Power-Limited (NPLFA) . . . . 760 Part II

   Power-Limited (PLFA) . . . . 760 Part III

Ducts . . . . 760.3(B)

Electrical Circuit Protective System, NPLFA . . . 760.176(F)(2)

GFCI Protection Prohibited. . . . . 760.41(B)

Grounding . . . . 250.112(I)

Health Care Facilities . . . . 517 Part VI

   See Standard for Health Care Facilities, NFPA 99 . .NFPA 99

   See Life Safety Code, NFPA 101 . . . . NFPA 101

Identification of Circuits 760.30

Installation in Buildings 760.135

Installation with Conductors of Other Systems . . . . 760.3(G)

Listing of Cables 760.176, 760.179

   Non-Power Limited Fire Alarm Cables. 760.176

   Power Limited Fire Alarm Cables 760.154

Location, Hazardous . . . . 760.3(C)

Non-Power-Limited Circuits . . . . 760 Part II

   Cable Marking 760.176

   Conductors 760.49

   Conductors of Different Circuits in Same Raceway . . 760.48

   Multiconductor Cable 760.53

Number of Conductors and Cables in Raceways . . 760.3(J)

Number of Conductors in Raceway, Derating 760.51

Overcurrent Protection 760.43

   Location of 760.45

Plenums . . . . .760.53(B)(2)

Wiring Methods. . . . . 760.53(A)

   Application of Listed Cables . . . . 760.53(B)

   As Multiconductor Cable 760.53

Not Covered by Article 640 . . . . 640.1(B)

Plenums . . . . 760.3(B)

Power-Limited Circuits . . . . 760 Part III

   Cable Markings 760.154

   Cable Substitutions . . . . Table 760.154(A)

   Circuit Markings 760.124

   Installation 760.133

   Line-Type Fire Detectors 760.179

   Plenums . . . . .760.135(C)

   Power Sources 760.121

   Separation of Conductors 760.136

   Substitute Cables 760.154

   Wiring Methods and Materials

      Load Side 760.130

      Supply Side 760.127

Raceways and Sleeves Exposed to Different Temperatures . . . . .760.3(H)

Raceway Bushings . . . . .760.3(K)

Vertical Support for Fire Rated Cables and Conductors 760.3(I)

See Life Safety Code, NFPA 101 . . . . .NFPA 101

See National Fire Alarm Code, NFPA 72 . . . . NFPA 72

FIRE LADDERS

Clearance for Conductors Not Over 1000 Volts . . . 225.19(E)

Clearance for Service Conductors 230.9

Over 1000 Volts, *See Life Safety Code, NFPA 101* . . NFPA 101

FIRE PROTECTIVE SIGNALING CABLE

   See (HNGV) . . . .*UL Product Spec*

FIRE PUMPS . . . . .Art. 695

Connection Ahead of Mains . . . . 695.3(A)(1)

   Grouping of Disconnects. . . . . 230.72(B)

   Overload Protection . . . . 230.90 Ex. 4

   Permitted on Supply Side of Service Disconnect . .230.82(5)

   Prohibited If Emergency System 700.12

   Relative Location of Overcurrent Device . . . . . 230.94 Ex. 4

F

F

Continuity of Power 695.4

Control Wiring 695.14

   Arrangement . . . . 695.14(A)

   Engine Drive Control . . . . 695.14(D)

   Wiring Methods. . . . . 695.14(E)

Disconnecting Means . . . . 695.4(B)

   Marking Requirements, Controller . . . . . .695.4(B)(3)(d)

   Marking Requirements, Fire Pump . . . . . .695.4(B)(3)(c)

   Supervision . . . . .695.4(B)(3)(e)

Emergency Power Supply . . . . Art. 700

Equipment Location. 695.12

Feeder Sources . . . . 695.5(C)

   Overcurrent Protection. . . . . 695.5(B)

Fire Rated Assembly (2 hour) to Protect Pump Circuit . . . . .695.6(A)(2)(d)(3)

Ground-Fault Protection of Equipment, Service . . . . 230.95(C) Info. Note 2

   Building or Structural, Not Required . . . . . . .240.13(3)

On-Site Power Production Facility. . . . . 695.3(A)(2)

Overcurrent Protection

   Conductors . . . . 430.72(B) Ex. 1

   Control Circuit Transformer. . . . . 430.72(C) Ex.

   Motor. 430.31

Power Sources to 695.3

Power Wiring 695.6

   Circuit Conductors . . . . 695.6(B)

   Fire Pump Motors and Other Equipment . . . . 695.6(B)(1)

   Fire Pump Motors Only . . . . 695.6(B)(2)

   Ground Fault Protection . . . . 695.6(G)

   Junction Boxes. . . . . 695.6(I)

   Listed Electrical Circuit Protective Systems . . . . . 695.6(H)

   Loads Supplied by Controller and Transfer Switch . 695.6(E)

   Mechanical Protection . . . . 695.6(F)

   Overload Protection . . . . 695.6(C)

   Pump Wiring . . . . 695.6(D)

   Raceway Terminations . . . . 695.6(J)

   Service Conductors. . . . . 695.6(A)

   Voltage Drop. 695.7

Remote Control Circuits 430.72

Separate Service . . . . 230.2(A)(1)

   For Emergency Systems . . . . 700.12(D)

   Sufficiently Remote . . . . 230.72(B)

   Utility Service Connection. . . . . 695.3(A)(1)

Service Equipment Overcurrent Protection. . . 230.90(A) Ex. 4

Surge Protection 694.15

Transfer of Power within Pump Room. . . . . 695.3(F)

Transformers 695.5

See Standard for the Installation of Stationary Fire Pumps for Fire Protection . . . .

FIRE RATED

Assemblies . . . . .300.11(A)(1)

Cables and Conductors . . . . 300.19(B)

Circuit Integrity Cables . . . . 725.3(I)

Circuit Protective Systems, see (FHIT) . . . . .*UL Product Spec*

Critical Operations Power Systems (COPS). . . 708.10(C)(2)(3)

Emergency Systems . . . . .700.10(D)(1)(4)

Non-Fire-Rated Assemblies. . . . . .300.11(A)(2)

FIRE-RESISTIVE CABLE SYSTEMS

Boxes . . . . 728.5(E)

Cable Trays . . . . 728.5(D)

Communication Circuits . . . . .800.179(G)(2)

Definitions 728.2

General 728.4

Grounding 728.60

Installations. 728.5

Marking 728.120

Mounting . . . . 728.5(A)

Optical Fiber Cables . . . . 770.179(E)(2)

Other Articles 728.3

Pulling Lubricants . . . . 728.5(F)

Raceway Fill . . . . 728.5(C)

Scope 728.1

Splices . . . . .728.5(H)

Support . . . . 728.5(B)

   Vertical . . . . 728.5(G)

FIRE SPREAD, PREVENTION OF

CATV and Radio Systems 820.26

   Installation of Cables 820.110

Class 1, 2 & 3 Remote Control Systems . . . . 725.3(B)

Communication Circuits 800.110

Fire Alarm Systems . . . . 760.3(A)

Network-Powered Broadband Systems 830.26

   Installation of Cables 830.110

Optical Fiber Cables and Raceways 770.26

Wiring Methods, Spread of Fire or Products of Combustion 300.21

FIRE STOPS **300.21**
  Busways Barriers and Seals . . . . .368.234(B)
  See FIRE SPREAD, PREVENTION OF . . . . . Ferm's Finder

FIREWALLS, WIRING THROUGH
  See FIRE SPREAD, PREVENTION OF . . . . . Ferm's Finder
  See (BXRH) .UL Product Spec

FITTINGS . . . . **Art. 314**
  Conduit Bodies 314.16
  Definition of . . . . Art. 100 Part I
  Drainage Openings, Field Installed 314.15
  Expansion
    For Rigid PVC Conduit 352.44
    Underground Subject to Ground Movement . . . .
    . . . . 300.5(J) Info. Note
  Insulated Fittings Required . . . . 300.4(G)
  Separable Attachment Fitting. 314.27

FIXED ELECTRIC HEATING EQUIPMENT FOR PIPELINES & VESSELS . . . . **Art. 427**
  Branch-Circuit Sizing 427.4
  Control & Protection . . . . .427 Part VII
  Disconnecting Means 427.55
    Disconnect, Locked in Open Position . . . . . . 427.55(A)
  Expansion Joints 427.16
  Free Conductor at Boxes . . . . 427.18(A)
  Ground-Fault Protection of Equipment 427.22
  Grounding, Induction Heating 427.29
  Grounding, Resistance Heating Elements 427.23
  Grounding, Skin-Effect Heating 427.48
  Identification — Caution Signs 427.13
  Impedance Heating . . . . 427 Part IV
  Induction Heating . . . . 427 Part V
  Installation . . . . 427 Part II
  Resistance Heating Elements . . . . 427 Part III
  Skin-Effect Heating . . . . 427 Part VI

FIXED ELECTRIC SPACE HEATING EQUIPMENT . . . **Art. 424**
  See ELECTRIC HEAT (SPACE) . . . . Ferm's Finder

FIXED EQUIPMENT
  Bulk Storage Plants. . . . . 515.7(A)
  Electric Vehicle Charging System . . . . 625.44(C)
  Health Care Facilities . . . . 517.20(A)
  Motor Fuel Dispensing Facility. 514.2

  Sensitive Electronic Equipment. . . . . 647.4(D)(1)
  Swimming Pools 680.2
  See GROUNDING Fixed Equipment . . . . Ferm's Finder

FIXED OUTDOOR ELECTRIC DEICING AND SNOW MELTING EQUIPMENT . . . . **Art. 426**
  See DEICING AND SNOW MELTING . . . . . . Ferm's Finder

FIXED RESISTANCE AND ELECTRODE INDUSTRIAL PROCESS HEATING EQUIPMENT . . . . **ART. 425**
  Approval 425.9
  Boilers . . . . Art 425 Part VI and VII
  Branch Circuits. 425.3
  Control and Protection . . . . 425 Part III
  Disconnecting Means 425.19
  Fixed Industrial Process Duct Heaters. . . . . . .Art 425 Part V
  Fixed Industrial Process Electrode-Type Boilers. . Art 425 Part VII
  Fixed Industrial Process Resistance-Type Boilers . Art 425 Part VI
  Listed Equipment 425.6
  Locations 425.12
  Infrared Lamp Industrial Heating Equipment 425.14
  Marking of Heating Equipment . . . . 425 Part IV
  Overcurrent Protection 425.72
  Overpressure Limit Control. 425.74
  Overtemperature Limit Control 425.73
  Special Permission 425.10

(FIXTURE) Luminaire WHIPS
  Armored Cable (Type AC) . . . . 320.30(D)
  Conductor Sizes and Ampacity . . . . .210.19(A)(4)
  Flexible Metal Conduit . . . . 348.30(A) Ex. 3
  Flexible Metallic Tubing . . . . 360.20(A) Ex. 2
  Length of . . . . 410.117(C)
  Liquidtight Flexible Metal or Conduit . . . . . 350.30(A) Ex. 3
  Liquidtight Flexible Nonmetallic Conduit. . . . . . 356.30(2)
  Manufactured Wiring Systems . . . . . 604.100(A)(2) and (3)
  Metal-Clad Cable (Type MC) . . . . 330.30(D)(2)
  Nonmetallic-Sheathed Cable . . . . .334.30(B)(2)
  Protection. 240.4(B)(2)

(FIXTURE) Luminaire WIRE . . . . **Art. 402**
  Ampacity of, Tapped to Branch Circuits . . . . . 240.4(B)(2)
    Allowable . . . . 402.5 & Table
  Overcurrent Protection of 240.4
    Overcurrent Protection (General). 402.14

F

Supplementary Protection 240.10

Taps . . . . .210.19(A)(4)

   Length . . . . .410.117(C)

   Manufactured Wiring Systems . . . 604.100(A)(2) and (3)

Types . . . . Table 402.3

Wiring of . . . . 410 Part VI

Whips, see (FIXTURE) Luminaire WHIPS . . . . Ferm's Finder

See (ZIPR) .UL Product Spec

FIXTURES (LUMINAIRES) FOR POOLS . . . . Art. 680

Storable Pools 680.33

See SWIMMING POOLS . . . . Ferm's Finder

See (WBDT) .UL Product Spec

FIXTURES (LUMINAIRES) LIGHTING . . . . Art. 410

As a Raceway 410.64

Ballast Type (Electric Discharge)

   1000 Volts or Less . . . . 410 Part XIII

   Calculations, Inductive and LED Lighting Loads . 220.18(B)

   Conductors within 3" of a Ballast Must Be Rated Not Lower
Than 90°C 410.68

     Note: For Special Application of Type THW, See
Application

     Provision Table 310.104(A) 310.104

   Cord-Connected . . . . .410.62(B) & (C)

   Fixture (Luminaire) Mounting. 410.136

   For Signs and Outline Lighting . . . . Art. 600

   More than 1000 Volts . . . . 410 Part XIII

   Thermal Protection . . . . .410.130(E)

     High-Intensity Discharge (Fixtures) Luminaires 410.130(F)

   Voltage Limitations

     Branch Circuits 210.6

     Dwellings, Open-Circuit Voltage Exceeding 300 Volts . . .
. . . . .410.135

     Lighting Equipment Installed Outdoors 225.7

     Operating 1000 Volts or Less . . . . .410.130(A)

     Operating More than 1000 Volts 410.140

Bathtub and Shower Areas . . . . 410.10(D)

Branch-Circuit Ratings to (Fixtures) Luminaires . . . .
. . . . .210.19(A)(4) Ex. 1&2

   Maximum Load 220.18

   Overcurrent Protection 210.20

   Permissible Loads 210.23

   To Lampholders . . . . 210.21(A)

   Breaker Rated "SWD" for Switching Fluorescent . . 240.83(D)

Breaker Rated "HID" for Switching High Intensity Discharge
. . . . 240.83(D)

See (DIVQ) . . . . .UL Product Spec

Calculations, Recessed Luminaires . . . . 220.14(D)

Canopies . . . . 410 Part III

Clearance Required

   Bathtubs & Showers . . . . 410.10(D)

   Clothes Closet Light 410.16

   Hot Tubs and Spas, Indoors . . . . 680.43(B)

   Hot Tubs and Spas, Outdoors . . . . 680.22(B)

   Over Combustible Materials 410.12

   Recessed (Fixtures) Luminaires, From Combustible
Materials . . . . 410.116(A)(1)&(2)

   Recessed (Fixtures) Luminaires, From Thermal Insulation. .
. . . . .410.116(B)

Clothes Closet (Restrictions) 410.16

Cord-Connected . . . . 410.24(A)

   Adjustable Luminaires (Fixtures) . . . . 410.62(B)

   Listed Electric-Discharge and LED Luminaires (Fixtures) . .
. . . . 410.62(C)

   Unit Equipment Emergency Systems . . . . 700.12(F)

   See PENDANTS . . . . Ferm's Finder

Covering of Combustible Material at Outlet Boxes . . . 410.23

Disconnecting Means Required . . . . 410.130(G)

Decorative Lighting and Similar Accessories 410.160

Electric-Discharge Lighting

   See FIXTURES (LUMINAIRES) LIGHTING, Ballast Type. .
. . . . Ferm's Finder

Festoon Lighting

   See FESTOON LIGHTING . . . . Ferm's Finder

(Fixture) Luminaire Wires

   Taps

     See (FIXTURE) Luminaire WHIPS . . . . . Ferm's Finder

   Whips

     See (FIXTURE) Luminaire WHIPS . . . . . Ferm's Finder

     See (ZIPR) . . . . .UL Product Spec

     See (FIXTURE) Luminaire WIRE . . . . . . Ferm's Finder

Flush and Recessed Lighting Luminaires (Fixtures) 410 Part XI

   Clearance Required 410.116

   Supports to 410.36

   Taps to Junction Box (Whip)

     See (FIXTURE) Luminaire WHIPS . . . . . Ferm's Finder

   Temperature Limits

     Combustible Materials . . . . 410.115(A)

     Conductors in Outlet Boxes 410.21

Construction of (Fixtures) Luminaires. 410.118

    Near Combustible Materials 410.11

    Where Recessed in Fire-Resistant Material . . . 410.115(B)

Grounded (Neutral) Conductor Must Be Connected

    Polarization of Luminaires 410.23

    Screw Shell Lampholders 410.90

    Shell of Screw Shell Lampholders . . . . . . 200.10(C) & (D)

Grounding . . . . 250 Part VI

    Connected to an Equipment Grounding Conductor . . . . .
    . . . . 410.42

    (Fixtures) Luminaires and Lighting Equipment . . . .
    . . . . .410 Part V

    Health Care, Patient Care Spaces . . . .517.13(B) Ex. 2 to (3)

    Methods of Equipment Grounding . 250 Part VII and 410.44

Lampholders . . . . .410 Parts VIII & IX

    Circuits and Equipment, at Less Than 50 Volts 720.5

    Double-Pole Switched 410.93

    Heavy Duty (Rating of) . . . . 210.21(A)

        Permissible on 30-ampere Branch Circuits . . . 210.23(B)

        Permissible on 40- and 50-ampere Branch Circuits . . . .
        . . . . 210.23(C)

    Voltage Limitations

    See FIXTURES (LUMINAIRES) LIGHTING, Voltage
    Limitations . . . . Ferm's Finder

    Infrared Heating, Construction 422.48

        Branch-Circuits, 40- and 50-ampere Rating. . . 210.23(C)

        Branch-Circuit Requirements. . . . . 424.3(A)

        Overcurrent Protection . . . . 422.11(C)

    Infrared Lamp Industrial Heating Appliances 425.14

    Lamps Only (No Plug Fuses) 410.90

    Mechanical Strength of Luminaires and Parts . . 410 Part VII

    Medium Base

        Branch Circuits. . . . . 210.23(A)

        Not Permitted in Clothes Closets. . . . . 410.16(B)

    Multiwire Branch Circuits, Disconnects Required . . . . . .
    . . . . .410.130(G)(2)

    Overcurrent Protection

        Ampacity of (Fixture) Luminaire Wires . . . . Table 402.5

        Branch-Circuit Ratings . . . . 210.19(A)(4)

        Outlet Device Ratings, Lampholders. . . . . . 210.21(A)

        Outlet Devices . . . . 210.20(D)

        Permissible Loads 210.23

        Protection of Conductors 240.5

    Polarization

        Identification of Terminals . . . . 200.10(C) & (D)

Installation of Luminaires (Lampholders) . 410 Part VIII

    Of (Fixtures) and Luminaires (Lampholders). . . . 410.50

Signs & Outline Lighting . . . . 600.4(B)

Supports . . . . 410 Part IV

Wet & Damp Locations . . . . 410.10(A)

    To Be Weatherproof Type 410.96

LED Luminaires, Closets 410.16

Lighting Track . . . . 410 Part XIV

    Calculated Load for . . . . 220.43(B)

    Connected Load. . . . . 410.151(B)

    Definition . . . . Article 100, Part 1

    Fastening. 410.154

    Grounding .410.155(B)

    Heavy-Duty Track. 410.153

    Installation. . . . . 410.151(A)

    Locations Not Permitted . . . . 410.151(C)

        Bathtub and Shower Areas . . . . 410.10(D)

    Support. . . . . 410.151(D)

Locations . . . . 410 Part II

    Aircraft Hangars Class I Locations 513.4

        Not Within Class I Locations 513.7

    Commercial Garages Class I Locations 511.4

        Over Class I Locations. . . . . 511.7(B)

    Corrosive. . . . . 410.10(B)

    Hazardous (Classified) . . . . Art. 500

        Anesthetizing Locations (Above) . . . . 517.61(B)

        Anesthetizing Locations (Within) . . . . 517.61(A)

        Class I, Division 1 . . . . .501.130(A)

        Class I, Division 2 . . . . .501.130(B)

        Class I, Zone 0, 1, and 2 Locations . . . . Art. 505

        Class II, Division 1 . . . . .502.130(A)(1)

        Class II, Division 2 . . . . .502.130(B)

        Class III, Division 1 & 2 . . . . .503.130

        In Clothes Closets 410.16

        In Ducts & Hoods, Commercial Cooking Hoods Only . .
        . . . . 410.10(C)

        In Ducts for Dust, Loose Stock, or Vapor, Prohibited . . .
        . . . . 300.22(A)

        In Ducts or Plenums for Environmental Air . . 300.22(B)

        Zone 20, 21, and 22 Locations 506.20

    In Show Windows. 410.14

    In Trees. . . . . 410.36(G)

    Near Combustible Material 410.11

    Other Space for Environmental Air . . . . 300.22(C)

F

F

Outdoors 225.7

    Lampholders, Wet and Damp Locations 410.96

    Location Below Energized Conductors 225.25

    Support by Trees . . . . 410.36(G)

    Wet or Damp Locations . . . . 410.10(A)

Over 1000 Volts — Electric Discharge Type . . 410 Part XIII

Over 1000 Volts — Lockable Disconnecting Means . . . . . .

   . . . . 410.141(B)

Over Bath Tubs . . . . 410.10(D)

    Hydromassage Bathtubs 680.72

    Mobile Homes . . . . 550.14(D)

    Park Trailers . . . . 552.54(B)

    Recreational Vehicles . . . . 551.53(B)

Over Combustible Material 410.12

Spas & Hot Tubs

    Indoors . . . . 680.43(B)

    Outdoors . . . . 680.22(C)

    Outdoors (General) . . . . 680.22(C)

    Swimming Pools . . . . 680.22(C)

    Underwater 680.23

    Therapeutic Pools & Tubs

        General 680.60

        Permanently Installed 680.61

        Tubs (Hydrotherapeutic Tanks) . . . . 680.62(F)

        Underwater 680.23

    Wet & Damp . . . . 410.10(A)

    See HAZARDOUS (CLASSIFIED) LOCATIONS . . . Ferm's Finder

Low-Voltage Lighting . . . . Art. 411

Medium Base Lampholder

    (Not Over 120 Volts Between Conductors) . . . . 210.6(B)

Mogul Base Lampholder

    (Not Over 277 Volts to Ground) . . . . 210.6(C)

    Outdoors 225.7

Not Over 120 Volts (Dwellings) . . . . 210.6(A)

Not Over 600 Volts Between Conductors . . . . . . 210.6(D)

    Outdoor Lighting 225.7

Outlet Box must be Accessible Under

    Surface Mounted Electric Discharge and LED (Fixture) Luminaires . . . . 410.24(B)

    Suspended Ceiling, Securely Fastened . . . . . . 410.36(B)

Outline Lighting . . . . Art. 600

    1000 Volts or Less . . . . 410 Part XIII

    More Than 1000 Volts . . . . 410 Part XIII

Overcurrent Protection

    For Conductors, (Fixture) Luminaire Wires . . . . 210.20(B)

    For (Fixture) Luminaire Wires 240.5

    For Lampholders . . . . 210.21(A)

    For Rated Ampacity . . . . Table 402.5

    Permissible Load 210.23

Pendants

    Aircraft Hangars . . . . 513.7(B)

    Commercial Garages . . . . 511.7(A)(2)

    Conductors for Incandescent Lamps 410.54

    Hazardous (Classified) Locations

        Class I, Division 1 Locations . . . . 501.130(A)(3)

        Class I, Division 2 Locations . . . . 501.130(B)(3)

        Class II, Division 1 Locations . . . . 502.130(A)(3)

        Class II, Division 2 Locations . . . . 502.130(B)(4)

        Class III, Division 1 & 2 Locations . . . . 503.130(C)

        Hospitals (Hazardous Anesthetizing Locations) . . . . . .

        . . . . 517.61(B)(3) Ex. 2

    Not in Clothes Closets . . . . 410.16(C)

    Not in Theater Dressing Rooms 520.71

    Not Over Bathtubs . . . . 410.10(D)

    Show Windows 210.62, 410.14

Retrofit Kits

    Defined . . . . Art. 100

    Listing Requirements for Luminaires, Lampholders and Lamps 410.6

Roof Decking

    Installed Under . . . . 410.10(F)

Supports . . . . 410 Part IV

    Boxes for . . . . 314.27(A)

    Ceiling-Suspended (Paddle) Fans, Including Lights 314.27(C)

    Class I, Division 1 Locations . . . . 501.130(A)(4)

    Class II, Division 1 Locations . . . . 502.130(A)(4)

    Swimming Pool Areas . . . . 680.22(B)

Taps

    See (FIXTURE) Luminaire WHIPS . . . . Ferm's Finder

Temperature Limits

    On Conductors in Outlet Boxes 410.21

    Special Provisions for Flush and Recessed 410.115

Track Lighting

    Track Lighting (Defined) . . . . Art. 100

    See LIGHTING TRACK . . . . Ferm's Finder

Used as a Raceway 410.64

Voltage Limitations

   Not Over 120 Volts Between Conductors (Dwellings) . . . . 210.6(A) & (B)

   Not Over 150 Volts Between Conductors

      Swimming Pool Underwater Lights . . . . 680.23(A)(1), (4), and (5)

   Not Over 277 Volts to Ground. . . . . 210.6(C)

      Lighting Equipment Outdoors . . . . 225.7(C)

   Not Over 600 Volts Between Conductors . . . . 210.6(D)

      Lighting Equipment Outdoors. . . . . 225.7(D)

   Whips, (Fixture) Luminaire

      See (FIXTURE) Luminaire WHIPS . . . . Ferm's Finder

   Wire within 3" of a Ballast Must Be Rated Not Lower Than 90°C 410.68

   Wired Fixture (Luminaire) Sections . . . . 410.137(C)

   Wires, (Fixture) Luminaire

      See (FIXTURE) Luminaire WIRES . . . . Ferm's Finder

   Wiring of . . . . 410 Part VI

FLASH PROTECTION (Warning Labels) **110.16**
   See . . . .*Standard for Electrical Safety in the Workplace*
   See . . . . *Product Safety Signs and Labels*

FLASHERS, TIME SWITCHES **404.5**
. . . . **.600.6(B)**

FLAT CABLE ASSEMBLIES (Type FC) . . . . **Art. 322**
   Definition 322.2

   Installation . . . . 322 Part II

   Listing Requirements 322.6

   Protective Covers . . . . 322.10(3)

   Rating of Branch Circuit . . . . 322.10(1)

   Terminal Block Identification . . . . 322.120(C)

   Uses Not Permitted 322.12

   Uses Permitted 322.10

   See (GQKT). . . . .*UL Product Spec*

   See (GQRS) . . . .*UL Product Spec*

FLAT CONDUCTOR CABLE (Type FCC) . . . . **Art. 324**
   Branch-Circuit Ratings . . . . 324.10(B)

   Conductor Identification . . . . .324.120(B)

   Definitions 324.2

   Installation . . . . 324 Part II

      Alterations . . . . 324.56(A)

      Anchoring 324.30

      Cable Connections and Insulating Ends . . . . . 324.40(A)

      Connections to Other Systems . . . . 324.40(D)

      Coverings for Floors 324.30

      Crossings 324.18

      Enclosure and Shield . . . . 324.40(C)

      Receptacles . . . . 324.42(A)

      Receptacles and Housings . . . . 324.42(B)

   Listing Requirements 324.6

   Shields . . . . 324.40(C)

   System Height . . . . 324.10(G)

   Transition Assemblies . . . . 324.56(B)

   Uses Not Permitted 324.12

   Uses Permitted 324.10

   See (IKKT) . . . .*UL Product Spec*

   See (IKMW) . . . .*UL Product Spec*

FLEXIBLE CORD & CABLE . . . . **Art. 400**
   See CORDS . . . . Ferm's Finder

FLEXIBLE METAL CONDUIT (GREENFIELD) . . . . . **Art. 348**
   Angle Connectors (Not Concealed) 348.42

   Bends 348.24

   Bonding

      Equipment Bonding Jumper 348.60

      In Hazardous (Classified) Locations 250.100

      Required If Service Raceway. . . . . 230.43(15)

      Signs . . . . 600.7(B)(4)

      Where Used as Equipment Grounding Conductor 250.118(5)

   Definition of 348.2

   Fittings Listed 348.6

   Grounding . . . . 250.118(5)

      Permitted as Equipment Grounding Conductor . 250.118(5)

   Listing Requirements 348.6

   Maximum and Minimum Sizes 348.20

   Number of Conductors in, General 348.22

      Number of, in Metric Designator 12 (3/8") . . . Table 348.22

      Same Size in . . . . Informative Annex C . . . . Table C.3

      Same Size, Compact Conductors . . . Informative Annex C . . . . Table C.3A

   Raceway for Service-Entrance Conductors . . . . . 230.43(15)

   Support of 348.30

   Uses Not Permitted 348.12

   Uses Permitted 348.10

      1.8 m (6 ft) Maximum Length . . . . .348.20(A)(2)

F

Class I, Division 2 Locations for Flexible Connection. . . . . 501.10(B)(2)(2)

Elevators, Dumbwaiters, Escalators, etc.620.21(A)(1) through (A)(3)(a)

Enclosing Motor Leads . . . . .430.245(B)

(Fixture) Luminaire Taps . . . . 348.20(A)(2)(c)

Intrinsically Safe Locations. 504.20

Metric Designator 12 (3/8") Flex (Uses Permitted) 348.20(A)

Part of Listed Assembly. . . . . .348.20(A)(5)

Utilizing Equipment . . . . 348.20(A)(2)(a)

Wired Luminaire (Fixture) Sections . . . . . . .410.137(C)

See FLEXIBLE METAL CONDUIT . . . . Ferm's Finder

See (DXUZ). . . . .*UL Product Spec*

FLEXIBLE METALLIC TUBING . . . . Art. 360

Bends 360.24

Radii for Fixed Bends. . . . . Table 360.24(B)

Radii for Flexing Use . . . . Table 360.24(A)

Fittings Listed 360.6

Grounding 360.60

Permitted as Grounding Means . . . . 250.118(7)

Listing Requirements 360.6

Maximum and Minimum Size 360.20

Number of Conductors 360.22

Metric Designator 16 (1/2-in.) & 21 (3/4-in.) Trade Size . . . . 360.22(A)

Metric Designator 12 (3/8-in.) Trade Size . . . . . 360.22(B)

Splices and Taps 360.56

Uses Not Permitted 360.12

Uses Permitted 360.10

3/8" Permitted

Ducts or Plenums for Environmental Air . . . . 300.22(B)

For Approved Assemblies or Luminaires   360.20(A) Exc. 2

Other Space for Environmental Air . . . . . . 300.22(C)

Tap Conductors to Flush or Recessed Luminaires . . . . .410.117(C)

See (ILJW) . . . .*UL Product Spec*

FLOATING BUILDINGS . . . . Art. 553

Bonding of Non-Current-Carrying Parts 553.11

Covered by *Code* . . . . 90.2(A)(1)

Definition of 553.2

Feeder Conductors 553.6

Grounding . . . . 553 Part III

Insulated Neutral Required 553.9

Service Conductors 553.5

Service Equipment Location 553.4

Services and Feeders, Installation 553.7

FLOODPLAIN PROTECTION . . . . 708.10(C)(3)

FLOOR BOXES

For Receptacle Spacing . . . . 210.52(A)(3)

For Receptacle Use . . . . 314.27(B)

Grounding . . . . 250.146(C)

FLOOR RECEPTACLES

Grounding of . . . . 250.146(C)

In Wet Locations (Protection) . . . . 406.9(D)

May Count as Required Wall Receptacles . . . . .210.52(A)(3)

Meeting Rooms. . . . . .210.71(B)(2)

Used with Listed Boxes . . . . 314.27(B)

FLUORESCENT LIGHTING LUMINAIRES (FIXTURES)

1000 Volts or Less . . . . 410 Part XII

Auxiliary Equipment, Remote from . . . . 410.137(A)

Ballast Protection Required . . . . 410.130(E)

Circuit Breakers Used to Switch . . . . 240.83(D)

Clothes Closets, Permitted in . . . . .410.16(A)(2)

Mounting Location . . . . 410.16(C)

Connection of 410.24

Cord-Connected 410.62

Disconnecting Means Required . . . . .410.130(G)

Load Calculations, Value . . . . 220.14(D)

More than 1000 Volts . . . . 410 Part XIII

Raceways 410.64

Snap Switches for . . . . .404.14(A)(1) and (B)(2)

FLUSH LIGHTS, *See* **FIXTURES (LUMINAIRES) LIGHTING, Flush Lights . . . . Ferm's Finder**

FOREIGN MATERIALS (PAINT, PLASTER,CLEANERS, ABRASIVES, ETC) . . . . 110.12(B)

FORMAL INTERPRETATIONS 90.6

FORMING SHELLS, UNDERWATER POOL LIGHTS

Bonding of . . . . 680.26(B)

Definition 680.2

No-Niche Luminaires (Fixtures) . . . . 680.23(D)

Underwater Audio Equipment . . . . 680.27(A)

Wet-Niche Luminaires (Fixtures) . . . . 680.23(B)

FOUNTAINS . . . . **680 Part V**

Applicability of Article 680 . . . . 680.1

   Self-Contained, Portable Less Than 1.5 m (5 ft) 680.50

Bonding (Equipotential Bonding) . . . . 680.26(B)

   Of Piping Systems 680.53

Cord- and Plug-Connected 680.56

Ground-Fault Circuit-Interrupter Protection . . . . 680.51(A)

   For Cord- and Plug-Connected . . . . 680.56(A)

Grounding, Equipment Required to be 680.54

Junction Boxes and Other Enclosures 680.52

Lighting Luminaires (Fixtures), Submersible Pumps, etc. 680.51

Methods of Grounding 680.55

Signs, at Fountains 680.57

See SWIMMING POOLS . . . . Ferm's Finder

FOYERS, Dwelling Unit (Receptacles) . . . . .210.52(I)

FUEL CELL SYSTEMS . . . . **Article 692**

Connection to Grounded System . . . . .200.3 Ex.

Connection to Other Circuits . . . . Art. 692 Part VII

Definition 692.2

Electric Vehicle (draw current from) 625.2

Emergency Systems . . . . 700.12(E)

Health Care Facilities . . . . 517.30(B)

Installation 692.4

Listing Requirement 692.6

Grounding . . . . Art. 692 Part V

Installed by Qualified Persons . . . . 692.4(C)

Modular Data Systems 646.17

Optional Standby System . . . . 701.12(F)

Output Characteristics 692.61

Outputs Over 1000 Volts . . . . .Art. 692 Part VIII

Power Production Equipment . . . . 705.2 Info Note

Service, Supply Side . . . . .230.82(6)

Unbalanced Connections 692.64

Utility-Interactive Point of Connection 692.65

Wiring Methods . . . . .Art. 692 Part IV

FUEL DISPENSING SEE GASOLINE . . . . **Ferm's Finder**

FULL-LOAD CURRENT, MOTORS

Alternating Current

   Single-Phase . . . . Table 430.248

   Three-Phase . . . . Table 430.250

   Two-Phase . . . . Table 430.249

   Direct Current . . . . Table 430.247

FURNACES, *See* **HEATING EQUIPMENT, SPACE** . . . .
. . . . **Ferm's Finder**

FUNCTIONALLY GROUNDED PHOTOVOLTAIC SYSTEM . . **690.2**

FUSES

Ampere Ratings for Fuse and Inverse Time Circuit Breakers . .
. . . . Table 240.6(A)

Arc Energy Reduction 240.67

Cable Limiters, Supply Side at Service . . . . .230.82(1)

Cable Limiters, Supply of Circuits Over 150 V to Ground 240.40

Cartridge . . . . 240 Part VI

   Maximum Voltage, 300-Volt Type . . . . 240.60(A)

Classification of 240.61

Disconnect Ahead of 240.40

Electronically Actuated Fuse

   Feeders, Additional Requirements 240.101

   Over 1000 Volts (Defined) . . . . Art. 100, Part II

   Transformers, Overcurrent Protection Table 450.3(A) Note 4

   Under 600 Volts (Defined) . . . . Art. 100, Part I

Ground-Fault Protection, Services If Fused Switch Used . . . .
. . . . 230.95(B)

Locked or Sealed 230.92

   Rooms or Enclosures . . . . 110.26(F)

Lower Voltage Permitted 240.61

Marking of

   Cartridge Fuses . . . . 240.60(C)

   Plug Fuses . . . . 240.50(B)

Mounting Height of Switches . . . . 404.8(A)

Next Higher Size Permitted (800 Amps or Less) . . . . 240.4(B)

Not in the Grounded Conductor, (Generally) . . . . 230.90(B)

   Fuses Used as Motor Overload Protection 430.36

   Provisions for Connecting in Grounded Conductor . 240.22

Over 1000 Volts . . . . 240 Part IX

Parallel 240.8

Plug . . . . 240 Part V

   Not Over 125 Volts Between Conductors . . . .240.50(A)(1)

   Not Over 150 Volts to Ground . . . . .240.50(A)(2)

   Not To Be Installed in Lampholders 410.90

   Replacement Only, Edison Base . . . . 240.51(B)

   Screw Shell Connected to Load Side . . . . 240.50(E)

   Type S Required for New Work 240.52

Protection from Tampering, Specific Circuits 230.93

Readily Accessible 240.24

Renewable Fuses . . . . 240.60(D)

Access to Occupants, Service Equipment . . . . . 230.72(C)

    Fused Switches . . . . 404.8(A)

Semiconductor . . . . .430.52(C)(5)

Service Equipment Overcurrent Protection. . . . . 230.90(A)

Standard Ratings 240.6

Transformers, Fuse Ratings 450.3

    1000 Volts and Less . . . . .Table 450.3(B)

    Over 1000 Volts . . . . Table 450.3(A)

Voltage Ratings 240.61

Wet or Damp Locations 240.32

    Enclosures for 312.2

    Switch Enclosures for 404.4

See OVERCURRENT PROTECTION . . . . . . Ferm's Finder

See SHORT-CIRCUIT CURRENT AVAILABLE . Ferm's Finder

See (JCQR) . . . .*UL Product Spec*

GAGES (AWG), CONDUCTORS 110.6

Conductor Properties . . . . Chapter 9, Table 8

GALVANIC ACTION

Electrical Metallic Tubing 358.14

Intermediate Metal Conduit 342.14

Rigid Metal Conduit 344.14

GARAGES (COMMERCIAL) . . . . Art. 511

Battery Charging Equipment . . . . 511.10(A)

Class I Locations

    Defined in 511.3

    Group Classification (Atmosphere) . . . . 500.5(A)

Definitions

    Major Repair Garage 511.2

    Minor Repair Garage 511.2

Electric Vehicle Charging . . . . 511.10(B)

Elevators & Escalators In 620.38

Fuels, Heavier-Than-Air. . . . . . .511.3(C) and Table 511.3(C)

Fuels, Lighter-Than-Air . . . . . . 511.3(D) and Table 511.3(D)

Fuel Dispensing Equipment. . . . . 511.4(B)(1)

Ground-Fault Circuit-Interrupter Protection, Receptacles . . .
. . . . 511.12

Grounding & Bonding . . . . Art. 250

    Additional Requirements Class I Locations 501.30

    At Service . . . . 250.92(B)

    Bonding Conductors and Jumpers 250.102

    General 511.16

    In Hazardous (Classified) Locations 250.100

Lightning Protection 250.106

    Surge Arresters . . . . Art. 280

    Surge Protection. 501.35

    Surge Protective Devices [Transient Voltage (TVSS)] Art. 285

    See Standard for the Installation of Lightning Protection Systems, NFPA 780 . . . . NFPA 780

Portable Lighting Equipment (Hand Lamps) . . . . 511.4(B)(2)

Sealing 501.15

    Horizontal As Well As Vertical Boundaries 511.9

Wiring Methods

    Above Class I Locations 511.7

        Equipment above. . . . . 511.7(B)

    In Class I Locations (General) . . . . Art 501

        For Garages 511.4

    Rigid Nonmetallic Conduit Permitted . . . . 511.4(A)

    Underground Wiring 511.8

See HAZARDOUS (CLASSIFIED) LOCATIONS Ferm's Finder

See Standard for Parking Structures, NFPA 88A . . .NFPA 88A

See Code for Motor Fuel Dispensing Facilities and Repair Garages, NFPA 30A . . . . NFPA 30A

GARAGES (NONDWELLING)

GFCI Protection . . . . 210.8(B)(8)

GARAGES (RESIDENTIAL)

Floor Area Not Included for Lighting Load Calculations 220.12

Garage Branch Circuits . . . . .210.11(C)(4)

Grade-Level Accessory Buildings . . . . 210.8(A)(2)

Ground-Fault Circuit-Interrupter Protection Requirements . .
. . . . 210.8(A)(2)

Grounding Requirements If Remote 250.32

Lighting Outlets Required. . . . . 210.70(A)(2)

Receptacles Required . . . . 210.52(G)(1)

GAS PIPE BONDED .250.104(B)

See National Fuel Gas Code, NFPA 54 . . . . NFPA 54

GAS PIPE NOT AS GROUNDING ELECTRODE . 250.52(B)(1)

GAS TUBE SIGN AND IGNITION CABLE

Signs and Outline Lighting . . . . 600.32(B)

See (ZJQX) . . . .*UL Product Spec*

GAS TUBE SIGN TRANSFORMERS

Signs and Outline Lighting 600.21, 600.23

See (PWIK) . . . .*UL Product Spec*

GASOLINE BULK STORAGE PLANTS . . . . **Art. 515**

See BULK STORAGE PLANTS. . . . . Ferm's Finder

GASOLINE (MOTOR FUEL) DISPENSING . . . . **Art. 514**

Aboveground Fuel Storage . . . . 514.3(A)(3)

Boatyard and Marinas

    Classification of Locations . . . . 514.3(C)

    Hazardous (Classified) Locations 555.21

Circuit Disconnects (General) 514.11

    Attended Self-Service Stations . . . . 514.11(B)

    Unattended Self-Service Stations . . . . 514.11(C)

Class I Locations

    Group Classification (Atmosphere) . . . . 500.6(A)

    Extent of Locations . . . . 514.3(B)(1) & (2)

Conductors (Gas & Oil Resistant) 501.20

    See (ZLGR) . . . .*UL Product Spec*

Definition 514.2

Dispensing at Bulk Storage Plants 515.10

Dispensing at Marinas and Boatyards 555.21

Dispensing Equipment, Provisions to Remove All External

    Voltage Sources During Maintenance and Servicing . 514.13

Grounding & Bonding . . . . Art. 250

    Additional Requirements Class I Locations 501.30

    At Service . . . . 250.92(B)

    Equipment Bonding Jumpers 250.102

    General 514.16

    In Hazardous (Classified) Locations 250.100

Hand Lamps . . . . 511.4(B)(2)

Intrinsically Safe Systems . . . . Art. 504

Lightning Protection (Surge) 250.106

    Surge Arrestors . . . . Art. 280

    Surge Protection. 501.35

    See *Standard for the Installation of Lightning Protection Code*

Marinas and Boatyards

    Classification of Locations . . . . 514.3(C)

    Hazardous (Classified) Locations 555.21

Sealing 501.15

    At Dispenser . . . . 514.9(A)

    Horizontal As Well As Vertical Boundaries . . . . . 514.9(B)

Switch for Dispensing or Pumping Equipment . . . . 514.11(A)

Handle Ties (Not Permitted) . . . . 514.11(A)

Wiring Methods

    Above Class I Locations 514.7

    Below Class I Locations (Underground) 514.8

    Within Class I Locations 514.4

    See . . . *Code for Motor Fuel Dispensing Facilities and Repair Garages*

    See Chapter 13, Farms and Remote Sites, NFPA 30A-2003 . . . .*NFPA 30A-2003*

    See . . .Tables 514.3(B)(1) & (2) for Location Classifications

See Code for Motor Fuel Dispensing Facilities and Repair Garages

See GARAGES (COMMERCIAL) . . . . Ferm's Finder

See HAZARDOUS (CLASSIFIED) LOCATIONS Ferm's Finder

See (ZLGR) . . . .*UL Product Spec*

GENERAL CARE (CATEGORY 2) PATIENT SPACES. . . **517.18**

Definitions 517.2

See HEALTH CARE FACILITIES . . . . Ferm's Finder

GENERAL REQUIREMENTS FOR WIRING METHODS . . **Art. 300**

Boxes or Fittings, Where Required 300.15

Changing Raceway or Cable to Open Wiring 300.16

Conductors 300.3

    Different Systems . . . . 300.3(C)

        1000 Volts or Less . . . . 300.3(C)(1)

        Restrictions for Class 2 & 3 Circuit Conductors300.3(C)(1) Info. Note 1

    Installation with Other Systems (Nonelectrical) 300.8

    Insulating Bushings for Raceways . . . . 300.4(G)

    Number and Sizes of, in 300.17

    Of Same Circuit . . . . 300.3(B)

        Enclosures (Auxiliary Gutters) . . . . 300.3(B)(4)

        Grounding and Bonding Conductors . . . . 300.3(B)(2)

        Nonferrous Wiring Methods . . . . 300.3(B)(3)

        Paralleled Installations . . . . 300.3(B)(1)

    Supporting of Conductors in Vertical Raceways . . . 300.19

Exhaust and Ventilating Ducts 300.22

Feed-Through Neutral Connections . . . . 300.13(B)

Fire Rated Cables and Conductors, Support of . . . . 300.19(B)

Free Length of Wire at Outlets 300.14

Induced Currents Ferrous Metal Enclosures or Ferrous Metal Raceways 300.20

Mechanical and Electrical Continuity

    Conductors . . . . 300.13(A)

    Raceways and Cables 300.12

Raceways and Enclosures. 300.10

Over 1000 Volts . . . . 300 Part II

Aboveground Wiring Methods 300.37

Aboveground Wiring Methods within raceways in Wet Locations 300.38

Braid-Covered Insulated Conductors–Open Installation. 300.39

Conductor Bending Radius 300.34

Conductors of Different Systems . . . . 300.3(C)(2)

Covers Required 300.31

Insulation Shielding 300.40

Moisture or Mechanical Protection Metal-Sheathed Cables 300.42

Protection Against Induction Heating 300.35

Underground Installations . . . . 300.50(A)

Minimum Cover Requirements . . . . Table 300.50

Protection Against

Corrosion 300.6

Physical Damage 300.4

Raceways as a Means of Support . . . . 300.11(B)

Raceways Exposed to Different Temperatures 300.7

Expansion Joints . . . . 300.7(B)

Sealing Raceways, Change in Temperature . . . . . 300.7(A)

Securing and Supporting . . . . 300.11(A)

Spread of Fire or Products of Combustion 300.21

Through Metal Framing Members . . . . 300.4(B)

Through Wood Studs, Joists, Rafters . . . . 300.4(A)

Underground Installations 300.5

Minimum Cover Requirements . . . . Table 300.5

Voltage Limitations 300.2

Wiring in Ducts, Plenums, Air-handling Spaces 300.22

GENERATORS . . . . **Art. 445**

Ampacity of Conductors 445.13

Connection Supply Side of Service Permitted. . . . . 230.82(5)

Critical Operations Power Systems

Generator Set . . . . 708.20(F)

Outdoor, Permanently Installed . . . . 708.20(F)(5)(a)

Outdoor, Portable . . . . 708.20(F)(5)(b)

Disconnecting Means and Shutdown 445.18

Disconnecting Means. . . . . 445.18(A)

Generators Installed in Parallel . . . . 445.18(C)

Shutdown of Prime Mover . . . . 445.18(B)

Emergency Systems . . . . Art. 700

See EMERGENCY SYSTEMS . . . . Ferm's Finder

Ground-Fault Circuit-Interrupter Protection

Receptacles, 15kW or Smaller Portable Generators . . 445.20

Bonded Neutral Generators. . . . . 445.20(B)

Unbonded (Floating Neutral) Generators . . . . 445.20(A)

Grounding

AC Systems 250.20

Conductor to be Grounded 250.26

Separately Derived Systems 250.30

As Source If Separately Derived System . . . . . . 250.20(C)

Equipment (Fixed) 250.112

Objectionable Currents. 250.6

Over 1000 Volts . . . . 250 Part X

Impedance Grounded Neutral Systems 250.187

Permanently Installed 250.35

Portable and Vehicle-Mounted . . . . 250.34(A)&(B)

In Class I, Division 1 Locations . . . . 501.125(A)

In Class I, Division 2 Locations . . . . 501.125(B)

Interconnected Electric Power Production Sources . . Art. 705

Legally Required Standby Systems . . . . Art. 701

Nameplate, Stationary Generators Over 15kW 445.11

Neutral Bonded to Frame

Field Modifications 445.11

Marked by Manufacturer 445.11

Optional Standby Systems. . . . . Art. 702

Outdoor, Permanently Installed . . . . 702.12(A)

Outdoor, Portable . . . . 702.12(B)

Power Inlets Rated at 100 Amperes or Greater. . . 702.12(C)

Overcurrent Protection

Shall Be Provided 445.12

Where Generator Equipped . . . . 445.13(B)

Permanently Installed, Grounding 250.35

Portable Generators 250.34

Separately Derived Systems 250.30

Premises Wiring System Derived From . . . . 250.20(B)

DC Systems 250.162

Point of Connection 250.164

Size of DC Grounding Electrode Conductor . . . 250.166

Recreational Vehicles 551.30

Pre-Wiring. . . . . 551.47(R)

Supply Conductors . . . . 551.30(E)

See TRANSFER SWITCHES . . . . Ferm's Finder

GOOSENECKS, SERVICE CABLES **230.54**

"GREENFIELD" . . . . **Art. 348**
    See FLEXIBLE METAL CONDUIT . . . . Ferm's Finder

GRAIN HANDLING & STORAGE AREAS
    Bonding . . . . 502.30(A)
        At Service Equipment 250.92
        Equipment Bonding Jumpers 250.102
        In Hazardous (Classified) Locations 250.100
    Class II Area Location Classification . . . . . 500.5(C)(1) & (2)
    Class II Group Classifications . . . . 500.6(B)
    Flexible Cords 502.140
    General Requirements . . . . Art. 502
    Grounding and Bonding . . . . Art. 250
        Additional Requirements 502.30
    Lighting Luminaires (Fixtures) in 502.130
    Lightning Protection (Surge) 250.106
        Surge Arrestors . . . . Art. 280
        Surge Protection. 502.35
    See Standard for the Installation of Lightning Protection Systems, NFPA 780 . . . . NFPA 780
    Motors & Generators
        In Class II, Division 1 Locations. . . . . .502.125(A)
        In Class II, Division 2 Locations. . . . . .502.125(B)
    Receptacles in 502.145
    Sealing 502.15
    Switches in 502.115
    Wiring Methods
        Class II, Division 1 . . . . 502.10(A)
        Class II, Division 2 . . . . 502.10(B)
    See Recommended Practice for the Classification of . . . . Combustible Dusts and of Hazardous (Classified) Locations for Electrical Installations in Chemical Process Areas
    See HAZARDOUS (CLASSIFIED) LOCATIONS Ferm's Finder

GROMMETS REQUIRED . . . . **300.4(B)(1)**
    For Flexible Cords and Cables 400.14

GROOVES, SHALLOW, CABLES AND RACEWAYS INSTALLED
. . . .**300.4(F)**

IN GROUND BAR, EQUIPMENT **408.40**
    Feeder Conductor Grounding Means 215.6
    Isolated Ground Receptacles . . . . 250.146(D)

GROUND CLAMPS **250.70**
    Connection to Be Accessible . . . . 250.68(A)
    Connection to Be Clean 250.12
    Connection of Grounding and Bonding Equipment
        Permitted Methods 250.8
    One Wire Only to a Ground Clamp 250.70
    Protection of Clamp 250.10
    See (KDER). . . . .*UL Product Spec*

GROUND DETECTORS
    AC Systems 50 to 1000 Volts Not Grounded . . . . . 250.21(B)
        Required on All Ungrounded Systems 250.21
    Electric Cranes in Class III Locations, Power Supply 503.155(A)
    High-Impedance Grounded Neutral Systems. 250.36
    Isolated Power Systems in Health Care Facilities
        Line Isolation Monitor . . . . .517.160(B)
        Optional for Critical Care Spaces . . . . 517.19(E)
        Within Hazardous (Classified) Anesthetizing Locations . . .
        . . . . .517.61(A)(2)
    Portable or Mobile Equipment over 1000 Volts. . . 250.188(D)
    See ISOLATING TRANSFORMERS . . . . Ferm's Finder

GROUND-FAULT CIRCUIT INTERRUPTERS (GFCI)
    Accessory Buildings, Dwellings . . . . 210.8(A)(2)
    Appliances
        Accessibility 422.5
        Drinking Water Coolers, Electric . . . . 422.5(A)(2)
        High-Pressure Spray Washers . . . . 422.5(A)(3)
        Tire Inflation Machines (For Public Use). . . . . 422.5(A)(4)
        Type and Location . . . . 422.5(B)
        Vacuum Machines (Automotive for Public Use). 422.5(A)(1)
        Vending Machines . . . . 422.5(A)(5)
    Basements, Unfinished, Dwelling Units . . . . 210.8(A)(5)
    Bathrooms
        Dwellings . . . . 210.8(A)
        Other Than Dwelling Units . . . . 210.8(B)
        Patient Care, Health Care Facilities 517.21
    Bathtubs, Hydromassage 680.71
    Bathtubs and Shower Stalls . . . . 210.8(A)(9)
    Boathouses . . . . 210.8(A)(8)
    Boat Hoists . . . . 210.8(C)
    Carnivals, Circuses, Fairs, etc. 525.23
    Commercial Garages 511.12
    Conductive Heated Floors of Bathrooms, Kitchens, and
    Hydromassage Bathtub Locations . . . . 424.44(E)

G

G

Construction Sites 590.6

Cord Sets (Temporary Installations) . . . . 590.6(A)(1)

Crawl Spaces, at or below Grade Level, Dwellings . 210.8(A)(4)

Crawl Space Lighting Outlets . . . . 210.8(E)

Definition . . . . Art. 100 Part I

Deicing and Snow-Melting Equipment, Impedance, Heating 426.32

Dishwasher Outlets (Dwelling Units) . . . . 210.8(D)

Determining Distance (Receptacle) 210.8

Dwellings . . . . 210.8(A)

Elevators, etc. 620.85

Feeders 215.9

Fountains

    Cord- and Plug-Connected Equipment. 680.56

    Signs . . . . 680.57(B)

Garages, Commercial 511.12

Garages, Dwellings. . . . . 210.8(A)(2)

Garages, Nondwelling . . . . 210.8(B)(8)

Generators (Portable), Receptacles, 15kW or Smaller . . 445.20

Health Care Facilities, Wet Locations . . . . 517.20(A)

    Pool and Tubs for Therapeutic Use . . . . 680 Part VI

    Therapeutic Tubs (Hydrotherapeutic Tanks) . . . 680.62(A)

        Receptacles within 1.5 m (5 ft.) . . . . 680.62(E)

High Pressure Spray Washers . . . . 422.5(A)(3)

Hydromassage Bathtub 680.71

Indoor Wet Locations, Other than Dwelling Units 210.8(B)(6)

Kitchens, Dwelling Units . . . . 210.8(A)(6)

Kitchens, Other Than Dwelling Units . . . . 210.8(B)(2)

Laundry Areas . . . . .210.8(A)(10)

Locker Rooms . . . . 210.8(B)(7)

Marinas & Boatyards . . . . 210.8(A)(8)

Mobile Home Service Equipment, Additional Receptacles . . . . 550.32(E)

Mobile Homes . . . . 550.13(B)

    Pipe Heating Cable Outlet . . . . 550.13(E)

Other Than Dwelling Units . . . . 210.8(B)

    Basements (Unfinished/Non-Habitable) . . . .210.8(B)(10)

    Bathrooms . . . . 210.8(B)(1)

    Crawl Spaces. . . . . 210.8(B)(9)

    Garages and Service Bays. . . . . 210.8(B)(8)

    Kitchens . . . . 210.8(B)(2)

    Locker Rooms . . . . 210.8(B)(7)

    Outdoors . . . . 210.8(B)(4)

    Rooftops . . . . 210.8(B)(3)

Showering Facilities. . . . . 210.8(B)(7)

Sinks . . . . 210.8(B)(5)

Wet Locations (Indoor). . . . . 210.8(B)(6)

Outdoors, Dwelling Units . . . . 210.8(A)(3)

Outdoors, Nondwelling . . . . 210.8(B)(4)

Park Trailers, Where Required . . . . 552.41(C)

    Pipe Heating Cable Outlet . . . . 552.41(D)

Pipeline and Vessel Heating, Impedance, Heating . . . 427.27

Readily Accessible Location 210.8

Receptacle Replacement . . . . 406.4(D)

    Note: Where replacements are made at receptacle locations
that are required to be GFCI types, the replacements must be
GFCI protected.

Receptacles

    Dwellings . . . . 210.8(A)

    Other Than Dwellings . . . . 210.8(B)

Replacement of . . . . 406.4(D)

Recreational Vehicle Parks 551.71

Recreational Vehicles

    Receptacle Locations, Required . . . . 551.41(C)

    Shower Luminaires (Fixtures) . . . . 551.53(B)

    With One Branch Circuit. . . . . 551.40(C)

Residential Occupancies . . . . 210.8(A)

Rooftop Receptacles, Nondwelling. . . . . 210.8(B)(3)

Signs (Outdoor Portable) . . . . 600.10(C)(2)

Sink

    Dwelling Units. . . . . 210.8(A)(7)

    Nondwelling. . . . . 210.8(B)(5)

Spas & Hot Tubs

    Indoor Installations

        Lighting Luminaires (Fixtures), Outlets, and Paddle Fans . . . . .680.43(B)(2)

        Receptacles Providing Power to . . . . . . 680.43(A)(3)

        Receptacles within 3.0 m (10 ft.) . . . . . . .680.43(A)(2)

    Outdoor . . . . .680.42(A)(2)

    Outlet Supplying Self-Contained or Package Units . . 680.44

Swimming Pools

    Electrically Operated Pool Covers . . . . .680.27(B)(2)

    Motors, Other Than Dwelling Units . . . . . .680.21(A)(1)

    Protection of Wiring in Enclosures . . . . . . .680.23(F)(3)

    Requirement for Luminaires, Paddle Fans . . . .680.22(B)(4)

    Requirement for Receptacles . . . . .680.22(A)(4)

    Storable Pools 680.32

    Types Allowed 680.5

Underwater Luminaires, Relamping . . . . . . .680.23(A)(3)

Therapeutic Pools & Tubs . . . . 680.62(A)

Receptacles within 1.5 m (6 ft) . . . . 680.62(E)

Tire Inflation Machines (For Public Use) . . . . . 422.5(A)(4)

Unfinished Basements . . . . 210.8(A)(5)

Vacuum Machines (Automotive For Public Use) . 422.5(A)(1)

Vending Machines . . . . 422.5(A)(5)

Wet Locations

Indoor Locations, Nondwelling . . . . 210.8(B)(6)

See (KCXS) . . . . .UL Product Spec

GROUND FAULT CURRENT PATH ART.100

Ground-Fault Current Paths, Examples . . Art. 100, Info. Note

GROUND-FAULT CURRENT PATH, EFFECTIVE . . . ART. 100

GROUND-FAULT DETECTION, DIRECT-CURRENT SYSTEMS

Grounded . . . . 250.167(B)

Marking . . . . 250.167(C)

Ungrounded . . . . 250.167(A)

GROUND-FAULT PROTECTION OF EQUIPMENT

Boatyards and Marinas 555.3

Building or Structure Main Disconnecting Means 240.13

Definition of . . . . Art. 100 Part I

Emergency Systems, Signals . . . . .700.6(D)

Feeders 215.10

Fixed Outdoor Deicing and Snow-Melting Equipment

Impedance Heating 426.32

Resistance Heating 426.28

Fuses . . . . 230.95(B)

Health Care Facilities 517.17

Legally Required Standby Systems, Not Required 701.26

Marinas and Boatyards 555.3

Orderly Shutdown (Branch Circuit) . . . . 210.13 Ex. 1

Orderly Shutdown (Feeder) . . . . 215.10 Ex. 1

Orderly Shutdown (Service) . . . . 230.95 Ex.

Performance Testing . . . . 230.95(C)

Pipeline and Vessel Heating

Impedance Heating 427.27

Resistance Heating 427.22

Settings . . . . 230.95(A)

Service Equipment 230.95

Signs and Outline Lighting, Transformers and Electronic

Power Supplies (Secondary-Circuit Ground Fault Protection)
. . . . 600.23(B)

See (KDAX) .UL Product Spec

GROUND-FAULT SENSING AND RELAYING EQUIPMENT

See (KDAX) .UL Product Spec

GROUND RING, ELECTRODE . . . . 250.52(A)(4)

Size of Conductor to . . . . 250.66(C)

GROUND RODS . . . . 250 Part III

25 Ohms or Less Resistance to Ground . . . . 250.53(A)(2)EX.

CATV and Radio Distribution Systems 820.100

At Mobile Homes — Grounding and Bonding . . . 820.106

Communication Circuits (Primary Protector) 800.100

At Mobile Homes 800.106

Intersystem Bonding Termination . . . . 250.94(A), 800.100(B),
. . . . .820.100(B)

Lightning Protection Systems, Required Bonding 250.106

Use of Strike Termination Devices (Air Terminals) . . 250.60

Network-Powered Broadband Systems 830.100

At Mobile Homes 830.106

Maximum No. 6 Ground Wire to a Ground Rod . . . 250.66(A)

Multiple Rods Distance Apart . . . . . 250.53(A)(3) Info. Note

Radio and Television Equipment . . . . 810.21(F)

Size, Length & Depth to Be Driven . . . . 250.53(G)

Auxiliary CATV and Radio Distribution Systems . . 820.100

Communication Circuits . . . . .800.100(B)

Network-Powered Broadband Systems . . . . . . .830.100(B)

Radio and Television Equipment . . . . 810.21(F)

Grounding Electrodes 250.54

Permitted 250.54

See (KDER) .UL Product Spec

See (KDSH) .UL Product Spec

GROUNDED

Circuit and System, AC . . . . 250 Part II

Circuit and System, DC . . . . 250 Part VIII

Conductor to Service Equipment . . . . 250.24(C)

Conductors

Continuity of Grounded Conductor . . . . 200.2(B)

Delta Connected Service . . . . .250.24(C)(3)

Feeder Identification 215.12

Grouping for Multiple Circuits . . . . 210.4(D)

Grouping with Same Circuit . . . . 200.4(B)

Identification 200.6

Installation .200.4(A)

Multiple Circuits . . . . 200.4(B)

Not Used for Grounding Equipment . . . . . . .250.142(B)

Not Used for Grounding . . . . .250.24(A)(5)

Sizing of . . . . Table 250.102(C)(1)

Switches Controlling Lighting Loads . . . . 404.2(C)

Theaters, Extra-Hard Usage Cords . . . . 520.44(C)

To Be Grounded, AC Systems 250.26

To Be Grounded, DC Systems 250.162

Use for Grounding Permitted

    At Separate Buildings or Structures . . 250.32(B)(1) Ex.(2)

    Load-Side Equipment . . . . .250.142(B), Ex. 1–4

    Separately Derived Systems . . . . 250.30(A)

    Supply-Side Equipment . . . . .250.142(A)

Definition of . . . . .Art. 100 Part I

Direct-Current Systems, Ground-Fault Detection . .250.167(B)

Effectively

    Effective Ground-Fault Current Path . . . . . . 250.4(A)(5)

    Metal In-Ground Support Structure . . . . . .250.52(A)(2)

Equipment . . . . 250 Part VI

Lighting Systems 30 Volts or Less

    Secondary Circuits Not Permitted to Be Grounded   411.6(A)

    Secondary Circuits Not Permitted to Be Grounded 250.22(4)

Location of System Connections, AC . . . . 250.24(A)

Other Conductor and Enclosures 250.86

Overcurrent Device Permitted in Grounded Conductor . . . .
. . . . 230.90(B)

Point of Connection, DC 250.164

Power Systems in Anesthetizing Locations 517.63

Separately Derived Systems 250.30

Service Enclosures and Raceways 250.80

Sizing, Grounded Conductor . . . . Table 250.102(C)(1)

Use & Identification of Grounded Conductors . . . . Art. 200

    For Branch Circuits . . . . 210.5(A)

    Identification of . . . . 310.110(A)

    Means of Identification 200.6

See NEUTRAL OR GROUNDED CONDUCTOR Ferm's Finder

GROUNDING . . . . **Art. 250**

Agricultural Buildings . . . . 547.5(F)

Air-Conditioning (outdoor roof) 440.9

Air-Conditioning, Room 440.61

Alternating Current Systems 250.20

Anesthetizing Locations 517.62

Antenna 810.21

Appliances (General) . . . . 250 Part VI

Clothes Washers 250.114

Dishwashers 250.110

    Cord- and Plug-Connected (If Permitted). . . . 250.114

Existing Counter Mounted Cooking Units 250.140

Freezers 250.114

In Mobile Homes . . . . .550.16(B)(3)

In Park Trailers 552.56

In Recreational Vehicles 551.55

Ranges 250.140

Wall Mounted Ovens 250.140

Audio Signal Processing, Amplification & Reproduction . 640.7

Bars (In Panelboards) 408.40

Feeder Conductor Grounding Means 215.6

Boxes 250.86

Attachment of Conductors to Boxes 250.148

Equipment Grounding . . . . 250 Part VI

Metal Boxes 314.4

Methods of Equipment Grounding . . . . 250 Part VII

Other Conductor Enclosures 250.86

CATV Systems, To Other Systems 250.94

Cable Grounding 820.100

Conductive Shield of Coaxial Cable 820.93

Equipment Grounding 820.103

Intersystem Bonding Termination . . . . .820.100(B)

Separately Derived Systems 250.30

Circuits (AC) . . . . 250 Part II

Circuits (DC) . . . . 250 Part VIII

Clothes Dryers 250.140

Clothes Washers 250.114

Communications Systems (Methods) . . . . 800 Part IV

Bonding for Communication Systems 250.94

Cable and Primary Protector . . . . 800.100(A)

Cable and Primary Protector at Mobile Homes . 800.106(A)

Devices, Listing Required 800.180

Intersystem Bonding Termination . . . . .800.100(B)

Conductors

Aluminum or Copper-Clad Aluminum Not Permitted Near
the Earth or on Masonry Walls (Equipment Grounding). . .
. . . . .250.120(B)

    Grounding Electrode Conductors . . . . 250.64(A)

    Physical Damage . . . . 250.64(B)

Definition (GROUNDED or GROUNDING)   Art. 100 Part I

Equipment Grounding Conductors . . . . . . 250 Part VI

Continuity. 250.124

Identification of .250.119

Installation 250.120

Size of 250.122

Types. 250.118

Line-Side of Service Equipment 250.66

   Minimum . . . . Table 250.66

   Sizing .250.102(C)

Load-Side of Service Equipment 250.122

   Adjustment for Increase in Phase Conductor Size . . . . .250.122(B)

   Flexible Cord and (Fixture) Luminaire Wires. .250.122(E)

   Minimum . . . . Table 250.122

   Motor Circuits . . . . 250.122(D)

   Multiple Circuits, Same Raceway . . . . . . .250.122(C)

   Parallel Conductors . . . . .250.122(F)

   Sizing 250.122

   Material for Grounding Electrode Conductor . . . 250.62

Objectionable Current Over 250.6

Conductor Connections

   Boxes, to and in 250.148

   Clean Surfaces. 250.12

   Conductors and Equipment 250.8

   Grounding Electrode, to 250.68

   Grounding Electrode, Means of Connection. 250.70

   Protection of Attachment 250.10

   Solder Connections Must be Mechanically Secure 110.14(B)

   Wiring Device Terminals, Identification of 250.126

Conductor to Be Grounded. 250.26

Conductor Required. 250.64

   General. 250.4

   Swimming Pool Circuits (Specific) . . . . Art. 680

   Note: Installing supplementary equipment grounding conductors in metal raceways is no substitute for effectively bonding those raceways . . . . 250.96(B) Info. Note

Connections . . . . 250.8(A) & (B)

Cranes & Hoists 610.61

   Class III, Division 1 & 2 Locations 503.30

Direct Current Systems 250.162

   Point of Connection 250.164

   Separately Run from Circuit Conductors . 250.134(B) Ex. 2

   Size 250.166

   Use of Grounded Conductor (Load-side Equipment) . . . . 250.142(B) Ex. 3

Dishwashers, Permanently Connected. 250.110

Dishwashers, Cord- and Plug-connected 250.114

Dryers (Clothes) 250.140

   Mobile Homes. 550.16

Earth Return Not Permitted . . . . 250.4(A)(5)

Earth Return Not Permitted . . . . 250.4(B)(4)

   (Supplementary) Auxiliary Electrodes 250.54

   Note: Supplementary grounding electrodes shall be permitted to augment the equipment grounding conductors specified in Section 250.118. The earth shall not be used as an effective ground-fault current path..

Electrode Conductor

   Connection of, to Electrode 250.68

      Clean Surfaces 250.12

      Methods. 250.70

   Definition of . . . . Art. 100

   Enclosures and Raceways for . . . . 250.64(E)

   Note: Metal enclosures protecting the grounding electrode conductors must be bonded at both ends to the grounding electrode conductor.

   Installation of 250.64

      DC Systems 250.164

      Separately Derived AC Systems (Grounded) . . . . 250.30(A)(3) and (4)

      Separately Derived AC Systems (Ungrounded) 250.30(B)

      Service-supplied AC Systems 250.24

   Protection of Connection Accessibility . . . . 250.68(A)

   Size of Required, AC Systems 250.66

   Size of Required, DC Systems 250.166

   Splice of Not Generally Permitted . . . . 250.64(C)

      Busbar Splice Permitted . . . . .250.64(C)(2)

      Irreversible Compression Connector or Exothermic Welding or Riveting Permitted. . . . . 250.64(C)

      Multiple Enclosure Services, Permitted for . . . 250.64(D)

   Taps Permitted . . . . 250.64(D)

Electrodes . . . . 250 Part III

   Aluminum Electrodes Not Permitted . . . . . .250.52(B)(2)

   Auxiliary Grounding Electrodes 250.54

   Bonding Together

      Air Terminals. 250.60

      All Electrodes Bonded Together to Form System. . 250.50

      CATV Systems . . . . .820.100(B) & (D)

      Common Electrode 250.58

      Conductor Taps. . . . . 250.64(D)(1)

      For Communications Circuits . . . . . .800.100(B) & (D)

G

For Radio and Television Equipment . . . 810.21(F) & (J)

In Agricultural Buildings . . . . 547.9(A)(5)

Lightning Protection Systems. 250.106

Made (Installed) Rod, Pipe, and Plate and Other Electrodes
. . . . 250.52

Metal Well Casing Permitted as Electrode. . .250.52(A)(8)

Network-Powered Broadband Systems . 830.100(B) & (D)

Bonding for Communication Systems 250.94

Two or More Buildings from Common Service 250.32(A)

Underground Gas Line Not Permitted. . . . .250.52(B)(1)

Burial Depth, Ground Rings . . . . 250.53(F)

Burial Depth, Plate Electrodes. . . . . 250.53(H)

Burial Depth, Rod and Pipe . . . . 250.53(G)

Types of, Permitted to Be Used for System . . . . 250.52(A)

Types of, Not Permitted to Be Used for System . . 250.52(B)

Definition of Grounding Electrode . . . . Art. 100

Enclosures and Raceways, Existing Installations . . 250.86 Ex. 1

Branch-Circuit Extensions . . . . 250.130(C)

Equipment . . . . 250 Part VI

Cord- and Plug-Connected 250.114

Fastened in Place (Fixed) 250.110

Fixed (Specific) 250.112

Nonelectric 250.116

Faceplates, See FACEPLATES, Grounding Required . . . Ferm's Finder

Fixed Equipment . . . . 250 Part VI

Effectively Grounded 250.136

Methods of Grounding . . . . 250 Part VII

Fastened in Place. 250.134

Swimming Pool 680.6

Wet-Niche, Dry-Niche, and No-Niche. . . . . .680.23(F)(2)

Flexible Metal Conduit

See FLEXIBLE METAL CONDUIT . . . . Ferm's Finder

Freezers 250.114

Generators

Fastened in Place 250.110

Portable and Vehicle-Mounted 250.34

Separately Derived Systems . . . . 250.30(A)5 and 6

Hazardous (Classified) Locations 250.100

See HAZARDOUS (CLASSIFIED) LOCATIONS . . . .
. . . . Ferm's Finder

Health Care Facilities

See HEALTH CARE FACILITIES . . . . Ferm's Finder

High Impedance Grounded Neutral 250.36

Separately Derived Systems . . . . 250.30(A)

High Voltage System . . . . 250 Part X

See OVER 1000 VOLTS, NOMINAL . . . . . Ferm's Finder

Information Technology Equipment

Equipment Grounding and Bonding 645.15

System Grounding 645.14

Insulated Ground Wire

Identification .250.119

Insulation Integrity 110.7

Marinas and Boatyards, Branch Circuits and Feeders . . . .
. . . . 555.15(B)

Panelboards, In Patient Care Spaces 517.14

Patient Bed Location Receptacles [Critical Care (Category 1)]
. . . . 517.19(B)

Patient Bed Location Receptacles [General Care
(Category 2)]. . . . . 517.18(B)

Patient Care Spaces . . . . 517.13(B)

Pool Luminaires (Fixtures) and Related Equipment . . . . .
. . . . .680.23(F)(2)

Pool Motors 680.21

Wet-Niche Luminaires (Fixtures) with NM Conduit . . . . .
. . . . .680.23(B)(2)

Insulated (Isolated) Grounds

Counted in Conductor Fill for Boxes . . . . . . .314.16(B)(5)

For Receptacles (IG) . . . . 250.146(D)

Identification of Receptacles and Cover Requirements . . . .
. . . . 406.3(D)

Receptacles for Audio Signal Processing, etc. . . . . 640.7(C)

Receptacles in Patient Care Vicinity (not allowed). . .517.16(A)

Receptacles outside Patient Care Vicinity . . . . . 517.16(B)

Where Used . . . . 250.96(B) & Info. Note

Liquidtight Flexible Metal Conduit

See LIQUIDTIGHT FLEXIBLE METAL CONDUIT Ferm's
Finder

Luminaires (Lighting Fixtures) 410.40

Metal Boxes

Continuity and Attachment to. 250.148

Electrical Continuity 300.10

For Service Conductors. 250.80

Other Than for Service Conductors 250.86

Outlet, Device, Junction Boxes, etc. 314.4

Over 1000 Volts . . . . 250 Part X

Metal Elbows, Underground in Nonmetallic Conduit Run

Other Than Service Connected to EGC. . . . . . 250.86 Ex. 3

Service Raceways Connected to Grounded Service

Conductor . . . . 250.80 Ex.

Metal Enclosures . . . . 250 Part IV

   1000 Volts and Higher 250.190

   See CONTINUOUS DUTY . . . . Ferm's Finder

Metal Frames of Buildings

   As Grounding Electrode . . . . .250.52(A)(2)

      For Separately Derived System Grounding Electrode . . . . .250.30(A)(6)(2)

   Required Bonding Where Not Used As Electrode 250.104(C)

Metal Gas Piping, Aboveground, Upstream of Shutoff. . . . . .250.104(B)

   Underground Not Permitted As Grounding Electrode . . . . .250.52(B)(1)

Metal Piping

   Gas Piping . . . . .250.104(B)

   Other Piping. . . . . .250.104(B)

   Water Piping

      For Separately Derived Systems. . . . . . . .250.30(A)(6)

      Required Bonding Where Not Used As Electrode . . . . 250.104(D)

      Use As Grounding Electrode . . . . .250.52(A)(1)

      Note: Interior metal water piping located more than 1.52 m (5 ft) from the point of entrance to the building cannot be used as a part of the grounding electrode system or as a conductor to interconnect electrodes that are part of the grounding electrode system. . . . . .250.68(C)(1)

Metal Well Casings

   As Part of Grounding Electrode System . . . . .250.52(A)(8)

   Required Grounding With Submersible Pump . 250.112(M)

Metallic Entrance Conduits Containing

   Communication Circuits. 800.49

   Community Antenna Television and Radio Distribution Systems. 820.49

   Network-Powered Broadband Communications Systems 830.49

   Optical Fiber Cables 770.49

   Premises-Powered Broadband Communications Systems 840.49

Meters

   Continuity around Water Meters . . . . 250.53(D)(1)

      Effective Grounding Path . . . . 250.68(B)

   Instruments, Relays and . . . . 250 Part IX

      In Class I Locations 501.105

   On Load-Side of Service . . . . .250.142(B)

Methods

   Common Grounding Electrode 250.58

Conductor Connections, Grounded System . . . 250.130(A)

Conductor Connections, Ungrounded System . .250.130(B)

Cord- and Plug-Connected Equipment 250.138

Effective Ground-Fault Current Path, Definition . . Art. 100

   For Grounding Electrode Conductor . . . . . . 250.68(B)

Equipment Considered Effectively Grounded 250.136

Fixed Equipment 250.134

   Note: Fixed equipment grounding conductors must be run in the raceway with the circuit conductors or in the case of direct burial conductors right with them in the trench.

Frames of Ranges and Clothes Dryers 250.140

Main Bonding Jumper 250.28

Path at Services 250.24

Raceways, Short Sections of 250.132

System Bonding Jumper 250.28

Underground Service Cable 250.84

Use of Grounded Circuit Conductor

   Load-Side Equipment . . . . .250.142(B)

   Supply-Side Equipment . . . . 250.142(A)

   Note: Connections that depend on solder not permitted.

Mobile Homes 550.16

Motors, Grounding All Voltages . . . . 430 Part XIII

   At Swimming Pools . . . . 680.6(3)

   Connection at Terminal Housings . . . . 430.12(E)

   Equipment Grounding . . . . 250 Part VI

Multiple Circuit Connections 250.144

   Equipment Bonding Jumper In Parallel . . . . . 250.102(C)

   Single Equipment Grounding Conductor . . . . 250.122(A)

Neutral (Grounded Conductor) to Main Service Equipment . . . . 250.24(C)

   Connection to Equipment Grounding Conductor . 250.130

Objectionable Current. 250.6

Optical Fiber Cables 770.106

   Length of Conductor . . . . .770.100(A)(4)

   Listing Requirements 770.180

Other Systems

   See GROUNDING, Electrodes, Bonding Together . . . . Ferm's Finder

Over 250 Volts to Ground 250.97

Over 1000 Volts . . . . Article 250 Part X

Panelboards

   General. 408.40

   In Critical Care (Category 1) Spaces . . . . 517.19(E)

   In Patient Care Spaces 517.14

Method of, for Swimming Pools . . . . 680.25(A)

Required Grounding for Swimming Pools . . . . 680.6(7)

Used as Service Equipment . . . . 408.3(C)

Ranges 250.140

    Mobile Homes . . . . 550.16(B)

Receptacles 406.3

    Circuit Extensions . . . . 250.130(C)

    Connection to Boxes 250.146

    General, Identification, Use, Grounding Poles . . 406.10(B)

    Isolated Ground . . . . 406.3(D)

        For Audio Signal Processing Equipment . . . . . 640.7(C)

    Replacements . . . . 406.4(D)

Recreational Vehicles

    Bonding of Non-Current-Carrying Parts 551.56

    General Requirements 551.54

    Insulated Neutral . . . . 551.54(C)

    Interior Equipment 551.55

    Receptacles to Be Grounding Type 551.52

Recreational Vehicle Parks 551.75

    Supply Configurations (Receptacles) 551.81

    Supply Equipment 551.76

Refrigerating Equipment (outdoor rooftops) 440.9

Sealtight Flexible Metal Conduit

    See LIQUIDTIGHT FLEXIBLE METAL CONDUIT . Ferm's Finder

Separate Buildings 250.32

    Agricultural Buildings . . . . 547.9(B)(3)

    Class I Locations . . . . 501.30(A) Ex.

    Class II Locations . . . . 502.30(A) Ex.

    Class III Locations . . . . 503.30(A) Ex.

    For Swimming Pool Equipment 680.6

    Panelboards as Service Equipment . . . . 408.3(C)

    Panelboards 408.40

Separately Derived Systems 250.30

    Means of 250.30

    With 60/120 Volts to Ground . . . . 647.6(A)

Service Equipment

    Alternating Current Systems, Service-Supplied 250.24

    Bonding of Services 250.92

        Methods of . . . . 250.92(B)

    Break the Grounded Conductor in the Main Disconnect 230.75

    Common Grounding Electrode 250.58

    Concentric and Eccentric Knockouts . . . . 250.92(B)

Continuity of Raceways and Enclosures 300.10

Enclosures 250.80

    All Service Enclosures . . . . 250.92(A)

    Continuity of 300.10

    Methods . . . . 250.92(B)

Exposed Structural Steel, Bonding of . . . . 250.104(C)

    Connection to Equipment Grounding Conductor 250.130

    Main Bonding Jumper and System Bonding Jumper 250.28

    Main Disconnect . . . . 250.24(A)(1)

    Grounding Electrode Conductor . . . . 250 Part III

    See GROUNDING, *Electrode Conductor* . . Ferm's Finder

    Grounding Electrodes

        See GROUNDING, Electrodes . . . . Ferm's Finder

Solar Photovoltaic Systems 690.41

Symbol . . . . 250.126 Info. Note Figure

Unnecessary Bends and Loops Avoided 250.4(A)(1) Info. Note

Wind Electric Systems 694.40

GROUNDING CONNECTIONS

Location of System Grounding Connections

    Arrange to Prevent Objectionable Current . . . . . 250.6(A)

Equipment Bonding Jumper Line-Side . . . . 250.102(C)

Equipment Bonding Jumper Load-Side . . . . 250.102(D)

    Point of Connection for DC Systems . . . . . . 250.164(A)

    Service Supplied AC Systems, Grounded . . . . 250.24(A)

    Service Supplied AC Systems, Ungrounded . . . . 250.24(E)

Main and System Bonding Jumper(s) 250.28

    Grounded Conductor (Neutral) Must Be Bonded to Service Equipment . . . . 250.24(C)

    Installation . . . . 250.24(A)(4)

    Material . . . . 250.28(A)

    Metallic Piping and Exposed Structural Steel . . . . 250.104(B) & (C)

    Minimum Size Load Side, Equipment Bonding Jumper . . . . Table 250.122

        Size of, on Supply Side of Service . . . . 250.102(C)

    Minimum Size, Supply Side Equipment Bonding . . . . Table 250.122

        Jumper (12.5% rule) . . . . Table 250.102(C)(1)

    Multiple Raceways, Load-Side, Equip. Bonding Jumper . . . . 250.102(D)

    Multiple Raceways, Supply-Side Bonding Jumper . . . . 250.102(C)

    Size . . . . 250.28(D)

Supplemental Ground Required . . . . 250.53(D)(2)

Use of Grounded Circuit Conductor . . . . .250.142(A)

Use of Grounded Circuit Conductor on

    Electrode-Type Boilers Over 1000 Volts . . . . . 490.72(E)

    Grounding for Electrode-Type Boilers 490.74

    Load Side of Mains . . . . .250.142(B)

Water Line, Bond Around Unions in . . . . . . 250.53(D)(1)

    For Effective Grounding Path . . . . 250.68(B)

Water Meters & Filters, Bond Around . . . . . 250.53(D)(1)

    For Effective Grounding Path . . . . 250.68(B)

Water Pipe Used to Ground a System Shall Be Supplemented
. . . . 250.53(D)(2)

Signs 600.7

Solar Photovoltaic Systems . . . . 690 Part V

Specific Equipment 250.112

Supplementary Grounding, Auxiliary Grounding Electrode . .
. . . . 250.54

    Permitted to Connect to Equipment Grounding Conductor
. . . . 250.54

Swimming Pools

    Equipment to Be Grounded 680.6

    Methods of Grounding 680.6

    Wet-Niche Luminaires (Fixtures) . . . . 680.23(B)

    See SWIMMING POOLS, Bonding & Grounding . . Ferm's Finder

Terminal Bar 408.40

Transformers 450.10

    Grounding Autotransformers 450.5

GROUNDING ELECTRODE CONDUCTORS

Burial Depth . . . . .250.64(B)(4)

Definition . . . . Art. 100

Installation 250.64

Location, Common Location . . . . 250.64(D)(3)

Securing and Protection from Physical Damage . . . 250.64(B)

See GROUNDING, Electrode Conductors . . . . Ferm's Finder

Taps . . . . 250.64(D)(1)

GROUNDING ELECTRODES

Definition . . . . Art. 100

Direct-Current Sizing 250.166

Not Permitted As . . . . 250.52(B)

Types

    Concrete-Encased Electrode . . . . .250.52(A)(3)

    Ground Ring . . . . .250.52(A)(4)

    Local Metal Underground Systems or Structures 250.52(A)(8)

    Metal In-Ground Support Structure . . . . . . .250.52(A)(2)

    Metal Underground Water Pipe . . . . .250.52(A)(1)

    Other Listed Electrodes . . . . .250.52(A)(6)

    Plate Electrodes . . . . .250.52(A)(7)

    Rods and Pipes Electrodes . . . . .250.52(A)(5)

See GROUNDING, Electrodes . . . . Ferm's Finder

GROUPING OF CONDUCTORS

MC Cable – Single Cables Grouped . . . . 330.80(B)

Multiwire Branch Circuits in Panelboards . . . . 210.4(B)

GROUPING OF DISCONNECTS

Outside Feeders and Branch Circuits 225.34

Services 230.72

GUARDING, GUARDS

Circuit-Breaker Handles . . . . 240.41(B)

Circuit Breakers and Fuses During Operation . . . . 240.41(A)

Construction Sites, Over 1000 Volts 590.7

Elevators, Dumbwaiters, Escalators, etc., Machine Room 620.71

Generators 445.15

Live Parts, General 110.27

    Over 1000 Volts 110.34

Motors and Motor Controllers 430.232

    For Attendants 430.233

    Portable Motors Over 150 Volts to Ground 430.243

    Solar Photovoltaic Systems . . . . 690.33(B)

Storage Batteries 480.9

Transformers 450.8

Wind Electric Systems . . . . . 694.10(C) Informational Note

X-Ray Installations 517.78

GUEST ROOMS and GUEST SUITES

Arc-Fault Circuit-Interrupter Protection . . . . 210.12(C)

Bathrooms (overcurrent devices not located) . . . . . 240.24(E)

Cooking (permanent provisions) 210.17

Fixed Multioutlet Assemblies . . . . 220.14(H)

Lighting Outlets . . . . 210.70(B)

Overcurrent Device (location) . . . . 240.24(B)(1)(2)

Receptacle Placement 210.60

    Tamper-Resistant Receptacles . . . . 406.12(2)

Voltage Limitations (Branch-Circuit) . . . . 210.6(A)

G

H

GUTTERS, AUXILIARY . . . . Art. 366

Ampacity of Conductors

In Nonmetallic . . . . 366.23(B)

In Sheet Metal . . . . 366.23(A)

Extension Beyond Equipment . . . . 366.12(2)

No Restriction on Length for Elevators 620.35

Permitted Length for Elevators . . . . 366.12 Ex.

Grounding, Connected to an ECG 366.60

Indoor and Outdoor Use

Nonmetallic . . . . 366.10(B)(1) and (2)

Sheet Metal . . . . 366.10(A)(1) and (2)

Number of Conductors in

For Elevators 620.33

Nonmetallic . . . . 366.22(B)

Sheet Metal . . . . 366.22(A)

Supports

Nonmetallic . . . . 366.30(B)

Sheet Metal . . . . 366.30(A)

Wire Bending Space . . . . 366.58(A)

H

HALLWAY

AFCI Protection . . . . 210.12(A)

Lighting Outlet . . . . 210.70(A)(2)

Mobile Home . . . . 550.13(D)

Outlets (Dwelling Units) . . . . 210.52(H)

Switches (Grounded Conductor) . . . . 404.2(C)

HAND LAMPS/PORTABLE LIGHTING EQUIPMENT

Commercial Garages (Unswitched & Insulated) . . . 511.4(B)(2)

General, Portable Luminaires (Formerly Hand Lamps) . 410.82

Grounding Not Required with Isolating Transformer . . . . . .
. . . . 250.114(4)(g) Ex.

Grounding Required . . . . 250.114(4)(e)

HANDHOLE ENCLOSURES . . . .

Size, Over 1000 Volts 314.71

Systems 1000 Volts and Less 314.30

Systems over 1000 Volts . . . . 314.70(C)

HANDLE TIES

Feeder Disconnecting Means . . . . 225.33(B)

Multiwire Branch Circuits . . . . 240.15(B)(1)

Service Disconnecting Means . . . . 230.71(B)

HANGARS, AIRCRAFT . . . . Art. 513

See AIRCRAFT HANGARS . . . . Ferm's Finder

HARMONICS

Cablebus .368.258

Design Consideration for Neutral Currents (Branch Circuit) . .
. . . . 210.4(A) Info. Note 1

Electrical Duct Banks . . . . Informative Annex B, Figure Notes

Existing Neutral Overheating . . . . 310.10(H)Ex.2 Info. Note

Feeder or Service Neutral, Consideration of . . . .
. . . . 220.61(C)(2) Info. Note

Neutral Considered Current-Carrying, Due to   310.15(B)(5)(c)

Non-Linear Loads in Excess of 50 percent 400.5

Non-Linear Loads Major Portion . . . .
. . . . Table 520.44(C)(3)(a) Note

Temperature Limitations internally due to . . . .
. . . . 310.15(A)(3) Info. Note 1

See NONLINEAR LOAD . . . . Ferm's Finder

HAZARDOUS (CLASSIFIED) LOCATIONS . . . . Art. 500

Approval for Class and Properties (Equipment) . . . . 500.8(A)

Bonding and Grounding 250.100

Class I Locations 501.30

Class II Locations 502.30

Class III Locations 503.30

Cable Seals

Class I, Division1 . . . . 501.15(D)

Class I, Division 2 . . . . 501.15(E)

Zone 0 . . . . .505.16(A)(2)

Zone 1 . . . . .505.16(B)(7)

Zone 2 . . . . .505.16(C)(2)

Classification of Group (Atmosphere)

Class I, Groups A, B, C, and D . . . . 500.6(A)

Class I, Groups IIA, IIB, and IIC (in Zone Locations) . . 505.6

Class II, Groups E, F, and G . . . . 500.6(B)

Classification of Locations, Rooms, Sections and Areas . . 500.5

Note: Each room, section, or area of an occupancy hall should
be considered individually in determining its classification.

Class I Locations . . . . 500.5(B)

Division 1 . . . . 500.5(B)(1)

Division 2 . . . . 500.5(B)(2)

Zone 0 . . . . 505.5(B)(1)

Zone 1 . . . . 505.5(B)(2)

Zone 2 . . . . 505.5(B)(3)

See Recommend Practice for the Classification of Flammable
Liquids, ... Gases, or

Vapors and of Hazardous (Classified) Locations for Electrical Installations in Chemical Process Areas

Class II Locations . . . . 500.5(C)

    Division 1 . . . . 500.5(C)(1)

    Division 2 . . . . 500.8(C)(2)

    See . . . . . Recommended Practice for the Classification of Combustible Dusts and of Hazardous (Classified) Locations for Electrical Installations in Chemical Process Areas

Class III Locations . . . . 500.5(D)

    Division 1 . . . . 500.5(D)(1)

    Division 2 . . . . 500.5(D)(2)

Class I Locations (Zones) . . . . Art. 505

Class I Locations . . . . Art. 501

    Bonding in . . . . 501.30(A)

        At Service 250.92

        General 250.100

    Chemicals by Groups . . . . 500.6(A)

        For Zone 0, 1, & 2 . . . . 505.6

        See . . . . Recommend Practice for the Classification of Recommended Practice for the Classification of Flammable Liquids, Gases, or Vapors and of Hazardous (Classified) Locations for Electrical Installations in Chemical Process Areas

    Conductor Insulation 501.20

    See (ZLGR) . . . . UL Product Spec

    Control Transformers & Resistors 501.120

    Definitions (as applied to Hazardous Locations) . . Art. 100

    Documentation Required . . . . 500.4(A)

    Dual Classifications of Areas . . . . 505.7(B)

    Dual Classifications of Areas . . . . 506.7(B)

    Equipment Temperature . . . . 500.8(C)(4)

    Flexible Connections

        Division 1 . . . . 501.10(A)(2)

        Division 2 . . . . 501.10(B)(2)

    Flexible Cords

        For Flexibility Division 2 Locations . . . . . 501.10(B)(2)

        For Process Control Instruments (Division 2) . . . . 501.105(B)(6)

        Use of 501.140

    Grounding 501.30

        At Service 250.92

        General 250.100

        Zone 0, 1, & 2 Locations 505.25

        Zone 20, 21, & 22 Locations 506.25

    Health Care Facilities, In . . . . 517 Part IV

Live Parts Not Exposed 501.25

Luminaires (Lighting Fixtures) 501.130

Meters, Instruments, and Relays 501.105

Motors and Generators 501.125

Multiwire Branch Circuits, Prohibited . . . . 210.4(B)

Optical Fiber Cable

    Division 1 . . . . 501.10(A)(1)(e)

    Division 2 . . . . 501.10(B)(1)(7)

Protection Techniques 500.7

Receptacles and Attachment Plugs 501.145

Reciprocating Engine-Driven Generators and Compressors . . . . 501.125(B) IN

Reclassification of Areas, Zone 0, 1, and 2 Locations 505.7(C)

Reclassification of Areas, Zone 20, 21, and 22 Locations . . . . 506.7(C)

Sealing & Drainage 501.15

Signaling, Alarm, Remote Control & Communication 501.150

Special Precautions 505.7

Specific Locations . . . . Art. 510

Spray Application, Dipping, Coating, and Printing Processes Using Flammable Combustible Materials . . . . Article 516

Supervision of Work, Qualified Person,

    Class I, Zone 0, 1, and 2 Locations . . . . 505.7(A)

        Special Precautions 506.7

Surge Arresters, Over 1 kV . . . . Art. 280

    See Standard for the Installation of Lightning Protection Systems, NFPA 780 . . . . NFPA 780

    Types and Installation 501.20

Switches, Circuit Breakers, Motor Controllers & Fuses . 501.115

Transformers & Capacitors 501.100

Utilization Equipment 501.135

Wiring Methods 501.10

    Aircraft Hangars 513.4

    Bulk Storage Plants 515.4

        Underground Wiring 515.8

    Class I, Division 1 . . . . 501.10(A)

    Class I, Division 2 . . . . 501.10(B)

    Class I, Zone 0 . . . . 505.15(A)

    Class I, Zone 1 . . . . 505.15(B)

    Class I, Zone 2 . . . . 505.15(C)

    Commercial Garages 511.4

    Definitions

        Major Repair Garage 511.2

        Minor Repair Garage 511.2

H

Gasoline (Motor Fuel) Dispensing and Service Stations 514.4

    Underground Wiring. 514.8

Health Care, within Hazardous Anesthetizing Locations 517.61

Major Repair Garage Classification . . . . 511.3(D)

Minor Repair Garage Classification . . . . 511.3(C)

Spray Application, Dipping, and Coating Processes 516.6

Class II Locations . . . . Art. 502

Bonding in . . . . 502.30(A)

    At Service . . . . 250.92(B)

    General 250.100

Control Transformers & Resistors. 502.120

Documentation Required . . . . 500.4(A)

Dusts by Group . . . . 500.6(B)

See . . . . . Recommended Practice for the Classification of Combustible Dusts and of Hazardous (Classified) Locations for Electrical Installations in Chemical Process Areas

Flexible Connections

    Division 1 .502.10(A)(2)

Flexible Cords

    Division 1 Locations . . . . .502.10(A)(2)(5)

    Division 2 Locations . . . . .502.10(B)(2)

    Installation . . . . .502.140(B)

    Luminaries (Lighting Fixtures) 502.130

    Permitted Uses . . . . .502.140(A)

Grounding 502.30

    At Service 250.92

    General 250.100

Live Parts, Not Exposed 502.25

Luminaires (Lighting Fixtures) 502.130

Motors and Generators 502.125

Optical Fiber Cable

    Division 1 . . . . .502.10(A)(1)(4)

    Division 2 . . . . .502.10(B)(1)(8)

Receptacles and Attachment Plugs 502.145

Sealing 502.15

Signaling, Alarm, Remote Control & Communication and

    Meters, Instruments, and Relays 502.150

Special Precautions 505.7

Special Precautions 506.7

Surge Arresters . . . . Art. 280

    Types and Installation 502.35

See Standard for the Installation of Lightning Protection

Systems, NFPA 780 . . . . NFPA 780

Switches, Circuit Breakers, Motor Controllers & Fuses 502.115

Transformers & Capacitors 502.100

Utilization Equipment 502.135

Ventilation Piping. 502.128

Wiring Methods

    Class II, Division 1 . . . . 502.10(A)

    Class II, Division 2 . . . . 502.10(B)

Class III Locations . . . . Art. 503

Bonding in . . . . 503.30(A)

    At Service 250.92

    General 250.100

Control Transformers & Resistors 503.120

Cranes & Hoists 503.155

    Documentation Required . . . . 500.4(A)

    Special Requirements 610.3

    See CRANES AND HOISTS . . . . Ferm's Finder

Fibers or Flyings, Easily Ignitable . . . . 500.5(D)

Flexible Connections . . . . .503.10(A)(3)

Flexible Cords 503.140

Grounding 503.30

    At Service 250.92

    General 250.100

Live Parts Not Exposed 503.25

Luminaires (Lighting Fixtures) 503.130

Motors and Generators 503.125

Operating Temperature (Dust) 503.5

Receptacles. 503.145

Signaling, Alarm, Remote Control & Communication 503.150

Storage Battery Charging Equipment 503.160

Switches, Circuit Breakers, Motor Controllers & Fuses 503.115

Transformers & Capacitors 503.100

Utilization Equipment 503.135

Ventilating Piping. 503.128

Wiring Methods

    Class III, Division 1 . . . . 503.10(A)

    Class III, Division 2 . . . . 503.10(B)

Classified (Specific Locations) . . . . Art. 510

Aircraft Hangars . . . . Art. 513

    See AIRCRAFT HANGARS. . . . . Ferm's Finder

Bulk Storage Plants . . . . Art. 515

See BULK STORAGE PLANTS. . . . . . . Ferm's Finder

Commercial Garages . . . . Art. 511

   See COMMERCIAL GARAGES . . . . . . Ferm's Finder

Finishing Processes . . . . Art. 516

   See FINISHING PROCESSES. . . . . Ferm's Finder

Health Care Facilities . . . . Art. 517

   See HEALTH CARE FACILITIES . . . . . Ferm's Finder

Motor Fuel Dispensing Facilities . . . . Art. 514

   See GASOLINE (MOTOR FUEL) DISPENSING. . . . . .

   . . . . Ferm's Finder

Spray Application, Dipping & Coating . . . . Art. 516

   See SPRAY APPLICATION, DIPPING & COATING, ETC.
Ferm's Finder

Luminaires (Fixtures) & Fittings

   Class I, Division 1 . . . . 501.130(A)

   Class I, Division 2 . . . . 501.130(B)

   Class I, Zones 0, 1, and 2 . . . . 505.20

   Class I, Zones 20, 21, 22 . . . . 506.20

   Class II, Division 1 . . . . 502.130(A)

   Class II, Division 2 . . . . .502.130(B)

   Class III, Divisions 1 and 2 . . . . 503.130

   Fixture (Luminaires) Fittings *See* (IGIV) . .*UL Product Spec*

   Fixtures (Luminaires) Paint Spray Booth

      See (IFYJ) . . . . *UL Product Spec*

   Fixtures, (Luminaires) Recessed Type

      See (IGBW) . . . .*UL Product Spec*

   Fixtures, (Luminaires), see (IFUX). . . . .*UL Product Spec*

   Spray Applications, Booths, etc. . . . . 516 Part III

   Note: Equipment subject to accumulation of residue or dusts
is not permitted in spray areas unless specifically listed for the
application.. . . . . 516.6(B)4

Ignition Temperature Information . . . . 500.8(C)

   NFPA 325, *Guide to Fire Protection Hazard Properties of
Flammable Liquids, Gases, and Volatile Solids contained
in the NFPA "Fire Protection Guide to Hazardous
Materials˙–2001 edition"*

   *See Recommended Practice for the Classification of Flammable
Liquids, Gases, or Vapors and of Hazardous (Classified) Loca-
tions for Electrical Installations in Chemical Process Areas* . .
. . . . NFPA 497

   *See Recommended Practice for the Classification of
Combustible Dusts and of Hazardous (Classified) Locations
for Electrical Installations in Chemical Process Areas* . . . . .
. . . . NFPA 499

Intrinsically Safe Systems . . . . Art. 504

   As Protection Technique . . . . 500.7(E)

See INTRINSICALLY SAFE SYSTEMS. . . . . Ferm's Finder

Identification of Occupancies 500.9

Protection Techniques, General 500.7

   Class I, Zone 0, 1, and 2 Locations 505.8

   Class I, Zone 20, 21, and 22 Locations 506.8

Reference Standards

   Class I, II, and III, Divisions 1 and 2 Locations . . . 500.4(B)

   Class I, Zone 0, 1, and 2 Locations . . . . 505.4(B)

   Class I, Zone 20, 21, and 22 Locations . . . . 506.4(B)

   Suitability — Equipment . . . . 500.8(A)

Wiring under Hazardous Areas

   Aircraft Hangars 513.8

   Bulk Storage Tanks 515.8

   Commercial Garages 511.4

   Motor Fuel Dispensing Facilities 514.8

See ZONE 0, CLASS 1 HAZARDOUS (CLASSIFIED)
LOCATIONS . . . . Ferm's Finder

See ZONE 20, 21, 22 CLASS 1 HAZARDOUS (CLASSIFIED)
LOCATIONS . . . . Ferm's Finder

HDPE TYPE CONDUIT . . . . Art. 353

Class I, Division 1 . . . . .501.10(A)(1)(a) Ex.

Commercial Garages. . . . . .511.8 Ex.

Conduit and Tubing Fill Tables. . . . . . .Informative Annex C

Joints, Made by Heat Fusion, Electrofusion or Mechanical

Fittings . . . . 353.48 Info. Note

Motor Fuel Dispensing . . . . 514.8 Ex. No. 2

Services

   Recreational Vehicles. . . . . 551.80(B)

   Service-Entrance . . . . 230.43(17)

   Underground Wiring Method. . . . . .230.30(B)(4)

HEADERS

Cellular Concrete Floor Raceways . . . . 372.18(A)

   Connections to Cabinets and Other Enclosures . . 372.18(B)

   Inserts . . . . 372.18(D)

   Maximum Number of Conductors 372.22

   Splices and Taps 372.56

Cellular Metal Floor Raceways 374.1

   Maximum Number of Conductors 374.22

   Splices and Taps 374.56

Definition of (Headers)

   For Cellular Concrete Floor Raceways 372.2

   For Cellular Metal Floor Raceways 374.2

H HEADROOM & WORKING CLEARANCE AT EQUIPMENT

600 Volts, Nominal, or Less 110.26

  Clear Spaces . . . . 110.26(B)

  Depth of Working Space . . . . .110.26(A)(1)

  Entrance to Working Space . . . . 110.26(C)

  Height of Working Space. . . . . .110.26(A)(3)

  Width of Working Space . . . . .110.26(A)(2)

Over 1000 Volts 110.32

  Depth of Working Space . . . . 110.34(A)

  Entrance and Access to Work Space 110.33

  Work Space about Equipment 110.34

HEALTH CARE FACILITIES . . . . Art. 517

Ambulatory Health Care Facility

  Definition of 517.2

  Essential Electrical System 517.45

  Wiring and Protection . . . . 517 Part II

  Essential Electrical System 517.25

  Wiring and Protection . . . . 517 Part II

  See Standard for Health Care Facilities, NFPA 99. . . NFPA 99

  Communications . . . . 517 Part VI

Definition of 517.2

Essential Electrical System 517.30

  Alternate Power Sources

    Fuel Cell Systems . . . . .517.30(B)(2)

    Generating Units . . . . .517.30(B)(1)

  Capacity of Systems . . . . 517.31(D)

  Coordination . . . . 517.31(G)

  Feeders from Alternate Power Sources . . . . . . 517.31(F)

  Optional Loads . . . . .517.31(B)(1)

  Sources of Power 517.30

  Transfer Switches . . . . 517.31(B)

Fire Alarm Systems . . . . 517 Part VI

General . . . . Art. 760

  See FIRE ALARM SYSTEMS . . . . Ferm's Finder

  See Standard for Health Care Facilities, NFPA 99 . . NFPA 99

  See Life Safety Code, NFPA 101 . . . . .NFPA 101

  See National Fire Alarm Code, NFPA 72 . . . . . . NFPA 72

Governing Body, Definition 517.2

Grounding

  Certain Spaces, Nonapplicability . . . . .517.10(B)(1)

  Definitions of Patient Equipment and Reference Point . 517.2

  Feeders, Critical Care Spaces . . . . 517.19(E)

  Hospitals . . . . 517 Part II

Anesthetizing Locations 517.62

Critical Care (Category 1) Spaces . . . . 517 Part II

  Specific Requirements 517.19

General Care (Category 2) Spaces . . . . 517 Part II

  Specific Requirements 517.18

Patient Care Spaces . . . . 517 Part II

  Critical Care (Category 1) 517.19

  General Care (Category 2) 517.18

Panelboards 517.14

  Receptacles and Fixed Equipment 517.13

Therapeutic Pools & Tubs . . . . 680 Part VI

X-Ray Area 517.78

Nursing Homes and Limited Care Facilities . . . . 517 Part II

  Nonapplicability, Certain Spaces . . . . .517.10(B)(2)

  Panelboards . . . . 517.19(E)

Ground-Fault Circuit-Interrupter Protection

  Not Required Certain Critical Care (Category 1) Spaces . . .
. . . . 517.21

Therapeutic Equipment . . . . 680.62(A)

Therapeutic Pools & Tubs . . . . 680 Part VI

  Receptacles within 6 ft . . . . 680.62(E)

  Therapeutic Tubs (Hydrotherapeutic Tanks) . . 680.62(A)

Wet Procedure Locations, Receptacles and Fixed Equipment
. . . . 517.20

  Wet Procedure Locations Defined (under Patient Care
  Space) 517.2

Ground-Fault Protection of Equipment

  Feeders 215.10

    Additional Level Required (Applicability) . . . 517.17(A)

    Where Protection Provided . . . . 517.17(B)

  Not Required for Emergency Systems 700.31

  Selectivity . . . . 517.17(C)

  Services 230.95

  Signal Devices, Emergency Systems . . . . 700.6(D)

  Testing . . . . 517.17(D)

Hazardous (Classified) Locations . . . . 517 Part IV

  See HAZARDOUS (CLASSIFIED) LOCATIONS . . . .
. . . . Ferm's Finder

  See Standard for Health Care Facilities, NFPA 99 . . NFPA 99

Hospitals

  Critical Branch, Selected Equipment 517.33

  Definition of 517.2

  Essential Electrical System 517.30

    Branches of (Life Safety Branch and Critical Branch) . . .
. . . . 517.31

Capacity of Systems . . . . 517.31(D)

Coordination . . . . 517.31(G)

Equipment System Branch

    Equipment System Connection to Alternate Power . .

    . . . . 517.35

        Separation of Circuits . . . . .517.31(C)(1)

Feeders from Alternate Power Sources . . . . . 517.31(F)

Mechanical Protection . . . . .517.31(C)(3)

Optional Loads . . . . .517.31(B)(1)

Sources of Power 517.30

Transfer Switches . . . . 517.31(B)

Wiring Requirements . . . . 517.31(C)

Legally Required Standby . . . . Art. 701

Life Safety Branch, Selected Equipment 517.33

See Standard for Health Care Facilities, NFPA 99. . . NFPA 99

Inhalation Anesthetizing Location . . . . 517 Part IV

See Standard for Health Care Facilities, NFPA 99. . . NFPA 99

Isolated Grounding Receptacles, Not Used In Patient Care

Vicinity . . . . 517.16(B)

Isolating Transformers

Critical Care (Category 1) Spaces (Optional) . . 517.19(F) & (G)

Isolated Power Systems 517.160

Low-Voltage Circuits . . . . 517.64(C)

Wet Procedure Locations 517.20

See Standard for Health Care Facilities, NFPA 99. . . NFPA 99

Medical Office (Dental Office), Definition 517.2

Nursing Homes and Limited Care Facilities

Definitions, Both 517.2

Essential Electrical Systems 517.25

Capacity of System . . . . 517.42(C)

Connection to Equipment Branch 517.44

Connection to Life Safety Branch 517.43

Emergency Systems, General . . . . Art. 700

Legally Required Standby . . . . Art. 701

Separation from Other Circuits . . . . 517.42(D)

Sources of Power 517.41

See Standard for Health Care Facilities, NFPA 99. . . NFPA 99

Panelboards (Bonding & Grounding) 517.14

Critical Care (Category 1) Spaces . . . . 517.19(E)

Patient Care Space

Critical Care (Category 1) Space

Grounding of Receptacles and Fixed Equipment . . 517.13

Requirements for 517.19

Definitions 517.2

General Care (Category 2) Space

Grounding of Receptacles and Fixed Equipment . . 517.13

Requirements for 517.18

Grounding of Receptacles and Fixed Equipment . . 517.13

See Standard for Health Care Facilities, NFPA 99. . . NFPA 99

Ground-Fault Circuit-Interrupter Protection 517.21

Wet Procedure Locations 517.20

Receptacle(s)

Above Hazardous Locations . . . . 517.61(B)

Covers That Limit Pediatric Access . . . . 517.18(C)

Exemption from, Certain Critical Care (Category 1) Spaces

. . . . 517.21

Explosionproof . . . . 517.61(A)(3) & (5)

Ground-Fault Circuit-Interrupter 517.20

Grounding

Connecting Grounding Terminal to Box 250.146

Critical Care (Category 1) Spaces . . . . 517.19(B)

General Care (Category 2) Spaces . . . . 517.18(B)

General 517.13

Hospital Grade, Required

Above Hazardous Locations . . . . .517.61(B)(5)

Critical Care (Category 1) Spaces . . . . 517.19(B)

General Care (Category 2) Spaces . . . . 517.18(B)

In Other Than Hazardous Locations . . . . .517.61(C)(2)

Note: Non-hospital grade receptacles must be replaced with hospital-grade receptacles upon any modifications of use, renovation, or as existing receptacles need replacement.

Insulated Equipment Grounds 517.13

Covers . . . . 406.3(D)(2)

Critical Care (Category 1) Patient Bed Location 517.19(B)

General Care (Category 2) Patient Bed Location 517.18(B)

Isolated Ground . . . . 250.146(D)

Use and Identification of . . . . 406.3(D)(1)

Isolated Power Systems 517.160

Isolated Grounding Receptacles, Not Used Inside Patient Care

Vicinity . . . . 517.16(A)

Low Voltage . . . . 517.64(F)

Number of (Hospitals)

Operating Rooms . . . . 517.19(C)

Patient Bed Locations, Critical Care (Category 1) . . . . .

. . . . 517.19(B)

Patient Bed Locations, General Care (Category 2) . . . . .

. . . . 517.18(B)

Receptacles, 50- and 60-ampere, 250 Volts

Above Hazardous Locations . . . . .517.61(B)(6)

In Other Than Hazardous Locations . . . . . .517.61(C)(3)

Sealing Fittings . . . . .517.61(B)(4)

Tamper Resistant . . . . 517.18(C)

Therapeutic Pools & Tubs . . . . 680 Part VI

   Bonding . . . . 680.62(B)

   Methods of Bonding . . . . 680.62(C)

   Grounding . . . . 680.62(D)

     Methods of . . . . 680.62(D)

   Ground-Fault Circuit-Protection, for Equipment . 680.62(A)

     For Receptacles . . . . 680.62(E)

   Luminaires (Lighting Fixtures)

     Indoor Areas . . . . 680.22(B)

     Permanently Installed Pools . . . . 680.61 Ex.

     Tub Areas . . . . 680.62(F)

     Underwater 680.23

Wiring Methods . . . . 517 Part II

   Insulated Equipment Grounding Conductor 517.13

     Critical Care (Category 1) Space Bed Location Receptacles

     . . . . 517.19(B)

     General Care (Category 2) Space Bed Location Receptacles

     . . . . 517.18(B)

   Mechanical Protection of Essential Electrical System . . . . .

   . . . . .517.31(C)(2)

X-RAY Equipment . . . . 517 Part V

Note: Radiation safety and performance requirements of

several classes of x-ray equipment are regulated under Public

Law 90-602 and are enforced by the Department of Health

and Human Services . . . . 517.70 Info. Note 1

See Standard for Health Care Facilities, NFPA 99 . . . . NFPA 99

HEAT DETECTING CIRCUIT INTERRUPTER . . . . . .440.65(3)

HEAT PUMPS . . . . Art. 440

Branch-Circuit Conductors . . . . 440 Part IV

Branch-Circuit Short-Circuit and Ground-Fault Protection . .

. . . . 440 Part III

Calculations

   See ELECTRIC HEAT (SPACE), Calculations of Load Ferm's
   Finder

Controllers for . . . . 440 Part V

Definitions 440.2

Disconnecting Means . . . . 440 Part II

Motor-Compressor & Branch-Circuit Overload Protection 440
Part VI

HEATING APPLIANCES . . . . Art. 422

Central Heating Equipment (Other Than Electric) 422.12

Flexible Cords for 422.16

Infrared Lamp Type 425.14

   Lampholder Types and Ratings 422.48

Signals for 422.42

Subdivision of Load . . . . 422.11(F)

HEATING CABLES . . . . 424 Part V

See ELECTRIC HEAT (SPACE), Cables . . . . . Ferm's Finder

HEATING EQUIPMENT, SPACE (Fixed) . . . . .Art. 424

Mobile Home Outside, Provisions for . . . . 550.20(B)

See DEICING AND SNOW-MELTING . . . . . Ferm's Finder

See DUCT HEATERS . . . . Ferm's Finder

See ELECTRIC HEAT (SPACE) . . . . Ferm's Finder

See FIXED ELECTRIC HEATING EQUIPMENT FOR

PIPELINES AND VESSELS . . . . Ferm's Finder

See HEAT PUMPS . . . . Ferm's Finder

See INDUCTION AND DIELECTRIC HEATING Ferm's Finder

See INFRARED LAMP HEATING . . . . Ferm's Finder

HEATING PANELS AND HEATING PANEL SETS . . 424 Part IX

For Pipeline and Vessel Heating . . . . 427.23(B)

See ELECTRIC HEAT (SPACE), Panels and Sets . Ferm's Finder

HEIGHT OF WORKING SPACE . . . . 110.26(A)(3)

HERMETIC REFRIGERANT MOTOR COMPRESSORS . Art. 440

Ampacity and Rating 440.6

Branch-Circuit Conductors . . . . 440 Part IV

Branch-Circuit Short-Circuit and Ground-Fault Protection . .

. . . . 440 Part III

Controllers for Motor-Compressors . . . . 440 Part V

Compressor and Branch-Circuit Overload Protection . . . . . .

. . . . 440 Part VI

Defined . . . . Art. 100

Disconnecting Means . . . . 440 Part II

Room Air Conditioners . . . . 440 Part VII

   Protection Devices 440.65

     Arc-fault circuit interrupter (AFCI) . . . . .440.65(2)

     Heat Detecting Circuit Interrupter (HDCI) . . . .440.65(3)

     Leakage-Current Detector-Interrupter (LCDI) . .440.65(1)

H.I.D. LAMP TYPE LUMINAIRES (FIXTURES)

See (IEWX) . . . .*UL Product Spec*

See (IEXT) . . . .*UL Product Spec*

HIGH IMPEDANCE GROUNDED NEUTRAL 250.36

AC Systems 50 to 1000 Volts Not Required To Be Grounded . . 250.21

Equipment Bonding Jumper . . . . 250.36(E)

Grounding Electrode Conductor Connection Location . . . . . 250.36(F)

Grounding Impedance Location . . . . 250.36(A)

Grounded System Conductor . . . . 250.36(B)

Marked Legibly and Permanently . . . . 408.3(F)(3)

Neutral Point to Grounding Impedance Conductor Routing . . 250.36(D)

Separately Derived Systems . . . . 250.30(A) Ex.

System Grounding Connection . . . . 250.36(C)

1kV and Over 250.187

   Equipment Grounding Conductors . . . . . . 250.187(D)

   Grounding Impedance Location . . . . 250.187(A)

   Neutral Identified and Insulated . . . . 250.187(B)

   System Neutral Connection . . . . 250.187(C)

HIGH-LEG (STINGER or WILD LEG)

Caution Signs . . . . 408.3(F)(1)

Feeder Identification 110.15

Marking of in Switchboards and Panelboards. . . . . 408.3(F)

Marking of, General 110.15

   No Delta Breakers in Single-Phase Panels . . . . 408.36(C)

Phase Arrangement, Switchboards and Panelboards. . 408.3(E)

Plug Fuses Permitted. . . . . 240.50(A)(2)

Service Conductor Identification. 230.56

Signage Requirements, Caution . . . . 408.3(F)(1)

Switchboard or Panelboard Permanently Field Marked 408.3(F)

HIGH VOLTAGE, OVER 1000 VOLTS NOMINAL

Busways . . . . 368 Part IV

Capacitors . . . . 460 Part II

Definitions (Over 1000 Volts, Nominal) . . . . Art. 100 Part II

Equipment . . . . 490 Part II

Grounding . . . . 250 Part X

Medium Voltage Cable: Type MV . . . . Art. 328

Motors. . . . . 430 Part XI

Outside Branch Circuits and Feeders . . . . 225 Part III

Overcurrent Protection . . . . 240 Part IX

Portable Cables. . . . . 400 Part III

Pull and Junction Boxes . . . . 314 Part IV

Requirements for Electrical Installations . . . . . . 110 Part III

Resistors and Reactors . . . . 470 Part II

Services . . . . 230 Part VIII

Solar Photovoltaic Systems . . . . 690 Part IX

Solar Photovoltaic Systems (Large Scale) . . . . Art. 691

Transformers, see TRANSFORMERS . . . . . . Ferm's Finder

Tunnel Installations . . . . 110 Part IV

Wind Electric Systems. . . . . 694 Part VIII

Wiring Methods . . . . 300 Part II

See OVER 1000 VOLTS, NOMINAL. . . . . . . Ferm's Finder

HOIST, STAGE LIGHTING

Defined 520.2

Wiring Information 520.40

HOISTS AND CRANES . . . . Art. 610

See CRANES & HOISTS . . . . Ferm's Finder

HOISTWAY (ELEVATOR) CABLE

See (MSZR) . . . . UL Product Spec

HOISTWAYS

Definition of . . . . Art. 100 Part I

Door Interlock Wiring. . . . . 620.11(A)

Wiring in

   Class 2, or 3 Remote Control and Signaling . . . . 725.136(I)

   Lightning Protection Conductors . . . . 620.37(B)

   Location of and Protection for Cables 620.43

   Main Feeders . . . . 620.37(C)

   Power-Limited (PLFA) Circuits in Hoistways . . . 760.136(F)

   Suspension of Traveling Cables 620.41

   Uses Permitted. . . . . 620.37(A)

Wiring Methods, General 620.21

   Elevators, Between Risers, Limit Switches, etc.620.21(A)(1)(a)

   For Class 2 Power-Limited Circuits . . . . . . 620.21(A)(1)(a)

   Wiring Methods. . . . . 620.21(A)(1)(c)

HOODS & DUCTS

See DUCTS & HOODS . . . . Ferm's Finder

HOSPITALS

See HEALTH CARE FACILITIES . . . . Ferm's Finder

HOT TUBS & SPAS . . . . 680 Part IV

Definitions 680.2

Disconnecting Means for Equipment — Simultaneous . 680.13

Electrically Powered Pool Lift. . . . . 680 Part VIII

   Bonding 680.83

I

Defined 680.2

Listed 680.81

Emergency Switch Required, User Access to 680.41

Ground-Fault Circuit-Interrupter Protection Required . . . . .
. . . . .680.42(A)(2)

Indoor Installations 680.43

Bonding . . . . 680.43(D)

Methods of . . . . 680.43(E)

Disconnecting Means, Equipment 680.13

Disconnecting Means, Motors . . . . 430 Part IX

Electric Heaters 680.10

Grounding . . . . 680.43(F)

Methods of 680.6

Lighting Luminaires (Fixtures) and Ceiling Fans . 680.43(B)

Ground-Fault Circuit-Protection . . . . .680.43(B)(1)

Receptacles . . . . 680.43(A)(2)

Ground-Fault Circuit-Protection, within 3.0 m (10 ft.) . .
. . . . 680.43(A)

Location . . . . .680.43(A)(1)

Outlet Box Hood . . . . 406.9(B)(1)

Tamper-Resistant 406.12

That Provide Power to Spas and Hot Tubs . .680.43(A)(3)

Weather-Resistant . . . . 406.9(A) and (B)

Switches [1.5 m (5 ft.) away] . . . . 680.43(C)

Outdoor Installations 680.42

Bonding . . . . 680.42(B)

Flexible Connections . . . . 680.42(A)

Wiring Per Article 680 Parts I, II, and IV . . . . . . Art. 680

Storable Hot Tub (defined) 680.2

See SPAS AND HOT TUBS . . . . Ferm's Finder

See SWIMMING POOLS . . . . Ferm's Finder

See (WBYQ) . . . . .UL Product Spec

HOTELS & MOTELS

Arc-Fault Circuit-Interrupter Protection . . . . . . 210.12(C)

Assembly Occupancies (finish rating) . . . . 518.4(C)

Branch-Circuit Limitations . . . . 210.6(A)

General Lighting Loads . . . . Table 220.12

Demand Factors . . . . Table 220.42

GFCI for Bathrooms, Kitchens . . . . 210.8(A), 210.18, 210.60

Lighting Outlets Required . . . . 210.70(B)

Meeting Rooms 210.71

Receptacle

Loads 220.44

Receptacle Placement . . . . 210.60(B)

Receptacles Required 210.52

Tamper-Resistant 406.12

See Life Safety Code, NFPA 101 . . . . NFPA 101

HOUSEBOATS . . . . **Art. 553**

See FLOATING BUILDINGS . . . . Ferm's Finder

HVAC Equipment (Air Conditioning and Refrigerator) Art. 440

HYBRID SYSTEM

Defined . . . . Art. 100

Example, Photovoltaic Systems . . . . Figure 690.1(b)

Unbalanced Interconnections, Unbalanced Voltage . . 705.100

Utility-Interactive Inverters, Interconnection 705.82

HYDROMASSAGE BATHTUBS . . . . **680 Part VII**

Accessibility 680.73

Bonding 680.74

GFCI Protection Required for Circuit 680.71

Other Electrical Equipment 680.72

See (NCHX) . . . . .UL Product Spec

I

IDENTIFICATION OF

Branch Circuits on Panel Doors . . . . 408.4(A)

Conductors

Branch Circuit, General 210.5

For General Wiring 310.10

High (Delta) Leg

For Conductors or Busbar 110.15

For Services 230.56

General 110.15

Intrinsically Safe Systems . . . . 504.80(C)

Motor Control Centers . . . . 430.97(B)

Phase Arrangement, Switchboards and Panelboards . . .
. . . . 408.3(E)

Sensitive Electronic Equipment . . . . 647.4(C)

Ungrounded, Multiwire Branch Circuits 110.15

Disconnecting Means 110.22

Panelboard Circuits and Modifications 408.4

Emergency System Wiring . . . . 700.10(A)

Equipment Grounding Conductor 250.119

Feeders

Direct-Current Systems, Ungrounded Conductors . . . . . .
. . . . .215.12(C)(2)

Equipment Grounding Conductor . . . . 215.12(B)

Grounded Conductor. . . . . 215.12(A)

Supplied From More Than One Nominal Voltage System . .
. . . . .215.12(C)(1)

(Fixture) Luminaire Wires, Grounded Conductor 402.8

Flexible Cords

    Equipment Grounding Conductor 400.23

    Grounded Conductor. 400.22

    Luminaire (Fixture) Wires, Grounded Conductor. . . . 402.8

Grounded Conductor . . . . Art. 200

    Conductors of Different Systems . . . . 200.6(D)

    Conductors for General Wiring . . . . 310.110(A)

    For Branch Circuits . . . . 210.5(A)

    In Flexible Cord . . . . 200.6(C)

    In Multiconductor Cables . . . . 200.6(E)

    Sizes Larger Than 4 AWG . . . . 200.6(B)

    Sizes 6 AWG or Smaller . . . . 200.6(A)

    Terminals. 200.10

    Use of Color, General . . . . 200.7(A)

        Circuits 50 Volts or More . . . . 200.7(C)

        Circuits Less Than 50 Volts . . . . 200.7(B)

Identification of Terminals

    Aluminum, for . . . . 110.14(A)

    Devices Connected to Grounded Conductor, for . . . 200.10

    Grounding-type Receptacles, Adapters, etc. . . . . 406.10(B)

    Intrinsically Safe Systems . . . . 504.80(A)

    More Than One Conductor, for . . . . 110.14(A)

Intrinsically Safe System Wiring . . . . 504.80(B)

Isolated Ground Receptacles . . . . 406.2(D)

Isolated Power Systems, Health Care Facilities . . 517.160(A)(5)

Panelboard Circuits 408.4

Receptacles Connected to Critical Branch, Hospitals . . . . . .
. . . . 517.34(A)

Service Disconnecting Means . . . . 230.70(B)

Ungrounded Conductors . . . . .310.110(C)

See Also CONDUCTORS, Identification of . . . . Ferm's Finder

ILLUMINATION ABOUT ELECTRICAL EQUIPMENT . . . .
. . . .**110.26(D)**

ILLUMINATION FOR EMERGENCY SYSTEMS. **700.16**

IMMERSION DETECTION OF APPLIANCES **422.41**

IMMERSION HEATERS **422.44**

IMPEDANCE GROUNDING

Grounded Neutral System, 1 kV and Over 250.187

Grounded Neutral System, High-Impedance 250.36

See HIGH IMPEDANCE GROUNDED NEUTRAL . . . .
. . . . Ferm's Finder

IN SIGHT FROM

Definition of . . . . Art. 100

Disconnecting Means For

    Air-Conditioning Equipment 440.14

    Air-Conditioning Unit, Single-Phase Room, Attachment Plug
. . . . 440.63

    Appliances, Motor Operated Rated over 1/8 HP. . 422.31(C)

    Appliances, Permanently Connected Over 300 VA 422.31(B)

    Duct Heaters 424.65

    Electric Discharge Lighting, Over 1000 Volts . . . .
. . . . .410.141(B)

    Electrically Driven or Controlled Irrigation Machines . . . .
. . . . 675.8(B)

    Electric Signs . . . . 600.6(A)

    Fixed Electric Space Heating Equipment 424.19

    Induction and Dielectric Heating Equipment 665.12

    Mobile Home Service Equipment . . . . 550.32(A)

    Motors . . . . 430 Part IX

        Control Circuits 430.74

        Controller . . . . 430.102(A)

        Motor and Driven Machinery. . . . . .430.102(B)

    Phase Converters . . . . 455.8(A)

    Shore Power Connections . . . . 555.17(B)

    Swimming Pool, Spa, and Hot Tub Equipment 680.13

        Emergency Switch for Spas and Hot Tubs 680.41

INCANDESCENT LAMPS . . . . **Art. 410**

Aircraft Hangers . . . . 513.7(C)

Clearance of Luminaires (Fixtures) 410.116

Clothes Closets, In 410.16

Dressing Rooms of Theaters 520.72

Garages . . . . 511.7(B)

Lamp Wattage Marking 410.120

Medium and Mogul Bases 410.103

Recessed. 410.115

INCIDENTAL METAL PARTS

Not Likely to Become Energized . . . . 422.15(C)

I

INDEPENDENT

Emergency Lighting Branch Circuits 700.17

Means of Support for Wiring above Ceilings . . . . . 300.11(A)

    Fire-Rated Assemblies . . . . .300.11(A)(1)

    Non-Fire-Rated Assemblies . . . . .300.11(A)(2)

Supports for Service Drops 230.29

Wiring, Emergency Circuits . . . . 700.10(B)

Note: *See* specific occupancy or system for further information on independent wiring, sources of supply, etc.

INDIVIDUAL BRANCH CIRCUIT

Appliances . . . . 422.10(A)

Definition of . . . . .Art. 100 Part I

Electric Sign or Outline Lighting. . . . . 600.5(A)

Electrode-Type Boiler Over 1000 Volts . . . . . . 490.72(A)

Elevator Car Lighting, HVAC 620.22

Fixed Electric Space-Heating Equipment . . . . . . 424.3(A)

Hydromassage Bathtubs. 680.71

Marinas and Boatyards . . . . .555.19(A)(3)

Motor Circuits 430.52

Office Furnishings . . . . 605.9(B)

Permissible Loads 210.22

Receptacles on . . . . .210.21(B)(1)

    Permissible Load 210.23

INDUCTION (ARRANGE WIRING TO PREVENT HEATING BY)

Busbar Arrangements . . . . 408.3(B)

For Three-Way and Four-Way Switching . . . . . . 404.2(A)

General . . . . 300.3(B)

Impedance Heating Systems 426.33

In Metal Enclosures or Raceways 300.20

Over 1000 Volts 300.35

Single Conductor Type UF Cable . . . . .340.10(2)

Single Conductors in Cable Trays . . . . 392.20(D)

Underground Installations . . . . 300.5(I)

INDUCTION & DIELECTRIC HEATING EQUIPMENT Art. 665

Ampacity of Supply Conductors 665.10

Definitions 665.2

Disconnecting Means 665.12

Grounding, Guarding & Labeling . . . . Art. 665 Part II

Industrial & Scientific Application . . . . Art 665 Part 1

Output Circuit 665.5

Overcurrent Protection 665.11

Remote Control 665.7

INDUSTRIAL CONTROL EQUIPMENT

See (NIMX) . . . .*UL Product Spec*

INDUSTRIAL CONTROL PANELS . . . . ART. 409

Arc-Flash Hazard Warning, Marking 110.16

Busbars and Conductors 409.102

Conductor, Minimum Size and Ampacity 409.20

Defined . . . . Article 100

Disconnecting Means 409.30

Enclosures 409.100

Enclosure Type, Marking 110.28

Grounding 409.60

Installation . . . . Art. 409, Part II

Marking. 409.110

More Than One Power Source, Marking. 409.110

Overcurrent Protection 409.21

Service Equipment 409.108

Short-Circuit Current Rating 409.22

    Documentation . . . . 409.22(B)

    Installation . . . . 409.22(A)

Spacing between Uninsulated Parts 409.106

Wire Space 409.104

See (NITW) . . . .*UL Product Spec*

INDUSTRIAL MACHINERY . . . . Art. 670

Clearance, Working Space . . . . 670.1 Info. Note 2

Conductor Size . . . . 670.4(A)

Definition of 670.2

Exceeds Available Fault Current 670.5

Disconnecting Means . . . . 670.4(B)

Fixed Resistance and Electrode Industrial Process Heating

Equipment . . . . Art. 425

    Boilers . . . . Art 425 Part VI and VII

    Branch Circuits 425.3

    Control and Protection . . . . 425 Part III

    Disconnecting Means. 425.19

    Listed Equipment 425.6

    Locations. 425.12

    Infrared Lamp Industrial Heating Equipment 425.14

    Marking of Heating Equipment . . . . 425 Part IV

    Process Duct Heaters . . . . 425 Part V

    Process Electrode-Type Boilers . . . . 425 Part VII

    Process Resistance-Type Boilers . . . . 425 Part VI

        Overcurrent Protection 425.72

        Overpressure Limit Control. 425.74

Overtemperature Limit Control 425.73

Machine Nameplate Data 670.3

Overcurrent Protection . . . . 670.4(C)

See Electrical Standard for Industrial Machinery . . . . NFPA 79

Short-Circuit Current Rating 670.5

Surge Protection. 670.6

INFORMATION TECHNOLOGY EQUIPMENT . . . . . . Art. 645

Abandoned Cables . . . . 645.5(G)

Ampacity of Branch-Circuit Conductors . . . . 645.5(A)

Cable Routing Assemblies. . . . . 645.3(F)

Cables under Raised Floors . . . . 645.5(E)

    Air-handling Spaces . . . . 300.22(D)

Connecting Cables to Branch Circuit . . . . 645.5(B)

Critical Operations Data System 645.2

Dedicated Zones for Disconnecting Means 645.10

Definition 645.2

Disconnecting Means 645.10

Engineering Supervision 645.25

Grounding, Equipment 645.15

Grounding, System. 645.14

Interconnecting Cables . . . . 645.5(C)

Marking of Equipment 645.16

Neutral Load

    Conductor Considered Current-Carrying . . . . 310.15(B)(5)

    Feeder or Service 220.61

    Multiwire Branch Circuits . . . . 210.4(A) Info. Note 2

Optical Fiber Cables . . . . 645.3(H)

Penetrations of Fire-Resistant Room Boundary . . . . 645.3(A)

Physical Protection . . . . 645.5(D)

Plenums . . . . 645.3(B)

Power Distribution Unit 645.17

Remote Disconnect Control 645.2

Room, Definition 645.2

Securing in Place . . . . 645.5(F)

Selective Coordination 645.27

Special Requirements for Room 645.4

Surge Protection 645.18

Under Raised Floors . . . . 645.5(E)

    Branch Circuits . . . . 645.5(E)(1)

    Cords, Cables, Grounding Conductors . . . . . 645.5(E)(2)

    Optical Fiber Cables . . . . 645.5(E)(3)

    Table- Cables Installed Under Raised Floor . Table 645.10(B)(5)

Uninterruptible Power Supplies (UPS) 645.11

See Definition of Nonlinear Load . . . . Art. 100 Part I

Zone 645.2

Zones, Identified for Disconnect 645.10

    Remote Disconnect Controls . . . . 645.10(A)

Critical Operations Data Systems . . . . 645.10(B)

INFORMATIONAL NOTES . . . . 90.5(C)

INFORMATIVE ANNEXES . . . . 90.5(D)

Informative ANNEX A, Product Safety Standards . . . Annex A

Informative ANNEX B, Application Information for Ampacity Calculation . . . . Annex B

Informative ANNEX C, Conduit and Tubing Fill Tables

    For Conductors and Fixture Wires of the Same Size Annex C

Informative ANNEX D, Examples . . . . Annex D

Informative ANNEX E, Types of Construction (see 334.10) . . . . Annex E

Informative ANNEX F, Availability and Reliability for Critical Operations Power Systems; and Development and Implementation of Functional Performance Tests (FPTs) for Critical Operations Power Systems . . . . Annex F

Informative ANNEX G, Supervisory Control and Data Acquisition (SCADA) . . . . Annex G

Informative ANNEX H, Administration and Enforcement . . . . Annex H

Informative ANNEX I, Recommended Tightening Torque Tables . . . . Annex I

Informative ANNEX J, ADA Standards for Accessible Design . . . . Annex J

INFRARED LAMP HEATING APPLIANCES

Branch Circuits

    Fixed Electric Space-Heating . . . . 424.3(A)

    Industrial Heating Appliances 425.14

    Permissible Load . . . . 210.23(C)

Industrial Heating 422.48

Overcurrent Protection . . . . 422.11(C)

INHIBITOR REQUIRED ON

Aluminum Connections If Required by Listing or Manufacturer . . . . 110.3(B)

Not to Adversely Affect 110.14

See (DVYW) . . . . *UL Product Spec*

INNERDUCT

Coaxial Cables . . . . 820.110(A)(3)

Communication Wires and Cables. . . . . 800.110(A)(3)

I

Definition . . . . Art. 100

Installed Within Listed Metal Raceway . . . . . . .770.113(E)

Network-Powered Broadband Communication Cables . . . . .
. . . . .830.110(A)(3)

Optical Fiber Cables . . . . .770.110(A)(3)

Risers in Metal Raceways . . . . .820.113(E)

INSERTS

Cellular Concrete Floor Raceways . . . . 372.18(D)

Cellular Metal Floor Raceways . . . . 374.18(C)

Underfloor Raceways 390.14

INSPECTIONS AND TESTS

Equipment Over 1000 Volts, Nominal

    Outside Branch Circuits and Feeders 225.56

    Pre-energization and Operating Tests. . . . . . . 110.41(A)

    Test Reports . . . . 110.41(B)

INSTALLATION AND USE INSTRUCTIONS . . . . . . 110.3(B)
See (AALZ) . . . . .UL Product Spec

INSTITUTIONS, EMERGENCY LIGHTING . . . . . . .Art. 700
See Life Safety Code, NFPA 101 . . . . .NFPA 101

**INSULATED (ISOLATED) EQUIPMENT GROUNDING
CONDUCTOR**
See GROUNDING, Insulated Ground Wire . . . . Ferm's Finder

INSULATED FITTINGS & BUSHINGS

Cabinets, Cutout Boxes and Meter Socket Enclosures . 312.6(C)

Required for Conductors 4 AWG and Larger . . . . . 300.4(G)

Underground Installations . . . . .300.5(H)

INSULATED (ISOLATED) GROUND RECEPTACLES

Audio Signal Processing, Amplification, and Reproduction. . .
. . . . 640.7(C)

Conductor Fill in Outlet, Device & Junction Boxes . . . . . .
. . . . .314.16(B)(5)

Connecting Receptacle Grounding Conductor to Box . . . . .
. . . . 250.146(D)

Continuity and Attachment of Conductor to Boxes . . . .
. . . . 250.148 Ex.

Faceplates for . . . . 406.3(D)(2)

Identification of Receptacles . . . . 406.3(D)

Insulated from Mounting Means, Reduction of Noise . . . . . .
. . . . 250.146(D)

In Health Care Facilities . . . . 517.16(A)

    Inside Patient Care Vicinity . . . . 517.16(A)

Outside Patient Care Vicinity . . . . 517.16(B)

    Special-Purpose Receptacles. . . . . 517.19(H)

Patient Care Vicinity . . . . 517.16(A)

    Inside . . . . 517.16(A)

    Outside. . . . . 517.16(B)

Reduction of Electrical Noise . . . . 250.96(B)

Sensitive Electronic Equipment . . . . 647.7(B)

INSULATING DEVICES & MATERIALS

Insulating Tape

    See (OANZ) . . . . .UL Product Spec

Insulation, Equivalent to Conductors . . . . 110.14(B)

INSULATION

Conductors

    Construction and Application 310.104

    Corrosive Conditions, Suitable for . . . . 310.10(G)

    Dry Locations . . . . 310.10(A)

    Dry and Damp Locations . . . . 310.10(B)

    Exposed to Direct Sunlight. . . . . 310.10(D)

    General Requirement for 310.1

    Identification 310.110

    Temperature Limitations . . . . 310.15(A)(3)

    Wet Locations . . . . 310.10(C)

Equipment . . . . 110.3(A)(4)

Luminaire (Fixture) Wire Construction and Application . 402.3

Flexible Cord Construction Specifications . . . . . 400 Part II

    Type and Usage 400.4

Integrity of 110.7

Service Conductors

    Overhead Service Conductors. 230.22

    Service-Entrance Conductors 230.41

    Underground Service Conductors. 230.30

Shielding — Over 1000 Volt Cables, Grounding 300.40

Splices and Joints . . . . 110.14(B)

    In Flexible Cord to Retain Insulation Properties. . . 400.13

Thermal

    Branch-Circuit Wiring above for Space-Heating Cables . . .
. . . . 424.36

    Within 75 mm (3 in.) of Recessed Luminaires (Fixtures). . .
. . . . .410.116(B)

**INTERCONNECTED ELECTRIC POWER PRODUCTION
SOURCES . . . . .Art. 705**
Definitions 705.2

Directory 705.10

Disconnecting Means

    Device 705.22

    Equipment 705.21

    Interactive System. 705.23

    Sources 705.20

Equipment Approval. 705.6

Generators . . . . Art. 705 Part III

Ground-Fault Protection 705.32

Grounding 705.50

Interactive Inverters . . . . Art. 705 Part II

Interrupting and Short-Circuit Current Rating. 705.16

Loss of Primary Source 705.40

Loss of 3-Phase Primary Source 705.42

Microgrid Systems . . . . Art. 705 Part IV

Other Articles 705.3

Overcurrent Protection 705.30

    Location, Supply Side 705.31

Point of Connection 705.12

Scope 705.1

System Installation 705.6

Unbalanced Interconnections 705.100

Utility-Interactive Inverters. . . . . Art. 705 Part II

Warning Labels (load side) . . . . .705.12(B)(2)

INTEGRATED ELECTRICAL SYSTEMS . . . . Art. 685

INTEGRATED GAS SPACER CABLE . . . . Art. 326

Ampacity of 326.80

Bends

    Number of 326.26

    Radius 326.24

Conductors 326.104

Conduit 326.116

    Dimensions . . . . Table 326.116

Definition 326.2

Insulation 326.112

Uses Not Permitted 326.12

Uses Permitted 326.10

INTERCOMMUNICATIONS SYSTEMS . . . . .Art. 800

INTERCONNECTORS

Nonmetallic-Sheathed Cable . . . . 334.40(B)

INTERMEDIATE METAL CONDUIT . . . . Art. 342

Bends

    How Made 342.24

    Number of 342.26

Bushings 342.46

Construction - Made of 342.100

Couplings and Connectors

    Running Threads Not Permitted . . . . 342.42(B)

    Threadless . . . . 342.42(A)

Definition 342.2

Dimensions and Percent Area of . . . . .Chapter 9 Table 4 (IMC)

Dissimilar Metals. 342.14

Marking [Note 1.5 m (5 ft.) Intervals] 342.120

Minimum and Maximum Sizes 342.20

Not To Be Used as a Means of Support for Cables or

    Class 2 and 3 Circuit Conductors 725.143

    Communications Circuits . . . . 800.133(B)

    Community Antenna TV & Radio Distribution Systems. . .
    . . . . .820.133(B)

    Fire Alarm Circuit Conductors 760.143

    Network-powered Broadband Systems . . . . . . 830.133(B)

    Nonelectrical Equipment (General). . . . . 300.11(B)

Number of Conductors in 342.22

    Combinations of Conductors (General) . . . .
    . . . . Chapter 9, Table 1, Notes to Tables

        Dimension of Conductors in . . . . . . Chapter 9 Table 5

        Compact Stranded . . . . Chapter 9 Table 5A

        Same Size . . . . Table C4 and C4(A)

Reaming and Threading 342.28

Securing and Supports 342.30

Splices and Taps 342.56

Standard Lengths. 342.130

Uses Permitted 342.10

Wet Locations . . . . 342.10(D)

See RIGID METAL CONDUIT. . . . . Ferm's Finder

See (DYBY) . . . . .UL Product Spec

INTERRUPTING CAPACITY OF BREAKERS AND FUSES

Circuit Breakers, Series Ratings 240.86

Circuit Impedance, Short-Circuit Current Ratings and Other
Characteristics 110.10

Contribution from Interconnected Power Sources 705.16

Individual Pole Consideration, Circuit Breakers . . . .
. . . . 240.85 Info. Note

Interrupting Ratings, Sufficient for. 110.9

I

Marking

    Cartridge Fuses and Fuseholders . . . . 240.60(C)

    Circuit Breakers . . . . 240.83(C)

INTERSYSTEM BONDING TERMINATION

Definition of . . . . Art. 100

Communication Circuits . . . . .800.100(B)

CATV Systems .820.100(B)

Installation 250.94

Network Powered Broadband Communication Systems. . . . .
. . . . .830.100(B)

Radio and Television Equipment . . . . 810.21(F)

INTRINSICALLY SAFE SYSTEMS . . . . Art. 504

Bonding 504.60

Conductors, Separation of 504.30

Definitions 504.2

Enclosures. . . . . 504.10(C)

Equipment Listed 504.4

Equipment Installation 504.10

Grounding 504.50

Hazardous (Classified) Locations Protection Technique. . . . .
. . . . 500.7(E)

    Class I, Zone 0, 1, and 2 Locations . . . . 505.8(C)

Identification 504.80

    Color Coding . . . . 504.80(C)

    Terminals. 504.80(A)

    Wiring . . . . 504.80(B)

Sealing 504.70

Separation. 504.30

    From Different Intrinsically Safe Circuit Conductors . . . . .
. . . . 504.30(B)

    From Grounded Metal . . . . 504.30(C)

    From Nonintrinsically Safe Circuit Conductors . . 504.30(A)

Simple Apparatus

    Control Drawing . . . . 504.10(A)

    Definition . . . . Art. 100

    Enclosures . . . . 504.10(C)

    Installation. . . . . 504.10(D)

    Location . . . . 504.10(B)

Wiring Methods 504.20

INVERTER

Connected to Grounded System . . . . 200.3 Ex

Definition of 690.2

Definition of Multimode Inverter 705.2

Recreation Vehicles 551.32

Used with Fuel Cell Systems . . . . Art. 692

Used with Interconnected Electric Power Production Sources .
. . . . Art. 705

Used with Solar Photovoltaic Systems . . . . Art. 690

Used with Wind Electric Systems . . . . Art. 694

Utility-Interactive, Definition. . . . . Art. 100

IRRIGATION MACHINES . . . . Art. 675

Bonding 675.14

Branch-Circuit Conductors 675.9

Center-Pivot Irrigation Machines . . . . 675 Part II

    Continuous-Current Rating . . . . 675.22(A)

    Equivalent Current Rating 675.22

    Locked-Rotor Current . . . . 675.22(B)

Collector Rings 675.11

Conductors, More Than Three in Raceway or Cable . . . 675.5

Connectors 675.17

Control Panel Marking 675.6

Definitions 675.2

Disconnecting Means

    For Individual Motors and Controllers . . . . 675.8(C)

    Main Controller . . . . 675.8(A)

    Main Disconnecting Means . . . . 675.8(B)

Energy from More Than One Source 675.16

Grounding 675.12

    Methods of. 675.13

Irrigation Cable 675.4

    See (OFFY). . . . .*UL Product Spec*

Irrigation Machines

    Continuous Current Rating . . . . 675.7(A)

    Equivalent Current Ratings 675.7

    Locked-Rotor Current . . . . 675.7(B)

Lightning Protection 675.15

    Grounding Electrode System . . . . 250 Part III

    *See Standard for the Installation of Lightning Protection
Systems, NFPA 780.* . . . . .NFPA 780

Lockable Disconnect. . . . . 675.8(B)

Several Motors on One Branch Circuit 675.10

ISLAND COUNTERTOP RECEPTACLE SPACES . . 210.52(C)(2)

Separate Spaces, Islands . . . . .210.52(C)(4)

ISLANDING, LOSS OF INTERCONNECTED POWER . . . . . .
. . . .**705.40 Info. Note 1**

ISOLATED

Arcing or Suddenly Moving Parts 240.41

Capacitors, Isolating Means, Over 1000 Volts. . . . . 460.24(B)

Conductor Enclosures and Raceways . . . . 250.86 Ex. 3

Definition of (as applied to location). . . . . . . Art. 100 Part I

Electric Snow-Melting and Deicing 426.12

Elevators and Similar Equipment. . . . . 620.5(B)

Equipment Ground, Technical Power System. . . . 640.2 (Def.)

Ground Receptacle, Reduction of Electrical Noise . 250.146(D)

Impedance Heating 426.30

Isolating Means, Equipment Over 1000 Volts. 490.22

Live Parts Guarded Against Accidental Contact . . . 110.27(A)

Motors and Controllers Over 50 Volts. . . . . 430.232(3)

Other Than Service Raceways . . . . 250.86 Ex. 3

Phase Conductors, in Close Proximity. . . . . . . 300.5(I) Ex. 2

Resistors and Reactors. . . . . 470.18(B)

Service Raceways Underground — Metal Elbows . . 250.80 Ex.

Short Sections of Raceway 250.132

Sign and Outline Lighting Parts, Grounding 600.7

Metal Fittings at Swimming Pools, Exempt from Bonding . . .
. . . . .680.26(B)(5)

Water Pipe, Multi-occupancy Buildings . . . . . .250.104(A)(2)

ISOLATED (INSULATED) GROUND RECEPTACLES

Inside Patient Care Vicinity. . . . . 517.16(A)

Outside Patient Care Vicinity. . . . . 517.16(B)

See INSULATED (ISOLATED) GROUND RECEPTACLES . .
. . . . Ferm's Finder

ISOLATED POWER SYSTEMS

Cranes and Hoists Over Class III Locations. . . . . .503.155(A)

Critical Care (Category 1) Patient Space (Optional) . 517.19(F)

Individual Circuits for Certain Critical Branch Equipment. .
. . . . .517.31(C)(2)

System Grounding . . . . 517.19(G)

Wet Locations, Permitted in Lieu of GFCI Protection . . . .
. . . . 517.20(A)

Electrolytic Cells, Portable Equipment. . . . . 668.21(A)

Health Care Facilities 517.160

Impedance Heating Systems 426.31

Induction and Dielectric Heating Equipment 665.5

Swimming Pool Transformers and Power Supplies 680.23(A)(2)

ISOLATING TRANSFORMERS

AC Systems 50 to 1000 Volts Not Required to Be Grounded . .
. . . . 250.21

Crane and Hoist, Using Track As Circuit Conductor . . . . . .
. . . . .610.21(F)(2)

Electrolytic Cells, Portable Equipment . . . . 668.20(B)

Power Supply and Receptacles. . . . . 668.21(A)

Health Care Facility Installations . . . . .517.160(A)(1)

Restriction on Rooms Served . . . . .517.160(A)(4)

Impedance Heating Systems 426.31

Lighting Systems 30 Volts or Less . . . . 411.6(B)

Swimming Pool Use . . . . .680.23(A)(2)

J

JOINTS

Expansion

Busways, Over 1000 Volts, Nominal 368.244

Earth Movement 1000 Volts and Less. . . . . 300.5(J)

Earth Movement Over 1000 Volts, Nominal . . . . 300.50(C

Electric Space Heating Cables in Concrete or Poured

Masonry Floors 424.44

Fixed Electric Heating for Pipelines and Vessels . . . 427.16

Fixed Outdoor Electric Deicing and Snow-Melting. . . . . .
. . . . 426 Part III

Heating Panels & Heating Panel Sets . . . . 424.98(C)

Metal Raceways 250.98

Nonmetallic Auxiliary Gutters 366.44

Nonmetallic Wireways 378.44

Raceways Exposed to Different Temperatures . . . . 300.7(B)

Rigid PVC Conduit

Expansion Characteristics Tables. . . . . Table 352.44

Securing and Supporting, Provisions for 352.30

To Be Provided 352.44

RTRC Conduit. . . . . Table 355.44

Grounding Electrode Conductor . . . . 250.64(C)

Insulating, at Luminaires (Fixtures) . . . . 410.36(D)

Insulation of . . . . 110.14(B)

Strain at, Flexible Cords 400.14

JOISTS (WOOD or METAL)

Air-Handling Space . . . . 300.22(C) Ex.

Armored Cable

Exposed 320.15

J

In Accessible Attics 320.23

Through or Parallel to Framing Members 320.17

Boxes on. 314.23

Cables and Raceways Parallel to . . . . 300.4(D)

Concealed Knob-and-Tube Wiring 394.23

Through or Parallel to Framing Members 394.17

Electric Space-Heating Cables . . . . .424.41(I) & (J)

In Concrete or Poured Masonry Floors. . . . . . 424.44(C)

Holes Through or Notches in 300.4

Nonmetallic-Sheathed Cable . . . . 334.15(C)

Open Wiring

Crossing . . . . 398.15(C)

In Attics 398.23

Through 398.17

JUMPERS, BONDING

Definition of .Art. 100 Part I

Equipment

Attachment .250.102(B)

Definition of . . . . Art. 100

Installation. 250.102(E)

Load Side of Service . . . . 250.102(D)

Material . . . . 250.102(A)

Supply Side of Service. . . . . 250.102(C)

Expansion Joints, Raceways 250.98

Grounding Electrode System . . . . 250.53(C)

Grounding Electrodes 250.50

Grounding-Type Receptacles 250.146

Hazardous (Classified) Locations

Class I Locations 501.30

Class II Locations 502.30

Class III Locations 503.30

Intrinsically Safe Systems 504.60

Zone 0, 1, and 2 Locations 505.25

Zone 20, 21, and 22 Locations 506.25

Health Care Facilities (Patient Care Vicinity)   .517.19(D) & (E)

High-Impedance Grounded Neutral Systems . .250.36(E) & (G)

Intersystem Bonding Termination 250.94

Main

AC Systems (Grounded) 250.28

DC Systems .250.168

Definition . . . . Art. 100

Other Systems 250.94

Piping Systems

Metal Water Piping . . . . .250.104(A)

Other Metal Piping . . . . .250.104(B)

Separately Derived Systems . . . . 250.30(A)(1) & (2)

Service Equipment . . . . 250.92(B)

Service Supplied AC Systems, Wire or Busbar . . 250.24(A)(4)

Structural Metal, Exposed. . . . . 250.104(C)

System Bonding Jumper 250.28

System Bonding Jumper . . . . .250.30(A)(1)

Definition . . . . Art. 100, Part I

JUNCTION AND PULL BOXES . . . . Art. 314

Accessible. 314.29

Accessible after Electric-Discharge and LED Luminaires (Fixtures) Installed

. . . . 410.24(B)

Boxless Devices

See BOXLESS DEVICES . . . . Ferm's Finder

Ceiling-Suspended (Paddle) Fan Support . . . . . . 314.27(C)

Conductors

Entering Boxes (General). . . . . 300.4(G)

Entering Boxes and Conduit Bodies 314.17

From Electrical Nonmetallic Tubing 362.46

From Intermediate Metal Conduit 342.46

From High Density Polyethylene Conduit. 353.46

From Nonmetallic Underground Conduit with Conductors

. . . . 354.46

From Reinforced Thermosetting Resin Conduit . . 355.46

From Rigid Metal Conduit 344.46

From Rigid PVC Conduit 352.46

Conduit Bodies

Cross-sectional Area of. . . . . .314.16(C)(1)

Dimensions of for Pulls. 314.28

Over 1000 Volts. 314.71

General 314.1

Marked Capacity of . . . . .314.16(C)(2)

Number of Conductors in . . . . 314.16(C)

Support of .314.16(C)(2)

Where Required 300.15

Continuity of Metal Enclosures

At Services . . . . 250.92(A)

Boxes 314.4

Electrical Continuity 300.10

Hazardous (Classified) Locations, General. 500.8

Class I Locations 501.30

Class I, Zone 0, 1, and 2 Locations 505.25

Class I, Zone 20, 21, and 22 Locations 506.25

Class II Locations 502.30

Class III Locations 503.30

Intrinsically Safe Systems . . . . .504.50 & .60

In Hazardous (Classified) Locations 250.100

Mechanical Continuity 300.12

Other Enclosures 250.96

Over 250 Volts. 250.97

Covers

Completed Installations 314.25

Compatible with Construction . . . . 314.28(C)

Extensions from . . . . 314.22 Ex.

Manholes . . . . 110.75(D)

Marking of . . . . 110.75(E)

Material 314.41

Over1000 Volts . . . . 314.72(E)

Marking . . . . 314.72(E)

Required 300.31

Suitable for Expected Handling . . . . 314.72(F)

Emergency Systems, Separation of Wiring . . . . . . 700.10(B)

Essential Electrical Systems. Separation of Wiring

Hospitals . . . . 517.31(C)

Nursing Homes . . . . 517.42(D)

Extension Rings

Box Volume Calculations. . . . . 314.16(A)

Exposed Extensions 314.22

Floor Boxes . . . . 314.27(B)

For Cellular Concrete Floor Raceways . . . . . . 372.18(C)

Splices and Taps in 372.56

For Cellular Metal Floor Raceways . . . . 374.18(B)

Splices and Taps in 374.56

For Underfloor Raceways 390.13

Splices and Taps in 390.6

Free Length of Conductors In (General) 300.14

Deicing and Snow-Melting Equipment (Embedded) . . . . .
. . . . 426.22(E)

Deicing and Snow-Melting Equipment (Exposed) 426.23(A)

For Electric Space-Heating Cables . . . . 424.43(B)

Pipeline and Vessel Heating . . . . 427.18(A)

Grounding

See GROUNDING, Boxes . . . . Ferm's Finder

High Voltage Systems, Over 1000 Volts . . . . 314 Part IV

See OVER 1000 VOLTS, NOMINAL. . . . . . Ferm's Finder

Identification of

For Emergency Systems . . . . 700.10(A)

For Intrinsically Safe Systems . . . . 504.80(C)

For Underground Locations 314.29

Luminaire (Fixture) Support 410.30

Weight Limits for Support of Luminaires (Lighting Fixtures)
. . . . .314.27(A) & (B)

Metallic Boxes

Conductors Entering . . . . 314.17(B)

Grounding of

See GROUNDING, Boxes . . . . Ferm's Finder

Sealing Unused Openings . . . . 110.12(A)

Thickness of Metal 314.40

Mounting . . . . 110.13(A)

In Concrete, Tile or Other Noncombustible 314.20

Repairing Noncombustible Surfaces 314.21

Supports 314.23

From Cable Tray Systems . . . . 392.18(G)

Nonmetallic, Permitted 314.3

Grounding Conductors . . . . .250.148(B)

Sealing Unused Openings . . . . 110.12(A)

Support 314.23

Provisions for 314.43

Number of Conductors in 314.16

Required 300.15

Round Boxes (Not Permitted) 314.2

Sizing of Pull & Junction Boxes (Standard) 314.16

Dimensions 314.28

Over 1000 Volts 314.71

Unused Openings (Closed) . . . . 110.12(A)

Volume Required Per Conductor . . . . Table 314.16(B)

Warning Sign "Danger - High Voltage - Keep Out" . 314.72(E)

Wet Locations

General 300.6

Prevent Moisture Entering or Accumulating. 314.15

See SWIMMING POOLS . . . . Ferm's Finder

See (BGUZ) . . . . .UL Product Spec

K

K

KITCHENS

Appliance Load 220.53

Arc-Fault Circuit-Interrupter Protection . . . . 210.12(A)

Branch Circuits Required in Dwelling Units . . . .210.11(C)(1)

   Mobile and Manufactured Homes . . . . 550.12(B)

   Recreational Vehicles 551.42

   Park Trailers 552.46

Connection of

   Dishwasher and Trash Compactor . . . . . . .422.16(B)(2)

   Waste Disposal . . . . .422.16(B)(1)

Definition of . . . . Art. 100, Part I

Disconnection of Appliances in . . . . 422 Part III

GFCI Protection of Receptacle Outlets in Dwelling Units . . .
. . . . .210.8(A)

   Dishwasher Outlet . . . . .210.8(D)

   Mobile and Manufactured Homes. . . . . 550.13(B)

   Park Trailers . . . . 552.41(C)

   Recreational Vehicles . . . . 551.41(C)

GFCI Protection of Receptacle Outlets Other Than

   Dwelling Units . . . . 210.8(B)(2)

Grounding of Appliances in Cord- and Plug-Connected

   Fastened in Place or Connected by Permanent Wiring . . . .
. . . . .250.114

      Methods. 250.110

      Ranges 250.140

      Specific Equipment 250.112

Installation of Appliances . . . . 422 Part II

Kitchen Equipment Load, Other Than Dwelling Units . 220.56

Lighting Outlet, Wall Switch-Controlled in . . . . 210.70(A)(1)

Receptacle Outlets Required for

   Countertops . . . . 210.52(C)

      Position . . . . 406.5(E)

   General Provisions . . . . 210.52(A)

   Small Appliances . . . . 210.52(B)

      Mobile and Manufactured Homes . . . . 550.12(B)

      Park Trailers 552.41

      Recreational Vehicles 551.41

Range Load Household 220.55

Sinks. . . . . 210.8(A)(7)

Small Appliance Branch-Circuit Load, Dwelling Unit . . . . . .
. . . . 220.52(A)

   Mobile and Manufactured Homes . . . . . . .550.18(A)(2)

KNIFE SWITCHES

600 to 1000 Volts 404.13

Damp or Wet Locations 404.4

Enclosures . . . . 404.3(A)

Mounting Height 404.8

Position and Connection of 404.6

Ratings

   General-Use . . . . 404.13(C)

   Isolating Switches . . . . 404.13(A)

   Motor-Circuit . . . . 404.13(D)

   To Interrupt Current . . . . 404.13(B)

See SWITCHES . . . . Ferm's Finder

KNOB-&-TUBE WIRING (CONCEALED) . . . . Art. 394

Boxes, Wiring Entering

   Metal Boxes . . . . 314.17(B)

   Nonmetallic Boxes . . . . 314.17(C)

Clearance

   General . . . . 394.19(A)

   Limited Conductor Space . . . . 394.19(B)

   Piping, Exposed Conductors . . . . 394.19(C)

Conductor Supports . . . . 394.30(A)

Conductors 394.104

Definition of 394.2

In Unfinished Attic and Roof Spaces 394.23

Insulation in Area of . . . . .394.12(5)

Splices 394.56

Through Walls, Floors, etc. 394.17

Tie Wires . . . . 394.30(B)

Uses Not Permitted 394.12

Uses Permitted 394.10

KNOCKOUTS

Concentric, Eccentric, or Oversized, Bonding Around

   Bonding at Service . . . . 250.92(B)

   Over 250 Volts. . . . . 250.97 Ex.

Grommets Required At Metal Studs . . . . 300.4(B)(1)

Openings to Be Closed

   General . . . . 110.12(A)

   In Cabinet, Cutout Boxes and Meter Socket Enclosure . . . .
. . . . 312.5(A)

Through Which Conductors Enter. . . . . 314.17(A)

L

LABELED (Definition of) . . . . Art. 100 Part I

Manufactured and Mobile Homes

Manufactured Home Service Equipment . . . . . .550.32(B)(7)

Mobile Home Service Equipment, 125/250-Volt Receptacle . .
. . . . 550.32(G)

Outside Heating/Air-Conditioning Equipment. . . . 550.20(B)

Park Trailers

    Outside Heating/Air-Conditioning Equipment . . 552.59(B)

    Prewired for Air-Conditioning . . . . .552.48(P)(3)

    Service Equipment . . . . 552.44(D)

Recreational Vehicles

    Prewired for Air-Conditioning . . . . 551.47(Q)(3)

    Prewired for Generator . . . . .551.47(R)(4)

    Service Equipment . . . . 551.46(D)

LABELS

Cable Trays Containing Conductors Over 600 Volts   392.18(H)

    Industrial Establishments . . . . 392.18(H) Ex.

Cable Trays, Service Conductors 230.44

Circuit Directories 110.22

Direct-Current Ground-Fault Detection 250.167

Elevators, Etc.. 620.3(A)

Equipment Grounding Conductors 250.119

Field-Applied Hazard . . . . 110.21(B)

Fixed Electric Space-Heating Equipment . . . . . . 424.92(C)

Flexible Cords 400.20

In Panelboards . . . . 408.4(A)

    Source of Supply. . . . . 408.4(B)

Induction and Dielectric Heating Equipment 665.25

Intrinsically Safe Systems, Identification. 504.80

Manufacturer's Markings . . . . 110.21(A)

Recreational Vehicles

    Air-Conditioning, Pre-Wring . . . . 551.47(Q)

    Branch Circuits, Pre-Wiring . . . . 551.47(S)

    Designed . . . . 551.4(C)

    Electrical Entrance . . . . 551.46(D)

    Generator, Pre-Wiring . . . . 551.47(R)

Service, Supply Side 230.82

Signs, Markings and Listings . . . . 600.4(C) and (D)

Solar Photovoltaic Systems

    Direct Current on or Inside a Building . . . . . . 690.31(G)

    Rapid Shutdown Systems. . . . . 690.56(C)

See ANSI Z535.4-2011, Product Safety Signs and Labels . ANSI
. . . . Z535.5

LABEL ON CABLE TRAYS

Containing Conductors Rated Over 600 Volts . . . . 392.18(H)

Where Service and Non-Service Conductors are Present . . . .
. . . . 230.44 Ex.

LACQUERS AND PAINTS

Application of . . . . Art. 516

Classification of Atmospheres . . . . 500.6(B)

Class I Locations, General . . . . 500.5(B)

    Requirements in. . . . . Art. 501

    Zone 0, 1, and 2 Locations . . . . Art. 505

To Be Removed for Grounding Continuity 250.12

Not to Contaminate Equipment, Integrity of Equipment . . . .
. . . . 110.12(B)

LAMPHOLDERS . . . . 410 Parts VIII & XI

Circuits and Equipment, at Less Than 50 Volts 720.5

Combustible Materials, near 410.97

Cord-Connected . . . . 410.62(A)

Damp or Wet Locations 410.96

Double-Pole Switched 410.93

Heavy Duty (Rating of) . . . . 210.21(A)

Infrared Lamp Industrial Heating Appliances 425.14

Mogul Base 410.103

Outdoor 225.24

Outlet Boxes . . . . 314.27(A)

Over Combustible Material, Unswitched Type 410.12

Pendant

    Bathtub and Shower Areas . . . . 410.10(D)

    Not Permitted in Clothes Closets . . . . 410.16(B)

    Not Permitted in Theater Dressing Rooms 520.71

Permissible on 30-ampere Branch Circuits . . . . . . 210.23(B)

Permissible on 40- and 50-ampere Branch Circuits . 210.23(C)

Raceway Supported Enclosures for. . . . . 314.23(F)

Screw Shell Type 410.90

Voltage Limitations . . . . 210.6(B)(C)(D)

**LARGE-SCALE PHOTOVOLTAIC (PV) ELECTRIC POWER PRO-
DUCTION FACILITY** . . . . **Art. 691**

Applicable PV Systems (no less than 5000 kW) 691.1

Arc-Fault Mitigation 691.10

Conformance of Construction to Engineered Design . . 691.7

Definitions. 691.2

L

Direct Current Operating Voltage 691.8

Disconnection of Photovoltaic Equipment. 691.9

Engineered Design 691.6

Equipment Approval 691.5

Fence Grounding 691.11

Special Requirements. 691.4

LAUNDRY RECEPTACLE OUTLETS, DWELLINGS

Arc-Fault Circuit-Interrupter Protection . . . . 210.12(A)

Branch-Circuit Load. . . . . 220.52(B)

Mobile and Manufactured Homes. . . . . 550.18(A)(3)

Laundry Area, Definition of 550.2

Receptacles, GFCI Protected . . . . 210.8(A)(10)

Required Branch Circuit . . . . .210.11(C)(2)

Mobile and Manufactured Homes . . . . 550.12(C)

Requirement for Receptacle . . . . 210.52(F)

Mobile and Manufactured Homes . . . . 550.13(D)(7)

Within 6 ft of Appliance . . . . 210.50(C)

LEAKAGE-CURRENT DETECTOR-INTERRUPTER (LCDI) . . . .
. . . .**440.65**

Definition of 440.2

Room Air Conditioners 440.65

LED SIGN ILLUMINATION SYSTEM. 600.33

Definition of 600.2

LEGALLY REQUIRED STANDBY SYSTEMS . . . . Art. 701

Batteries. . . . . 701.12(A)

Capacity and Rating 701.4

Circuit Wiring . . . . 701 Part II

Definition of 701.2

Ground-Fault Protection of Equipment (Not Required) . . . . . .
. . . . 701.26

Maintenance . . . . 701.3(C)

Overcurrent Protection . . . . 701 Part IV

Accessible to Authorized Persons Only 701.25

Selective Coordination 701.27

Signals 701.6

Ground-Fault Indication . . . . 701.6(D)

Signs 701.7

Sources of Power . . . . 701 Part III

Tests and Maintenance 701.3

Transfer Equipment

Electrically Operated, Mechanically Held 701.5

Listing . . . . 701.5(C)

Short-Circuit Current Rating (documented) . . . . 701.5(D)

LENGTHS

Busways

Maximum of Cord or Cable from Plug-In Device368.56(B)(2)

Maximum, Reduction without Overcurrent Device 368.17(B)

Conduit Bodies. . . . . 314.28(A)

Conduit Bodies and Handhole Enclosures, Over 1000 Volts
. . . . 314.71

Conduit and Tubing

Note: *See* article for the specific type of conduit or tubing

Flexible Cord, Specific Appliances . . . . 422.16(B)

Free Conductor at Outlets, Junctions, and Switches . . . 300.14

Deicing and Snow-Melting, Nonheating Leads . . 426.23(A)

Nonheating Leads of Resistance Elements, Pipelines and
Vessels . . . . 427.18(A)

Nonheating Leads of Space-Heating Cable . .424.43(B) & (C)

Pull and Junction Boxes. 314.28

Over 1000 Volts, Nominal 314.71

Space-Heating Cable, Nonheating Leads 424.34

Taps

Branch Circuit . . . . 210.19(A)(4) Ex. 1

Feeder . . . . 240.21(B)

Motor Feeders 430.28

Single Motor . . . . .430.53(D)(2)&(3)

Supervised Industrial Installations . . . . 240 Part VIII

Transformer Secondary Conductors . . . . 240.21(C)

LIFE SAFETY BRANCH

Definition of 517.2

Essential Electrical Systems

Hospitals 517.33

Separation from Other Circuits. . . . . .517.31(C)(1)

Nursing Homes and Limited Care Facilities 517.42

Separation from Other Circuits. . . . . 517.42(D)

LIFE SUPPORT EQUIPMENT, ELECTRICAL . . . . . 517.45(B)

Defined 517.2

Essential Electrical Systems

Hospitals and Health Care Facilities 517.29

Nursing Homes and Limited Care Facilities 517.45

Ground-Fault Protection 517.17

LIGHTING

Airfield Lighting Cable . . . . 310.10(F)Ex. 2

Branch Circuits, Calculations of Loads 220.12

    Inductive and LED Loads . . . . 220.18(B)

    See CALCULATIONS . . . . Ferm's Finder

Cove 410.18

Crawl Spaces-GFCI Protection . . . . 210.8(E)

Decorative 410.160

Demand Factors 220.42

    See DEMAND FACTORS . . . . Ferm's Finder

Electric Discharge Lighting

    Connection of Luminaires 410.24

    Cord-Connected . . . . 410.62(C)

    Definition . . . . Art. 100

    Hazardous (Classified) Locations

        Class I, Div. 2 . . . . 501.130(B)(6)

        Class II, Div. 2 . . . . 502.130(B)(5)

    Lamp Auxiliary Equipment 410.104

Energy Code, Designed and Constructed . . . . . . 220.12 Ex.

Feeders, Calculation of Loads 220.42

    Show Window and Track Lighting 220.43

Festoon Lighting

    Conductor Size . . . . 225.6(B)

    Definition . . . . Art. 100 Part I

    Portable Stage Equipment 520.65

Fixtures *See* LUMINAIRES . . . . Ferm's Finder

LED Lighting

    Connection of Luminaires 410.24

    Cord Connected . . . . 410.62(C)

Lighting Assembly

    Cord-and-Plug Connected . . . . 680.33(A)(B)

        Definition 680.2

    Through-Wall . . . . 680.23(E)

        Definition 680.2

Lighting Outlets

    All Occupancies . . . . 210.70(C)

    Crawl Spaces . . . . 210.8(E)

    Definition . . . . Art. 100 Part I

    Dwelling-Type Occupancies . . . . 210.70(A)

    Emergency Systems . . . . Art. 700

    Equipment Over 1000 Volts, Nominal . . . . . . 110.34(D)

    Guest Rooms or Guest Suites . . . . 210.70(B)

    Heating, Air-Conditioning and Refrigeration Equipment . . . . 210.70(C)

    Motor Control Centers . . . . 110.26(D)

    Permanently Installed Pool Locations . . . . 680.22(B)

    Service Equipment . . . . 110.26(D)

    Spa and Hot Tub Locations . . . . 680.43(B)

    Switchboards & Panelboards . . . . 110.26(D)

    See Life Safety Code, NFPA 101 . . . . NFPA 101

Loads for Specified Occupancies 220.12

LIGHTING SYSTEMS, LOW VOLTAGE . . . . Art. 411

Branch Circuit 411.7

Class 2 Power Source (Connected to) 411.1

Definition 411.3

Hazardous, (Classified) Locations 411.8

Listing Required 411.4

Location Requirements 411.5

Rating 411.3

Scope 411.1

Secondary Circuits

    Bare Conductors . . . . 411.6(C)

    Insulated Conductors . . . . 411.6(D)

    Isolating Transformer Required . . . . 411.6(B)

    Not to Be Grounded . . . . 411.6(A)

    Pools, Spas, and Fountains — Horizontal Clearance 411.5(B)

    Walls, Floors, and Ceilings (Conductors Installed In) . . . . 411.5(A)

LIGHTING TRACK . . . . 410 Part XIV

Calculated Load for . . . . 220.43(B)

Connected Load . . . . 410.151(B)

Construction Requirements . . . . 410.155(A)

Definition . . . . Art. 100

Fastening 410.154

Grounding . . . . 410.155(B)

Heavy-Duty Track 410.153

Installation . . . . 410.151(A)

Locations Not Permitted . . . . 410.151(C)

Support . . . . 410.151(D)

See (IFFR) . . . . *UL Product Spec*

LIGHTNING PROTECTION SYSTEM (GROUND TERMINALS)

Bonding to Grounding Electrode System 250.106

Irrigation Machines 675.15

Separation of Communications Wires 800.53

Use of Strike Termination Devices 250.60

See Standard for the Installation of Lightning Protection Systems . . . . NFPA 780

L

LIGHTNING, SURGE ARRESTERS . . . . **Art. 280**
  Antenna Discharge Units Receiving Stations 810.20
  Antenna Discharge Units Transmitting Stations 810.5728
  Circuits Requiring Primary Protectors
    Communication Circuits . . . . 800.90(A)
      General Requirements for Protective Devices   800 Part III
      Installation of Conductors 800.50
    Network-Powered Broadband Systems 830.90
      Grounding Methods . . . . 830 Part IV
      Premises-Powered Broadband Communications
    Systems 840.90
        Grounding Methods . . . . 840 Part IV
  Class I, Division 1 and 2 . . . . 501.35
  Class II, Division 1 and 2 . . . . 502.35
  Community Antenna TV . . . . 820 Part III
  Connection of . . . . 280 Part III
  Definition . . . . Art. 100 Part 1
  Grounding Electrode Conductor in Metal Enclosures . . 280.25
  Installation . . . . 280 Part II
  Number Required 280.3
  Selection of 280.4
  Services Over 1000 Volts 230.209
  See Standard for the Installation of Lightning Protection Systems,
  NFPA 780 . . . . NFPA 780
  See (OVGR) . . . .*UL Product Spec*
  See . . . . *Soares Book on Grounding and Bonding*

LIMITED ACCESS WORKING SPACE . . . . **110.26(A)(4)**

LIMITED CARE FACILITY
  Definition of 517.2
  Essential Electrical System 517.40
  Wiring and Protection . . . . 517 Part II

LIMITED POWER (LP) CABLES . . . . **725.179(I)**
  Transmission of Power and Data . . . . .725.144(B)

LINE ISOLATION MONITOR . . . .**517.160(B)**
  Definition 517.2
  See(OWLS) . . . .*UL Product Spec*

LIQUIDTIGHT FLEXIBLE METAL CONDUIT . . . . **Art. 350**
  Angle Connectors (Not Concealed) 350.42
  Bends 350.24
    Number of 350.26
  Bonding

    Equipment Bonding Jumper 350.60
    In Hazardous (Classified) Locations 250.100
    Required If Service Raceway . . . . .230.43(15)
    Where Used As Equipment Grounding Conductor250.118(6)
  Definition of 350.2
  Fittings 350.6
  Grounding .250.118(6)
    Permitted As Grounding Means 350.60
      Listing 350.6
  Maximum and Minimum Sizes 350.20
  Number of Wires in, General 350.22
    Number of Wires in 3/8" Size . . . . 350.22(B)
    Same Size Conductors, Compact . . . .
     . . . . Informative Annex C, Table C7A
    Same Size, in . . . . Informative Annex C, Table C7
  Support of 3/8 in. Size . . . . 350.20(A) Ex.
  Trimming (Rough Edges) 350.28
  6 ft. Maximum Length . . . . . . 350.30(A) Ex. No. 3 and 4
  Elevators, Dumbwaiters, Escalators, etc. . . . . .620.21(A)(1)
  Enclosing Motor Leads . . . . .430.245(B)
  Uses Not Permitted 350.12
  Uses Permitted 350.10
    As Service and Feeders for Floating Buildings . . . . 553.7(B)
    As Service Entrance . . . . .230.43(15)
  See (DXHR) . . . .*UL Product Spec*

LIQUIDTIGHT FLEXIBLE NONMETALLIC CONDUIT . **Art. 356**
  Angle Connectors (Not Concealed) 356.42
  Bends 356.24
    Number of 356.26
  Definitions
    Type LFNC-A . . . . 356.2(1)
    Type LFNC-B . . . . 356.2(2)
    Type LFNC-C . . . . 356.2(3)
  Encasement in Concrete . . . . 356.10(7)
  Equipment Grounding 356.60
  Hazardous Location Installation . . . . 356.12(4)
  Listing 356.6
  Maximum and Minimum Size 356.20
  Number of Wires in, General 356.22
    Type LFNC-A
      Same Size Conductors, Compact . . . .
       . . . . Informative Annex C, Table C6(A)
      Same Size, in . . . . Informative Annex C, Table C6

Type LFNC-B

    Same Size Conductors, Compact . . . .
. . . . Informative Annex C, Table C5(A)

    Same Size, in . . . . Informative Annex C, Table C5

Type LFNC-C

    Manufacturer's information on internal area will have to be
used to apply percent of cross-sectional fill area using . .
. . . . Chapter 9 Table 1

Securing and Support 356.30

Uses Not Permitted 356.12

Uses Permitted 356.10

    As Service Entrance . . . . 230.43(16)

    As Services and Feeders for Floating Buildings . . . 553.7(B)

    Class I, Division 2 Locations . . . . 501.10(B)(2)(4)

    Class II, Division 1 & 2 Locations . . . .
. . . . 502.10(A)(2)(3) and (B)(2)

    Class III, Division 1 & 2 Locations . . . . . 503.10(A)(3)(3)

    Elevators, Dumbwaiters, Escalators, etc. 620.21

    Lengths Over 1.8 m (6 ft.) for Type LFNC-B . . . . .356.10(5)

    Neon Secondary Conductors Over 1000 Volts . . . .
. . . . .600.32(A)(1)

See (DXOQ) . . . . *UL Product Spec*

LISTED

Armored Cable: Type AC 320.6

Assembly Type Cord . . . . 400.10(A)(11)

Audio System Equipment Near Bodies of Water . . . 640.10(B)

Circuit Breakers for SWD Duty . . . . 240.83(D)

Circuit Breakers for HID Duty . . . . 240.83(D)

Definition of . . . . Art. 100

Electrical Metallic Tubing 358.6

Electrical Nonmetallic Tubing 362.6

Electric Discharge Lighting Systems of More Than 1000 Volts .
. . . . .410.140(A)

Electric Signs and Outline Lighting 600.3

Electric Vehicle Charging Systems 625.5

Electrified Truck Parking Spaces, Various Equipment . Art. 626

Electrodes . . . . .250.52(A)(5)(b)

Enforcement of Code 90.4

    Approval 110.2

Examination . . . . 110.3(A)

    Installation and Use . . . . 110.3(B)

Examination of Equipment for Safety 90.7

Extension Cord Sets . . . . 240.5(B)(3)

Field Assembled Extension Cord Sets . . . . 240.5(B)(4)

Fixed Electric Space-Heating Equipment 424.6

Flat Conductor Cable 324.6

Flexible Metal Conduit 348.6

    For Grounding . . . . 250.118(5)

    Flexible Metallic Tubing 360.6

    Fittings for Grounding . . . . 250.118(7)

    Fuel Cell Systems 692.6

High Density Polyethylene Conduit 353.6

Intermediate Metal Conduit 342.6

Lighting Systems Operating at 30 Volts or Less 411.3

Liquidtight Flexible Metal Conduit 350.6

    For Grounding . . . . 250.118(6)

        Liquidtight Flexible Nonmetallic Conduit 356.6

        Luminaires as Raceways . . . . 410.64(A)

Luminaires and Lampholders 410.6

Manufactured Wiring Systems 604.6

Mobile Homes . . . . 550.4(D)

Nonmetallic Auxiliary Gutters 366.6

Nonmetallic Extensions 382.6

Nonmetallic-Sheathed Cable 334.6

Nonmetallic Underground Conduit with Conductors . . . 354.6

Nonmetallic Wireways 378.6

Optical Fiber Cables 770.179

Other Listed Electrodes — Chemical, Enhanced . . . .
. . . . .250.52(A)(6)

Panelboards, Maximum Number of Overcurrent Devices . . .
. . . . 408.54

Reinforced Thermosetting Resin Conduit 355.6

Rigid Metal Conduit 344.6

Rigid Polyvinyl Chloride Conduit 352.6

Single Conductor Cables in Cable Trays . . . . 392.10(B)(1)(a)

Solar Photovoltaic Systems

    General Requirements . . . . 690.4(B)

    Over 1000 Volts 691.5

Storage Batteries (and Equipment) 480.3

Strut-Type Channel Raceway 384.6

Surface Metal Raceways 386.6

Surface Nonmetallic Raceways 388.6

Swimming Pool Double Insulated Pumps . . . . 680.21(B)

Underground Feeder and Branch-Circuit Cable 340.6

Wind Electric Systems . . . . 694.7(A)(B)

LISTED & MARKED — ZONE LOCATIONS

Class I Locations 501.5

L

Class I, Zone 0, 1, and 2, General 505.9

Class I, Zone 0 . . . . 505.20(A)

Class I, Zone 1 . . . . 505.20(B)

Class I, Zone 2 . . . . 505.20(C)

Class II Locations 502.6

Class II, Zone 20, 21, and 22, General 506.9

    Zone 20. . . . . 506.20(A)

    Zone 21. . . . . 506.20(B)

    Zone 22. . . . . 506.20(C)

Class III Locations 503.6

LIVE PARTS

Appliances 422.4

Capacitors . . . . 460.2(B)

Definition of . . . . Art. 100 Part I

Equipment, Specific, Over 1000 Volts . . . . 490 Part III

Exposed 110.26

Generators 445.14

Guarding 110.27

Hazardous (Classified) Locations

    Class I, Division 1 & 2 . . . . 501.25

    Class II, Division 1 & 2 . . . . 502.25

    Class III, Division 1 & 2 . . . . 503.25

Luminaires, Lampholders, and Lamps 410.5

Lighting Systems, Electric Discharge

    1000 Volts or Less . . . . 410 Part XII

    More than 1000 Volts . . . . 410 Part XIII

Motion Picture and Television Studios, in . . . . . . 530.15(A)

Motors and Controllers . . . . Art. 430 Part XII

Over 1000 Volts, Work Space and Guarding . 110.34(A)(D)(E)

    Outdoor Installations . . . . 110.31(C)

Theaters, in 520.7

Transformers, Guarding . . . . 450.8(C)

LOADS

Appliances, Household Cooking 220.55

Branch Circuits

    Calculations . . . . Art. 220

    Continuous Loads on . . . . 210.20(A)

    Maximum 220.18

    Permissible 210.23

    Summary of . . . . Table 210.24

Continuous (Definition of) . . . . Art. 100 Part I

    Branch Circuits, on . . . . 210.20(A)

Feeders 215.3

Service-Entrance Conductors . . . . 230.42(A)

See CONTINUOUS LOAD . . . . Ferm's Finder

Demand

    Appliances, 4 or More, Dwelling Units 220.53

    Clothes Dryers 220.54

    Electric Heating 220.51

    General Lighting 220.42

    Household Cooking Appliances 220.55

    Marinas and Boatyards 555.12

    Mobile Homes 550.31

    Motors 430.26

    Receptacles, Other Than Dwellings . . . . 220.14(I)

    Recreational Vehicles 551.73

    Stage Set Lighting 530.19

    Use of Optional Calculations . . . . 220 Part IV

    See DEMAND FACTORS . . . . Ferm's Finder

Electric Cooking Appliances in Dwellings and Household Cooking

Appliances Used in Instructional Programs 220.55

Electric Vehicle . . . . Art. 625

    Other Applicable Articles . . . . Table 220.3

Farm . . . . 220 Part V

Feeder . . . . 220 Part III

Household Cooking Appliances Used in Institutional Programs

. . . . 220.14(B)

Inductive

    Lighting . . . . 220.18(B)

    Signs, Disconnects . . . . 600.6(B)

    Switches, Snap Switch Ratings 404.14

    See NONLINEAR LOADS . . . . Ferm's Finder

        Kitchen Equipment, Other Than Dwelling Units . . 220.56

Laundry, Dwellings . . . . 220.52(B)

Lighting, Energy Code . . . . 220.12 Ex.

Marinas and Boatyards 555.12

Mobile Home Parks 550.31

Mobile Homes 550.18

Motors, Conductors . . . . 430 Part II

Motor Outlets . . . . 220.14(C)

Nonlinear (Definition of) . . . . Art. 100 Part I

    See NONLINEAR LOADS . . . . Ferm's Finder

Other Loads, All Occupancies 220.14

    Banks and Office Buildings . . . . 220.14(K)

    Dwelling Occupancies . . . . 220.14(J)

Electric Dryers & Electric Cooking Appliances in Dwellings and Household Cooking Appliances Used in Instructional Programs . . . . 220.14(B)

Fixed Multioutlet Assemblies . . . . 220.14(H)

Heavy-Duty Lampholders . . . . 220.14(E)

Luminaires . . . . 220.14(D)

Motor Outlets . . . . 220.14(C)

Other Outlets . . . . 220.14(L)

Receptacle Outlets. . . . . 220.14(I)

Show Windows . . . . 220.14(G)

Sign and Outline Lighting . . . . 220.14(F)

Specific Appliances or Loads . . . . 220.14(A)

Park Trailers 552.47

Permissible

Branch Circuits 210.22

Multiple-Outlet Branch Circuits. 210.23

Recreational Vehicle Parks 551.73

Small Appliances, Dwellings . . . . 220.52(A)

Specific Appliances or Loads . . . . 220.14(A)

Stage Equipment 520.41

LOAD FACTOR . . . . *See* **Informative Annex B**
(For ampacities calculated under engineering supervision)

Application of Tables. . . . Informative Annex B, 310.15(B)(2)

Criteria Modifications . . . Informative Annex B, 310.15(B)(3)

Examples Showing Use of Figure B-310.15(B)(2)(1) . . . . .Informative Annex B, 310.15(B)(7)

Interpolation Chart . . . . .Fig. B., 310.15(B)(2)(1)

See Load Factor. . . . . *Ferm's Charts and Formulas*

LOCKABLE DISCONNECTING MEANS **110.25**

Air-Conditioning and Refrigerating Equipment 440.14

Appliances . . . . 422.31(B)

Carnivals, Circuses, Fairs and Similar Events

Rides, Tents, Concessions 525.21

Services 525.10

Cranes and Hoists . . . . 610.31 and 610.32

Electric-Discharge Lighting, More than 1000 Volts . . . . .410.141(B)

Electric Vehicle Charging System 625.43

Electrically Driven or Controlled Irrigation Machines . . . . 675.8(B)

Electrified Truck Parking Spaces

Parking Space . . . . 626.24(C)

Supply Wiring . . . . 626.22(D)

Transport Refrigerated Units. 626.31

Elevators, etc.

Car Light, Receptacle(s), and Ventilation Disconnecting Means 620.53

Disconnects, General 620.51

Heating and Air-Conditioning Disconnecting Means 620.54

Utilization Equipment Disconnecting Means 620.55

Equipment Over 1000 Volts, Circuit Breakers 490.46

Equipment Over 1000 Volts, Interrupter Switches 490.44

Feeder Disconnecting Means . . . . 225.52(C)

Fire Pumps 695.4

Fixed Electric Space-Heating Equipment . . 424.19(A) and (B)

Fixed Outdoor Electric Deicing and Snow-Melting Equipment . . . . 426.51(A) and (D)

Generators 445.18

Induction and Dielectric Heating Equipment. 665.12

Motors. . . . . 430.102(A) and (B)

Motors, Over 1000 Volts. 430.227

Motors with More Than One Source of Power 430.113

Outdoor Lamps. 225.25

Sensitive Electronic Equipment, Lighting Equipment . . . . 647.8(A)

Signs . . . . 600.6(A)

Transfer Equipment 702.5

Transformers 450.14

LOCKER ROOMS, GFCI PROTECTION . . . . **210.8(B)(7)**

LOCKNUTS (DOUBLE)

Bonding At Service, Not Permitted for . . . . 250.92(B)

Bonding Over 250 Volts to Ground 250.97

Continuity of Metal Raceways 300.10

Hazardous Areas (Bonding), Not Permitted for 250.100

Class I Locations . . . . 501.30(A)

Class II Locations . . . . 502.30(A)

Class III Locations . . . . 503.30(A)

Intrinsically Safe Systems . . . . 504.60(A)

Zone 0, 1, and 2 Locations . . . . 505.25(A)

Zone 20, 21, and 22 Locations . . . . 506.25(A)

Mobile Homes . . . . 550.15(F)

Park Trailers . . . . 552.48(B)

Recreational Vehicles . . . . 551.47(B)

Under Insulating Bushings . . . . 300.4(G)

L

LOW-VOLTAGE FIXED ELECTRIC SPACE-HEATING EQUIPMENT
Branch Circuits 424.104

Energy Sources 424.101

Installation. 424.103

Listed Equipment 424.102

Scope 424.100

LOW VOLTAGE LIGHTING SYSTEMS . . . . Art. 411
(Note: operating at no more than 30 volts ac or 60 volts dc- see 411.1 Scope)
Branch Circuit 411.7

Class 2 Power Source (Connected to) 411.1

Hazardous, (Classified) Locations 411.8

Listing Required 411.4

Location Requirements 411.5

Pools, Spas, and Fountains — Horizontal Clearance . 411.5(B)

Rating 411.3

Scope 411.1

Secondary Circuits

Bare Conductors . . . . 411.6(C)

Insulated Conductors . . . . 411.6(D)

Isolating Transformer Required . . . . 411.6(B)

Not to Be Grounded . . . . 411.6(A)

Pools, Spas, and Fountains — Horizontal Clearance . 411.5(B)

Walls, Floors, and Ceilings (Conductors Installed In) . . . . . .
. . . . 411.5(A)

LOW-VOLTAGE SUSPENDED CEILING POWER DISTRIBUTION SYSTEMS
Circuits not to be Grounded . . . . .250.22(6)

Conductor Sizes and Types 393.104

Connections 393.57

Connectors . . . . 393.40(A)

Definitions 393.2

Disconnecting Means 393.21

Enclosures . . . . 393.40(B)

Grounding 393.60

Installation 393.14

Interconnection of Power Sources . . . . 393.45(B)

Listing Requirements 393.6

Overcurrent Protection . . . . 393.45(A)

Reverse Polarity . . . . 393.45(C)

Scope 393.1

Securing and Supporting 393.30

Splices 393.56

Uses Not Permitted 393.12

Uses Permitted 393.10

LOW-VOLTAGE SYSTEMS
Audio Signal Processing, Amplification & Reproducing. . . . .
. . . . Art. 640

Circuits and Equipment Operating at Less Than 50 Volts . . . .
. . . . Art. 720

Class 1, 2 & 3 Systems . . . . Art. 725

See CLASS 1, 2 & 3 REMOTE CONTROL CIRCUITS. . . .
. . . . Ferm's Finder

Communications Circuits. . . . . Art. 800

See COMMUNICATIONS CIRCUITS . . . . . Ferm's Finder

Community Antenna TV & Radio Distribution Systems . . . .
. . . . Art. 820

See COMMUNITY ANTENNA TV & RADIO DISTRIBU-
TION SYSTEMS. . . . . Ferm's Finder

Different Systems in Same Enclosure

See CONDUCTORS, Different Systems in Same Enclosure .
. . . . Ferm's Finder

Fire Alarm Systems . . . . Art. 760

See FIRE ALARM SYSTEMS. . . . . Ferm's Finder

Grounding, AC Systems Less than 50 Volts . . . . . 250.20(A)

Health Care Facilities, Equipment and Instruments . . . 517.64

Lighting . . . . Art. 411

Motor Control Circuits . . . . 430 Part VI

Network-Powered Broadband Communications Systems . . . .
. . . . Art. 830

Park Trailers . . . . 552 Part II

Premises-Powered Broadband Communications Systems . . .
. . . . Art. 840

Radio & TV Equipment . . . . Art. 810

Recreational Vehicles . . . . 551 Part II

Definition 551.2

LUGS & TERMINAL CONNECTIONS
Aluminum to Copper (Permitted if Listed) 110.14

Connection of Grounding and Bonding Equipment 250.8

Fine Stranded Conductors 110.14

Identification of Wiring Device Terminals

Equipment Grounding Terminals 250.126

Receptacles, Adapters, Connectors, Plugs . . . . 406.10(B)

Grounded Conductor Connections 200.10

No Conductor Larger Than 10 AWG Under a Binding Screw .
. . . . 110.14(A)

Not More Than One Conductor Under a Binding Screw . . . .
. . . . 110.14(A)

Solar Photovoltaic Wiring Systems . . . . . 690.31(E) and (F)

Splices . . . . 110.14(B)

Suitable for the Purpose (Listed) 110.14

　Note: Use oxide inhibitor on aluminum conductor terminations where required.

　　Temperature Limitations . . . . 110.14(C)

See Aluminum Conductor Terminations . . . .
. . . . *Ferm's Charts and Formulas*

See Tightening Torque Information . . . .
. . . . *Ferm's Charts and Formulas*

See (DVYW) . . . .*UL Product Spec*

See (ZMVV) . . . .*UL Product Spec*

LUMINAIRES . . . . **Art. 410**

As a Raceway 410.64

Ballast Type (Electric Discharge and LED)

　1000 Volts or Less . . . . 410 Part XII

　Calculations, Inductive and LED Loads . . . . . . 220.18(B)

　Conductors within 3" of a Ballast Must Be Rated Not Lower Than 90°C 410.68

　　Provision Table 310.104(A) 310.104

　Cord-Connected . . . . .410.62(B) & (C)

　For Signs and Outline Lighting . . . . Art. 600

　Luminaire Mounting 410.136

　More than 1000 Volts . . . . 410 Part XIII

　Thermal Protection . . . . 410.130(E)

　　High-Intensity Discharge Luminaires (Fixtures) . . . . . .
. . . . .410.130(F)

　Voltage Limitations

　　Branch Circuits 210.6

　　Dwellings, Open-Circuit Voltage Exceeding 300 Volts. . .
. . . . .410.135

　　Lighting Equipment Installed Outdoors 225.7

　　Operating 1000 Volts or Less . . . . 410.130(A)

　　Operating More than 1000 Volts . . . . 410.140(B)

　See Ballast Data Charts . . . . . . *Ferm's Charts and Formulas*

Bathtub and Shower Areas . . . . 410.10(D)

Branch-Circuit Ratings to Luminaires . . . 210.19(A)(4) Ex. 1

　Maximum Load 220.18

　Overcurrent Protection. 210.20

　Permissible Loads 210.23

　To Lampholders . . . . 210.21(A)

Breaker Rated "SWD" for Switching Fluorescent . . 240.83(D)

Breaker Rated "HID" for Switching High Intensity Discharge
. . . . 240.83(D)

See (DIVQ) . . . .*UL Product Spec*

Calculations, General . . . . 220.14(D)

　Inductive and LED Loads, Maximum . . . . . . 220.18(B)

Canopies . . . . 410 Part III

Clearance Required

　Bathtubs & Showers . . . . 410.10(D)

　Clothes Closet Light 410.16

　Hot Tubs and Spas, Indoors . . . . 680.43(B)

　Hot Tubs and Spas, Outdoors . . . . 680.22(B)

　Over Combustible Materials 410.12

　Recessed Luminaires, From Combustible Materials . . . . .
. . . . 410.116(A)(1) and (2)

　Recessed Luminaires, From Thermal Insulation .410.116(B)

Clothes Closet (Restrictions) 410.16

Cord-Connected . . . . 410.24(A)

　Adjustable Luminaires . . . . 410.62(B)

　Fountain Luminaires 680.51

　Listed Electric-Discharge and LED Luminaires . . 410.62(C)

　Storable Swimming Pool Luminaires 680.33

　Unit Equipment, Emergency Systems . . . . . . 700.12(F)

　Unit Equipment, Legally Required Standby Systems . . . . .
. . . . 701.12(G)

　See PENDANTS . . . . Ferm's Finder

Covering of Combustible Material at Outlet Boxes . . . 410.23

Crawl Space Outlets

　All Occupancies . . . . 210.70(C)

　Dwelling Units . . . . 210.70(A)

　GFCI Protection . . . . 210.8(E)

Definition (Luminaire) . . . . Art. 100 Part I

Directly Controlled (Emergency Systems) 700.24

Disconnecting Means Required . . . . 410.130(G)

Electric-Discharge Lighting

　See (FIXTURES) LUMINAIRES, Ballast Type . Ferm's Finder

Festoon Lighting

　See FESTOON LIGHTING . . . . Ferm's Finder

(Fixture) Luminaire Wires

　See (FIXTURE) WIRE . . . . Ferm's Finder

　Taps

　　See (FIXTURE) WHIPS . . . . Ferm's Finder

　Whips

　　See (FIXTURE) WHIPS . . . . Ferm's Finder

　　See (ZIPR) . . . .*UL Product Spec*

Flush and Recessed Luminaires . . . . 410 Part X

　Clearance Required 410.116

L

Supports to 410.36

Taps to Junction Box (Whip)

See (FIXTURE) WHIPS . . . . Ferm's Finder

Temperature Limits

Combustible Materials. . . . . 410.115(A)

Conductors in Outlet Boxes. 410.21

Construction of Luminaires. 410.118

Near Combustible Materials 410.11

Where Recessed in Fire-Resistant Material . . .410.115(B)

Grounded (Neutral) Conductor Must Be Connected

Polarization of Luminaires 410.50

Screw Shell Lampholders 410.90

Shell of Screw Shell Lampholders . . . . . 200.10(C) & (D)

Grounding . . . . 250 Part VI

Connected to an Equipment Grounding Conductor . . . . .

. . . . 410.42

Health Care, Patient Care Spaces . . . .517.13(B) Ex. 2 to (3)

Luminaires and Lighting Equipment . . . . 410 Part V

Methods of Equipment Grounding . . . . 250 Part VII

Infrared Heating, Construction. 422.48

Branch-Circuits, 40- and 50-Ampere Rating . 210.23(C)

Branch-Circuit Requirements. . . . . 424.3(A)

Overcurrent Protection . . . . 422.11(C)

Infrared Heating, Installation. 425.14

Lamps Only (No Plug Fuses). 410.90

LED Luminaires, Closets 410.16

Locations . . . . .410 Part II

Aircraft Hangars Class I Locations 513.4

Not Within Class I Locations 513.7

Commercial Garages Class I Locations 511.4

Over Class I Locations. . . . . 511.7(B)

Corrosive. . . . . 410.10(B)

Hazardous (Classified) . . . . Art. 500

Anesthetizing Locations (Above) . . . . 517.61(B)

Anesthetizing Locations (Within) . . . . 517.61(A)

Class I, Division 1 . . . . 501.130(A)

Class I, Division 2 . . . . .501.130(B)

Class I, Zone 0, 1, and 2 Locations . . . . Art. 505

Class II, Division 1 . . . . .502.130(A)(1)

Class II, Division 2 . . . . .502.130(B)

Class III, Division 1 & 2 . . . . .503.130

Zone 20, 21, and 22 Locations 506.20

In Clothes Closets. 410.16

In Ducts & Hoods, Commercial Cooking Hoods Only . . . .

. . . . 410.10(C)

In Ducts for Dust, Loose Stock, or Vapor, Prohibited . . . . .

. . . . 300.22(A)

In Ducts or Plenums for Environmental Air . . . . 300.22(B)

In Show Windows 410.14

In Trees or Other Vegetation. . . . . 410.36(G)

Near Combustible Material 410.11

Other Space for Environmental Air . . . . 300.22(C)

Outdoors 225.7

Lampholders 410.96

Location Below Energized Conductors 225.25

Support by Trees . . . . 410.36(G)

Wet or Damp Locations . . . . 410.10(A)

Over 1000 Volts — Electric Discharge Type . . 410 Part XIII

Over 1000 Volts — Lockable Disconnecting Means. . . . . .

. . . . .410.141(B)

Over Bath Tubs . . . . 410.10(D)

Hydromassage Bathtubs 680.72

Mobile Homes . . . . 550.14(D)

Park Trailers . . . . 552.54(B)

Recreational Vehicles . . . . 551.53(B)

Over Combustible Material 410.11

Spas & Hot Tubs

Indoors . . . . 680.43(B)

Outdoors . . . . 680.22(B)

Outdoors (General) . . . . 680.22(B)

Swimming Pools. . . . . 680.22(B)

Underwater 680.23

Therapeutic Pools & Tubs

General 680.60

Permanently Installed 680.61

Tubs (Hydrotherapeutic Tanks) . . . . 680.62(F)

Underwater 680.23

Wet & Damp. . . . . 410.10(A)

See Hazardous Areas (Defined) . *Ferm's Charts and Formulas*

See HAZARDOUS (CLASSIFIED) LOCATIONS . . . Ferm's Finder

Low-Voltage at Swimming Pools . . . . .680.22(B)(6)

Low Voltage Lighting . . . . Art. 411

Mechanical Strength of Luminaires and Parts . . . 410 Part VII

Medium Base

Branch Circuits . . . . 210.23(A)

Not Permitted in Clothes Closets . . . . 410.16(B)

Medium Base Lampholder

    (Not Over 120 Volts Between Conductors) . . . . . 210.6(B)

Mogul Base Lampholder

    (Not Over 277 Volts to Ground) . . . . 210.6(C)

    Outdoors 225.7

Multiwire Branch Circuits, Disconnects Required 410.130(G)(2)

Not Over 120 Volts (Dwellings) . . . . 210.6(A)

Not Over 600 Volts Between Conductors . . . . 210.6(D)

    Outdoor Lighting 225.7

Outlet Box must be Accessible Under

    Surface-Mounted Electric-Discharge and LED Luminaire . .

    . . . . 410.24(B)

        Suspended Ceiling, Securely Fastened . . . . . 410.36(B)

Outline Lighting . . . . Art. 600

    1000 Volts or Less . . . . 410 Part XII

    More Than 1000 Volts . . . . 410 Part XIII

Overcurrent Protection

    Ampacity of Fixture Wires . . . . Table 402.5

    Branch-Circuit Ratings . . . . .210.19(A)(4)

    For Conductors, Luminaire (Fixture) Wires . . . . 210.20(B)

    For Luminaire (Fixture) Wires 240.5

    For Lampholders . . . . 210.21(A)

    For Rated Ampacity . . . . Table 402.5

    Outlet Device Ratings . . . . 210.21(A)

    Outlet Devices . . . . 210.20(D)

    Permissible Load 210.23

    Protection of Conductors . . . . 240.5(B)(2)

Pendants

    Aircraft Hangars . . . . 513.7(B)

    Commercial Garages . . . . 511.7(A)(2)

    Conductors for Incandescent Lamps 410.54

    Hazardous (Classified) Locations

        Class I, Division 1 Locations . . . . .501.130(A)(3)

        Class I, Division 2 Locations . . . . .501.130(B)(3)

        Class II, Division 1 Locations . . . . .502.130(A)(3)

        Class II, Division 2 Locations . . . . .502.130(B)(4)

        Class III, Division 1 & 2 Locations . . . . . . .503.130(C)

        Hospitals (Hazardous Anesthetizing Locations) . . . . . .

        . . . . 517.61(B)(3) Ex. 2

    Not in Clothes Closets . . . . 410.16(B)

    Not in Theater Dressing Rooms 520.71

    Not Over Bathtubs . . . . 410.10(D)

    Show Windows 410.14

Polarization

Identification of Terminals . . . . 200.10(C) & (D)

Installation of Lampholders 410.90

Of Luminaires (Fixtures) and Lampholders 410.50

Retrofit Kits

    Defined . . . . Art. 100

    Listing Requirements for Luminaires, Lampholders and

    Lamps 410.6

Roof Decking

    Installed Under . . . . 410.10(F)

Signs & Outline Lighting . . . . 600.4(B)

Supports . . . . 410 Part IV

    Boxes for . . . . 314.27(A)

    Ceiling-Suspended (Paddle) Fans, Including Lights . . . . . .

    . . . . 314.27(C)

    Class I, Division 1 Locations . . . . 501.130(A)(4)

    Class II, Division 1 Locations . . . . 502.130(A)(4)

    Swimming Pool Areas . . . . 680.22(B)

Taps

    Armored Cable (Type AC) . . . . 320.30(D)

    Conductor Sizes and Ampacity . . . . .210.19(A)(4)

    Flexible Metal Conduit . . . . 348.30(A) Ex. 3

    Flexible Metallic Tubing . . . . 360.20(A) Ex. 2

    Length of . . . . .410.117(C)

    Liquidtight Flexible Metal or # Conduit . . . 350.30(A) Ex. 3

    Liquidtight Flexible Nonmetallic Conduit . . . . . .356.30(2)

        Size . . . . .356.20(A)(2)

    Manufactured Wiring Systems . . 604.100(A)(1) & (2) Ex. 1

    Metal-Clad Cable (Type MC) . . . . . . 330.30(D)(2) and (3)

    Nonmetallic-Sheathed Cable . . . . .334.30(B)(2)

    Protection . . . . 240.5(B)(2)

Temperature Limits

    On Conductors in Outlet Boxes 410.21

    Special Provisions for Flush and Recessed 410.115

Track Lighting

    See LIGHTING TRACK . . . . Ferm's Finder

Used as a Raceway 410.64

Voltage Limitations

    Not Over 120 Volts Between Conductors (Dwellings) . . . .

    . . . . 210.6(A) & (B)

    Not Over 150 Volts Between Conductors

        Swimming Pool Underwater Lights . . . . . .680.23(A)(4)

        Low Voltage Contact Limit, Definition 680.2

        Fountain Luminaires . . . . 680.51(B)

        GFCI Protection, Relamping . . . . . . .680.23(A)(3)

L

General Compliance . . . . .680.23(A)(8)

Junction Box Location . . . . .680.24(A)(2)

Storable Pool Luminaires . . . . 680.33(A)&(B)

Not Over 277 Volts to Ground . . . . 210.6(C)

Lighting Equipment Outdoors . . . . 225.7(C)

Not Over 600 Volts Between Conductors . . . . . . 210.6(D)

Lighting Equipment Outdoors . . . . 225.7(D)

Wet & Damp Locations . . . . 410.10(A)

To Be Weatherproof Type 410.96

Wire within 3" of a Ballast Must Be Rated Not Lower Than 90°C
. . . . 410.64

Wired Luminaire Sections . . . . 410.137(C)

Wires, Luminaires (Fixture)

See (FIXTURE) LUMINAIRE WIRES . . . . . Ferm's Finder

Wiring of . . . . 410 Part VI

LUMINAIRES FOR POOLS . . . . Art. 680

See SWIMMING POOLS . . . . Ferm's Finder

See (WBDT) . . . . .UL Product Spec

MACHINE ROOMS AND SPACES, ELEVATOR, ESCALATOR, ETC. . . . . 620 Part VIII

Branch Circuit for Lighting and Receptacles 620.23

Flexible Cords Permitted . . . . . 620.21(A)(2)(d)(4)and(3)(e)

Guarding Equipment 620.71

Wiring in .620.21(A)(3)

MACHINE SCREWS (32 THREADS PER INCH)

Covers and Canopies 314.25

Receptacles 406.5

Switches . . . . 404.10(B)

Note: The use of sheet metal screws or other screws not listed for devices, covers or canopies are not allowed.

MACHINE TOOL WIRE

Ampacity of . . . . 310.15(A)(1) Info. Note 2

See Electrical Standard for Industrial Machinery, NFPA 79 . . .
. . . . NFPA 79

See (ZKHZ) . . . . .UL Product Spec

MANDATORY RULES . . . . 90.5(A)

MAIN BONDING JUMPER 250.28

More Than One Service Enclosure . . . . 250.28(D)(2)

Sizing . . . . 250.28(D)

When Used at Service Panels . . . . 250.24(B)

Industrial Control Panels 409.108

Motor Control Centers 430.95

Switchboards and Panelboards . . . . 408.3(C)

Table for Sizing . . . . Table 250.102(C)(1)

MANHOLES and OTHER ELECTRIC ENCLOSURES INTENDED FOR PERSONNEL ENTRY . . . . 110 Part V

Access to Vaults and Tunnels 110.76

Access to 110.75

Cabling Work Space 110.72

Conductor Bending Space 110.74

Conductors Racked, Subsurface Enclosures 110.74

1000 Volts, Nominal, or Less . . . . 110.74(A)

Over 1000 Volts, Nominal . . . . 110.74(B)

Equipment Work Space 110.73

General Requirements 110.70

Using Appropriate Engineering Requirements and Practices
. . . . 110.71 Info. Note

Note: National Electrical Safety Code, ANSI C-2 contains design and installation requirements applicable to this type of enclosure.

Over 1000 Volts, Conductors of Different Systems . . . .
. . . . .300.3(C)(2)(e)

Separation of Class 1 and Power Supply Circuits . .725.48(B)(3)

Separation of Class 2 & 3 Circuits . . . . . . .725.136(A)&(F)

MANUFACTURED BUILDING . . . . Art. 545

Bonding and Grounding 545.11

Boxes 545.9

Component Interconnections 545.13

Definition of 545.2

Grounding Electrode Conductor Provisions for 545.12

Protection of Conductors and Equipment 545.8

Receptacle or Switch with Integral Enclosure 545.10

Service Entrance Conductors

As Service Conductors 545.5

Installation 545.6

Service Equipment Location 545.7

Wiring Methods 545.4

MANUFACTURED HOMES . . . . **Art. 550**

Appliances 550.14

Arc-Fault Protections 550.25

Branch Circuits. 550.12

Calculations. 550.18

Definition 550.2

Disconnecting Means 550.11

Feeders 550.33

Ground-Fault Circuit Interrupters . . . . 550.13(B)

Grounding 550.16

Listed and Labeled . . . . 550.4(D)

Luminaires 550.14

Not Intended as a Dwelling Unit . . . . 550.4(A)

Power Supply 550.10

Receptacle Outlets 550.13

Service Equipment . . . . 550.32(A)

Testing. 550.17

Wiring Methods 550.15

See MOBILE HOMES . . . . Ferm's Finder

MANUFACTURED WIRING SYSTEMS . . . . **Art. 604**

Construction, Cable or Conduit Types . . . . .604.100(A)

Definition of 604.2

Installation 604.7

Listing Requirements 604.6

Uses Not Permitted 604.12

Uses Permitted 604.10

Of Flexible Cord As Part of Listed Assembly . 604.100(A)(3)

See (QQVX) . . . . .UL Product Spec

MANUFACTURER'S MARKING . . . . **110.21(A)**

MARINAS & BOATYARDS . . . . **Art. 555**

Branch Circuits . . . . 555.19(A)(3)

Cable, Marina and Boatyard

See (PDYQ) .UL Product Spec

Disconnecting Means 555.17

Dwellings (applicable) 555.1

Electrical Connections, Decks and Docks. 555.9

Equipment Grounding Conductor, Type of Conductor . . . . .
. . . . 555.15(B)

Feeder and Service Demand Factors. 555.12

Gasoline (Motor Fuel) Dispensing Stations

Classification of Locations . . . . 514.3(C)

Hazardous (Classified) Locations 555.21

Ground-Fault Circuit-Interrupter Protection . . .555.19(B)(1)

Ground-Fault Protection 555.3

Grounding

Branch-Circuit Equipment Grounding Conductor 555.15(D)

Equipment Grounding Conductor, Insulated Conductor . .
. . . . 555.15(B)

Equipment Grounding Conductors, Size . . . . . . 555.15(C)

Equipment to Be Grounded . . . . 555.15(A)

Feeder Equipment Grounding Conductors . . . . 555.15(E)

Motor Fuel Dispensing Stations

Classification of Locations . . . . 514.3(C)

Hazardous (Classified) Locations 555.21

Occupancy Types 555.1

Receptacles, Requirements for 555.19

Service Equipment Location 555.11

Signage 555.24

Swimming (risk of) 555.24

Wiring Methods 555.13

Wiring Over and Under Navigable Water . . . . . .555.13(B)(3)

See FLOATING BUILDINGS. . . . . Ferm's Finder

See Fire Protection Standard for Marinas and Boatyards,
. . . . .NFPA 303

MARKING AND LABELING REQUIREMENTS

Agricultural Buildings, Distribution Point . . . .
. . . . 547.9(A)(10)&(D)

Arc-Flash Hazard Warning 110.16

Available Fault Current 110.24

Cable Trays, Over 600 Volts. . . . . 392.18(H)

Industrial Establishment . . . . 392.18(H) Ex.

Cords

Optional . . . . 400.6(B)

Standard . . . . 400.6(A)

Critical Operations Power Systems, Receptacle Identification .
. . . . .708.10(A)(2)

Direct-Current Ground-Fault Detection 250.167

Directory, Interconnected Electric Power 705.10

Disconnecting Means, General . . . . 110.22(A)

Disconnecting Means, Engineered Series . . . . . . 110.22(B)

Disconnecting Means, Tested Series . . . . 110.22(C)

Disconnecting Means (Wind) . . . . .694.22(A)(4)

Electric-Discharge Lighting Systems of More Than 1000 Volts .
. . . . .410.146

Electric Vehicles 625.15

Electrolytic Cells, Isolating Transformer Receptacles 668.21(C)

Field-Applied Hazard Marking . . . . 110.21(B)

Fire Alarm Systems, Branch Circuit Identification . 760.41(B) &
. . . . .760.121(B)

Fire Pump, Disconnecting Means . . . . .695.4(3)(c)

Fuel Cells, Stand Alone . . . . 692.10(C)

Fuel Cells, Stored Energy 692.56

Fuel Cells, Switch and Circuit Breakers 692.17

Generators

   Neutral Bonded to Frame, Manufacturer Marking . . 445.11

   Neutral Bonded to Frame, Field Modified Marking . 445.11

Health Care Facilities, Receptacle Identification . . . .
. . . . 517.31(E)4 and 517.41(E)

High-Impedance Grounded Neutral . . . . 408.3(F)(3)

High Leg Marking 110.15

Identification, Grounded Conductor . . . . 210.5(A)

Identification of Power Sources (PV) 690.56

Identification of Power Sources (Wind) 694.54

Inverter Output Connection . . . . 705.12(B)(3)

Marinas and Boatyards, Other Than Shore Power Receptacles
. . . . .555.19(B)(2)

Marking, Boxes and Conduit Bodies. 314.44

Marking, Circuit Breakers. 240.83

Marking, Conductors 310.120

Marking, Field Applied Hazard Markings. . . . . . . 110.21(B)

Marking, Fuel Cells . . . . 692 Part VI

Marking, Fuses . . . . 240.60(C)

Marking, Industrial Control Panels 409.110

Marking, Luminaries 410.74

Marking, Lamp Wattage for Luminaries. 410.120

Marking, Manufacturer . . . . 110.21(A)

Marking, PV Systems . . . . 690 Part VI

Marking, Manhole Covers . . . . 110.75(E)

Marking, Panelboards 408.58

Marking, Product . . . . 110.21(A)

Marking, Switches 404.20

Marking, Transformer Disconnects 450.14

Marking, Wind Systems . . . . 694 Part VI

Mobile Home, Service Equipment, Receptacle . . . . 550.32(G)

Natural and Artificially Made Bodies of Water . . . . 682.14(A)

Outdoor Deicing and Snow Melting Equipment 426.13

Phase Converters, Conductors . . . . 455.6(B)

Recreation Vehicle, Supply Equipment . . . . 551.77(F)

Service Equipment, Disconnecting Means . . . . . . 230.70(B)

Service Equipment, Supply Side 230.82

Stand Alone System (PV) . . . . 690.10(C)

Substations 490.48

Switches 404.20

Surface Metal Raceways 386.120

Surface Nonmetallic Raceways 388.120

Transformer

   General . . . . 450.11(A)

   Source Marking (Reverse Feeding) . . . . 450.11(B)

Ungrounded Systems . . . . 250.21(C)

Wind Systems, Disconnecting Means . . . . .694.22(C)(2)

MAST-TYPE SUPPORTS

CATV Aerial Coaxial Cable Support. . . . . 820.44(C)

Outside Feeders and Branch Circuits Support 225.17

Power Service-Drop Support 230.28

Radio and TV Equipment. 810.12

MEANS OF EGRESS, ILLUMINATION

Hospitals . . . . 517.33(A)

Nursing Homes and Limited Care Facilities. . . . . 517.43(A)

See Life Safety Code, NFPA 101 . . . . .NFPA 101

MECHANICAL EXECUTION OF WORK

Circuits and Equipment Less Than 50 Volts. 720.11

Class 1, 2 and 3 Remote Control, Signaling, Etc. 725.24

Communications Circuits 800.24

Community Antenna Television and Radio Distribution . . . .
. . . . 820.24

Fire Alarm Systems 760.24

Optical Fiber Cables and Raceway 770.24

Workmanship 110.12

MEDIUM VOLTAGE CABLE, TYPE MV . . . . Art. 328

Installed by Qualified Person 328.14

Listing 328.6

See (PITY) . . . .*UL Product Spec*

Support 328.30

Uses Permitted 328.10

Uses Not Permitted 328.12

MEETING ROOMS

Fixed Wall Receptacle Outlets . . . . .210.71(B)(1)

Floor Receptacle Outlets . . . . .210.71(B)(2)

Square Foot Requirements . . . . 210.71(A)

MESSENGER SUPPORTED WIRING . . . . Art. 396

Ampacity 310.15

Conductor Splices and Taps 396.56

Equipment Grounding Conductor . . . . 396.30(C)

Insulated Conductor, Definition 396.2

Messenger Grounding 396.60

Messenger Support 396.30

Neutral Conductor . . . . 396.30(B)

Uses Not Permitted 396.12

Uses Permitted 396.10

   Cable Types . . . . 396.10(A)

   Hazardous Locations . . . . 396.10(C)

   In Industrial Establishments . . . . 396.10(B)

METAL BOXES

See BOXES AND FITTINGS, Metallic Boxes . . Ferm's Finder

See (QCIT) . . . .*UL Product Spec*

See (BGUZ) . . . .*UL Product Spec*

METAL DUSTS & POWDERS (Combustible)

Class II Group Classification . . . . 500.6(B)(1)

Class II Locations . . . . 500.5(C)

Enclosures Specifically Approved for Locations . . .502.115(A)

Requirements for Class II Locations . . . . Art. 502

Transformers and Capacitors Prohibited . . . . .502.100(A)(3)

See HAZARDOUS (CLASSIFIED) LOCATIONS Ferm's Finder

METAL FRAME OF BUILDING

Bonding . . . . 250.104(C)

Equipment Grounding Conductor, Not Permitted as . . . . . .

. . . . .250.136(A)

Grounding Electrode . . . . 250.52(A)(2)

   For Separately Derived Systems . . . . 250.104(D)

METAL HALIDE LAMPS

Containment requirements . . . . 410.130(F)(5)

METAL IN-GROUND SUPPORT STRUCTURE(S) . . 250.52(A)(2)

METAL PARTS IN VICINITY OF TRANSFORMERS . 450.10(B)

METAL PIPING

Bonding . . . . 250.30(A)(8)

Gas Piping . . . . 250.104(B)

Other Metal Piping . . . . 250.104(B)

Water . . . . 250.104(A)

METAL RACEWAYS (MAINTAIN CONTINUITY)

See CONDUIT, Continuity of Run . . . . Ferm's Finder

See RACEWAYS . . . . Ferm's Finder

METAL SIDING, GROUNDING OF . . . . 250.116 (Info. Note)

METAL STRUCTURES, OVER 1000 VOLTS . . . . . 250.194(B)

METAL SURFACE RACEWAY . . . . .Art. 386

See SURFACE METAL RACEWAY . . . . Ferm's Finder

METAL UNDERGROUND WATER PIPE

As a Grounding Electrode . . . . 250.52(A)(1)

METAL WATER PIPE AND STRUCTURAL STEEL . . 250.68(C)

METAL WELL CASINGS

Grounding Electrode . . . . 250.52(A)(8)

Grounding Equipment . . . . 250.112(M)

METAL WIREWAYS, *See* **WIREWAYS, METAL** . . **Ferm's Finder**

METAL WORKING MACHINE TOOLS . . . . Art. 670

Machine Tool Wire, Type MTW . . . . Table 310.104(A)

See Electrical Standard for Industrial Machinery . . . .

. . . . NFPA 79

See INDUSTRIAL MACHINERY . . . . Ferm's Finder

See (ZKHZ) . . . .*UL Product Spec*

METAL-CLAD CABLE, TYPE MC . . . . .Art. 330

Ampacity 330.80

   Conductors Rated 0-2000 Volts 310.15

   Conductors Rated 2001 to 35,000 Volts 310.60

   Of Sizes 18 AWG and 16 AWG 330.80

   Where Installed in Cable Tray . . . . 330.80(A)

Bending Radius 330.24

   Interlocked-Type Armor or Corrugated Sheath . . 330.24(B)

   Shielded Conductors . . . . 330.24(C)

   Smooth Sheath . . . . 330.24(A)

Exposed Work 330.15

Grounding 330.108

Installation . . . . 330 Part II

Insulated Conductor Types 330.112

Listing Requirements 330.6

Support of 330.30

Uses Not Permitted 330.12

Uses Permitted 330.10

Aircraft Hangars . . . . 513.7(A)

Bulk Storage Plants . . . . 515.7(A)

Cable Trays, in 392.10

    Rated Over 1000 Volts . . . . 392.18(H)

Class I, Division 1 Locations (Specific Restrictions) . . . . . .
. . . . 501.10(A)(1)(c)

Class I, Division 2 Locations . . . . 501.10(B)(1)(6)

Class II, Division 1 Locations (Specific Restrictions) . . . . .
. . . . 502.10(A)(1)(3)

Class II, Division 2 Locations . . . . 502.10(B)(1)(3)

Class III, Division 1 & 2 Locations . . . . . 503.10(A)(1)(4)

Commercial Garages . . . . 511.7(A)(1)

Cranes and Hoists 610.11

Ducts or Plenums Used for Environmental Air . . 300.22(B)

Elevators, Dumbwaiters, Escalators, etc. 620.21

Equipment Grounding Conductor, As . . . . . . 250.118(10)

Health Care Facilities, Patient Care Spaces . . . . 517.13(A)

    Outer Metal Armor to Be Identified As Ground Return
    Path . . . . 517.13(A)

    See Grounding Use (PJAZ) . . . . *UL Product Spec*

Information Technology Equipment, Raised Floors . . . . .
. . . . 645.5(E)(2)

Manufactured Wiring Systems . . . . . . 604.100(A)(2)(3)

Messenger Supported Wiring, As . . . . . . Table 396.10(A)

Motion Picture and TV Studios 530.11

Motor Fuel Dispensing Facilities 514.4

Other Spaces Used for Environmental Air . . . . 300.22(C)(1)

Outside Branch Circuits and Feeders 225.10

Places of Assembly . . . . 518.4(A)

Safety-Control Equipment, Class 1, Wiring . . . . 725.31(B)

Service-Entrance Conductors . . . . 230.43(13)

Spray Application, Dipping, and Coating Processes 516.7(A)

Swimming Pool Motors . . . . 680.21(A)(1)

Theaters, Audience Areas of Motion Picture & TV . 520.5(A)

See (PJAZ) . . . . *UL Product Spec*

METER FITTINGS
See (PJVV) . . . . *UL Product Spec*

METER MOUNTING EQUIPMENT
See (PJSR) . . . . *UL Product Spec*

METER SOCKETS . . . . Art. 312
Conductors Entering Enclosures 312.5

Damp, Wet, or Hazardous (Classified) Locations 312.2

Deflection of Conductors 312.6

Disconnects . . . . 230.82(3)

Grounding 250.142

Individual, Not Service Equipment 230.66

Supply Side of Service Disconnect . . . . 230.82(2)

Supply Side of Service Overcurrent Devices . . . . 230.94 Ex. 5

See (PJYZ) . . . . *UL Product Spec*

METERING TRANSFORMER CABINETS . . . . Art. 312
See METER SOCKETS . . . . Ferm's Finder

See (PJXS) . . . . *UL Product Spec*

METERS
Class I Locations 501.105

Grounding 250.142

    Cases of, at 1000 Volts and Over 250.176

    Cases of, at 1000 Volts or less 250.174

Supply Side of Service Disconnect . . . . 230.82(2)

Supply Side of Service Overcurrent Devices . . . . 230.94 Ex. 5

See (PJSR) . . . . *UL Product Spec*

Note: Type, location & mounting height should always be checked with the serving agency.

METRIC SYSTEM 90.9
Metric Designators and Trade Sizes . . . . 300.1(C)

Numerical Designation for

    Electrical Metallic Tubing . . . . 358.20(B) (Info. Note)

    Flexible Metal Conduit . . . . 348.20(B) (Info. Note)

    Flexible Metallic Tubing . . . . 360.20(B) (Info. Note)

    Intermediate Metal Conduit . . . . . 342.20(B) (Info. Note)

    Liquidtight Flexible Metal Conduit . . 350.20(B) (Info. Note)

    Liquidtight Flexible Nonmetallic Conduit . . . .
    . . . . 356.20(B) (Info. Note)

    Nonmetallic Underground Conduit with Conductors . . . .
    . . . . 354.20(B) (Info. Note)

    Rigid Metal Conduit . . . . 344.20(B) (Info. Note)

    Rigid PVC Conduit . . . . 352.20(B) (Info. Note)

    RTRC Conduit, Fiberglass . . . . . . 355.20(B) (Info. Note)

Threaded Conduit, Hazardous (Classified) Locations . . . . . .
. . . . 500.8(E)(2)

See METRIC SYSTEM, Measurements and Conversions . . . .
. . . . Ferm's Finder

MINERAL-INSULATED, METAL-SHEATHED CABLE . . Art. 332
Ampacity of 332.80

Ampacity of 310.15

Bends 332.24

Conductor Material 332.104

Emergency Systems . . . . 700.10(D)(1)

Fire Pumps 695.6

Fittings . . . . 332.40(A)

Insulation Material 332.112

Listing Requirements 332.6

Outer Sheath 332.116

    For Equipment Grounding Purposes 332.108

Places of Assembly . . . . 518.4(A)

Single Conductors 332.31

Supports 332.30

Terminal Seals . . . . 332.40(B)

Through Joists, Studs or Rafters . . . . 332.30(A)

Uses Not Permitted 332.12

Uses Permitted 332.10

Wet Locations . . . . 332.10(3)

See (PPKV) . . . . *UL Product Spec*

MOBILE HOMES . . . . **Art. 550**

Note: The term "mobile home" includes "manufactured homes" that are similar structure(s) designed to be used with or without a permanent foundation. *See* Definitions of both terms in 550.2

Appliances

    Accessibility . . . . 550.14(B)

    Fastened During Transit . . . . 550.14(A)

    Grounding Frames of 550.16

Branch Circuits 550.12

Calculations

    Park Electrical Wiring System 550.30

        Demand Factors . . . . Table 550.31

    Supply-Cord and Distribution Panelboard Load . 550.18(B)

Definitions 550.2

Disconnecting Means . . . . 550.11(A)

    Mounting Height, Outdoor Disconnecting Means 550.32(F)

Disconnecting Means and Branch-Circuit Protection 550.11(B)

Distribution System 550.30

    Demand Factors 550.31

Feeder (Four Insulated Conductors) . . . . 550.10(I)(1)

    Capacity, Minimum Rating 100 Amperes . . . . . 550.33(B)

    Minimum Size Permitted . . . . 310.15(B)(7)

    Size . . . . 215.2(A)(3)

    Type, Identification, Equipment Ground . . . . . 550.33(A)

Ground-Fault Circuit-Interrupter Protection . . . . 550.13(B)

    For Pipe Heating Cable Outlet, Where Installed. . 550.13(E)

    Receptacles At Service Equipment . . . . 550.32(E)

Grounding & Bonding 550.16

    Bonding of Non-Current-Carrying Metal Parts . . 550.16(C)

    Equipment Grounding Means . . . . 550.16(B)

    Insulated Grounded Conductor (Neutral) . . . . . 550.16(A)

Interconnection of Multiple-Section Mobile Home Units 550.19

Listing and Labeling . . . . 550.4(D)

Neutral Must Be Isolated from Enclosure in . . . . . 550.16(A)

Not Intended as a Dwelling Unit, Requirements for . . 550.4(A)

Outdoor Outlets, Luminaires (Fixtures), Air-Cooling Equipment, etc. 550.20

Power Supply . . . . 550.10(B)

    Equipment Grounding 550.16

    Feeders 550.33

Receptacle Outlets, Where Required or Permitted 550.13

    At Service Equipment . . . . 550.32(D)

    Pipe Heating Cable Outlet . . . . 550.13(E)

Services and Feeders . . . . 550 Part III

Service Equipment, Manufactured Home . . . . 550.32(B)

Service Equipment . . . . 550.32(A)

    Ground-Fault Circuit-Interrupter Protection . . . 550.32(E)

    Marking of 125/250-Volt Receptacle Used in . . . 550.32(G)

    Minimum Size Permitted . . . . .310.15(B)(7)

    Rating of . . . . 550.32(C)

    Size . . . . 215.2(A)(3)

Testing

    Continuity, Operational, and Polarity Checks . . . 550.17(B)

    Dielectric Strength . . . . 550.17(A)

Wiring Methods & Materials 550.15

    Boxes, Fittings, and Cabinets . . . . .550.15(I)

    Component Interconnections . . . . 550.15(K)

    For Ranges, Clothes Dryers, or Similar Appliance 550.15(E)

    Metal and Nonmetallic Cable Protection through Studs . . . . 550.15(C)

    Nonmetallic Cable Protection Where Exposed . . 550.15(B)

    Ratings of Switches . . . . 550.15(G)

    Under Chassis Wiring . . . . 550.15(H)

MOBILE X-RAY EQUIPMENT . . . . **Art. 660**

Connection to Supply Circuit . . . . 660.4(B)

Definition 660.2

Grounding 660.48

Manual Control Device 660.21

MODULAR DATA CENTERS

Cable Routing Assemblies. . . . . 646.3(F)

Definitions 646.2

Emergency Lighting Circuits 646.17

Equipment 646.10

Field-Wiring Compartments 646.8

Flexible Power Cords and Cables. 646.9

Installation and Use 646.14

Lighting

    Emergency. 646.16

    General Illumination 646.15

Listing 646.4

Nameplate Data 646.5

Other Articles 646.3

Overcurrent Protection 646.6

Plenums. . . . . 646.3(B)

Receptacles 646.12

Scope 646.1

Short-Circuit Current Rating 646.7

Supply Conductors. 646.6

Transformers 646.11

Working Space for ITE 646.20

Workspace

    Battery Installations. 646.21

    Entrance to and Egress 646.19

    General 646.18

    Service and Maintenance. 646.22

MODULE, SOLAR PHOTOVOLTAIC (Definition of) . . . 690.2

Module use in Solar Photovoltaic Devices. . . . . . . Art. 690

MOGUL BASE LAMPHOLDERS

Branch-Circuit Voltage Limitations . . . . 210.6(C)(3)

Ratings 410.103

MOTELS AND HOTELS

AFCI Requirements . . . . 210.12(C)

General Lighting Load . . . . Table 220.12

Ground-Fault Circuit-Interrupter Requirements. . . . 210.8(A)

    For Other Than Dwelling Units . . . . 210.8(B)

Lighting Load Demand Factors . . . . Table 220.42

Receptacle Load Demand Factors, Other Than Dwelling Unit . . . . Table 220.44

Receptacle Outlets, General . . . . 210.60(A)

Receptacle Outlets, Required 210.52

Receptacle Outlets, Placement of . . . . 210.60(B)

Tamper-Resistant Receptacles . . . . 406.12(2)

See Life Safety Code, NFPA 101 . . . . NFPA 101

MOTION PICTURE PROJECTORS . . . . Art. 540

Audio Signal Equipment, etc. 540.50

Definitions 540.2

    Nonprofessional Projector 540.2

    Professional-Type Projector 540.2

Nonprofessional Projectors . . . . 540 Part III

    Listing of Equipment 540.32

    Projection Room Not Required If Safety Film Used. . 540.31

Professional Type Equipment . . . . 540 Part II

    Emergency System Control . . . . 540.11(C)

    Listing of Equipment 540.20

    Location of Associated Electrical Equipment . . . 540.11(A)

    Projection Room Required. 540.10

    Work Space 540.12

MOTION PICTURE & TELEVISION STUDIOS . . . . . . Art. 530

Cellulose Nitrate Film Storage Vaults . . . . 530 Part V

Definitions 530.2

Dressing Rooms . . . . 530 Part III

Feeder Conductor Sizing, General . . . . 530.19(A)

    Demand Factors Permitted. . . . . Table 530.19(A)

    Demand Factors, Portable Feeders . . . . 530.19(B)

Grounding 530.20

Lamps, Portable 530.16

Lamps, Portable Arc Lamp 530.17

Live Parts, Enclosing and Guarding 530.15

Overcurrent Protection 530.18

Stage or Set . . . . 530 Part II

    Plugs and Receptacles. 530.21

    Single-Pole Separable Connectors. 530.22

    Stage Lighting and Effects Control 530.13

    Wiring

        Permanent. 530.11

        Portable 530.12

Substations . . . . 530 Part VI

See Also: THEATERS, AUDIENCE AREAS OF MOTION . . . PICTURE AND TELEVISION STUDIOS AND SIMILAR LO- CATIONS . . . . Ferm's Finder

MOTOR CONTROL CENTERS . . . . 430 Part VIII

Available Fault Current 430.99

Busbars and Conductors 430.97

Dedicated Equipment Space . . . . 110.26(E)

Definition of .Art. 100 Part I

Grounding 430.96

Overcurrent Protection 430.94

Service-Entrance Equipment, Use As 430.95

Spaces About 110.26

Spacings. .Table 430.97(D)

Wire Bending Space, Minimum . . . . 430.97(C)

See (NJAV) . . . .*UL Product Spec*

MOTOR CONTROLLERS . . . . **430 Part VII**

Auxiliary Devices

See (NKCR) . . . .*UL Product Spec*

Combination Fuseholder and Switch As. 430.90

Combination Motor Controllers

See (NKJH) . . . .*UL Product Spec*

Copper Conductors . . . . 430.9(B)

Definition, of (Controller). 430.2

Design 430.82

Disconnect Means Permitted in Same Enclosure As . . 430.103

Enclosure Types (Environmental Conditions) 110.28 and Table

Float & Pressure-operated

See (NKPZ) . . . .*UL Product Spec*

Location of Disconnecting Means . . . . 430.102(A)

Magnetic

See (NLDX) . . . .*UL Product Spec*

See (NLRV) . . . .*UL Product Spec*

Motor Not in Sight of Controller 430.102

Need Not Open All Conductors Unless Also Disconnect 430.84

Number of Motors Served by 430.87

Number of Overload Units 430.37

Over 1500 Volts

See (NJHU) . . . .*UL Product Spec*

Permitted to Serve As Overload Protection 430.39

Portable Motor 1/3 Horsepower or Less. . . . . . . 430.81(B)

Ratings 430.83

Stationary Motors, 2 Horsepower or Less . . . . . 430.83(C)

Torque Motors. 430.83(D)

Voltage Rating . . . . 430.83(E)

Stationary Motor, 1/8 Horsepower or Less . . . . . 430.81(B)

Torque Requirements . . . . 430.9(C)

Wire Bending Space 430.10

See (NJOT) . . . .*UL Product Spec*

MOTOR FUEL DISPENSING

Circuit Disconnects

Attended Self-Service Motor Fuel . . . . 514.11(B)

Emergency Electrical Disconnect . . . . 514.11(A)

Unattended Self-Service Motor Fuel . . . . 514.11(C)

Classification of Locations 514.3

Boatyards and Marinas . . . . 514.3(C)

Classified Areas . . . . 514.3(B)

Unclassified Areas. . . . . 514.3(A)

Definitions 514.2

Figures for Area Classification

Adjacent to Dispensers . . . . Figure 514.3

Adjacent to Storage Tanks . . . . Figure 514.3(B)

Grounding and Bonding 514.16

Maintenance 514.13

Sealing

At Boundary. . . . . 514.9(B)

At Dispenser. . . . . 514.9(A)

Tables

Class I Locations . . . . Table 514.3(B)(1)

Electrical Equipment . . . . Table 514.3(B)(2)

Underground Wiring 514.8

Wiring and Equipment

Above Class I Locations 514.7

In Class I Location 514.4

See GASOLINE (MOTOR FUEL) DISPENSING. . . . .
. . . . *Ferm's Finder*

MOTORS . . . . **Art. 430**

Adjustable Speed Drive Systems . . . . .Art. 100 Part I

Air-Conditioning Units . . . . 430.1 Info. Note 1

Appliances, Motor-Driven 422.3

Ampacity and Motor Rating Determination 430.6

Automatic Restarting 430.43

Branch-Circuit Overload Protection . . . . 430 Part III

Continuous-Duty Motors 430.32

Intermittent-Duty Motors 430.33

Number of Overload Units Required . . . . . Table 430.37

Branch-Circuit Short-Circuit & Ground-Fault Protection . . .
. . . . 430 Part IV

Individual Motor 430.52

Maximum Rating or Setting of . . . . Table 430.52

Several Motors or Loads on One Branch-Circuit . . . 430.53

Not Over 1 Hp Each . . . . 430.53(A)

Other Group Installations . . . . 430.53(C)

Single Motor Taps . . . . 430.53(D)

Smallest Motor Protected . . . . 430.53(B)

Use of Tables 430.148 to 150 to Determine Value 430.6(A)(1)

Calculations – *See* Example D8 . . . . . Informative Annex D

Capacitors 430.27

Conductor Ampacity . . . . 460.8(A)

Disconnecting Means. . . . . 460.8(C)

Overcurrent Protection. . . . . 460.8(B)

Rating or Setting of Motor Overload Device 460.9

See CAPACITORS . . . . Ferm's Finder

Code Letters (Locked Rotor Indicating) . . . . .Table 430.7(B)

Compressor Motors . . . . Art. 430

Hermetic Refrigerant Motor-Compressor . . . . . . Art. 440

See AIR-CONDITIONING & REFRIGERATING EQUIP-MENT . . . . Ferm's Finder

Conductors for Motors . . . . 430 Part II

Conductors for General Wiring 310.1

Constant Voltage Direct-Current – Power Resistors . 430.29

Controllers and Control Circuit Devices . . . . . . 430.9(B)

Determining Ampacity of . . . . 430.6(A)(1)

Feeder Demand Factor Permitted 430.26

Feeder Tap Conductors. 430.28

Integral Parts of Equipment . . . . 300.1(B)

Multimotor and Combination-load Equipment 430.25

Several Motors or a Motor(s) & Other Load(s) 430.24

Single Motor 430.22

Conductors for Small Motors

18 AWG Copper . . . . 430.22(G)(1)

16 AWG Copper . . . . 430.22(G)(2)

Note: Always use tables to size conductors and use

nameplate to size overload protection.

Control Centers . . . . 430 Part VIII

Control Circuits . . . . 430 Part VI

Class 1, 2, and 3 Circuits . . . . 725.3(F)

Copper Conductors At Terminals . . . . 430.9(B)

Disconnection. 430.75

Electrical Arrangement of 430.74

For Fire Pumps 695.14

Grounding

Arrange So Accidental Ground Won't Start 430.73

Circuits Permitted but Not Required to Be Grounded . . .
. . . . .250.21(A)(3)

Ungrounded Circuits Permitted 685.14

Overcurrent Protection. 430.72

For Specific Conductor Applications. . . . . . . 240.4(G)

Maximum Rating of . . . . Table 430.72(B)

Orderly Shutdown 430.44

System Coordination 240.12

Transformer . . . . 430.75(B)

In Controller Enclosure 430.74

Requirements . . . . Art. 450

Separately Derived Systems 250.30

Controllers . . . . 430 Part VII

See MOTOR CONTROLLERS . . . . Ferm's Finder

See NEMA Sizes . . . . *Ferm's Charts and Calculations*

Cord- and Plug-Connected . . . . 430.42(C)

Disconnecting Means for. . . . . .430.109(F)

Controller for 1/3 Horsepower or Less . . . . 430.81(B)

Cranes & Hoists . . . . Art. 610

DC Motors

Full-Load Current. . . . . Table 430.247

Power Resistors 430.29

Conductor Rating Factors. . . . . Table 430.29

Design B, C, and D

Conversion Table for Selecting Disconnecting Means . Table
. . . . .430.251(B)

Disconnecting Means. . . . . .430.109(A)(1)

Instantaneous Circuit Breaker Trip Setting. . . . .
. . . . 430.52(C)(3) Ex. 1

Note: Also applies to Design B motors

Listed Self-Protected Combination Controller. .430.52(C)(6)

Note: Also applies to Design B motors

Marking on Motors . . . . 430.7(A)(9)

Maximum Rating or Setting . . . . Table 430.52

Motor Controllers. . . . . .430.83(A)(1)

Motor Short-Circuit Protector. . . . . .430.52(C)(7)

Disconnecting Means . . . . 430 Part IX

A Group of Motors Served by a Single Disconnect . . . . . .
. . . . 430.112 Ex.

For Combination Loads . . . . 430.110(C)

Ampere Rating of 430.110

Cord- and Plug-Connected . . . . 430.109(F)

Rating of. 430.42(C)

Damp or Wet Locations 404.4

Disconnect Both Motor & Controller. 430.101

Disconnect in Sight from Motor and Driven Machinery . . .
. . . . .430.102(B)

Disconnect Must Be in Sight from Controller . . 430.102(A)

Grounded Conductor. 430.105

Motor Not in Sight from Controller. . . . .

. . . . 430.102(B) Ex. to (1) and (2)

    In Sight from, Definition of . . . . .Art. 100 Part I

Power from Two Sources. 430.113

Readily Accessible. 430.107

Single Disconnect for Each Motor. 430.112

Switch or Circuit Breaker As Both

    Controller & Disconnect 430.111

To Be Indicating. 430.104

Type, Every Switch in Circuit to Comply 430.108

    Ampere Rating and Interrupting Capacity 430.110

Feeder Taps 430.28

Overcurrent Protection. . . . . 240.21(F)

Single Motor Tap . . . . 430.53(D)

Feeders . . . . 430 Part II

Feeder Demand Factor 430.26

Feeder Taps 430.28

Multimotor and Combination-Load Equipment . . . 430.25

Several Motors or a Motor(s) and Other Load(s) . . . 430.24

Short-Circuit and Ground-Fault Protection . . . . 430 Part V

    Rating or Setting – Motor Load. 430.62

    Rating or Setting – Power and Light Loads 430.63

Full-Load Running Current 430.6

Direct-Current Motors . . . . Table 430.247

Single-Phase Alternating Current . . . . Table 430.248

Three-Phase Alternating Current . . . . Table 430.250

Two-Phase Alternating Current . . . . Table 430.249

Ground-Fault Protection, Branch-Circuit . . . . . 430 Part IV

Ground-Fault Protection, Feeder. . . . . 430 Part V

Grounding . . . . 430 Part XIII

Enclosures for Controllers 430.244

Equipment Grounding and Conductors . . . . . 250 Part VI

Means for Equipment Grounding Connection . . 430.12(E)

Method of Grounding 430.245

Methods of Equipment Grounding . . . . 250 Part VII

Stationary Motors 430.242

Group Installations

Ampacity of Conductors 430.24

Number of Controllers 430.87

Overload Protection 430.42

Short-Circuit and Ground-Fault Protection 430.53

Single Disconnect Permitted for Group . . 430.102(A) Ex. 2

Hazardous (Classified) Locations

Class I Locations 501.125

Class II Locations 502.125

Class III Locations 503.125

High Voltage (Over 1000 Volts, Nominal) . . . . 430 Part XI

    See OVER 1000 VOLTS, NOMINAL . . . . . Ferm's Finder

Highest Rated or Smallest Rated 430.17

In Sight from (Definition of) . . . . Art. 100

Industrial Machinery . . . . Art. 670

    See INDUSTRIAL MACHINERY . . . . Ferm's Finder

Location of Motors 430.14

Protected Against Dust 430.16

Protected Against Liquids 430.11

    See HAZARDOUS (CLASSIFIED) LOCATIONS . . . .

. . . . Ferm's Finder

Locked-Rotor Currents . . . . Table 430.251(A) and 430.251(B)

Code Letters (Locked Rotor Indicating) . . . .Table 430.7(B)

Motor Control Centers . . . . 430 Part VIII

    See MOTOR CONTROL CENTERS . . . . . Ferm's Finder

Orderly Shut Down of 430.44

Generator Considered Vital to Operation . . . 445.12(E) Ex.

Integrated Electrical Systems . . . . Art. 685

Power Loss Hazard . . . . 240.4(A)

System Coordination 240.12

Over 1000 Volts, Nominal . . . . 430 Part XI

Engineering Supervision, Protective Device Settings . . . . .

. . . . 430.225(B)(1)

    See OVER 1000 VOLTS, NOMINAL . . . . . Ferm's Finder

Overcurrent Protection

Branch Circuits . . . . 430 Part IV

    Individual Motor 430.52

    Maximum Rating of . . . . .Table 430.52

    Several Motors on One Branch Circuit 430.53

Feeders . . . . 430 Part V

    Rating or Setting – Motor Load. 430.62

    Rating or Setting – Power and Light Loads 430.63

Use Tables 430.247 through 250 for Determining Value of. .

. . . . 430.6(A)(1)

Overload Protection . . . . 430 PART III

Adjustment for Capacitors 460.9

Continuous-Duty Motor 430.32

Intermittent-Duty Motor. 430.33

Number of Overload Units

    Fuses. 430.36

Other Than Fuses 430.37

    Number and Location . . . . Table 430.37

    Number of Conductors Opened, by Other Than Fuses

    or Thermal Protectors 430.38

    Use of Nameplate Values for Separate Overload . . . .

    . . . . 430.6(A)(2)

Overtemperature Protection 430.126

Phase Converters . . . . Art. 455

Protection of Live Parts . . . . 430 Part XII

    Guards for Attendants 430.233

    Required If 50 Volts or More 430.232

Restarting, Automatic 430.43

Setting of Branch-Circuit Protective Device 430.6

    Maximum Rating or Setting . . . . Table 430.52

    Short-Circuit and Ground-Fault . . . . 430 Part IV

Short-Circuit & Ground-Fault Protection

    Branch Circuit . . . . 430 Part IV

      Maximum Rating or Setting of . . . . Table 430.52

    Feeder . . . . 430 Part V

    Use of Tables 430.247 through 250 to Determine . . . .

    . . . . 430.6(A)(1)

Small Motor Conductors

    18 AWG Copper . . . . .430.22(G)(1)

    16 AWG Copper . . . . .430.22(G)(2)

Starters . . . . 430 Part VII

Tables — Motor Information

    Duty Cycle Service . . . . Table 430.22(E)

    Feeders 430.28

    Full Load Current

      Three-Phase AC Motors . . . . Table 430.250

      Two-Phase AC Motors . . . . Table 430.249

      Single-Phase AC Motors . . . . Table 430.248

    Locked-Rotor Current, Conversion Single-Phase . . . .

    . . . . Table 430.251(A)

    Locked-Rotor Current, Conversion Polyphase . . . .

    . . . . Table 430.251(B)

    Locked-Rotor Indicating Letter . . . . .Table 430.7(B)

    Maximum Rating or Setting of Protective Devices . . . Table

    . . . . 430.52

    Number of Overload Units Required . . . . . . Table 430.37

    Other Articles . . . . Table 430.5

    Secondary Conductor . . . . Table 430.23(C)

    Single Motor Taps . . . . 430.53(D)

Terminal Housings 430.12

Three Overload Devices, Three-Phase . . . . Table 430.37

Valve Actuator Motor (VAM) Assemblies, Definition of . 430.2

Ventilation . . . . 430.14(A)

Water Pumps, Motor Operated . . . . .250.112(L)

Welders, Arc, Motor-Generator . . . . 630 Part II

Wire-Bending Space . . . . 430.10(B)

MOTORS & GENERATORS FOR USE IN CLASS I, GROUPS C & D; CLASS II, GROUPS E, F & G

See (PSPT) . . . .*UL Product Spec*

See (PTDR) . . . .*UL Product Spec*

See(PTKQ) . . . .*UL Product Spec*

See (PUCJ) . . . .*UL Product Spec*

See (PTHE) . . . .*UL Product Spec*

MOUNTING OF EQUIPMENT (General) . . . . 110.13(A)

Mounting of Snap Switches 404.10

Outlet, Device, Pull, and Junction Boxes 314.23

Switches and Circuit Breakers 404.8

MOUNTING POSTS AND PEDESTALS FOR DISTRIBUTION EQUIPMENT

See (PUPR) . . . .*UL Product Spec*

MOVING WALKS . . . . Art. 620

See ELEVATORS . . . . Ferm's Finder

MULTI-FAMILY DWELLINGS

Definition . . . . Art. 100

Disconnecting Means, in Separate Enclosures . . . 230.40 Ex. 2

    Access to Occupants . . . . 230.72(C)

    Appliances . . . . 422 Part III

      Cord- and Plug-Connected 422.33

      With Unit Switches . . . . 422.34(A)

    Electric Heat, with Unit Switches . . . . .424.19(C)(1)

    Location 230.70

    Maximum Number for Sets of Service-Entrance Conductors

    . . . . 230.71(A)

    Service Overcurrent Devices, Access to . . . . . 240.24(B)

Overcurrent Protection

    Access to Devices Protecting Conductors Supplying . . . . .

    . . . . 240.24(B)

    Access to Occupants, Service . . . . 230.72(C)

    Location in Circuit 240.21

    Locked Service Overcurrent Devices 230.92

    Service Equipment, Rating . . . . 230.90(A)

Type NM Cable (Romex) Not Permitted 334.12

Type NM Cable (Romex) Permitted 334.10

Services

   Access to Devices Protecting Conductors Supplying . . . . .
. . . . 240.24(B)

   Access to Disconnecting Means . . . . 230.72(C)

   Additional Permitted . . . . 230.2(B)(1)

   Location of Disconnecting Means. 230.70

   Locked Service Overcurrent Devices 230.92

   Maximum Number . . . . 230.71(A)

   Number of Service-Entrance Conductor Sets . . 230.40 Ex. 4

   See CALCULATIONS . . . . Ferm's Finder

   See SERVICES . . . . Ferm's Finder

MULTIMODE INVERTER

Interconnected Electric Power Production Sources (defined). .
. . . . 705.2

Microgrid Systems . . . . 705.170(3) Info Note

Photovoltaic Systems (defined) 690.2

MULTIOUTLET ASSEMBLY . . . . **Art. 380**

Calculations . . . . 220.14(H)

   See CALCULATIONS . . . . Ferm's Finder

Definition . . . . Art. 100 Part I

Insulated Conductors . . . . 380.23(A)

Pull Boxes . . . . 380.23(B)

Through Partitions 380.76

Uses Not Permitted 380.12

Uses Permitted 380.10

See (PVGT) . . . . *UL Product Spec*

MULTIOUTLET BRANCH-CIRCUIT

Ampacity . . . . .210.19(A)(2)

Branch-Circuit Requirements – Summary 210.24

Greater Than 50 Amperes, Industrial Premises . . . 210.3 Ex.

Next Higher Standard Overcurrent Device Not Permitted . . .
. . . . 240.4(B)(1)

Outlet Devices 210.21

Permissible Loads 210.23

MULTIPLE CIRCUITS

Equipment Bonding Jumper on Load Side of Service . . . . . .
. . . . 250.102(D)

Multiple Branch Circuits, Simultaneously Disconnect . . . 210.7

Multiple Circuit Connections, Grounding Means . . . 250.144

Multiwire Branch Circuit Considered Multiple Circuits . . . .
. . . . 210.4(A)

Rating 210.3

Size of Equipment Grounding Conductors . . . . . 250.122(C)

MULTIPLE-OCCUPANCY BUILDING

Disconnecting Means, in Separate Enclosures . . . 230.40 Ex. 2

   Access to Occupants . . . . 230.72(C)

   Appliances . . . . 422 Part III

      Cord- and Plug-Connected 422.33

      With Unit Switches. . . . . 422.34(D)

   Electric Heat, with Unit Switches . . . . .424.19(C)(4)

   Location 230.70

   Maximum Number for Sets of Service-Entrance

      Conductors . . . . 230.71(A)

   Service Overcurrent Devices, Access to . . . . . . 240.24(B)

Overcurrent Protection

   Access to Devices Protecting Conductors Supplying . . . . .
. . . . 240.24(B)

   Access to Occupants, Service . . . . 230.72(C)

   Location in Circuit 240.21

   Locked Service Overcurrent Devices 230.92

   Service Equipment, Rating. . . . . 230.90(A)

Type NM Cable (Romex) Not Permitted 334.12

Type NM Cable (Romex) Permitted 334.10

Services

   Access to Devices Protecting Conductors Supplying . . . . .
. . . . 240.24(B)

   Access to Disconnecting Means . . . . 230.72(C)

   Additional Permitted . . . . 230.2(B)(1)

   Location of Disconnecting Means. . . . . 230.70(A)

   Locked Service Overcurrent Devices 230.92

   Maximum Number . . . . 230.71(A)

   Number of Service-Entrance Conductor Sets . . 230.40 Ex. 4

   See CALCULATIONS . . . . Ferm's Finder

   See SERVICES . . . . Ferm's Finder

MULTIPLE RACEWAYS

Installation — Equipment Bonding Jumper . . 250.102(C)(2),
. . . . .250.122(F)

Minimum Size of Bonding Jumper, Load Side . . . 250.122(D)

Minimum Size of Bonding Jumper, Supply Side . . 250.102(C)

Size Equipment Bonding Jumper, Supply Side . . . 250.102(C)

Size of Equipment Bonding Jumper, Load Side . . 250.102(D)

MULTIPLE SEPARATELY DERIVED SYSTEMS . . 250.30(A)(6)

N

MULTIWIRE BRANCH CIRCUITS

Branch Circuits Permitted to Be Multiwire . . . . . . 210.4(A)

Definition of . . . . Art. 100

Emergency Systems, Branch Circuits 700.19

Grouping of Conductors in Panelboard . . . . 210.4(D)

    Disconnecting Means. . . . . 210.4(B)

    Disconnecting Means, Luminaires . . . . 410.130(G)

    Disconnecting Means, Location of Luminaires 410.130(G)(3)

Neutral Continuity Must Not Be Dependent on Device

    Connections . . . . 300.13(B)

Not Permitted, Freestanding-Type Partitions,

    Cord- and Plug-Connected . . . . 605.9(D)

Requirements for in Class I, Division 1 Locations . . . 210.4(B)

Requirements for in Class II, Division 1 Locations. . . 210.4(B)

Tie Bars Required (Line-to-Line Loads)

    Devices on Same Yoke 210.7

    Disconnecting Means Temporary Circuits . . . . . . 590.4(E)

    Dwelling Units, Simultaneous Disconnection . . . . 210.4(B)

    Permission to Supply Line-to-Line Loads . . . 210.4(C) Ex. 2

Ungrounded Conductors Tapped from Grounded 210.10

N

NATURAL AND ARTIFICIALLY MADE BODIES OF WATER . . . . **Art. 682**

Bonding and Grounding . . . . 682 Part III

Definitions of 682.2

Electrical Connections. 682.12

Electrical Equipment and Transformers. 682.12

Equipotential Plane 682.33

    Areas Not Requiring . . . . 682.33(B)

    Areas Requiring . . . . 682.33(A)

    Bonding of . . . . 682.33(C)

Ground-Fault Circuit Interrupter Protection 682.15

Submersible or Floating Equipment 682.14

NEAT AND WORKMANLIKE

Audio Signal Processing, Amplification, and Reproduction. . . . . 640.6(A)

CATV and Radio Distribution 820.24

Class 1, 2, and 3 Circuits 725.24

Communication Circuits 800.24

Fire Alarm Systems 760.24

General 110.12

Less than 50 Volts 720.11

Network-Powered Broadband Communications Systems 830.24

Optical Fiber Cables and Raceways 770.24

Premises-Powered Broadband Communications Systems 840.24

NEON

Neon Secondary-Circuit Wiring, 1000 Volts or Less, Nominal 600.31

Neon Secondary-Circuit Wiring, Over 1000 Volts, Nominal 600.32

Neon Tubing 600.41

    Definition of 600.2

NETWORK POWERED BROADBAND COMMUNICATIONS SYSTEMS. . . . . **Art. 830**

Abandoned Cables. 830.25

Access to Electrical Equipment Behind Panels 830.21

Burial Depth . . . . Table 830.47(C)

Cable Routing Assemblies . . . . 830.110(C)

Cable Ties and Accessories, Nonmetallic 830.24

Cables Outside and Entering Buildings . . . . 830 Part II

Definitions 830.2

Ducts, Wiring Within . . . . 830.3(B)

Grounding Devices, Required to be Listed 830.180

Grounding Methods. . . . . 830 Part IV

Grounding and Bonding at Mobile Homes 830.106

Installation Methods Within Buildings . . . . 830 Part V

Listing Requirements . . . . 830 Part VI

Mechanical Execution of Work. 830.24

Minimum Cover Requirements . . . . Table 830.47(C)

Output Circuits. . . . . 830.3(E)

Overhead (Aerial) Cables 830.44

Power Limitations 830.15

Protection (Electrical) . . . . 830 Part III

Raceway Types . . . . 830.110(A)

Underground Cables Entering Buildings 830.47

NEUTRAL OR GROUNDED CONDUCTOR

Bare (Permitted)

    Ampacity of Bare Conductors . . . . .310.15(B)(4)

        Table Value . . . . .Table 310.15(B)(21)

    Outside Branch Circuits and Feeders . . . . .225.4 Ex.

    Overhead Service Conductors . . . . .230.22 Ex.

Service Entrance. . . . . 230.41 Ex.

Solidly Grounded Systems 1kV and Over . . . .
. . . . .250.184(A)(1) Ex. 1 & 2 & 3

Underground Service Lateral . . . . 230.30 Ex.

Bonded to Service Equipment . . . . 250.24(C)

Separately Derived Systems . . . . 250.30(A)(1)

Two or More Buildings Supplied by Feeder or Branch Circuit
. . . . 250.32(B)

Within Service Disconnect Enclosure 250.28

Brought to Service Equipment . . . . 250.24(C)

Calculation of (Feeder or Service Load) 220.61

Considered Current-Carrying . . . . .310.15(B)(5)

Examples. . . . . Informative Annex D

Change in Size 240.23

Common Neutral Not Permitted (Generally)

Class I, Division 1 Locations . . . . 210.4(C)

Class I, Zone 1 Locations . . . . 210.4(C)

Class II, Division 1 Locations . . . . 210.4(C)

Freestanding-Type Partitions, Cord- and Plug-Connected. .
. . . . 605.9(D)

Zone 20 and 21 Locations . . . . 210.4(C)

Common Neutral Permitted

Feeders 215.4

Lighting Equipment Installed Outdoors . . . . . . 225.7(B)

Multiwire Branch Circuits 210.4

Definition of . . . . .Art. 100 Part I

Considered Current-Carrying . . . . .310.15(B)(5)

Examples. . . . . Informative Annex D

Contained within the Same Raceway, Cable Tray,

Trench, Cable or Cord . . . . 300.3(B)

Exceptions

Auxiliary Gutters. . . . . 300.3(B)(4)

Paralleled Installations. . . . . 300.3(B)(1) Ex.

Switch Loops . . . . 404.2(A) Ex.

Underground Installations . . . . 300.5(I) Ex. 1 & 2

Metal (Ferrous) Raceways . . . . 300.20(A)

Over 1000 Volts. 300.35

Underground Feeder and Branch-Circuit Cable. . 340.10(2)

Underground Installations . . . . 300.5(I)

Definition of Neutral Conductor . . . . .Art. 100 Part I

Definition of Neutral Point . . . . .Art. 100 Part I

Disconnection of, at Main Service 230.75

For More than one Branch Circuit, Neutral Conductor . . 200.4

Grouping Multiwire Circuits, Ungrounded Conductors210.4(D)

Grouping with Same Circuit . . . . 200.4(B)

Harmonics (Nonlinear Load)

Definition of . . . . .Art. 100 Part I

Feeder or Service Neutral . . . . 220.61(C) IN 2

Flexible Cords and Cables . . . . 400.5(A)

Multiwire Branch Circuits . . . . 210.4(A) IN

Neutral Considered Current-Carrying . . . . . .310.15(B)(5)

High Impedance Grounding 250.36

Identification & Marking of . . . . Art. 200

Conductors for General Wiring . . . . .310.110(A)

For Branch Circuits . . . . 210.5(A)

Means of Identifying Grounded Conductors 200.6

Impedance Grounded Neutral Systems 250.187

Installation . . . . 200.4(A)

Insulated, Required

1000 Volt Minimum Solidly Grounded Neutral Systems

1 kV and Over . . . . 250.184(A)

High Impedance Grounded System . . . . 250.36(B)

Messenger Supported Wiring . . . . 396.30(B)

Multiple Circuits . . . . 200.4(B)

Neutral Conductors (more than one branch circuit). . . . 200.4

Neutral (Current-Carrying Conductor) . . . . . . .310.15(B)(5)

Flexible Cords and Cables (Ultimate Insulation Temp) . . .
. . . . 400.5(B)

Neutral (Feeder Load) 220.61

Neutral (to Every Service) Must Not Be Smaller Than the

Required Grounding Electrode Conductor . .250.24(C)(1)

Not to Be Dependent on Device Connections for

Continuity on Multiwire Branch Circuits . . . . . 300.13(B)

Overcurrent Device Not Permitted in the Grounded Conductor
. . . . 230.90(B)

Exceptions

Fuse in Grounded Conductor 3 Wire, 3 Phase AC . . 430.36

Other Than Fuses . . . . Table 430.37

Simultaneously Opened . . . . 230.90(B)

Unless Conditions Met . . . . 240.22(1) & (2)

Reduction in Size. 240.23

Re-Identifying at Switches. . . . . 200.7(C)(1)

Size of Conductor

Minimum 250.66

Not Smaller Than Grounding Electrode Conductor. . . . . .
. . . . .250.24(C)(1)

Overhead Service Conductors . . . . 230.23(C)

Parallel Conductors . . . . .250.24(C)(2)

   Existing Installations, Under Engineering Supervision . . . . 310.10(H)(1) Ex. 2

Phase Conductors over 1100 kcmil Copper . . .250.24(C)(1)

Service Entrance. . . . . 230.42(C)

Table for Sizing . . . . Table 250.102(C)(1)

Underground Service . . . . 230.31(C)

Switch in Grounded Conductor Not Permitted. . . . . 404.2(B)

  Exceptions

    Circuit Breaker If Simultaneously Opens All

    Conductors . . . . 230.90(B)

    For Circuits through or to Motor Fuel Dispensers . . . . . 514.11(A)

      In Service Disconnecting Means 230.75

      Motor Controller 430.105

      Switches or Circuit Breakers (General) . . . . 404.2(B) Ex.

  Service Overcurrent Device . . . . 230.90(B)

  Wind Electric Systems 694.20

  Use of for Grounding Equipment

    Load Side . . . . .250.142(B)

      Agricultural Buildings . . . . 547.9(B)(3)

      Frames of Ranges, Dryers, Etc., Existing Installations 250.140

      In Separate Buildings . . . . 250.32(B)

      Mobile Homes 550.16

      Recreational Vehicle Site Supply, Not Permitted . . . . 551.76(C) & (D)

      Recreational Vehicles . . . . 551.54(C)

      Separately Derived Systems 250.30

    Supply Side. . . . . .250.142(A)(3)

  Wind Electric Systems 694.20

NEUTRAL CONDUCTOR
Definition of . . . . Art. 100

NEUTRAL POINT
Definition of . . . . Art. 100

NIGHTCLUBS . . . . Art. 518

NIPPLES & NIPPLE FILL (CONDUIT OR TUBING)
60 Percent Fill Allowed, Not Exceeding 600 mm (24 in.) . . . . Chapter 9 Table 1, Note 4

Approved for the Condition . . . . 300.6(C)

Class I Division 2- Seals . . . . .501.15(B)(1)

Class I Locations- Seals . . . . .501.15(A)(3)

Corrosion Protection . . . . 300.6(A)

  Supplementary . . . . 300.6(B)

Derating Factors Not Applicable, Raceways Not Exceeding 600 mm (24 in.) . . . . 310.15(B)(3)(a)(2)

Pole Luminaire . . . . .410.30(B)(2)

Zone 1 . . . . 505.16(B)(2)(2)(c)

NOMINAL VOLTAGE
See VOLTAGE . . . . Ferm's Finder

NONAUTOMATIC, DEFINED . . . . Art. 100

NONCOINCIDENT LOADS 220.60
Room Air Conditioners and Other Equipment on Same Circuit . . . . 440.62(C)

NONELECTRICAL EQUIPMENT, GROUNDING OF . 250.116

NONFERROUS METALS
Aluminum Rigid Conduit. 344.100

Electrical Metallic Tubing . . . . 358.10(B)

Faceplates, Receptacles . . . . 406.6(A)

Faceplates, Switches . . . . 404.9(C)

Fixed Outdoor Electric Deicing and Snow Melting Equipment 426.26

Grounding Electrodes . . . . .250.52(A)(7)

Grounding Electrode Conductor Enclosures . . . . . 250.64(E)

Markings, Corrosion Resistant 344.120

Metal-Clad Cable 330.31

Red Brass Conduit 344.100

Rigid Metal Conduit (Aluminum) 344.100

Stainless Steel Conduit. 344.100

Underfloor Raceways . . . . 390.3(B)

Wiring Methods . . . . 300.3(B)(3)

NONGROUNDING-TYPE RECEPTACLES, REPLACEMENT OF . . . . 406.4(D)

NONINCENDIVE CIRCUIT
Class I, Division 2 Locations

  Meters, Instruments, and Relays . . . .501.105(B)(1), Ex.(3)

  Signaling, Alarm, Communications, Remote Control . . . . 501.150(B)(1) Ex.(3)

  Wiring Methods. . . . . .501.10(B)(3)

Class II, Division 2 Locations

  Signaling, Alarm, Communications, Remote Control,

Meters, etc. . . . . .502.150(B)(1) Ex.

Wiring Methods. . . . . .502.10(B)(3)

Class III, Division 1 Locations

Wiring Methods. . . . . .503.10(A)(4)

Definitions of Nonincendive Words and Terms,

Specific to Article 506, Zone 20, 21, and 22 Locations . 506.2

Protection Techniques. . . . . .500.7(F)(G)(H)

Zone 20, 21, and 22 Locations . . . . 506.8(F)

NONINTERCHANGEABLE

Cartridge Fuseholders. . . . . 240.60(B)

Type S Fuses . . . . 240.53(B)

NONINSTANTANEOUS TRIP (Arc Energy Reduction)   240.87

NONLINEAR LOADS

Definition of . . . . .Art 100

Feeder or Service Neutral . . . . 220.61(C) IN

Flexible Cords and Cables. . . . . 400.5(A)

Multiwire Branch Circuits. . . . . 210.4(A) IN 1

Neutral Considered Current-Carrying . . . . . 310.15(B)(5)(c)

NONMETALLIC AUXILIARY GUTTERS . . . . Art. 366

Ampacity of Conductors . . . . 366.23(B)

Definition of 366.2

Listing Requirements 366.6

Marking 366.120

Number of Conductors . . . . 366.22(B)

Uses Permitted . . . . 366.10(B)

See AUXILIARY GUTTERS . . . . Ferm's Finder

NONMETALLIC BOXES

See BOXES & FITTINGS, Nonmetallic . . . . . Ferm's Finder

NONMETALLIC CONDUIT

See CONDUIT. . . . . Ferm's Finder

See High Density Polyethylene Conduit – Type HDPE Art. 353

See CONDUIT, High Density Polyethylene Conduit . Ferm's Finder

See Liquidtight Flexible Nonmetallic Conduit . . . . . Art. 356

See LIQUIDTIGHT FLEXIBLE NONMETALLIC CONDUIT. . . . . Ferm's Finder

See Nonmetallic Underground Conduit with Conductors. . . . . Art. 354

See NONMETALLIC UNDERGROUND CONDUIT WITH CONDUCTORS . . . . Ferm's Finder

See Reinforced Thermosetting Resin Conduit . . . . . Art. 355

See REINFORCED THERMOSETTING RESIN CONDUIT . . . . Ferm's Finder

See Rigid PVC Conduit . . . . Art. 352

See RIGID PVC CONDUIT . . . . Ferm's Finder

NONMETALLIC EXTENSIONS . . . . Art. 382

Bends 382.26

Boxes and Fittings 382.40

Concealable Exposed Runs . . . . 382.15(B)

Construction Specifications (Concealed Type Only) 382 Part III

Definition of 382.2

Devices, Receptacles and Housings 382.42

Exposed Runs. 382.15

Listing Requirements 382.6

Securing and Supporting 382.30

Splices and Taps 382.56

Uses Not Permitted 382.12

Uses Permitted 382.10

See (PXXT). . . . . .UL Product Spec

NONMETALLIC-SHEATHED CABLE: TYPE NM, NMC, and NMS

. . . . . .Art. 334

Accessible Attics 334.23

Ampacity Shall Be That of 60°C Conductors 334.80

Derating Permitted from 90°C Ampacity. 334.80

In Contact With Draft or Firestopping or Thermal Insulation 334.80

Sealed Within Thermal Insulation, Caulk, or Sealing Foam 334.80

Bending Radius 334.24

Conductors, Sizes and Type 334.104

Conductors Shall Be Rated 90°C 334.112

Construction Types, Sheath. 334.116

Type NM. . . . . 334.116(A)

Type NMC. . . . . 334.116(B)

Type NMS . . . . 334.116(C)

Definition. 334.2

Devices of Insulating Materials . . . . 334.40(B)

Devices with Integral Enclosures . . . . 334.40(C)

Devices without a Separate Outlet Box . . . . 334.30(C)

Entering Boxes 314.17

Cabinets, Cutout Boxes, and Meter Socket Enclosures . 312.5

Exposed Work 334.15

Installation of . . . . 334 Part II

Interconnectors . . . . 334.40(B)

Listing Required 334.6

Marking of . . . . 334.112 IN

Nonmetallic Outlet Boxes . . . . 334.40(A)

Protection of

   At Crawl Hole (Attics & Roof Spaces) 334.23

   Cables and Raceways Installed In or Under Roof Decking . .
. . . . 300.4(E)

   Closely Follow Surface . . . . 334.15(A)

   Exposed Work 334.15

   Metal Cabinets, Cutout Boxes, Meters 312.5

   Parallel to Framing Members and Furring Strips . . 300.4(D)

   Shallow Grooves, in . . . . 300.4(F)

   Through Bored Holes and Notches in Wood Framing

     Members . . . . 300.4(A)(1) & (2)

   Through Floors . . . . 334.15(B)

   Through Metal Framing Members . . . . . 300.4(B)(1) & (2)

   Through or Parallel to Wood or Metal Framing Members . .
. . . . 334.17

   Unfinished Basements and Crawl Spaces . . . . 334.15(C)

SE Cable, Interior Installations Comply with Article 334 . . . .
. . . . 338.10(B)(4)

Securing and Supporting 334.30

   Every 1.4 m (4 1/2 ft) 334.30

   In Unfinished Basements and Crawl Spaces . . . . 334.15(C)

   Within 300 mm (12 in.) of Metal Box 334.30

   Within 200 mm (8 in.) of Nonmetallic Box . . 314.17(C) Ex.

   Exceptions

     Concealed Work in Finished Buildings . . . . 334.30(B)(1)

     Wiring Devices without Separate Box . . . . . . 334.30(C)

     Within Accessible Ceilings (Whips) . . . . . 334.30(B)(2)

UF Cable Used for Interior Wiring Shall Comply with

   the Requirement of Article 334 . . . . 340.10(4)

Unfinished Basements and Crawl Spaces . . . . 334.15(C)

Uses Permitted (General, Types NM, NMC, and NMS) . 334.10

   Electric Discharge and LED Luminaires,

     Connection of . . . . 410.24(A)

   In Cable Trays, Identified for . . . . 334.10(4)

   In Nursing Homes and Limited Care Facilities . 517.10(B)(2)

   In Business Offices, Corridors, Waiting Rooms in Clinics,

     Medical and Dental Offices & Outpatient Facilities . . . .
. . . . 517.10(B)(1)

   In Places of Assembly, Not Fire-rated Construction 518.4(B)

   In Theaters, Motion Picture & Television Studios, etc.

     Not Fire-Rated Construction . . . . 520.5(C)

     (Note: Refer to 334.10(3) for building construction

      types permitted.)

   Multifamily Dwellings of Types III, IV, and V Construction
. . . . 334.10(2)

   One-and Two-Family Dwellings . . . . 334.10(1)

   Other Structures of Types III, IV, and V Construction . . . .
. . . . 334.10(3)

     See . Informative Annex E (for determination of building
     types)

     See Standard on Types of Building Construction) NFPA 220

     See . . . . also applicable building code)

   Spas and Hot Tubs . . . . 680.42(C)&(D)

   Swimming Pool Motors, Interior One-Family Dwellings

     and Another Building or Structure Associated with . . . .
. . . . 680.21(A)(1)

   Temporary Installations (No Height Limitation) . . 590.4(B)

Uses Not Permitted . . . . 334.12(A)(1)-(10)

Uses Not Permitted, Types NM and NMS . . . . . 334.12(B)

Uses Permitted (Specific)

   Type NM . . . . 334.10(A)

   Type NMC . . . . 334.10(B)

   Type NMS . . . . 334.10(C)

White Conductor 200.7

   See MULTIFAMILY DWELLINGS . . . . Ferm's Finder

   See MULTIPLE-OCCUPANCY BUILDING . . Ferm's Finder

   See (PWVX) . . . . *UL Product Spec*

NONMETALLIC-SHEATHED CABLE INTERCONNECTORS . . . . **334.40(B)**

NONMETALLIC UNDERGROUND CONDUIT WITH CONDUCTORS . . . . **Art. 354**

Aboveground Use, Encased in Concrete . . . . 354.10(5)

Bends

   How Made 354.24

   Number of 354.26

Bushings 354.46

Conductor Terminations 354.50

Construction of 354.100

Definition of 354.2

Installation of . . . . 354 Part II

Insulation Temperature Limitations . . . . 355.10(I)

Listing Requirements 354.6

Marking 354.120

Maximum and Minimum Size . . . . 354.20(A) & (B)

Number of Conductors 354.22

Trimming 354.28

Uses Not Permitted 354.12

Uses Permitted 354.10

See (QQRK) . . . . *UL Product Spec*

NONMETALLIC WIREWAYS

Dead Ends 378.58

Definitions 378.2

Expansion Fittings 378.44

Extensions 378.70

Grounding 378.60

Insulated Conductors 378.23

Listing 378.6

Marking 378.120

Number of Conductors 378.22

Parallel Conductors 378.20

Securing and Supporting 378.30

Size of Conductors 378.21

Splices and Taps 378.56

Uses Not Permitted 378.12

Uses Permitted 378.10

NON-POWER-LIMITED FIRE ALARM CIRCUIT . . . 760 Part II

Definition of 760.2

See FIRE ALARM SYSTEMS . . . . Ferm's Finder

NONREMOVABLE

Type S Fuse Adapters . . . . 240.54(C)

NONTAMPERABLE

Circuit Breakers 240.82

Type S Fuses . . . . 240.54(D)

NUMBER OF

Bends

EMT, Electrical Metallic Tubing 358.26

ENT, Electrical Nonmetallic Tubing 362.26

FMC, Flexible Metal Conduit 348.26

HDPE, High Density Polyethylene Conduit 353.26

IMC, Intermediate Metal Conduit 342.26

LFMC, Liquidtight Flexible Metal Conduit 350.26

LFNC, Liquidtight Flexible Nonmetallic Conduit . . 356.26

NUCC, Nonmetallic Underground Conduit with Conductors
. . . . 354.26

PVC, Rigid Polyvinyl Chloride Conduit 352.26

RTRC, Reinforced Thermosetting Resin Conduit . . . 355.26

RMC, Rigid Metal Conduit 344.26

See BENDS, Number of Bends Permitted in . . Ferm's Finder

Circuits Required . . . . 210.11(A)

Central Heating Equipment (Other Than Fixed Electric) . . .
. . . . 422.12

Computation of Loads to Determine 220.10

Dwelling Units . . . . 210.11(C)(1) – (3)

Elevator Hoistway Pit Lighting and Receptacles . . 620.24(A)

Elevator Machine Room/Machinery Space . . . . . 620.23(A)

Manufactured and Mobile Homes . . . . 550.12(A)-(E)

Marinas and Boatyards . . . . .555.19(A)(3)

Recreational Vehicles . . . . .551.42(A)-(D)

Signs . . . . 600.5(A)

Conductors in

See CONDUCTORS, Number of, in . . . . . . Ferm's Finder

Lighting Outlets Required

About Electric Equipment . . . . 110.26(D)

Over 1000 Volts . . . . 110.34(D)

All Occupancies . . . . 210.70(C)

Dwellings . . . . 210.70(A)

Guest Rooms and Guest Suites . . . . 210.70(B)

Overcurrent Devices (Panelboards) 408.36

Maximum Number in 408.54

Receptacle Outlets Required

All Occupancies, Wherever Flexible Cords with

Attachment Plugs Are Used . . . . 210.50(B)

Dwellings 210.52

Electrical Service Areas 210.64

Meeting Rooms 210.71

Service Disconnecting Means 230.71

Grouping of 230.72

Service-Entrance Conductor Sets 230.40

Services to a Building 230.2

Supplies to More Than One Building or Structure 225.30

Disconnecting Means for Each Supply 225.33

Grouping of Disconnects 225.34

NURSING HOMES AND LIMITED CARE FACILITIES

Definition, Limited Care Facility 517.2

Definition, Nursing Home 517.2

Essential Electrical System 517.40

Capacity of System . . . . 517.42(C)

Equipment Branch 517.44

Life Safety Branch 517.43

Power Sources . . . . 517.41(A)

Receptacle Identification . . . . 517.42(E)

Separation from Other Circuits . . . . 517.42(D)

Transfer Switches . . . . 517.42(B)

Wiring and Protection . . . . 517 Part II

Spaces Used Exclusively for Patient Sleeping Rooms . . . . .
. . . . .517.10(B)(2)

See HEALTH CARE FACILITIES . . . . Ferm's Finder

OFFICE FURNISHINGS . . . . Art. 605

Cords Permitted

   Freestanding-Type, Cord- and Plug-Connected . . 605.9(A)

   Lighting Accessories . . . . 605.6(B)

Definition 605.2

Fixed-Type Office Furnishings 605.7

Freestanding Type Office Furnishings

   Cord- and Plug-Connected 605.9

   Not Fixed 605.8

General Information 605.3

Hazardous (Classified) Locations . . . . 605.3(B)

Interconnections 605.5

Lighting Accessories 605.6

   Connection . . . . 605.6(B)

   Listed 605.6

   Receptacle Outlet in, Not Permitted . . . . 605.6(C)

   Support . . . . 605.6(A)

Multiwire Circuits Not Permitted in . . . . 605.9(D)

Office Furnishing Interconnections 605.5

Power Supply

   Fixed-Type Office Furnishings 605.7

   Freestanding-Type Office Furnishing, Cord- and
   Plug-Connected 605.9

   Freestanding-Type Office Furnishing, Not Fixed 605.8

Receptacles

   Located Not More Than 300 mm (12 in.) from Partition . . .
   . . . . 605.9(B)

   Maximum Number in Office Furnishings or Groups 605.9(C)

   Supplying Power to on Separate Circuit . . . . 605.9(B)

Uses Permitted . . . . 605.3(A)

Wireways 605.4

See (QAWZ) . . . . .UL Product Spec

See (QAXB) . . . . .UL Product Spec

OFFICE TRAILERS . . . . 550.4(A)

See MOBILE HOMES . . . . Ferm's Finder

OPEN BOTTOM EQUIPMENT

Mechanical Continuity of Raceways and Cables 300.12

OPEN KNOCKOUT (Wiring through) . . . . 300.4(G)

Boxes 314.17

OPEN WIRING . . . . Art. 398

Clearance from Piping, Exposed Conductors, etc. 398.19

Conductor Supports 398.30

Conductor Supports, Mounting . . . . 398.30(D)

Conductors, Type 398.104

Definition 398.2

Devices 398.42

Dry Locations . . . . 398.15(A)

Entering Spaces Subject to Wetness, Dampness or

   Corrosive Vapors . . . . 398.15(B)

Exposed to Physical Damage . . . . 398.15(C)

For Service Entrance . . . . 230.43(1)

   Entering Buildings or Other Structures 230.52

   Mounting Supports . . . . 230.51(C)

   Protection, Aboveground . . . . 230.50(B)

For Temporary Wiring, Prohibited (General) . . . 590.4(B)&(C)

   Exceptions

      Branch Circuits, Emergencies and Tests and

      90-day Maximum for Holiday Lighting, etc. 590.4(C) Ex.

      Feeders for Emergencies and Tests Only . . . . 590.4(B) Ex.

In Accessible Attics 398.23

Through Walls, Floors, Wood Cross-Members, etc. . . . 398.17

Tie Wires . . . . 398.30(E)

Uses Not Permitted 398.12

Uses Permitted 398.10

See OUTSIDE BRANCH CIRCUITS & FEEDERS Ferm's Finder

OPENINGS ADEQUATELY CLOSED

Conductors Entering Boxes, etc. . . . . 314.17(A)

Spread of Fire or Products of Combustion 300.21

Unused Openings, Boxes and Conduit Bodies . . . . 110.12(A)

   Cabinet Cutout Boxes and Meter Socket Enclosures 312.5(A)

OPENINGS, APPROVED FOR DRAINAGE (BOXES, ETC.).... . . . . .314.15

OPERATING ROOM RECEPTACLES . . . . 517.19(C)

OPTICAL FIBER CABLES AND RACEWAYS . . . . Art. 770

Applications of Listed Optical Fiber Cables 770.154

Cable Marking . . . . Table 770.179

Cable Routing Assemblies . . . . 770.110(C)(1) and (2)

Cable Substitutions. . . . . Table 770.154(b)

Cable Trays . . . . 770.113(H)

Circuit Integrity Cable. . . . . 770.179(E)(1)

Class 1, Division 1 . . . . 501.10(A)(1)(e)

Class 1, Division 2 . . . . 501.10(B)(1)(7)

Class 2, Division 1 . . . . 502.10(A)(1)(4)

Class 2, Division 2 . . . . 502.10(B)(1)(8)

Definitions . . . . .Art 100

Ducts for Dust, Loose Stock, or Vapor Removal . . . . 770.3(B)

Electrical Circuit Protective System, Defined 770.2

Field Assembled . . . . .770.179(F)

Fire Resistance, Listing for . . . . 770.179(A)

Fire-Resistive Cables. . . . . 770.179(E)(2)

Fire Spread 770.26

Grounding 770.93, 770.100

Intersystem Bonding Termination. . . . . . . 770.100(B)(2)

Length of Conductor . . . . 700.100(A)(4)

Listed or Part of Listed Equipment 770.180

Metallic Entrance Conduit. 770.49

Non-Current-Carrying Conductive Members 770.106

Hazardous Locations . . . . 770.3(A)

Innerduct, Defined. 770.2

Installation of Optical Fibers and Electrical Conductors 770.133

Listing, Marking, and Installation 770.113

Listing Requirements 770.179

Mechanical Execution of Work. 770.24

Overhead (Aerial) 770.44

Substitutions 770.154

Types 770.2

Underground Cables Entering Building 770.47

Unlisted Cables Entering Buildings 770.48

See (QAYK) . . . . .UL Product Spec

See(QAZM). . . . . .UL Product Spec

OPTIONAL STANDBY SYSTEMS . . . . Art. 702

Capacity and Rating of 702.4

Circuit Wiring 702.10

Definition 702.2

Equipment Load Selection 702.4

Generator Sets

Outdoor, Permanently Installed . . . . 702.12(A)

Outdoor, Portable . . . . 702.12(B)

Grounding, Portable Generators 702.11

Nonseparately Derived System . . . . 702.11(B)

Separately Derived System . . . . 702.11(A)

Outdoor Generator Sets 702.12

Permanently Installed. . . . . 702.12(A)

Portable- 15kW or Less. . . . . 702.12(B)

Portable- Greater the 15 kW . . . . 702.12(A)

Portable- Power Inlets, 100 Amperes or Greater. . 702.12(C)

Power Inlet . . . . 702.7(C)

Signals. 702.6

Signs . . . . 702.7(A)

At Grounding Location. . . . . 702.7(B)

At Power Inlet . . . . 702.7(C)

Transfer Equipment 702.5

Automatic . . . . 702.4(B)(2)

Manual . . . . 702.4(B)(1)

Short-Circuit Current Rating 702.5

ORDERLY SHUTDOWN

Coordination (Selective) . . . . Art.100 Part I

Electrical System Coordination 240.12

Ground-Fault Protection of Equipment (Branch Circuit) . . . . 210.13 Ex. 1

Ground-Fault Protection of Equipment (Feeder). . 215.10 Ex. 1

Ground-Fault Protection of Equipment (General) 240.13

Ground-Fault Protection of Equipment, (Not Applicable) . . . . 230.95 Ex. 1

Ground-Fault Protection of Equipment (Service) . . 230.95 Ex.

Integrated Electrical Systems . . . . 685 Part II

Insulation Level- 173 Percent . . . . . . .Table 310.104(E) Notes

Motor Overload Protection 430.44

Motor Overtemperature Protection . . . . .430.126(C)

Overcurrent Protection for Generators Deemed Essential . . . . 445.12 Ex.

Overcurrent Protection, Cranes and Hoists . . . . . . 610.53(B)

Overload Protection, Elevators, etc. . . . . . 620.61(B) Info. Note

O

Permanent Amusement Attractions 522.25

Power Loss Hazard . . . . 240.4(A)

ORGANS, PIPE . . . . **Art. 650**

Conductors 650.6

Definitions 650.2

Overcurrent Protection 650.8

Protection from Accidental Contact 650.9

Sources of Energy 650.4

OUTDOOR

Lighting

    Equipment Installed Outdoors 225.7

    Lampholders 410.96

    Location of Outdoor Lamps 225.25

    Outdoor Lampholders 225.24

    Supported by Trees . . . . 410.36(G)

    Wet and Damp Locations . . . . 410.10(A)

    See FESTOON LIGHTING . . . . Ferm's Finder

Receptacles

    Damp and Wet Locations . . . . 406.9(A)&(B)

    GFCI Requirements . . . . 210.8(A)(3)

    Required, One- and Two-Family Dwellings . . . . 210.52(E)

OUTDOOR, OVERHEAD CONDUCTORS, OVER 1000 VOLTS .

. . . . **Art. 399**

Defined 399.2

OUTLET

Definition of . . . . Art. 100 Part I

    Lighting Outlet, Definition of . . . . Art. 100 Part I

        See LIGHTING, Lighting Outlets . . . . . . Ferm's Finder

    Receptacle Outlet, Defined . . . . Art. 100

        See RECEPTACLE . . . . Ferm's Finder

OUTLET BOX . . . . **.314.27**

Ceiling . . . . .314.27(A)(2)

Ceiling Fan . . . . 314.27(C)

Extra Duty . . . . 406.9(B)

Floor . . . . 314.27(B)

Separable Attachment Fittings . . . . 314.27(E)

Utilization Equipment . . . . 314.27(D)

Vertical Surface . . . . .314.27(A)(1)

OUTLINE LIGHTING . . . . **Art. 600**

Definition . . . . Art. 100 Part I

Electric-Discharge Systems 1000 Volts or Less . . . 410 Part XII

Electric-Discharge Systems More than 1000 Volts . . . .

. . . . 410 Part XII

See SIGNS, ELECTRIC AND OUTLINE LIGHTING . . . . .

. . . . Ferm's Finder

OUTPUT CIRCUITS

Amplifiers . . . . 640.9(C)

Characteristics, Interconnected Power Production Source 705.14

Fuel Cell Systems . . . . Art. 692

Induction and Dielectric Heating Equipment 665.5

Solar Photovoltaic Systems . . . . Art. 690

OUTSIDE

Fire Pump Supply Conductors . . . . 695.6(A)

Service Conductors Considered 230.6

See OUTDOOR . . . . Ferm's Finder

OUTSIDE BRANCH CIRCUITS & FEEDERS . . . . . . **Art. 225**

Attached to Buildings or Structures 225.11

Clearance, Not over 1000 Volts

    Final Spans . . . . 225.19(D)

    From Buildings 225.19

    From Finish Grade, Sidewalks, or Platforms 225.18

    From Nonbuilding or Nonbridge Structures . . . . 225.19(B)

    Horizontal Clearances . . . . 225.19(C)

    Over Roofs . . . . 225.19(A)

    Over Swimming Pools 680.8

    Zone for Fire Ladders . . . . 225.19(E)

Clearance, Over 1000 Volts

    Over Buildings and Other Structures 225.61

    Over Roadways, Walkways, Rail, Water, and Open Land . . .

    . . . . 225.60

    See Life Safety Code, NFPA 101 . . . . .NFPA 101

Common Neutral, for Lighting . . . . 225.7(B)

Communications Systems . . . . 800 Part I

Conductor Covering 225.4

Conductor Size and Support 225.6

    Overhead Spans . . . . 225.6(A)

        Vegetation Such As Trees Not for Support 225.26

    Festoon Lighting . . . . 225.6(B)

Disconnecting Means

    Access 225.35

Construction 225.38

General 225.34

Identification 225.37

Over 1000 Volts, Location . . . . 225.52(A)

Over 1000 Volts, Not Readily Accessible . . . . . . 225.52(A)

Over 1000 Volts, Pre-Energization and Operating Tests . . . .
. . . . 225.56, 110.41

Overcurrent Protective Devices, Access 225.40

Rating 225.39

Type. 225.36

Entering a Building or Structure 225.11

Exiting a Building or Structure 225.11

Fire Alarm Circuits 760.32

Lampholders 225.24

More Than One Building or Other Structure . . . . . 225 Part II

Access to Overcurrent Protective Devices 225.40

Disconnecting Means. 225.31

Access to Occupants 225.35

Construction 225.38

Grouping 225.34

Identification 225.37

Location 225.32

Number 225.33

Rating 225.39

Suitable for Use as Service Equipment 225.36

Grounding 250.32

Number of Supplies 225.30

Over 1000 Volts . . . . 225 Part III

Open-Conductor Spacings 225.14

Size of Conductor 225.5

Wiring on Outside of Buildings or Other Structures . . 225.10

Raceways on Exterior of Buildings or Other Structures . . .
. . . . 225.22

Using Service Entrance Cable 225.21

Exterior Installations. . . . . 338.10(B)

OVENS & RANGES

Commercial

Branch-Circuit Ratings (General) . . . . 210.19(A)(4)

Calculated Load 220.56

Disconnecting Means (General). 422.30

Cord- and Plug-Connected . . . . 422.33(A)

Permanently Connected. . . . . 422.31(B)

Unit Switch(es) As Disconnecting Means . . . . 422.34(D)

Individual Branch Circuit Ratings . . . . 422.10(A)

Overcurrent Protection. . . . . 422.11(A)(D)(F)

Flexible Cord . . . . .422.16(B)(3)

Grounding of Frames 250.140

Use of Grounded Conductor . . . . .250.142(B) Ex.1

In Mobile Homes 550.16

In Park Trailers . . . . 552.55(C)

In Recreational Vehicles . . . . 551.54(C)

Household Appliances

Branch-Circuit Ratings (General) . . . . 210.19(A)(3)

Calculation of Load 220.55

Branch-Circuit Computations . . . . 220.14(B)

Demand Factors . . . . Table 220.55

Optional Demand Factors, Mobile Homes . . . .
. . . . 550.18(B)(4)(5)

Optional Demand Factors, Park Trailers . 552.47(B)(4)(5)

Disconnecting Means (General). 422.30

Cord- and Plug-Connected . . . . 422.33(A)&(B)

Permanently Connected. . . . . 422.31(B)

Unit Switch(es) as Disconnecting Means 422.34(A)(B)(C)

Individual Branch-Circuit Ratings . . . . 422.10(A)

Minimum Ampacity and Size . . . . 210.19(A)(3)

Feeder or Service Neutral Load. 220.61

Neutral Conductor. . . . . 210.19(A)(3), Ex. 2

Tap Conductors. . . . . 210.19(A)(3) Ex. 1

Overcurrent Protection . . . . 422.11(A)&(B)

Receptacle Ratings . . . . .210.21(B)(4)

See CALCULATIONS . . . . Ferm's Finder

OVER 1000 VOLTS, NOMINAL (High Voltage)

Aboveground Wiring Methods 300.37

Ampacity

Conductors to 2000 Volts 310.15

Allowable Ampacities . . . .Table 310.15(B)16 through 21

Conductors 2001 to 35,000 Volts 310.60

By Tables . . . . Table 310.60(C)67 through 86

Definitions 310.2

Modifications to Table Ambients and Burial Depths. . . .
. . . . .310.60(B)(2)

Under Engineering Supervision . . . . 310.60(C)

See Informative Annex B for examples of formula applications

See . . . . IEEE Standard Power Cable Ampacity
Tables . . . .

Bends (Conductor Radius) 300.34

Boxes, Junction and Pull . . . . 314 Part IV

   General. 314.70

   Size of

      Angle or U Pulls . . . . 314.71(B)

      Removable Sides . . . . 314.71(C)

      Straight Pulls . . . . 314.71(A)

   Suitable Covers . . . . 314.72(E)

Branch Circuits. . . . . 210.19(B)

Busways . . . . 368 Part II

Cable

   Medium Voltage Type MV. . . . . Art. 328

   Portable. . . . . 400 Part III

      Splices 400.36

   Radius of Bends 300.34

Cable Tray . . . . Art. 392

Capacitors . . . . 460 Part II

Clearance of Live Bare Parts 490.24

Clearances of Outside Branch Circuits and Feeders 225 Part III

   See OUTSIDE BRANCH CIRCUITS AND FEEDERS . . . .

   . . . . Ferm's Finder

Clearances of Service Conductors

   See Life Safety Code, NFPA 101 . . . . .NFPA 101

Conductors (General) 310.1

   Braid-Covered Insulated Conductors – Open Installation . . 300.39

   Direct Burial Conductors. . . . . 310.10(F)

      Above 2000 Volts. . . . . 310.10(F)

   Insulation and Jacket Thickness Nonshielded Solid Types RHH and RHW

      Dielectric Insulated Conductors Rated 2400 Volts . . . . .

      . . . . Table 310.104(D)

   Insulation Shielding 300.40

   Insulation Thickness, Nonshielded Dielectric Insulated Conductors

      Rated 2400 Volt. . . . . Table 310.104(D)

   Insulation Thickness Shielded Solid Dielectric

      Insulated Conductors 2001 to 35,000 Volts . . . .

      . . . . Table 310.104(E)

   Radius of Bends 300.34

   Shielding, Above 2000 Volts . . . . 310.10(E)

   Type MV, Conductor Application and Insulation . . . . . .

      . . . . Table 310.60(C)(67) thru 310.60(C)(86)

Conductors of Different Systems 300.32

Conductor Installations . . . . 110.74(B)

Definitions, General . . . . 100 Part II

High Voltage. 490.2

Disconnecting Means

   Equipment . . . . Art. 490

   Mobile and Portable Equipment . . . . 490.51(D)

   Outside Branch Circuits and Feeders . . . . 225 Part III

   Service 230.205

      Isolating Switches 230.204

      Location . . . . 230.205(A)

      Overcurrent Devices As 230.206

      Permitted to be Located Not Readily Accessible . 230.205

      Remote Control . . . . 230.205(C)

      Type . . . . 230.205(B)

      Doors . . . . .110.31(A)(3)

Electrode Type Boilers. . . . . 490 Part V

   Branch-Circuit Requirements 490.72

   Grounded Neutral Conductor . . . . 490.72(E)

   Bonding 490.74

   Supply System 490.71

Enclosure for Electrical Installations 110.31

   Conductor Installations 110.74

   Enclosed Equipment Accessible to Unqualified Persons . . .

   . . . . 110.31(D)

   Indoor Installations

      Accessible to Qualified Persons Only . . . . .110.31(B)(2)

      Accessible to Unqualified Persons . . . . . . .110.31(B)(1)

   Locked Rooms or Enclosures . . . . 110.34(C)

   Outdoor Installations

      Accessible to Qualified Persons Only . . . . .110.31(C)(2)

   Accessible to Unqualified Persons . . . . . . .110.31(C)(1)

   See Definition of Qualified Person . . . . Art. 100

Entrance and Access to Work Space 110.33

Equipment Over 1000 Volts

   Backfeed 490.25

   Circuit Breakers 490.45

   Circuit-Interrupting Devices. 490.21

      Circuit Breakers . . . . 490.21(A)

      Distribution Cutouts and Fuse Links, Expulsion Type . .

      . . . . 490.21(C)

      Load Interrupters . . . . 490.21(E)

      Oil-Filled Cutouts . . . . 490.21(D)

      Power Fuses and Fuseholders . . . . 490.21(B)

   Danger Signage

      Accessibility to Energized Parts 490.35

      Backfeed Installations 490.25

Cable Connections. Portable 490.55

Enclosures, Portable 490.53

Fuseholders . . . . .490.21(B)(6)

Definition Applying to Article 490.2

Door Stops and Cover Plates 490.38

Electrode-Type Boilers . . . . 490 Part V

Enclosures in Wet or Damp Locations . . . . 490.3(B)

Fused Interrupter Switches 490.44

Gas Discharge from Interrupting Devices 490.39

Grounding 490.36

Isolating Means 490.22

Metal-Enclosed Power Switchgear and Industrial Control
Assemblies . . . . 490 Part III

Minimum Space Separation 490.24

Mobile and Portable . . . . 490 Part IV

Oil-Filled Equipment . . . . 490.3(A)

Specific Provisions . . . . 490 Part II

Substations 490.48

Switchgear Used as Service Equipment 490.47

Visual Inspection Windows 490.40

Voltage Regulators 490.23

Warning Signage

Isolating Switches 490.22

Substations . . . . 490.48(B)

Fences (Metal), Grounding and Bonding . . . . . . 250.194(A)

General Installations . . . . 110 Part III

Grounding . . . . 250 Part X

Cable Shields 490.47

Connected to an Equipment Grounding Conductor . 490.36

Derived Neutral Systems 250.182

Equipment 250.190

Grounding Service-Supplied Alternating-Current Systems .
. . . . 250.186

Impedance Grounded Neutral Systems 250.187

Of Equipment, Fences and Enclosures, etc. 250.190

Of Systems Supplying Portable or Mobile Equipment 250.188

Solidly Grounded Neutral Systems 250.184

Illumination about Electrical Equipment . . . . . . 110.34(D)

Impedance Grounded Neutral Systems 250.187

Locking, Circuit Breaker Capability 490.46

Locks . . . . .110.31(A)(4)

Manholes and Other Enclosures Intended for Personnel Entry
. . . . 110 Part V

Mobile & Portable Equipment . . . . 490 Part IV

Moisture or Mechanical Protection for Metal-Sheathed Cables
. . . . 300.42

Motors . . . . 430 Part XI

Motor Disconnecting Means 430.227

Motor Grounding, Connected to EGC 430.245

Outside Branch Circuits and Feeders . . . . 225 Part III

Isolating Switches 225.51

Overcurrent Protection . . . . 240 Part IX

Feeders and Branch Circuits 240.100

Additional Requirements for Feeders 240.101

Services . . . . 230 Part VIII

Enclosed Devices . . . . 230.208(B)

Overcurrent Device as Disconnecting Means . . . 230.206

Protection Requirements 230.208

Transformers . . . . 450.3(A)

Protection against Induction Heating 300.35

Resistors & Reactors . . . . 470 Part II

Services . . . . 230 Part VIII

Signs, Warning

Distribution Cutouts and Fuse Links, Expulsion Type . . . .
. . . . .490.21(C)(2)

Fused Interrupter Switches . . . . 490.44(B)

High-Voltage Fuses . . . . 490.21(B)(7) Ex.

Load Interrupters . . . . 490.21(E)

Mobile and Portable Equipment Enclosures 490.53

Power Cable Connections to Mobile Machines 490.55

Pull and Junction Boxes . . . . 314.72(E)

Rooms and Enclosures . . . . 110.34(C)

Substations . . . . 490.48(B)

Vaults and Equipment Rooms . . . . .490.48(B)(1)

Structures (Metal), Grounding and Bonding . . . . .250.194(B)

Substations 490.48

Surge Arresters . . . . Art. 280

Services (Lightning Arresters) 230.209

Switching Mechanism, Lock Remains in Place . . . . 490.44(C)

Temporary Wiring, Guarding 590.7

Transformers . . . . Art. 450

Overcurrent Protection of . . . . 450.3(A)

Specific Provisions Applicable to Different Types . 450 Part II

Vaults . . . . .110.31(A)(5)

Tunnel Installations . . . . 110 Part IV

Underground Installations 300.50

Backfill . . . . 300.50(E)

Industrial Establishments . . . . 300.50(A)(2)

Minimum Cover Requirements . . . . Table 300.50

Other Nonshielded Cables . . . . 300.50(A)(3)

Protection from Damage . . . . 300.50(C)

Raceway Seal . . . . 300.50(F)

Shielded Cables and Nonshielded Cables in Metal-Sheathed Cable

    Assemblies . . . . 300.50(A)(1)

    Splices . . . . 300.50(D)

Vaults

    Conductors Considered Outside Building . . . . . . 230.6(3)

    Doors . . . . .110.31(A)(3)

    Floors . . . . .110.31(A)(2)

    General Requirements for . . . . 450 Part III

    Installations in 110.31

    Locks . . . . .110.31(A)(4)

    Separation from Low-Voltage Equipment . . . 110.34(B) Ex.

    Services Over 35,000 Volts 230.212

    Specific Provisions Applicable to Different Types of Transformers . . . . 450 Part II

        Transformers . . . . .110.31(A)(5)

        Walls and Roof . . . . .110.31(A)(1)

Warning Signs, Conductor Access in Conduit and Cable Systems 300.45

    Wet Locations

        Above Grade 300.38

        Underground . . . . 300.50(B)

Wiring Methods . . . . 300 Part II

Working Space

    About Equipment 110.32

    Clear Space . . . . 110.34(A)

    Entrance and Access to 110.33

OVERCURRENT DEVICES

Not In Bathrooms . . . . 240.24(E)

Not In Clothes Closets . . . . 240.24(D)

Not Over Steps . . . . 240.24(F)

OVERCURRENT PROTECTION . . . . Art. 240

Access to (Location of) . . . . 240 Part II

Circuit Breakers Used as Switches . . . . 404.8(A)

In Circuit 240.21

In or on Premises 240.24

More Than One Building or Structure 225.40

Multiple-Occupancy Building . . . . 230.72(C)

    By Each Occupant . . . . 240.24(B)

Locked Service Overcurrent Devices 230.92

Air-Conditioning & Refrigeration Equipment . . . . 240.4(G)

    Branch-Circuit Short-Circuit & Ground-Fault . . 440 Part III

    Location of 440.14

    Motor-Compressor & Branch-Circuit Overload . . 440 Part VI

Ampere Rating 240.6

    Adjustable-Trip Circuit Breakers . . . . 240.6(B)

    Fuses and Fixed-Trip Circuit Breakers . . . . . . 240.6(A)

    Restricted Access Adjustable-Trip Circuit Breakers . 240.6(C)

    Table-Standard Ampere Rating . . . . Table 240.6(A)

Appliances 422.11

Branch-Circuit Conductors and Equipment 210.20

    Overcurrent Protective Device, Branch-Circuit

    Definition of . . . . Art. 100

    Overcurrent Protective Device, Supplementary

    Definition of . . . . Art. 100

Branch-Circuit Taps . . . . 210.19(A)(4) Ex. 1

    General Requirements . . . . 240.21(A)

    Protection of Conductors 240.4

Breakers (Up Position Must Be On Position) 240.81

    Used As Switches 404.7

    See BREAKERS & FUSES . . . . Ferm's Finder

Busways 368.17

    Busway Taps . . . . 240.21(E)

    Feeders or Branch Circuits 368.17

    Feeders . . . . 368.17(A)

    Rating for Branch Circuit . . . . 368.17(D)

    Reduction in Size . . . . 368.17(B)

Capacitors . . . . 240.4(G)

    Conductors . . . . 460.8(B)

    For Units 460.25

    See Power Factor Correction Capacitors . . . . Ferm's Charts and Formulas

Cartridge Fuses . . . . 240 Part VI

    Classification of 240.61

    See FUSES . . . . Ferm's Finder

Class 1 Remote Control and Signaling Circuits 725.41

Class 2 and 3 Remote Control and Signaling Circuits . 725.121

    Conductors 240.4

    Limitations Chapter 9 . . . . Tables 11(A)&(B)

    Taps 240.21

Conductors from Generator Terminals . . . . 240.21(G)

Control Circuits

    Cranes 610.53

Elevators . . . . 620.61(A)

Motors 430.72

Others (General) 240.4

Specific Applications . . . . 240.4(G)

Cords (Flexible) 240.5

Ampacity to Be Used for Determining . Table 400.5(A)(1) &
Table 400.5(A)(2) . . . .

Cranes & Hoists . . . . 610 Part VI

Control Circuits, Creating Hazard . . . . 610.53(B)

Definition of

Overcurrent Protective Device, Branch-Circuit . . . Art. 100

Current-Limiting Overcurrent Protective Device 240.2

Overcurrent . . . . Art. 100 Part I

Deicing & Snow-Melting Equipment 426.4

Nonheating Leads . . . . 210.19(A)(4) Ex.1(e)

Devices (Fuses or Circuit Breakers) in Parallel 240.8

Devices Rated 800 Amperes or Less . . . . 240.4(B)

Devices Rated Over 800 Amperes . . . . 240.4(C)

Direct Current Systems (General) 240.1

Disconnecting Means Ahead of Fuses 240.40

Electrical System Coordination. 240.12

Ground-Fault Protection, Health Care Facilities. . . . . . .
. . . . .517.17(B) and (C)

Electric Vehicle Charging Systems 625.41

Electric Welders . . . . 240.4(G)

Arc Welders . . . . 630 Part II

For Conductors. . . . . 630.12(B)

For Welder . . . . 630.12(A)

Resistance Welders . . . . 630 Part III

For Conductors. . . . . 630.32(B)

For Welders . . . . 630.32(A)

Electroplating 669.9

Elevators, Dumbwaiters, Escalators, Moving Walks,

Wheelchair & Stairway Chair Lifts . . . . 620 Part VII

Emergency Systems . . . . 700 Part VI

Feeder Taps Not Over 3 m (10 ft). . . . . .240.21(B)(1)

Feeder Taps Not Over 7.5 m (25 ft) . . . . .240.21(B)(2)

Transformer (Primary Plus Secondary). . . . .240.21(B)(3)

Feeder Taps Over 7.5 m (25 ft) (High Bay Manufacturing) . . .
. . . . .240.21(B)(4)

Feeder Taps Outside, Unlimited Length . . . . .240.21(B)(5)

Feeders 240.4

General. 215.3

Taps. . . . . 240.21(B)

Fire Protective Signaling Systems . . . . 240.4(G)

NPLFA Circuit Conductors 760.43

Limitations . . . . Chapter 9 Tables 12(A) and 12(B)

Location of 760.45

Fire Pumps . . . . 695.4(B)(1)(a)(1)

Feeder Sources . . . . 695.5(C)(2)

Overload Protection . . . . 695.6(C)

Transformers Supplying . . . . 695.5(B)

(Fixture) Luminaire Wire 240.5

Ampacity To Be Used for Determining. . . . . . Table 402.5

General. 402.14

Supplementary Protection 240.10

Overcurrent Protective Device, Supplementary, Definition of
. . . . 100 Part I

Fuel Cell Systems. 692.9

Conductor Ampacity, Relative to . . . . 692.8(B)

Fuses, See FUSES. . . . . Ferm's Finder

Generators 445.12

Heating Equipment (Space) 424.22

Heating Equipment for Pipelines & Vessels 427.4

Heating Equipment, Induction & Dielectric 665.11

Industrial Machinery . . . . 670.4(B) & (C)

Irrigation Machines . . . . Art. 675

Lampholders . . . . 210.21(A)

Not for Plug Fuses. 410.90

Summary Requirements 210.24

Location of, in Circuit 240.21

Location of, in or on Premises

Circuit Breakers Used As Switches . . . . 404.8(A)

For Service Equipment . . . . 230 Part VII

General. 240.24

Location Related to Service Disconnecting Means . . 230.91

Not Exposed to Physical Damage . . . . 240.24(C)

Not Permitted in Clothes Closets or in Bathrooms . . . . . .
. . . . 240.24(D)&(E)

Protection of Specific Circuits 230.93

Locked, Sealed or Not Readily Accessible

More than One Building or Structure. 225.40

Service Overcurrent Device 230.92

Specific Circuits 230.93

Metal Working Machine Tools, etc. . . . . 670.4(C)

Motion Picture Studios 530.18

Feeders . . . . 530.18(B)

Lighting, Other Than Stage Set . . . . 530.18(G)

Location Boards . . . . 530.18(D)

Plugging Boxes . . . . 530.18(E)

Stage or Set Cables . . . . 530.18(A)

Substations, DC Generators 530.63

Motor Circuits & Feeders

Branch-Circuit Short-Circuit & Ground-Fault . . 430 Part IV

Feeder Short-Circuit & Ground-Fault . . . . . . 430 Part V

Motor and Branch-Circuit Overload Protection 430 Part III

Over 1000 Volts 430.225

Motor & Motor Control . . . . 240.4(G)

Control Circuits 430.72

Motor-Operated Appliances (General) . . . . 240.4(G)

Specific . . . . 422.11(B) through (G)

Multiple-Occupancy Buildings

See MULTIPLE-OCCUPANCY BUILDINGS . Ferm's Finder

See OVERCURRENT PROTECTION, Access to (Location of) . . . . Ferm's Finder

Next Higher Size Permitted . . . . 240.4(B)

Individual Motor Circuit . . . . 430.52(C)(1) Ex. 1 & 2

No Overcurrent Device in the Grounded Conductor

Fuses Used as Overload Protection 430.36

General Restriction 240.22

Service Equipment . . . . 230.90(B)

Not Located Over Steps of a Stairway . . . . 240.24(F)

Not Required Fire Pump Power Wiring, Short Circuit Only . . . . 695.6(C)

Fire Pump Transformer Secondary . . . . 695.5(B)

Generators . . . . 445.12 Ex.

Power Loss Hazard . . . . 240.4(A)

Selection . . . . 695.4(B)(2)

Orderly Shutdown

Ground-Fault Protection of Equipment . . . . . . 240.13(1)

Integrated Electrical Systems 685.10

Motors 430.44

Power Loss Hazard . . . . 240.4(A)

Selective Coordination (Emergency Systems) 700.32

Selective Coordination (Legally Required Standby Systems) 701.27

Services, GFPE . . . . 230.95 Ex.

System Coordination 240.12

Note: If immediate automatic shutdown of equipment would increase personnel hazard and equipment damage, it is permissible to connect the overload protective device to an alarm system instead of causing immediate interruption of the circuit, so corrective action

or an orderly shutdown can be initiated.

Organs (Pipe) 650.8

Outlet Devices 210.21

Rated Less Than 800 Amperes . . . . 240.4(B)(1)

Outside Branch Circuits and Feeders 225.3

Over 1000 Volts, Nominal . . . . 240 Part IX

Enclosed Devices . . . . 230.208(B)

Equipment Requirements . . . . Art. 490

Services, Overcurrent Device As Disconnecting Means 230.206

Transformers . . . . 450.3(A)

Panelboards 408.36

Maximum Number in Panelboards 408.54

Phase Converters (General) . . . . 240.4(G)

Supply Conductors and Converter 455.7

Pipe Organs 650.8

Places of Assembly, Power Outlets 518.5

Plug Fuses . . . . 240 Part V

Not in Lampholders 410.90

Power Loss Hazard . . . . 240.4(A)

Protection of Conductors 240.4

Readily Accessible Place

Accessibility . . . . 240.24(A)

Services 230.92

Switches and Circuit Breakers . . . . 404.8(A)

Receptacles 210.21

Conductors Feeding, Under 800 Amperes . . . . . 240.4(B)

Summary Requirements 210.24

Remote Control, Signaling, Power Limited . . . . . . 240.4(G)

Resistance-Type Boilers 424.72

Selective Coordination

Critical Operations Power Systems (COPS) 708.54

Elevators, Etc. 620.62

Emergency Systems 700.32

Legally Required Standby Systems 701.27

Selectivity, GFPE, Health Care Facilities . . . . . . 517.17(C)

Sensitive Electronic Equipment . . . . 647.4(A)

Separate Buildings or Structures 225.3

Separately Derived Systems . . . . 240.4(F)

Conductor Protection . . . . 240.21(C)

Panelboard Supplied through a Transformer . . . . 408.36(B)

Sensitive Electronic Equipment, 60 Volts to Ground 647.4(A)

Supervised Industrial Installations, Feeder Taps . . 240.92(B)

See SEPARATELY DERIVED SYSTEMS . . . . Ferm's Finder

Service Conductors

    Location of. 230.91

    Over 1000 Volts As Service Disconnect. 230.206

    Relative Location of Device 230.94

    Service Equipment 230.90

Services . . . . 230 Part VII

Signs & Outline Lighting, Maximum Rating for . . . . 600.5(B)

Small Conductors, 16 and 18 AWG . . . . 240.4(D)

Solar Photovoltaic Systems 690.9

Standard Ampere Ratings 240.6

    Adjustable-Trip Circuit Breakers . . . . 240.6(B)

    Fuses and Fixed-Trip Circuit Breakers . . . . 240.6(A)

    Restricted Access Adjustable-Trip Circuit Breakers   240.6(C)

Supervised Industrial Installations . . . . 240 Part VIII

    Definition 240.2

    Location in Circuit

        Feeder and Branch-Circuit Conductors . . . . . 240.92(A)

        Outside Feeder Taps . . . . 240.92(D)

        Protection by Primary Overcurrent Device . . . 240.92(E)

        Transformer Secondary Conductors, Separately

          Derived Systems . . . . 240.92(C)

Supplementary Overcurrent Protection

    Appliances with Resistance-Type Elements Over 48 Amperes

    . . . . 422.11(F)

    Fixed Electric Space-Heating 424.22

    Not As Substitute for Branch-Circuit Devices 240.10

    Tapped Motor Control Circuits . . . . 430.72(A)

Switchboards & Panelboards 408.36

    Protection of Instrument Circuits 408.52

Tap Conductors . . . . 240.4(E)

    Battery Conductor Taps . . . . 240.21(H)

    Busway Taps . . . . 240.21(E)

    Definition of 240.2

    From Generator Terminals. . . . . 240.21(G)

    Motor Circuit Taps . . . . 240.21(F)

    Service Conductor Taps . . . . 240.21(D)

    Transformer Secondary taps . . . . 240.21(C)

Theaters

    Dimmers 520.25

    Portable Equipment Other Than Switchboards . . 520.62(B)

    Portable Switchboards on Stage Overcurrent Protection . . .

    . . . . 520.53

    Receptacle Circuits . . . . 520.62(B)

    Road Show Connection Panel . . . . 520.50(C)

Thermal Devices Not Designed for Short-circuit Use . . . 240.9

Transformers 450.3

    1000 Volts or Less . . . . 450.3(B)

    Autotransformers, 1000 Volts or Less . . . . 450.4(A)

    Ground Reference for Fault Protection Devices . 450.5(B)(2)

    Grounding Autotransformers Three-Phase 4-Wire . . . . . .

    . . . . 450.5(A)(2)

    Over 1000 Volts . . . . 450.3(A)

    Panelboard Supplied from . . . . 408.3(C)

    Secondary Conductors (General) . . . . 240.4(F)

Secondary Conductors (Specific). . . . . 240.21(C)

    Secondary Ties . . . . 450.6(B)

    Supplying Transformer, Primary Plus Secondary Not Over

      7.5 m (25 ft) . . . . 240.21(B)(3)

    Voltage (Potential) Transformers . . . . 450.3(C)

Ungrounded Conductors 240.15

Vertical Position, Enclosures 240.33

Wet Locations 240.32

    Cabinets and Cutout Boxes 312.2

    Used As Switches 404.4

X-Ray Equipment

    Health Care Facilities 517.73

    Industrial, Nonmedical and Nondental Use 660.6

OVERLOAD

Definition . . . . Art. 100

Example- How Calculated. . Informative Annex D, Example D8

Protection

    Appliances- Motor Operated. . . . . 422.11(G)

    Cranes and Hoists. 610.43

    Devices (other than fuses) . . . . . . 430.37 and Table 430.37

    Elevators, Etc. 620.21(B)

    Fire Pumps- not have . . . . 695.6(C)

    Motor. . . . . 430 Part III

    Power Loss Hazard (created). . . . . 240.4(A)

    Service Conductors 230.90

Thermal Devices (not for protection of conductors) 240.9

P

PADDLE (CEILING-SUSPENDED) FANS

Bathtubs and Shower Areas above . . . . 410.10(D)

Outlet Box, Support of . . . . 314.27(C)

Separable Attachment Fitting . . . . 314.27(E)

Spare Separately Switched Ungrounded Conductors 314.27(C)

Spas and Hot Tubs, Indoor . . . . 680.43(B)

Support of 422.18

Swimming Pools . . . . 680.22(B)

See also CEILING-SUSPENDED (PADDLE) FANS . . . . . .
. . . . Ferm's Finder

PAINT SPRAYING . . . . **Art. 516**
See SPRAY APPLICATION, DIPPING, AND COATING . . .
. . . . Ferm's Finder

See (QEFY) . . . . *UL Product Speck*

PANELBOARDS, SWITCHGEAR & SWITCHBOARDS . **Art. 408**

Accessibility 240.24

Containing Switches or Circuit Breakers 404.8

Of Energized Parts over 1000 Volts 490.35

To Occupants . . . . 230.72(C)

Bare Metal Parts, Minimum Spacing 408.56

Barriers . . . . 312.11(D)

Conductors in Same Vertical Section . . . . . . 408.3(A)(3)

In Service Switchboards and Switchgear . . . . 408.3(A)(2)

Bending Space for Wire Within Panelboard Enclosure

Back Wire-Bending Space . . . . 408.55(C)

Side Wire-Bending Space . . . . 408.55(B)

Top and Bottom Wire-Bending Space . . . . . . 408.55(A)

Bonding, Health Care 517.14

Breakers (Up Position On) 240.81

In Enclosures 404.7

Cable Entering . . . . 312.5(C)

Deflection of Conductors 312.6

Clearances

Around Switchboards and Switchgear . . . . . . 408.18(B)

Clear Spaces . . . . 110.26(B)

From Ceilings, Switchboards and Switchgear . . . 408.18(A)

Clearance of Bare Live Parts

Auxiliary Gutters, In . . . . 366.100(E)

Bus Enclosures 408.5

Cabinets and Cutout Boxes, in . . . . 312.11(A)(3)

Minimum Spacings Bare Metal Parts 408.56

Over 1000 Volts 110.34

Minimum Space Separation 490.24

Under 600 Volts 110.26

Conductor Bending Space Within Panelboard Enclosure

Back Wire-Bending Space . . . . 408.55(C)

Side Wire-Bending Space . . . . 408.55(B)

Top and Bottom Wire-Bending Space . . . . . . 408.55(A)

Conductors Feeding through (General) . . . . 312.8(A)

Isolated Equipment Grounding Conductor . . . 250.146(D)

Not Required to Terminate in . . . . 408.40 Ex.

Conduit Risers Entering Bottom Shall Not Exceed 75 mm (3 in.)
. . . . 408.5

Damp or Wet Locations

Cabinets and Cutout Boxes 312.2

Containing Overcurrent Devices 240.32

Panelboards 408.37

Switchboards and Switchgear 408.16

Dead Front (Required) 408.38

Dedicated Equipment Space . . . . 110.26(E)

Over 1000 Volts . . . . 110.34(F)

Definition of (Panelboard, Switchboard, Switchgear) . . . . . .
. . . . Art. 100 Part I

Enclosure 408.38

Field Identification Required 408.4

Grounding . . . . 408.3(C)

Of Panelboards 408.40

Supplying Swimming Pool Equipment 680.25

Grounding Terminal Bar (Required) 408.40

Health Care Facilities 517.14

Critical Care (Category 1) Spaces . . . . 517.19(D)

High-Leg Identification . . . . 408.3(F)

High-Leg Marking 110.15

High-Leg Phase Arrangement . . . . 408.3(E)

Identification of Disconnecting Means 110.22

Circuits and Modifications 408.4

Illumination . . . . 110.26(D)

Over 1000 Volts . . . . 110.34(D)

Marking of Panelboards 408.58

See Marking Guide for Panelboards . . . . . *UL Product Spec*

Maximum Number of Overcurrent Devices 408.54

Minimum Spacing, Bare Minimum Parts 408.56

Mounting of (General Equipment) 110.13

Damp and Wet Locations 312.2

Position in Wall 312.3

No Delta Breakers . . . . 408.36(C)

Open Bottom Equipment, Mechanical Continuity of Raceways and Cables 300.12

Overcurrent Protection 408.36

Power Monitoring Equipment . . . . 312.8(B)

Readily Accessible

    Air-Conditioning or Refrigeration Equipment 440.14

    Location in or on Premises (General). 240.24

    Motor Disconnecting Means. 430.107

    Service Equipment . . . . 230.70(A)(1)

    Switches and Circuit Breakers . . . . 404.8(A)

Repairing Noncombustible Surfaces 312.4

Signs

    Caution, Meet These Requirements . . . . . . 110.21(B)

    Danger, Meet These Requirements . . . . 110.21(B)

    Field-Applied . . . . 110.21(A)

    Warning, Meet These Requirements . . . . 110.21(B)

Source of Power, Marking. . . . . 408.4(B)

Spare Circuits Identified as Spares 408.4

Splices in . . . . 312.8(A)

Split-Bus Panels (As Service Equipment) . . . . . 408.36 Ex. 1

Support of (General Equipment). . . . . 110.13(A)

    Damp, Wet, or Hazardous Locations 312.2

    Position in Wall 312.3

Taps to Conductors . . . . 312.8(A)

Terminals . . . . 408.3(D)

Wet or Damp Locations

    Cabinets and Cutout Boxes 312.2

    Containing Overcurrent Devices 240.32

    Panelboards 408.16

    Switchboards. 408.16

    Switchgear 408.16

Wire Bending Space

    At Terminals. 312.6(B)

    For Conductors Entering Bus Enclosures 408.5

    In Panelboards 408.55

        Back Wire-Bending Space. . . . . 408.55(C)

        Side Wire-Bending Space . . . . 408.55(B)

        Top and Bottom Wire-Bending Space . . . . . 408.55(A)

Working Clearance and Space . . . . 110.26(A)

    Access and Entrance to . . . . 110.26(C)

    Existing Dwelling Units . . . . 110.26(A)(3) Ex. 1

    Headroom . . . . .110.26(A)(3)

    Over 1000 Volts 110.32

        Entrance and Access to 110.33

        Clear Space 110.34

See (QEUY) . . . . .UL Product Spec

See Switchboards (WEIR) . . . . .UL Product Spec

PANEL, (SOLAR PHOTOVOLTAIC SYSTEMS)

Definition of 690.2

PANIC HARDWARE, LISTED

Over 1000 Volts . . . . .110.33(A)(3)

Storage Batteries 480.9

Under 1000 Volts . . . . .110.26(C)(3)

PARALLEL

Alternate Power Sources, Additional Service Permitted . . . . 230.2(A)(5)

    Interconnected Electric Power Production Sources . Art. 705

Breakers & Fuses Not Permitted in 240.8

    Fused Switches. 404.27

Cables and Raceways to Framing Members. . . . . . . 300.4(D)

    Type NM Cable 334.17

Conductors 1/0 AWG and Larger . . . . 310.10(H)

    Ampacity Adjustment (Derating) . . . . 310.10(H)4

    Cable Tray Installations. . . . . 392.20(C)

    Conductors of Same Circuit . . . . 300.3(B)(1)

    Conductors of Same Circuit Underground. . 300.5(I) Ex. 1–2

    Equipment Bonding Conductors . . . . 310.10(H)(5)

    Equipment Grounding Conductors . . . . 250.122(F)

    Exceptions to Minimum Size Rule . . 310.10(H)(1) Ex. 1–2

    General Requirements for Paralleled Conductors . 310.10(H)

    Run in Separate Raceways or Cables (Paralleled) . . . . 310.10(H)(3)

Elevator Traveling Cables . . . . .620.12(A)(1)

Equipment Bonding Jumpers. . . . . 250.102(D)

Equipment Grounding Conductors . . . . .250.122(F)

Frequencies 360 Hz and Higher . . . . . . 310.10(H)(1) Ex. 1

Grounded Neutral Conductors, Existing Installations

    Under Engineering Supervision . . . . . 310.10(H)(1) Ex. 2

Raceways

    Conductor and Installation Characteristics . . 310.10(H)(2)

    Conductors in Same . . . . 300.3(B)(1)

    Conductors in Same, Underground . . . . . 300.5(I) Ex. 1–2

    Same Physical Characteristics . . . . 310.10(H)(2)

Service-Entrance Conductors. . . . . 250.24(C)(2)

Stage Switchboard Feeders . . . . 520.27(A)

Supply-Side Bonding Jumper . . . . 250.102(C)(2)

Transformers

    Parallel Operation Permitted 450.7

    Secondary Ties 450.6

PARK TRAILERS . . . . Art. 552

Attachment Plug . . . . 552.44(C)

Bonding 552.57

Branch Circuits

    Determined- Number 552.46

    Protection 552.42

Calculations 552.47

Combination Electrical Systems 552.20

Conductors and Boxes 552.49

Cord 552.44

    Attachment Plugs . . . . 552.44(C)

    Cord Length . . . . 552.44(B)

    Labeling . . . . 552.44(D)

Definition of 552.2

Distribution Panelboard 552.45

    Grounded Conductor Insulated from Enclosure . 552.45(A)

Grounding 552.55

Interior Equipment Grounding 552.56

Labels 552.5

Low-Voltage Systems 552.10

Luminaires (Lighting Fixtures) 552.54

Nominal 120- or 120/240-Volt Systems 552.40

Outdoor Outlets, Luminaires (Fixtures), Equipment . . . 552.59

Power Supply 552.43

Receptacle Configuration . . . . Figure 552.44(C)(1)

Receptacle Outlets Not Permitted . . . . 552.41(F)

Receptacle Outlets Required 552.41

    Ground-Fault Circuit-Interrupter Protection . . . 552.41(C)

    Pipe Heating Cable Outlet . . . . 552.41(D)

    Outdoor Receptacle Outlets . . . . 552.41(E)

Switches 552.52

Tests Required (Factory) 552.60

Wiring Methods 552.48

PART-WINDING MOTORS 430.4

Code Letter Markings . . . . 430.7(B)(5)

Single Motor Conductors . . . . 430.22(D)

PATH, GROUNDING

Effective Ground Fault Current Path, Defined . . . . . Art. 100

    For Grounded Systems . . . . 250.4(A)(5)

    For Ungrounded Systems . . . . 250.4(B)(4)

To Grounding Electrode At Service . . . . 250.24(D)

PATIENT BED LOCATION

Critical Care (Category 1) Space 517.19

Definition of 517.2

General Care (Category 2) Space 517.18

Multiwire Branch Circuit Prohibited 517.18

PATIENT CARE SPACES

Definitions within Patient Care Space

    Basic Care (Category 3) Space 517.2

    Critical Care (Category 1) Space 517.2

    General Care (Category 2) Space 517.2

    Support (Category 4) Space 517.2

Critical Care (Category 1) Space 517.19

General Care (Category 2) Space 517.18

Wet Procedure Locations 517.20

PATIENT CARE VICINITY (Definition of) 517.2

Grounding and Bonding (Optional) . . . . 517.19(D)

PEDIATRIC LOCATIONS

Listed Tamper Resistant Receptacles or Covers Required . . . .

. . . . 517.18(C)

PENDANTS

See FIXTURES (LUMINAIRES) LIGHTING, Pendants . . . . .

. . . . Ferm's Finder

PENINSULA COUNTERTOP

Peninsula Countertop Locations, Receptacle Outlets 210.52(C)

PERFORMANCE TESTING

Ground Fault Protection of Equipment . . . . 230.95(C)

SCADA Systems . . . . Informative Annex G

PERMANENT AMUSEMENT ATTRACTIONS

Conductors

    Ampacity 522.22

    Overcurrent Protection 522.23

    Size 522.21

    Type 522.20

Control Circuits . . . . Art. 522 Part II

Control Systems . . . . Art. 522

Definitions 522.2

Ungrounded Control Circuits 522.25

Wet Locations 522.28

Wiring Methods, Control Circuits . . . . Art. 522 Part III

See Article 525 for Carnivals, Circuses, Fairs, and
Similar Events . . . . Ferm's Finder

PERMANENTLY INSTALLED GENERATORS

Grounding 250.35

PERMANENT WARNING SIGNS (REQUIRED)

See WARNING SIGNS . . . . Ferm's Finder

PERMISSIBLE LOADS

Individual Branch Circuits 210.22

Multiple-Outlet Branch Circuits 210.23

PERSON, QUALIFIED (Definition of) . . . . Art. 100

See QUALIFIED PERSON, WORK BY . . . . . . Ferm's Finder

PHASE CONVERTERS . . . . Art. 455

Capacitors 455.23

Conductors

   Ampacity. . . . . 455.6(A)

   Manufactured Phase Marking . . . . 455.6(B)

Definitions 455.2

Disconnecting Means 455.8

Equipment Grounding Connection 455.5

Marking (Nameplate Information) 455.4

Overcurrent Protection 455.7

Rotary-Phase Converter, Definition of 455.2

Single-Phase Loads Not Connected to Manufactured Phase . .
. . . . 455.9

Specific Provisions Applicable for Different Types of 455 Part II

   Disconnecting Means, Static-Phase Converter 455.20

   Power Interruption, Rotary-Phase Converter 455.22

   Start-Up, Rotary-Phase Converter 455.21

Static-Phase Converter, Definition of 455.2

Terminal Housings 455.10

PHOTOVOLTAIC SYSTEMS (SOLAR) . . . . Art. 690

Arc-Fault Circuit Protection (DC) 690.11

Auxiliary Grounding Electrode. . . . . 690.47(B)

Calculations for Maximum Current of Circuit . . . . . 690.8(A)

Charge Control. 690.72

Circuit Requirements . . . . Art. 690 Part II

Circuit Sizing. 690.8

Connection to Other Sources. 690.59

Connectors 690.33

Correction Factors . . . . Table 690.31(A)

Defined . . . . Article 100

Definitions Applicable to System 690.2

Disconnecting Means . . . . Art. 690 Part III

   Disconnect PV Equipment. 690.15

   Location . . . . 690.13(A)

   Marking . . . . 690.13(B)

   Maximum Number of . . . . 690.13(D)

   Not in Grounded Conductor 690.15

   Rapid Shutdown. 690.12

   Ratings . . . . 690.13(E)

   Suitable for Use . . . . 690.13(C)

   Type of Disconnect . . . . 690.13(F)

Disconnect Type 690.15

Electric Vehicle Charging . . . . Art. 690 Part X

Energy Storage Systems 690.71

Equipment- Not Located in Bathrooms . . . . 690.4(E)

Functional Grounded PV System 690.2

General Requirements. 690.4

Ground-Fault Protection . . . . 690.41(B)

Grounding . . . . Art. 690 Part V

Grounding Electrode System 690.47

Identification of Power Systems 690.56

Interrupting Rating . . . . 690.15(B)

Large-Scale Photovoltaic (PV) Electric Power Production
Facility. . . . . Art. 691

   Applicable PV Systems (no less than 5000 kW) 691.1

   Arc-Fault Mitigation 691.10

   Conformance of Construction to Engineered Design. . 691.7

   Definitions. 691.2

   Direct Current Operating Voltage. 691.8

   Disconnection of Photovoltaic Equipment 691.9

   Engineered Design 691.6

   Equipment Approval 691.5

   Fence Grounding 691.11

   Special Requirements 691.4

Listed Equipment . . . . 690.4(B)

Locations Not Permitted . . . . 690.4(E)

Marking . . . . Art. 690 Part VI

Modules- Alternating-Current (ac) 690.6

Multiple Inverters . . . . 690.4(D)

Over 1000 Volts . . . . Art. 690 Part IX

Overcurrent Protection 690.9

Qualified Personnel . . . . 690.4(C)

Rapid Shutdown 690.12

　Labels . . . . 690.56(C)

Serving a Building with an Electrical Supply System . . 690.4(A)

Stand-Alone Systems 690.10

Storage Batteries . . . . Art. 690 Part VIII

Temperature Correction Factors . . . . Table 690.31(A)

Wiring Methods . . . . Art. 690 Part IV

See SOLAR PHOTOVOLTAIC SYSTEMS . . . . Ferm's Finder

See (QHWJ) . . . . .UL Product Spec

See (QIGU) . . . . .UL Product Spec

PHYSICAL PROTECTION

Agricultural Buildings . . . . 547.5(E)

Bushing . . . . 300.5(H)

Conductors, Raceways, and Cables 300.4

Cables, Raceways and Boxes Installed Under Roof Decking . . . . 300.4(E)

Electrical Metallic Tubing (EMT) 358.2

Fixed Electric Heating Equipment for Pipelines and Vessels 427.11

Furring Strips . . . . 300.4(D)

Information Technology Equipment . . . . 645.5(D)

Insulated Fittings . . . . 300.4(G)

Intermediate Metal Conduit (IMC) 342.2

Notches in Wood . . . . 300.4(A)(2)

Parallel to Framing Members . . . . 300.4(D)

Park Trailers- Low-Voltage Wiring . . . . .552.10(C)(1)

Raceway (Minor Damage) . . . . 300.4 Info Note

Rigid Metal Conduit (RMC) 344.2

Safety-Control Equipment . . . . 725.31(B)

Shallow Grooves . . . . 300.4(F)

Transformer Secondary Conductors . . . . .240.92(C)(3)

PIN AND SLEEVE TYPE PLUGS, RECEPTACLES AND CABLE CONNECTORS

See (QLGD) . . . . .UL Product Spec

PIPE ELECTRODES . . . . 250.52(A)(5)

Connection of Grounding Electrode Conductor to . 250.66(A)

Installation of . . . . 250.53(G)

Physical Protection 250.10

Resistance of . . . . 250.53(A)(2) Ex.

See GROUNDING ELECTRODES . . . . Ferm's Finder

PIPE ORGANS . . . . Art. 650

Abandoned Cable 650.7

Conductors 650.6

　Installation 650.7

Definitions 650.2

Electronic Organ Equipment . . . . 650.3(A)

Electronic Organs and Other Musical Instruments . . . 640.1

Grounding 650.5

Optical Fiber Cables . . . . 650.3(B)

Overcurrent Protection 650.8

Protection from Accidental Contact 650.9

Sources of Power 650.4

PIPELINES AND VESSELS, HEATING . . . . Art. 427

Continuous Load 427.4

Control and Protections . . . . 427 Part VII

Definitions 427.2

Disconnecting Means 427.55

Identification 427.13

Induction Heating . . . . 427 Part V

Impedance Heating . . . . 427 Part IV

Overcurrent Protection 427.57

Protected from Physical Damage 427.11

Resistance Heating Elements . . . . 427 Part III

Skin-Effect Heating . . . . 427 Part VI

Thermal Protection 427.12

See FIXED ELECTRIC HEATING EQUIPMENT FOR PIPE-LINES AND VESSELS . . . . Ferm's Finder

PIPING SYSTEMS, BONDING 250.104

PLACES OF ASSEMBLY . . . . Art. 518

Examples of . . . . 518.2(A)

General Classifications 518.2

　Multiple Occupancies . . . . 518.2(B)

　Theatrical Areas . . . . 518.2(C)

Portable Switchboards and Power Outlets 518.5

Temporary Wiring, Exhibition Halls . . . . 518.3(B)

Wiring Methods (General) . . . . 518.4(A)

　For Use in Nonrated Construction . . . . 518.4(B)

　For Use in Spaces with Finish Rating . . . . 518.4(C)

PLANTS

Bulk Storage . . . . Art. 515

Cleaning and Dyeing . . . . 500.5(B)(1), Info. Note 1(6)

    Class I Location . . . . Art. 501

Clothing Manufacturing . . . . .500.5(D)(1), Info. Note 1

    Class III Location . . . . Art. 503

Woodworking . . . . .500.5(D)(1), Info. Note 1

    Class III Location . . . . Art. 503

PLATE GROUNDING ELECTRODES . . . . 250.52(A)(7)

Connection of Grounding Electrode Conductor to . 250.66(A)

Installation of . . . . 250.53(H)

Resistance of . . . . 250.53(H)

PLAQUES   See LABELS. . . . . Ferm's Finder

PLENUM

Cable Ties and Cable Accessories (Nonmetallic) . .300.22(C)(1)

Communication Circuits within Plenum . . . . . 800.170(C)

Communication Circuit Support. 800.24

Definition of . . . . Art. 100 Part I

Low Smoke and Heat Release Properties . . . .300.22(C)(1) IN

Wiring in 300.22

    Cable Tray Systems . . . . .300.22(C)(2)

    Community Antenna Television and Radio Distribution Systems 820.24

    Network-Powered Broadband Communications Systems 830.24

    Equipment . . . . .300.22(C)(3)

    Information Technology Equipment . . . . 300.22(D)

    Wiring Methods. . . . . .300.22(C)(1)

See DUCTS & HOODS . . . . Ferm's Finder

POLARITY

Adapters. . . . . .406.10(B)(3)

Cord- and Plug-Connected Appliances 422.40

Flat Conductor Cable: Type FCC. . . . . 324.40(B)

Identification of Terminals 200.10

Lampholders, Screw-Shell Type 410.90

Of Connection 200.11

Of Luminaires (Fixtures) 410.50

Portable Luminaires . . . . 410.82(A)

PORTABLE LUMINAIRES & LIGHTING EQUIPMENT (FORMERLY HAND LAMPS) . . . . 410.82, 511.4(B)(2)

PORTABLE POWER CABLES

Flexible Cords and Cables . . . . Art. 400

See (QPMU) .UL Product Spec

POTENTIAL TRANSFORMERS . . . . .450.3(C)

POTTING COMPOUNDS FOR USE AT POOLS

Flush Deck Boxes . . . . 680.24(A)(2)(c)(1)

Swimming Pool, Wet-Niche Luminaires (Fixtures) . . . . 680.23(B)(2)(b)

See (WCRY) .UL Product Spec

POWER & CONTROL TRAY CABLE (TYPE TC) . . . . . Art. 336

Ampacity 336.80

Bends 336.24

Between Cable Tray and Equipment . . . . .336.10(7)

Construction . . . . Art. 336 Part III

Definition of 336.2

Dwelling Units- Use . . . . .336.10(9)

Installation . . . . Art. 336 Part II

Listing Requirements 336.6

Jacket, Flame Retardant 336.116

Marking 336.120

Uses Not Permitted 336.12

Uses Permitted 336.10

See (QPOR) . . . . .UL Product Spec

POWER CONVERSION EQUIPMENT

Branch-Circuit Short-Circuit and Ground-Fault Protections

    Several Motors or Loads 430.131

    Single Motor Circuits. 430.130

POWER DISTRIBUTION BLOCKS . . . . 314.28(E)

Conductors Not to Obstruct . . . . .376.56(B)(5)

In Metal Raceways . . . . 376.56(B)

Installation . . . . .376.56(B)(1)

Live Parts . . . . .376.56(B)(4)

Size of Enclosure . . . . .376.56(B)(2)

Splices and Taps . . . . 376.56(A)

Wire Bending Space . . . . .376.56(B)(3)

POWER ELECTRONIC DEVICES . . . . 430.52(C)(5)

POWER FACTOR

Use of in Examples . . . . .Informative Annex D

POWER INLET . . . . .702.7(C)

Optional Standby Systems. 702.12

Signs Required . . . . 702.7(C)

POWER-LIMITED CIRCUIT CABLE

See (QPTZ) . . . .*UL Product Spec*

POWER-LIMITED FIRE ALARM (PLFA) CIRCUITS

Fire Alarm Systems . . . . 760 Part III

See FIRE ALARM SYSTEMS . . . . Ferm's Finder

POWER-LIMITED TRAY CABLE (TYPE PLTC) 725.135

Cable Trays . . . . 725.135(H)

Class I, Division 2 Locations . . . . 501.10(B)(1)(3)

Class I, Zone 2 Locations . . . . .505.15(C)(1)(d)

Class II, Division 2 Locations . . . . 502.10(B)(1)(4)

Cross-Connect Arrays . . . . 725.135(I)

Definition 725.2

Fabricated Ducts Used for Environmental Air . . . .725.135(B)

Industrial Establishments . . . . 725.135(J)

Listing and Marking of . . . . .725.135(A)

Multifamily Dwellings . . . . .725.135(L)

One- and Two-Family Dwellings . . . . 725.135(M)

Other Building Locations . . . . 725.135(K)

Plenums . . . . 725.135(C)

Risers

    Fireproof Shafts . . . . 725.135(F)

    Metal Raceways . . . . 725.135(E)

    One-and Two-Family Dwellings . . . . 725.135(G)

    Vertical Runs . . . . 725.135(D)

POWER MONITORING EQUIPMENT . . . . .312.8(B)

POWER OUTLETS & FITTINGS

Assembly Occupancies 518.5

Definition of . . . . Art. 100 Part I

Electric Vehicle Supply Equipment. 625.2

Electrified Truck Parking Spaces (permitted disconnect) . . . .
. . . . 626.31(B)

Enclosure type number (Marked) 110.28

Marina and Boatyard Power Outlets 555.2

    Disconnecting Means (permitted). . . . . 555.17(B)

    Manual Operation. 555.11

    Shore Power Receptacles . . . . .555.19(A)(1)

Mobile Homes- Service Equipment . . . . 550.32(C)

Recreational Vehicle Site Supply Equipment 551.2

Grounding Electrode (not required) . . . . 551.75(B)

Temporary Wiring . . . . 590.4(C) and (E)

Theaters, Motion Pictures, TV Studios 520.51

See Informative Annex A- Product Standard Name

See (QPYV) . . . .*UL Product Spec*

PREASSEMBLED CABLE IN NONMETALLIC CONDUIT . . . . .
. . . . **Art. 354**

See NONMETALLIC UNDERGROUND CONDUIT WITH
CONDUCTORS . . . . Ferm's Finder

See (QQRK). . . . .*UL Product Spec*

**PREMISES-POWERED BROADBAND COMMUNICATION
SYSTEMS.** . . . . **Art. 840**

Abandoned Cable 840.25

Definitions 840.2

Ducts, Wiring Within . . . . 840.3(B)

Grounding

    Grounding Devices, Required to be Listed 840.180

    Grounding, Metallic Entrance Conduits 840.49

    Mobile Homes 840.106

    Network Terminal and Cable Grounding. 840.100

    Not Leaving the Building. 840.101

Installation Requirements . . . . .840.3(D)

Installation Methods Within Buildings . . . . . . 840 Part V

Listing Requirements 840.170

    Accessory Equipment. . . . . 840.170(H)

    Communication Equipment . . . . .840.170(C)

    Network Terminal. . . . . .840.170(A)

Mechanical Execution of Work 840.24

Optical Fiber Cables

    Overhead. 840.44

    Underground 840.47

Other Articles 840.3

Overhead (Aerial) Coaxial Cable) 840.46

Overhead (Aerial) Communication Wires & Cables . . . 840.45

Premise Power over Communication Cables 840.160

    Powering Circuits 840.160

Power Source (Limitations) . . . . .840.170(G)

Raceways and Cable Routing Assemblies 840.110

Underground Wires and Cables 840.47

Unlisted Wires and Cables 840.48

PREMISES WIRING (SYSTEM)

Branch Circuits (more than one nominal voltage) . 210.5(C)(1)

Connection to Grounded System. 200.3

Critical Operations Power Systems (COPS). 708.1

Definition of . . . . Art. 100 Part I

Electric Vehicle Supply Equipment (to vehicle). 625.2

Feeders (more than one nominal voltage) . . . . . .215.12(C)(1)

Floating Building (has a system) 553.2

Fuel Cell System (feeder to the). . . . . 692.8(B)

Grounded Conductors. 200.1

Microgrid System 705.2

Optional Standby Systems. 702.1

Photovoltaic System (disconnect from) 690.13

Pool Lifts (connected to) 680.82

Service Conductors (simultaneously disconnect) 230.74

Service Point . . . . Art 100 Part 1

Site Isolation Device- Agricultural . . . . 547.9(A)(3)

Stand-Alone Systems 710.15

Surge Arrestors- Over 1000 Volts. 280.1

Surge-Protective Devices- 1000 Volts and Less 285.1

System Grounding Connections

    Alternating-Current System . . . . 250.24(A)

    Ungrounded System . . . . 250.24(E)

PRESSURE CONNECTORS

Agricultural Building Concrete Embedded Elements 547.10(B)

Disconnection of Grounded Conductor 230.75

Listed

    Connecting to Grounding Electrodes. 250.70

    Grounding Conductors and Equipment 250.8

Separately Installed, Temperature Rating . . . . .110.14(C)(2)

Service Conductors to Terminals 230.81

Swimming Pool Equipotential Bonding Grid 680.26

Terminals, Electrical Connections . . . . 110.14(A)

See (ZMVV) . . . . .UL Product Spec

PRINTING PROCESSES . . . . **Article 516**

PRODUCT CERTIFICATION OF EQUIPMENT **110.3**

PRODUCT SAFETY STANDARDS . . . . **Informative Annex A**

PROTECTION

Combustible Material, Appliances 422.17

Corrosion

Boxes, Metal (Over 1000 Volts) . . . . 314.72(A)

Cable Trays . . . . 392.10(C)

Conductors 310.10

Electrical Metallic Tubing . . . . 358.10(B)

Enamel Coated . . . . 300.6(A)(1)

Ferrous Metal Equipment . . . . 300.6(A)

Protection (suitable) 300.6

General Equipment 300.6

Intermediate Metal Conduit . . . . 342.10(B)

    Supports, Hardware, Etc., Wet Locations . . . . 342.10(D)

Metal-Clad Cable: Type MC 330.12

Mineral-Insulated, Metal-Sheathed Cable: Type MI. . . . . .

. . . . .332.10(9) and(10)

Nonmetallic-Sheathed Cable: Type NMC . . . .334.10(B)(1)

    Construction, Type NMC . . . . .334.116(B)

Nonmetallic Wireways . . . . .378.10(2)

Rigid Metal Conduit . . . . 344.10(B)

    Nonferrous Corrosion-Resistant, Marking 344.120

    Protected by Enamel Only. . . . . .344.10(A)(4)

    Supports, Hardware, Etc., Wet Locations . . . . 344.10(D)

Rigid PVC Conduit . . . . 352.10(B)

Strut-Type Channel Raceway . . . . .384.100(B)

Underfloor Raceways . . . . 390.3(B)

Underground Feeder and Branch-Circuit: Type UF. . . . . .

. . . . .340.10(3)

Hazardous (Classified) Locations, Techniques 500.7

    Class I, Zone 0, 1, and 2 Locations 505.8

Liquids, Motors 430.11

Live Parts 110.27

    Generators 445.14

    Transformers. . . . . 450.8(C)

Motor Overload . . . . 430 Part III

Overcurrent, See OVERCURRENT PROTECTION . . . .

. . . . Ferm's Finder

Physical Damage, from

    Armored Cable: Type AC 320.15

    Busways . . . . 368.10(C)(2) and 368.12(A)

    Cable Trays. 392.12

    Conductors 300.4

        Over 1000 Volts. . . . . 300.50(C)

    Electrical Equipment . . . . 110.27(B)

    Electrical Metallic Tubing . . . . 358.12(1)

    Electrical Nonmetallic Tubing . . . . .362.12(9)

    Flat Cable Assemblies: Type FC . . . . .322.10(3)

P

P

Flexible Metal Conduit . . . . .348.12(7)

Flexible Metallic Tubing . . . . .360.12(5)

Grounding Conductor

    CATV Systems . . . . 820.100(A)(6)

    Communication Circuits . . . . .800.100(A)(6)

    Network-Powered Broadband Communications Systems
. . . . .830.100(A)(6)

    Radio and Television Equipment . . . . 810.21(D)

Grounding Electrode Conductor . . . . 250.64(B)

    Burial Depth . . . . .250.64(B)(4)

Ground Clamps and Fittings 250.10

Instrumentation Tray Cable: Type ITC . . . . 727.4(5)

Lamps, Electric Discharge Lighting More Than 1000 Volts. .
. . . . .410.145

Lighting Track . . . . .410.151(C)(1)

Liquidtight Flexible Metal Conduit . . . . 350.12(1)

Liquidtight Flexible Nonmetallic Conduit . . . . . 356.12(1)

Luminaire (Fixture) Wiring 410.48

Metal-Clad Cable: Type MC . . . . 330.12(1)

Metal-Sheathed Cables over 1000 Volts 300.42

Metal Wireways . . . . 376.12(1)

Mineral-Insulated Metal-Sheathed Cable: Type MI 332.12(1)

    Underground Runs . . . . 332.10(10)

Multioutlet Assembly . . . . 380.12(2)

Network-Powered Broadband Communications Systems

    Attached to Buildings . . . . 830.44(G)(4)

    Underground Circuits Entering Buildings . . . . . 830.47(C)

        Wiring within Buildings. . . . . 830.47(C)

Nonmetallic-Sheathed Cable. . . . . 334.15(B)

Nonmetallic Wireways . . . . 378.12(1)

Non-Power-Limited Fire Alarm Cables (NPLFA) . . . .
. . . . 760.53(A)(1)

Open Conductors and Cables (Services) 230.50

Open Wiring on Insulators. . . . . 398.15(C)

Overcurrent Devices . . . . 240.24(C)

Power and Control Tray Cable: Type TC . . . . . . 336.12(1)

Power-Limited Fire Alarm Cables (PLFA) . . . 760.130(B)(1)

Raceways .300.5(D)

    Over 1000 Volts. . . . . 300.50(C)

Rigid PVC Conduit . . . . 352.10(F)

RV Park, Underground Branch Circuits and Feeders . . . . .
551.80(B)

Safety Control Equipment Circuits . . . . 725.31(B)

Space-Heating Systems . . . . 424.12(A)

Surface Metal Raceways . . . . 386.12(1)

Surface Nonmetallic Raceways . . . . 388.12(2)

Transformers. . . . . 450.8(A)

Underground Branch-Circuit & Feeder Cable: Type UF . . .
. . . . .340.12(10)

Underground Installations

    Conductors, Cables, and Raceways Over 1000 Volts . . . .
. . . . 300.50(C)

    Conductors, Cables, and Raceways. . . . . 300.5(D)

    Protection from Ground Movement . . . . 300.5(J)

    Service-Entrance Conductors. 230.50

PROTECTOR, COMMUNICATION SYSTEMS

Antenna 810.6

Application . . . . 800.90(A)

Bonding 800.100

Critical Operations Power Systems (COPS). . . . . .708.14(4)

Figure 800(a) and (b) 800.1

Grounding 800.100

Hazardous (Classified) Locations (not located in) . . 800.90(C)

Installation 800.50

Listed . . . . .800.170(A)

Location. 800.90(B)

Mobile Homes, At 800.106

Modular Data Centers . . . . 646.3(C)

Network-Powered Broadband Systems 830.90

Primary Protector Requirements – Listed 800.170

Primary Protector 800.90

Secondary Protector Requirements . . . . 800.90(D)

Short as Practicable- Length . . . . 800.100(A)(4)

Unlisted Cables. 800.48

See ANSI/UL 497B. Protectors for Data Communications

PUBLIC ADDRESS SYSTEMS . . . . Art. 640

Class 1, 2, & 3 Remote Control, Signaling Systems . . Art. 725

Communication Circuits . . . . Art. 800

PULL BOXES & JUNCTION BOXES

See BOXLESS DEVICES. . . . . Ferm's Finder

See JUNCTION AND PULL BOXES . . . . . . Ferm's Finder

PULLOUT SWITCHES DETACHABLE TYPES

See (WGEU) . . . .*UL Product Spec*

PUMPS

Water, Motor-Operated . . . . .250.112(L)

PUMP HOUSES

See GROUNDING, Fixed Equipment . . . . . . Ferm's Finder

See MOTORS . . . . Ferm's Finder

See Submersible Pump Cable (YDUX) . . . . .UL Product Spec

See UNDERGROUND WIRING . . . . Ferm's Finder

PV SYSTEMS . . . . Art. 690

See PHOTOVOLTAIC SYSTEMS (SOLAR) . . . Ferm's Finder

See Large-Scale Photovoltaic (PV) Electric Power Production
Facility. . . . . Ferm's Finder

PVC (ELECTRICAL NONMETALLIC TUBING) . . . . . . Art. 362

See ELECTRICAL NONMETALLIC TUBING . Ferm's Finder

PVC (RIGID POLYVINYL CHLORIDE CONDUIT) . . . . Art. 352

See RIGID PVC CONDUIT. . . . . Ferm's Finder

See (DZYR) . . . . .UL Product Spec

Q

QUALIFIED PERSON, Definition of . . . . . . Art. 100 Part I

QUALIFIED PERSON, WORK MUST BE PERFORMED BY OR ACCESSIBLE ONLY TO

Aboveground Wiring Methods, Over 1000 Volts. 300.37

AC Systems 50 to 1000 Volts Not Required to Be Grounded . .
. . . . .250.21(A)(3)b

Amusement Attractions- Control Systems 522.7

Arc-Flash Hazard Warning 110.16

Available Fault Current, Marking Requirements . 110.24(B) Ex.

Branch Circuits from Autotransformers. . . . . . . 210.9 Ex. 2

Branch Circuits Over 600 Volts. . . . . 210.19(B)(2)

Branches from Busways by Cord and Cable Assemblies. . . . .
. . . . 368.56(B)(2) Ex.

Cable Trays

   Airfield Lighting. . . . . 392.10(E)

   Grounding and Bonding- Metal Tray . . . . 392.60(A)

   Support of Raceways and Cables . . . . 392.18(G)

   Temporary Wiring . . . . 518.3(B) Ex.

   Wiring Methods in Industrial Establishments . . . 392.10(B)

   Warning Notices. . . . . 392.18(H) Ex.

Capacitors, Accidental Contact. . . . . 460.2(B)

Carnivals, Circuses and Fairs (Guarding) . . . . 525.10(A)

Cartridge Fuses. 240.40

Circuit Breakers Indoors, over 1000 Volts. . . .490.21(A)(1)(a)

Class I, Zone 0, 1, and 2 Locations . . . . 505.7(A)

Wiring Methods, Zones 1 and 2 . . . . . 505.15(1)(b) & (c)

Flexible Cords, Zones 1 and 2 . . . . 505.17

Communication System Test Equipment . . . . 800.18 Ex.

Cords and Cables (Splices)- over 600 Volts 400.36

Cranes and Hoists (Disconnect) . . . . 610.31 Ex.

Critical Operations Data Systems . . . . .645.10(B)(2)

Critical Operations Power Systems (COPS). . . . . . . 708.5(B)

Depth of Working Space, 600 Volts, Nominal or Less . . . . . .
. . . . .110.26(A)(1)(c)

Direct-Current Switchboards, Not Required Deadfront . . . . .
. . . . 530.64(A)

Disconnecting Means, Air-Conditioning Equipment . . . . . .
. . . . 440.14 Ex. 1

Enclosures, Rooms, or Areas, Over 1000 Volts 110.31

Energy Storage Systems

   Batteries . . . . .706.30(B) and (C)

   Charge Control 706.23

   Fuses . . . . 706.21(E)

Equipment Over 1000 Volts

   Circuit Breakers . . . . .490.21(A)(1)

   Enclosures 490.53

   Guarding 490.32

Feeder Taps- over 25 feet long . . . . 240.21(B)(4)(1)

Feeders from Autotransformers . . . . 215.11 Ex. 2

Feeders over 600 Volts . . . . 215.2(B)(3)

Fixed Electrostatic Equipment, Restricted Access . . . .
. . . . .516.10(A)(8)(3)

Flexible Cords and Cables- Industrial 400.17

Fuel Cell Systems. . . . . 692.4(C)

Fuseholders, Over 1000 Volts . . . . 490.21(B)(6) Ex.

Grounded Conductor of Multiconductor Cables 200.6(E) Ex. 1

Ground-Fault Protection for Receptacles . . . .
. . . . .210.8(B)(4) Ex. 2 to (4)

Ground-Fault Protection of Equipment . . . . 230.95(C)

Guarding of High-Voltage Parts within a Compartment . . . .
. . . . 490.32

Guarding of Live Parts. . . . . 110.27(A)

High-Impedance Grounded Neutral Systems . . . . 250.36(1)

Identification of Equipment Grounding Conductors . . . . . .
. . . . .250.119(B)

Indoor Installations, Over 1000 Volts . . . . .110.31(B)(2)

Installation of Optical Fibers and Electrical Conductors

   Composite Optical Fiber Cables and Over 1000 Volts . . . .
. . . . 770.133(A) Ex. 4

   Nonconductive Optical Fiber Cables and Over 1000 Volts . .

Q

. . . . 770.133(A) Ex. 3

Instrument Transformer Cases 250.172

Instrumentation Tray Cable: Type ITC, Uses Permitted . . 727.4

Integrated Electrical Systems . . . . 685.1(2)

Interconnected Electric Power Production Sources . . . .
. . . . .705.12(C)(2)

Interior Metal Water Pipe As Grounding Electrode . . . .
. . . . 250.68(C)(1) Ex.

Isolating Switches, Services Over 1000 Volts . . . . 230.204(C)

Large-Scale Photovoltaic Electric Power Production Facility . .

Disconnect for Isolation 691.9

Location of Switchboards 408.20

Locked Electrical Equipment Room or Enclosures

1000 Volts or Less . . . . 110.26(F)

Over 1000 Volts . . . . 110.34(C)

Low-Voltage Suspended Ceiling Power Distribution Systems. .
. . . . 393.14 Info. Note

Manholes & Enclosures Intended for Personnel Entry . . . . .
. . . . 110.70 Ex.

Means of Identification of Terminals . . . . 200.9 Ex.

Medium Voltage Cable: Type MV, Installation of 328.14

Messenger-Supported Wiring, Industrial Establishments . . . .
. . . . 396.10(B)

Metallic Cable Trays as Equipment Grounding Conductor . . .
. . . . 392.60(A)

Motor Controllers, Speed Limitation . . . . . . 430.89 Ex. (2)

Multioutlet Branch Circuits Greater Than 50 Amperes 210.3 Ex.

Neon Tubing . . . . 600.41(D)

Non-Power-Limited Fire Alarm (NPLFA) Circuits

Branch Circuit. . . . . 760.41(B)

Oil-Insulated Transformers Installed Indoors . . . 450.26 Ex. 5

Open Wiring Supports, Industrial Establishments . . 398.30(C)

Outdoor Installations, Over 1000 Volts . . . . . .110.31(C)(2)

Panelboard Enclosures Other Than Deadfront . . . . 408.38 Ex.

Portable Stage and Studio Equipment, Temporary Use . . 530.6

Portable Switchboards on Stage. 520.53

Power Cable Connections to Mobile Machines Over 1000 Volts
. . . . 490.55

Power and Control Tray Cable: Type TC, Uses Permitted . . . .
. . . . .336.10(7)

Power-Limited Fire Alarm (PLFA) Circuits

Branch Circuits . . . . .760.121(B)

Power-Limited Tray Cable (PLTC) . . . . 725.135(J)

Receptacles for 60/120-Volt Technical Power . . .647.7(A) Ex.

Reconditioned Equipment- Industrial . . . . . 110.21(A)(2) Ex.

Restricted Access Adjustable-Trip Circuit Breakers 240.6(C)(3)

Selective Coordination

Critical Operations Power Systems (COPS) 708.54

Emergency Systems 700.32

Interconnected Electric Power Production Systems. . . 705.8

Legally Required Standby Systems 701.27

Sensitive Electronic Equipment, General . . . . 647.3(2)

Services Exceeding 1000 Volts

Isolating Switches 230.204

Solar Photovoltaic Systems . . . . 690.4(C)

Splices (Cords)- over 600 Volts 400.36

Substations 490.48

Definition . . . . Article 100

Supervised Industrial Installations . . . . . Art. 240, Part VIII

Definition . . . . 240.2(1)

Switchboards and Panelboards- live parts 408.20

Temporary Wiring for Receptacles, Industrial . . . 590.6(A) Ex.

Temporary Wiring Over 600 Volts 590.7

Temporary Wiring, Use of Single Conductors for Feeders. . . .
. . . . .590.4(B) Ex.

Terminations (Cords) - over 600 Volts. 400.36

Theaters, Motion Pictures and TV . . . . 520.54(K)

Time Switches, Flashers, and Similar Devices . . . . 404.5 Ex.

Transformer Overcurrent Protection Over 1000 Volts. . . . . .
. . . . Table 450.3(A), Note 3

Transformer Secondary Conductors

Industrial Installations- Taps not over 25 feet . .240.21(C)(3)

Taps over 25 feet. . . . . .240.21(C)(4)

Transformer Vault Door Locks . . . . 450.43(C)

Transformers, Accessibility 450.13

Transformers, Exposed Energized Parts . . . . 450.8(C)

Underground Installations

Industrial Establishments . . . . .Table 300.50 Note 3

Over 1000 Volts 300.50

Wind Electric Systems. 694.7

Fuses 694.26

Working Clearances, Elevator Equipment 620.5

X-Ray Equipment (Disconnect) . . . . 660.5 Ex.

Zone 20, 21, and 22 Locations Wiring Methods 506.15

RACEWAYS ABOVEGRADE, WET LOCATIONS

1000 Volts or Less 300.9

Over 1000 Volts 300.38

Arrange to Drain

   On Exterior Surfaces of Buildings or Other Structures 225.22

   Service Suitable for Use in Wet Locations 230.53

Arrange So Water Will Not Enter . . . . 230.54(G)

Bonding

   Class I Locations . . . . 501.30(A)

   Class II Locations . . . . 502.30(A)

   Class III Locations . . . . 503.30(A)

   Service and Other Raceways . . . . 250 Part V

Busways . . . . Art. 368

   See BUSWAYS . . . . Ferm's Finder

Cellular Concrete Floor . . . . Art. 372

   See CELLULAR CONCRETE FLOOR RACEWAYS . . . . .

   . . . . Ferm's Finder

Cellular Metal Floor . . . . Art. 374

   See CELLULAR METAL FLOOR RACEWAYS Ferm's Finder

Class I Locations . . . . 501.30(A)

Class II Locations . . . . 502.30(A)

Class III Locations . . . . 503.30(A)

Complete Runs . . . . 300.18(A)

Continuity of Run

   Bonding in Hazardous Locations 250.100

   Bonding Loosely Jointed Metal Raceways 250.98

   Bonding of Other Enclosures . . . . 250.96(A)

   Bonding of Service Raceways . . . . 250.92(B)

   Bonding Over 250 Volts 250.97

   Electrical Continuity Metal Raceways and Enclosures 300.10

   Electrical Metallic Tubing 358.42

   Intermediate Metal Conduit 342.42

   Isolated Grounding Circuits . . . . 250.96(B)

   Mechanical Continuity 300.12

   Method of Bonding at Service . . . . 250.92(B)

   Rigid Metal Conduit 344.42

   Threaded Conduit Hazardous Locations . . . . . . 500.8(E)

Definition of Bonding . . . . Art. 100

Different Systems in Same Enclosure . . . . 300.3(C)

   1000 Volts, Nominal or Less . . . . 300.3(C)(1)

   Cable Trays

      Cables Over 1000 Volts . . . . 392.20(B)

      Multiconductor Cables 1000 Volts or Less . . . 392.20(A)

   CATV and Radio Distribution Systems . . . . . . Art. 820

   Class 1 Remote Control, Signaling Circuits 725.48

   Class 2 & 3 Remote Control, Signaling Circuits . . . 725.133

   Communications Circuits . . . . Art. 800

   Elevators, Dumbwaiters, etc. . . . . Art. 620

   Emergency System Wiring . . . . 700.10(B)

   Grounded Conductors . . . . 200.6(D)

   Intrinsically Safe Systems . . . . Art. 504

   Network-Powered Broadband Communications Systems . .

   . . . . Art. 830

   Nonelectrical Systems Prohibited 300.8

   Nonpower-Limited Fire Alarm (NPLFA) Circuits 760.48(A)

   Optical Fiber Cables 770.133

   Optional Standby Wiring 702.10

   Over 1000 Volts, Nominal . . . . 300.3(C)(2)

      Requirements for 300.32

   Power-Limited Fire Alarm (PLFA) Circuits 760.136

   Prohibition of with Service Conductors 230.7

   Seal

      Outside Branch Circuits and Feeders 225.27

   Solar Photovoltaic Systems . . . . 690.31(B)

   Surface Metallic Raceways 386.70

   Surface Nonmetallic Raceways 388.70

   Wiring Legally Required Standby Wiring 701.10

Electrical Metallic Tubing . . . . Art. 358

   See ELECTRICAL METALLIC TUBING . . . Ferm's Finder

Electrical Nonmetallic Tubing . . . . Art. 362

   See ELECTRICAL NONMETALLIC TUBING . . . .

   . . . . Ferm's Finder

Emergency Circuits (Independent) . . . . 700.10(B)

Expansion Joints

   Bonding Loosely Jointed Metal Raceways 250.98

   Coefficient of Expansion, Steel Conduit 300.7(B), Info. Note

   Earth Movement . . . . 300.5(J) IN

   In Rigid PVC Conduit 352.44

   Nonmetallic Auxiliary Gutters 366.44

   Provided Where Necessary . . . . 300.7(B)

Exposed to Different Temperatures 300.7

Field-Cut Threads . . . . 300.6(A) Info. Notes

Flexible Metal Conduit . . . . Art. 348

   See FLEXIBLE METAL CONDUIT . . . . . . Ferm's Finder

Flexible Metallic Tubing . . . . Art. 360

   See FLEXIBLE METALLIC TUBING . . . . . Ferm's Finder

R

Grounding and Bonding of

    Class I Locations . . . . 501.30(A)

    Class II Locations . . . . 502.30(A)

    Class III Locations . . . . 503.30(A)

    Equipment Grounding . . . . 250 Part VI

    Methods of . . . . 250 Part VII

    Service, Enclosures and Other Raceways . . . 250 Part IV

High Density Polyethylene Conduit Type (HDPE) . . Art. 353

Indoor, Wet Locations . . . . 300.6(D)

Induced Currents in

    Enclosures for Grounding Electrode Conductors . 250.64(E)

    Group Conductors . . . . 300.20(A)

    Protection against Induction Heating 300.35

Inserting Conductors in

    Complete Runs . . . . 300.18(A)

    Conductors of the Same Circuit . . . . 300.3(B)

    Equipment Grounding Conductor in Same Raceway . . . . .250.134(B)

    Number and Size 300.17

    Stranded Conductors . . . . .310.106(C)

Installation of

    Complete Runs . . . . 300.18(A)

    Welding . . . . 300.18(B)

Installed in Shallow Grooves . . . . 300.4(F)

Insulating Fittings (Bushings) . . . . 300.4(G)

    In Lieu of Box or Termination Fitting . . . . 300.16(B)

Intermediate Metal Conduit . . . . Art. 342

    See INTERMEDIATE METAL CONDUIT . . Ferm's Finder

Liquidtight Flexible Metal Conduit . . . . Art. 350

    See LIQUIDTIGHT FLEXIBLE METAL CONDUIT Ferm's Finder

Liquidtight Flexible Nonmetallic Conduit . . . . . . Art. 356

    See LIQUIDTIGHT FLEXIBLE NONMETALLIC CONDUIT . . . . Ferm's Finder

Luminaires (Lighting Fixtures) As 410.64

Metal Surface Raceways . . . . Art. 386

    See SURFACE METAL RACEWAYS . . . . . Ferm's Finder

No Splices in 300.15

    See SPLICES AND TAPS . . . . Ferm's Finder

Number and Size of Conductors in 300.17

    See CONDUCTORS, Number of, in . . . . . . Ferm's Finder

On Rooftops, Raceways and Cables . . . . 310.15(B)(3)(c)

Outside 225.22

    Services 230.53

Parallel Runs . . . . 310.10(H)(1)

    Underground . . . . 300.5(I) Ex. 1-2

Rigid Metal Conduit . . . . Art. 344

    See RIGID METAL CONDUIT . . . . Ferm's Finder

Rigid Polyvinyl Chloride Conduit . . . . Art. 352

    See RIGID PVC (POLYVINYL CHLORIDE) CONDUIT . . . . Ferm's Finder

Sealing of

    Class I Locations . . . . 501.15(A)

    Class I, Zone 0, 1, and 2 Locations . . . . 505.16(A)

    Class II Locations 502.15

    Exposed to Different Temperature . . . . 300.7(A)

    Intrinsically Safe Systems 504.70

    Service Raceways 230.8

    Spare or Unused . . . . 300.5(G)

    Underground Installations (General) . . . . 300.5(G)

    Zone 20, 21, and 22 Locations 506.16

Strut-Type Channel . . . . Art. 384

    See STRUT-TYPE CHANNEL RACEWAYS . . Ferm's Finder

Support for Nonelectrical Equipment . . . . 300.11(B)

Support of 300.11

Supporting Conductors, Vertical 300.19

Surface Metal Raceways . . . . Art. 386

    See SURFACE METAL RACEWAYS . . . . . Ferm's Finder

Surface Nonmetallic Raceways . . . . Art. 388

    See SURFACE NONMETALLIC RACEWAYS Ferm's Finder

Temperature Changes of 300.7

Under Roof Decking . . . . 300.4(E)

Underfloor, *See* UNDERFLOOR RACEWAYS . . Ferm's Finder

Underground

    See UNDERGROUND WIRING . . . . Ferm's Finder

    Definition of . . . . Art. 100

    Indoors . . . . 300.6(D)

    Underground . . . . 300.5(B)

    Use of PVC Conduit . . . . 352.10(G)

    Wet Locations

        1000 Volts or Less . . . . 300.5(B)

        Over 1000 Volts . . . . 300.50(B)

Wireways, Metal . . . . Art. 376

Wireways, Nonmetallic . . . . Art. 378

    See WIREWAYS, METAL & WIREWAYS, NONMETALLIC Ferm's Finder

RADIO & TELEVISION DISTRIBUTION (CATV) . . . . Art. 820
See COMMUNITY ANTENNA TELEVISION AND RADIO
DISTRIBUTION SYSTEMS. . . . . Ferm's Finder

RADIO & TELEVISION EQUIPMENT . . . . Art. 810
Amateur Transmitting & Receiving – Antennas . . 810 Part III
Antenna Discharge Units 810.20
Antenna Lead-In Protectors 810.6
Clearances. 810.18
Grounding Devices to be Listed 810.7
Grounding Means 810.21
Intersystem Bonding Termination . . . . 810.21(F)
Receiving Equipment – Antenna Systems . . . . . . 810 Part II
Supports. 810.12
    Grounding 810.15

RADIUS OF BENDS
Cables
    Armored: Type AC 320.24
    High Voltage Cable 300.34
    Integrated Gas Spacer Cable 326.24
    Metal-Clad Cable: Type MC 330.24
    Mineral-Insulated Metal-Sheathed: Type MI Cable . . 332.24
    Nonmetallic-Sheathed Type NM (Romex) 334.24
    Service-Entrance Cable: Type SE 338.24
Conductors
    Auxiliary Gutters, in . . . . 366.58(A)
    Bending Radius, Over 1000 Volts 300.34
    Enclosures for Motor Controllers and Disconnects, in . . . .
    . . . . 430.10(B)
    Examination of Equipment . . . . 110.3(A)(3)
    Pull and Junction Boxes Not Over 1000 Volts, in . . . 314.28
    Pull and Junction Boxes Over 1000 Volts, in 314.71
    Metal Wireways, in . . . . 376.23(A)
    Nonmetallic Wireways, in . . . . 378.23(A)
    Switch or Circuit-Breaker Enclosures, in . . . . 404.3(A)
    Switchboards, Switchgear or Panelboards, in. . . . . 408.3(F)
        Clearance Entering Bus Enclosures. 408.5
        Provisions for. 408.55
        Terminals of Cabinets, Cutout Boxes, Meter Sockets   312.6
Conduit and Tubing
    Electrical Metallic Tubing 358.24
    Electrical Nonmetallic Tubing 362.24
    Flexible Metal Conduit 348.24
    Flexible Metallic Tubing 360.24

Intermediate Metal Conduit 342.24
High Density Polyethylene Conduit Type HDPE . . . 353.24
Nonmetallic Underground Conduit with Conductors   354.24
Radius of Conduit and Tubing Bends . . Chapter 9, Table 2
Rigid Metal Conduit 344.24
Rigid PVC Conduit 352.24
Table 2 . . . . Chapter 9

RAILROAD TRACKS
    Clearance for Overhead Conductors . . . . 225.18(5)

RAILWAY
Light and Power Not Connected 110.19
Motors and Controls 555.23
Not Covered by Code . . . . 90.2(B)
Outside Branch Circuits and Feeders . . . . .225.18(5)
Service Conductor Clearance . . . . .230.24(B)(5)

RAINTIGHT, RAINPROOF, OR WEATHERPROOF
Boxes, Conduit Bodies, and Fittings 314.15
Cabinets, Cutout Boxes, and Meter Socket Enclosures . . 312.2
Definition
    Rainproof . . . . Art. 100
    Raintight . . . . Art. 100
    Watertight . . . . Art. 100
    Weatherproof . . . . Art. 100
Motor Control Enclosures Selection . . . . .Table 110.28
Switch Enclosures, Weatherproof in Damp or Wet Locations. .
. . . . 404.4
See WEATHERPROOF . . . . Ferm's Finder

RANGE HOODS . . . . 422.16(B)(4)
See CALCULATIONS . . . . Ferm's Finder
See OVENS AND RANGES. . . . . Ferm's Finder

RAPID SHUTDOWN OF SOLAR PHOTOVOLTAIC SYSTEMS
Rapid Shutdown of PV Systems on Buildings. 690.12
    Controlled Conductors. . . . . 690.12(A)
    Controlled Limits . . . . 690.12(B)
        Inside the Array Boundary . . . . .690.12(B)(2)
        Outside the Array Boundary . . . . .690.12(B)(1)
    Equipment . . . . 690.12(D)
    Initiation Device . . . . 690.12(C)
Identification of Power Systems
    Building with Rapid Shutdown Plaques and Directories . . .
    . . . . 690.56(C)

R

R

Label Notification

    Array and Conductors Leaving the Array. . . . . Figure 690.56(C)(1)(a)

    Only Conductors Leaving the Array . . . . Figure 690.56(C)(1)(b)

    More Than One Type . . . . .690.56(C)(2)

    Rapid Shutdown Switch . . . . .690.56(C)(3)

    Type. . . . . .690.56(C)(1)

RATED LOAD CURRENT

Definition of 440.2

Marking on Hermetic Refrigerant Motor-Compressors . . 440.4

REACTORS . . . . **Art. 470**

READILY ACCESSIBLE

See ACCESSIBLE (READILY ACCESSIBLE) . . Ferm's Finder

REBAR (CONCRETE ENCASED ELECTRODE) . . . 250.52(A)(3)

Concrete Encased Electrode . . . . .250.52(A)(3)

    Accessible (not required) . . . . .250.68(A) Ex. No. 1

    Connections . . . . 250.66(B)

    Direct-Current Sole Connection. . . . . 250.166(D)

    Existing Building or Structures . . . . 250.50 Ex.

    Rebar (Consist of and Size). . . . . .250.52(A)(3)

    Rebar Extension . . . . .250.68(C)(3)

    Swimming Pool (not allowed for Grounding Electrode) . . . . .250.52(B)(3)

RECEPTACLES

Anesthetizing Locations, Low-Voltage . . . . 517.64(F)

Appliances (GFCI to be Readily Accessible) 422.5

Arc-Fault Circuit-Interrupter

    Branch Circuit Protections. . . . . 406.4(D)(4)

    Dormitory Units. . . . . 210.12(C)

    Dwelling Units . . . . 210.12(A)

    Extensions and Modifications . . . . 210.12(B)

    Readily Accessible Location . . . . 406.4(D)

    Replacement . . . . 406.4(D)

Attachment Methods (Screws) 406.5

Baseboard Heaters, in 424.9

    As Required Outlet for Wall Space 210.52

Bathtubs, Within 6 feet, GFCI-Protected . . . . . 210.8(A)(9)

Branch Circuits. 210.7

    Required in Dwelling Units 210.52

Calculations . . . . .220.14(A)-(L)

Demand Factors – Non-Dwelling Units 220.44

    Marinas and Boatyards 555.19

    See CALCULATIONS . . . . Ferm's Finder

    See Notes under Table 220.12 . . . . 220.14(J) and (K)

Child Care Facilities, Tamper Resistant . . . . 406.12(3)

    Definition (Child Care Facility) 406.2

CO/ALR Marking Required If Aluminum Wire Is Used . . . . 406.3(C)

    See (RTRT) . . . . *UL Product Spec*

Configurations

    Mobile Home Power Supply . . . . 550.10(C)

    Park Trailer Power Supply . . . . 552.44(C)

    Recreational Vehicle Power Supply . . . . 551.46(C)

        Ratings. 551.81

Connected to an Equipment Grounding Conductor . . 406.4(B)

Controlled

    Building Automation . . . . 406.3(E)

    Energy Management . . . . 406.3(E)

    Marking . . . . Figure 406.3(E)

Countertop Applications, Not Face-Up Position . . . . 406.5(G)

Critical Branch, Health Care Facilities. . . . . 517.34(A)

Critical Care (Category 1), Patient Bed Locations .517.19(B)(1)

Damp or Wet Locations, Weather Resistant Required . 406.9(A)

Decks, Dwelling Units . . . . .210.52(E)(3)

Definition of (Selected Receptacles) 517.2

Demand Factors (Non-Dwelling Feeders) 220.44

    Marinas and Boatyards . . . . Art. 555

    Permitted to Use Lighting Load Demand Factors . . . . Table 220.42

Disconnecting Means

    Cord- and Plug-Connected Appliances. 422.16

    Cord- and Plug-Connected Motors . . . . .430.109(F)

Dormitories. 210.60

Electrical Service Areas 210.64

Faceplates

    Completely Cover Opening 406.6

    Grounding . . . . 406.6(B)

    Insulated Material. . . . . 406.6(C)

    Integral Night Light and/or USB Charger . . . . . . 406.6(D)

    Means of Grounding, Patient Care Spaces . . 517.13(B) Ex. 1

    Metal . . . . 406.6(A)

    Nonmetallic Plate on Isolated Ground Receptacles

        Nonmetallic Boxes . . . . 406.3(D)(2)

    Position of Receptacle Faces . . . . 406.5(G)

Required on Boxes . . . . 314.28(C)

Thickness (Metal) . . . . 406.6(A)

Wet or Damp Locations, Flush with Faceplate . . . 406.9(E)

Face-up Position (Not Permitted)

Countertops and Similar Work Surfaces . . . . . . 406.5(G)

Mobile Home Countertops . . . . 550.13(F)(2)

Park Trailers Countertops . . . . 552.41(F)(2)

Recreational Vehicle, Countertops or Similar Surfaces . . . .
. . . . 551.41(D)

Floor

Boxes to Be Listed for the Application . . . . . . 314.27(B)

Meeting Room . . . . 210.71(B)(2)

Protection for Floor Receptacle . . . . 406.9(D)

Seating Areas . . . . 406.5(H)(4)

Within 18 in. of Wall . . . . 210.52(A)(3)

Foyer, Dwelling Unit . . . . 210.52(I)

General Care (Category 2), Patient Bed Locations . . 517.18(B)

Ground-Fault Circuit-Interrupter, Protection of

See GROUND-FAULT CIRCUIT-INTERRUPTERS . . . . .
. . . . Ferm's Finder

Grounding

Connecting Receptacle Terminal to Box 250.146

Nongrounding Replacement or Circuit Extension . . . . . .
250.130(C)

Receptacles and Cord Connectors . . . . 406.4(A)

Receptacles, Adapters, Cord Connectors, Plugs 406.4

Guest Rooms and Suites of Hotels and Motels, Tamper-Resistant
. . . . 406.12(B)

Hazardous (Classified) Locations

Class I Locations 501.145

Connections for Process Control Instruments . . . .
. . . . 501.105(B)(6)

Class II Locations 502.145

Class III Locations 503.145

Health Care Facilities

Above Hazardous (Classified) Anesthetizing Locations . . .
. . . . 517.61(B)(5)

Critical Branch

Receptacle Identification . . . . 517.31(E)

Selected Receptacles Supplied by . . . . 517.34(A)

Ground-Fault Circuit-Interrupter

Not Required, Certain Critical Care (Category 1) Spaces .
. . . . 517.21

Wet Procedure Locations . . . . 517.20(A)

Grounding

Critical Care (Category 1) Spaces 517.19

General Care (Category 2) Spaces 517.18

Insulated (Isolated) Receptacles . . . . 517.160(A)(5)

Isolated Ground Receptacles . . . . 250.146(D)

Patient Care Spaces 517.13

Hospital Grade Receptacles

Critical Care (Category 1) Patient Bed Location 517.19(B)

General Care (Category 2) Patient Bed Location 517.18(B)

Operating Rooms . . . . 517.19(C)(2)

Note: It is not intended that there be a total, immediate
replacement of existing non-hospital-grade receptacles. It
is intended, however, that non-hospital-grade receptacles
be replaced with hospital-grade receptacles upon
modification of use, renovation, or as existing receptacles
need replacement . . . . 517.18(B)(Info. Note)

Hospital Use Type

Above Hazardous Anesthetizing Locations . . 517.61(B)(5)

Other-Than-Hazardous Anesthetizing Locations . . . . . .
. . . . 517.61(C)(2)

Insulated Equipment Grounding Conductor . . . 517.13(B)

Connection Grounding Terminal to Box 250.146

Critical Care (Category 1) Space Bed Locations, Required
. . . . 517.19(B)

General Care (Category 2) Space Bed Locations, Required
. . . . 517.18(B)

Insulated Grounding Terminals, Outside Patient Care
Vicinity . . . . 517.16(B)

Permitted, for Reduction of Electrical Noise . . 250.96(B)

Laundry Areas

AFCI Protection . . . . 210.12(A)

GFCI Protection . . . . 210.8(A)(10)

Low-Voltage Circuits . . . . 517.64(F)

Number of, in Hospitals

Certain Rooms and Spaces Exempt from 517.18(B) Ex. 1&2

Critical Care (Category 1) Space . . . . 517.19(B)

General Care (Category 2) Space . . . . 517.18(B)

Operating Rooms . . . . 517.19(C)

Other-Than-Hazardous Anesthetizing Locations . 517.61(C)

Special Purpose, Grounding . . . . 517.19(H)

Tamper-Resistant Cover (Listed) Pediatric Locations . . . . .
. . . . 517.18(C)

Tamper-Resistant Receptacles (Listed) Pediatric Locations .
. . . . 517.18(C)

Within Hazardous (Classified) Anesthetizing Locations . . .
. . . . 517.61(A)(5)

Heating, Air-Conditioning, and Refrigeration Equipment

R

R

Rooftops, Attics and Crawl Spaces 210.63

Hotels & Motels (Non-Dwellings)

    Arc-Fault Circuit-Interrupter . . . . 210.12(C)

    GFCI Bathroom and Rooftop . . . . 210.8(B)

    Guest Rooms, Number of . . . . 210.60(A)

    Placement of . . . . 210.60(B)

    Lighting Loads- General (Unit Load) . . . . . . Table 220.12

    Lighting Outlets . . . . 210.70(B)

    Load Calculations for . . . . 220.14(I)

    Permitted Demand Factors 220.44

    Receptacle Load Permitted to Apply Lighting Demands . . . . Table 220.42

    Tamper-Resistant . . . . .406.12(2)

    Voltage Not Exceed 120 Volts . . . . 210.6(A)

Hydromassage Bathtubs . . . . 680 Part VII

    Accessibility of Receptacle 680.73

    Bonding .680.74(A)(5)

    GFCI Protected- within 6 ft. 680.71

    Individual Branch Circuit 680.71

In Damp or Wet Locations . . . . 406.9(A) and (B)

Installation

    Connecting Receptacle Ground Terminal to Box . . 250.146

    Dwelling Units 210.52

    Methods of Equipment Grounding 250.130

    Multiple Branch Circuits on Same Yoke 210.7

    Required Outlets, General 210.50

Insulated Equipment Grounding Conductor . . . . . 517.13(B)

    Connection Grounding Terminal to Box . . . . . 250.146(D)

    Critical Care (Category 1) Space Bed Locations, Required . . . . 517.19(B)

    General Care (Category 2) Space Bed Locations, Required . . . . 517.18(B)

    Isolated Grounding Receptacles (Patient Care Vicinity) . . . . 517.16(A)

    Inside Patient Care Vicinity . . . . 517.16(A)

    Outside Patient Care Vicinity . . . . 517.16(B)

    Isolated Ground Receptacles . . . . 406.3(D)

    Permitted, for Reduction of Electrical Noise . . . . 250.96(B)

Kitchens, Dwelling Units . . . . 210.8(A)(6)

Kitchens, Other Than Dwelling Units . . . . 210.8(B)(2)

Loads . . . . 210.21(B)

    Maximum Cord- and Plug-Connected . . Table 210.21(B)(2)

    Maximum 220.18

    Other Loads – All Occupancies 220.14

Permissible 210.23

Ratings for Various Size Circuits . . . . . Table 210.21(B)(3)

Summary 210.24

Locations

    General 210.50

    Dwelling Units 210.52

        Required Outlets in Addition to Those Part of a Luminaire (Fixture) or Appliance or in Cabinets or Cupboards 210.52

    Electrical Service Areas 210.64

    Guest Rooms 210.60

    HACR Equipment Outlet 210.63

    Show Windows 210.62

Marinas and Boatyards 555.19

Maximum Cord- and Plug-Connected Load to . . . . Table 210.21(B)(2)

Maximum Height [Dwellings 1.7 m (5 1/2 ft)] . . . . 210.52(4)

Meeting Rooms 210.71

Mounting 406.5

    On Countertops . . . . 406.5(E)

    On Covers . . . . 406.5(C)

    Orientation . . . . 406.5(G)

    Work Surfaces . . . . 406.5(F)

Multioutlet Assembly . . . . Art. 380

    Calculations . . . . 220.14(H)

Multiwire Branch-Circuit 210.4

    See MULTIWIRE BRANCH CIRCUITS . . . . Ferm's Finder

Non-Grounding-Type, Replacement of . . . . 406.4(D)(2)

    Connection of Equipment Grounding Conductor . . 250.130

Nursing Homes, Identification . . . . 517.41(E)

Operating Rooms . . . . 517.19(C)

Outdoors (Dwellings)

    Ground-Fault Circuit-Interrupter Protection Required . . . 210.8(A)(3)

    Outlet Required . . . . 210.52(E)

Outdoors (Damp or Wet Locations) 406.8

Outlet Assemblies . . . . .210.52(C)(5) and D

Outlet Box Hood, Definition 406.2

    Damp or Wet Locations 314.15

    Wet Locations (Extra-Duty) . . . . 406.9(B)

Overcurrent Protection 210.20

    Maximum Cord- and Plug-Connected Load . . . . Table 210.21(B)(2)

    Summary of Branch-Circuit Requirements . . Table 210.24

Ratings (Receptacles) . . . . .210.21(B)(3)

In Motion Picture and TV Studios 530.21

Receptacles for Various Size Circuits . . . Table 210.21(B)(3)

Receptacles, Cord Connectors, and Attachment Plugs . . . .
. . . . 406.3

Summary Requirements 210.24

Replacements . . . . 406.4(D)

Arc-Fault Circuit-Interrupter Protection . . . . . 406.4 (D)(4)

Ground-Fault Circuit-Interrupters . . . . 406.4(D)(3)

Grounding-Type Receptacles . . . . 406.4(D)(1)

Non-Grounding Type Receptacles . . . . 406.4(D)(2)

Tamper-Resistant Receptacles . . . . 406.4(D)(5)

Weather-Resistant Receptacles . . . . 406.4(D)(6)

Connection of Equipment Grounding Conductor . . . . . .
. . . . .250.130(C)

Note: AFCI, GFCI, Tamper-Resistant and Weather-Resistant
protected receptacles must be provided where replacements
are made at receptacle outlets that are required be so protected elsewhere in the *NEC*.

Required in Dwellings (General) 210.50

Every 3.6 m (12 ft) or 1.8 m (6 ft) from a Point .210.52(A)(1)

Hydromassage Bathtubs . . . . 680 Part VII

Locations. 210.52

Motels & Hotels 210.60

Required in Occupancies . . . . 210 Part III

Rooftop Receptacles. 210.63

Show Windows 210.62

Spas and Hot Tubs Indoors . . . . 680.43(A)

Swimming Pools . . . . 680.22(A)

See GROUND-FAULT CIRCUIT-INTERRUPTER PROTEC-
TION . . . . Ferm's Finder

Seating Areas . . . . 406.5(H)

Separable Attachment Fitting (see Receptacle) . . . . . Art. 100

Ceiling Fan. .422.18(2)

Disconnection Means. 422.33

Outlet Box . . . . 314.27(E)

Separately Derived Systems 60 Volts to Ground 647.1

Show Windows, Required, ... 210.62

In Elevated Floors of Show Windows . . . . . 314.27(B) Ex.

Shower Stalls, Within 6 feet, GFCI-Protected. . . . 210.8(A)(9)

Spas and Hot Tubs . . . . 680.43(A)

Swimming Pools . . . . 680.22(A)

Tamper Resistant (Pediatric Locations) . . . . 517.18(C)

Tamper Resistant Type

Assembly Occupancy Areas . . . . .406.12(6)

Child Care Facilities . . . . 406.12(3)

Clinics, Medical, and Dental Offices . . . . .406.12(5)

Dormitories . . . . .406.12(7)

Dwelling Units . . . . 406.12(1)

Guest Rooms and Guest Suites (Hotel, Motels) . . 406.12(2)

Identified Receptacle Types . . . . 406.12 Info. Note

Locations- Not Required . . . . . . .406.12 Ex. to (1) thru (7)

Preschools and Elementary Educational . . . . . .406.12(4)

Temporary Installations

Ground-Fault Circuit-Interrupter Requirements 590.6

Installation of . . . . 590.6(A)

Wet Locations, Receptacles. . . . . 590.4(D)(2)

Terminals, Identification . . . . 200.10(B)

Theaters

Control and Overcurrent Protection of Circuits. . . . .
. . . . .520.21(3)

For Equipment and Luminaires (Fixtures) on Stage . . . . .
. . . . 520.45

Torque of Connections . . . . 110.14(D)

USB Charger . . . . 406.3(F)

Faceplate . . . . 406.6(D)

Voltage Between Adjacent Devices . . . . 406.5(J)

Weather-Resistant Type . . . . 406.9(A) and (B)

Wet or Damp Locations 406.9

Work Surfaces . . . . 406.5(F)

See (RTDV) . . . .*UL Product Spec*

See (RTRT) . . . .*UL Product Spec*

RECEPTACLES & PLUG COMBINATIONS, HAZARDOUS (CLASSIFIED) LOCATIONS

See (RRAT) . . . .*UL Product Spec*

RECESSED LUMINAIRES

Clearances, Installation 410.116

Clothes Closets, in 410.16

Electric Radiant Heating Panels (separation) . . . .424.93(A)(3)

Insulation, Clearance from . . . . .410.116(B)

Raceways, Identified for Through-Wiring . . . . . . 410.64(B)

Swimming Pools- Indoor . . . . 680.43(B)(1)(1)

Thermal Protection of Incandescent-Type . . . . . .410.115(C)

Used as Raceways 410.64

Wiring. 410.117

RECIPROCALS, *See* **Formula** . *Ferm's Charts and Information*

RECONDITIONED EQUIPMENT . . . . 110.21(a)(2)

R

RECREATIONAL VEHICLES . . . . **Art. 551**
Air Conditioning, Pre-Wiring . . . . 551.47(Q)
Branch Circuit, Pre-Wiring . . . . 551.47(S)
Branch Circuits Required 551.42
Combination Systems . . . . 551 Part II
Definitions 551.2
Energy Management System . . . . 551.42(C) Ex. 2
Factory Tests . . . . 551 Part V
Generator, Pre-Wiring. . . . . 551.47(R)
Labels . . . . 551.4(C)
    At the Electrical Entrance . . . . 551.46(D)
Nominal 120- or 120/240-Volt Systems . . . . . . 551 Part IV
Other Power Sources . . . . 551 Part III
Parks (RV) . . . . 551 Part IV
    Calculated Load. 551.73
    Clearance for Overhead Conductors 551.79
    Demand Factors. . . . . .Table 551.73(A)
    Distribution System. 551.72
    Grounding 551.75
    Overcurrent Protection. 551.74
    Protection of Equipment 551.78
    Receptacles. 551.81
    Supply Equipment Location 551.77
        Grounding 551.76
    Type of Receptacles Provided 551.71
    Underground Conductors 551.80
Receptacle Configuration Types . . . . . Figure 551.46(C)(1)
Receptacle Outlets Required 551.41
    Rooftop Decks. . . . . .551.41(B)(4)
Supply Conductors. . . . . 551.30(E)
Wiring Methods 551.47
See MOBILE HOMES . . . . Ferm's Finder
See PARK TRAILERS . . . . Ferm's Finder

RECREATIONAL VEHICLE PARKS . . . . **Art. 551**
Calculation of Loads 551.73
Definitions 551.2
Demand Factors . . . . .Table 551.73(A)
Disconnecting Means . . . . 551.77(B)
Distribution System 551.72
    50-Ampere Receptacles from 120/240-Volt, or 208Y/120-Volt System 551.72
    Neutral Conductors. . . . . 551.72(D)
    Receptacles. . . . . 551.72(C)

Systems. . . . . 551.72(A)
Three-Phase Systems . . . . 551.72(B)
Grounding (General) 551.75
    Exposed Non-Current-Carrying Metal Parts . . . 551.76(A)
    Grounding Electrode. . . . . 551.75(B)
    Neutral Conductor Not to Be Used As Equipment Ground . . . . 551.76(C)
    No Ground Connection on Load Side of Service . . . . 551.76(D)
    Secondary Distribution Systems . . . . 551.76(B)
    Site Supply Equipment 551.76
Marking of Site Equipment . . . . 551.77(F)
Outdoor Equipment, Protection of 551.78
Overcurrent Protection 551.74
Overhead Conductors, Clearance of 551.79
Pre-Wiring . . . . .551.47(Q), (S)
Receptacle Outlets 551.71
    20-Ampere. . . . . 551.71(A)
    30-Ampere. . . . . 551.71(B)
    50-Ampere. . . . . 551.71(C)
    50-ampere installation requires a 30-ampere. . . . 551.71(C)
    Additional Receptacles . . . . 551.71(E)
    Configuration of Supply Receptacles 551.81
    Ground-Fault Circuit-Interrupter Protection . . . 551.71(F)
    Tent Sites . . . . 551.71(D)
Site Equipment, Location of . . . . 551.77(A)
Underground Service, Feeder and Branch Circuits . . . 551.80
See UNDERGROUND SERVICE & WIRING . . Ferm's Finder

RECTIFIER
AC Systems 50 to 1000 Volts Not Required to Be Grounded . . . . .250.21(A)(2)
Belowground-protected from physical damage. 110.55
Class I, Division 1 Locations 501.55
Class II, Division 1 Locations. . . . . .502.150(A)(2)
Motion Picture Projection Rooms 540.11
    Listed Enclosures 540.20
Motors- nominal voltage 430.18
    Single Motor. 430.22
Two-Wire DC Systems, Derived from . . . . . 250.162(A) Ex. 2
Wind Electric Systems
    Components (Interactive System) . . . . . Figure 694.1(a)
    Components (Stand-Alone System). . . . . Figure 6914.1(b)
    Wind Turbine Output Circuit 694.2

REFRIGERATION & AIR CONDITIONING . . . . **Art. 440**
See AIR-CONDITIONING & REFRIGERATING
EQUIPMENT . . . . Ferm's Finder

REINFORCING THERMOSETTING RESIN CONDUIT (FIBER-GLASS) (TYPE RTRC) . . . . **Art. 355**

REINFORCING-BAR GROUNDING ELECTRODES . . . .
. . . . **250.52(A)(3)**
See RTRC . . . . Ferm's Finder

RELAYS
Overload, Motor Overcurrent Protection 430.40
Overload, Motor-Compressor and Branch-Circuit   440 Part VI
Reverse-Current, Transformers. . . . . 450.11(B)

REMOTE CONTROL CIRCUITS . . . . **Art. 725**
Access to Electrical Equipment 725.21
Grounding . . . . 250.112(I)
Motors, Control Circuits . . . . 430 Part VI
Safety-Control Equipment 725.31
See CLASS 1, 2, & 3 REMOTE CONTROL CIRCUITS . . . . .
. . . . Ferm's Finder
See CONTROL CIRCUITS . . . . Ferm's Finder
See DIFFERENT SYSTEMS IN SAME ENCLOSURE . . . . . .
. . . . Ferm's Finder
See Power-Limited Circuit Cable (QPTZ) . . . . UL Product Spec

REPAIR GARAGES (MAJOR AND MINOR) . . . . **Art. 511**
See Commercial Garages . . . . Ferm's Finder

REPAIRING NONCOMBUSTIBLE SURFACES **312.4**
Cabinets, Cutout Boxes, Meter Enclosures 312.4
Outlet, Device, Pull and Junction Boxes. 314.21

RESISTANCE
Appliances . . . . Art. 422
Fixed Electric Heating Equipment for Pipelines and Vessels . .
. . . . Art. 427
Fixed Electric Space-Heating Equipment . . . . Art. 424
Fixed Outdoor Electric Deicing and Snow-Melting Equipment
. . . . Art. 426
Fixed Resistance and Electrode Industrial Process Heating
Equipment . . . . Art. 425
Low Contact Resistance, Wet-Niche Luminaires . . 680.23(B)(5)
Of Conductors, Direct-Current . . . . Chapter 9, Table 8
Of Made Electrodes 25 Ohms or Less . . . . . 250.53(A)(2) Ex.
Three Single Conductors in Conduit, Alternating-Current . . .
. . . . .Chapter 9, Table 9
Welders . . . . 630 Part III

RESISTIVELY GROUNDED DC SYSTEMS
Caution Signage . . . . 408.3(F)(5)

RESISTORS & REACTORS . . . . **Art. 470**
Combustible Material within 305 mm (12 in.), Thermal Barrier
. . . . 470.3
Conductor Insulation 470.4
Location, Not Subject to Physical Damage 470.2
Over 1000 Volts, Nominal . . . . 470 Part II

RETROFIT KIT
Defined . . . . Art. 100
Field-Installed Secondary Wiring, Signs 600.12
Installation Instructions. . . . . 600.4(E)
Listing Requirements for Luminaires, Lampholders and Lamps
410.6
Listing Requirements for Signs 600.3
Sign Installations Instructions . . . . 600.4(F)

REVERSE FEEDING TRANSFORMERS . . . . **450.11(B)**

RHEOSTATS
Motion Picture and TV Studios . . . . 530.15(C)
Motor Controllers . . . . 430.82(C)
Theaters and Audience Areas
Dimmers 520.25
Installed in Cases or Cabinets 520.7

RIGID METAL CONDUIT . . . . **Art. 344**
Aluminum, Must Be Suitable for the Condition . . . .
. . . . 300.6, 344.10(A)(3), (B)(2)
Shall Not Be Used in Concrete or Earth Burial
See (DYWV) . . . . UL Product Spec
Bends
How Made 344.24
Number of 344.26
Radius of . . . . Chapter 9, Table 2
Couplings and Connectors 344.42
Bushings. 344.46
Conductors 4 AWG and Larger . . . . 300.4(G)
Corrosive Environments . . . . 344.10(B)
Couplings and Connectors, Threadless . . . . 344.42(A)
Definition 344.2

R

R

Dimensions & Percent Area of . . . . Chapter 9 Table 4

Dissimilar Metals. 344.14

Field-Cut Threads . . . . 300.6(A) Info. Notes

Listing 344.6

Marking 344.120

Material of Construction 344.100

Minimum and Maximum Sizes 344.20

Not to Be Used As a Means of Support for Cables or

    Nonelectrical Equipment (General). . . . . 300.11(B)

    CATV and Radio Distribution Systems. 820.24

    Class 2 and 3 Circuit Conductors 725.143

    Communications Circuits . . . . .800.133(B)

    Fire Alarm Circuit Conductors 760.143

    Network-Powered Broadband Systems . . . . . . 830.133(B)

Number of Conductors in 344.22

    Combinations of Conductors (General) . Chapter 9 Table 1

        Compact Stranded . . . . Chapter 9 Table 5A

        Dimensions of Conductors in. . . . . Chapter 9 Table 5

    Same Size. . . . . . Informative Annex Tables C8 and C8(A)

Reaming & Threading 344.28

Red Brass RMC . . . . 344.10(A)(2)

Running Threads Not Permitted . . . . 344.42(B)

Securing and Supporting of. 344.30

Sizes

    Minimum . . . . 344.20(A)

    Maximum . . . . 344.20(B)

Splices and Taps 344.56

Stainless Steel- only with Stainless Steel fittings. 344.14

Supporting Enclosures. . . . . 314.23(E) & (F)

Types

    Aluminum . . . . .344.100(2)

    Red Brass. . . . . .344.100(3)

    Stainless Steel . . . . .344.100(4)

    Steel with Protective Coatings . . . . .344.100(1)

Uses Permitted 344.10

See (DYIX) . . . .*UL Product Spec*

RIGID PVC CONDUIT . . . . **Art. 352**

Ambient Temperature Limitations . . . . 352.12(D)

Bends

    How Made 352.24

    Number of 352.26

    Radius of . . . . Chapter 9 Table 2

Boxes and Fittings 352.48

Bushings 352.46

Conductors 4 AWG and Larger . . . . 300.4(G)

Construction 352.100

Definition 352.2

Dimensions and Percent Area of . . . . . . Chapter 9 Table 4

Expansion Fittings 352.44

    Expansion Characteristics of Fiberglass Reinforced . . . . .

    . . . . Table 352.44

    Expansion Characteristics of PVC . . . . . . Table 352.44

Exposed, Protection from Physical Damage . . . . . 352.10(F)

Grounding (Equipment) 352.60

    See GROUNDING, Fixed Equipment. . . . . Ferm's Finder

Hazardous (Classified) Location Installation . . . . . 352.12(A)

Installation . . . . 352 Part II

Insulation Temperature Limitations . . . . .352.10(I)

Listed 352.6

Marking (Including Material Type) 352.120

Minimum and Maximum Sizes 352.20

Not to Be Used As a Means of Support for Cables or

    CATV and Radio Distribution Systems. . . . . . 820.133(B)

    Class 2 and 3 Circuit Conductors 725.143

    Communications Circuits 800.24

    Fire Alarm Circuit Conductors 760.143

    Network-Powered Broadband Systems . . . . . .830.133(B)

    Nonelectrical Equipment (General). . . . . 300.11(B)

Number of Conductors in, Schedule 40 and HDPE Conduit . .

. . . . 352.22

    Combinations of Conductors (General) . Chapter 9 Table 1

        Compact Stranded . . . . .Chapter 9 Table 5A

        Dimension of Conductors in . . . . . . Chapter 9 Table 5

    Same Size. . . . . Informative Annex Tables C10 and C10(A)

Number of Conductors in, Schedule 80 (Same Size) . . . . . .

Informative Annex Table C9

    Combinations of Conductors (General) . Chapter 9 Table 1

        Compact Stranded . . . . Chapter 9 Table 5A

        Dimension of Conductors in . . . . . . Chapter 9 Table 5

    Same Size . . . . . Informative Annex Tables C9 and C9(A)

Number of Conductors in, ... 352.22

    Combinations of Conductors (General) . Chapter 9 Table 1

        Compact Stranded . . . . Chapter 9 Table 5A

        Dimensions of Conductors in. . . . . . Chapter 9 Table 5

    Same Size. . . . . Informative Annex Tables C11 and C11(A)

Number of Conductors in, Type EB (Encased Burial in Concrete). 352.22

    Combinations of Conductors (General) . Chapter 9 Table 1

Compact Stranded . . . . Chapter 9 Table 5A

Dimensions of Conductors in. . . . . . Chapter 9 Table 5

Same Size . . . . Informative Annex Tables C12 and C12(A)

Securing and Supporting 352.30

   Other Support Spacings Included in Listing . . . . 352.30(B)

Sizes

   Maximum . . . . 352.20(B)

   Mimimum . . . . 352.20(A)

Splices and Taps 352.56

Uses Permitted 352.10

   Above Class I Locations

      Commercial Garages. . . . . 511.7(A)(1)

   Essential Electrical System Hospitals, Schedule 40 . . . . . .

   . . . . .517.31(C)(2)

   Essential Electrical System Hospitals, Schedule 80 . . . . . .

   . . . . .517.31(C)(3)(1)

   Motor Fuel Dispensing Facilities . . . . . . 514.8, Ex. No. 2

   Places of Assembly

      If Encased in 50 mm (2 in.) of Concrete . . . . . 518.4(A)

      Nonrated Construction . . . . 518.4(B)

      In Certain Spaces with 15-minute Finish Rating . 518.4(C)

   Protection of Service Cables, Suitable for Location

   Schedule 80 . . . . 230.50(B)(1)(3)

   Protection of Underground Conductors, Schedule 80

      1000 Volts and Below . . . . 300.5(D)(4)

      Over 1000 Volts. . . . . 300.50(C)

   Recreational Vehicle, Underground Conductors

      Protection of, Schedule 80. . . . . 551.80(B)

   Support of Conduit Bodies Only . . . . 352.10(H)

   Theaters and Audience Areas 520.5

   Under Hazardous Areas

      Bulk Storage Plants. 515.8

      Class I, Division 1 . . . . .501.10(A)(1)(a) Ex.

      Commercial Garages. . . . . 511.7(A)(1)

      Motor Fuel Dispensing Facilities 514.8 Ex.2

Uses Not Permitted 352.12

   Ambient Temperatures Over 50°C Unless Listed . 352.12(D)

   Branch-Circuit Wiring, Patient Care Areas 517.13

   Conductor Insulation Temperatures Exceeding

      Ambient Temperatures . . . . 352.12(D)

   Ducts, Plenums, and Other Air-Handling Spaces . . . 300.22

   Hazardous (Classified) Locations (Except As Permitted in

   Ch. 5 Art.) . . . . 352.12(A)

   Support of Luminaires (Fixtures) and Other Equipment . . .

. . . . 352.12(B)

Where Subject to Physical Damage Unless Identified . . . .

. . . . 352.12(C)

See Reinforced Thermosetting (DZKT) . . . . .*UL Product Spec*

See Schedule 40 & 80, PVC Type RTRC (DZYR) . . . .

. . . .*UL Product Spec*

See Underground, PVC Type (EAZX) . . . . . .*UL Product Spec*

ROMEX (NONMETALLIC-SHEATHED CABLE) . . . . Art. 334
See NONMETALLIC-SHEATHED CABLE. . . . Ferm's Finder

ROOF DECKING
Cables, Raceways and Boxes Installed Under, Physical

Protection. . . . . 300.4(E)

Luminaires (Fixtures) Installed Under, Physical Protection . . .

. . . . 410.10(F)

ROOF ON BUILDING BEFORE INSTALLING EQUIPMENT . . .
. . . . . .110.11
Dry Locations, Definition of . . . . Art. 100 Part I

Nonmetallic-Sheathed Cable, Type NM – Uses Permitted. . . .

. . . . 334.10(A)

ROOF TOPS
Raceways and Cables Exposed to Sunlight .310.15(B)(3)(c) and

Table 310.15(B)(2)(a) and (b)

RTRC TYPE CONDUIT . . . . Art. 355
Ambient Temperature Restrictions. . . . . 355.12(D)

Bends 355.24

Bushings. 355.46

Conductors- Number of. 355.22

Construction .355.100

Definition 355.2

Expansion Fittings 355.44

Grounding 355.60

Joints 355.48

Listing 355.6

Securing and Supporting 355.30

Sizes

   Maximum . . . . 355.20(B)

   Minimum . . . . 355.20(A)

Splices and Taps. 355.56

Trimming 355.28

Uses Not Permitted 355.12

Uses Permitted 355.10

S

RUNNING THREADS (NOT PERMITTED)

Intermediate Metal Conduit on Connections, Couplings . . . .
. . . . 342.42(B)

Rigid Metal Conduit on Connections, Couplings . . 344.42(B)

S

(SCADA) Supervisory Control & Data Acquisition . . . . . .
. . . . **Info. Annex G**

Definition 708.2

SAFETY AND EXAMINATION OF EQUIPMENT **90.7**

SCHOOLS

Branch-Circuit, Feeder, & Service Calculations . . . . . Art. 220

General Lighting Load . . . . Table 220.12

Optional Method 220.86

Tamper-Resistant Receptacles

Preschool and Elementary Education Facilities . . .406.12(4)

See CALCULATIONS . . . . Ferm's Finder

SCREW SHELLS

Identification of Terminals, Screw Shells . . . . . . 200.10(C)

Screw Shell Devices with Leads . . . . 200.10(D)

Lampholders, Installation . . . . 410 Part VIII

Polarization of Luminaires (Fixtures) 410.50

SCREWS

Covers and Canopies, Drywall Type Not to be Used . . . 314.25

Receptacles, Drywall Type Not to be Used 406.5

Switches, Drywall Type Not to be Used . . . . 404.10(B)

Under Roof Decking- Damage by Screws

Cables, Raceways and Boxes . . . . . 300.4(E) and Info. Note

Luminaires . . . . 410.10(F)

SEALING, HAZARDOUS (CLASSIFIED) LOCATIONS

Accessible, Class I, Divisions 1 and 2 . . . . 501.15(C)(1)

Accessible, Class II, Divisions 1 and 2 . . . . 502.15

Cable Systems, Class I, Division 1 . . . . 501.15(D)

Cable Systems, Class I, Division 2 . . . . 501.15(E)

Class II, Divisions 1 and 2, Methods of 502.15

Compound Thickness . . . . .501.15(C)(3)

Conductor or Optical Fiber Fill Not More Than 25% 501.15(C)(6)

Conduit Systems, Class I, Division 1 . . . . 501.15(A)

Conduit Systems, Class I, Division 2 . . . . 501.15(B)

Optical Fiber Cables . . . . 500.8(F)

Splices Not Permitted in Seal Fittings . . . . . . .501.15(C)(4)

Zones

Class I, Zone 2 . . . . .505.15(C)(1)(6)

Optical Fiber Cable . . . . 505.9(F)

Sealing 505.16

Class I, Zones 0, 1, and 2 . . . . 505.16(D)

Zone 0 . . . . 505.16(A)

Zone 1 . . . . 505.16(B)

Zone 2 . . . . 505.16(C)

Zone 20, 21, and 22 . . . . 506.16

See HAZARDOUS (CLASSIFIED) LOCATIONS . . . .
. . . . Ferm's Finder

SEALING RACEWAY FROM WARM TO COLD . . . . . .300.7(A)

Busway Sections, Barriers and Seals 368.234

SEALING UNDERGROUND RACEWAY

1000 Volts and Less . . . . 300.5(G)

Over 1000 Volts . . . . 300.50(F)

Service Raceways 230.8

SEALTIGHT, LIQUIDTIGHT FLEXIBLE METAL CONDUIT . . . .
. . . . **Art. 350**

See LIQUIDTIGHT FLEXIBLE METAL CONDUIT . . . . . .
. . . . Ferm's Finder

See(DXHR) . . . .*UL Product Spec*

SEALTIGHT, LIQUIDTIGHT FLEXIBLE NONMETALLIC CONDUIT . . . .**Art. 356**

See LIQUIDTIGHT FLEXIBLE NONMETALLIC CONDUIT
. . . .*UL Product Spec*

See(DXOQ) . . . .*UL Product Spec*

SEATING AND OTHER SIMILAR AREAS

Receptacle Requirements . . . . 406.5(H)

SECTIONED EQUIPMENT BONDING CONDUCTORS . . . . . .
. . . .**310.10(H)(5)**

SECURING AND SUPPORTING

Armored Cable, Type AC 320.30

Boxes 314.23

Nonmetallic 314.43

Busways 368.30

Cabinets, Cutout Boxes, and Meter Socket Enclosures

Of Cables to . . . . 312.5(C)

Cables & Raceways above Access Panels. . . . . 300.4(C)

   CATV Systems. 820.21

   Class 1, 2 and 3 Remote Control Circuits. 725.21

   Communications Circuits 800.21

   Fire Alarm Systems 760.21

   Network-Powered Broadband Systems 830.21

   Optical Fiber Cables and Raceways 770.21

Ceiling-Suspended (Paddle) Fans . . . . 314.27(D)

   Boxes . . . . 314.27(C)

   Canopies for Wire Space 422.19

   Exposed Ceiling Finish, Combustible. 422.21

   Outlet Boxes to Be Covered 422.20

   Specific Weight Limitations 422.18

Conductors in Vertical Raceways. 300.19

Electrical Metallic Tubing. 358.30

Electrical Nonmetallic Tubing 362.30

Equipment, General . . . . 110.13(A)

Fire-Rated Floor/Ceiling or Roof/Ceiling Assembly . . . .
. . . . .300.11(A)(1)

Flat Cable Assemblies, Type FC 322.30

Flexible Cords

   Branches from Busways . . . . 368.56(B)

   For Underwater Lighting, Strain Relief . . . . . . 680.24(E)

   Securing at Terminals. 400.10

Flexible Metal Conduit 348.30

Intermediate Metal Conduit 342.30

Liquidtight Flexible Metal Conduit 350.30

Liquidtight Flexible Nonmetallic Conduit. 356.30

Luminaires . . . . 410 Part IV

   Class I, Division 1 Locations . . . . .501.130(A)(4)

   Class II, Division 1 Locations . . . . 502.130(A)(4)

   Outlet Boxes for . . . . 314.27(A)

   Suspended Ceilings, By. . . . . 410.36(B)

   Swimming Pools, Outdoor Spas and Hot Tubs. . . 680.22(B)

Messenger Supported Wiring. . . . . Art. 396

   Messenger Supports. . . . . 396.30(A)

Metal-Clad Cable, Type MC 330.30

Non-Fire-Rated Floor/Ceiling or Roof/Ceiling Assembly . . . .
. . . . .300.11(A)(2)

Nonmetallic-Sheathed Cable (Romex)

   300 mm (12 in.) from Metal Boxes 334.30

   200 mm (8 in.) from Plastic Boxes . . . . 314.17(C) Ex.

   Every 1.4 m (4 1/2 ft) 334.30

   In Unfinished Basements and Crawl Spaces . . . . 334.15(C)

Open Wiring on Insulators 398.30

Paddle, Ceiling-Suspended Fans . . . . 314.27(D)

   Canopies for Wire Space 422.19

   Exposed Ceiling Finish, Combustible. 422.21

   Outlet Boxes to Be Covered 422.20

   Specific Weight Limitations 422.18

Panelboards, General . . . . 110.13(A)

   Busbars and Conductors in . . . . 408.3(A)(1)

   Of Cables to . . . . 312.5(C)

Radio and Television, Antennas and Lead-in 810.12

Rigid Metal Conduit 344.30

Rigid PVC Conduit 352.30

Service Overhead Spans . . . . 230 Part II

   By Service Masts. 230.28

   Note: Only power service-drop conductors are permitted to
   be attached to a service mast. See also. . . . . . . 820.44(C)

Strut-Type Channel Raceways 384.30

Wireways

   Metal 376.30

   Nonmetallic 378.30

SELECTIVE COORDINATION

Critical Operations Power Systems (COPS). 708.54

Definition . . . . Art. 100

Elevators 620.62

Emergency Systems 700.32

Fire Pumps . . . . 695.3(C)(3)

Information Technology Equipment. 645.27

Legally Required Standby Systems 701.27

SELECTIVITY

Critical Operations Power Systems. . . . . 708.52(D)

Health Care Facilities 517.17

SELF-CONTAINED DEVICES . . . . 334.40(B)

SEMICONDUCTOR FUSES

Individual Motor Circuits. . . . . .430.52(C)(5)

Motors with Power Conversion Equipment. . . . 430.130(A)(4)

SENSITIVE ELECTRONIC EQUIPMENT

Sensitive Electronic Equipment. . . . . Art. 647

Disconnecting Means, Luminaire, Lockable . . . . . 647.8(A)

Grounding of 647.6

Lighting Equipment 647.8

Receptacles 647.7

Three-Phase Systems. 647.5

Voltage Line-to-Line, Line-to-Ground. 647.1

Wiring Methods 647.4

SEPARABLE ATTACHMENT FITTINGS . . . . 314.27(E)

SEPARATE BUILDINGS OR OTHER STRUCTURES
Disconnecting Means

    Access to Occupants 225.35

    Construction of 225.38

    Grouping of 225.34

    Identification of 225.37

    Location 225.32

    Maximum Number of Disconnects for Each Supply . 225.33

    Number of Supplies. 225.30

    Rating of 225.39

    Suitable for Use as Service Equipment 225.36

Grounding of 250.32

    Agricultural Buildings 547.9

    Grounding Electrode System . . . . 250 Part III

    Panelboards 408.40

Mobile Home Services. 550.32

Overcurrent Protection

    Access to Protective Devices 225.40

    Location in Circuit 240.21

    Panelboards 408.36

Panelboards. . . . . 408 Part II

SEPARATELY DERIVED SYSTEMS
Bonding Jumper, System . . . . 250.30(A)(1)

    Size of . . . . 250.28(D)

Definition of . . . . Art. 100 Part I

Disconnecting Means 240.21

    Location of. 404.8

For Ungrounded Direct-Current Systems 250.169

Grounded Systems . . . . 250.30(A)

    Bonding . . . . 250.30(A)(8)

    Grounded Conductor. . . . . 250.30(A)(3)

    Grounding Electrode . . . . 250.30(A)(4)

    Grounding Electrode Conductor, Multiple System . . . . . .
    . . . . .250.30(A)(6)

    Grounding Electrode Conductor, Single System . . . . . .
    . . . . .250.30(A)(5)

    Installation . . . . 250.30(A)(7)

Supply-Side Bonding Jumper . . . . 250.30(A)(2)

System Bonding Jumper . . . . 250.30(A)(1)

Not Required to Be Grounded 250.21

Outdoor Source . . . . 250.32(C)

Overcurrent Protection of

    Generators 445.12

    In Supervised Industrial Installations . . . . . 240 Part VIII

        Location of Overcurrent Protection 240.92

    Location in Circuit 240.21

    Motor Control Circuit . . . . 430.72(A)

    Not Required If Power Loss Hazard Created . . . . 240.4(A)

    Panelboard Supplied Through Transformer . . . . 408.36(B)

    Requirement for. . . . . 240.15(A)

    Transformer Secondary Conductors by Primary OCD . . . .
    . . . . 240.4(F)

    Transformers. 450.3

Required to Be Grounded . . . . 250.20(D)

Systems with 60 Volts to Ground. 647.3

Ungrounded Systems . . . . 250.30(B)

    Bonding Path and Conductor. . . . . .250.30(B)(3)

    Grounding Electrode . . . . .250.30(B)(2)

    Grounding Electrode Conductor. . . . . .250.32(B)(1)

SERIES/PARALLEL CIRCUITS . . . . Ferm's Finder

SERVICE AREA, ELECTRICAL
Receptacle Requirements 210.64

SERVICE CABLES
See SERVICE-ENTRANCE CABLE . . . . Ferm's Finder

SERVICE CONDUCTORS
Over 1000 Volts, Ground-Fault Circuit Conductors Brought to
Service Point

    With a Grounded Conductor . . . . 250.186(A)

    Without an Grounded Conductor. . . . . 250.186(B)

Overhead

    Clearances 230.24

    Insulation and Covering 230.22

    Means of Attachment. 230.27

    Point of Attachment. 230.26

    Service Masts as Supports 230.28

    Size and Rating 230.23

    Supports over Buildings 230.29

Underground

Installation . . . . 230.30(A)

Size and Rating 230.31

Protection Against Physical Damage 230.32

Spliced Conductors 230.33

Wiring Methods . . . . 230.30(B)

SERVICE DROPS . . . . **230 Part II**

Ampacity of Conductors 230.23

Attachment to Service Mast 230.28

Clearances

    Above Roofs . . . . 230.24(A)

    From Building Openings . . . . 230.9(C)

    From Buildings 230.9

    From Final Grade or Earth . . . . 230.24(B)

    Over 1000 Volts see *Life Safety Code, NFPA 101* . . NFPA 101

    Swimming Pools 680.8

    Vegetation as Support 230.10

Definition of . . . . Art. 100 Part I

Means of Attachment 230.27

Number of, to a Building 230.2

Overhead Service Locations 230.54

Point of Attachment 230.26

Service Masts

    Attachment . . . . 230.28(B)

        As Support 230.28

        Strength . . . . 230.28(A)

Size and Rating 230.23

Rated 60°C through 90°C . . . . Table 310.15(B)17

Rated 150°C through 250°C . . . . Table 310.15(B)19

Support Over Buildings 230.29

SERVICE ENTRANCE CABLE

Bending Radius 338.24

Construction 338.100

Definition 338.2

Exterior Installations . . . . 338.10(B)(4)(b)

Interior Installations . . . . 338.10(B)(4)(a)

Listing Requirements 338.6

Marking 338.120

Uses Not Permitted 338.12

Uses Permitted 338.10

SERVICE ENTRANCE CONDUCTORS

Cable Trays 230.44

Conductors Entering Building or Structure 230.52

Higher Voltage to Ground 230.56

Insulation 230.41

Minimum Size and Rating 230.42

Mounting Supports 230.51

Number Per Set 230.40

Overhead Service Locations 230.54

Protection Against Physical Damage 230.50

Raceways to Drain 230.53

Spliced Conductors 230.46

Wiring Methods for 1000 Volts, Nominal, or Less 230.43

SERVICE EQUIPMENT

Bonding 250.92

Disconnect, Supply Side 230.82

Equipment Connected to Supply Side 230.82

Ground-Fault Protection of Equipment 230.95

    Additional Level Required . . . . 517.17(B)

    Definition of . . . . Art. 100

    Emergency Systems . . . . 700.6(D)

    Fire Pumps . . . . 695.6(G)

    Optional Standby Systems Not Required 701.26

    Performance Testing . . . . 230.95(C)

Illumination of Service Equipment

    1000 Volts, Nominal or Less . . . . 110.26(D)

    Over 1000 Volts, Nominal . . . . 110.34(D)

        Note: Additional lighting luminaires (fixtures) are not intended where the

    workspace is illuminated by an adjacent light source.

Location of Service Equipment . . . . 230 Part VI

    Floating Buildings 553.4

    General 110.26

    Manufactured Homes . . . . 550.32(B)

    Mobile Homes . . . . 550.32(A)

    Nearest the Point of Entrance of the Service Conductors . . . . 230.70(A)(1)

    Over 1000 Volts . . . . 110 Part III

    Overcurrent Device 240.24

Main Disconnects . . . . 230 Part VI

    Combined Rating of 230.80

    Grouped . . . . 230.72(A)

    Hazardous (Classified) Locations (*See* Chap. 5) . . 230.70(C)

S

S

High Voltage Systems . . . . 230 Part VIII

    Location and Type 230.205

    Overcurrent Device as 230.206

Location on Premises 240.24

Locked or Sealed 230.92

    Specific Circuits 230.93

Marked Suitable for 230.66

    Suitable for Prevailing Conditions . . . . 230.70(C)

Marked As Service Disconnect . . . . 230.70(B)

Minimum Size & Rating 230.79

More Than One Building or Other Structure 225.33

Mounting Height . . . . 240.24(A)

No Mains Smaller Than 15 Amperes 230.79

Not More Than Six

    For Each Service 230.71

    To Be Grouped 230.72

    For Service-Entrance Conductor Sets 230.40

Provisions for Breaking the Grounded Conductor . . 230.75

Provisions to Bond the Grounded Conductor 250.26

Rating of Disconnect 230.79

Readily Accessible Place . . . . 230.70(A)(1)

    Accessible to Occupants . . . . 230.72(C)

Minimum Size & Rating

    Combined Rating of Disconnects 230.80

    Dwelling Unit Service and Feeder Conductors . 310.15(B)(7)

    Service Disconnect 230.79

    Service-Drop Conductors 230.23

    Service-Entrance Conductors . . . . 230.42(A)

    Service-Lateral Conductors, Underground 230.31

Overcurrent Protection of . . . . 230 Part VII

    Location 230.91

    Permitted Rating for Dwelling Services . . . 230.90(A) Ex. 5

Panelboards 408.36

    Service Conductors . . . . 230.90(A)

    General 240.22

    No Overcurrent Device in Grounded Conductor. . . . .

    . . . . 230.90(B)

Individual Residential Occupancy Only for Existing Installations . . . . 408.36 Ex. 3

Split Bus Panels Permitted as Main Service Equipment in an

Suitable for Available Short-Circuit Current 110.9

    Cartridge Fuses . . . . 240.60(C)(3)

    Circuit Breakers . . . . 240.83(C)

    Circuit Impedance and Other Characteristics 110.10

Surge Arresters (Over 1000 Volts) 230.209

Working Space about

    See WORKING SPACE . . . . Ferm's Finder

SERVICE LATERALS . . . . 230 Part III

Ampacity of Conductors . . . . Table 310.15(B)16

Bare Permitted for Grounded Conductor . . . . . 230.30(A) Ex.

Bushing or Terminal Fitting on Open End of Conduit 300.5(H)

Definition of . . . . Art. 100 Part I

Direct Burial 300.5

    Over 1000 Volts, Nominal 300.50

    Identified for Use . . . . 310.10(F)

    See OVER 1000 VOLTS, NOMINAL . . . . . Ferm's Finder

Insulation of 230.30

Protection Against Damage 230.32

Sealing Underground Raceway 230.8

    General . . . . 300.5(G)

    Over 1000 Volts . . . . 300.50(F)

Size and Rating 230.31

UF, Type . . . . Art. 340

Under Buildings . . . . 300.5(C)

    Where Considered Outside the Building 230.6

USE, Type . . . . Art. 338

USE and UF . . . . Table 310.104(A)

See UNDERGROUND WIRING . . . . Ferm's Finder

SERVICE POINT

Definition of . . . . Art. 100 Part I

Distribution Point (Agricultural Buildings) 547.2

Grounded Conductor 250.186

Premises Wiring, Definition of . . . . Art. 100 Part I

Service Conductors, Definition of . . . . Art. 100 Part I

Shall Not Apply 230.200

SERVICE STATIONS, GASOLINE (Motor Fuel Dispensing Facilities) . . . . Art. 514

See GASOLINE (MOTOR FUEL) DISPENSING. Ferm's Finder

SERVICE-ENTRANCE CABLE . . . . Art. 338

Bends 338.24

Definition of 338.2

Feeder or Branch-Circuit Wiring . . . . .338.10(B)(4)

    Entering, Exiting, or Attached to Buildings or Structures . .

    . . . . 225.11

    In Messenger Supported Wiring 396.10

Use of Grounded Conductor for Equipment 250.142

Wiring on Buildings or Other Structures 225.10

Grounding Frames of Ranges and Dryers 250.140

Installation Methods

    Exterior . . . . 338.10(4)(b)

    Interior . . . . 338.10(4)(a)

Physical Protection

    Aboveground . . . . 230.50(B)

    Underground . . . . 230.50(A)

Service-Entrance Conductors, As . . . . 338.10(A)

Temperature Limitations . . . . 338.10(B)(3)

Underground 338.100

Uses Not Permitted, Type SE 338.12

USE Type, Underground or Outside Only . . . . . 338.12(B)(4)

See (TXKT) . . . . *UL Product Spec*

SERVICE-ENTRANCE CONDUCTORS . . . . 230 Part IV

Bare Permitted for Grounded Conductor . . . . . . 230.41 Ex.

Connections at Weatherhead 230.54

Definition of (Overhead and Underground Systems) . Art. 100 Part I

Drip Loops . . . . 230.54(F)

Identification of Higher Voltage to Ground Conductor . 230.56

Insulation of 230.41

High-Leg Marking 110.15

    Mounting Supports 230.51

Number of Sets 230.40

Overcurrent Protection . . . . 240.21(D)

Protection of Open Conductors

    Aboveground . . . . 230.50(B)

    Underground . . . . 230.50(A)

Raceways to Drain 230.53

Size and Rating 230.42

Splices, Permitted in 230.46

Wiring Methods 230.43

SERVICES . . . . Art. 230

Bonding of 250.92

    See BONDING, Service Equipment . . . . . . *Ferm's Finder*

Calculations for Size of . . . . Art. 220

    Examples . . . . Informative Annex D

    See CALCULATIONS . . . . *Ferm's Finder*

Conductors

    Considered Outside of Building 230.6

Example for Sizing . . . . Informative Annex D7

For Fire Pumps . . . . 695.6(A)

One Building Not to Be Supplied through Another . . 230.3

Other Conductors Not in Service Raceway 230.7

Overcurrent Protection of . . . . 230 Part VII

    Dwelling Services . . . . 310.15(B)(7)

        Overhead Service Conductors . . . . Art. 100

        Underground Service Conductors . . . . . . Art. 100

Dedicated Space for Equipment

    1000 Volts, Nominal or Less . . . . 110.26(E)

    Over 1000 Volts, Nominal . . . . 110.34(F)

Grounded Conductor to . . . . 250.24(C)

Grounding . . . . Art. 250

    Conductors . . . . 250 Part III

    Connections . . . . 250 Part III

    Electrode System . . . . 250 Part III

    High-Voltage Systems (Over 1 kV) . . . . 250 Part X

    Methods of Equipment Grounding . . . . 250 Part VII

    Raceways and Enclosures . . . . 250 Part IV

    System . . . . 250 Part II

    See BONDING, Service Equipment . . . . . . *Ferm's Finder*

    See GROUNDING, Service Equipment . . . . *Ferm's Finder*

High-Leg Color Coding

    General Marking Requirements 110.15

    Phase Arrangement and Busbar Arrangement . . . 408.3(E)

    Service Conductor 230.56

High Voltage Service . . . . 230 Part VIII

    See OVER 1000 VOLTS, NOMINAL . . . . . . *Ferm's Finder*

Identification of Other Services, Feeders and Circuits . 230.2(E)

Manufactured Home . . . . 550.32(B)

Mast Type 230.28

    Note: Only power service-drop conductors are permitted

    to be attached to a service mast. Antennas are not permitted

    to be attached to the electric service mast 810.12

    See Drawing SM-1 & SM-2 . . . . *Ferm's Charts and Formulas*

Mobile Home Service . . . . 550.32(A)

    Additional Outside Electrical Equipment . . . . . 550.32(D)

    Additional Receptacles . . . . 550.32(E)

    Marking . . . . 550.32(G)

    Mounting Height . . . . 550.32(F)

    Rating . . . . 550.32(C)

    See MOBILE HOMES . . . . *Ferm's Finder*

Multiple Occupancy Building

    Access to Occupants . . . . 230.72(C)

S

Access to Overcurrent Device . . . . 240.24(B)

Additional Permitted 230.2

Number of Disconnects at One Location 230.71

Number of Service-Entrance Conductor Sets . . . . 230.40 Exceptions

See CALCULATIONS . . . . Ferm's Finder

Multiple Service for Separate Loads . . . . 230.2(A)

  Service-Entrance Conductor Sets . . . . 230.40 Ex. 2

Neutral (Grounded Conductor) to Every Service Disconnect . . . . 250.24(C)

No Other Conductors in Service Raceway or Cable 230.7

No Solder Lugs in Main Service 230.81

Number of

  Drops or Laterals to a Building 230.2

  Main Disconnects 230.71

    Additional Disconnects . . . . 230.72(B)

    Combined Rating 230.80

  Number of Supplies, More than One Building 225.30

    Number of Disconnects for Each Supply 225.33

  Service-Entrance Conductor Sets 230.40

    Floating Buildings 553.5

  Service-Entrance Conductors Supplied 230.40

  Services to a Building 230.2

Over 1000 Volts . . . . 230 Part VIII

  See OVER 1000 VOLTS, NOMINAL . . . . . Ferm's Finder

Over 35,000 Volts 230.212

Overhead Service Conductors . . . . 230 Part II

  Defined . . . . Art. 100

  Service-Entrance Conductors . . . . 230 Part IV

Raceways for Use at Services 230.43

  Floating Buildings . . . . 553.7(B)

Raceways to Drain 230.53

Rating of Disconnect 230.79

  Combined Ratings 230.80

Recreational Vehicles Parks . . . . 551 Part VI

Relative Location of Equipment and Overcurrent Device 230.94

Remote Control of Disconnect, Over 1000 Volts . . 230.205(C)

Remote Disconnecting Means . . . . 230.72(B)

Sealing Raceway from Warm to Cold . . . . 300.7(A)

  Busways 368.234

Sealing Underground Raceway 230.8

  1000 Volts or Less . . . . 300.5(G)

  Over 1000 Volts . . . . 300.50(F)

Separate Building or Structure . . . . 225 Part II

Separate Service Permitted

  Capacity Requirements . . . . 230.2(C)

  Different Characteristics . . . . 230.2(D)

  Special Conditions . . . . 230.2(A)

  Special Occupancies . . . . 230.2(B)

Service-Entrance Cable . . . . Art. 338

  See (TXKT) . . . . *UL Product Spec*

Service Head (Location)

  Clearance from Building Openings 230.9

  Overhead Service Locations 230.54

  Point of Attachment 230.26

  Physical Protection

    Aboveground . . . . 230.50(B)

    Underground . . . . 230.50(A)

Size & Rating

  Combined Rating of Disconnects 230.80

  Disconnecting Means 230.79

    Mobile and Manufactured Homes . . . . 550.32(C)

  Dwelling Unit Service and Feeder Conductors   310.15(B)(7)

  Example, Service Conductors for Dwellings . . . Informative Annex D7

  Overhead Service-Drop Conductors 230.24

  Service-Entrance Conductors 230.42

  Service-Lateral Conductors 230.30

Splices Permitted in Conductors 230.46

Split Bus Panels 408.36

Tap Ahead of Mains

  Equipment Permitted 230.82

  Fire Pumps 695.3

  Interconnected Power Production Sources 705.12

  Legally Required Standby Systems . . . . 701.12(E)

  Solar Photovoltaic Systems 690.59

Taps Permitted 230.46

Underground Service . . . . 230 Part III

  Conductors Connected at Supply End Only 230.2

  Considered Outside Building 230.6

Underground Service Conductors

  Defined . . . . Art. 100

Vertical Clearances of Service Conductors From Final Grade or Earth . . . . 230.24(B)

Wiring Methods for Service Conductors 230.43

  Floating Buildings . . . . 553.7(B)

  Over 1000 Volts . . . . 230.202(B)

Working Space about

See WORKING SPACE. . . . . Ferm's Finder

SETTING (of Circuit Breaker)

Adjustable-Trip Circuit Breaker . . . . 240.6(B)

Arc Energy Reduction. 240.87

Branch-Circuit Overcurrent Protection 210.20

Branch-Circuit Rating 210.3

Critical Operations Power Systems (COPS). . . . . . 708.24(E)

Definition of (Circuit Breaker, Setting) . . . . . Art. 100 Part I

Emergency Systems . . . . 700.5(E)

Feeders and Branch Circuits, Over 1000 Volts, Nominal . . . .
. . . . .240.100

Feeders, Over 1000 Volts 240.101

Ground-Fault Protection of Equipment . . . . 230.95(A)

Inspections and Test

    Feeders 225.56

    Over 1000 Volts 110.41

Legally Required Standby Systems . . . . .701.5(D)

Optional Standby Systems. 702.5

Restricted Access Adjustable-Trip Circuit Breakers . . 240.6(C)

Service Equipment, Over 1000 Volts, Nominal 230.208

Service Equipment Overcurrent Protection. . .230.90, Part VII

Service Ground-Fault Protection of Equipment 230.95

Transformer Overcurrent Protection . . Table 450.3(A) and (B)

SHEET METAL SCREWS

Covers and Canopies, Not to be Used 314.25

Grounding and Bonding Equipment, Not to be Used . . . . . .
. . . . 250.8(A)(6)

Receptacles, Not to be Used 406.5

Switches, Not to be Used . . . . 404.10(B)

SHIELDING OF CONDUCTORS . . . . 310.10(E)

Ampacity Values for Shielded Cables . . . . 310.60(B)(1)

Bending Radius, Over 1000 Volts 300.34

Bending Radius, Type MC Cable 330.24

CATV Cable Grounding 820.100

Direct Burial Conductors Over 2001 Volts . . . .310.10(F) Ex.1

Insulation Shielding Over 1000 Volts 300.40

Intrinsically Safe Systems . . . . 504.50(B)

Pull and Junction Boxes, Over 1000 Volts, Nominal . . 314.71

Sealing of Conductors, Class I, Division 1 Locations . . . . . .
. . . . 501.15(D)(1) Ex.

Sealing of Conductors, Class I, Division 2 Locations . . . . . .

. . . . 501.15(E)(1) Ex. 2

Splices of Underground Conductors . . . . 300.50(D)

See OVER 1000 VOLTS, NOMINAL . . . . . . Ferm's Finder

Type FCC Cable . . . . Art. 324

Type PLTC Cable . . . . 725.179(E)

SHORT-CIRCUIT CURRENT AVAILABLE

Circuit Impedance, Short-Circuit Current Ratings and Other
Characteristics 110.10

Definition of (Short-Circuit Current Rating) . . . . . Art. 100

Disconnect

    Feeder . . . . 225.52(B)

    Service (in excess of 1000 V). . . . . .230.205(B)

    Service (not in excess of 1000 V) . . . . .230.82(3)

Equipment to Be Rated for 110.9

Marking of, for Fuses . . . . 240.60(C)

Marking of, for Circuit Breakers . . . . 240.83(C)

Series Rated Systems 240.86

    Marking of for End Use Equipment . . . . 240.86(B)

    Motor Contributions . . . . 240.86(C)

    Selected Under Engineering Supervision . . . . . 240.86(A)

Note: Contact the serving utility company for short-circuit
current available at service point, and be able to calculate it up
to the service/feeder equipment.

SHOW WINDOWS

Branch Circuits, Load Calculations for . . . . 220.14(G)

Definition of . . . . Art. 100 Part I

Electric Signs and Outline Lighting . . . . Art. 600

Feeders, Load Calculations for . . . . 220.43(A)

Flexible Cords, Types Permitted 400.15

Floor Boxes for Use in Elevated Show Windows   314.27(B) Ex.

Luminaires, Types Permitted 410.14

Receptacle Spacing for 210.62

    In Floor Boxes . . . . 314.27(B)

SHOWCASES (CORD-CONNECTED) 410.59

Cord Requirements . . . . 410.59(A)

No Other Equipment Permitted . . . . 410.59(D)

Receptacles, Connectors, and Attachment Plugs . . . 410.59(B)

Secondary Circuit(s) of Ballasts . . . . 410.59(E)

Support of Cords . . . . 410.59(C)

SHOWER STALLS

Receptacles Within 6 feet of Bathtub or Shower Stall, GFCI
Protection . . . . 210.8(A)(9)

S

S

SIGNALING CIRCUITS . . . . **Art. 725**
Class 1, Class2 and Class 3 Remote-Control, Signaling, and
Power-Limited Circuits . . . . Art. 725

Energy Management Systems. . . . . Art. 750

Fire Alarm Systems . . . . Art. 760

    See FIRE ALARM SYSTEMS. . . . . Ferm's Finder

See CLASS 1, 2 & 3 REMOTE CONTROL,

SIGNALING, AND POWER-LIMITED CIRCUITS . . . .
See **CIRCUITS** . . . . Ferm's Finder

SIGNS, ELECTRIC AND OUTLINE LIGHTING . . . . . **Art. 600**
Applications of Power Limited Cable . . . . Table 600.33(A)(1)

Ballasts 600.22

    Class 2 Power Sources 600.21

    Listing Required . . . . 600.22(A)

    Thermal Protection Required . . . . 600.22(B)

    Ballasts, Transformers and Electronic Power Supplies . 600.21

    Accessibility . . . . 600.21(A)

    Attic and Soffit Locations . . . . 600.21(E)

    Location . . . . 600.21(B)

    Suspended Ceilings . . . . 600.21(F)

    Working Space . . . . 600.21(D)

Branch Circuits 600.5

    Computed Load . . . . 220.14(G)

    Rating . . . . 600.5(B)

    Required . . . . 600.5(A)

    Wiring Methods. 600.5(C)

Cable Substitutions. . . . . Table 600.33(A)(2)

    Applications of Power Limited Cable . . . Table 600.33(A)(1)

    Conductors . . . . 600.33(A)

    Power Sources 600.24

    Secondary Lighting 600.33

Connected to an Equipment Grounding Conductor . 600.7(A)

Definitions 600.2

Definition of Outline Lighting . . . . Art. 100 Part I

Disconnecting Means 600.6

Dwelling Occupancies, Voltage Restrictions . . . . . 600.32(I)

Electric-Discharge Lighting, Definition . . . . Article 100 Part I

Electrode Connections 600.42

Equipment Grounding Conductor

    Connected to . . . . 600.7(A)(1)

    Size . . . . 600.7(A)(2)

Enclosures 600.8

Field-Installed Secondary Wiring 600.12

Field-Installed Skeleton Tubing and Wiring . . . . 600 Part II

Grounding and Bonding 600.7

In Fountains 680.57

Installation Instructions . . . . 600.4(E)

Listing Requirements 600.3

    Location of 600.9

    Marking Requirements 600.4

        Durability . . . . 600.4(D)

        Portable Signs Exempted . . . . 600.4(E) Ex.

        Visibility. 600.4(C)

Neon Secondary-Circuit Conductors, 1000 Volts or Less 600.31

Neon Secondary-Circuit Conductors, Over 1000 Volts . 600.32

    Length of High-Voltage Cable . . . . 600.32(J)

Neon Tubing 600.41

Photovoltaic (PV) Powered Sign 600.34

    Definition 600.2

Portable or Mobile Signs 600.10

    GFCI Protection Required . . . . 600.10(C)(2)

Retrofit Kit

    Defined . . . . Article 100

    Field-Installed Secondary Wiring, Signs 600.12

    Listing Requirements for Signs 600.3

    Marking . . . . 600.4(B)

    Sign Installations Instructions . . . . 600.4(E)

Remote Metal Parts, Bonding . . . . .600.7(B)(1) Ex

Section Signs, Definition of 600.2

Transformers and Electronic Power Supplies 600.23

    Listing Required . . . . 600.23(A)

    Marking Required . . . . 600.23(F)

    Rating of Secondary Current . . . . 600.23(D)

    Secondary Connections . . . . 600.23(E)

    Secondary-Circuit Ground-Fault Protection. . . . 600.23(B)

    Voltage Limitations . . . . 600.23(C)

See the IAEI book on *NEON LIGHTING*

See Signs (UXYT) . . . .*UL Product Spec*

See Skeletal Neon Sign and Outline Lighting (UZBL). . . . . .
. . . .*UL Product Spec*

SIGNS AND LABELS
Caution, Meet These Requirements . . . . 110.21(B)

Danger, Meet These Requirements . . . . 110.21(B)

Field-Applied . . . . 110.21(B)

Warning, Meet These Requirements . . . . 110.21(B)

See ANSI Z535.4-2011, Product Safety Signs and Labels . . . . .

. . . . ANSI Z535.4

See WARNING SIGNS . . . . Ferm's Finder

SIMPLE APPARATUS

Definition . . . . Art. 100

Installation . . . . 504.10(D)

SINKS

Dwelling Units . . . . 210.8(A)(7)

Other than Dwelling Units . . . . 210.8(B)(5)

Receptacle Outlet Locations . . . . 210.52(C)(5)

Separate Spaces . . . . 210.52(C)(4)

SKELETON TUBING . . . . **600 Part II**

See SIGNS, ELECTRIC AND OUTLINE LIGHTING . . . . . .

. . . . Ferm's Finder

See (UZBL) . . . .*UL Product Spec*

SKID MOUNTED EQUIPMENT

Equipment Grounding Conductor, Connected to . 250.112(K)

SKIN EFFECT HEATING

Fixed Electric Heating for Pipelines and Vessels . . . .

. . . . .Art. 427 Part VI

Fixed Outdoor Electric Deicing and Snow Melting Equipment

. . . . Art. 426 Part V

Skin Effect Heating Systems, Defined . . . . . 426.2 and 427.2

SMOKE ALARM

AFCI Protection of Outlet . . . . 210.12(A)

Installed in Dwelling Unit . . . . 210.12(A) IN 2

See International Residential Code (IRC) Chapter 3- R314

See NFPA 72, 2013, National Fire Alarm and Signaling Code . .

. . . . NFPA 72

SMOKE DETECTOR . . . .**645.4(2)(3)**

SNAP SWITCHES

Accessibility and Grouping 404.8

Location . . . . 404.8(A)

Voltage between Adjacent Switches . . . . 404.8(B)

Definition of (General-Use Snap) . . . . Art. 100 Part I

Motors, Stationary 2 HP or Less

Permitted As Controller . . . . .430.83(C)(2)

Permitted As Disconnect . . . . .430.109(C)(2)

Mounting of 404.10

Panelboards Containing Switches 30 Amperes or Less 408.36(A)

Provisions for Faceplates . . . . 404.9(A)

Grounding . . . . 404.9(B)

Position of . . . . 404.9(A)

Ratings 404.14

Relative Arrangement of Switches and Fuses 408.39

See Snap Switches (WJQR) . . . .*UL Product Spec*

SOLAR PHOTOVOLTAIC SYSTEMS . . . . **Art. 690, Art. 691**

Alternating-Current Modules 690.6

Arc-Fault Circuit Protection, Direct Current 690.11

Back-Fed Circuit Breakers . . . . 710.15(E)

Circuit and Equipment Overcurrent Protection 690.9

Circuit Requirements . . . . 690 Part II

Circuit Routing . . . . 690.31(G)

Circuit Sizing & Current 690.8

DC-to-DC Converter Output Circuit Current . . 690.8(A)(6)

Component Identification . . . . Figure 690.1(a) and (b)

Conductors of Different Systems . . . . 690.31(B)

Connection to Other Sources 690.59

Supply Side of Service Equipment . . . . 230.82(6)

Definition of (Photovoltaic Systems) . . . . . . Art. 100 Part I

Definitions Applicable to System 690.2

Disconnecting Means . . . . 690 Part III

Equipment Disconnecting Means . . . . 690.15(D)

Interrupting Rating . . . . 690.15(B)

Isolating Device . . . . 690.15(C)

Types of Disconnects . . . . 690.13(F)

Energy Storage Systems

General 690.71

Self-Regulated PV Charge Control 690.72

Flexible Cords and Cables . . . . 690.31(E)

Flexible, Fine Stranded Cables, Listed Connectors Required 690.31(H)

Functional Grounded PV System 690.2

General Requirements 690.4

Ground-Fault Protection, DC Modules . . . . 690.41(B)

Grounding and Bonding . . . . 690 Part V

Building or Structures Supporting a PV Array . . . 690.47(A)

Additional Auxiliary Electrodes for Array Grounding . . . . 690.47(B)

Identification of Components in Common Configurations . . .

. . . . Figure 690.1(b)

Identification of System Components . . . . . . Figure 690.1(a)

Inverters (Multiple) . . . . .690.4(D)

Large-Scale Photovoltaic Systems . . . . Art. 691

    Accessible 691.4

    Approval 691.5

    Arc-Fault Mitigation 691.10

    Conformance of Construction of Engineered Design. . 691.7

    Definitions 691.2

    Direct Current Operating Voltage. 691.8

    Disconnection of Photovoltaic Equipment 691.9

    Engineered Design 691.6

    Fence Grounding 691.11

    Field-Applied Hazard Labels. . . . . 691.4(2)

    Not Installed on Buildings . . . . 691.4(5)

    Qualified Personnel . . . . 691.4(1)

Listing and Identification Required — Equipment . . 690.4(B)

Marking . . . . 690 Part VI

Maximum Voltage 690.7

Multiple Inverters . . . . 690.4(D)

Not Permitted (Bathrooms) . . . . 690.4(E)

Stand-Alone Systems 690.10

Overcurrent Protection 690.9

    Circuits and Equipment . . . . 690.9(A)

    Power Transformers . . . . 690.9(D)

Qualified Persons to Perform Work . . . . 690.4(C)

Rapid Shutdown of PV Systems on Buildings. 690.12

    Controlled Conductors . . . . 690.12(A)

    Controlled Limits . . . . 690.12(B)

    Equipment . . . . 690.12(D)

    Initiation Device. . . . . 690.12(C)

    Plaques and Directories . . . . 690.56(C)

Scope 690.1

Separation and Marking Requirements . . . . 690.31(B)

Wiring Methods . . . . 690 Part IV

See (QIIO). . . . . .UL Product Spec

SOLDERING LUGS & WIRE CONNECTORS

Electrical Connections. 110.14

Equipment Grounding Conductors to Boxes 250.148

Fire Pumps- Pump Wiring . . . . 695.6(D)

Grounding Electrode Conductor- Not Permitted 250.70

Knob-And-Tube Wiring (Splices and Taps). 394.42

Low-Voltage Suspended Ceiling Power Distribution Systems. .
. . . . 393.40(A)

Service Conductors- Not Permitted 230.81

Solder Not Permitted in Grounding or Bonding Connection

SOUND-RECORDING AND SIMILAR EQUIPMENT . . **Art. 640**

See . . . . AUDIO SIGNAL PROCESSING, AMPLIFICATION,
AND REPRODUCTION EQUIPMENT . . . . . Ferm's Finder

SPACE HEATING EQUIPMENT, FIXED ELECTRIC. . . . **Art. 424**

See FIXED ELECTRIC HEATING EQUIPMENT FOR PIPE-
LINES AND VESSELS. . . . . Ferm's Finder

See FIXED ELECTRIC SPACE-HEATING EQUIPMENT . . .
. . . . Ferm's Finder

See FIXED OUTDOOR ELECTRIC DEICING AND
SNOW-MELTING EQUIPMENT . . . . Ferm's Finder

See HEAT PUMPS . . . . Ferm's Finder

See INDUCTION & DIELECTRIC HEATING. . Ferm's Finder

See INFRARED LAMP HEATING APPLIANCES . . . . . .
. . . . Ferm's Finder

See (ZMVV) . . . . .UL Product Spec

SPAS & HOT TUBS . . . . **680 Part IV**

See HOT TUBS & SPAS. . . . . Ferm's Finder

See SWIMMING POOLS . . . . Ferm's Finder

See (WBYQ). . . . . .UL Product Spec

**SPRAY APPLICATION DIPPING, COATING, AND PRINTING
PROCESSES**

Classification of Locations

    Open Containers 516.4

    Membrane Enclosures 516.18

    Painting, Dipping, and Coating Processes 516.29

    Spray Application Processes 516.5

Definitions 516.2

Grounding 516.16

Special Equipment 516.10

Wiring and Equipment

    Class I Locations 516.6

Not Within Classified Locations 516.7

SPECIAL PERMISSION (Definition of) . . . . . **Art. 100 Part I**

Electric Signs and Outline Lighting 600.3

Enforcement 90.4

Fixed Electric Space-Heating Equipment 424.10

Fixed Industrial Process Heating Equipment 425.10

Fixed Outdoor Electric Deicing and Snow-Melting Equipment
. . . . 426.14

For Certain Utility Installations Exempted from Code
Requirements . . . . 90.2(C)

Knob-And-Tube Use Permitted 394.10

Number of Services 230.2

Surge Arrester- Over 1000 Volts . . . . 280.24(C)

Note: Many *Code* sections contain alternate methods that may be used if special permission is granted by the AHJ.

SPECIAL PURPOSE GROUND-FAULT CIRCUIT-INTERRUPTER (SPGFCI)

Temporary Installations . . . . 590.6(B)(2)

SPLICES AND TAPS

Auxiliary Gutters 366.56

Boxes Not Required . . . . 334.40(B)

Boxes Required 300.15

    Temporary Wiring . . . . 590.4(G)

    See BOXLESS DEVICES . . . . Ferm's Finder

Cabinets and Cutout Boxes . . . . 312.8(A)

Cable Trays, Permitted to Project Above Side Rails . . . 392.56

Carnivals, Circuses, Fairs and Similar Events . . . . 525.20(D)

Cellular Concrete Floor Raceways 372.56

Cellular Metal Floor Raceways 374.56

Concealed Knob-and-Tube 394.56

Conduit Bodies (General) 300.15

    When Permitted . . . . .314.16(C)(2)

Construction Sites . . . . 590.4(G)

Deicing and Snow-Melting . . . . 426.24(B)

Direct Burial Cable . . . . 110.14(B)

    Box Not Required . . . . 300.5(E)

    Box Not Required, Over 1000 Volts . . . . 300.50(D)

Feeder Taps (General) . . . . 240.21(B)

    Over 1000 Volts . . . . .240.101(B)

    Supervised Industrial Installations . . . . 240 Part VIII

Flat Cable Assemblies (Splices) . . . . 322.56(A)

    Taps. . . . . 322.56(B)

Flexible Cords

    General 400.13

    On Construction Sites . . . . 590.4(G)

General Requirements 110.14

Grounding Electrode Conductor 250.64

    Method of Splicing . . . . 250.64(C)

        Splices in Busbars Permitted . . . . .250.64(C)(2)

    Taps. . . . . 250.64(D)(1)

Heating Cables

    For Pipelines and Vessels . . . . 427.23(A)

    Outdoor Deicing and Snow-Melting . . . . 426.24(B)

    Space-Heating Cables, Cannot Alter Length 424.40

    Space-Heating Cables, Embedded . . . . 424.41(D)

Insulation of . . . . 110.14(B)

Messenger Supported Wiring 396.56

Motor Feeders 430.28

Panelboards, in . . . . 312.8(A)

Power Distribution Blocks . . . . 376.56(B)

Power Monitoring Equipment . . . . 312.8(B)

Raceways, Not in (Generally) . . . . 300.13(A)

    Note: Refer to appropriate raceway article for further

        information and see also . . . . 300.15(A)

Sealing Fittings, Not in . . . . .501.15(C)(4)

Service-Entrance Conductors 230.46

Swimming Pool Lighting Ground Wire, Splice Not Permitted . 680.23(F)(2)

Transformers . . . . 240.21(C)

Underground, Listed . . . . 110.14(B)

Wireways, in

    Metal 376.56

    Nonmetallic 378.56

    Power Distribution Blocks (Metallic Wireways). . 376.56(B)

Note: Use oxide inhibitor on aluminum terminations where required by listing or manufacturer.

See Aluminum Conductor Terminations . . . *Ferm's Charts and Formulas*

See Tightening Torque Information *Ferm's Charts and Formulas*

See (DVYW) . . . .*UL Product Spec*

SPLIT-BUS PANELBOARDS 408.36

SPRAY APPLICATION, DIPPING, COATING & PRINTING PROCESSES . . . . Art. 516

See FINISHING PROCESSES. . . . . Ferm's Finder

STAGE

Equipment, Defined 520.2

Lighting Hoist, Defined 520.2

Lighting Hoist, Wiring Method 520.40

Switchboard 520.2

See . . . . Article 520

STAND-ALONE SYSTEMS Laura- Need Formatting Help

Back-Fed Circuit Breaker . . . . 710.15(E)

Conductor Sizing . . . . 710.15(B)

Equipment Approval 710.6

Premises Wiring System 710.15

Supply Output. 710.15(A)

S

S

STANDBY SYSTEMS . . . . **Art. 700**
  Back-Fed Circuit Breaker . . . . 710.15(E)
  Conductor Sizing . . . . 710.15(B)
  Equipment Approval 710.6
  Premises Wiring System 710.15
  Supply Output . . . . 710.15(A)

STATIC
  Antenna, Radio and Television 810.57
  Bulk Storage Plants . . . . 515.16 Info. Note
  Electric Discharges (Spray Applications) 516.40
  Hazardous (Classified) Locations . . 500.4(B) Info. Note 1 and 3
  Painting in Aircraft Hangers . . . . . . 513.3(C)(2) Info. Note
  Zones 0, 1and 2 . . . . 505.4(B) IN 1 and 3
  Zones 20, 21 and 22 . . . . 506.4(B) IN

STEEL TUBE
  See ELECTRICAL METALLIC TUBING . . . . . Ferm's Finder
  See FLEXIBLE METALLIC TUBING . . . . . . Ferm's Finder

STORABLE SWIMMING POOLS . . . . **680 Part III**
  Ground-Fault Circuit-Interrupter Required 680.32
  Lighting (Fixtures) Luminaires 680.33
  Pumps 680.31
  See SWIMMING POOLS . . . . Ferm's Finder
  See (WCSX) . . . .*UL Product Spec*
  See (WBDT) . . . .*UL Product Spec*

STORAGE BATTERIES . . . . **Art. 480**
  Aircraft, Special Equipment 513.10
  Audio Signal Processing, Amplification, & Reproduction
    Auxiliary Power Supply Wiring . . . . 640.9(B)
  Battery and Cell Terminations 480.4
  Battery System, Defined . . . . Art 100 Part I
  Charging Equipment, Class III Locations 503.160
  Corrosion Prevention . . . . 480.4(A)
  DC Disconnect Methods 480.7
  Definitions 480.2
  Electric Vehicles
    Ventilation Not Required . . . . 625.52(A)
    Ventilation Required . . . . 625.52(B)
  Emergency Systems
    As Alternate Power Source, Health Care Facilities . . . . . .
    . . . . .517.30(B)(1)
    (*See* 517.2 for definition of *Alternate Power Source*)

  As Power Source . . . . 700.12(A)
    Unit Equipment . . . . 700.12(F)
  Equipment 480.3
  Garages, Special Equipment 511.10
  IEEE Standards . . . . 480.1 Info. Note
  Insulation Support 480.8
  Listing Requirement 480.3
  Location 480.10
  Nominal Voltage, (Battery or Cell) Defined 480.2
  Racks and Trays (Support Structure) 480.9
  Recreational Vehicles . . . . 551.4(B)
  Solar Photovoltaic Systems . . . . 690 Part VIII
  Support Systems 480.9
  Ventilation . . . . 480.10(A)
  Vents (Cells) 480.11

STRIKE TERMINATION DEVICES **250.60**
  Electrode Location and Placement . . . . 250.53(B)
  Lightning Protection System 250.106
  Radio Receiving Stations . . . . 810.18(I) Info. Note 1
  See NFPA 780-2011, Standard for the Installation of Lightning Protection Systems . . . . NFPA 780

STRUCTURAL JOINT, EXPANSION AND DEFLECTION . . . . .
. . . . **300.4(H)**

STRUCTURAL STEEL
  As a Grounding Electrode . . . . 250.52(A)(2)
  Bonding . . . . 250.52(A)(6)
  Bonding Piping Systems and Structural Metal 250.104
  Metal In-Ground Support Structure(s) . . . . . .250.52(A)(2)

STRUCTURES (METAL), OVER 1000 VOLTS . . . . . **250.194(B)**

STRUT-TYPE CHANNEL RACEWAYS . . . . **Art. 384**
  Busways . . . . .368.56(A)(14)
  Definition of 384.2
  Grounding of 384.60
  Listing 384.6
  Marking 384.120
  Number of Conductors 384.22
  Size of . . . . Table 384.22
  Size of Conductors 384.21
  Support of 384.30
  Uses Not Permitted 384.12
  Uses Permitted 384.10

See (RIUU). . . . .*UL Product Spec*

SUBMERSIBLE PUMP CABLE
See PUMP HOUSES. . . . . Ferm's Finder

See Underground Branch Circuit and Feeder Cable (YDUX) .
. . . .*UL Product Spec*

SUBSTATION **490.48**
Covered by Code, Industrial . . . . 90.2(A)(2)

Definition . . . . Art 100 Part I

Design, Documentation, and Required Diagrams 490.48

Feeders, Inspection and Test . . . . 225.56(A)(6), 110.41

Fences and Other Metal Structures, Grounding and Bonding .
. . . . .250.194

Grounding for AC Substations 250.191

High-Voltage Fuses . . . . .490.21(B)(7)

Indoor Installations . . . . .110.31(B)(1)

Inspections and Test 110.41

Large-Scale Photovoltaic (PV) Electric Power Production
Facility. 691.2

Mobile and Portable Equipment 490.51

Motion Picture Productions, Feeders . . . . 530.18(B)

Motion Picture and Television Studios and Similar Locations .
. . . . 540 Part VI

Not Covered by Code, Utility . . . . 90.2(A)(4)

Portable or Mobile Equipment, Grounding Exemption 250.188

Supervised Industrial Installations, Exclusion 240.2

Television Studio Sets, Feeder Sizing. 530.19

Tunnels . . . . 110.51(A)

Warning Signs . . . . 490.48(B)

See ANSI/IEEE 80-2000, IEEE Guide for Safety in AC Substation Grounding

SUBSURFACE ENCLOSURES . . . . **110.12(B)**
Manholes and Enclosures for Personnel Entry . . . 110 Part V

SUNLIGHT ON ROOFTOPS
Raceways and Cables Exposed . . . . .Table 310.15(B)(3)(c)

SUPERVISED INDUSTRIAL INSTALLATIONS . . **Art. 240 VIII**

SUPERVISORY CONTROL AND DATA ACQUISITION (SCADA)
. . . . **Informative Annex G**
See SCADA . . . . Ferm's Finder

SUPPLEMENTARY OVERCURRENT PROTECTION . . **240.10**
Bathrooms, Permitted in . . . . 240.24(E)

Class I, Division 2, Fuses Internal to (Fixtures) Luminaires . .
. . . . 501.115(B)(4)

Electric Heating Appliance . . . . 422.11(F)

Electric Heating Equipment Disconnecting Means . 424.19(A)

Electric Heating Equipment Overcurrent Protection 424.22(C)

Motor Control Circuits . . . . 430.72(A)

Not Required to Be Readily Accessible . . . . . . 240.24(A)(2)

Solar Photovoltaic Source and Output Circuits . . . . 690.9(D)

Supplementary Overcurrent Protective Device (Definition of)
. . . . Art. 100, Part I

SUPPLY CONDUCTORS
Ungrounded Conductors . . . . 250.102(C)(2) Info. Note

SUPPLY SIDE BONDING JUMPER, DEFINED **250.2**
Sizing . . . . Table 250.102(C)(1)

SUPPORTS
See SECURING AND SUPPORTING. . . . . . Ferm's Finder

SURFACE EXTENSIONS **314.22**
Grounding . . . .
250.86 . . . .

SURFACE METAL RACEWAYS **Art.386**
Combination, Signaling, Lighting and Power Circuits . 386.70

Conductors

    Number of 386.22

    Size of 386.21

Extension through Walls and Floors . . . . 386.10(4)

General . . . . 386 Part I

Grounding 386.60

Marking 386.120

Splices and Taps 386.56

Uses Not Permitted 386.12

Uses Permitted 386.10

See RACEWAYS . . . . Ferm's Finder

See (RJBT) . . . .*UL Product Spec*

SURFACE NONMETALLIC RACEWAYS . . . .**Art. 388**
Combination 388.70

Conductors

    Number of 388.22

    Size of 388.21

Construction 388.100

Extension through Walls and Floors . . . . 388.10(2)

S

S

General . . . . 388 Part I

Marking 388.120

Securing and Supporting 388.30

Splices and Taps 388.56

Uses Not Permitted 388.12

Uses Permitted 388.10

   See (RJTX) . . . . *UL Product Spec*

SURGE PROTECTION (LIGHTNING ARRESTERS)
See LIGHTNING, SURGE ARRESTERS . . . . . Ferm's Finder

SURGE ARRESTORS, OVER 1000 Volts . . . . Art. 280

Connection . . . . 280 Part III

Definition of . . . . Art. 100 Part I

Emergency Systems 700.8

Grounding Electrode Conductor. 280.25

Installation . . . . Art. 280 Part II

Interconnections 280.24

Location. 280.11

Number Required 280.3

Routing of Grounding Conductors. 280.14

Selection. 280.4

Uses Not Permitted 280.12

SURGE-PROTECTIVE DEVICES, 1000 VOLT OR LESS . Art. 285

Connecting of 285.21

Definition . . . . Article 100 Part I

Emergency Systems 700.8

Grounding Electrode Conductor. 285.28

Installation . . . . Art. 285 Part II

Listing 285.6

Location. 285.11

   of Connection Installation . . . . 285.23(A)

Number Required 285.4

Routing of Connections 285.12

Short Circuit Current Rating 285.7

See (XUPD) . . . . *UL Product Spec*

Type 1 . . . . 285.23

Type 2 . . . . 284.24

Type 3 . . . . 285.25

Type 4 and Other Component Type 285.13

Uses Not Permitted 285.3

SWIMMING POOLS . . . . Art. 680

Applicability of Article 680 . . . . 680.1

Approval of Equipment 680.4

Branch Circuit Wiring. . . . . 680.23(F)(1)

Bonding 680.26

   Equipotential Bonding Grid . . . . 680.26(B)

   Potting Compound Used for Wet-Niche (Fixtures)
   Luminaires . . . . 680.23(B)(2)(b)
   . . . .

   Reinforcing Steel . . . . 680.26(B)(1)(a)

   Water Heaters . . . . 680.26(B)(6)(b)

   See BONDING . . . . Ferm's Finder

   See (WCRY) . . . . *UL Product Spec*

Conductor Clearances

   Not Covered by Article 680 . . . . 225.18 & 19

   Overhead 680.8

   Underground 680.11

   See also *Life Safety Code, NFPA 101* . . . . NFPA 101

Cord- and Plug-Connected Equipment 680.8

   Methods of Grounding 680.6

   Receptacles for . . . . 680.22(5)

Corrosive Environment 680.14

   Chapter 3 (Noncorrosive Environments). . . . . 680.21(A)(1)

Covers (Electrically Operated)

   Location of Motors and Controllers . . . . . . 680.27(B)(1)

   Wiring Methods . . . . 680.21(A)

   Note: *See* 680.27(B)(1) Info. Notes 1, 2, & 3 for other
   applicable sections

Deck Area Heating . . . . 680.27(C)

   Permanently Wired Radiant Heaters . . . . . . 680.27(C)(2)

   Radiant Heating Cables Not Permitted Above   680.27(C)(2)

   Radiant Heating Cables Not Permitted Below Deck. . . . .
   680.27(C)(3)

   Unit Heaters . . . . 680.27(C)(1)

Decorative Fireplaces . . . . 680.22(B)(7)

Definitions 680.2

Disconnecting Means (Maintenance) 680.13

Double Insulated Pumps . . . . 680.21(B)

   Bonding Not Required (Other Provisions Required) . . . . .
   . . . . 680.26(B)(6) Ex.

Emergency (Shut-Off) Switch for Spas and Hot Tubs . . 680.41

Electric Pool Water Heater 680.10

   Bonding & Grounding . . . . 680.26(B)(6)

Electrically Powered Pool Lifts

   Approval 680.81

   Bonding 680.83

   Definition 680.2

Nameplate Marking 680.85

Protection 680.82

Switching Devices 680.84

See ELECTRICALLY
POWERED POOL LIFTS . . . . Ferm's Finder

Enclosures for Transformers, GFCIS or Similar Devices . . . .
. . . . 680.24(B)

Grounding Terminals . . . . 680.24(D)

Location and Mounting Height . . . . .680.24(B)(2)

Protection . . . . 680.24(C)

Sealing of Conduits . . . . .680.24(B)(1)(3)

Strain Relief . . . . 680.24(E)

Equipment Rooms & Pits 680.12

Equipotential Bonding

Perimeter Surfaces, Pools . . . . 680.26(B)

Perimeter Surfaces, Spas and Hot Tubs . . . . . 680.42(B)

Pool Water . . . . 680.26(C)

Feeder Wiring Methods . . . . 680.25(A)

Fire Pits (Low Voltage) . . . . .680.22(B)(7)

Fountains . . . . 680 Part V

See FOUNTAINS . . . . Ferm's Finder

Forming Shell, Definition of 680.2

Bonding of . . . . .680.26(B)(4)

Gas-Fired Luminaires . . . . .680.22(B)(7)

Gas-Fired Water Heater 680.28

Grounding and Bonding Terminals 680.7

Ground-Fault Circuit-Interrupter Protection

Fountains

For Signs in . . . . 680.57(B)

See FOUNTAINS . . . . Ferm's Finder

Hydromassage Bathtubs . . . . 680 Part VII

Bonding 680.74

See HYDROMASSAGE BATHTUBS . . . . Ferm's Finder

Motors (Cord- and Plug-Connected) . . . . . . 680.22(A)(2)

No Other Conductors in Boxes or Raceways . .680.23(F)(3)

Spas & Hot Tubs . . . . .680.43(A)(2)

See HOT TUBS & SPAS . . . . Ferm's Finder

Swimming Pool Area

Luminaires [Lighting Luminaires (Fixtures) above Water] .
. . . . 680.22(B)(4)

Luminaires [Lighting Luminaires (Fixtures) below Water]
. . . . .680.23(A)(3)

Pool Covers, Electrically Operated . . . . . .680.27(B)(2)

Receptacles . . . . .680.22(A)(5)

Storable Pools 680.32

Therapeutic Pools, Permanently Installed 680.61

Therapeutic Tubs (Hydrotherapeutic Tanks) 680.62

Types of GFCI Protection Permitted 680.5

See (KCXS) . . . .*UL Product Spec*

Grounding (General) 680.6

Methods of Grounding (Feeders) . . . . 680.25(A)

Use of Potting Compound on Connections . 680.23(B)(2)(b)

Water Heaters . . . . .680.26(B)(6)

GFCI Protection

Area Receptacles . . . . .680.22(A)(4)

Ceiling Fans . . . . .680.22(B)(4)

Hydromassage Bathtubs 680.71

Lighting . . . . .680.22(B)(4)

Outlets, Receptacle or Direct Connection . . . . 680.21(C)

Pool Pump Motors . . . . 680.21(A)(B)(C)

Relamping, Pool Luminaires, Underwater . . . 680.23(A)(3)

Storable Pools-Equipment 680.32

Storable Pools - Pump Motors 680.31

Hydromassage Bathtubs . . . . 680 Part VII

See HYDROMASSAGE BATHTUBS . . . . . . Ferm's Finder

Junction Boxes, Underwater Lighting 680.24

Bonding 680.26

Grounding Terminals

Continuity Between Raceways . . . . . . .680.24(B)(1)(4)

Number Required . . . . 680.24(D)

Methods of Grounding . . . . 680.24(F)

Location and Mounting Height . . . . .680.24(B)(2)

Potting Compound, Flush Boxes Low Voltage Contact
Limit or Less . . . . .680.24(A)(2)(c)

Protection . . . . 680.24(C)

Strain Relief for Cord . . . . 680.24(E)

Threaded Conduit Hubs or Bosses . . . . . . .680.24(B)(1)

Transformers, GFCI Enclosures, etc. . . . . 680.24(B)

See (WCEZ) . . . .*UL Product Spec*

Listed 680.4

Low Voltage Contact Limit, Defined 680.2

Low-Voltage Gas-Fired Equipment

Decorative Fireplace . . . . .680.22(B)(7)

Fire Pits . . . . .680.22(B)(7)

Luminaires . . . . .680.22(B)(7)

Similar Equipment . . . . .680.22(B)(7)

Luminaires (Lighting Fixtures)

Gas-Fired . . . . .680.22(B)(7)

General Lighting (above Water Level) . . . . . . 680.22(B)

S

Ground-Fault Circuit-Interrupter Protection 680.22(B)(4)

Grounding .680.23(F)(2)

   Methods . . . . 680.23(F)(2) (a) and (b)

Low-Voltage . . . . 680.22(B)(6) & (7)

Switching Devices . . . . 680.22(C)

Underwater (below Water Level) 680.23

   Dry-Niche . . . . 680.23(C)

   GFCI Protection — Relamping . . . . 680.23(A)(3)

   Junction Boxes for . . . . 680.24(A)

   No-Niche . . . . 680.23(D)

   Transformers, Enclosures . . . . 680.24(B)

   Wet-Niche. . . . . 680.23(B)

   See (WBDT) . . . .*UL Product Spec*

Marking Guidelines for Swimming Pool Equipment

   See UL Swimming Pool Marking Guide, Appendix A . . . . .
. . . .*UL Product Spec*

Motors

   Corrosive Environments . . . . .680.21(A)(1)

   Electrically Operated Pool Covers . . . . 680.27(B)

   (Note: *See* Info. Notes 1, 2, and 3 for other applicable sections)

   GFCI Receptacles Providing Power to . . . . . . 680.22(A)

   Methods of Grounding — 12 AWG Conductor 680.21(A)(1)

   See MOTORS . . . . Ferm's Finder

Panelboards 680.25

Pools and Tubs for Therapeutic Use . . . . 680 Part VI

   See THERAPEUTIC POOLS AND TUBS . . . Ferm's Finder

Receptacles . . . . 680.22(A)

   Circulation and Sanitation Systems . . . . . 680.22(A)(2)

   Ground-Fault Circuit-Protection . . . . 680.22(A)(4)

   Motors (Supplied by Outlets) . . . . 680.21(C)

   Motors (Supplied by Receptacles) . . . . 680.22(B)

     Location of . . . . 680.22(A)(1)–(5)

   Other Receptacles. . . . . 680.22(A)(3)

   Required, General Purpose . . . . 680.22(A)(1)

     Maximum Mounting Height . . . . 680.22(A)(1)

Storable Pools

   See STORABLE SWIMMING POOLS . . . . . Ferm's Finder

Switching Devices [Not within 1.5 m (5 ft)] . . . . . 680.22(C)

Transformers (Swimming Pool) . . . . 680.23(A)(2)

   Enclosures for . . . . 680.24(B)

   See (WDGV). . . . .*UL Product Spec*

Underground Wiring 680.11

Underwater Audio Equipment . . . . 680.27(A)

   Forming Shell and Metal Screen . . . . 680.27(A)(3)

Speakers . . . . 680.27(A)(1)

Wiring Methods. . . . . 680.27(A)(2)

Underwater Luminaires 680.23

   Dry-Niche (Fixtures) Luminaires . . . . 680.23(C)

   Grounding . . . . .680.23(F)(2)

   Junction Boxes Directly Connected to Forming Shell. . . . .
. . . . .680.23(F)(2)(b)

   Methods of Grounding . . . . .680.23(F)(2)

   No-Niche Luminaires . . . . 680.23(D)

   Other Enclosures Directly Connected to Forming Shell . . .
. . . . .680.23(F)(2)

   Storable Swimming Pools 680.33

   Wet-Niche (Fixtures) Luminaires . . . . 680.23(B)

   See (WBDT) . . . .*UL Product Spec*

Wiring Methods

   Dry-Niche (Fixtures) Luminaires . . . . .680.23(F)(1)

   Feeders 680.25

   Motors . . . . 680.21(A)

   No-Niche (Fixtures) Luminaires . . . . .680.23(F)(1)

   Other Equipment . . . . 680.27(A)(2)

   Panelboards 680.25

   Pool Covers . . . . 680.21(A)

   Underground Wiring 680.11

   Underwater Audio . . . . .680.27(A)(2)

   Wet-Niche (Fixtures) Luminaires . . . . .680.23(B)(2)

     ENT and EMT Permitted In or On Buildings 680.23(F)(1)

     Flexible Connections . . . . 680.23(F)(1) Ex.

     For Grounding . . . . .680.23(F)(2)

SWITCHBOARDS, SWITCHGEAR & PANELBOARDS

Arc-Flash Hazard Warning 110.16

Available Fault Current 110.24

Equipment Over 1000 Volts, Nominal . . . . Art. 490 Part III

Field Identification Required 408.4

Signs, Field Applied . . . . 110.21(B)

   High-Impedance Grounded Neutral AC System 408.3(F)(3)

   High-Leg Identification . . . . 408.3(F)(1)

   Resistively Grounded DC Systems . . . . 408.3(F)(5)

   Ungrounded AC Systems . . . . 408.3(F)(2)

   Ungrounded DC Systems . . . . 408.3(F)(4)

Working Space . . . . 110.26(A)

See PANELBOARDS & SWITCHBOARDS . . . Ferm's Finder

See SWITCHGEAR . . . . Ferm's Finder

SWITCHES . . . . **Art. 404**

AFCI Protection- Dwelling Units 210.12

Attachment Methods (Screws) . . . . 404.10(B)

Accessibility and Grouping 404.8

    For Busway Installations . . . . 404.8(A) Ex. 1

Agricultural Buildings 547.6

Both as Controller and Disconnecting Means 430.111

Box Not Required . . . . 334.40(B)

Breakers Used to Switch Fluorescent Lights Must Be Marked

    "SWD" . . . . 240.83(D)

Breakers Used to Switch High-Intensity Discharge Lights

    Marked "HID" . . . . 240.83(D)

Cascading (Switch to Switch) Enclosure Not Used as Junction

Box 312.8

CO/ALR Marking Required If Aluminum Wire Is Used . . . .

    . . . . 404.14(C)

    See (WJQR) . . . .*UL Product Spec*

Construction – Faceplates . . . . 404.9(C)

Damp or Wet Locations 404.4

Definitions, 1000 Volts and Less . . . . Art. 100

Definitions, Over 1000 Volts . . . . Art. 100 Part II

Disconnecting Means, More Than One Building 225.33

Double Pole (all conductors including grounded) to Fuel Dis-

pensing . . . . 514.11(A)

    Tie Bars Not Permitted for Single-Pole Breakers . 514.11(A)

Electronic Lighting Control Switches 402.22

    Number on Branch Circuit. . . . . .404.2(C) Ex.

    Number on Feeder . . . . .404.2(C) Ex.

Emergency Lighting Circuits (Control) . . . . . . 700 Part V

Enclosures 404.3, 404.12

Faceplates

    Grounding (General) 250.110

        For Snap Switches . . . . 404.9(B)

        Mobile and Manufactured Homes . . . . 550.15(D)

        Of Enclosures. 404.12

        Patient Care Spaces . . . . 517.13(B) Ex. 1

    In Completed Installations 314.25

    Position for Snap Switches . . . . 404.9(A)

For Busways. 368.239

Four-Way Switching . . . . 404.2(A)

Gravity to Open Switches . . . . 404.6(A)

    Indication of Position 404.7

    Up Position to Be On (Breakers Used As Switches) . 240.81

Grounded Conductor (not required) . . . . 404.2(C)

Hazardous (Classified) Locations

    Class I, Division 1 . . . . 501.115(A)

    Class I, Division 2 . . . . 501.115(B)

        Part of Luminaires (Fixtures) or Lampholders 501.130(B)(5)

    Class II, Division 1 . . . . 502.115(A)

    Class II, Division 2 . . . . 502.115(B)

        For Utilization Equipment to Be Dusttight . 502.135(B)(3)

    Class III 503.115

        For Utilization Equipment . . . . 503.135(C)

Heights Not to Exceed 2.0 m (6 ft 7 in.) (Generally) . . 404.8(A)

Horsepower Rated 430.109

    Marking 404.20

Identification of

    As Disconnecting Means. 110.22

    Circuit Directory in Panelboards . . . . 408.4(A)

    Source of Supply . . . . 408.4(B)

Knife Switches

    Marking 404.20

    Position and Connection. 404.6

    Rated 600 to 1000 Volts. 404.26

    Ratings 404.13

    To Be Indicating. 404.7

Lighting Load, Grounded Conductor . . . . 404.2(C)

Location at Tubs and Showers 404.4

Marking 404.20

Motor Controllers 430.83

Multiple Snap Switches . . . . 404.8(C)

Not Connected to Equipment Grounding Conductor . . . . . .

. . . . 404.9(B) Ex.2 to (B)

Over 1000 Volts

    Isolating Means 490.22

    Isolating Switches 230.204

    Load Interrupters . . . . 490.21(E)

Rating of 600 to 1000 Volt Knife Switches 404.26

Rating & Use of Snap Switches 404.14

    Mobile and Manufactured Homes . . . . 550.15(G)

    Motor Disconnecting Means 430.109

    See (WJQR) . . . .*UL Product Spec*

Required

    For Lighting Outlets 210.70

    Theater Dressing Rooms (with Pilot Light) 520.73

Switching to Be Done in Ungrounded Conductors . . 404.2(B)

    Exception . . . . 404.2(B) Ex.

S

Dispensing Equipment . . . . 514.11(A)

Motor Circuit Disconnects (Grounded Conductors). 430.105

Theater Dressing Rooms 520.73

Three-Way Switching . . . . 404.2(A)

Time Switches, Flashers, and Similar Devices 404.5

Transfer Switches

    See TRANSFER SWITCHES . . . . Ferm's Finder

Up Position to Be On 240.81

    Indication of Position 404.7

Voltage Limitations (Snap Switches)

    Between Adjacent Switches . . . . 404.8(B)

    Between Switches and Receptacles . . . . 404.8(B)

    Rating and Use 404.14

Wet Locations 404.4

Wire Bending Space, Deflection 312.6

    At Terminals 404.3

See DISCONNECTING MEANS . . . . Ferm's Finder

See SERVICE EQUIPMENT, Main Disconnects Ferm's Finder

Note: The wiring space and current-carrying capacity of switches are based on the use of 60°C wire where wire sizes 14 AWG through 1 AWG are used and 75°C wire where wire sizes 1/0 and larger are used.

See Switches, Pull Out Type (WFXV) . . . . . .*UL Product Spec*

SWITCHGEAR . . . . **Art. 408**

AC Phase Arrangement . . . . 408.3(E)

Accessible to Unqualified Persons, Over 1000 Volts   110.31(B)

Arc-Flash Hazard Warning 110.16

Auxiliary Gutter

    Metallic 366.2

    Nonmetallic 366.2

Available Fault Current 110.24

Barriers for Service Use . . . . 408.3(A)(2)

Bonding, Building of Multiple Occupancy . . . . 250.104(A)(2)

Buss Arrangement . . . . 408.3(E)

Construction 408.50

Critical Care (Category 1) Spaces, Equipment Grounding and Bonding . . . . 517.19(E)

DC Bus Arrangement . . . . 408.3(E)(2)

Damp Locations 408.16

Dedicated Equipment Space . . . . 110.26(E)

Defined . . . . Art. 100

Disconnects, Branch Circuits and Feeders, No More than Six 225.33

Disconnects, Service, No More than Six . . . . 230.71(A)

Emergency Systems, Wiring . . . . 700.10(B)(5)(b)

Entrances, Over 1000 Volts . . . . 110.33(A)

Enclosure Types 110.28

Equipment Grounding Conductor, Connected . . 250.112(A)

Equipment Grounding Conductor, Devices Over 1000 Volts 490.37

Equipment Grounding Conductor, Equipment Over 1000 Volts 490.36

Equipment Over 1000 Volts . . . . Art. 490 Part III

Field-Applied Hazard Markings . . . . 110.21(B)

Field Identification Required 408.4

Fire Pumps, Utility Service Connection . . . . . . 695.3(A)(1)

Gang Operated Switch, High Voltage Fuses . . . . .490.21(B)(7)

Grounded Conductor Disconnection Means, Feeders . . . . 225.38(C)

Grounded Conductor Disconnection Means, Service . . 230.75

High-Leg Identification . . . . 408.3(F)(1)

Illumination . . . . 110.26(D)

Industrial Installation Secondary Conductors Not over 25 Feet Long . . . . .240.21(B)(3)

Instruments, Meters, and Relays, Grounding . Art. 250 Part IX

Legally Required Standby Systems, Ahead of Service Disconnect . . . . 701.12(E)

Location to Easily Ignitable Material 408.17

Marking 110.21

Photovoltaic Systems, Bipolar . . . . 690.31(I)

Protection from Foreign Materials . . . . 110.34(F)

Taps Not over 10 Feet Long . . . . 240.21(B)(1)(2)

Transformer Secondary Conductors Not over 10 Feet Long . . . . 240.21(C)(2)(2)

Types (Defined) . . . . Article 100 Info. Note

Reconditioned Equipment . . . . .110.21(A)(2)

Service, Constructed of Substantial Metal, Over 1000 Volt 230.211

Service, Over 35,000 Volts 230.212

Service Equipment, Used as . . . . 408.3(C)

Service Equipment Over 1000 Volts, Used as 490.47

Signs

    Field Applied . . . . 110.21(B)

    High-Impedance Grounded Neutral AC System 408.3(F)(3)

    High-Leg Identification . . . . 408.3(F)(1)

    Resistively Grounded DC Systems . . . . 408.3(F)(5)

    Ungrounded AC Systems . . . . 408.3(F)(2)

    Ungrounded DC Systems . . . . 408.3(F)(4)

Signage for Identification of Systems . . . . 408.3(F)

Substations, Documentation 490.48

Supervised Industrial Installations, Outside Feeder Taps . . . . 240.92(D)

Supervised Industrial Installations, Overload Protection . . . . .240.92(C)(2)

Temporary Installations, Branch Circuits . . . . 590.4(C)

Unused Openings 408.7

Wet Locations 408.16

Wire Bending Space . . . . 408.3(G)

Wind Electric Systems, Number of Disconnects   694.22(C)(4)

Working Space, 1000 Volts and Below . . . . 110.26(A)

Working Space, above 1000 Volts. . . . . 110.34(A) Ex.

See, Switchgear, Over 1000 Volts . . . . Ferm's Finder

See (WVDA) . . . . UL Product Spec

See SWITCHBOARDS, SWITCHGEAR & PANELBOARDS . . . . Ferm's Finder

SYMBOL

Controlled Receptacle Marking . . . . 406.3(E) Figure

Grounding . . . . 250.126 Info. Note Figure

Grounding-Pole Identification . 406.10(B)(4) Info. Note Figure

Termination Point- Equipment Grounding Conductor . . . . 406.10(B)(4) Info. Note Figure

SYSTEM BONDING JUMPER

Controlled Lighting Loads . . . . .404.2(C) Exception

Critical Operations Powers Systems, No Need To Ground . . . . 708.20(C) Ex.

Definition . . . . Art. 100

Direct Current System 250.168

Grounded System 250.28

Separately Derived AC Systems. . . . . .250.30(A)(1)

Sizing . . . . Table 250.102(C)(1)

SYSTEM ISOLATION EQUIPMENT . . . . 430.109(A)(7)

Definition of 430.2

T

TABLES

AC Resistance and Reactance . . . .   Chapter 9 Table 9

Air-Conditioning and Refrigeration Equipment, Other Art . . . . Table 440.3(D)

Ambient Correction Factors . . . . Table 310.15(B)(2)(b)

Ambient Temperature Adjustment, Rooftop Conduits Raceways

and Cables . . . . .Table 310.15(B)(3)(c)

Ampacity of

Conductors 0 through 2000 Volts, 60°C through 90°C

Bare Conductors . . . . .Table 310.15(B)(21)

In Free Air. . . . . .Table 310.15(B)(17)

In Raceways . . . . .Table 310.15(B)(16)

Supported on Messenger . . . . . . .Table 310.15(B)(20)

Conductors 0 through 2000 Volts, 150°C through 250°C

In Free Air . . . . .Table 310.15(B)(19)

In Raceways . . . . .Table 310.15(B)(18)

Conductors 2001 to 35,000 volts . . . . . Table 310.60(C)(4)

Cords and Cables for Border Lights . . . . 520.44(C)

Correction Factors, Solar Photovoltaic Systems — Flexible Cords and Cables . . . . 690.31(E)

Crane & Hoist Conductors . . . . 610.14(A)

(Fixture) Luminaire Wire . . . . Table 402.5

Flexible Cord and Cables . . . . . Table 400.5(A)(1) & (2)

Adjustment Factors 400.5

High Voltage Conductors, 2001 through 35,000 Volts   Tables . . . . 310.60(C)(67) through (86)

Integrated Gas Spacer Cable 326.80

Note: For more than Three Current-Carrying Conductors in a raceway or cable, see . . . . .Table 310.15(B)(3)(a)

Application & Insulation of Conductors

Under 1000 Volts (see Table Note 1) . . . . Table 310.104(A)

Bare Metal Parts, Spacings between Switchboards and Panelboards 408.56

Bonding Jumper Sizing . . . . Table 250.102(C)(1)

Boxes, Fill (Metal) . . . . Table 314.16(A)

Volume Allowance Required Per Conductor   Table 314.16(B)

Branch-Circuit Requirements (Summary) 210.24

Branch Circuits, Specific-Purpose 210.2

Bulk Storage Plants. . . . . .Table 515.3

Cabinets & Cutout Boxes

Width of Wiring Gutters . . . . Table 312.6(A)

Wire Bending Space at Terminals . . . . . . Table 312.6(B)

Conductor Does Not Enter Opposite Its Terminal . . . . 312.6(B)(1)

Conductor Enters Opposite Its Terminal . . . 312.6(B)(2)

Cable Markings/Listing Requirements

Class 1, 2 and 3 Remote Control and Signaling . . . . .725.179(K) and Table

Communications 800.113

Community Antenna Television and Radio 820.113

Fire Alarm

NPLFA. . . . . 760.176(G)

PLFA. 760.179

Optical Fiber 770.113

Cable Substitutions

Class 2 and 3 Remote Control and Signaling . . 725.154(A)

Communications 800.154

Community Antenna Television and Radio Table 820.154(b)

Fire Alarm . . . . 760.154(A)

Network-Powered Broadband Communications . . . . Table . . . . .830.154(b)

Optical Fiber 770.154

Cable Tray Fill

Multiconductor Cables in Ladder, Ventilated Trough, or Solid Bottom 392.22

Multiconductor Cables in Solid Channel . . . . . 392.22(3)

Multiconductor Cables in Ventilated Channel . . 392.22(2)

Single Conductor, Ladder or Ventilated Trough Trays . . . . 392. 22(B)

Cable Tray for Grounding 392.60

Cable Tray, Wiring Methods Permitted . . . . . . 392.10(A)

Calculation of Feeder Lighting Load by Occupancies . 220.42

Chapter 9 (Tables)

AC Resistance and Reactance for 600-Volt Cables . . Table 9

Class 2 and 3 AC Power Source Limitations . . Table 11(A)

Class 2 and 3 DC Power Source Limitations . . Table 11(B)

Conductor Properties . . . . Table 8

Conductor Stranding . . . . Table 10

Compact Copper and Aluminum Wire Dimensions . . . . Table 5A

Dimensions of Insulated Conductors and Fixture Wire . . . . Table 5

Dimensions and Percent Area of Conduit and Tubing. . . . . Table 4

LFA AC Power Source Limitations. . . . . . . Table 12(A)

LFA DC Power Source Limitations . . . . . . Table 12(B)

Percent of Cross-Sectional Area . . . . Table 1

Radius of Conduit and Tubing . . . . Table 2

See   Notes to Tables (1) thru (10) . . . .

Circuit Breakers (Inverse Time)- Standard Ampere Ratings . . . . Table 240.6(A)

Class 1, Class 2, and Class 3 Remote-Control, Signaling, and Power-Limited Circuits

Ampacities . . . . Table 725.144

Applications . . . . Table 725.154

Cable Marking. . . . . .Table 725.179(J)

Cable Substitutions . . . . Table 725.154(A)

Clearance of

Bare Live Parts, Over 1000 Volts above Working Space. . . . . 110.34(E)

Bare Live Parts Over 1000 Volts, Field-fabricated . . . 490.24

Bare Metal Parts in Motor Control Centers . . . . 430.97(D)

Bare Metal Parts in Switchboards and Panelboards . 408.56

Conductors Entering Bus Enclosures 408.5

Over 1000 Volts

Over Buildings and Other Structures 225.61

Over Roadways, Walkways, Rail, Water, and Open Land 225.60

Service Conductors and Surfaces — Cables/Open Conductor . . . . 230.51(C)

Working Space

Over 1000 Volts, Nominal . . . . 110.34(A)

Under 1000 Volts . . . . 110.26(A)(1)

Communication Antenna Television and Radio Distribution Systems

Coaxial Cable in Buildings. . . . . Table 820.154(a)

Coaxial Cable Marking. . . . . Table 820.179

Coaxial Cable Use and Permitted Substitution. . . . . Table 820.154(b)

Communication Circuits

Cable Markings . . . . Table 800.179

Cable Routing Assemblies . . . . Table 800.154(c)

Cable Routing Assembly Marking. . . . . . Table 800.182(a)

Cable Substitutions . . . . Table 800.154(d)

Communication Raceways in Buildings . . Table 800.154(b)

Communication Raceway Marking . . . . . Table 800.182(b)

Wires and Cables in Buildings. . . . . . . Table 800.154(a)

Conductors

Application & Insulation

(Fixture) Luminaire Wires 402.3

Overcurrent Protection, Specific Conductor Applications . . . . 240.4(G)

Under 1000 Volts (see Note 1 below table) . . . . . Table . . . . .310.104(A)

Boxes, Number in

Metal . . . . Table 314.16(A)

Volume Allowance Required Per Conductor . . . . Table 314.16(B)

Clearances for, Entering Bus Enclosures 408.5

Combination of, in Raceways

Areas of Conduit or Tubing . . . . Chapter 9, Table 4

Compact Aluminum Building Wire Dimensions. . . . . .Chapter 9, Table 5A

Conductor Properties . . . . Chapter 9, Table 8

Dimensions of Conductors & Luminaire (Fixture) Wires . . . . .Chapter 9, Table 5

Percent of Cross Section for Conductors and Cables (General) . . . . Chapter 9, Table 1

Conductors based on 30 degrees C (86 degree F) . . . . Table . . . . 310.15(B)(32)(a)

Conduit and Tubing, Fill for (All the Same Size)   Informative Annex C Tables

Contact Conductor Supports, Cranes and Hoists . 610.14(D)

Deflection, Minimum Bending Space

Conductor Does Not Enter Opposite Its Terminal . . . . 312.6(B)(1)

Conductor Enters Opposite Its Terminal . . . 312.6(B)(2)

Terminals of Enclosed Motor Controllers . . . . 430.10(B)

Dimensions

Compact or Copper Aluminum Building Wire   Chapter 9, Table 5A

Conductor Properties . . . . Chapter 9, Table 8

Insulated, and (Fixture) Luminaire Wires . . . . .Chapter 9, Table 5

Rubber and Thermoplastic Covered . . Chapter 9, Table 5

Direct Burial (Cover Requirements) 300.5

Over 1000 Volts, Nominal. 300.50

(Fixture) Luminaire Wires . . . . Chapter 9, Table 5

Flexible Cords and Cables 400.4

Ampacity . . . . Tables 400.5(A)(1) & (A)(2)

Adjustment Factors 400.5

Grounded Conductor . . . . Table 250.102(C)(1)

Grounding, Size

Equipment Grounding Conductor 250.122

System, Alternating-Current 250.66

Insulations

Under 1000 Volts (see note 1 below table). . . . . Table 310.104(A)

Main Bonding Jumper . . . . Table 250.102(C)(1)

Maximum Number . . . . Chapter 9, Table 1 & Notes

Maximum Number in (All the Same Size) . . . . .Informative Annex C Tables

Electrical Metallic Tubing . . . . Table C.1

Compact Conductors . . . . Table C.1(A)

Electrical Nonmetallic Tubing . . . . Table C.2

Compact Conductors . . . . Table C.2(A)

Flexible Metal Conduit . . . . Table C.3

Compact Conductors . . . . Table C.3(A)

Metric Designator 12 (3/8") Flexible Metal Conduit 348.22

Intermediate Metal Conduit . . . . Table C.4

Compact Conductors . . . . Table C.4(A)

Liquidtight Flexible Metal Conduit. . . . . Table C.7

Compact Conductors . . . . Table C.7(A)

Metric Designator 12 (3/8") Liquidtight Flexible Metal Conduit 348.22

Liquidtight Flexible Nonmetallic Conduit (LFNMC-A) . . . . .Table C.6

Compact Conductors . . . . Table C.6(A)

Liquidtight Flexible Nonmetallic Conduit (LFNMC-B) . . . . .Table C.5

Compact Conductors . . . . Table C.5(A)

PVC Conduit, Type EB . . . . Table C.12

Compact Conductors . . . . Table C.12(A)

Rigid Metal Conduit . . . . Table C.8

Compact Conductors . . . . Table C.8(A)

Rigid PVC Conduit, Schedule 80 . . . . Table C.9

Compact Conductors . . . . Table C.9(A)

Rigid PVC Conduit, Schedule 40 & HDPE . . . Table C.10

Compact Conductors . . . . Table C.10(A)

Rigid PVC Conduit, Type A. . . . . Table C.11

Compact Conductors . . . . Table C.11(A)

Minimum Size. . . . . Table 310.106(A)

Over 1000 Volts to 35,000 Volts

See TABLES, Ampacity of . . . . Ferm's Finder

Overcurrent Protection, Low-Voltage Wiring, Park Trailers . . . . .552.10(E)(1)

Properties of . . . . Chapter 9, Table 8

Size of Amateur Station Outdoor Antenna Conductors 810.52

Size of Receiving Station Outdoor Antenna Conductors . . . . 810.16(A)

Conduit and Tubing

Combination of Conductors . . . . Chapter 9, Table 4

Compact Conductors (Aluminum) . . . Chapter 9, Table 5A

Conductor Fill, All the Same Size . . . Informative Annex C Tables

Dimensions of Insulated Conductors & (Fixture) Luminaire Wires . . . . Chapter 9, Table 5

Fiberglass Reinforced, Expansion Characteristics . . . 355.44

Flexible Metal Conduit, Metric Designator 12 (3/8") Size 348.22

Integrated Gas Spacer Cable, Dimensions 326.116

Paper Spacer Thickness 326.112

Radii of Bends 326.24

Liquidtight Flexible Metal Conduit, Metric Designator 12 (3/8") Size 348.22

Metric Designator and Trade Sizes . . . . 300.1(C)

Percent of Cross Section . . . . Chapter 9, Table 1

PVC Rigid, Expansion Characteristics 352.44

Radius of Bends (General) . . . . Chapter 9, Table 2

Flexible Metallic Tubing, Fixed . . . . 360.24(B)

Flexible Metallic Tubing, Infrequent Flexing . . 360.24(A)

Nonmetallic Underground Conduit with Conductors 354.24

Supports — Rigid Metal Conduit . . . . 344.30(B)(2)

Rigid PVC Conduit . . . . 352.30(B)

Cooking Appliances, Dwelling Units 220.55

Other than Dwelling Units 220.56

Cranes & Hoists

Ampacities of Conductors, Short-Time Rated . . 610.14(A)

Demand Factors . . . . 610.14(E)

Secondary Conductor Rating Factors . . . . . . 610.14(B)

Demand Factors

Commercial Cooking Equipment 220.56

Cranes & Hoists . . . . 610.14(E)

Elevators 620.14

Farm Loads, Other Than Dwelling Units 220.102

Total Farm Loads 220.103

Household Clothes Dryers 220.54

Household Ranges 220.55

Lighting Load Feeders 220.42

Marinas and Boatyards 555.12

Mobile Home Park (Feeders & Service Conductors) . 550.31

Multifamily Dwellings, Optional (Service) 220.84

Receptacle Loads (Non-Dwelling Feeders) 220.44

Recreational Vehicle Park (Service & Feeders) 551.73

Restaurants, New (Optional) 220.88

Schools (Service Conductors), Optional 220.86

Stage Set Lighting . . . . 530.19(A)

Dwelling Service Conductor Sizing . . . . Example D7

Electric Signs and Outline Lighting

Class 2 Cable Substitutions . . . . Table 600.33(A)(2)

Power Limited Cable . . . . Table 600.33(A)(1)

Electric Vehicle Charging Systems

Minimum Ventilation Required . . . . . 625.52(B)(1) & (2)

Elevator Feeder Demand Factors 620.14

Electrified Truck Parking Spaces

Demand Factors . . . . Table 626.11(B)

Elevator Feeder Demand Factors 620.14

Enclosure Selection . . . . Table 110.28

Equipment Grounding Conductors 250.122

Fire Alarm Systems

Cable Markings . . . . Table 760.179(I)

Cable Substitutions . . . . Table 760.154(A)

NPLFA Cable Markings . . . . Table 760.176(G)

PLFA Cables in Buildings . . . . Table 760.154

(Fixture) Luminaire Wires (Same Size) in Conduit and Tubing . . . . Informative Annex C Tables

(Fixture) Luminaire Wire (Types) 402.3

Flexible Cords and Cables 400.4

Ampacity . . . . Tables 400.5(A)(1) & (A)(2)

Adjustment Factors 400.5

Fuses (Standard Ampere Rating) . . . . Table 240.6(A)

General Lighting Unit Load by Occupancies 220.12

Grounded Conductor . . . . Table 250.102(C)(1)

Grounding, Application of Other Articles 250.3

Grounding, General Requirements 250.1

Grounding Conductor Sizing . . . . . . Table 250.102(C)(1)

Grounding Electrode Conductors 250.66

Hazardous (Classified) Locations

Bulk Storage Plants 515.3

Class I, Zone 0, 1, and 2

Gas Classification Groups . . . . 505.9(C)(1)(2)

Maximum Surface Temperature, Group II Equipment . . . . 505.9(D)(1)

Minimum Distance of Obstructions, Flange Openings . . . . 505.7(D)

Types of Protection Designation . . . . . . 505.9(C)(2)(4)

Motor Fuel Dispensing Facilities and Commercial Garages . . . . 514.3(B)(1)

Classified Areas Adjacent to Dispensers . . . . Figure 514.3

Classified Areas for Dispensing Devices (Gases) . . . . 514.3(B)(2)

Safe Operating Temperatures

Class I, Identification Numbers . . . . 500.8(C)

Class II . . . . 500.8(D)(2)

High Voltage Conductors (Over 1000 Volts, Nominal)

Bare Live Parts, Over 1000 Volts above Working Space . . . . 110.34(E)

Bare Live Parts Over 1000 Volts, Field-fabricated . . 490.24

Thickness of Insulation . . . . . . Table 310.104(B) and (D)

Household Clothes Dryers 220.54

Household Ranges and Other Cooking Appliances . . . 220.55

Information Technology Equipment

    Cables Under Raised Floors . . . . Table 645.10(B)(5)

Integrated Electrical Systems, Application of Other Articles 685.3

Interconnected Electric Power Production Sources

    Other Articles — Interconnected Electric Power Production 705.3

Lighting Loads by Occupancy 220.12

Lighting Load (Feeder Demand Factor) 220.42

Limitations for Network-Powered Broadband Communication Systems 830.15

Live Parts, Separation

    Air Separation, Indoors 490.24

        Elevation . . . . 110.34(E)

    From Fences, Over 1000 Volts 110.31

    Working Space, Over 1000 Volts, Nominal . . . . 110.34(A)

        Maximum 1000 Volts . . . . 110.26(A)(1)

Main Bonding Jumper Sizing . . . . Table 250.102(C)(1)

Marinas and Boatyards (Demand Factors) 555.12

Maximum Appliance Loads at Receptacles . . . .210.21(B)(2)

    Summary 210.24

Messenger Supported Wiring, Permitted Cable Types 396.10(A)

Metric Designators and Trade Sizes . . . . . . .Table 300.1(C)

Minimum Cover Requirements, 0 to 1000 Volts 300.5

Minimum Cover Requirements, Over 1000 Volts 300.50

Minimum Cover Requirements, Network-Powered Broadband Systems . . . . 830.47(C)

Minimum Size of Conductors . . . . 310.106(A)

Minimum Wire Bending Space

    Conductor Does Not Enter Opposite Its Terminal . 312.6(A)

    Conductor Enters Opposite Its Terminal . . . . . . 312.6(B)

    Terminals of Enclosed Motor Controllers . . . . . 430.10(B)

Mobile Home Parks (Demand Factor) 550.31

Motor Fuel Dispensing

    Electrical Equipment . . . . Table 514.3(B)(2)

    Facilities . . . . Table 514.3(B)(1)

Motors

    Conductor Rating Factors, Power Resistors 430.29

    Conductors for Small Motors . . . . 430.22(G)

        16 AWG Copper . . . . 430.22(G)(2)

        18 AWG Copper . . . . 430.22(G)(1)

    Control Circuit Overcurrent Protection . . . . . . 430.72(B)

Control Center Spacing between Bare Metal Parts . . 430.97

Controller Enclosure Type . . . . 110.28 and Table

Direct-Current Motor-Rectified Supplied . . . . . 430.22(A)

Duty Cycle Service . . . . Table 430.22(E)

    Secondary Conductor (Wound Rotor). . . Table 430.23(C)

Full-Load Current in Amperes

    DC Motors . . . . Table 430.247

    Single-Phase AC Motors . . . . Table 430.248

    Two-Phase AC Motors . . . . Table 430.249

    Three-Phase AC Motors . . . . Table 430.250

Locked-Rotor Current, Conversions .Tables 430.251(A)&(B)

Locked-Rotor Indicating Letters . . . . 430.7(B)

Maximum Rating or Setting of Protective Devices . . 430.52

Multispeed Motor . . . . 430.22(B)

Other Articles 430.5

Overload Units Required 430.37

Part-Winding Motors . . . . 430.22(D)

Terminal, Spacing and Housing

    Terminal Spacings, Fixed . . . . Table 430.12(C)(1)

    Usable Volumes, Fixed Terminals . . . Table 430.12(C)(2)

    Wire-to-Wire Connections . . . . Table 430.12(B)

Wire Bending Space, Controllers . . . . . . Table 430.10(B)

Wye-Start, Delta-Run Motor . . . . 430.22(C)

Multifamily Dwellings (Demand Factor), Optional . . . 220.84

Multiplying Factors from DC Resistance to AC Resistance . . . Chapter 9, Table 9

Network-Powered Broadband Communications System

    Cables in Buildings . . . . Table 830.154(a)

    Cable Substitutions . . . . Table 830.154(b)

    Cover Requirements (Underground) . . . . .Table 830.47(C)

    Limitations. . . . . .Table 830.15

Notes to Tables (Chapter 9) . . . . Notes

Optical Fiber Cables

    Cable Markings . . . . Table 770.179

    Cable Substitutions . . . . Table 770.154(b)

    In Buildings . . . . Table 770.154(a)

Optional Load Calculations

    Multifamily Dwelling Units 220.84

    Restaurants, New 220.88

    Schools 220.86

Outside Branch Circuits and Feeders, Other Articles . . . 225.3

    Over 1000 Volts

        Over Buildings and Other Structures 225.61

        Over Roadways, Walkways, Rail, Water, and Open Land .

T

. . . . 225.60

Overcurrent Protection, Other Articles 240.3

    Specific Conductor Applications . . . . 240.4(G)

Overcurrent Protective Device, Maximum Rating . . 430.72(B)

Park Trailer Low-Voltage Overcurrent Protection . 552.10(E)(1)

Percent of Cross Section of Conduit and Tubing for Conductors and Raceways. . . . . Chapter 9, Table 1

Power Limitations

    AC Class 2 & 3 Circuits. . . . . Chapter 9, Table 11(A)

    DC Class 2 & 3 Circuits . . . . Chapter 9, Table 11(B)

    Network-Powered Broadband Systems 830.15

    PLFA AC Fire Protective Circuits . . Chapter 9, Table 12(A)

    PLFA DC Fire Protective Circuits . . . Chapter 9, Table 12(B)

Properties of Conductors . . . . Chapter 9, Table 8

PVC Expansion Rate. . . . . Table 352.44

PVC Support . . . . Table 352.30

Radio and Television Equipment

    Outdoor Antenna Conductors. . . . . Table 810.52

    Receiving Station Conductors . . . . Table 810.16(A)

Radius of Conduit Bends (General) . . . . . Chapter 9, Table 2

Rating Factors for Power Resistors 430.29

Receptacle Ratings & Load

    Demand Factors, Other Than Dwelling Units 220.44

    Maximum Cord- and Plug-Connected Load. . . 210.21(B)(2)

    Receptacle Ratings . . . . 210.21(B)(3)

    Shore Power, Marinas and Boatyards, for. 555.12

    Summary. 210.24

Recreational Vehicle Park (Demand) 551.73

Reinforced Thermosetting Resin Conduit Expansion Rate Table 355.44

Reinforced Thermosetting Resin Conduit Support Table 355.30

Repair Garages

    Major and Minor Fuel Heavier-Than-Air. . . .Table 511.3(C)

    Major Fuel Lighter-Than-Air . . . . Table 511.3(D)

Resistance of Conductors . . . . Chapter 9, Tables 8 & 9

Restaurants, Optional Load Calculations for New . . . 220.88

Rigid Metal Conduit Support. . . . . Table 344.30(B)(2)

Services . . . . Figure 230.1

    Support and Clearance . . . . 230.51(C)

Schools (Service and Feeder Conductors), Optional . . 220.86

Signs and Outline Lighting

    Class 2 Cable Substitutions. . . . . Table 600.33(A)(2)

    Power Limited Cable . . . . Table 600.33(A)(1)

Solar Photovoltaic Systems

    Ambient Temperature Correction. . . . . 690.31(A)

    PV Wire Strands- Minimum. . . . . 690.31(E)

    Voltage Correction Factors, Silicon Modules. 690.7

Standard Ampere Rating for Fuses and Inverse Time Circuit Breakers . . . . Table 240.6(A)

Strut-Type Channel Raceway, Size and Inside Diameter 384.22

Supply-Side Bonding Jumper Sizing . . . . Table 250.102(C)(1)

Sunlight on Rooftop, Adjustments . . . .Table 310.15(B)(3)(c)

Supports for

    Conductors in Vertical Raceways . . . . 300.19(A)

    Rigid Metal Conduit . . . . .344.30(B)(2)

    Rigid PVC Conduit 352.44

Swimming Pools

    Overhead Conductor Clearances 680.8

    Underground Burial Depths . . . . .Table 300.5

System Bonding Jumper Sizing . . . . . Table 250.102(C)(1)

Theaters, Motion Pictures and TV Studios, and Similar Locations

    Cords and Cables . . . . Table 520.44(C)(3)

    More than Three Current-Carrying Conductors . . . . Table 520.44(C)(3)(a)

Transformers

    Overcurrent Protection, 1000 Volts and Less. . . . 450.3(B)

    Overcurrent Protection, Over 1000 Volts. . . . . . 450.3(A)

Ventilation Required, Electric Vehicle Charging Systems . . . . 625.52(B)(1) & (2)

Welders

    Duty Cycle Factors for Arc Welders . . . . 630.11(A)

    Duty Cycle Factors for Resistance Welders . . .630.31(A)(2)

Wind Electric Systems

    Working Spaces 694.7

Wire Bending Space

    Conductor Does Not Enter Opposite Its Terminal . 312.6(A)

    Conductor Enters Opposite Its Terminal . . . . . . 312.6(B)

    Terminals of Enclosed Motor Controllers . . . . . 430.10(B)

Working Clearances

    Over 1000 Volts, Nominal . . . . 110.34(A)

    Under 1000 Volts . . . . .110.26(A)(1)

Working Spaces. . . . . Table 110.26(A)(1)

    Wind Electric Systems . . . . .Table 694.7

TAMPERABILITY

Cartridge Fuses. . . . . 240.60(D)

Circuit Breakers 240.82

Edison-Base Fuses . . . . 240.51(B)

Lighting Track Systems . . . . .410.155(A)

Service Conductors Supplying Specific Load 230.93

Type S Fuses . . . . 240.54(D)

    Mobile Homes 550.11

TAMPER-RESISTANT RECEPTACLES

Assembly Occupancies (such as transportation waiting areas, gymnasiums, skating rinks, and auditoriums) . . . . .406.12(6)

Business Offices, Corridors, Waiting Rooms (in clinics, medical and dental offices, and outpatient facilities) . . . . . .406.12(5)

Child Care Facilities . . . . 406.12(3)

Dormitories. . . . . .406.12(7)

Dwelling Units . . . . 406.12(1)

Guest Rooms and Guest Suites of Hotels and Motels 406.12(2)

Preschools and Elementary Education Facilities . . . .406.12(4)

Receptacles or Covers, Designated General Care Pediatric Locations . . . . 517.18(C)

Replacements . . . . 406.4(D)(5)

TAPS

Battery Conductors . . . . 240.21(H)

Box Not Required . . . . 334.40(B)

Branch-Circuit Taps 210.19

    Conductor Overcurrent Protection, General. . . . 210.20(B)

    Motor Branch Circuit Taps. . . . . 240.21(F)

    Over 1000 Volts . . . . 240.100(A)

    Overcurrent Protection, Flexible Cords and Cables 240.5(B)

    Protection of Conductors . . . . 240.4(E)

    Single Motor Taps . . . . 430.53(D)

    Summary Requirements 210.24

    Tap Conductors . . . . 240.21(A)

Busway Taps . . . . 240.21(E)

    Branch Circuits, Overcurrent Protection Rating. . 368.17(D)

    Branches from Busways 368.56

    Feeder or Branch Circuits . . . . 368.17(C)

    Feeder Overcurrent Protection . . . . 368.17(A)

    Reduction in Ampacity Size of Busway . . . . . 368.17(B)

Cascading (Switch to Switch) 312.8

Feeders . . . . 240.21(B)

    3 m (10 ft.) Tap Rule . . . . .240.21(B)(1)

        Motor Feeder . . . . 430.28(1)

        Transformer Secondary Conductors . . . . .240.21(C)(2)

    7.5 m (25 ft.) Tap Rule . . . . .240.21(B)(2)

Motor Feeder Tap . . . . 430.28(2)

    Single Motor Taps . . . . 430.53(D)

    Transformer Secondary Conductors . . . . . .240.21(C)(6)

    Transformer Secondary Conductors, Industrial Installations. . . . . .240.21(C)(3)

30 m (100 ft.) Tap Rule (High Bay Manufacturing Building) . . . . .240.21(B)(4)

    Motor Feeder Taps . . . . 430.28 Ex.

Over 1000 Volts . . . . .240.101(B)

Outside Taps of Unlimited Length . . . . .240.21(B)(5)

Supervised Industrial Installations . . . . 240 Part VIII

    Branch-Circuit and Feeders (General). . . . . . 240.92(A)

    Outside Feeder Taps . . . . 240.92(B)

    Transformer Secondary Conductors of Separately Derived Systems . . . . 240.92(C)

Transformer Feeder . . . . 240.21(B)

    Outside Secondary Conductors . . . . .240.21(C)(4)

    Primary Plus Secondary Not Over 7.5 m (25 ft.) . . . . .240.21(B)(3)

    Secondary Conductors from Feeder Tapped .240.21(C)(5)

    Secondary Conductors . . . . 240.21(C)

    Secondary Conductors Not Over 7.5 m (25 ft.) . . . . .240.21(C)(6)

Generator Terminal Taps . . . . 240.21(G)

    Ampacity of Conductors 445.13

Grounding Electrode Conductor Taps . . . . 250.64(D)

    Separately Derived Systems . . . . 250.30(A)(6)

Luminaires (Fixtures) . . . . 210.19(A)(4) Ex. 1

(Fixture) Luminaire Wires and Flexible Cords . . . . 210.19(A)(4) Ex. 2

    Overcurrent Protection of . . . . 240.5(B)

Flexible Metal Conduit . . . . 348.20(A)(2)(c)

Liquidtight Flexible Metal Conduit . . . . . . 350.30(A) Ex. 3

Liquidtight Flexible Nonmetallic Conduit . . . 356.20(A)(2)

Manufactured Wiring Systems . . . . . .604.100(A)(2) Ex. 1

Wiring . . . . 410.117(C)

Motor Circuit Taps . . . . 240.21(F)

    Feeders 430.28

    Single Motor Tap, Branch Circuit . . . . 430.53(D)

Outside Feeder Taps

    Supervised Industrial Installations . . . . 240.92(D)

    Transformer Secondary Conductors . . . . . .240.21(C)(4)

    Unlimited Length . . . . 240.21(B)(5)

Service Conductors . . . . 240.21(D)

    Spliced or Tapped Permitted 230.46

Equipment Allowed . . . . 230.82(5)

Supervised Industrial Installations, Feeder Taps . . . 240.92(B)

Ungrounded Conductors from Grounded Systems 215.7

See CONDUCTORS, Splices of or in. . . . . . . Ferm's Finder

See OVERCURRENT PROTECTION . . . . . Ferm's Finder

See SPLICES AND TAPS . . . . Ferm's Finder

TASK ILLUMINATION

Critical Branch (control of) . . . . 517.34(B)

Definition of 517.2

Generator Set Locations

    Life Safety Branch- Hospitals . . . . 517.33(E)

    Life Safety Branch- Nursing Home and Limited Health Care
Facilities . . . . 517.43(F)

Hospitals . . . . 517.34(A)

Hospital, Life Safety Branch, Generator Set and Transfer Switch
517.34(A)

Nursing Homes. . . . . 517.44(A)(1)

Other Health Care Facilities . . . . 517.45(C)

TELEPHONE EQUIPMENT 800.18
See COMMUNICATIONS CIRCUITS . . . . . . Ferm's Finder

TELEVISION & MOTION PICTURE STUDIOS . . . . . . Art. 530
See MOTION PICTURE & TELEVISION STUDIOS . . . . . .
. . . . Ferm's Finder

See THEATERS, ETC. . . . . Ferm's Finder

TELEVISION & RADIO EQUIPMENT . . . . Art. 810
See Community Antenna Television and Radio Distribution
Systems . . . . Art. 820

See COMMUNITY ANTENNA TELEVISION AND RADIO
DISTRIBUTION SYSTEMS. . . . . Ferm's Finder

See RADIO & TELEVISION EQUIPMENT . . . Ferm's Finder

TEMPERATURE [AT LUMINAIRES (LIGHTING FIXTURES)]
Conductors in Outlet Boxes 410.21

Flush and Recessed Luminaires (Fixtures) 410.115

Underwater Luminaires (Lighting Fixtures) . . . 680.23(A)(7)

TEMPERATURE, AMBIENT
TEMPERATURE, AMBIENT *See* AMBIENT TEMPERATURE
. . . . Ferm's Finder

TEMPERATURE CLASSIFICATIONS
Hazardous (Classified) Locations . . . . 500.8(C)(4)

    Class I, Zone 0, 1, and 2 Locations . . . . 505.9(D)

TEMPERATURE CORRECTION FACTORS . . . .
. . . . Tables 310.15(B)(2)(a)&(b)
See Informative Annex B for Examples of Formulas . . . .
. . . . Informative Annex B

TEMPERATURE OF CONDUCTOR INSULATION   310.15(A)(3)
0 to 2000 Volts . . . . Table 310.104(A)

See CONDUCTORS, Temperature Rating of Insulation . . . . .
. . . . Ferm's Finder

TEMPORARY INSTALLATIONS . . . . Art. 590
Approval Required . . . . 590.2(B)

Branch Circuits Protection . . . . 590.4(C)

    Type SE Cable . . . . 590.4(C)(2)

Carnival, Circuses, Fairs, and Similar Events . . . . . Art. 525

Connected to an Equipment Grounding Conductor
(Receptacles) . . . . 590.4(D)

Cords and Cable Assemblies (Not Extension Cords) . 590.4(J)

Disconnecting Means . . . . 590.4(E)

Exhibition Halls . . . . 518.3(B)

Feeders . . . . 590.4(B)

    Type SE Cable . . . . 590.4(A)(2)

Ground-Fault Protection for Personnel 590.6

    Assured Equipment Grounding Conductor Program . . . .
. . . . 590.6(B)(2)

    Other Outlets . . . . 590.6(B)

    Receptacles, 15-, 20-, & 30-Ampere, 125-volt, Single-Phase
. . . . 590.6(A)

    SPGFCI Protection . . . . 590.6(B)(2)

Grounding (General) . . . . Art. 250

High Voltage Systems, Guarding 590.7

Lamp Protection . . . . 590.4(F)

Protection from Accidental Damage . . . . 590.4(H)

Receptacles to Be Grounding Type . . . . 590.4(D)

    Not Permitted on Lighting Circuits . . . . 590.4(D)

Services (per Article 230) . . . . 590.4(A)

Splices . . . . 590.4(G)

Support . . . . 590.4(J)

    By Vegetation Such As Trees Prohibited 225.26

Termination(s) at Devices . . . . 590.4(I)

Time Constraints 590.3

TERMINAL BAR (GROUNDING)
For Panelboards 408.40

    Isolated Ground Receptacles . . . . 250.146(D)

Swimming Pool Equipment . . . . 680.25(B)

    Junction Boxes and Enclosures 680.24

    Underwater Luminaires (Fixtures) 680.23

Transformer. . . . . 450.10(A)

TERMINAL HOUSINGS (MOTORS) **430.12**

TERMINALS

Connections to . . . . 110.14(A)

    Conductors and Equipment 250.8

    Grounding Electrode 250.70

CO/ALR Marking

    Receptacles . . . . 406.3(C)

    Switches . . . . 404.14(C)

Electric Discharge Tubing, Neon Electrode Conductors, Signs
. . . . 600.42

Flat Cable Assemblies . . . . 322.120(C)

Identification of

    Grounding-Pole of Receptacles . . . . 406.10(B)

    Motors and Controllers . . . . 430.9(A)

    Polarity. . . . . 200.9 & 10

    Switches . . . . 404.6(C)

    Wiring Device 250.126

Receptacles, Grounding Terminal . . . . 406.10(B)

    Connection to Boxes 250.146

    See (RTDV) . . . . .UL Product Spec

Switches . . . . 404.6(C)

    See (WJQR) . . . . .UL Product Spec

    Note: Use oxide inhibitor on aluminum conductors
    where required by manufacturer . . . . 110.3(B)

Temperature Limitations . . . . 110.14(C)

See Conductor Termination Compounds (DVYW) . . . .
. . . . .UL Product Spec

See(AALZ) .UL Product Spec

TESTING

Assured Equipment Grounding Conductor Program . . . . . .
. . . . 590.6(B)(2)

Emergency Systems 700.3

Equipment for Safety 90.7

Feeders Over 1000 Volts, Pre-Energization and Operating . . .
. . . . 225.56(A)

Ground-Fault Protection of Equipment . . . . 230.95(C)

    In Health Care Facilities . . . . 517.17(D)

Inspections and Tests 225.56, 110.41

Feeders 225.56,

    Over 1000 Volts, (complete electrical system design) . 110.41

Insulation Resistance, Space-Heating Cable 424.45

Legally Required Standby Systems 701.3

Mobile Homes 550.17

Park Trailers 552.60

Performance Tested . . . . 225.56(A)

Pre-energization and Operating Tests 110.41

Recreational Vehicles 551.60

Temporary Installations, Permitted for . . . . 590.3(C)

Transformers Used for Research, Development, etc. 450.1 Ex. 8

Wiring Integrity 110.7

THEATERS, AUDIENCE AREAS OF MOTION PICTURE AND TELEVISION STUDIOS, AND SIMILAR LOCATIONS . Art. 520

Construction 520.53

    Interior Conductors. . . . . 520.53(E)

    Neutral Terminal . . . . 520.53(B)

    Pilot Light . . . . 510.53(A)

    Single-Pole Separable Connector . . . . 520.53(C)

    Supply Feed-Through. . . . . 520.53(D)

Definitions 520.2

Dressing Rooms . . . . 520 Part VI

    Lamp Guards 520.72

    Pendant Lampholders Prohibited 520.71

    Pilot Lights Required 520.74

    Switches Required 520.73

Emergency Systems . . . . Art. 700

Grounding 520.81

Luminaire Supply Cords. . . . . 520.68(A)(3)

Portable Equipment Used Outdoors 520.10

Stage Equipment

    Defined. 520.2

    Fixed, Other Than Switchboards . . . . 520 Part III

    Portable, Other Than Switchboards . . . . 520 Part V

Stage Lighting Hoist

    Defined. 520.2

    Wiring Information. 520.40

Supply Conductors. 520.54

Switchboards

    Defined. 520.2

    Constant Power . . . . 520.26(D)

    Fixed . . . . 520 Part II

    Intermediate. 520.26(C)

Manual . . . . 520.26(A)

Portable . . . . 520 Part IV

Remotely Controlled . . . . 520.26(B)

Wiring Methods . . . . 520.5(A)

Nonrated Construction . . . . 520.5(C)

Portable Equipment . . . . 520.5(B)

THERAPEUTIC EQUIPMENT . . . . 517.73(B)

THERAPEUTIC POOLS & TUBS . . . . 680 Part VI

Application of Article 680 Part VI 680.60

Permanently Installed Pools. 680.61

Note: Permanent Installations to comply with 680 Parts I & II

See Exception for Luminaires . . . . 680.61 Ex.

Portable Therapeutic Appliances . . . . Art. 422

Therapeutic Tubs (Hydrotherapeutic Tanks) 680.62

Bonding . . . . 680.62(B)

Methods . . . . 680.62(C)

Ground-Fault Circuit-Interrupter Protection

Listed Units . . . . 680.62(A)(1)

Other Units . . . . 680.62(A)(2)

Outlets . . . . 680.62(A)

Receptacles . . . . 680.62(E)

Grounding . . . . 680.62(D)

Luminaires . . . . 680.62(F)

Exception from Limitations . . . . 680.61 Ex.

In Area to Be Totally Enclosed Type . . . . . . 680.62(F)

See THERAPEUTIC POOLS & TUBS . . . . . . Ferm's Finder

THERMAL DEVICES 240.9

Fluorescent Luminaires . . . . 410.130(E)

High-Intensity Discharge Luminaires . . . . 430.130(F)

Motors

Continuous-Duty . . . . 430.32(A)(2) and (B)(2)

Recessed Incandescent Luminaires. . . . . .410.115(C)

Thermal Protector(s) (Motors), Definition . . . . . 100 Part I

THERMALLY PROTECTED

Definition of, (as applied to motors) . . . . Art. 100

Fluorescent Lamp Ballasts . . . . .410.130(E)

High-Intensity Discharge Luminaires (Fixtures) . . .410.130(F)

Luminaires (Fixtures), Recessed Incandescent . . . .410.115(C)

THERMOSTATS

Appliances . . . . Art. 422

Cables Green Color, Okay – Not as Equipment Ground . . .

. . . . 250.119 Ex. 1

Installation (Class 2 Wiring) . . . . Art. 725 Part III

Fixed Electric Space-Heating Equipment

As Switching Devices 424.20

Loads Permitted . . . . 424.3(B)

See ELECTRIC HEAT (SPACE) . . . . Ferm's Finder

THREADS (CONDUITS)

Explosionproof Equipment

Divisions Metric- (5 fully engaged) . . . . 500.8(E)(2)

Divisions NPT- (5 fully engaged) . . . . 500.8(E)(1)

Zones Metric- (5 fully engaged) . . . . 505.9(E)(2)

Zones NPT- (5 fully engaged) . . . . 505.9(E)(1)

FIELD-CUT (other than at the factory) . . 300.6(A) Info. Note

Running

Intermediate Metal Conduit . . . . 342.42(B)

Rigid Metal Conduit . . . . 344.42(B)

THREE OVERLOAD UNITS, MOTORS . . . . . . Table 430.37

TIE BARS (Circuit-Breaker Handle Ties)

Circuit Breaker as Overcurrent Device . . . . 240.15(B)

Disconnecting Means, Temporary Wiring . . . . . . 590.4(E)

Feeders . . . . 225.33(B)

Mobile Homes . . . . 550.11(C)

Multiple Branch Circuits 210.7

Multiwire Branch Circuits . . . . .240.15(B)(1)

Service Disconnects . . . . 230.71(B)

Simultaneous Opening of Poles 230.74

Ungrounded Conductors Tapped from Grounded System . . .

. . . . 210.10

Screw Tightness . . . . Informative Annex I

TIRE INFLATION MACHINES (For Public Use) . . 422.5(A)(4)

TOOLS

Cord- and Plug-Connected, Double Insulated . . . 250.114 Ex.

Industrial Machinery . . . . Art. 670

Motor-Operated, Hand-Held, Grounding . . . . 250.114(4)(c)

TORQUING INFORMATION

Electrical Connections . . . . 110.14(D)

Motor Controller Terminals . . . . 430.9(C)

Recommended Tightening Torque Tables   Informative Annex I

Tightness of Screws . . . . Informative Annex I

TRACK, LIGHTING . . . . **410 Part XIV**

Defined (Lighting Track) . . . . Article 100

See FIXTURES (LUMINAIRES) LIGHTING, Lighting Track. . Ferm's Finder

TRAFFIC SIGNALS

Ungrounded Signal Conductors with Green Insulation Permitted . . . . 250.119 Ex. 3

TRAILERS, TYPES OF

Park Trailers . . . . Art. 552

Recreational Vehicles . . . . Art. 551

Travel Trailers, Definition 551.2

TRANSFER SWITCHES

Definition of . . . . Art. 100 Part I

Emergency Systems

Documentation . . . . 700.5(E)

Electrically Operated and Mechanically Held . . . . 700.5(C)

Fire Protection of . . . . 700.10(D)

Identified as Component of Emergency System . 700.10(A)

Inadvertent Parallel Operation Shall be Avoided . . 700.5(B)

Maintenance and Repair . . . . 700.3(F)

Normal Power Wiring Permitted in . . . . 700.10(B)

Provided for Generator Set. . . . . .700.12(B)(1)

Shall Supply Only Emergency Loads . . . . .700.5(D)

To Be Listed for Emergency System Use . . . . . . 700.5(A)

Essential Electrical Systems

Ambulatory Health Care Centers 517.45

Clinics, Medical and Dental Offices, etc. 517.25

Hospitals

Equipment Branch Connection to Alternate Source 517.35

Illumination of Means of Egress (Life Safety Branch) . . .
. . . . 517.33(A)

Location of Components 517.30

Maximum Time for Transfer (10 Seconds) 517.31

Note: For typical systems, *See* . . . . .Info. Notes
. . . . Figures 517.31(a) & (b)

Number of Transfer Switches . . . . 517.31(B)

Optional Loads from Separate Transfer Switches . . . . .
. . . . .517.31(B)(1)

Separation of Wiring. . . . . .517.31(C)(1)

Subdivision of Critical Branch . . . . 517.34(C) Info. Note

Nursing Homes and Limited Care Facilities

Connection to Equipment Branch 517.44

Illumination of Means of Egress (Life Safety Branch) . . .

. . . . 517.43(A)

Location of Components . . . . 517.41(C)

Note: For typical systems, *See* . . . .
. . . . Figure 517.42(a) & (b)

Number of Transfer Switches . . . . 517.42(B)

Separation of Wiring . . . . 517.42(D)(1)

Relative Location of Switches and Ground-fault Protection .
. . . . 517.17(B)

Fire Pumps

Continuity of Power 695.4

Equipment Location 695.12

Equipment to Be Listed for Fire Pump Service 695.10

No Other Loads Permitted to be Supplied from . . 695.6(E)

Remote Devices, not to prevent operation of . . . 695.14(C)

Fuel Cell Systems 692.59

Health Care Facilities (General)

Critical Care (Category 1) Spaces

Patient Bed Location Branch Circuits . . . 517.19(A) Ex. 2

Patient Bed Location Receptacles . . . . . 517.19(B)(1)(2)

General Care (Category 2) Areas Patient Bed Location
Circuits . . . . 517.18(A) Ex. 3

Legally Required Standby

Electrically Operated and Mechanically Held . . . . 701.5(C)

Inadvertent Parallel Operation Shall be Avoided . . 701.5(B)

Provided for Generator Set . . . . .701.12(B)(1)

To Be Automatic and Identified for the Use . . . . 701. 5(A)

Optional Standby Power Systems

Transfer Equipment. 702.5

See (WPTZ) . . . .*UL Product Spec*

TRANSFORMER VAULTS

Doorways 450.43

Fire Ratings . . . . 450.43(A)

Locks and Panic Hardware . . . . 450.43(C)

Sill or Curb Required . . . . 450.43(B)

Drainage 450.46

Enclosures and Access 110.31

Fire Resistivity, Over 1000 Volts . . . . 110.31(A)

Illumination . . . . 110.34(D)

Location of 450.41

Storage in, Prohibited 450.48

Ventilation Openings 450.45

Walls, Roofs and Floors, Construction and Fire Rating . 450.42

Water Pipes and Accessories 450.47

T

Working Space, Entrance and Access 110.33

Working Space and Guarding. 110.34

TRANSFORMERS AND TRANSFORMERS VAULT . . . Art. 450

Access (Limited Working Space) . . . . .110.26(A)(4)

Alternating Current Systems to Be Grounded 250.20

Alternating Current Systems Not Required to Be Grounded 250.21

(Arc) Electric Welders . . . . Art. 630

Askarel-Insulated, Indoors 450.25

Autotransformers, 1000 Volts or Less 450.4

   Audio Signal Processing . . . . 640.9(D)

   Ballasts 410.138

   Branch-Circuits 210.9

   Feeders 215.11

   For Grounding 3-Phase, 3-Wire Systems 450.5

   Motor Starting. 430.82(B)

   Overcurrent Protection. . . . . 450.4(A)

   Prohibited in Park Trailers . . . . 552.20(E)

   Prohibited in Recreational Vehicles . . . . 551.20(E)

   Transformer Field-Connected as Autotransformer . . . . 450.4(B)

Buck & Boost . . . . 210.9 Ex. 1 & 2

   Common Use for Autotransformers 450.4

Calculations for, *See* CALCULATIONS . . . . . . Ferm's Finder

Carnivals, Circuses, Fairs, and Similar Events . . . . 525.10(B)

Definitions 450.2

Disconnecting Means 450.14

Dry-Type

   Indoors

      Not Over 112 1/2 kVA . . . . 450.21(A)

      Over 112 1/2 kVA . . . . 450.21(B)

      Over 35,000 Volts to Be in Vault . . . . 450.21(C)

   Outdoors. 450.22

Electrically Actuated Fuse . . . . Table 450.3(A) Note 4

Fire Pumps, for 695.5

   Feeder Source . . . . 695.5(C)

   Overcurrent Protection of . . . . 695.5(B)

   Sizing . . . . 695.5(A)

Fuse, Electrically Actuated . . . . Table 450.3(A) Note 4

Grounding of

   Dry-Type Transformer Enclosures . . . . 450.10(A)

   Exceptions from, for Certain Systems . . 250.30(A)(4) Ex 2.

   Metal Parts, Fences, Guards, Etc. . . . . 450.10(B)

Other Metal Parts . . . . 450.10(B)

   Outside Transformer Supplying Service . . . . 250.24(A)(2)

Guarding 450.8

Hazardous (Classified) Locations

   Class I Locations 501.100

      Control Transformers 501.120

   Class II Locations 502.100

      Control Transformers 502.120

      Signaling, Alarm, Etc. Systems 502.150

   Class III Locations 503.100

      Control Transformers 503.120

High Leg

   Feeders 110.15

   See HIGH LEG . . . . Ferm's Finder

Installation of 450.13

   Specific Provisions Applicable to Different Types of Transformers. 450 Part II

Isolating Transformers

   Class III Locations . . . . 503.155(A)

   Electrolytic Cells . . . . 668.20(B)

      Power Supply Circuits, Portable Equipment. . . 668.21(A)

   Induction and Dielectric Heating 665.5

   Integrated Electrical System, Control Circuits 685.14

   Isolated Power Systems, Health Care Facilities. . . . 517.160

   Lighting Systems 30 Volts or Less 411.7

   Optional Protective Technique, Critical Care (Category 1) Spaces. . . . . 517.19(F)

   Runway Tracks As Circuit Conductor . . . . . .610.21(F)(2)

   Systems Not Required to Be Grounded 250.21

   Underwater Luminaires (Lighting Fixtures) . . 680.23(A)(2)

   Wet Procedure Locations, Health Care Facilities . . . 517.20

Less-Flammable, Liquid-Insulated

   Indoor Installations . . . . 450.23(A)

   Outdoor Installations . . . . 450.23(B)

Location of 450.13

Marking of

   General . . . . 450.11(A)

   Source Marking (Reverse Feed) . . . . 450.11(B)

Modification of Existing Transformers 450.28

Motor Control Circuit 430.74

Nonflammable Fluid-Insulated 450.24

Oil-Insulated

   Indoor Installations 450.26

   Outdoor Installations 450.27

Overcurrent Protection of. 450.3

   1000 Volts or Less . . . . 450.3(B)

   Autotransformers, 1000 Volts or Less . . . . 450.4(A)

   Control Circuit Secondary Conductors. 430.74

   Electrically Actuated Fuse . . . . Table 450.3(A) Note 4

   Ground Reference for Fault Protection Devices . . . . .

   . . . . 450.5(B)(2)

   Grounding Autotransformers Three-Phase 4-Wire . . . . . .

   . . . . 450.5(A)(2)

   Over 1000 Volts . . . . 450.3(A)

     Current Transformers . . . . 240.100(A)(1)

   Panelboard Supplied from . . . . 408.36(B)

   Secondary Conductors (General) . . . . 240.4(F)

     Secondary Conductors (Specific). . . . . 240.21(C)

   Secondary Ties . . . . 450.6(B)

   Solar Photovoltaic Systems . . . . 690.9(F)

   Supervised Industrial Installations . . . . . . 240 Part VIII

   Supplying Fire Pumps . . . . 695.5(B)

   Supplying Transformer, Primary Plus Secondary

     Not Over 7.5 m (25 ft.) . . . . 240.21(B)(3)

   Voltage (Potential) Transformers . . . . 450.3(C)

   Wind Electric Systems . . . . 694.15(B)

Parallel Operation 450.7

Park Trailer Combination Systems . . . . 552.20(B)

Potential (Voltage) . . . . 450.3(C)

Power-Limited and Signaling Circuits

   Class 1 Circuits . . . . 725.41(A)(1)

   Class 2 and 3 Circuits . . . . 725.121(A)(1)

   Recreational Vehicle Combination Systems . . . . . 551.20(B)

   Autotransformers . . . . 551.20(E)

Remote Control, Circuits for

   Control Transformer in Controller Enclosure . . . 430.75(B)

   Class 1 Circuits . . . . 725.41(A)(1)

   Class 2 and 3 Circuits . . . . 725.121(A)(1)

Research and Development Use, Exempt . . . . . . 450.1 Ex. 8

Reverse Feeding . . . . 450.11(B)

Secondary Ties 450.6

Separately Derived Systems 250.30

   See SEPARATELY DERIVED SYSTEMS . . . . Ferm's Finder

Short-Circuit Current Available

   Circuit Impedance 110.10

Signs and Outline Lighting

   Ballasts, Transformers and Electronic Power Supplies and

   Class 2 Power Sources 600.21

   Enclosures 600.8

   Transformers and Electronic Power Supplies 600.23

Specific Provisions for Different Types . . . .

. . . . 450 Part II

Supplied from Feeders, Ampacity of Conductors. . 215.2(B)(1)

Taps, See TAPS . . . . Ferm's Finder

Terminal Bar Not Installed over Vented Area 450.10

Terminal Wiring Space 450.12

Three-Wire to Three-Wire . . . . 240.4(F)

Two-Winding, Underwater Lighting . . . . 680.23(A)(2)

Two-Wire to Two-Wire . . . . 240.4(F)

Vaults . . . . 450 Part III

Vented Portion, Terminal Bar not Installed 450.10

Ventilation of 450.9

Voltage (Potential) . . . . 450.3(C)

Working Space . . . . 110.26(A)

   Limited Access. . . . . 110.26(A)(4)

See Transformers (includes many types of) (XNWX) . . . . . .

. . . . .UL Product Spec

TRAVEL TRAILERS, RECREATIONAL VEHICLES, AND VEHICLE PARKS . . . . **Art. 551**

   Definition 551.2

   See RECREATIONAL VEHICLE . . . . Ferm's Finder

TRAY CABLE, POWER AND CONTROL, TYPE TC . . . **Art. 336**

   Ampacity of 336.80

   Bends of 336.24

   Conductors

     Class 1 Circuits . . . . .336.104(C)

     Fire Alarm Systems . . . . .336.104(A)

     Thermocouple Circuits . . . . .336.104(B)

   Construction of . . . . 336 Part III

   Definition of 336.2

   Installation and Support 336.10

   Jacket (flame retardant) 336.116

   Listing 336.6

   Marking 336.120

   Uses Not Permitted 336.12

   Uses Permitted 336.10

   See Instrumentation Tray Cable, Type ITC . . . . Art. 727

TREES

   Not for Support of Overhead Conductor Spans 225.26

   Permitted for Support of Outdoor Lighting Luminaires

(Fixtures) . . . . 410.36(G)

Support, Holiday Lighting Branch Circuits . . . . 590.4(J) Ex.

Vegetation as Support 230.10

TUBING

Electric Discharge, Signs, etc. (Neon) 600.41

Electrical Metallic . . . . Art. 358

    See ELECTRICAL METALLIC TUBING. . . . Ferm's Finder

Electrical Nonmetallic . . . . Art. 362

    See ELECTRICAL NONMETALLIC TUBING . . . .
. . . . Ferm's Finder

Field-Installed Skeleton . . . . 600 Part II

Flexible Metallic . . . . Art. 360

    See FLEXIBLE METALLIC TUBING . . . . . Ferm's Finder

Neon, Definition of 600.2

Skeleton, Definition 600.2

TURBINE *See* **WIND ELECTRIC SYSTEMS** . . . . **Ferm's Finder**

**TV AND MOTION PICTURE STUDIOS AND SIMILAR
LOCATIONS** . . . . **Art. 530**
    See THEATERS, AUDIENCE AREAS OF MOTION PICTURE
AND TELEVISION STUDIOS, AND SIMILAR LOCATIONS
Ferm's Finder

TV AND RADIO DISTRIBUTION . . . . **Art. 820**
    See COMMUNITY ANTENNA TELEVISION AND RADIO
DISTRIBUTION . . . . Ferm's Finder

TV AND RADIO EQUIPMENT . . . . **Art. 810**
    See RADIO AND TELEVISION EQUIPMENT. Ferm's Finder

TYPES OF CONSTRUCTION . . . . **Informative Annex E**

UF WIRE (Direct Burial) . . . . **Art. 340**
See UNDERGROUND FEEDER AND BRANCH-CIRCUIT
CABLE . . . . Ferm's Finder

UFER GROUND (Concrete-Encased Electrode) . . **250.52(A)(3)**
See Rebar . . . . Ferm's Finder

UNBALANCED INTERCONNECTIONS

Energy Storage Systems . . . . 706.8(D)

Fuel Cell Systems 692.64

Interconnected Electric Production Sources

    Single Phase . . . . 705.100(A)

    Three Phase . . . . 705.100(B)

Solar Photovoltaic Systems 705.100

Wind Electric Systems 705.100

UNDER BUILDINGS

Cables to Be in Raceway . . . . 300.5(C)

Service Conductors 230.6

UNDERFLOOR RACEWAYS . . . . **Art. 390**

Ampacity of Conductors 390.17

Connections to Cabinets, Wall Outlets 390.15

Covering 390.4

Dead Ends 390.11

Definition 390.2

Discontinued Outlets 390.8

Inserts 390.14

Junction Boxes 390.13

Laid in Straight Lines 390.9

Markers at Ends 390.10

Maximum Number of Conductors 390.6

Size of Conductors 390.5

Splices & Taps 390.7

Uses Not Permitted . . . . 390.3(B)

Uses Permitted . . . . 390.3(A)

UNDERGROUND CABLES

Optical Fiber Cables 770.47

Type MC . . . . 300.5(C) Ex. 2

Type MI . . . . 300.5(C) Ex. 1

UNDERGROUND ENCLOSURES

Manholes . . . . 110 Part V

Handhole Enclosures 314.30

    Over 1000 Volts . . . . 314.70(C)

Subsurface Enclosures, Accessibility 314.29

**UNDERGROUND FEEDER AND BRANCH-CIRCUIT CABLE,
TYPE UF** . . . . **Art. 340**

Ampacity of 340.80

Bending Radius 340.24

Conductor Construction and Applications . . Table 310.104(A)

Construction . . . . 340 Part III

Definition 340.2

Ground Movement . . . . 300.5(J)

Installed as Nonmetallic-Sheathed Cable . . . . 340.10(4)

Listing Requirements 340.6

Protection of 300.5

Uses Not Permitted 340.12

Uses Permitted 340.10

See (YDUX) . . . . *UL Product Spec*

UNDERGROUND, RACEWAYS, WET LOCATIONS

1000 Volts or Less . . . . 300.5(B)

Over 1000 Volts . . . . 300.50(B)

UNDERGROUND SERVICE

Entrance Cable Type USE . . . . Art. 338

UNDERGROUND SERVICE CONDUCTORS . . . . . 230 Part III

See Service Conductors, Underground . . . . . *Ferm's Finder*

UNDERGROUND WIRING

Aluminum Conduit (Not Permitted without Supplementary

   Corrosion Protection) . . . . 344.10(A)(3) and (B)(2)

   See (DYWV) . . . . *UL Product Spec*

Ampacity of Conductors Underground

   0 to 2000 Volts . . . . .Table 310.15(B)(16)

     Under Engineering Supervision — Formula . . 310.15(C)

   2001 to 35,000 Volts. Tables 310.60(C)(77) to 310.60(C)(86)

     Application of Tables 310.60

   Note: For examples of formulas, *See*. . Informative Annex B

Buried Conductors (Direct Burial)

   1000 Volts or Less 300.5

   Conductor Application and Insulation . . . Table 310.104(A)

   Identified for Use . . . . 310.10(F)

   Over 1000 Volts 300.50

   Type UF . . . . 340.10(1)

   Type USE 338.2

Concrete Encased (Raceways) . . . . Table 300.5 Note 2

Conductor Types in Wet Locations . . . . 310.10(C)

Cover Requirements

   1000 Volts or Less . . . . Table 300.5

   Over 1000 Volts . . . . Table 300.50

Earth Movement . . . . 300.5(J)

   Over 1000 Volts . . . . 300.50(C)

Electrical Metallic Tubing . . . . 358.10(B)

   Supplementary Corrosion Protection Required

See (FJMX) . . . .*UL Product Spec*

High Density Polyethylene Conduit (HDPE) . . . . 353.10(4)

Installation, 1000 Volts and Less 300.5

   Backfill . . . . 300.5(F)

   Definition of Cover . . . . Table 300.5 Note 1

   Minimum Cover Requirements . . . . Table 300.5

Installation, Over 1000 Volts 300.50

   Backfill . . . . 300.50(E)

   Definition of Cover . . . . Table 300.50 Note [a]

   Minimum Cover Requirements . . . . Table 300.50

Intermediate Metal Conduit . . . . 342.10(B)

Lighting System- Low Voltage . . . . Table 300.5 Note[a]

Liquidtight Flexible Metal Conduit . . . . 350.10(3)

Liquidtight Flexible Nonmetallic Conduit. . . . . . 356.10(4)

Listed Low-Voltage Lighting System . . . . . . Table 300.5 Note[b]

Nonmetallic Underground Conduit with Conductors . . 354.10

Over 1000 Volts, Nominal 300.50

   See OVER 1000 VOLTS, NOMINAL . . . . . . *Ferm's Finder*

Pool, Spa, and Fountain Lighting. . . . . Table 300.5 Note[b]

Protection of . . . . 300.5(D)

   Over 1000 Volts . . . . 300.50(C)

Recreational Vehicle Parks 551.80

Reinforced Thermosetting Resin Conduit . . . . . 355.10(G)

Rigid Metal Conduit . . . . 344.10(B)

   Aluminum (Not Permitted without Supplementary Corrosion

   Protection)

     See (DYWV) . . . . *UL Product Spec*

Rigid PVC Conduit . . . . 352.10(G)

   See RIGID PVC CONDUIT . . . . *Ferm's Finder*

Rock Encountered (reduction of depth) . . . Table 300.5 Note 5

"S" Loops . . . . 300.5(J) IN

Services . . . . 230 Part III

   Protection against Physical Damage . . . . 230.50(A)

Splices and Taps . . . . 110.14(B)

   1000 Volts or Less . . . . 300.5(E)

   Over 1000 Volts . . . . 300.50(D)

Swimming Pool Area 680.11

Under Hazardous (Classified) Areas

   Aircraft Hangars 513.8

     Sealing 513.9

   Bulk Storage Plant 515.8

     Sealing 515.9

   Class I, Division 1 . . . . 501.10(A) Ex.

   Commercial Garages, Major 511.8

U

Commercial Garages, Minor. 511.8

Motor Fuel Dispensing Facilities 514.8

   Sealing. 514.9

Wet Locations . . . . 310.10(C)

Definition of . . . . Art. 100

Listing for . . . . 300.5(B)

   Over 1000 Volts. . . . . 300.50(B)

Note: Installations underground, in concrete slabs, or in direct contact with the earth are "Locations, Wet". . Art. 100

UNGROUNDED

Definition of . . . . Art. 100

UNGROUNDED SYSTEMS

3-Phase and 2-Phase Systems . . . . .240.15(B)(3)

3-Wire Direct Current Circuits. . . . . .240.15(B)(4)

AC Systems Not Required to Be Grounded 250.21

AC Systems, Signage . . . . 408.3(F)(2)

Circuits Not to Be Grounded 250.22

Cranes and Hoists . . . . .610.21(F)(2)

Critical Care (Category 1) Spaces (Optional) . . . . . 517.19(F)

   Isolated Power System Grounding. . . . . 517.19(G)

DC Systems . . . . 250.162(A) Ex.

DC System, Signage . . . . 408.3(F)(4)

Direct-Current Ground-Fault Detection . . . . . . 250.167(A)

Electric Cranes, Hoists, Class III Locations . . . . . 503.155(A)

Electrolytic Cells . . . . Art. 668

Equipment Grounding Conductor Connections . . .250.130(B)

Feeder Identification

   Alternating-Current Systems, Ungrounded Conductors . . . . .215.12(C)(1)

   Direct-Current Systems, Ungrounded Conductors . . . . .215.12(C)(2)

General Requirements . . . . 250.4(B)

Ground Detectors

   AC Systems 50 to 1000 Volts. . . . . 250.21(B)

   Critical Care (Category 1) Spaces (Optional) . . . 517.19(F)

   Electric Cranes and Hoists, Class III Locations . 503.155(A)

   Isolated Power Systems . . . . 517.160(B)

   Wet Procedure Locations, Hospitals, etc. . . . . . 517.20(B)

Ground-Fault Detections . . . . 250.167(A)

Induction and Dielectric Heating, Generator Output . . . 665.5

Integrated Electrical Systems, DC 685.12

   Control Circuits 685.14

Isolated Power Systems, Hospitals . . . . 517 Part VII

Circuits in Anesthetizing Locations . . . . 517.63(F)

Inhalation Anesthetizing Locations . . . . 517.61(A)(1)& (2)

Location of Isolated Power Systems . . . . 517.63(E)

Marking of . . . . 250.21(C)

Lighting Systems Operating at 30 Volts or Less . . . . 411.6(A)

Separately Derived Systems, AC . . . . 250.30(B)

Separately Derived Systems, DC 250.169

Swimming Pool Luminaire (Lighting Fixture) Transformers . . . . .680.23(A)(2)

Switchboards and Panelboards . . . . 408.3(F)

Voltage to Ground (Definition of) . . . . Art. 100 Part I

Wet Procedure Locations, Hospitals, etc. . . . . 517.20(B)

UNINTERRUPTIBLE POWER SUPPLY EQUIPMENT

Critical Operations Power Systems. . . . . 708.20(G)

Definition 708.2

Emergency System Power Supply . . . . 700.12(C)

Information Technology Equipment 645.11

Legally Required Standby Systems . . . . 701.12(C)

See (YEDU) .UL Product Spec

UNIT EQUIPMENT

Battery-Powered Lighting Units 517.2

Emergency Systems . . . . 700.12(F)

   Components . . . . .700.12(F)(1)

   Installation . . . . .700.12(F)(2)

Legally Required Standby Systems . . . . 701.12(G)

Modular Data Systems. 646.17

UNIT SUBSTATIONS

See SERVICE EQUIPMENT . . . . Ferm's Finder

See (YEFR) . . . . .UL Product Spec

See (Over 1000 Volts, Nominal) (YEFV) . . . .UL Product Spec

UNUSED OPENINGS TO BE CLOSED . . . . 110.12(A)

Cabinets, Cutout Boxes, and Meter Socket Enclosures . . . . . 312.5(A)

Outlet, Device, Pull and Junction Boxes, Conduit Bodies . . . . 314.17(A)

USB CHARGER

Faceplate . . . . 406.6(D)

Receptacle. . . . . 406.3(F)

USE OF EQUIPMENT. 110.3

USE WIRE (Direct Burial) **338.2**

See SERVICE ENTRANCE CABLE . . . . Ferm's Finder

See (TYLZ) . . . .*UL Product Spec*

UTILITY, ELECTRIC

Connections, Meter Enclosures 230.82

Fire Pump . . . . 695.3(A)(1)

Ground-Fault Protection for Personnel 590.6

Installations Covered by *NEC* . . . . 90.2(A)

Installation Not Covered by *NEC*. . . . . .90.2(B)

Meter Sockets (not required to be listed) . . . . . . 230.66 Ex

Point of Demarcation (see Service Point) . . Art. 100 Info Note

Special Permission .90.2(C)

Transfer Equipment 702.5

UTILITY-INTERACTIVE INVERTER

Definition of . . . . Art. 100

Energy Storage Systems

    Charge Control . . . . .706.23(B)(3)

    Inverter Output Circuit (Defined). 706.2

    Loss of Power . . . . 706.8(C)

Fuel Cell Systems, Point of Connection 692.65

    Output Circuit (Defined). 692.2

Interconnected Electric Power Production Sources . . . 705.12

    Energy Storage. 705.80

    Hybrid Systems 705.82

    Mounted in Not-Readily-Accessible Locations 705.70

    Output Circuit, Interactive Inverter

        Definition of 705.2

        Maximum Current Rating. . . . . 705.60(A)(2)

    Overcurrent Protection. 705.65

Permitted Without Grounded Conductor . . . . . . .200.3 Ex.

Solar Photovoltaic Systems

    Diversion Charge Controller (Defined) 690.27

    Mounted in Not-Readily-Accessible Locations . . 690.15(A)

    Output Circuit. 690.6(B)

Wind Electric Systems . . . . Art. 694

    Inverter Output Circuit (Defined). 694.2

UTILIZATION EQUIPMENT

Aircraft Hangars, Portable Utilization Equipment 513.10(E)(2)

Boxes

    Depth of 314.24

    For Support of . . . . 314.27(D)

Branch Circuits, Permissible Loads 210.23

Bulk Storage Plants, Portable Utilization Equipment . 515.7(C)

Class I Locations 501.135

Class II Locations 502.135

Class III Locations 503.135

Definition of . . . . Art. 100

Spray Areas, Class I Locations . . . . 516.6(D)

Utilization Equipment, Device Fill in Boxes . . . .314.16(B)(4)

UL's STANDARDS FOR SAFETY CATALOG OF STANDARDS

All published and proposed STANDARDS FOR SAFETY are listed both alphabetically and by UL subject number in UL's CATALOG OF STANDARDS FOR SAFETY. Issued January and July of each year, the catalog includes the latest edition and revision dates of all standards, description of UL's Revision Subscription Service, and a listing of UL standards covering specific product areas that are available as Sets.

UL's Product Spec tells what products are covered by each UL standard, and which UL standard covers what products. Over 500 generic product categories are listed, and the index gives more than 3,000 examples from the 12,000 specific product types covered in the scope of UL's standards. There is also an alphabetical listing of keywords from the titles of all UL standards. It is available online at productspec.ul.com/.

STANDARDS GLOSSARY

UL's STANDARDS GLOSSARY is a compilation of terms and their definitions taken from the glossary sections of UL standards.

V

VACUUM MACHINES

Central Units Within Single Family Dwellings 422.15

GFCI Protection . . . . 422.5(A)(1)

VAPORS, FLAMMABLE

See HAZARDOUS (CLASSIFIED) LOCATIONS Ferm's Finder

VAULTS

Access to 110.76

Capacitors . . . . 460.2(A)

Equipment Work Space 110.73

Film Storage . . . . 530 Part V

General . . . . 110 Part V

Over 1000 Volts, Nominal, Enclosures for Installations . 110.31

Electrical Vaults . . . . 110.31(A)

Service Conductors Over 35,000 Volts. 230.212

Services Considered Outside the Building . . . . . . 230.6(3)

Strength, of Structure 110.71

Transformer . . . . 450 Part III

Specific Provisions for Different Types of Transformers . 450 Part II

Ventilation 110.77

Guarding of Ventilating Grating 110.78

VEHICLES

Commercial Garages, Repair and Storage . . . . Art. 511

Covered by Code. . . . . 90.2(A)(1)

Garage (for storage of)

Definition . . . . Art. 100

GFCI Protection

Dwelling Units . . . . 210.8(A)

Other Than Dwelling Units . . . . 210.8(B)(8)

Receptacle Outlet . . . . .210.52(G)(1)

Not Covered by Code . . . . 90.2(B)(1)

See ELECTRIC VEHICLES. . . . . Ferm's Finder

See Electrified Truck Parking Spaces . . . . . . Ferm's Finder

See RECREATIONAL VEHICLES. . . . . Ferm's Finder

VENDING MACHINES

Ground-Fault Circuit-Interrupter to be Readily Accessible . . . . 422.5(A)(5)

See ANSI/UL 541-2010, Standard for Refrigerated Vending Machines, or ANSI/UL 751-2010, Standard for Vending Machines

VENTILATED (Definition of) . . . . Art. 100 Part I

VENTILATING DUCTS, WIRING IN Ducts, Plenums, etc. 300.22

Spread of Fire or Products of Combustion 300.21

VENTILATING PIPING FOR MOTORS

Class II Locations 502.128

Class III Locations 503.128

VENTILATION

Aircraft Hangars . . . . 513.3(B) and (D)

Ammonia (Refrigerant Machinery Rooms) . . . .

Class and Division . . . . 500.5(A)

Zones . . . . 505.5(A)

Battery Locations 480.10

Bulk Storage Plants. . . . . Table 515.3

Commercial Garages, Repair & Storage . . . . 511.3(C) and (D)

Electric Vehicles 625.52

Minimum Required Cubic Feet Per Minute (CFM) . . . . Table 625.52(B)(1)(b)

Minimum Required Cubic Meters Per Minute (m³/min) . . . . Table 625.52(B)(1)

Required Markings . . . . 625.15(B) and (C)

Equipment, General . . . . 110.13(B)

Information Technology, under Raised Floors . . . . 645.5(E)

Motors . . . . 430.14(A)

Exposed to Dust Accumulations 430.16

Motor Fuel Dispensing Facilities . . Table 514.3(B)(1) and (2)

Spray Application, Dipping & Coating. 516.5

Spray Booth (Defined) . . . . .516.2 Info. Note

Spread of Fire 300.21

System Controls, Tunnels, Over 1000 Volts 110.57

Transformers 450.9

Vaults 450.45

Ventilation to Open Air 110.77

Guarding of Ventilation Grating 110.78

Zone 0, 1, and 2 Locations . . . . Art. 505

Zone 20, 21, and 22 Locations . . . . Art. 506

VERTICAL SURFACES (BOXES) . . . . 314.27(A)(1)

VESSELS & PIPELINES, HEATING . . . . .Art. 427

See FIXED ELECTRIC HEATING EQUIPMENT FOR PIPELINES AND VESSELS . . . . Ferm's Finder

VISIBLE (IN SIGHT FROM, WITHIN SIGHT) . . . . . . ART. 100

VOLTAGE

Branch Circuit, Limitations 210.6

Considered 110.4

Definition of

High Voltage 490.2

Low Voltage 551.2

Low Voltage Contact Limit 680.2

Photovoltaic System Voltage 690.2

Voltage (Nominal) . . . . Art. 100 Part I

Voltage (of a Circuit) . . . . Art. 100 Part I

Voltage for Calculations . . . . 220.5(A)

Voltage to Ground . . . . Art. 100 Part I

Drop

See VOLTAGE DROP . . . . Ferm's Finder

Electric Vehicle Charging System, Nominal 625.4

Elevator Equipment Working Clearances . . . . . . 620.5(D)

Less than 50 Volts . . . . Art. 720

    Class 1, 2, & 3 Remote Control, Signaling Circuits . Art. 725

    Grounding of . . . . 250.20(A)

Lighting Equipment Installed Outdoors 225.7

Limitations . . . . 300.2(A)

    Between Adjacent Snap Switches . . . . 404.8(B)

    Between Adjacent Receptacles/Devices. . . . . 406.5(J)

    Electric-Discharge Lighting Systems (Over 1000 Volts) . . .
    . . . . 410 Part XIII

    Electric-Discharge Lighting Systems (Under 1000 Volts) . .
    . . . . 410 Part XII

    Elevators, Etc. (Article 620) 620.3

    Rating and Use, Snap Switches. 404.14

    See (WJQR). . . . . *UL Product Spec*

    Swimming Pool Luminaires (Lighting Fixtures) . . . .
    . . . . .680.23(A)(4)

Outdoor Overhead Conductors over 1000 Volts . . . . Art. 399

Over 1000 Volts, Nominal

    See OVER 1000 VOLTS, NOMINAL . . . . . . Ferm's Finder

    Photovoltaic System Voltage, Maximum . . . . . 690.7(A)

VOLTAGE DROP

AC Resistance and Reactance . . . . Chapter 9 Table 9

Branch Circuit 3% Recommended . . . 210.19(A) Info. Note 4

Conductors 0-2000 Volts, General . . 310.15(A)(1) Info. Note 1

DC Resistance of Conductors . . . . Chapter 9 Table 8

Feeder 3% (Feeder Plus Branch Circuit 5%) . . . .
. . . . 215.2(A)(1)(b) Info. Note 2

Fire Pumps 695.7

Sensitive Electronic Equipment. . . . . 647.4(D)

See Voltage Drop Tables . . . . . . *Ferm's Charts and Formulas*

Note: When conductors are adjusted in size, such as to

    compensate for voltage drop, equipment ground wires, where

    required, shall be adjusted proportionately in size according

    to circular mil areas. *See* . . . . 250.122(B)

See Voltage Drop Section

    See Ampere-feet Method. . . . . *Ferm's Charts and Formulas*

    See Equipment Grounding Conductor Adjustment. . . . . .
    . . . . *Ferm's Charts and Formulas*

    See Voltage Drop Formulas . . . .
    . . . . *Ferm's Charts and Formulas*

VOLTAGE (POTENTIAL) TRANSFORMER . . . . . . .450.3(C)

VOLTAGE VARIATIONS

See Multiplier Formula . . . . *Ferm's Charts and Formulas*

See Multiplier Table . . . . *Ferm's Charts and Formulas*

VOLT-AMPERES

Class 1 Power-Limited Circuits . . . . 725.41(A)(2)

Class 2 & 3 AC Power-Limited Circuits   Chapter 9 Table 11(A)

Class 2 & 3 DC Power-Limited Circuits   Chapter 9 Table 11(B)

Lighting Track, 150 Volt-Amperes Per 600 mm (2 ft) 220.43(B)

Power-Limited Fire Alarms, AC, PLFA . Chapter 9 Table 12(A)

Power-Limited Fire Alarms, DC, PLFA . Chapter 9 Table 12(B)

    See CLASS 1, 2 & 3 REMOTE CONTROL CIRCUITS . . .
    Ferm's Finder

Receptacle Load, Nondwelling Use 180 Volt-amperes 220.14(I)

Used for Load Calculations . . . . Art. 220

WADING POOLS (Definition of) 680.2

Applicability of Article 680 to. 680.1

WARNING RIBBON

Underground Conductors

    Over 1000 Volts (Direct-Buried Cables). . . . .
    . . . . Table 300.50 Note b and d

    Under 1000 Volts (Service Conductors). . . . . 300.5(D)(3)

WARNING SIGNS

Aircraft Hangers

    Aircraft Battery Charging and Equipment . . . . 513.10(B)

    External Power Sources for Energizing Aircraft . . . .
    513.10(C)(2)

    Mobile Servicing Equipment with Electrical Components . .
    . . . . 513.10(D)

    Mobile Stanchions . . . . 513.7(F)

ANSI Standard

    See . . . *ANSI Z535.4-2011, Product Safety Signs and Labels*

Arc-Flash Hazard Warning 110.16

Assembly Occupancies (Temporary Wiring in Cable Trays) . .
. . . . 518.3(B) Ex.

Available Fault Current (Non-Dwelling Units) 110.24

Boilers

    Fixed Electric Space Heating Equipment . . . . . . .424.86(5)

    Fixed Resistance and Electrode Industrial Process Heating
    Equipment . . . . .425.86(5)

Cable Trays

Containing Conductors Over 600 Volts . . . . . 392.18(H)

Containing Service Conductors 230.44

Capacitors, Isolating or Disconnecting Switches with No Interrupting Rating . . . . 460.24(B)(2)

Disconnecting Means, Series Rated Combination Systems 110.22

Electrically Heated Pipelines and Vessels 427.13

Electroplating 669.7

Electrostatic Spraying Equipment . 516.10(A)(8), 516.10(B)(4)

Elevators, Escalators, etc.

More Than One Driving Machine in a Machine Room . . . . 620.51(D)

Power Circuits (Exceeding 1000 Volts) . . . . 620.3(A)

Power from More Than One Source . . . . 620.52(B)

Emergency Sources . . . . 700.7(A)

Grounding Connection . . . . 700.7(B)

Enclosure for Electrical Installations In Places Accessible to Unqualified Persons

(Indoors) .110.31(B)(1)

Entrances to Rooms and Other Guarded Locations . 110.27(C)

Feed-Through Conductors in Switch and Overcurrent Device Enclosures. 312.8(A)

Field-Applied Hazard Markings . . . . 110.21(B)

Fire Pumps

Disconnect . . . . 695.4(B)(3)

Electric Utility Service Connection . . . . 695.3(A)(1)

Fuel Cell Systems

Disconnecting Means 692.17

Point of Connection . . . . 692.65, 705.12(D)(2)

Stand-Alone Systems . . . . 692.10(C)

Stored Energy 692.56

Generator, Power Inlet Use . . . . 702.7(C)

Hazardous (Classified) Locations

Class 1 Locations

Meters, Instruments, and Relays (Cord-and-Plug Connection) . . . . 501.105(B)(6)

Induction and Dielectric Heating Equipment 665.23

Interconnected Electric Power Production Sources

Disconnect Device 705.22

Inverter Output Connection . . . . 705.12(B)

Intrinsically Safe Wiring . . . . 504.80(B)

Knife Switches (Energized in the Open Position). . 404.6(C) Ex

Legally Required Standby Systems . . . . 701.7(A)

Remote Grounding Connection. . . . . 701.7(B)

Marinas and Boatyards

Electric Shock Hazard- Swimming. 555.24

Wiring Over and Under Navigable Water. . . . . .555.13(B)(3) Info Note

Mobile Home

Outside Heating/Air-Conditioning Equipment . . 550.20(B)

Mobile Home Service Equipment (Grounding Electrode) . . . . .550.32(B)(7)

Mobile Home Service Equipment (125/250-Volt Receptacle) . . . . 550.32(G)

Motion Picture Projection Rooms [Cellulose Acetate (Safety) Film]. . . . . 540.11(B) Ex No 1

Motors

Control Circuits (Disconnection) . . . . . 430.75(A) Ex No 1

Controller Disconnecting Means (Over 1000 Volts) . . . . .430.102(A) Ex 1

Energy from More Than One Source 430.113

Optional Standby Systems. . . . . 702.7(A)

Remote Grounding Connection. . . . . 702.7(B)

Outdoor Electric Deicing and Snow-Melting Equipment 426.13

Outside Heating/Air-Conditioning Equipment . . . 552.59(B)

Prewiring for Air-Conditioning . . . . 552.48(P)

Over 1000 Volts, Nominal

Conductor Access in Conduit and Cable Systems . . 300.45

Distribution Cutouts and Fuse Links, Expulsion Type . . . . .490.21(C)(2)

Fused Interrupter Switches (Backfeed) . . . . . . 490.44(B)

High-Voltage Fuses (More Than One Source) . . . . 490.21(B)(7) Ex.

Load Interrupters (More Than One Switch) . . . . 490.21(E)

Mobile and Portable Equipment Enclosures 490.53

Outside Branch Circuit or Feeder Disconnecting

Means (Fused Cutouts) . . . . 225.52(B) Ex

Power and Cable Connections to Mobile Machines. . 490.55

Pull and Junction Boxes . . . . 314.72(E)

Rooms and Enclosures . . . . 110.34(C)

Substations 490.48

Transformer with Exposed Live Parts . . . . 450.8(D)

Park Trailer

Electrical Entrance (Correct Ampere Rating) . . . 552.44(D)

Outdoor Heating and Air Conditioning Outlets. . 552.59(B)

Prewiring for Air-Conditioning . . . . 552.48(P)

Prewiring for Other Circuits . . . . 552.48(Q)

Power Inlet, Portable Generator Use . . . . 702.7(C)

Recreational Vehicles

Electrical Entrance (Correct Ampere Rating) . . . 551.46(D)

Prewiring for Air-Conditioning . . . . 551.47(Q)

Prewiring for Branch Circuits . . . . 551.47(S)

Prewiring for Generators . . . . 551.47(R)

Site Supply Equipment . . . . 551.77(F)

Signage Requirements . . . . 110.21(B)

Signs

Disconnect . . . . 600.6(A)(1) Ex 2

Retrofit Illumination Systems . . . . 600.4(B)

Servicing Purposes . . . . 600.6(A)(2)

Spas and Hot Tubs (Emergency Switch) 680.41

Sensitive Electronic Equipment (Technical Power). 647.7(A)(2)

Solar Photovoltaic Systems

AC PV Modules 690.52

DC PV Power Source 690.53

DC PV Source and Output Circuits Inside a Building

(Wiring Methods and Enclosures Containing PV Circuits)

. . . . .690.31(G)(3)

Bipolar Source and Output Circuits . . . . 690.7(C)

Disconnecting Means . . . . 690.13(B)

Equipment Disconnecting Means . . . . 690.15(D)

Modules 690.51

Stand-Alone Systems, 120 Volts . . . . 710.15(C)

Spray Application, Dipping, and Coating Processes . . . .

. . . . .516.10(A)(8)

Handle (Grounding of Persons) . . . . 516.10(B)(3)

Stand-Alone Systems . . . . 710.15(C)

Switches, Position and Connection (Energized) . 404.6(C) Ex.

Temporary Wiring, Cable Trays in Exhibition Halls (Cable

Trays) . . . . 518.3(B) Ex.

Theaters, Motion Picture and Television Studios

Single-Pole Separable Connectors, Internal Parallel

Connections . . . . 530.22(C)

Single Primary Stage Switchboard (Dimmer Bank) . . . . .

. . . . .520.27(A)(3)

Transformers

Guarding of Transformers . . . . 450.8(D)

Remote Disconnecting Means 450.14

Voltage Warning (Exposed Live Parts) . . . . 450.8(D)

Welding Cable in Cable Trays. . . . . 630.42(C)

Wind Electric Systems

Disconnecting Means . . . . 694.22(A)

See ANSI Z535.4-2011 . . . . ANSI Z535.4

Note: It is important to pay careful attention to these references, as they provide a form of visual written instructions that are designed to keep people from getting injured or electrocuted.

See PERMANENT WARNING SIGNS (REQUIRED) . . Ferm's Finder

WASHERS, HIGH-PRESSURE SPRAY . . . . 422.5(A)(3)

WATER HEATERS, STORAGE OR INSTANTANEOUS-TYPE

Branch-Circuit Rating 125% . . . . 422.10(A)

Continuous Load 422.13

Swimming Pool Water Heaters 680.10

Controls 422.47

Disconnecting Means . . . . 422 Part III

Cord- and Plug-Connected 422.33

Permanently Connected 422.31

Unit Switch(es) 422.34

Grounding 250.110

See GROUNDING, Fixed Equipment. . . . . . Ferm's Finder

Overcurrent Protection 422.11

Rated More Than 48 Amperes, ASME Rated Vessel . . . . .

. . . . 422.11(F)

Swimming Pool Water Heaters 680.10

WATER METERS, FILTERING DEVICES, AND SIMILAR EQUIPMENT

Bond around to Maintain Continuity . . . . . . 250.53(D)(1)

WATER PIPE USED AS GROUNDING ELECTRODE. . . . .

. . . . . .250.52(A)(1)

Interior and Connected Within 5 feet . . . . 250.68(C)

Must be Supplemented . . . . 250.53(D)(2)

See GROUNDING, Electrodes. . . . . Ferm's Finder

WATER PUMPS

Motor-Operated . . . . 250.112(L)

Swimming Pools

Double Insulated . . . . .680.26(B)(6)

Receptacle Location. . . . . .680.22(A)(2)

WEATHERHEAD, ABOVE POWER COMPANY

Point of Attachment . . . . 230.54(C)

WEATHERPROOF

Definition of . . . . Art. 100 Part I

Agricultural Buildings

Equipment Enclosures, Boxes, Conduit Bodies, and Fittings

Installed in Damp or Wet Locations . . . . . . 547.5(C)(2)

Cabinets, Cutout Boxes, and Meter Socket Enclosures . 312.2

Carnivals, Circuses, Fairs and Similar Events

Portable Distribution or Termination Boxes . . . . 525.22(A)

Services . . . . 525.10(B)

Circuit Breaker (Surface-Mounted) . . . . 404.4(A)

Enclosure Types, Motor Controllers . . . . Table 110.28

Enclosures for Overcurrent Devices 240.32

Enclosures for Switches or Circuit Breakers. . 404.4(A) and (B)

Fixed Electric Heating Equipment for Pipelines and Vessels

Impedance Heating 427.25

Fixed Outdoor Electric Deicing and Snow-Melting Equipment

Impedance Heating 426.30

Marinas and Boatyards

Receptacles, Shore Power. . . . . 555.19(A)

Panelboards 408.37

Park Trailers, Direct Wired . . . . 552.48(O)(2)

Receptacles in Damp or Wet Locations 406.9

Recreational Vehicles, Direct Wired . . . . .551.47(P)(2)

Roof on Building before Installing the Equipment . . . 110.11

Switch (Surface-Mounted) . . . . 404.4(A)

Switchboards 408.16

Transformers, Dry-Type Installed Outdoors 450.22

Tunnel Installations over 1000 Volts (Enclosures) 110.59

WELDERS . . . . **Art. 630**
Arc Welders . . . . 630 Part II

Ampacity of Supply Conductors

Group of Welders . . . . 630.11(B)

Individual . . . . 630.11(A)

Disconnecting Means 630.13

Duty Cycle . . . . Table 630.11(A)

Overcurrent Protection

For Conductors. . . . . 630.12(B)

For Welders . . . . 630.12(A)

Listing 630.6

Resistance Welders . . . . 630 Part III

Ampacity of Supply Conductors

Groups of Welders . . . . 630.31(B)

Individual Welders, General . . . . 630.31(A)(1)

Individual Welder, Specific Operation . . . . 630.31(A)(2)

Disconnecting Means. 630.33

Duty Cycle . . . . Table 630.31(A)(2)

Overcurrent Protection

For Conductors. . . . . 630.32(B)

For Welders . . . . 630.32(A)

Welding Cable . . . . 630 Part IV

Cable Tray Installation 630.42

WELDING
Of or to Metal Raceways Not Permitted . . . . . . 300.18(B)

Splices . . . . 110.14(B)

WELDING CABLE
Cable Support . . . . 630.42(A)

Conductors 630.41

Fire Spread and Products of Combustion . . . . . . 630.42(B)

Installation in Cable Tray 630.42

Signage- Cable Tray . . . . 630.42(C)

See (ZMAY) . . . .*UL Product Spec*

WELDING, EXOTHERMIC
Concrete-Encased Electrode . . . . .250.52(3)

Connection of Grounding and Bonding Equipment . . 250.8

Equipotential Bonding Grid Connection . . . . . . 680.26(B)

Swimming Pools. . . . . 680.26(B)

Natural and Artificial Made Bodies of Water. . . . 682.33(C)

Fireproofed Structural Metal . . . . 250.68(A) Ex. 2

Grounding Conductor Connection to Electrodes 250.70

Hold-Down Bolts (to Concrete-Encased Electrode)250.68(C)(2)

Multiple Separately Derived Systems. . . . . 250.30(A)(6)(c)(3)

Natural and Artificial Made Bodies of Water . . . . . 682.33(C)

Splice in Grounding Electrode Conductor Permitted . . . . . .
. . . . .250.64(C)(1)

Swimming Pools . . . . 680.26(B)

WELLS
See GROUNDING, Fixed Equipment . . . . . . Ferm's Finder

See MOTORS . . . . Ferm's Finder

See PUMP HOUSES. . . . . Ferm's Finder

Thermoplastic-Insulated (ZLGR) . . . . . .*UL Product Spec*

Thermoset-Insulated(ZKST). . . . .*UL Product Spec*

Underground Feeder and Branch-Circuit Cable (YDUX). .
. . . .*UL Product Spec*

See UNDERGROUND WIRING . . . . Ferm's Finder

WET PROCEDURE LOCATIONS, HEALTH CARE FACILITIES . .
. . . .**517.20**

Definition 517.2

Isolated Power Systems . . . . 517.20(B)

Receptacles and Fixed Equipment . . . . 517.20(A)

WET LOCATIONS

Audio Signal Processing, Flexible Cords and Cables . 640.42(E)

Above Grade — Raceways, Interior of

    1000 Volts and Less 300.9

    Over 1000 Volts 300.38

Auxiliary Gutters (Nonmetallic) . . . . 366.6(A)(2)

Boxes in 314.15

Cabinets, Cutout Boxes & Meter Socket Enclosures in . . 312.2

Cables and Conductors in Raceways or Enclosures Underground. . . . . 300.5(B)

Class 1, Class 2, and Class 3 Circuits . . . . 725.3(L)

Class 1, 2, 3 Remote Control . . . . 725.179(E)

Conductors, Types . . . . 310.10(C)

    Applications . . . . Table 310.104(A)

    See Thermoplastic-Insulated (ZLGR) . . . . . *UL Product Spec*

    See Thermoset-Insulated (ZKST) . . . . *UL Product Spec*

    See Underground Feeder and Branch-Circuit Cable (YDUX)

    . . . . *UL Product Spec*

Critical Operations Power Systems, Floodplain Protection . . . . .708.10(C)(3)

Definition of . . . . Art. 100 Part I

    For Health Care Facilities, Patient Care Spaces 517.2

    Deteriorating Agents 110.11

    Electric Welders, Cord Assemblies . . . . 626.32(B)

Drainage Openings, Field Installed (Boxes, etc.) 314.15

Electrical Metallic Tubing, in . . . . 358.10(C)

Enameled Equipment . . . . 300.6(A)(1)

Fire Alarm . . . . 760.3(D)

(Fixtures) Luminaires in . . . . 410.10(A)

Flexible Metal Conduit, in (not permitted) . . . . . . 348.12(1)

Health Care Facilities, Wet Procedure Locations 517.20

Indoors . . . . .300.6(D)

Intermediate Metal Conduit, in . . . . 342.10(D)

Irrigation Cable .675.4(A)

Liquidtight Flexible Metal Conduit, in . . . . 350.10(1)

Liquidtight Flexible Nonmetallic Conduit, in. . . 356.10(2), (3)

Metal Clad Cable. . . . . .330.10(A)(11)

Metal Wireways, in . . . . 376.10(3)

Mineral-Insulated, Metal-Sheathed Cable. . . . . . .332.10(3)

Mounting of Equipment in . . . . 300.6(A) through (D)

Natural and Artificial Made Bodies of Water, Wiring Methods 682.13

Nonmetallic Wireways. . . . . 378.10(3)

NPLFA Cables 760.176

Neon, Electrode Enclosures. . . . . 600.42(H)(2)

Neon Secondary Conductors in Raceways . . . . . 600.42(G)

PLFA Cables 760.179

Other Than Dwelling Units . . . . 210.8(B)(6)

Outdoors, Dwelling Units . . . . 210.8(A)(3)

Outside Branch Circuits and Feeders 225.4

Panelboards, in 408.37

Raceways, Exterior Surfaces. 225.22

Raceways, Interior Surfaces

    Abovegrade (1000 Volts or Less) 300.9

    Abovegrade (Over 1000 Volts) 300.38

    Underground (1000 Volts or Less) . . . . 300.5(B)

    Underground (Over 1000 Volts) . . . . 300.50(B)

Receptacles in . . . . 406.9(B)

Rigid Metal Conduit, in . . . . 344.10(D)

Rigid PVC Conduit, in . . . . 352.10(D)

Service Heads . . . . 230.54(A)&(B)

Signs and Outline Lighting . . . . 600.9(D)

Switchboards, in 408.16

Switches, in 404.4

See WEATHERPROOF . . . . Ferm's Finder

Note: (Location, Wet) Installations underground or in concrete slabs in direct contact with the earth shall be classed "wet location." . . . . Art. 100 Part I

Underground — Raceways, Interior of

    1000 Volts and Less . . . . 300.5(B)

    Over 1000 Volts . . . . 300.50(B)

WIND ELECTRIC SYSTEMS . . . . Art. 694

Circuit Requirements 694.10

Circuit Sizing & Current 694.12

Components

    Interactive . . . . Figure 694.1(a)

    Stand-Alone . . . . Figure 694.1(b)

Definitions Applicable to System 694.2

Disconnecting Means . . . . 694 Part III

Diversion Load Controllers . . . . 694.7(C)

Energy Storage or Backup Power System Requirements. . . . . Art. 480

Flexible Cords and Cables . . . . 694.30(B)

Grounding and Bonding . . . . 694 Part V

    Equipment in General . . . . 694.40(A)

    Tower . . . . 694.40(B)

Guy Wires . . . . 694.40(B)(4)

Identification of Power Sources 694.54

Installation 694.7

Listing and Identification Required — Equipment . . . 694.7(B)

Marking . . . . 694.22(A), 694.22(C)(2)

Maximum Voltage 690.7

Overcurrent Protection 694.15

   Circuits and Equipment 694.12

Raceways, Tower Supports used as . . . . 694.7(F)

Receptacle (for Maintenance) . . . . 694.7(E)

Stand-Alone Systems 694.10

Storage Batteries . . . . Article 480

Supply Side of Service Equipment . . . . 230.82(6)

Surge Protective Device . . . . 694.7(D)

Systems Over 1000 Volts . . . . 694 Part VII

Tower Grounding . . . . 694.40(B)

Turbine Disabling 694.56

Turbine Shutdown 694.23

Wind Turbine Output Circuits . . . . 694.10(A)

Wiring Methods . . . . 694 Part IV

Working Clearances . . . . 694.7(G)

   Working Spaces . . . . .Table 694.7

See (ZGEN) . . . .*UL Product Spec*

WIRE

See CONDUCTORS . . . . Ferm's Finder

See (ZGZX) . . . .*UL Product Spec*

WIRELESS POWER TRANSFER EQUIPMENT . . Art. 625, Part IV

Charger Power Converter 625.2

Construction 625.102

Definitions 625.2

Electric Vehicle Coupling 625.16

Grounding 625.101

Installation (Charger Power Converter) . . . . .625.102(B)

Primary Pad .625.102(C)

Protection of Pad Output Cable . . . . 625.102(D)

WIRE BENDING SPACE

Auxiliary Gutters . . . . 366.58(A) and (B)

Back Wire-Bending Space . . . . 408.55(C)

Bare Metal Part, Minimum Spacing 408.56

Bending Radius Over 1000 Volts 300.34

Enclosures for Motor Controllers and Disconnects . 430.10(B)

Examination of Equipment . . . . 110.3(A)(3)

Manholes 110.74

Metal Wireways . . . . 376.23(A)

Motor Control Centers . . . . 430.97(C)

Motor Terminal Housings . . . . .430.12(B) & (C)

Nonmetallic Wireways . . . . 378.23(A) and (B)

Pull and Junction Boxes Not Over 1000 Volts 314.28

Pull and Junction Boxes Over 1000 Volts 314.71

Side Wire-Bending Space . . . . 408.55(B)

Switchboards and Panelboards . . . . 408.3(G)

   Clearance Entering Bus Enclosures 408.5

   Provisions for 408.55

Switch or Circuit Breaker Enclosures . . . . 404.3(A)

   How Measured 404.28

Terminals of Cabinets, Cutout Boxes, Meter Sockets . . . 312.6

Top and Bottom Wire-Bending Space . . . . 408.55(A)

Transformers 450.12

WIRE CONNECTORS

Direct Burial Use . . . . 110.14(B)

Electrical Connections 110.14

   Terminal . . . . 110.14(A)

   Splices . . . . 110.14(B)

Examination of Equipment 110.3

Fire Pump (shall not be permitted) . . . . 695.6(D)

See TERMINALS . . . . Ferm's Finder

See (ZMKQ) . . . .*UL Product Spec*

WIRE, Luminaire (FIXTURE) . . . . Art. 402

See FIXTURE WIRES, Fixture . . . . Ferm's Finder

WIRED LUMINAIRE (FIXTURE) SECTIONS . . . . 410.137(C)

WIREWAYS, METAL . . . . Art. 376

Conductors, Size 376.21

   Number of 376.22

Conductors Connected in Parallel 376.20

Dead Ends 376.58

Definition of 376.2

Deflected Insulated Conductors 376.23

Electrical and Mechanical Continuity . . . . 376.100(A)

Extensions from 376.70

Extensions through Walls . . . . 376.10(4)

Live Parts Required to be Covered . . . . 376.56(B)(4)

Marking 376.120

Power Distribution Blocks . . . . 376.56(B)

Listed For Line Side of Service Equipment . . 376.56(B)(1)

Smooth Rounded Edges . . . . 376.100(C)

Splices and Taps 376.56

Substantial Construction . . . . 376.100(B)

Supports

    Horizontal . . . . 376.30(A)

    Vertical . . . . 376.30(B)

Use

    Not Permitted 376.12

    Permitted 376.10

WIREWAYS, NONMETALLIC . . . . **Art. 378**

Conductors, Size 378.21

    Number of 378.22

Conductors Connected in Parallel 378.20

Dead Ends 378.58

Definition of 378.2

Deflected Insulated Conductors 378.23

Expansion Fittings 378.44

Extensions from 378.70

Extensions through Walls . . . . 378.10(4)

Grounding 378.60

Listed Required 378.6

Marking 378.120

Splices and Taps 378.56

Supports

    Horizontal . . . . 378.30(A)

    Vertical . . . . 378.30(B)

Use

    Not Permitted 378.12

    Permitted 378.10

WIRING METHODS

Agricultural Buildings 547.5

Audio Systems . . . . Art. 640

Boxes (Required) 300.15

    See BOXLESS DEVICES . . . . Ferm's Finder

Cables

    See CABLES . . . . Ferm's Finder

Carnivals, Circuses, Fairs, and Similar Events . . . 525 Part III

Corrosion Protection 300.6

Cranes and Hoists 610.11

Ducts, Plenums, and Other Air-Handling Spaces 300.22

Electric Vehicle Charging Systems . . . . 625 Part II

Electroplating 669.6

Elevators, Dumbwaiters, etc. 620.21

Emergency Systems . . . . 700 Part II

Fire Alarm Systems

    Non Power Limited Fire Alarm (NPLFA) Circuits . . 760.46

    Power Limited Fire Alarm (PLFA) Circuits

        Load Side of Power Source 760.130

        Supply Side of Power Source 760.127

Fire Pumps

    Control Wiring . . . . 695.14(E)

    Generator Control . . . . 695.14(F)

    Power Wiring 695.6

Floating Buildings, Services or Feeders . . . . 553.7(B)

Fuel Cell Systems . . . . 692 Part IV

General . . . . Art. 300

Hazardous (Classified) Locations

    See . . . . HAZARDOUS (CLASSIFIED) LOCATIONS for

    Specific Items or Locations . . . . Ferm's Finder

Health Care Facilities . . . . 517 Part II

Information Technology Equipment 645.5

Intrinsically Safe Systems 504.20

Limitations 300.2

Manufactured Buildings 545.4

Marinas and Boatyards 555.13

Mobile and Manufactured Homes 550.15

Motion Picture and Television Studios. . . . . Art. 530

Over 1000 Volts

    See OVER 1000 VOLTS. . . . . Ferm's Finder

Park Trailers

    Low-Voltage . . . . 552.10(C)

    120 or 120/240-Volt Systems 552.48

Places of Assembly 518.4

Planning 90.8

Raceways

    See RACEWAYS . . . . Ferm's Finder

Recognized As Suitable 110.8

Recreational Vehicles

    Low-Voltage 551.40

    120 or 120/240-Volt Systems 551.47

Remote-Control, Signaling, and Power-Limited Circuits

    Class 1 . . . . 725.46

    Class 2 or 3

        Load Side of Power Source 725.130

Supply Side of Power Source 725.127

Sensitive Electronic Equipment 647.4

Signs and Outline Lighting . . . . 600.5(C)

Solar Photovoltaic Systems . . . . 690 Part IV

Swimming Pools, Fountains, and Similar Installations. Art. 680

Temporary 590.2

Theaters, Audience Areas 520.5

Underground Installations . . . . 300.5(B)

　　See UNDERGROUND WIRING . . . . Ferm's Finder

X-Ray Equipment 660.4

WOODEN PLUGS (Not Permitted) . . . . 110.13(A)

WOODWORKING PLANTS . . . . . . 500.5(D)(1) Info. Note 1
Class III Locations . . . . Art. 503

See HAZARDOUS (CLASSIFIED) LOCATIONS Ferm's Finder

WORKING SPACE
1000 Volts and Less 110.26

　　Clear Spaces . . . . 110.26(B)

　　Depth of Working Space . . . . 110.26(A)(1)

　　Entrance to and Egress from Working Space . . . 110.26(C)

　　Headroom . . . . 110.26(E)

　　Height of Working Space . . . . 110.26(A)(3)

　　Illumination . . . . 110.26(D)

　　Limited Access. . . . . .110.26(A)(4)

　　Locked Electrical Equipment Rooms or Enclosures . . . 110.26(F)

　　Outdoors . . . . .110.26(E)(2)

　　Personnel Doors . . . . .110.26(C)(3)

　　Separation from High-Voltage Equipment . . . .110.26(A)(5)

　　Width of Working Space . . . . .110.26(A)(2)

Over 1000 Volts . . . . 110 Part III

　　Depth of Working Space . . . . 110.34(A)

　　Entrance to Enclosures and Access to Work Space . . 110.33

　　Enclosure for Electrical Installations 110.31

　　Personnel Doors . . . . .110.33(A)(3)

　　Work Space about Equipment 110.34

　　See Life Safety Code, NFPA 101 . . . . .NFPA 101

WORKMANLIKE INSTALLATION
CATV and Radio Distribution Systems 820.24

Circuits and Equipment Operating at Less Than 50 Volts 720.11

Class 1, 2, and 3 Remote Control, Signaling Circuits . . 725.24

Communications Circuits 800.24

Fire Alarm Systems 760.24

General 110.12

Less Than 50 Volts 720.11

Low-Voltage Suspended Ceiling Power Distribution Systems. . . . . 393.14(A)

Network-Powered Broadband Systems 830.24

Optical Fiber Cables and Raceways 770.24

Sign Illumination Systems- Class 2 . . . . .600.33(B)(1)

X

X-RAY EQUIPMENT
Health Care Facilities . . . . 517 Part V

　　Applicability 517.70

　　Connection to Supply Circuit 517.71

　　Control Circuit Conductors 517.74

　　Disconnecting Means 517.72

　　Equipment, Approved Type 517.75

　　Guarding & Grounding 517.78

　　High-Tension Cables 517.77

　　Operating at more than 1000 Volts . . . . 517.71(C)

　　Overcurrent Protection. 517.73

　　Rating of Supply Conductors 517.73

　　Transformers and Capacitors 517.76

Industrial, Nonmedical and Nondental Use. . . . . . . Art. 660

　　Capacitors 660.36

　　Connection to Supply Circuit 660.4

　　Control . . . . 660 Part II

　　Definitions 660.2

　　Disconnecting Means 660.5

　　Equipment, Approved Type 660.10

　　Guarding & Grounding . . . . 660 Part IV

　　Hazardous Locations 660.3

　　Minimum Size of Conductors 660.9

　　Operating at more than 1000 Volts . . . . 660.4(C)

　　Overcurrent Protection 660.6

　　Rating of Supply Conductors 660.6

　　Transformers 660.35

　　Wiring Terminals 660.7

Note: Radiation safety and performance requirements of several classes of X-ray equipment are regulated under Public Law 90-602 and are enforced by the Department of Health and Human Services. . . . . 660.1 Info. Note 1

Note: information on radiation protection by the National Council on Radiation Protection and Measurements is published as *Reports of the National Council on Radiation Protection and Measurement.* These reports can be obtained from NCRP Publications,7910 Woodmont Ave., Suite 1016, Bethesda, MD 20814. . . . . 660.1 Info. Note 2

Y

YOKE

Device or Equipment Fill, Boxes . . . . .314.16(B)(4)

Grounding by Contact Devices or Yokes . . . . . . 250.146(B)

Provisions for . . . . 404.9(B) Ex. 1 & Ex. 2

Surface Mounted Box . . . . 250.146(A)

Load Calculations for Multiple Receptacles on Same 220.14(I)

Multiple Branch Circuits, All Occupancies, Disconnect for
Devices or Equipment on Same 210.7

Nonmetallic Type, No Equipment Grounding Conductor Required . . . . .404.9(B) Ex. 2

Receptacle, Definition of . . . . Art. 100 Part I

Receptacle Mounting 406.5

Snap Switches, Mounting of, in Box . . . . 404.10(B)

Utilization Equipment . . . . 314.27(D) Ex.

Vertical Surface Outlets . . . . 314.27(A)(1) Ex.

Z

ZONE

Ammonia, Refrigerant Machinery Rooms
Zone 0, 1, and 2 Locations . . . . 505.5(A)

Bathtubs and Showers . . . . 410.10(D)

Receptacles, Shower Zone, Dwellings. . . . . . 406.9(B)(2)

Receptacles, Shower Zone, Mobile Homes . . . . 550.13(F)

Receptacles, Shower Zone, Recreational Vehicles 552.41(F)(1)

Capacitor Overcurrent Protection . . . . 460.25(D)

See   NSI/IEEE 18 Shunt Power Capacitors for Definition of Safe Zone

Dedicated Equipment Space . . . . 110.26(E)

Definitions
Zone 0, 1, and 2 Locations 505.2

Zone 20, 21, and 22 Locations 506.22

Electrolytic Cell Line Working 668.10

Definition of 668.2

Grounding Not Required in . . . . 668.3(C)(3)

Fire Ladders, for, Outside Branch Circuits and Feeders . . . . .
. . . . 225.19(E)

Information Technology Equipment Rooms 645.10

Process, Fixed Electrostatic Equipment, Signs .516.10(A)(8)(1)

ZONE 0, CLASS I HAZARDOUS (CLASSIFIED) LOCATIONS   .
Art. 505

Note for All Class I, Zone 0, 1, and 2 Applications: All persons involved in the design, construction and inspection of installations using the zone classifications are advised to pay careful attention to the information and referenced standards contained in fine print notes throughout Article 505.

Classification of Area . . . . 505.5(B)(1)

Classification of Locations, General . . . . 505.5(A)

Documentation Required . . . . 505.4(A)

Drainage . . . . 505.16(E)

Dual Classification of Areas . . . . 505.7(B)

Equipment, Group Marking . . . . 505.20(D)

Equipment Listed and Marked for Use in . . . . . . 505.20(A)

Grounding and Bonding 505.25

Implementation of Zone Classification System . . . . . 505.7(A)

Listing, Marking, and Documentation, Equipment Suitability .
505.9

Manufacturer's Instructions. . . . . 505.20(E)

Marking of Equipment for . . . . 505.9(C)

Material Groups (Atmospheres) 505.6

Protection Techniques 505.8

Designation . . . . Table 505.9(C)(2)(4)

Note: Intrinsic Safety Only Protection Technique Permitted in Zone 0

Qualified Person Required . . . . 505.7(A)

Reclassification Permitted . . . . 505.7(C)

Sealing . . . . 505.16(A)

Seals, General . . . . 505.16(D)

Spray Application, Dipping, Coating, and Printing Processes Using Flammable

Combustible Materials 516.5

Threading . . . . 505.9(E)

Wiring Methods for . . . . 505.15(A)

ZONE 1, CLASS I HAZARDOUS (CLASSIFIED) LOCATIONS . .
Art. 505

Available Short-Circuit Current for Type of Protection "e" . . .
. . . . 505.7(F)

Classification of Area . . . . 505.5(B)(2)

Classification of Locations, General . . . . 505.5(A)

Documentation Required . . . . 505.4(A)

Drainage . . . . 505.16(E)

Dual Classification of Areas . . . . 505.7(B)

Equipment, Group Marking . . . . 505.20(D)

Equipment Listed for Use in . . . . 505.20(B)

Flexible Cords 505.17

Grounding and Bonding 505.25

Implementation of Zone Classification System . . . . 505.7(A)

Increased Safety "e" Motors and Generators. 505.22

    Copper Conductors Required . . . . 505.18(A)

Listing, Marking, and Documentation, Equipment Suitability
. . . . 505.9

Manufacturer's Instructions. . . . . 505.20(E)

Marking of Equipment for . . . . 505.9(C)

Material Groups (Atmospheres) 505.6

Optical Fiber Cable . . . . 505.15(B)(1)(h)

Protection Techniques 505.8

    Designation . . . . Table 505.9(C)(2)(4)

Qualified Person Required . . . . 505.7(A)

Reclassification Permitted . . . . 505.7(C)

Sealing . . . . 505.16(B)

Seals, General . . . . 505.16(D)

Spray Application, Dipping, Coating, and Printing Processes
Using Flammable

Combustible Materials . . . . 516.5(A)(2)

Threading . . . . 505.9(E)

Wiring Methods for . . . . 505.15(B)

ZONE 2, CLASS I HAZARDOUS (CLASSIFIED) LOCATIONS . Art. 505

Classification of Area . . . . 505.5(B)(3)

Classifications of Locations, General . . . . 505.5(A)

Documentation Required . . . . 505.4(A)

Drainage . . . . 505.16(E)

Dual Classification of Areas . . . . 505.7(B)

Equipment, Group Marking . . . . 505.20(D)

Equipment Listed for Use in . . . . 505.20(C)

Flexible Connections . . . . .505.15(C)(2)

Flexible Cords and Connections 505.17

Grounding and Bonding 505.25

Implementation of Zone Classification System . . . . 505.7(A)

Instrumentation Connections . . . . 505.17(B)

Listing, Marking, and Documentation, Equipment Suitability
. . . . 505.9

Manufacturer's Instructions. . . . . 505.20(E)

Marking of Equipment for . . . . 505.9(C)

Material Groups (Atmospheres) 505.6

Optical Fiber Cable . . . . .505.15(C)(1)(h)

Protection Techniques 505.8

    Designation . . . . Table 505.9 (C)(2)(4)

Qualified Person Required . . . . 505.7(A)

Reclassification Permitted . . . . 505.7(C)

Sealing . . . . 505.16(C)

Seals, General . . . . 505.16(D)

Spray Application, Dipping, Coating, and Printing Processes
Using Flammable

Combustible Materials 516.5

Threading . . . . 505.9(E)

Wiring Methods for . . . . 505.15(C)

ZONE 20, 21, and 22 LOCATIONS FOR COMBUSTIBLE DUSTS, FIBERS, AND FLYINGS . . . . Art. 506

Definition of

    Zone 20 Hazardous (Classified) Location 506.2

    Zone 21 Hazardous (Classified) Location 506.2

    Zone 22 Hazardous (Classified) Location 506.2

ZONE 20, CLASS I HAZARDOUS (CLASSIFIED) LOCATIONS

Classification of Area . . . . 506.5(A)

Classifications of Locations, General . . . . 506.5(B)

    Specific . . . . 506.5(B)(1)

Dual Classification of Areas . . . . 506.7(B)

Equipment, Group Marking 506.6

Equipment Listed for Use in . . . . 506.20(A)

Equipment Temperature Classification . . . . 506.9(D)

Grounding and Bonding 506.25

Implementation of Zone Classification System . . . . 506.7(A)

Listing, Marking, and Documentation, Equipment Suitability .
506.9

Manufacturer's Instructions. . . . . 506.20(E)

Marking of Equipment for . . . . 506.9(C)

Protection Techniques. 506.8

    Designation . . . . Table 506.9(C)(2)(3)

Qualified Persons. . . . . 506.7(A)

Reclassification Permitted . . . . 506.7(C)

Sealing 506.16

Simultaneous Presence of Flammable Gases and Combustible

    Dusts or Fibers/Flyings . . . . 506.7(D)

Spray Application, Dipping, Coating, and Printing Processes
Using Flammable

Combustible Materials 516.5

Threading . . . . 506.9(E)

Wiring Methods for . . . . 506.15(A)

ZONE 21, CLASS I HAZARDOUS (CLASSIFIED) LOCATIONS

Classification of Area . . . . 506.5(A)

Classifications of Locations, General . . . . 506.5(B)

   Specific . . . . 506.5(B)(2)

Dual Classification of Areas . . . . 506.7(B)

Equipment, Group Marking 506.6

Equipment Listed for Use in . . . . 506.20(B)

Equipment Temperature Classification . . . . 506.9(D)

Grounding and Bonding 506.25

Implementation of Zone Classification System . . . . 506.7(A)

Listing, Marking, and Documentation, Equipment Suitability .
. . . . 506.9

Manufacturer's Instructions . . . . 506.20(E)

Marking of Equipment for . . . . 506.9(C)

Protection Techniques 506.8

   Designation . . . . Table 506.9(C)(2)(3)

Qualified Persons . . . . 506.7(A)

Reclassification Permitted . . . . 506.7(C)

Sealing 506.16

Simultaneous Presence of Flammable Gases and Combustible
   Dusts or Fibers/Flyings . . . . 506.7(D)

Spray Application, Dipping, Coating, and Printing Processes
Using Flammable

Combustible Materials 516.5

Threading . . . . 506.9(E)

Wiring Methods for . . . . 506.15(B)

ZONE 22, CLASS I HAZARDOUS (CLASSIFIED) LOCATIONS

Classification of Area . . . . 506.5(A)

Classifications of Locations, General . . . . 506.5(B)

   Specific . . . . 506.5(B)(3)

Dual Classification of Areas . . . . 506.7(B)

Equipment, Group Marking 506.6

Equipment Listed for Use in . . . . 506.20(C)

Equipment Temperature Classification . . . . 506.9(D)

Grounding and Bonding 506.25

Implementation of Zone Classification System . . . . 506.7(A)

Listing, Marking, and Documentation, Equipment Suitability .
. . . . 506.9

Manufacturer's Instructions . . . . 506.20(E)

Marking of Equipment for . . . . 506.9(C)

Protection Techniques 506.8

   Designation . . . . Table 506.9(C)(2)(3)

Qualified Persons . . . . 506.7(A)

Reclassification Permitted . . . . 506.7(C)

Sealing 506.16

Simultaneous Presence of Flammable Gases and Combustible
   Dusts or Fibers/Flyings . . . . 506.7(D)

Spray Application, Dipping, Coating, and Printing Processes
Using Flammable

Combustible Materials 516.5

Threading . . . . 506.9(E)

Wiring Methods for . . . . 506.15(C)

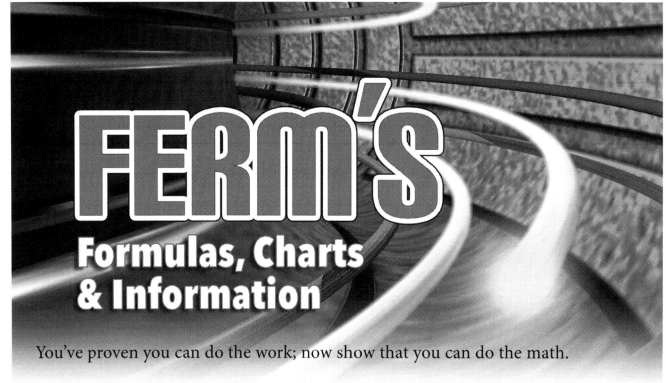

5 New Articles

Energy Storage Systems, Article 706
Large-Scale PV Electric Power Production, Article 691
Stand-Alone Systems, Article 710
Direct-Current Microgrids, Article 712
Fixed Industrial Process Heating, Article 425

5 Improvements

Single-Phase Dwelling Services & Feeders, 310.15(B)(7)
GFCI Protection for Non-Dwelling Units, 210.8(B)
Reconditioned Equipment, ID & Traceability, 110.21(A)(2)
Short-Circuit Current Documentation, 9 locations throughout
Limited Access Working Space Requirement, 110.26(A)(4)

255 Reported Changes

Be the first to learn the most essential changes to the 2017 NEC®. Written by industry experts who sit on the NEC® code-making panels, this comprehensive book is a must-have resource you will reference throughout the years.

Ferm's Fast Finder Index
Fourteenth Edition

CEO: David Clements

Director of Education: L. Keith Lofland

Technical Advisor: Joseph Wages, Jr.

Director of Marketing: Melody Schmidt

Director of Publishing: Kathryn Ingley

Creative Director / Cover Design: John Watson

Project Manager: Laura L. Hildreth

Technical Edit and Review:
Laura L. Hildreth
L. Keith Lofland
Joseph Wages, Jr.

Composed at IAEI in Minion Pro LT Standard by Adobe˚ and Arial Narrow by TrueType˚.
Printed by Walsworth Print Group on 70# Book. Bound in 12 pt. Cover.